THE BIBLICAL RESOURCE SERIES

Available

John J. Collins *The Apocalyptic Imagination*, Second Edition

Frank Moore Cross, Jr., and David Noel Freedman,
Studies in Ancient Yahwistic Poetry

S. R. Driver, *A Treatise on the Use of the Tenses in Hebrew
and Some Other Syntactical Questions*

Joseph A. Fitzmyer, S.J., *The Semitic Background of the New Testament*
(combined edition of *Essays on the Semitic Background
of the New Testament* and *A Wandering Aramean*)

Joseph A. Fitzmyer, S.J., *To Advance the Gospel*, Second Edition

Birger Gerhardsson, *Memory and Manuscript* with
Tradition and Transmission in Early Christianity

Roland de Vaux, *Ancient Israel: Its Life and Institutions*

MEMORY AND MANUSCRIPT

*Oral Tradition and Written Transmission in
Rabbinic Judaism and Early Christianity*

——————— *with* ———————

TRADITION AND TRANSMISSION
IN EARLY CHRISTIANITY

BIRGER GERHARDSSON

Foreword by
Jacob Neusner

WILLIAM B. EERDMANS PUBLISHING COMPANY
GRAND RAPIDS, MICHIGAN

DOVE BOOKSELLERS
LIVONIA, MICHIGAN

Originally published in two volumes by
C.W.K. Gleerup, Lund, Sweden
and Ejnar Munksgaard, Copenhagen, Denmark
under the titles
*Memory and Manuscript: Oral Tradition and Written Transmission
in Rabbinic Judaism and Early Christianity*
Volume XXII in the series *Acta Seminarii Neotestamentici Upsaliensis*
© 1961 Birger Gerhardsson
(Translated from author's Swedish manuscript by Eric J. Sharpe)
and *Tradition and Transmission in Early Christianity*
Volume XX in the series *Coniectanea Neotestamentica*
© 1964 Birger Gerhardsson
(translated by Eric J. Sharpe)

Combined edition with a new preface
© 1998 Birger Gerhardsson

Published jointly 1998 by
Wm. B. Eerdmans Publishing Company
255 Jefferson Ave. S.E., Grand Rapids, Michigan 49503
and Dove Booksellers
30633 Schoolcraft Road, Suite C, Livonia, Michigan 48150

Printed in the United States of America

01 00 99 98   7 6 5 4 3 2 1

Library of Congress Cataloging-in-Publication Data

Gerhardsson, Birger.
Memory and manuscript: oral tradition and written transmission in rabbinic Judaism
and early Christianity; with Tradition and transmission in early Christianity /
Birger Gerhardsson; translated by Eric J. Sharpe.
p.   cm.
First work originally published: Lund, Sweden: C. W. K. Gleerup; Copenhagen, Denmark:
E. Munksgaard, © 1961. (Acta Seminarii Neotestamentici Upsaliensis; 22);
2nd work originally published: Lund, Sweden: C. W. K. Gleerup; Copenhagen, Denmark:
E. Munksgaard, © 1964. (Coniectanea Neotestamentica; 20). With new preface.
Includes bibliographical references and index.
ISBN 0-8028-4366-2 (paper: alk. Paper)
1. Rabbinical literature – History and Criticism. 2. Tradition (Judaism)
3. Transmission of texts. 4. Bible. N.T. – Criticism, Form. 5. Tradition (Theology)
I. Sharpe, Eric J., 1933-   .
II. Gerhardsson, Birger. Tradition and transmission in early Christianity.
III. Title. IV. Title: Tradition and transmission in early Christianity.
BM495.5.G37 1998
225.6'63 – dc21   97-18990
                                                              CIP
                                                              r97

Till min Mor
Till minnet av min Far

Contents

Preface

Memory and Manuscript appeared in 1961,[1] and a new, very slightly corrected edition followed in 1964. The book has been out of print for some twenty-five years. When now, after a proposal from Professor Jacob Neusner and an invitation from the Wm. B. Eerdmans Publishing Company, I publish the book again, the follow-up booklet *Tradition and Transmission in Early Christianity* from 1964 is reprinted in the same volume.

There is something strange about reprinting a scholarly work thirty-five years after its original publication; it cannot possibly fit smoothly into the present stage of research. I am, nevertheless, bold enough to think that my approach as a whole and many of the individual points made are worthy of serious discussion today. As an aid to adequate understanding I shall therefore explain in this Preface both how I wish my book to be read and how my work on tradition has proceeded after the first appearance of the basic book. I will give a brief account of the origin of this book, say something in passing about the stage of research when it was written, make clear what it is about and not about, stress some of my basic terms and working definitions, comment upon a number of common misunderstandings, and, finally, mention pertinent literature and draw special attention to a few important contributions to the international discussion on the early Christian tradition published since 1961.

The reason for taking up the theme in the 1950s was that gospel research had for forty years tried to elucidate the origins and preservation of the Synoptic tradition, and yet not a single contribution provided a concrete picture of how the carriers of the Synoptic tradition had set

1. (ASNU 22; Lund: Gleerup, and Copenhagen: Munksgaard), in this Preface abbreviated *MM*. My other publications on the subject are here abbreviated as follows: *TT = Tradition and Transmission in Early Christianity* (CN 20; Lund: Gleerup, and Copenhagen: Munksgaard, 1964, now Stockholm: Almqvist & Wiksell International); *OGT = The Origins of the Gospel Traditions* (Philadelphia: Fortress, 1979, and London: SCM Press, 1980); *WE* = "Der Weg der Evangelientradition," in *Das Evangelium und die Evangelien*, ed. P. Stuhlmacher (WUNT 28; Tübingen: Mohr, 1983, 79-102); *GT = The Gospel Tradition* (ConBNT 15; Lund: Gleerup, 1986, now Stockholm: Almqvist & Wiksell International), also published as a contribution to *The Interrelations of the Gospels* (BETL 95), ed. D. L. Dungan (Leuven: Leuven University Press & Peeters, 1990), 497-545.

about transmitting their tradition, technically speaking. The approach applied did not even raise the issue. Similarly, Old Testament research (not least in Uppsala), though in quite different ways, had worked much with the problem of oral tradition in ancient Israel and the surrounding cultures for nearly thirty years, without trying to clarify the technical side of the transmission of the oral texts. I became curious and decided to attempt to address this deficiency.

The milieu in which Jesus and the earliest church worked was that of Jewish culture in Hellenistic times. As far as I could see, there existed within this culture only a single setting from which we could obtain a reasonably broad, coherent, and clear picture of the methods of transmission: the Pharisaic-rabbinic mainstream within Judaism (for the sake of simplicity, I used the shortened term "Rabbinic Judaism," *MM* 30-32; cf. the clarification in *TT* 9 and 11-21). The preserved material from other Jewish factions during roughly the same period is fragmentary and meager for our purpose. I would, of course, pay much more attention to these circles today than I did in 1961; findings and research during the latest decades have given us a far richer and more vivid picture of ancient Jewish pluralism than we had before. A rapid survey of the source material from Greco-Roman antiquity outside Judaism suggested that even there we would receive rather limited help for our inquiry (the research in this field after 1961 has not changed that situation very much, though the literary techniques of the schools of rhetoric have been well elucidated during the last decades).

Therefore I began with Pharisaic teachers and early rabbis, fully aware that this Jewish stream of tradition could not be isolated from the Hellenistic culture with which Jews since 300 years before Christ had been surrounded. Rabbinic specialists had written much about the Mishnah and the Talmud as well as midrashic and targumic material. In this vast secondary literature, however, there were only incidental comments on the techniques of transmission. Nobody gave a broad picture of the technical side of the transmission process, not even the foremost expert on the rabbinic tradition, Wilhelm Bacher. Therefore, I had to try to clarify the matter myself. The task was formulated as follows on p. 30:

"... to attempt to give a concrete picture of how, *from the purely technical point of view*, the sacred Torah was transmitted during these centuries."

The part of tradition that I wanted to elucidate first of all was the *oral* Torah (the expression taken in its widest meaning), and the aspect was its *transmission* (cf. *MM* 14-15, 30, and 71-72). I discussed, however, the transmission of written Torah as well, and that for two reasons: written and oral Torah interact so widely, and they show interesting similarities in structure.

Nomenclature was a problem. I could have chosen modern terms (written tradition, oral tradition, etc.), but I preferred, in order to preclude anachronism, basic terms from rabbinic literature: Torah, written Torah, oral Torah, mishnah, talmud, midrash, halakah, haggadah, and so on. Since all these Hebrew words have many meanings, I stated with working definitions how I intended to use them in this book. A few examples: I mean by Torah not the Law but that which I, with italics, stated in this way: *"In this investigation we shall use the term Torah, without qualification, as a collective designation for the Jews' sacred authoritative tradition (doctrine) in its entirety"* (*MM* 21). By written Torah I do not mean the Pentateuch (alone or together with the Prophets and the Writings), but Torah whose authoritative transmission is in written form (*MM* 19-32 and 33-42). By oral Torah I do not mean the Mishnah, but Torah whose authoritative transmission is oral (*MM* 19-32 and 71-78; cf. *GT* 19); thus even these two terms are in my usage wide and open. I allow myself to use the word "mishnah" to denote "that which is repeated": a short, terse, basic text, intended for memorization, regardless of its content (*MM* 26-28; cf., e.g., 82-83 and 145), etc. By verbal tradition, I do not mean only text tradition that is verbally fixed, but articulated tradition in general, in free as well as fixed wording (*TT* 7); I stress the interaction between fixed text and traditional yet fluid interpretation over and over in my presentation (*MM*, esp. 19-21, 41-42, 71-78, and 79-84). If these working definitions and programmatic declarations are ignored and the basic terms understood in more conventional ways, my presentation cannot be rightly understood.

The rabbinic material is fascinating but not easy to penetrate. The rabbis themselves formulated a number of rules on how to compose the material for successful transmission, how to proceed with teaching and transmission, how to retain memorized tradition in memory, and the like. I soon detected, however, certain pitfalls and took precautions to protect myself. I noted in particular that such rules normally codified an already existing practice. The rules themselves are thus later than a good deal of the transmitted material that appears to conform with them; furthermore, we cannot always be sure that the formulated rules were applied in practice. Therefore we cannot confine our attention to (1) these rules for teaching and transmission; we must also look for (2) illustrations of practice that corresponded with them, and search for (3) indications that the material preserved for us was in reality transmitted according to these principles. With the aid of this three-pronged approach, which I devised myself (*MM* 122), I tried to work out a broad, historically probable picture of the processes of transmission. I hoped that my pioneering attempt would be followed by more thorough studies by well-informed experts, especially scholars in Jewish studies.

One crux was the problem of dating, a perpetual headache for those who want to use rabbinic material in historical studies. That most of the material is older than the earliest written documents, in many cases even older than the first discernible redactions, was a universal conviction. But how early a dating is justified? Around 1960, scholars generally had greater confidence than we do today in the information the rabbis themselves have left us about who made a dictum or did what a rabbinic narrative relates. It was clear to me that the rabbinic material – the records and the rules for transmission that it contained – could not readily be traced further back than to the fall of the temple in A.D. 70 and the destruction of Jerusalem in A.D. 135; for my part, I noted that the work of Rabbi Aqiba represented a significant boundary (*MM*, e.g., 77-78 and 111-12; cf. *TT* 11-16, *OGT* 19-24, and *WE* 89-91). But I always made a point of distinguishing between Tannaitic and Amoraic rabbis and mentioned the name of the rabbi to whom a text was attributed so that the reader could date this piece of information roughly; and I pointed out repeatedly that development had taken place.

The total program for the transmission of material was not worked out during the time of the temple; the pedagogic techniques were refined and made more methodic, efficient, and general after 70 and 135. The individual guiding principles – "the essentials of the rabbinic method of transmission," as I called them (*MM* 76-78) – are, however, mostly old, in many cases very old indeed: memorization; the principle "first learn, then understand"; terseness; abridgment of material into short, pregnant texts; poetic artifices; rhythm; cantillation; mnemonic devices; use of written notes; diligent repetition, and so on (cf. *TT* 16-21). Therefore, it cannot be totally anachronistic to allow the later, fully developed technique to constitute the total picture, but to take the basic principles for transmission (see especially *MM* 122-70, cf. 111-12, *TT* 13-21, *OGT* 16-

19, and *WE* 90-91) one by one and ask if they were not applied already during the period of the temple by early Christian teachers, perhaps even by Jesus himself; as New Testament exegetes we must of course try to force our way back that far. We would not even need to discuss the question if the total scheme existed before the fall of the temple; but of course it did not (cf. *MM* 76-78, *TT* 13-21, *OGT* 15-26, and *WE* 87-91).

Many critics, however, believed and said that I simply tried to read back into the period before 70 the developed rabbinic technique of about A.D. 200, and that I imposed the academic methods of the rabbis on the popular preachers of early Christianity; they rejected my whole argument, without further discussion, as anachronistic and inadequate. This is not a correct account of my standpoint or method; nor is it a fruitful way of discussing a complex problem.

Memory and Manuscript was received in different ways. Numerous scholars were appreciative of my approach to the problem of tradition, especially Jewish and Catholic scholars, but also Protestant exegetes of a conservative bent. The rabbinic part of my study (*MM* 17-189) did not provoke many objections, apart from that of too early dating. The controversial section was that on the New Testament (191-35), generally only the tentative final chapter (324-35). Numerous New Testament scholars, first of all radical exegetes in the US and Germany, dismissed my principal thesis in this chapter and with it, without further ado, the entire study from beginning to end. I had written somewhat pointedly and provocatively; perhaps that also took its toll. I shall not here comment on the positive reception, nor on those points where well-founded criticism and continued research have led me to adopt more nuanced views on matters dealt with in my dissertation. I shall simply clarify my approach with a few comments on the most common negative reaction I received, a reaction widely represented in footnotes as well as in introductions to the New Testament and surveys of Gospel research or Jesus research.

As a young author, I was disappointed that so few critics took the trouble of presenting my thesis correctly and making it the point of their discussion. Some renowned reviewers, above all Dr. Morton Smith,[2] dis-

---

2. M. Smith's "A Comparison of Early Christian and Early Rabbinic Tradition," in *JBL* 82 (1963), 169-76, was the most critical review that my book received — and also the most widely cited.

missed the book completely after having summarized it in a caricatured and misleading way. This misrepresentation, and Smith's rather simplistic counterarguments, were repeated, in even more simplified forms, by countless critics who could not possibly have read the book themselves (they repeated the same misreadings); it was common for my approach to be simply dismissed with a reference to Dr. Smith's article. Some scholars do so even today.[3] The explanation which I gave in the introduction of *Memory and Manuscript* of the nature of my study, the numerous definitions and specifications which are to be found in the book, as well as the observations, clarifications, and further contributions that I have made since its publication, have been ignored by numerous critics (though not, it is true, by everyone).

In 1964 I published the supplement *Tradition and Transmission in Early Christianity*, which is reprinted in the present volume. There I tried to clarify the issue and correct basic misunderstandings. I regret the tone I took in the book; it was written by an offended young man, disappointed that scholarly discussion was not carried out in the careful way he had expected. I have also tried to remove misunderstandings in other ways, including a popular presentation of my approach (see below). I have further developed and expanded my approach with a series of other studies, mentioned in the footnotes to this Preface.

*   *   *

In *Memory and Manuscript*, my interest was mainly on the acts of transmission themselves. These I depicted as specific acts within the framework of what I called Early Christianity's "work with the word of the Lord," an activity which was both preservative and creative. In my opinion, there was in the Early Christian mother community in Jerusalem, and in other early churches as well, a *collegium*, formed by leading men (not some "rabbinic academy" [M. Smith]), which preserved, studied, discussed, and adapted the oral texts and formulated new texts ("words") on the basis of the Holy Scriptures and memories of Jesus. Both the texts with which they worked and the products of their reworking had firm *and*

---

3. Recently C. A. Evans, "Source, Form and Redaction Criticism," in *Approaches to the New Testament*, ed. S. E. Porter and D. Tombs; JSNTSup 120 (Sheffield: Sheffield Academic Press, 1995), 28-29.

flexible elements (*MM* 324-35;[4] cf. *TT* 35-47, *OGT* 67-91, *WE* 82, 85-91, and *GT* 28-57).

To my astonishment, my discussion of Early Christianity's "work with the word" after the departure of Jesus was hardly taken up in the debate by the majority of my critics. Instead they generally presupposed that I wanted to substantiate a thesis which my teacher Harald Riesenfeld had presented in a paper in 1957, to wit that the Christ-tradition was originally a "single, clearly-defined 'Holy word'" (if I may use W. D. Davies's formulation), which the early Christians preserved by reciting in the course of worship.[5] Thus the framework, including both preservation *and* creativity, which I had myself posited, and my many words about firmness *and* flexibility in tradition, were ignored; they were simply replaced by another view of the setting, character, and transmission of the Early Christian tradition.

After 1961 I began pursuing this "work with the word of the Lord" in Early Christianity: What happened when Jesus' "twelve" main disciples and other leading men in Early Christianity worked on the Jesus tradition — and the Holy Scriptures? The task demands a very large analytical work, and a variety of approaches. I can myself make only limited contributions. I started by analyzing a midrashic text from Early Christianity. I chose the long version of the narrative in which Jesus is put to the test by the devil after his baptism in *The Testing of God's Son* (1966). It was convenient to begin with this text because its degree of strict historicity must be low (Jesus is not surrounded by any witnesses:

---

4. I had given some hints of what the process may have involved in my account of how "the work with the word" is depicted and reflected in Acts and in the Pauline letters (*MM* 208-61 and 262-323 respectively).

5. W. D. Davies, "Reflections on a Scandinavian Approach to the 'Gospel Tradition,'" in *Neotestamentica et patristica*, Festschrift O. Cullmann (NovTSup 6; Leiden: Brill, 1962), 19. When Davies says (p. 17) that Riesenfeld and I have essentially the same picture of the Gospel tradition, he cannot give page references to my book, only three general "*op. cit.*," and, necessarily, he finds inconsistences in my usage. In my view, however, the Jesus-tradition was pluriform, and recitation in the worship of the community was *possibly* one of the *uses* of the Gospel tradition in Early Christianity, not the basic place of *transmission* proper (*MM* 335; cf. my comment in *TT* 40). Riesenfeld said in his paper "The Gospel Tradition and Its Beginnings," in *Studia Evangelica* 1 (TU 73) (1959), 51, that his own observations were "mainly based on considerations issuing from recent studies carried out in Uppsala," and refers in a footnote to my preparations for my dissertation. The footnote is missing in the separate edition of Riesenfeld's paper (London: Mowbray, 1957).

not any disciples, no human beings at all), and the text, for all its brevity, contains four quotations from the Holy Scriptures. Therefore, it is here especially easy to study how reflective and creative "work with the word of the Lord" has been carried out by the early Christian scribe who formulated the text.

I was, however, forced to interrupt this detailed analysis[6] in order to explore a new problem which that study had raised, the question what role Israel's creed of faith, the Shema', interpreted in a scribal way, came to play in Early Christianity's "work with the word of the Lord." I sensed immediately that this must be a central and fundamental issue for the content — and the form — of the Jesus tradition. Gradually, I could see the principle of the pertinent passages: Jesus himself, his unreceptive listeners and opponents, and his receptive listeners and adherents have all been *examined* with the triadic love-demand of the Shema' as the criterion. Not until 1996, however, could I bring this investigation to an end and present the seventeen most important of my partial studies, published separately in the period 1966-95, together in a volume with the title *The Shema in the New Testament*.[7] The passages analyzed show, all of them, that "the work with the word of the Lord" in Early Christianity could be both learned and acute.

In addition to the midrashic haggadah about the testing of Jesus after his baptism and the other Shema' passages, I have analyzed examples of most of the other types of text in the Gospels. I have studied representative parables and examined in detail all the narrative meshalim (parables) in the Gospels.[8] The same is true of the miracle narratives, to-

6. I published in 1966 the completed part of my study as *The Testing of God's Son (Matt 4:1-11 & Par): An Analysis of an Early Christian Midrash*, chaps. 1-4 (ConBNT 2; Lund: Gleerup, now Stockholm: Almqvist & Wiksell International). Afterward I have come to regret that I used the vague term "midrash." Today I would have written "midrashic haggadah." The substance of the most important of the remaining chapters of this study (chap. 7) is published in the article "Gottes Sohn als Diener Gottes," in *ST* 27 (1973), 73-106, repr. in my book *The Shema in the New Testament* (see next note), 139-72.

7. *The Shema in the New Testament: Deut 6:4-5 in Significant Passages* (Lund: Novapress, 1996).

8. "The Parable of the Sower and Its Interpretation," in *NTS* 14 (1967-68), 165-93, and "The Seven Parables in Matthew XIII," in *NTS* 19 (1972-73), 16-37, also in *The Shema in the New Testament*, 24-52, 53-74; and further, "Illuminating the Kingdom: Narrative Meshalim in the Synoptic Gospels," in *Jesus and the Gospel Tradition*, ed. H. Wansbrough (JSNTSup 64; Sheffield: JSOT Press, 1991), 266-309.

gether with all other texts dealing with the mighty deeds of Jesus in Matthew.[9] Furthermore, I have written about the birth and childhood narratives, as well as the passion and resurrection narratives, from various points of view.[10] The aphoristic meshalim (logia) remain to be analyzed one by one, a huge task to which I can make only limited contributions myself. The same is true of the complicated redactional measures which I think were operative in the transmission process in Early Christianity from the beginning until they took over the last phase of the Gospel tradition (e.g., *TT* 37-47, *WE* 88-89, *OGT* 85-86, and *GT* 34-57). As to the substance of the Early Christian message, I have primarily studied its ethical dimension, including specifically the ethical dimension of early Christology, a neglected issue.[11]

*　　*　　*

Much has happened since *Memory and Manuscript* appeared in 1961, within both early rabbinic and New Testament research. Rabbinic scholarship has not only given us a series of ameliorated text editions and translations, but has also taken up for further research and debate many of those problems which I tried to solve or draw attention to, as well as other questions. The greatest contribution has been made by Dr. Jacob Neusner, in studies both detailed and broad. He has illuminated the rabbinic tradition with approaches both old and new, in a career of unprecedented productivity. This is not the place to give an account of his achievements, nor do I think I need enumerate those studies of Dr. Neusner which are most pertinent from my point of view. I am pleased that he

---

9. *The Mighty Acts of Jesus according to Matthew*, in Scripta minora 1978-1979 in memoriam Gustavi Aulén (Scripta minora Regiae Societatis Humaniorum Litterarum Lundensis 1978-1979:5; Lund: Gleerup, 1979), supplemented with "Mighty Acts and Rule of Heaven: 'God is with us,'" in *The Shema in the New Testament*, 187-201.

10. See especially my articles "Gottes Sohn als Diener Gottes"; "Kristi uppståndelse – de bibliska vittnesbörden," in *Din uppståndelse bekänner vi*, ed. E. Franck (Stockholm: Verbum, 1988), 24-61; "Mark and the Female Witnesses," in *Dumu-E₂-Dub-ba-a*, Festschrift Å. W. Sjöberg, ed. H. Behrens et al. (Philadelphia: Occasional Publications of the S. N. Kramer Fund, 11, 1989), 217-26, and a number of other contributions in Swedish.

11. See *The Shema in the New Testament*, above all 173-86, 272-85, and 300-318. See further my book *The Ethos of the Bible* (Philadelphia: Fortress, 1981, and London: Darton, Longman and Todd, 1982).

has, in spite of our disagreements, wanted to write a preface to this reprint of my dissertation.

Within Gospel research, the present situation is quite different from that in the 1960s. Much of what leading scholars maintained at that time is called into question now. Today uncertainty prevails, and, with it, more openness to new approaches. I may perhaps take the recent interest in reprinting *Memory and Manuscript*, expressed from more than one source in the US, where the negative attitude toward my work has been most common, as an indication that even my approach may be taken up for serious discussion today.

A list of reviews of *Memory and Manuscript* and *Tradition and Transmission* is to be found at the end of this preface.[12] For broad, exhaustive discussions of studies on tradition since 1961, I can refer to Dr. Rainer Riesner's dissertation *Jesus als Lehrer* (3d ed. 1988; a fourth edition is expected) and Dr. Samuel Byrskog's *Jesus the Only Teacher* (1994), to which I will shortly return. Let me mention, very briefly, a few works which have special relevance for my approach to questions of tradition or which are important to the debate for other reasons.

Dr. Werner Kelber's book *The Oral and the Written Gospel* (1983)[13] is a fresh contribution to New Testament tradition research. The author is very critical of my approach, though he takes it seriously. I have criticized his own position in other contexts, particularly his oversimplified, general notion of Orality, the simplistic contrast he draws between Orality and Textuality, and his underestimation of the role that writing played in Israel for many centuries before Christ, a factor which partly explains the similarities between oral and written Torah tradition which I had tried to elucidate (*GT* 28-57; cf. *MM* 19-121).[14] Here I will mention only the curious fact that he

12. Important reviews and other contributions are also listed in my booklet *Die Anfänge der Evangelientradition* (see below), most detailed in the German version, 65-69 (this list was compiled by R. Riesner). Cf. further P. H. Davids, "The Gospels and Jewish Tradition: Twenty Years after Gerhardsson," in *Gospel Perspectives*, vol. 1, ed. R. T. France and D. Wenham (Sheffield: JSOT Press, 1980), 75-99.

13. Werner H. Kelber, *The Oral and the Written Gospel: The Hermeneutics of Speaking and Writing in the Synoptic Tradition, Mark, Paul, and Q* (Philadelphia: Fortress, 1983).

14. See further S. Talmon, "Oral Tradition and Written Transmission, or the Heard and the Seen Word in Judaism of the Second Temple Period," in *Jesus and the Oral Gospel*, ed. H. Wansbrough (JSNTSup 64; Sheffield: JSOT Press, 1991), 121-58, and Ø. Andersen, "Oral Tradition," in *Jesus and the Oral Gospel*, 17-58. Cf. also *Semeia* 39 (1987), and J. Halverson, "Oral and Written Gospel: A Critique of Werner Kelber," in *NTS* 40 (1994), 180-95.

characterizes my view of Jewish and Early Christian tradition as "a model of passive transmission," in contrast to Rudolf Bultmann's "model of evolutionary progression."[15] Apparently not even he has noticed that in *Memory and Manuscript* I do not depict the Jewish tradition as simply a heritage to be preserved but as extraordinarily rich and living, variegated and variable, and freshly creative. To be sure, I concentrated on the task of studying more closely an interesting *partial phenomenon* within the dynamic, flexible, and luxuriant tradition: those firm elements which seem to have been preserved with care for the wording (*MM* 19-32, 33-42, 71-78, and 91-92), but I characterized not only the written but also the oral Torah as "texts with complementary interpretation" (*MM* 79-83) and dealt extensively with the interaction between firm text and flexible clarification. Many critics seem to be unaware that even the rabbis could rework their traditions, change formulations, cancel elements, and insert additions and new layers. I could mention this part of their activity only in passing in *Memory and Manuscript*, a limitation which I have often had reason to regret (see, e.g., *MM* 75-78, 97-98, 103-12, 120-21, 146-48, 152-53, and 180-81; cf. *TT* 38-40).

Thus it was mainly the core elements within the articulated part of the tradition that I treated in *Memory and Manuscript*. In later works I have specified more closely and worked out more explicitly the hints I gave concerning *the anatomy of tradition as a whole* (*MM* 71-78; cf. also 292-99). In my book *The Gospel Tradition* (1986) I have also presented a model for a many-sided analysis of this complicated phenomenon: there I make a basic distinction between "inner" and "outer" tradition, and distinguish within the "outer" tradition (a) verbal (articulated) tradition, (b) behavioral tradition, (c) institutional tradition, and (d) material tradition (cf. also *MM* 71-78, 290-94, *TT* 7, *OGT* 11-14, 29-32, and *WE passim*).

The reviews of *Memory and Manuscript* included two *Besprechungen*, written by the leading New Testament professors in Tübingen, dismissively by Ernst Käsemann, favorably by Otto Michel.[16] Dr. Michel later wrote (together with Dr. Klaus Haacker) the preface to my popular booklet *Die Anfänge der Evangelientradition* (1976). This book contains a series of lectures in which I presented my position to German students of theology in Holzhausen (not far from Marburg) in March 1976. My text in this book was, at others' initative, translated into Swedish, Danish,

15. Kelber, *The Oral and the Written Gospel*, 8-14 and 2-8 respectively.
16. E. Käsemann, in *VuF* 8 (1963), 85-87; O. Michel, in *ThLZ* 87 (1964), 835-37.

French, English, Italian, and Spanish in 1977-80. The most reliable version is (next to that in Swedish) that in English; it carries the title *The Origins of the Gospel Traditions*.[17]

In Tübingen, some years later (1981), Rainer Riesner's dissertation *Jesus als Lehrer* was published.[18] It is a thorough study of the problem of tradition in early Judaism and Christianity, and includes a well-informed survey of earlier research. Dr. Riesner is one of the few New Testament scholars who have been interested in the individual, concrete characteristics of teaching and transmission that I took up in *Memory and Manuscript*. He shows — contrary to the criticism leveled against my work — that many of the didactic tools which, according to my presentation, were older than the developed rabbinic technique, can be found in material from times long before the teaching of the rabbis. He demonstrates further that the rabbinic technique is not a sophisticated academic specialty; rather, it consists largely of popular devices, applied for centuries in homes and elementary school teaching, as well as in synagogal activities — connections which I, too, had considered, although very briefly and in passing (*MM* 56-66, 73-78, and 123-24 for popular usage; *MM* 41-42, 67-70, 140-48, and 163-68 for synagogal; cf. further *TT* 18-19).

In 1982 Professor Käsemann's successor Peter Stuhlmacher organized a symposium in Tübingen on the theme *Das Evangelium und die Evangelien*. The contributions were published the next year in a massive volume with the theme of the symposium as the title.[19] Here a number of scholars from Europe and America discuss the problem of tradition extensively and carefully: the gospel; the gospel in the proclamation and teaching of Jesus and that of the first Jerusalem community as well as Paul; gospel research; the gospel tradition; the sayings source; the written gospel; each of the four canonical Gospels; the noncanonical sayings of Jesus as well as Justin's Apomnemoneumata; and, finally, the peculiarity of the Gospels in relation to Greek biography. I myself presented, under the title "Der Weg der

---

17. (Philadelphia: Fortress, 1979, and London: SCM Press, 1980). The German version is *Die Anfänge der Evangelientradition* (GuD 119; Wupperthal: Brockhaus, 1977).

18. *Jesus als Lehrer. Eine Untersuchung zum Ursprung der Evangelien-Überlieferung* (WUNT 2:7; Tübingen: Mohr, 1981, 3d ed. 1988).

19. *Das Evangelium und die Evangelien. Vorträge vom Tübinger Symposium 1982*, ed. P. Stuhlmacher (WUNT 28; Tübingen: Mohr, 1983). The volume was translated into English as *The Gospel and the Gospels* (Grand Rapids: Eerdmans, 1991). Unfortunately, the translation of my article is inadequate, even — in a number of places — directly misleading. Reference should be made to the German original.

Evangelientradition," and after rejecting common misunderstandings, a survey of how I envisage the way the tradition was transmitted, starting with Jesus and ending with the written Gospels (pp. 79-102).

An international group of scholars held a symposium, divided into two parts, in Dublin in 1989 and Gazzada (Italy) in 1990, on the theme "Oral Tradition Before, In and Outside the Gospels." Various scholars treated a broad spectrum of topics: the general topic of Oral Tradition; then oral tradition in the Hellenistic world in antiquity, in the Old Testament, among the Jews at the time of the second temple, and in the Pharisaic-rabbinic tradition; Jesus as preacher and teacher; Jesus' aphoristic and narrative meshalim; the narrative Jesus tradition; oral tradition in John and Paul as well as behind the Didache. Finally, a scholar (Dr. Ben Meyer) discussed the historical and theological consequenses of my approach. My own contribution had the title "Illuminating the Kingdom: Narrative Meshalim in the Synoptic Gospels" and contained a detailed examination of all the parables in the Gospels with a discussion of what these texts reveal about the transmission and adaptation which took place before they received their final written form. The papers from the symposium, completed with an article on the passion narrative, were published in 1991 by Dom Henry Wansbrough under the title *Jesus and the Oral Gospel Tradition*.[20]

In 1994 my student Samuel Byrskog submitted his dissertation *Jesus the Only Teacher*.[21] Dr. Byrskog studies thoroughly how Jesus is presented as teacher in the Gospel of Matthew and how the treatment and presentation of the transmitted text material there has been influenced by the conviction that Jesus is "the Only Teacher" of the Church (cf. my own remarks in *MM* 332-33, *TT* 40-44, *OGT* 47-49, *WE* 79-82, 91-93, and *GT* 48). Dr. Byrskog bases his analysis on my multidimensional model (see above), though his work is replete with insights from fresh investigations of other types as well. He starts with a careful study of the

20. (JSNTSup 64; Sheffield: JSOT Press, 1991). Prof. B. F. Meyer's contribution, "Some Consequences of Birger Gerhardsson's Account of the Origins of the Gospel Tradition," is to be found on pp. 424-40.

21. *Jesus the Only Teacher: Didactic Authority and Transmission in Ancient Israel, Ancient Judaism and the Matthean Community* (ConBNT 24; Stockholm: Almqvist & Wiksell International, 1994). Cf. the work of three other students of mine: S. Westerholm, *Jesus and Scribal Authority* (ConBNT 10; Lund: Gleerup, 1978); B. Holmberg, *Paul and Power: The Structure of Authority in the Primitive Church as Reflected in the Pauline Epistles* (ConBNT 11; Lund: Gleerup, 1978; repr. Philadelphia: Fortress, 1980); and K. Kjær-Hansen, *Studier i navnet Jesus* (Aarhus: Menighetsfakultetet, 1982).

Old Testament and of somewhat later Jewish material, confining his attention to circles which followed a more or less charismatic teacher and preserved tradition from and about him. Then he scrutinizes the Gospel of Matthew against this historical and phenomenological background. The book brings the study of Early Christianity's "work with the word of the Lord," within which the basic transmission of the verbal Jesus tradition took place, a clear step forward.

Finally, a brief comment on another point, where my academic, historical studies of the anatomy of the Early Christian tradition and the problem of its transmission seem to cause some confusion. The approach of the form-critical school to the problem of tradition was historical and theological at the same time: the question of the origin and transmission of the text material was interwoven with the question of the content and meaning of the Early Christian message. The majority of reactions to my study of the transmission were also theological rather than historical. To me it is, however, important to keep the purely historical question of the origin and transmission of the material apart from theological questions of the content and meaning of the Early Christian message, even if the two questions are interrelated. In the first case one must go back to the concrete realm of history; and one cannot without further ado extend such an approach to questions of theology. In the second case, one must reasonably take as one's starting point "the faith vision," on which the message of Jesus and of Early Christianity was founded (cf., e.g., *TT* 5-11, *OGT* 7-10, 90-91, *WE* 91-93, and *GT* 10).[22]

If this reprint should start a renewed discussion of early Christian tradition, at a considerably later stage of research than it was written for, then the discussion would benefit if it could be more precise, specific, and concrete than the debate which my work inaugurated thirty-five years ago, but which widely lived a life of its own.[23]

Lund, February 1997
Birger Gerhardsson

22. Therefore I can say in *TT* 31: "The thesis 'in the beginning was the sermon (*kerygma*)' is brilliant as a point of departure for Christian theology. But as a historical statement it is simply incorrect." A reviewer apprehended these words as arrogant.

23. I wish to thank my friend Dr. Stephen Westerholm, who has again polished my English.

Reviews

Memory and Manuscript
first edition (1961)

C. K. BARRETT, *JTS* 14 (1963) 445-49; P. BENOIT, *RB* 70 (1963) 269-73; M. BLACK, *SOTS BL* (1963) 66-67; J. BLIGH, *HeyJ* 6 (1965) 189-90; B. BRINKMANN, *Schol* 37 (1962) 426-30; J. COPPENS, *ETL* 38 (1962) 104-5; J. G. DAVIES, *ET* 74 (1962-63); A. DUNSTONE, R. E. NIXON, AND I. H. MARSHALL, *TSFBull* 45 (1966) 3-12; J. DUPONT, *RyMo* 35 (1961) 279-80; F. FESTORAZZI, *RBibIt* 11 (1963) 433-36; J. A. FITZMYER, *TS* 23 (1962) 442-57; B. GÄRTNER, *KÅ* 61 (1961) 247-54; A. GOLDBERG, *JerusPost* 18/9 (1963) and *BibOr* 21 (1964) 223-25; E. M. B. GREEN, *Churchman* 77 (1963) 120-21; J. G. H. HOFFMANN, *RevRéf* 13 (1962-64) 30-34; E. KÄSEMANN, *VuF* 8 (1963) 85-87; P. A. KERRIGAN, *Anton* 43 (1963) 434-42; W. G. KÜMMEL, *TR* 31 (1965-66) 24-26; M. É. LAUZIERE, *RevThom* 64 (1964) 466-67; E. LOHSE, *ThZ* 18 (1962) 60-62; C. M. MARTINI, *Bib* 44 (1963) 379-82; E. MASSAUX, *RHE* 56 (1962) 1135-36; O. MICHEL, *TLZ* 87 (1964) 835-37; W. MUNDLE, *LuRbl* 15 (1967) 124-25; F. MUSSNER, *TTZ* 73 (1974) 190-91; J. RADERMAKERS, *NRT* 86 (1964) 786-87; J. SCHMID, *BZ* 8 (1964) 151-54; B. SCHWANK, *ErbA* 38 (1962) 340-41; M. SMITH, *JBL* 82 (1963) 169-76; A. VIARD, *RSPT* 46 (1962) 274-76; G. WIDENGREN, *Numen* 10 (1963) 42-83; K. WILHELM, *Mitteilungsblatt* 29 (1961) 29/9, 4; P. WINTER, *ATR* 45 (1963) 416-19.

A brief French version appeared also: Birger Gerhardsson, *Mémoire et manuscrits dans le Judaisme rabbinique et le Christianisme primitif.* Adaptation francaise condensée de G. H. HOFFMANN (*RevRéf,* No. 54, 14; 1963), 54 pp. Part of the final chapter (328-35) was reprinted under the title "Memory and Manuscript: Birger Gerhardsson," in *In Search of the Historical Jesus,* ed. H. K. McARTHUR (New York: Charles Scribner's Sons, 1969), 33-40.

Tradition and Transmission in Early Christianity
first edition (1964)

R. S. BARBOUR, *SJT* 19 (1966) 114-15; C. K. BARRETT, *JTS* 16 (1965)
488-89; J. BLIGH, *HeyJ* 6 (1965) 189-90; P. BLOCK, *KrilFörÅ* 8 (1964)
156-57; B. BRINKMANN, *Schol* 39 (1964) 587-88; C. BUTLER, *DowR*
83 (1966) 76-78; C. EDWARDS, *JR* 44 (1964) 183-84; J. A. FITZMYER,
TS 25 (1964) 685, and *CBQ* 26 (1964) 487; H. HAAG, *TübTQ* 145 (1965)
398; M. É. LAUZIERE, *RevThom* 64 (1964) 466-67; P. VAN LEEUWEN,
TTNij 6 (1966) 212-13; E. LOHSE, *TLZ* 91 (1966) 189; É. MASSAUX,
RHE 59 (1965) 1087-88; J. E. MÉNARD, *RHR* 60 (1966) 93-94; M. PEL-
LEGRINO, *RStorLettRel* 1 (1965) 317-18; J. SMIT SIBINGA, *VoxT* 35
(1965) 131; L. H. SILBERMAN, *JBL* 84 (1965) 459-60; V. TAYLOR, *ET*
76 (1964-65) 149; R. WILLIAMS, *JR* 45 (1965) 87; A. V. ZIEGLER, *MTZ*
18 (1967) 89-90.

Foreword

Jacob Neusner
University of South Florida and Bard College

THE REPRINT OF *Memory and Manuscript* came about in consequence of an act of graciousness by its author and forms an act of penance by this writer. When, in 1993, I was Visiting Research Professor at Åbo Akademi in Finland and in that connection was invited to Lund to give the keynote address at the Scandinavian Congress for Jewish Studies, Professor Gerhardsson and his wife invited my colleague, Professor Karl-Johan Illman, and me for supper. That was an act of special forbearance since, when *Memory and Manuscript* appeared three decades prior, I reviewed it in an uncomprehending and unappreciative, indeed dismissive way. But, as is his way, Professor Gerhardsson did not allow a difference of opinion to intervene, and he accorded that hospitality for which Lund, uniquely among the ancient universities in Sweden, is well known. When we were chatting on that memorable summer evening, he gently referred to my wrongheaded reading of his book, and I responded that in retrospect I recognize that I acted unfairly and proposed making amends by reprinting the work, with an introduction by me, in a series that I edit for Scholars Press. If a still more suitable imprint presented itself, that would be all to the good. And that – happily – is how matters have turned out.

A. *Why Gerhardsson Was Denied a Hearing*

In the new Preface, Gerhardsson clarifies the point at issue so long ago. He underscores not only what he does say, but also what he does not say. In referring to the Rabbinic materials, as he does amply and ably, he does not claim in these pages to know how the oral traditions of any Judaism were formulated and transmitted before A.D. 70. He simply outlines how the processes of oral tradition are described in one body of writings. He knows that these materials reached closure long after the first century, and he furthermore recognizes, through careful choice of words, that the age to which the Rabbinic writings attest and the age of which they speak rarely, if ever, correspond. He invokes the Rabbinic writings to provide an example, a model, a possibility – not a record of exactly how things were in the time of the Evangelists. He wished to describe, as a free-standing cultural phenomenon, the techniques of oral formulation and transmission now embedded within Rabbinic writings. He stressed that he portrayed techniques, laying no claim to how broadly or narrowly those techniques were utilized among various circles or Judaisms. He is clear about a highly critical, sophisticated approach to the matter. The new Preface only underscores what was stated, in so many words, in the original, as readers of the reprint will judge for themselves.

But readers missed his careful qualifications, his thoughtful word-choices. In giving the work a negative reading on grounds of an uncritical retrojection of techniques attested only much later on into the age of the Evangelists, I followed the lead of my then-teacher, Morton Smith, with whom I wrote my dissertation just before Gerhardsson's book appeared, and whom I extravagantly admired, but not without solid reason, for his powers of penetrating criticism. To understand Smith's influence we have to identify the particular traits that he cultivated. And to place in perspective Smith's reading of Gerhardsson, we have to take a second look at his principal critic, Morton Smith himself.

Like Arthur Darby Nock, but lacking his perspicacity and cultivation, Smith made his career as a ferocious critic of others. Smith thereby surrounded himself with a protective wall of violent invective; what he wished to hide, and for a while succeeded in hiding, was the intellectual vacuum within. Of his entire legacy one book survives today, quite lacking influence but still a model of argument, and a handful of suggestive but insufficient articles. In all Smith wrote three important contributions to scholarship, one a model of argument and analysis though broadly ignored in the field to which it was devoted, another a pseudo-critical but in fact intellectually slovenly and exploitative monograph, and the third an outright fraud. But in the early 1960s, when Gerhardsson's book became a target of opportunity to demonstrate his capacity to seize the jugular, no one could have known the reality. I took as my model his sharp pen and his analytical wit, not understanding that Smith had no constructive capacities and would never on his own write an honest and important book.

The model of argument comes first. His Th.D. dissertation, written at Harvard under the general supervision of Harry A. Wolfson, the greatest academic scholar of Judaism of modern times, on *Palestinian Parties and Politics That Shaped the Old Testament*, in my view remains a model of scholarly argument and insight. Smith completed that work in the late 1950s, and it would mark not the beginning but the apex of his contribution to learning. It was what he could do when a great mind guided him.

What he could do on his own suffers by comparison, being slovenly and poorly formulated. His prior Hebrew University Ph.D. dissertation, *Tannaitic Parallels to the Gospels*, presented at the Hebrew University, where at that time scholarship in the New Testament cannot be ranked as informed, was the work of an autodidact. No professor of New Testament criticized the Gospels part, and the Tannaitic parallels part pursued issues no professor of Rabbinics addressed — thus, self-instruction. As I have demonstrated in vast and accurate detail in *Are There Really Tannaitic Parallels to the Gospels? A Refutation of Morton Smith*,[1] Smith presented very dubious arguments in behalf of remarkably obtuse propositions.

As to the scholarly fraud, who speaks of it any more, or imagines that the work pertains to the study of the New Testament at all? I need not remind readers of this reprint of the scandal of Smith's "sensational discovery" of the Clement fragment, the original of which no one but Smith was permitted to examine. Purporting, in Smith's report, to demonstrate that the historical Jesus was "really" a homosexual magician, the work has not outlived its perpetrator. In the end many were silenced — who wanted to get sued? — but few were gulled.

Beyond these three major scholarly projects — as I said, a self-certified Ph.D. dissertation that no one in the degree-granting university could evaluate, an exemplary work done under the tutelage of a great scholar but lacking all consequence in scholarly discourse, and a forgery and a fraud, beyond occasional articles of uneven quality but occasional brilliance, Smith produced a few potboilers, on the one side, and a corpus of book reviews of a supercilious and misleading character. And one of these — alas! — dismissed and denied a hearing to *Memory and Manuscript*, as Gerhardsson says with complete justification, "in a caricatured and misleading way." And let me plead guilty to Gerhardsson's indictment: "This misrepresentation, and Smith's rather simplistic counter-arguments, were repeated, in even more simplified forms, by countless critics." I was one of these, and I apologize in word and, here, in deed.

1. Atlanta: Scholars Press for South Florida Studies in the History of Judaism, 1993.

B. *The Context*

But why did Smith's basic argument — the book invokes later materials to describe earlier facts, as though the third century Mishnah could tell us about how things were done in the first century — enjoy the hearing that it did? Smith's self-serving rhetoric of authority — "the only scholar of New Testament who knew anything about Rabbinic literature" is how, with his encouragement, he was billed — cannot account for the cordial reception of the criticism. Smith spoke to a receptive audience, looking everywhere for precisely the flaw that he identified here. Why so? The reason is that, at that very moment, in the 1960s, the critical program of academic study of Rabbinic literature for historical purposes was taking shape. As Smith's then-disciple, I heard what, for my part, I wanted to hear. Smith identified in Gerhardsson's work exactly that enormous act of gullibility — believe what the sources say, apply whatever they allege as fact in the setting of which they speak and so let the third century tell us about the first — that characterized the use of those same Rabbinic documents by all prior and then-active scholars of Judaism and the history of the Jews. Gerhardsson's careful qualifications were simply not noticed because, with Smith's ferocious curses ringing in my ears, I heard only what I wished to hear, not what Gerhardsson was saying, not why he was saying it. What I expected to find — because I found it everywhere else — Smith said he had found. And that sufficed for me to find it too.

Specifically, I found Smith's critique self-evidently devastating because it was exactly that critique that I framed of my own work — I believed it all, except what I chose not to believe — that was forcing me to rethink the foundations of the field that then was known as "the history of the Jewish people in the period of the Mishnah and the Talmud," and which I renamed "Judaism in late antiquity," that is, from the period of some writings to the period attested by all sources equally. My *Life of Yohanan ben Zakkai* (1962) would be subjected to scathing dismissal by my *Development of a Legend: Studies on the Traditions Concerning Yohanan ben Zakkai*.[2] My methods in the five-volume History of the Jews in Babylonia would be replaced by those worked out in *The Rabbinic Traditions about the Pharisees before 70*,[3] I-III and *Eliezer ben Hyrcanus: The Tradition and the Man*,[4] I-II.

2. Leiden: Brill, 1970.
3. Leiden: Brill, 1971.
4. Leiden: Brill, 1973.

In challenging the premises of a hundred years of "Talmudic history," which treated as facts whatever the sources alleged, so that if a saying was attributed to a sage, he really made that saying in the time in which he lived, and if a story was told, the event really happened in that way, in that language, I rendered obsolete and historically worthless several generations of work, not to mention that of my own contemporaries and their students. When in 1984, submitting my paper in advance, I told the Israel Historical Society that everything they had printed in their journal *Zion* in this area was null, I got myself disinvited from the conference at which I was to give the keynote address. No wonder, then, that for the first twenty years of my career I could not publish a book in the USA, and until Ephraim E. Urbach died, my books were kept along with pornography under lock and key in the library of the Hebrew University. (Only afterward were they liberated and some of them placed on the shelves of the relevant reading room.)

Gerhardsson then came along as a fine target of opportunity: look what these credulous, uncritical New Testament scholars do with the Rabbinic materials — what they would never, ever do with the Gospels, which is, take them all at face value. But that is not what Gerhardsson was doing, not at all. I missed his point because I was not paying attention; I was listening for the sounds of a different battle altogether. Smith spoke the natural sounds of that day.

C. *Oral Formulation and Oral Transmission: The State of the Debate*

Gerhardsson pointed to Rabbinic literature as a model of how oral tradition goes on. As a matter of fact, work on mnemonics did go forward. My own contribution was to demonstrate two facts. First, we can find clear-cut mnemonic patterns that strongly indicate that the Mishnah was formulated and transmitted orally, and we have extensive knowledge, now, of how that was done. These I summarize in *Oral Tradition in Judaism: The Case of the Mishnah*.[5] They were based on the detailed analysis of my *Rabbinic Traditions about the Pharisees before 70* and *Eliezer ben Hyrcanus*. Further work on the problem of mnemonics in the Mishnah is set forth in *A History of the Mishnaic Law of Purities*, XXI. *The Redaction and*

5. New York: Garland, 1987.

Formulation of the Order of Purities in the Mishnah and Tosefta.[6] Second, by the criterion established in the Mishnah's mnemonics, most of the other Rabbinic documents cannot be represented as having been formulated and transmitted orally. Quite the opposite, if the Mishnah shows what an oral document ought to look like, then no other document — beginning with the Tosefta! — conforms. This is not to say that memorization did not take place. Quite the opposite, individual sayings almost certainly were orally formulated and orally transmitted. Quite what to make of these remains subject to serious debate. One party takes up individual sayings episodically, the other insists that we start with the whole, the document, and work backward into the parts.

The two positions are those of David Weiss Halivni and this writer, respectively. Halivni, in the several volumes of *Meqorot uMesorot* (Sources and Traditions) has treated the free-standing saying as an entity in its own terms, subject to exegesis out of all documentary context. Because Halivni's important work is in Hebrew, I have spent much effort to secure for him a hearing in English. This will be found, inter alia, in the books I edited, *The Formation of the Babylonian Talmud: Studies on the Achievements of Late Nineteenth and Twentieth Century Historical and Literary-Critical Research,*[7] *The Modern Study of the Mishnah,*[8] and *Law as Literature,*[9] co-edited with William Scott Green = *Semeia: An Experimental Journal for Biblical Criticism,* vol. 27.

In my critique of Halivni's thesis, *Sources and Traditions: Types of Composition in the Talmud of Babylonia,*[10] I point to problems I find in his basic theory on the character of Rabbinic literature, constructing a null-hypothesis to test his approach and, alas, sustaining that null-hypothesis. (I regret to note that Halivni has never responded to my criticism or even acknowledged receiving from me the books and articles in which I printed it.)

D. *Gerhardsson's Vindication: The Age beyond Historicism*

In his rather modest way, what Gerhardsson was proposing, and now affirms, is that comparison and contrast need not be synchronic and may

6. Leiden: Brill, 1977.
7. Leiden: Brill, 1970.
8. Leiden: Brill, 1973.
9. Chico: Scholars Press, 1993.
10. Atlanta: Scholars Press for South Florida Studies in the History of Judaism, 1992.

under carefully controlled and justified circumstances take the route of diachrony. He went in search of a model of how oral formulation and oral tradition can have taken place. He did not claim that his model derived from, or attested to, the practice of the period of his principal interest. He sought only knowledge of possible techniques. So he did not mean to say that the way they produced the Mishnah in the late second and early third century tells us how they produced the Gospels a century and a half earlier. Accused of anachronism and an uncritical reading of the sources, Gerhardsson fell victim to the prevailing historicism of the time: what we want to know is what really happened that day. Whatever we invoke to provide information must then tell us what happened at that time (or before), and whatever attests to cultural traits of an indeterminate time and place bears no consequence or relevance. But, as the new Preface underscores, what Gerhardsson proposed to describe was another, distinct, free-standing system: that of Rabbinic Judaism, attested in its own documents.

Apart from malice, which I think animated nearly everything Morton Smith ever wrote or encouraged others to write (or indeed actually wrote for them, under their names), what prevented him and others then close to him from paying attention to the careful language Gerhardsson used? It was the assumption that the only valid scholarship answered the narrowest historical questions: did it really happen? did he really say it? and if so, what kind of history can we make of it all, meaning, what can we say about what really was said and done? Smith honestly believed that he could write *the* life of *the* historical Jesus, which is why the spurious Clement fragment would form the center of the scholarly oeuvre that would occupy nearly his whole active career — that and the *Jesus the Magician* that would convey his (self-)hatred for Jesus and for Christianity — and would therefore bring about an irreparable breach between him and me. Linked by the premises of historicism, he would conduct his campaign in his manner, and I would pursue mine in my way. Mine had to do with the use of the Talmudic and related Rabbinic writings for historical purposes. What I would find in the decades beyond *Memory and Manuscript* leads to a redefinition of what I conceived the Rabbinic corpus to convey: the questions I determined it could legitimately answer.

These are questions of structure and system, leading to the address of questions of comparison and contrast among kindred structures and systems: diachrony, not only synchrony, because what matters is not limited to what happened on a given day. Long perspectives concerning trends, possibilities, alternatives — these would recast the scholarly agenda. What Gerhardsson did wrong was to frame his inquiry in terms of intellectual delicacy such as would be grasped only a quarter-century later, and then by only some of his critics. He transcended hard-core positivism and moved onward to the comparison and contrast of structures (in this case, bodies of writing allegedly resting upon oral formulation and oral trans-mission), so violating the norms of that positivism embodied, in his way, in Smith, and, in my way, in the trajectory of work then underway.

E. *Paradigmatic versus Historical Thinking*

To understand what is at stake, let me place Gerhardsson's work in a much larger framework, namely, the character of the evidence on which we work when we study formative Christianity and Judaism. I speak of the movement of which he was a precursor from the study of history syn-chronically to the study of models or paradigms diachronically (in his case, models of oral tradition). And that movement rests upon the recog-nition that, to begin with, the documents on which we work never were read in a hard-core positivist historicist setting. *They represent a different culture from the one that historicism has fabricated for them.* It must follow that the questions we frame, and the manner in which we propose to in-vestigate them, must prove congruent with the character of the docu-ments on which we work. To the character of the evidence, what Yohanan ben Zakkai really said to Vespasian, or what the historical Jesus really, ac-tually enunciated, among the many statements attributed to him, proves monumentally irrelevant. And to ask questions of history to documents of an other-than-historical character closes off access to the character of those very documents.

Let me spell out what I conceive to be the character of the Rabbinic documents, which will then justify the judgment just set forth. All scholar-ship on the Hebrew Scriptures concurs that ancient Israel set forth its the-ology through the media of historical narrative and thought. The Hebrew Scriptures set forth Israel's life as history, with a beginning, middle, and end; a purpose and a coherence; a teleological system. All accounts agree that the Scriptures distinguished past from present, present from future, and composed a sustained narrative, made up of one-time, irreversible events. In Scripture's historical portrait, Israel's present condition ap-pealed for explanation to Israel's past, perceived as a coherent sequence of weighty events, each unique, all formed into a great chain of meaning. But that is not how for most of the history of Western civilization the Hebrew Scriptures have been read by Judaism and Christianity. The idea of history, with its rigid distinction between past and present and its careful sifting of connections from the one to the other, came quite late onto the scene of intellectual life. Both Judaism and Christianity for most of their histories have read the Hebrew Scriptures in an other-than-historical framework. They found in Scripture's words paradigms of an enduring present, by which all things must take their measure; they possessed no conception whatsoever of the pastness of the past.

Rabbinic Judaism formulated out of Scripture not only rules validated by appeal to arguments resting on facts recorded therein, such as Leviticus Rabbah yields. Rabbinic Judaism, like nascent Christianity, also invented an entirely new way to think about times past, to tell time, and to keep all time, past, present, and future, within a single framework. For that purpose, a model was constructed consisting of selected events held to form a pattern that imposes order and meaning on the chaos of what happens, whether past or present or future. Time measured in this paradigmatic manner is time formulated by a free-standing, (incidentally) atemporal model, not appealing to the course of the sun and moon, nor concerned with the metaphor of human life and its cyclicality. Not only so, but the paradigm obliterates distinctions between past, present, and future, between here and now and then and there. The past participates in the present, the present recapitulates the past, and the future finds itself determined, predetermined really, within the same free-standing structure comprised by God's way of telling time. I explain these matters in detail in *The Presence of the Past, the Pastness of the Present: History, Time, and Paradigm in Rabbinic Judaism.*[11]

Theological paradigms of time are set forth by neither nature on its own (by definition) nor natural history (what happens on its own here on earth); by neither the cosmos (sun and moon) nor the natural history of humanity (the life cycle and analogies drawn therefrom). Nature's time by itself is contingent, forming a chapter within the rhythms of Israel's holy life. But in the setting of Judaism and Christianity, paradigms are set forth in revelation, encompassing and imposing structure upon nature's time, utterly ignoring the historical measurement of sequential time alto-

11. Bethesda: CDL Press, 1996.

gether; they explain the Creator's sense of order and regularity, which is neither imposed upon, nor derived from, nature's time, a subordinated consideration, as I just said, not to be discovered through history's time. That is why to paradigmatic time, history is wildly incongruous, and considerations of linearity, temporality, and historical order beyond all comprehension. God has set forth the paradigms that measure time by indicators of an other-than-natural character: supernatural time, which of course is beyond all conception of time. But, as we shall see, God has created nature, and Israel will tell time through both media of divine engagement: nature and the paradigms of Israel's own life.

Accordingly, a paradigm forms a way of keeping time that invokes its own differentiating indicators, its own signifiers, not so much counterparts to the indicators of nature's time as primary measures imposed upon those of nature. To the eternal present of time in Judaism and Christianity, nature's time makes its contribution, but only on the terms of the paradigm. That is to say, nature defines time as that span which is marked off by one spell of night and day; or by one sequence of positions and phases of the moon; or by one cycle of the sun around the earth (in the pre-Copernican paradigm). History further defines nature's time by marking a solar year by reference to an important human event, for example, a reign, a battle, or a building. So history's time intersects with, and is superimposed upon, nature's time. Cyclical time forms a modification of history's time, appealing for its divisions of the aggregates of time to the analogy, in human life, to nature's time: the natural sequence of events in a human life viewed as a counterpart to the natural sequence of events in solar and lunar time.

So much for a theological formulation of matters. What, in this-worldly language, is to be said about the same conception? Paradigmatic thinking constitutes a mode of argument about the meaning of events, about the formation of the social order. Appealing to the pattern, parties to a debate, for instance about the meaning of an event or the interpretation of a social fact, frame their arguments within the limits of the pattern: that event corresponds to this component of the paradigm shared among all parties to the debate. Paradigms derive from human invention and human imagination, imposed on nature and on history alike. Nature is absorbed, history recast, through time paradigmatic; that is, time invented, not time discovered; time defined for a purpose determined by humanity (the social order, the faithful, for instance), time not discovered but determined and predetermined, time that is not natural or formed in correspondence to nature, or imposed upon nature at specified intersections; but time that is defined completely in terms of the prior pattern or the determined paradigm or fabricated model itself: time wholly invented for the purposes of the social order that invents and recognizes time.

Paradigmatic thinking presents a mode of making connections and drawing conclusions and is captured in its essence by two statements of Augustine:

> We live only in the present, but this present has several dimensions: the present of past things, the present of present things, and the present of future things. . . .
>
> Your years are like a single day . . . and this today does not give way to a tomorrow, any more than it follows a yesterday. Your today is Eternity. . . .

Augustine, *Confessions* 10:13

I cannot imagine a more accurate précis of sages' conception of time: the past is ever present, the present takes place on the same plane of existence as the past, the whole forming an eternal paradigm, altogether beyond time. For our sages of blessed memory, the Torah, the written part of the Torah in particular, defined a set of paradigms that served without regard to circumstance, context, or, for that matter, dimension and scale of happening. A very small number of models emerged from Scripture, captured in the sets (1) Eden and Adam, (2) Sinai and the Torah, (3) the land and Israel, and (4) the Temple and its building, destruction, and rebuilding.

What, exactly, I mean by "models" requires explanation. In the present context, by "model" I mean that which is exemplary and enduring, thus taking place time and again, hither and yon: not a singular, one-time event but a model by which diverse happenings may be understood; not a one-time, particular person but an example, for instance, of virtue. Such a "model" is comprised by Eden and the Fall, the passage through the Sea and Sinai, the figure of Abraham or of Jacob. The patriarchs then serve as models for the people Israel, and the tribal progenitors (as at Genesis 49 and Deuteronomy 33) constitute the patterns for those that followed. To give a single concrete case, the destruction of the first Temple and the return to Zion some generations later forms not a one-time event but a model of what happens when Israel sins, suffers, atones, and is forgiven; that model then is invoked to organize the data of the destruction of the Second Temple and will further define the interpretive framework for thinking about later catastrophes as well.

Now what is interesting is that the models of explanation, defining an enduring, ahistorical mode of thinking, may identify persons or happenings or locations as paradigmatic. Formed into a list, a sequence of such models or paradigms may mix types of things that we should keep separate, which for us would not fit on the same list; such a list may cover persons, historical events, religious obligations, holy days, and a variety of practices and beliefs. Here is such a list of models or paradigms:

V:i.1. A. "I am very dark, but comely, [O daughters of Jerusalem, like the tents of Kedar, like the curtains of Solomon]" (Song 1:5):

B. "I am dark" in my deeds.

C. "But comely" in the deeds of my forebears.

2. A. "I am very dark, but comely":

B. Said the Community of Israel, "'I am dark' in my view, 'but comely' before my Creator."

C. For it is written, "Are you not as the children of the Ethiopians to Me, O children of Israel? says the Lord" (Amos 9:7):

D. "as the children of the Ethiopians" — in your sight.

E. But "to Me, O children of Israel, says the Lord."

3. A. Another interpretation of the verse, "I am very dark": in Egypt.

B. "but comely": in Egypt.

C. "I am very dark" in Egypt: "But they rebelled against me and would not hearken to me" (Ezek. 20:8).

D. "but comely" in Egypt: with the blood of the Passover offering and circumcision, "And when I passed by you and saw you wallowing in your blood, I said to you, In your blood live" (Ezek. 16:6) — in the blood of the Passover.

E. "I said to you, In your blood live" (Ezek. 16:6) — in the blood of the circumcision.

4. A. Another interpretation of the verse, "I am very dark": at the Sea, "They were rebellious at the sea, even the Red Sea" (Ps. 106:7).

B. "but comely": at the Sea, "This is my God, and I will be comely for him" (Exod. 15:2).

5. A. "I am very dark": at Marah, "And the people murmured against Moses, saying, What shall we drink" (Exod. 15:24).

B. "but comely": at Marah, "And he cried to the Lord, and the Lord showed him a tree, and he cast it into the waters and the waters were made sweet" (Exod. 15:25).

6. A. "I am very dark": at Rephidim, "And the name of the place was called Massah and Meribah" (Exod. 17:7).

B. "but comely": at Rephidim, "And Moses built an altar and called it by the name 'the Lord is my banner'" (Exod. 17:15).

7. A. "I am very dark": at Horeb, "And they made a calf at Horeb" (Ps. 106:19).

B. "but comely": at Horeb, "And they said, All that the Lord has spoken we will do and obey" (Exod. 24:7).

8. A. "I am very dark": in the wilderness, "How often did they rebel against him in the wilderness?" (Ps. 78:40).

B. "but comely": in the wilderness at the setting up of the tabernacle, "And on the day that the tabernacle was set up" (Num. 9:15).

9. A. "I am very dark": in the deed of the spies, "And they spread an evil report of the land" (Num. 13:32).

B. "but comely": in the deed of Joshua and Caleb, "Save for Caleb, the son of Jephunneh the Kenizzite" (Num. 32:12).

10. A. "I am very dark": at Shittim, "And Israel abode at Shittim, and the people began to commit harlotry with the daughters of Moab" (Num. 25:1).

B. "but comely": at Shittim, "Then arose Phinehas and wrought judgment" (Ps. 106:30).

11. A. "I am very dark": through Achan, "But the children of Israel committed a trespass concerning the devoted thing" (Josh. 7:1).

B. "but comely": through Joshua, "And Joshua said to Achan, My son, give I pray you glory" (Josh. 7:19).

12. A. "I am very dark": through the kings of Israel.

B. "but comely": through the kings of Judah.

C. If with my dark ones that I had, it was such that "I am comely," all the more so with my prophets.

V:ii.5. A. As to the verse, "I am very dark, but comely," R. Levi b.
R. Haita gave three interpretations:

B. "'I am very dark': all the days of the week.

C. "'but comely': on the Sabbath.

D. "'I am very dark': all the days of the year.

E. "'but comely': on the Day of Atonement.

F. "'I am very dark': among the Ten Tribes.

G. "'but comely': in the tribe of Judah and Benjamin.

H. "'I am very dark': in this world.

I. "'but comely': in the world to come."

Song of Songs Rabbah to Song 1:5

The formal traits of this composite prove blatant. The base-verse is parsed in three clauses, and the same parsing recurs throughout. Then in each sequence, a different set of meanings is imputed: deeds, deeds of forebears; my view, my Creator's view; rebellion in Egypt, obedience in Egypt; rebellion at the Sea, obedience at the Sea; and so on. The items that are listed constitute models, by themselves bearing no meaning that on its own is necessarily cogent to the other items on the same list. *But by effecting a pattern over and over again, the various items are made to deliver a single message: the contrast of rebellion and obedience.* Do the several components bear that message? Horeb, Egypt, the Sea, the spies, and the days of the week and the Sabbath – none of these on its own bears the meaning that, all together, they convey. Is then some other message delivered by the listed items, Horeb, Egypt, and the Sea? I see none. To the contrary, the words Horeb, Egypt, and the Sea, by themselves stand for nothing that the composite contains; the words in combination with other words – again, Horeb, Egypt, and the Sea – likewise bear no clear sense. It is the joining of two sets of words, the components of the base-verse, "I am dark" "but comely," together with the sequence Horeb, Egypt, and the Sea, that contains the message. The combination is Horeb, Egypt, and the Sea; that produces no symbolic speech. The recombination is Horeb, Egypt, and the Sea with "I am dark" "but comely" – and that produces a powerful and well-crafted message. Why do I classify the delivery of the message as symbolic discourse? Because at no point is the message made explicit, propositionally let alone syllogistically. The message is contained within the recombinant contrasts; it is fully exposed through the symbols that gain meaning in the recombination and contrast; and the message then is conveyed wholly through the manipulation of otherwise opaque words: hence, symbols in verbal form.

These paradigms served severally and jointly, for example, Eden and Adam on its own but also superimposed upon the Land and Israel; Sinai and the Torah on its own but also superimposed upon the Land and Israel; and, of course, the Temple, embodying natural creation and its intersection with national and social history, could stand entirely on its own or be superimposed upon any and all of the other paradigms. In many ways, then, we have the symbolic equivalent of a set of two-, three-, or even four-dimensional grids. A given pattern forms a grid on its own, one set of lines being set forth in terms of, for example, Eden, timeless perfection, in contrast to the other set of lines, Adam, temporal disobedience; but upon that grid, a comparable grid can be superimposed, the Land and Israel being an obvious one; and upon the two, yet a third and fourth, Sinai and Torah, the Temple and the confluence of nature and history.

By reference to these grids, severally or jointly, the critical issues of existence, whether historical or contemporary, played themselves out in the system and structure of Rabbinic Judaism. In particular, we may identify four models by which, out of happenings of various sorts, consequential or meaningful events would be selected, and by reference to which these selected events would be shown connected ("meaningful") and explicable in terms of that available paradigmatic logic that governed both the making of connections and the drawing of conclusions.

Paradigmatic thinking is not static, making lists of things that together teach lessons, but dynamic. That is to say, it is a medium for making sense of what happens, identifying consequential events and interpreting their meaning, and a mode of pointing out of the present toward what is going to happen. Once, after all, we know to what pattern a given event adheres, we can also say what will happen next, in line with the familiar lines that the pattern adumbrates. To understand paradigmatic thinking, we have then to address the kinds of problems it chooses to solve, the tasks it undertakes.

Let me then specify some particular types of paradigms and the sort of events that they encompass. First is the paradigm of Israel's past, present, and future (= "History" in the counterpart structure of historical thinking): how shall we organize happenings into events? On the largest scale the question concerns the division into periods of not sequences but mere sets of happenings. Periodization involves explanation, of course, since even in a paradigmatic structure, once matters are set forth as periods, then an element of sequence is admitted into the processes of description and therefore analysis and explanation.

Second and equally critical is the paradigm that organizes events concerning Israel and its experience among the nations. Moving from large aggregates, bordering on abstraction, we turn to the very concrete question of how Israel relates to the rest of the world. This involves explaining not what happened this morning in particular, but what always happens, that is, defining the structure of Israel's life in the politics of this world, explaining the order of things in both the social, political structure of the world and the sequence of actions that may occur and recur over time (the difference, paradigmatically, hardly matters). Paradigmatic thinking, no less than historical, explains matters; but the explanation derives from the character of the pattern which governs historical explanation rather than the order of events. Connections then drawn between one thing and something else serve to define a paradigm, rather than to convey a temporal explanation based on sequences – first this, then that, therefore this explains why that happened. The paradigm bears a different explanation altogether, one that derives from its principle of selection, and therefore the kinds of explanations paradigmatic thinking sets forth, expressed through its principles of selection in making connections and drawing conclusions, will demand rich instantiation.

This brings us to how paradigmatic thinking moves from the past that is present to the future that – in the theory at hand – is going to recapitulate past and present. The single most important task of paradigmatic thinking about events pertains to the analysis of what happens in line with what has happened so as to delineate the future history of Israel. Just as studying the past is supposed to explain the present and point to the future, so paradigmatic thinking bears the same responsibility. That concerns not so much explaining the present as permitting informed speculation about what will happen in the future. And that speculation will appeal to those principles of order, structure, and explanation that the paradigm sets forth to begin with. So future history in historical thinking and writing projects out of past and present a trajectory over time to come, and future history in paradigmatic thinking forms projects along other lines altogether.

The purpose of paradigmatic thinking, as much as historical, points toward the future. History is important to explain the present as well as to help peer into the future; and paradigms serve precisely the same purpose. The choice between the one model and the other, then, rests upon which appeals to the more authentic data. In that respect Scripture, treated as paradigm, met no competition in linear history, and it was paradigmatic, not historical, thinking that proved compelling for a thousand years or more. The future history of Israel is written in Scripture, and what happened in the beginning is what is going to happen at the end of time. That sense of order and balance prevailed. It comes to expression in a variety of passages, of which a severely truncated selection will have to suffice:

2. A. Said R. Abin, "Just as [Israel's history] began with the encounter with four kingdoms, so [Israel's history] will conclude with the encounter with the four kingdoms.

B. " 'Chedorlaomer, king of Elam, Tidal, king of Goiim, Amraphel, king of Shinar, and Arioch, king of Ellasar, four kings against five' " (Gen. 14:9).

C. "So [Israel's history] will conclude with the encounter with the four kingdoms: the kingdom of Babylonia, the kingdom of Medea, the kingdom of Greece, and the kingdom of Edom."

Genesis Rabbah XLII:II.

Another pattern serves as well, resting as it does on the foundations of the former. It is the familiar one that appeals to the deeds of the founders. The lives of the patriarchs stand for the history of Israel; the deeds of the patriarchs cover the future historical periods in Israel's destiny.

This survey of the way in which paradigmatic thinking comes to expression now permits a more general statement of matters. As a medium of organizing and accounting for experience, history — the linear narrative of singular events intended to explain how things got to their present state and therefore why — does not enjoy the status of a given. Nor does historical thinking concerning the social order self-evidently lay claim to plausibility. It is one possibility among many. Historical thinking — sequential narrative of one-time events — presupposes order, linearity, distinction between time past and time present, and teleology, among data that do not self-evidently sustain such presuppositions. Questions of chaos intervene; the very possibility of historical narrative meets a challenge in the diversity of story lines, the complexity of events, the bias of the principle of selection of what is eventful, of historical interest, among a broad choice of happenings: why this, not that. Narrative history first posits a gap between past and present, but then bridges the gap; why not entertain the possibility that there is none to begin with? These and similar considerations invite a different way of thinking about how things have been and now are, a different tense structure altogether.

A way of thinking about the experience of humanity, whether past or contemporary, that makes other distinctions than the historical ones between past and present and that eschews linear narrative and so takes account of the chaos that ultimately prevails, now competes with historical thinking. Paradigmatic thinking, a different medium for organizing and explaining things that happen, deals with the same data that occupy historical thinking, and that is why when we refer to paradigmatic thinking, the word "history" gains its quotation marks: it is not a datum of thought, merely a choice; contradicting to its core the character of paradigmatic thinking, the category then joins its opposite, paradigm, only by forming the oxymoron before us: paradigmatic thinking about "history."

The category "history," as conventionally defined and as further realized in the Authorized History of Scripture, Genesis through Kings, therefore forms merely one way of addressing the past in order to find sense and meaning therein. Clearly, with its emphasis on linear, irreversible events and the division between past and present, history's is not the way taken by Rabbinic Judaism in organizing Israel's experience: selecting what matters and explaining that. We know that that is the fact because none of the indicators of historical writing and thinking comes to the surface in the documents under study. The very opposite traits predominate. Rabbinic literature contains no sustained historical or biographical narrative, only anecdotes, makes no distinction between past and present but melds them. But that writing, resting as it does on the Hebrew Scriptures, then presents a paradox. A set of writings of a one-sidedly historical character, the Hebrew Scripture deriving from ancient Israel finds itself expounded in an utterly ahistorical way by its heirs, both Judaic and Christian.

What Scripture ("written Torah," "Old Testament") yields for Rabbinic Judaism is not one-time events, arranged in sequence to dictate meaning, but models or patterns of conduct and consequence. These models are defined by the written Torah or the Old Testament (read in light of the perspective of the Oral Torah or the New Testament). No component of the paradigm we shall consider emerges from other than the selected experience set forth by Scripture. But the paradigms are at the same time pertinent without regard to considerations of scale and formulated without interest in matters of singular context. Forthrightly selective — this matters, that is ignored — the principle of selection is not framed in terms of sequence; order of a different sort is found.

The models or paradigms that are so discerned then pertain not to one time alone — past time — but to all times equally — past, present and future. Then "time" no longer forms an organizing category of understanding and interpretation. The spells marked out by moon and sun and fixed stars bear meaning, to be sure. But that meaning has no bearing upon the designation of one year as past, another as present. The meaning imputed to the lunar and solar marking of time derives from the cult, on the one side, and the calendar of holy time, on the other: seven solar days, a Sabbath; a lunar cycle, a new month to be celebrated, the first new moon after the vernal equinox, the Passover, and after the autumnal, Tabernacles. Rabbinic Judaism tells time the way nature does and only in that way; events in Rabbinic Judaism deemed worth recording in time take place the way events in nature do. What accounts for the difference between history's time and paradigmatic time as set forth here is a conception of time quite different from the definition of historical time that operates in Scripture: the confluence of nature's time and history's way of telling time: two distinct chronographies brought together, the human one then imposed upon the natural one.

Since sages did not see themselves as removed in time and space from the generative events to which they referred the experience of the here and now, they also had no need to make the past contemporary. They neither relived nor transformed one-time historical events, for they found another way to overcome the barrier of chronological separation. Specifically, if history began when the gap between present and past shaped consciousness, then we naturally ask ourselves whether the point at which historical modes of thought concluded and a different mode of thought took over produced an opposite consciousness from the historical one: not cycle but paradigm. For, it seems to me clear, the premise that time and space separated our sages of the Rabbinic writings from the great events of the past simply did not win attention. The opposite premise defined matters: barriers of space and time in no way separated sages from great events, the great events of the past enduring for all time. How then are we to account for this remarkably different way of encounter, experience, and, consequently, explanation? The answer has already been adumbrated.

Sages assembled in the documents of Rabbinic Judaism, from the Mishnah forward, all recognized the destruction of the Second Temple and all took for granted that that event was to be understood by reference to the model of the destruction of the first. For our sages of blessed memory, the destruction of the Temple in A.D. 70 did not mark a break with the past, such as it had for their predecessors some five hundred years earlier, but rather a recapitulation of the past. Paradigmatic thinking then began in that very event that precipitated thought about history to begin with, the end of the old order. But paradigm replaced history because what had taken place the first time as unique and unprecedented took place the second time in precisely the same pattern and therefore formed of an episode a series. Paradigmatic thinking replaced historical when history as an account of one-time, irreversible, unique events, arranged in linear sequence and pointing toward a teleological conclusion, lost all plausibility. If the first time around, history — with the past marked off from the present, events arranged in linear sequence, narrative of a sustained character serving as the medium of thought — provided the medium for making sense of matters, then the second time around, history lost all currency.

The real choice facing our sages was not linear history over against paradigmatic thinking, but rather paradigm over against cycle. For the conclusion to be drawn from the destruction of the Temple a second time, once history, its premises disallowed, yielded no explanation, can have taken the form of a theory of the cyclicality of events. As nature yielded spring, summer, fall, and winter, so the events of humanity or of Israel in particular can have been asked to conform to a cyclical pattern, in line, for example, with Qohelet's view that what has been is what will be. But our sages obviously did not take that position at all.

They rejected cyclicality in favor of a different ordering of events altogether. They did not believe the Temple would be rebuilt and destroyed again, rebuilt and destroyed, and so on into endless time. They stated the very opposite: the Temple would be rebuilt but never against destroyed. And that represented a view of the second destruction that rejected cyclicality altogether. Sages instead opted for patterns of history and against cycles because they retained that notion for the specific and concrete meaning of events that characterized Scripture's history, even while rejecting the historicism of Scripture. What they maintained, as we have seen, is that a pattern governed, and the pattern was not a cyclical one. Here, Scripture itself imposed its structures, its order, its system — its paradigm. And the Official History left no room for the conception of cyclicality. If matters do not repeat themselves but do conform to a pattern, then the pattern itself must be identified.

Paradigmatic thinking formed the alternative to cyclical thinking because Scripture, its history subverted, nonetheless defined how matters were to be understood. Viewed whole, the Official History indeed defined the paradigm of Israel's existence, formed out of the components of Eden and the Land, Adam and Israel, Sinai, then given movement through Israel's responsibility to the covenant and Israel's adherence to, or violation, of God's will, fully exposed in the Torah that marked the covenant of Sinai. Scripture laid matters out, and our sages then drew conclusions from that layout that conformed to their experience. So the second destruction precipitated thinking about paradigms of Israel's life such as came to full exposure in the thinking behind the Midrash-compilations we have surveyed. The episode made into a series, sages' paradigmatic thinking asked of Scripture different questions from the historical ones of 586 because our sages brought to Scripture different premises, and drew from Scripture different conclusions. But in point of fact, not a single paradigm set forth by sages can be distinguished in any important component from the counterpart in Scripture, not Eden and Adam in comparison to the land of Israel and Israel, and not the tale of Israel's experience in the spinning out of the tension between the word of God and the will of Israel.

Predictably, therefore, the only history our sages would deem worth narrating — and not in sustained narrative even then — is the story of the Temple cult through days and months and years, and the history of the Temple and its priesthood and administration through time and into eternity. We now fully understand that fact. It is because, to begin with, the very conception of paradigmatic thinking as against the historical kind took shape in deep reflection on the meaning of events: what happened before has happened again — to the Temple. Ways of telling time before give way, history's premises having lost plausibility here as much as elsewhere. Now Israel will tell time in nature's way, shaping history solely in response to what happens in the cult and to the Temple. That is to say, the

Temple cult will tell time by appeal to the phases of the moon, carefully calibrated to remain within the rhythm of the solar year. There is no other history because, to begin with, there is no history.

Seeing the Rabbinic literature and the Gospels alike as models of phenomena, we then take the sources for what they are and value them for what they contain and exemplify. Gerhardsson has asked us to examine the Rabbinic evidence as a model of *how* oral formulation and oral transmission of what was initially, originally, oral tradition can have taken place. That approach — congruent with the sources, as I have explained, to the sources — simply treats each set of sources as a free-standing portrait of a system that sets upon its own foundations an example, a possibility, an occasion for comparison and contrast. What can be wrong with that? To see what is right, read this book.

MEMORY AND MANUSCRIPT

Contents

8

PART TWO

The delivery of the gospel tradition in early Christianity

Introduction

A PARTICULARLY fruitful epoch for gospel research dawned in 1919, when Martin DIBELIUS published his little book *Die Formgeschichte des Evangeliums*, followed, two years later, by Rudolf BULTMANN's comprehensive work *Die Geschichte der synoptischen Tradition*.[1] These represented a bold and decisive step forward into that hitherto little-known region dividing the written Gospels from the Master from Nazareth. Their aim was to clarify the origins and first period of development of the gospel *tradition*; the method followed was to place the gospel material side by side with the life and the needs of the young Church in a fresh way, and to parallel the origins of the gospel tradition and the growth of the Church. By using this method, it was possible to show, more clearly than ever before, how conditions in the young Church throw a good deal of light on the problem of the origins of the gospel material. On the other hand, the form and contents of the gospel material reveal much of interest in the situation and problems of the young Church. The pioneer works of the form-critical school reported important results; later publications were to register further advances.

These are well-known facts. It is also a well-known fact that the two pioneer form-critics made use of somewhat different methods in their respective works. DIBELIUS, with his "constructive method", proceeds from the situation in the young Church to the gospel material; BULTMANN, in his "analytical method", follows the opposite path. The difference is however slight. Both scholars are conscious that they are working in a circle. "Conclusions must be drawn from the forms of the literary tradition concerning the motives of the common life, and those forms are to be understood from the common life", writes BULTMANN, and goes on to say that, just as DIBELIUS must have made a number of observations on the forms of the tradition before obtaining a clear impression of the motives of the life of the community, so his (BULTMANN's) analysis could not be made without having a picture—albeit a provisional picture—of the early Christian fellowship and its history.[2]

---

[1] The third pioneer work was K. L. SCHMIDT, *Der Ramen der Geschichte Jesu* (1919).

[2] "Aus den Formen der literarischen Überlieferung soll auf die Motive des

As BULTMANN himself points out, a circle of this kind is unavoidable in all historical research, but the inevitable dangers must be recognized and limited. It seems however as though the pioneer form-critics and their nearest disciples have been insufficiently aware of these dangers. It has in fact proved to be the case that they—and particularly the school of BULTMANN—have either ignored or rejected most of the criticism directed at their solution of these extensive problems. We can verify this statement by referring to the new editions which appeared in 1933 and 1931 respectively, and in particular to BULTMANN's supplementary volume to his third edition of 1958, as well as to the course of the debate as a whole.[1]

There is no doubt that this insensitivity to criticism is dependent in no small measure on this fact of their arguing in a circle. The form-critics build their own house, and consolidate their own tradition. It is easy to defend a tradition, if, when discussing the situation of the early Church, one be allowed to argue from one's own concept of the character of the gospel material, and to meet theories on the origins of the gospel material from one's own notion of the situation in the early Church. It is perhaps a little unjust to caricature the position of the most typical representatives of the form-critical school in this way, but the caricature is not without justification. It has in point of fact been remarked that form-criticism has begun to stagnate—an observation made by *inter alia* CONZELMANN[2] and IBER.[3]

Gemeinschaftslebens zurückgeschlossen werden, und aus dem Gemeinschaftsleben heraus sollen die Formen verständlich gemacht werden." — "Sowenig Dibelius eine deutliche Vorstellung von den Motiven des Gemeindelebens gewonnen hat, ohne dass er schon formale Beobachtungen gemacht hätte, so sehr schwebt mir bei meinen Analysen ein freilich noch vorläufiges Bild von der urchristlichen Gemeinde und ihrer Geschichte vor, das seine Bestimmtheit und Gliederung eben durch die Untersuchung gewinnen soll", *Geschichte* (4th ed. 1958), pp. 5 f.; cf. DIBELIUS, *Formgeschichte* (3rd ed. 1959), pp. 8 f.

[1] It is hardly necessary in this connection to give a summary of literature on the debate on form-criticism. The greater part of the literature is listed in J. SCHNIE-WIND, Zur Synoptiker-Exegese, in *Theol. Rundschau* N.F. 2 (1930), pp. 129 ff., and G. IBER, Zur Formgeschichte der Evangelien, *ibid.* 24 (1957–58), pp. 283 ff. In these works is also given a thorough presentation of the most important problems dealt with by the form-critical debate 1919–57.

[2] Review of M. DIBELIUS, Botschaft und Geschichte, in *Verkündigung und Forschung* (1957), pp. 151 f.

[3] *Op. cit.*, p. 285. In his *Nachtrag* to the 3rd edition of DIBELIUS, *Formgeschichte*, pp. 302 ff., IBER stresses the importance of the continuation of the form-critical

There is thus a fundamental connection between the two views—of the situation in the young Church and the origins of the gospel tradition. On these two main questions the attitude of DIBELIUS and BULTMANN was clear as early as 1920, and has altered little in subsequent editions of their works. A great deal has however happened since 1920 in the ranks of those scholars who have been less fast bound to the methods of the form-critics. There is a general unwillingness in these circles to accept the view of Jesus and early Christianity given by DIBELIUS and BULTMANN in 1920. It is therefore difficult—or at least it ought to be difficult—to accept the pioneer form-critics' solution of the problem of the origins of the gospel tradition.

We must however be content with some brief remarks on critical points. First, the form-critics' view of early Christian eschatology. DIBELIUS often argues that the early Church, in its first phase, consisted of men with an intensive faith in the future ("zukunftgläubige Männer"), who awaited an early consummation of all things and organized their whole lives accordingly.[1] It is not possible today to maintain that the history of the early Church is the history of the way in which a tense and powerful expectation of an imminent parousia gradually weakened, to be replaced by faith in a second coming in the remote future. It was more complicated than that. It is obvious that in the young Church— as well as outside its boundaries—there were different groups having somewhat different ways of thought, and that the intensity with which the parousia was expected also varied according to the situation in different areas and at different times. For example, there can be little doubt that it must have been considerably stronger in Palestine during the troubled sixties, with their "wars and rumours of wars", than during the previous decade.[2]

Another critical point—and undoubtedly the most central—is the picture of Jesus. When DIBELIUS and BULTMANN sketched their view of the origins of the gospel tradition they had a definite idea about the identity and the ministry of Jesus of Nazareth. (We need not go into the differences between their respective views.)[3] Since that time, intensive

debate: even such basic problems as the *Sitz im Leben* of the gospel material are still unsolved.

[1] E.g. *Formgeschichte*, pp. 10, 12, 28, 241. This point of view is not accorded the same importance by BULTMANN.

[2] On the eschatological problem, see e.g. O. CULLMANN, Parusieverzögerung und Urchristentum, in *Theol. Literaturzeit.* 83 (1958), col. 1 ff.

[3] See R. BULTMANN, *Jesus* (1929), M. DIBELIUS, *Jesus* (1939).

study has aimed at deciding, for example, how Jesus conceived of his own nature, the kind of figure he wished to be, and what he said and did. Great strides forward have been made here. To be sure, no consensus of opinion has been reached—on this question there are practically as many views as there are N.T. scholars[1]—but so much is clear: only the one who has a conception of Jesus *similar* to that produced by DIBELIUS and BULTMANN can accept their view of the origins of the gospel tradition without reservations.

The same applies to the self-estimation of the young Church, and to its actual organization and offices. DIBELIUS and BULTMANN consider the Church to have been some kind of "pneumatic" democracy, in which spiritual material *("geistiges Gut")* was produced from among an anonymous folk-mass and stabilized in certain sociologically determined styles and forms. Since this theory was first advanced, however, an extremely important reorientation has taken place, particularly through the contributions of K. L. SCHMIDT[2] and OLOF LINTON.[3] We have good reason for believing that the young Church in all its "enthusiasm" was both ordered and organized, and that it recognized some men—and not others—as doctrinal authorities. It is therefore hardly realistic today to maintain that "the twelve" and other leading doctrinal authorities, played little or no part in the shaping of the tradition about Christ.

A related question is that of the type and extent of the education received by Jesus, "the twelve" and the other leaders and teachers in the earliest Church. For DIBELIUS the early Church as a whole was made up of the non-literary, "unliterarische Männer".[4] BULTMANN, as usual, has a feeling for the multiple and for nuances; he even puts the question: "Has this prophet (Jesus) perhaps proceeded from the circle of the scribes?"[5] However, he does not credit the Apostles with having had any extensive learning. According to some sayings in the N.T. Jesus received no teaching (μὴ μεμαθηκώς), John 7.15, and the Apostles were unlearned men from among the people (ἄνθρωποι ἀγράμματοι καὶ ἰδιῶται),

---

[1] See the picture of different attitudes, given in the symposium *Der historische Jesus und der kerygmatische Christus* (1960).

[2] Die Kirche des Urchristentums, in *Festgabe für* A. DEISSMANN (1927), pp. 259 ff., and IDEM, ἐκκλησία, in *Theol. Wörterb.*, ed. G. KITTEL, III (1938), pp. 502 ff.

[3] *Das Problem der Urkirche in der neueren Forschung* (1932, reprinted 1957). See also N. A. DAHL, *Das Volk Gottes* (1941).

[4] See e.g. *Formgeschichte*, pp. 1 ff.

[5] *Jesus*, pp. 55 ff.; cf. *Geschichte*, p. 52.

Acts 4.13. But critical research can hardly build too much on these sayings, which are *distinctly dogmatic*.[1] Critical examination of the material preserved from Jesus and the early Christian doctrinal authorities leads our thoughts in another direction.[2] This material is certainly not "literary"; but it is "learned":[3] stamped to no small degree by that type of learning which was to be found in that milieu to which Jesus and his disciples belonged. To ascribe this "learned" character in its entirety to later teachers and traditionists—making those men who were of the highest repute in early Christianity into ignorant, romantic and shadowy figures, lacking any rationally understandable competence—is scarcely to work with that hypothesis which gives the easiest explanation of an obscure phenomenon.

This brings us to another critical point: the concept of tradition.[4] It is a remarkable fact that neither of the two pioneer works on the form-criticism of the gospel tradition makes any attempt to define the concept of tradition in early Christianity.[5] It is nevertheless a fact that Jesus exercised his ministry, and the early Church developed, in a milieu in which tradition was known and recognized for what it was. "Tradition", for different groups both in Judaism and in the Hellenistic world, was a concept, a deliberate concept, an important concept.[6] The same is true in early Christianity. As early as the oldest preserved documents of the young Church, the epistles of Paul, of which the majority were written in the fifties, we see that early Christianity had a tradition (παρά-δοσις) which was regarded as authoritative. Further, we can see that at least some collections of gospel material belonged to the material classified in this way.[7] These early references in the sources, which are quite genuine, are of particular importance to the historian. DIBELIUS and BULTMANN have naturally not ignored these passages, but they pay remarkably little attention to them.[8]

[1] Cf. H. WINDISCH, *Paulus und Christus* (1934), pp. 118 ff.

[2] See below.

[3] The alternative "literary–non-literary" is unfortunate. A more fruitful alternative is "learned–unlearned" (the terms are naturally taken in the meaning they had in the original milieu on which the examination concentrates).

[4] See H. RIESENFELD, The Gospel Tradition and its Beginnings, in *Texte und Unters.* 73 (1959), pp. 43 ff. Also printed separately (1957).

[5] See instead R. BULTMANN, *Theologie des N.T:s* (1953), pp. 464 ff.

[6] On this point, see the following examination.

[7] See below, Ch. 15 D–E.

[8] The minor role accorded to this by DIBELIUS is clear from his presentation, *Formgeschichte*, pp. 242 ff.

We find in these early sources not only that a concept of tradition existed in early Christianity, but also that at least a certain type of transmission was regarded as being such a distinct activity that a technical terminology was used in order to refer to it: παραδιδόναι, παραλαμβάνειν, παράδοσις, etc.[1] The sources here give us a glimpse of a deliberate didactic activity on the part of definite doctrinal authorities: the formulation of definite sayings, and the methodical delivery and reception of such sayings. The pioneer form-critics prefer, however, to talk about "the biology of the folk-tale" ("eine Biologie der Sage")—a sort of biological process, carried on according to various psychological natural laws among a non-literary, anonymous crowd: a process in which text material comes into existence, grows, declines, is reshaped, altered, and finally put on to parchment—or disappears.[2]

We may stop at this point. The pioneer form-critics work with a diffuse concept of tradition and give only vague hints as to how the early Christian gospel tradition was transmitted, technically speaking. DIBELIUS summarizes the various forms of early Christian activity in the concept of "preaching" (Predigt), and there finds the *Sitz im Leben* in which the gospel tradition originated and was passed on.[3] BULTMANN considers it to be impossible to summarize the activity of the young Church in any such concept as "preaching"; instead he reckons with various expressions of the life of the Church: apart from preaching and teaching, he counts apologetics and polemics, church establishment and discipline, together with specialist work on the Scriptures.[4] But he nevertheless fails to give us any concrete picture of how he considers, from the purely technical point of view, the gospel tradition to have been transmitted. This is merely a natural consequence of his basic viewpoint: the early Church transmitted by believing, by spreading propaganda for its faith, and by consolidating and defending that same faith.

The lack of clarity on this point still remains, despite more than a generation's intensive work on the pre-literary stage of the gospel tradition.[5] It seems therefore to be highly necessary to determine what

---

[1] The technical meaning of these terms was early pointed out by *inter alia* J. WEISS (*Der erste Korintherbrief*, 1910, p. 283), and G. KITTEL (*Die Probleme des palästinischen Spätjudentums*, 1926, pp. 62 ff.).

[2] DIBELIUS, *Formgeschichte*, pp. 1 ff. and elsewhere, BULTMANN, *Geschichte*, pp. 3 ff.

[3] E.g. *Formgeschichte*, pp. 8 ff.

[4] *Geschichte*, p. 64.

[5] Cf. K. STENDAHL, *The School of St. Matthew* (1954), pp. 13 ff.

was the technical procedure followed when the early Church *transmitted*, both gospel material and other material. This investigation will be devoted to an attempt in this direction.

As in all other historical research, it is convenient to begin by attempting to gain a picture of the corresponding situation in the surrounding milieu, which in this case is the Jewish milieu. For a number of reasons, we shall concentrate on the main current within Judaism, devoting only limited attention to the sectarian movements which were to be found on both sides of this main stream. We shall also widen our horizons to include something of the surrounding Hellenistic world. It would be highly desirable for someone to devote a detailed special examination to the technique of transmission within the various groups and movements of the Hellenistic world during the centuries around the dawn of the Christian era.

We shall proceed from the Jewish documents to the information provided by the traditions of the early Church, the Acts of the Apostles and the *corpus paulinum*, in order to try and estimate the material at our disposal on tradition and the act of transmission in the young Church. But this opens the wide horizons of the synoptic material, which must be scanned on a basis of the results arrived at in our previous investigation. We cannot however undertake the analysis of this material in the present work. We shall merely, in a concluding chapter, sketch in a number of the main outlines.

The object of this investigation will be defined in more detail at the beginning of each part, and each sub-section of what follows.

Since we are dealing with a material which we consider generally to have been given far too little recognition in the N.T. debate, we shall give comprehensive references to literature on a vast number of isagogical, philological, historical and exegetical problems in the Jewish traditional literature. These are all problems which must be considered in the course of an investigation into the problem of tradition among the Rabbis, and they often provide parallels to certain problems of N.T. research.

PART ONE

Oral Tradition and Written Transmission
in Rabbinic Judaism

CHAPTER 1

Written and Oral Torah

JEWISH PIETY, as it is seen during the centuries around the beginning of the Christian era, has been appropriately characterized as *torah-centric*.[1] The people of the Covenant knew that they had the incomparable privilege of being entrusted with God's holy *Torah* (תורה), the source of Life and Salvation; this was accorded an importance which can hardly be exaggerated, and played a central and essential role in the life of the people. This applies—with certain variations—to all the more important religious groups within Judaism of that time. In some circles the torah-centric feature is extremely characteristic.[2]

In the Torah were to be seen God's wisdom, God's purposes and God's will—in every aspect of these words[3]—distinctly revealed to Israel; to the Torah was therefore attributed an unlimited richness of content: everything was to be found in it.[4] It was considered that there was not a single element in the lives of the society or of the individual which had no message from the Torah: it applied to every part of life.

---

[1] The term coined by W. R. FARMER, *Maccabees, Zealots, and Josephus* (1956), p. 48.

[2] To this subject see F. WEBER, *Jüdische Theologie* (2nd ed. 1897), pp. 14 ff., E. SCHÜRER, *Geschichte des jüdischen Volkes* II (4th ed. 1907), pp. 545 ff., P. BILLERBECK, *Comm.* III (1926), pp. 126 ff., IV (1928), pp. 415 ff., G. F. MOORE, *Judaism* I (1927), pp. 235 ff., J. BONSIRVEN, *Le Judaïsme Palestinien* I (1934), pp. 247 ff. (these works mainly for Rabbinic Judaism); H. A. WOLFSON, *Philo* I (2nd ed. 1948), pp. 19 ff., 87 ff. (for Hellenistic Judaism) and H. BRAUN, *Spätjüdisch-häretischer und frühchristlicher Radikalismus* I–II (1957), (for sectarian groups); cf. E. BICKERMANN, *Der Gott der Makkabäer* (1937), Chapters 4–5. — See further below, Ch. 14 D.

[3] On the identification of Torah and the Divine Wisdom, see e.g. Sir. 24, Bar. 3.37 ff., 4.1 ff.

[4] What is perhaps the most pregnant of all formulations of this conviction is that well known saying of Hillel or one of his pupils (בן בג בג) in Ab. V. 22: הפך בה והפך בה דכלא בה ("Turn it this way and turn it that way, for all is therein"; Lowe's ms. adds וכלך בה, "and your all is therein".) Cf. also the commentary in the ed. of K. MARTI, G. BEER, pp. 155 f. From the sectarian documents we may quote the illustrative saying in CD XVI.2: תורת משה כי בה הכל מדוקדק ("... the Law of Moses, for in it everything can [by learned consideration] be learnt"). It is a known fact that sayings of this kind are numerous.

Hence it was possible confidently to draw teaching, advice and the norms of life from the Torah. In it were to be found warning and punishment; from it could be taken encouragement, comfort and joy.

We shall not stop to deal with these basic Jewish ideas on the nature of the Torah in more detail.[1] But one fact must be pointed out. When we consider the many late Jewish statements on the Torah, we must be aware of the comprehensive and many-sided concept with which we are faced: the term Torah is used in many different senses. Therefore we must make some simple introductory remarks concerning the way in which we shall use the main terms in this book. We shall, however, ignore certain variations of meaning which in this context are of little importance.[2]

The Torah, in its most usual meaning, denotes the Pentateuch. According to a basic and widespread idea, God laid down in these five books of Moses—explicitly or implicitly—all the wisdom he wished to reveal to Israel and all the teaching he wished to give his people. In relation to the Pentateuch, the other Jewish sacred writings are looked upon as tradition (קבלה)[3] or commentary (תלמוד, מדרש),[4] which also applies to that sacred doctrine transmitted by word of mouth (משנה in its widest meaning).[5]

But since God's revelation to, and teaching of, his people are also to be seen in the other sacred Scriptures (כתובים, נביאים), the term Torah

---

[1] For a consideration of this problem, see the works quoted p. 19, n. 2. — The thesis put forward by D. RÖSSLER, *Gesetz und Geschichte* (1960), that the Apocalyptic groups had a quite different conception of Torah than the Pharisaic Rabbis is exaggerated.

[2] For the meaning of the term Torah in the O. T. see G. ÖSTBORN, *Tōrā in the O. T.* (1945) and I. ENGNELL, *Israel and the Law* (2nd ed. 1954). For the use of the term in rabbinic linguistic practice, see L. BLAU, *Zur Einleitung in die Heilige Schrift* (1894), pp. 16 f., and W. BACHER, *Die exegetische Terminologie der jüdischen Traditionsliteratur* I–II (1899–1905, hereafter abbreviated to *Terminologie*), I, p. 197.

[3] See BACHER, *Terminologie* I, pp. 165 f., and IDEM, *Tradition und Tradenten in den Schulen Palästinas und Babyloniens* (1914, hereafter abbreviated to *Tradition*), pp. 2 f., and BLAU, *Zur Einleitung*, pp. 24 ff.

[4] For the terms, see BACHER, *Terminologie* I, pp. 103 ff., 199 ff., and below, p. 83 f.

[5] For a consideration of the term and the fact, see below, pp. 27 f. and 83 f. For the different technical terms in connection with transmission and tradition, see BACHER, *Tradition*, pp. 1 ff., and *Terminologie* I, sub vocibus. The actual noun קבלה is not used for the oral Torah in Tannaitic linguistic practice (see BACHER, *Terminologie* I, *ibid.*) but the verb קבל is used frequently.

can also be used to denote the whole of the Jews' sacred Scriptures
(מקרא, כתוב).[1]

In its widest meaning, the term Torah is used as a collective designation for the whole of the authoritative, sacred tradition (doctrine); not
merely that which is codified in sacred Scripture, but also that which is
carried forward in sacred oral tradition (משנה in a wide meaning)—in
fact everything which is understood as being God's sacred revelation to,
and authoritative teaching of, his Covenant people.[2]

Here we shall proceed on the basis of this broad concept of the Torah.
In this investigation we shall use the term Torah, without qualification, as a
collective designation for the Jews' sacred authoritative tradition (doctrine) in
its entirety.

However, according to reliable rabbinic tradition a distinction was
drawn as early as the time of Hillel and Shammai, if not earlier, between
written and oral Torah: תורה שבכתב was that part of the sacred authoritative tradition which was transmitted in writing; תורה שבעל פה that part
which was transmitted orally.[3] Josephus also shows himself aware of
this distinction;[4] in fact he says that the Sadducees wanted people to
regard only those rules (νόμιμα) to be obligatory which were written
(γεγραμμένα), but not those coming from the tradition of the forefathers
(τὰ ἐκ παραδόσεως τῶν πατέρων [νόμιμα]).[5]

---

[1] BACHER, *Terminologie* I, p. 197, BLAU, *Zur Einleitung*, pp. 16 ff. We do not
need to consider the question of the limitations of the "canon". As history shows,
the concept of "holy Scriptures" has not automatically meant the precise limitation
of the "canon".

[2] BACHER, *Terminologie* I, *ibid.* Cf. W. G. KÜMMEL, Jesus und der jüdische
Traditionsgedanke, in *Zeitschr. f. d. Neutest. Wiss.* 33 (1934), p. 110. See also p. 82, n. 5–6.

[3] b Shab. 31 a, Abot d. R. Natan I, 15 (cf. 29); Sifre Deut. ad 33.10 and elsewhere.
See further BACHER, *Tradition*, pp. 22 ff., IDEM, *Terminologie* I, pp. 89 and 197,
L. BLAU, Ursprung und Geschichte des technischen Ausdrucks „Mündliche Lehre",
in *Mechiltha*, translated by J. WINTER, A. WÜNSCHE (1909), pp. xviii ff., D. DAUBE,
Rabbinic Methods of Interpretation and Hellenistic Rhetoric, in *Hebr. Un. Coll.*
Ann. 22 (1949), pp. 239 ff.

[4] *Ant.* 13.10.6; cf. 10.4.1. In this context Philo's sayings are less useful, since his
thoughts on the Law often follow Hellenistic paths. On this subject, cf. I. HEINE-
MANN, Die Lehre vom ungeschriebenen Gesetz im jüdischen Schrifttum, in *Hebr.*
Un. Coll. Ann. 4 (1927), pp. 149 ff., IDEM, *Philons griechische und jüdische Bildung*
(1932), pp. 528 ff., with WOLFSON, *Philo* I, pp. 188 ff. — For the concept
ἄγραφος νόμος within the Greek Tradition, see R. HIRZEL, ΑΓΡΑΦΟΣ ΝΟΜΟΣ
(1900).

[5] To judge from the evidence, the synoptic tradition was not aware of the theoretical, technical distinction, although the practical distinction was drawn. When

Consciousness of an oral tradition which interprets and complements the written law is "natural" in every legally governed society; we may nevertheless wonder how the Rabbis' clear and marked distinction between written and oral Torah came about. DAUBE has pointed out its formal resemblance to the distinction in the Hellenistic *rhetor* tradition between νόμοι ἔγγραφοι (*ius scriptum*) and νόμοι ἄγραφοι (*ius non scriptum*), and maintains that the rabbinic distinction arose as a result of Hellenistic influence, which was strongest during the period 100 B.C.– 25 B.C.[1] It is possible that such was the case. But if that is so, on this point the influence has been absorbed indirectly, and not as a piece of direct borrowing; a not unimportant alteration of the Hellenistic distinction has also come about. Here we must supplement the picture in two respects. We must on the one hand refer to certain phenomena within Judaism during the first and second centuries B.C., phenomena which show that it must have been relatively "natural" to have this distinction formulated at that time. (There is no doubt that these phenomena are also linked with the fact that at that time Judaism was surrounded by Hellenism,[2] but we do not need to go into that question here.) On the other hand, we must point out that the rabbinic distinction is drawn from another point of view than the Hellenistic.

First we must remember the opposition between Pharisees and Sadducees. If this controversy included, *inter alia*, the fact that the Sadducees denied—in theory—the fully normative standing of the oral customary law, which the Pharisees maintained (see below), then this *status controversiae* implied the existence of the natural conditions for a

according to Mark 7.1 ff. (Matt. 15.1 ff.) Jesus accuses the Pharisees of neglecting the commandment of God (ἡ ἐντολὴ τοῦ θεοῦ; also ὁ λόγος τοῦ θεοῦ) in order to hold fast their tradition (ἡ παράδοσις τῶν πρεσβυτέρων, ἡ παράδοσις ὑμῶν) he treats ἡ παράδοσις τῶν πρεσβυτέρων as a concrete entity, distinct from ἡ ἐντολὴ τοῦ θεοῦ, i.e. the (written) Law itself. His polemic is thus directed not against a wrong interpretation of the Scriptures but an observation of traditional statutes which contradict certain definite commandments in the Scriptures. Here we have a simple and practical distinction between written and oral Torah, although the technical term for this distinction is not used. We might mention in passing that the rest of the terminology of this pericope is strikingly "learned" and "technical". See below, pp. 288 f.

[1] *Rabbinic Methods.* — Cf. S. ZEITLIN, The Halaka, in *Jew. Quart. Rev.* 39 (1948–49), pp. 1 ff.

[2] On this subject see—apart from the classical SCHÜRER, *Geschichte* II, pp. 27 ff.— the latest work, V. TCHERIKOVER, *Hellenistic Civilization and the Jews* (translated from the Hebr. 1959).

conscious and definite formulation of the distinction between written and oral Torah.

A further phenomenon, the implications of which are as yet not quite clear, is intimately connected with this; that is, the struggle of the Pharisaic doctrinal authorities against the written transmission of the oral legal tradition.[1] This struggle is clearly demonstrated from Tannaitic and Amoraic times, but there are considerable indications that it was programmatical within Pharisaism as early as the first century B.C., if not earlier. We have already mentioned Josephus' statement that the Sadducees regarded only those rules as binding, which were written, whilst the Pharisees also transmitted and maintained observances derived from the tradition of the forefathers.[2] There is no reason to doubt the truth of Josephus' statement. He is evidently well initiated, and it is difficult to see what reason he could have had in this case for distorting the facts as he knew them. The statement is, however, very brief, and is consequently rather difficult to interpret. It is convenient to interpret it to mean that the Sadducees rejected all additions to the laws in the Pentateuch. But this—as many scholars have pointed out—was not the attitude of the Sadducees.[3] They knew from experience, as well as did the Pharisees, that the concise and fragmentary laws in the Pentateuch, despite the richness of content which was ascribed to them, demanded not only to be authoritatively interpreted, but also complemented. For example, the Sadducean priests needed a thorough and detailed halakah dealing with the performance of the complicated Temple services: it is certain that no extensive improvisation was allowed there.[4] The importance of the contents of the tractate Tamid was not limited to the period after the fall of the Temple![5] Similar circum-

[1] The problem is also considered below, Ch. 11 E.

[2] The passage reads: νόμιμά τινα παρέδοσαν τῷ δήμῳ οἱ Φαρισαῖοι ἐκ πατέρων διαδοχῆς, ἅπερ οὐκ ἀναγέγραπται ἐν τοῖς Μωυσέως νόμοις, καὶ διὰ τοῦτο ταῦτα τὸ Σαδδουκαίων γένος ἐκβάλλει, λέγον ἐκεῖνα δεῖν ἡγεῖσθαι νόμιμα τὰ γεγραμμένα, τὰ δ'ἐκ παραδόσεως τῶν πατέρων μὴ τηρεῖν. Josephus' statements on the Pharisees and the Sadducees are conveniently put together by SCHÜRER, *op. cit.* II, pp. 449 ff.

[3] This was stressed even by A. GEIGER in *Urschrift und Übersetzungen der Bibel* (1857, 2nd ed. 1928), pp. 133 ff.

[4] See also MOORE, *Judaism* I, pp. 251 ff.

[5] A. BRODY, *Der Mišna-Traktat Tamid* (1936), pp. 9 f., has good grounds for holding that the tractate Tamid was in its original form written by a priest as a handbook for priests. Cf. L. GINZBERG, Tamid the Oldest Treatise of the Mishnah, in *Journ. of Jew. Lore and Philos.* 1 (1919), pp. 33 ff., 197 ff., 265 ff. Note that the tractate was not *originally* an officially sanctioned σύγγραμμα but a "scroll of secrets" (see below).

stances apply in other fields. Josephus relates in another context that the Sadducees, for the sake of the people, observed the Pharisees' halakah to a great extent.[1] And from more or less reliable quotations, taken from various sources, we are acquainted with a number of the elements of the Sadducees' own specific doctrinal tradition.[2] Bearing all this in mind, we are inclined to agree with LAUTERBACH's thesis, that the Sadducees did not *per se* reject every complement to the Pentateuch laws, but that they did deny the fully normative standing of such orally transmitted rules.[3]

This position was tenable in many fields. But in certain areas it was absolutely necessary to have complementary laws, binding in character, for example in the penal code. The Sadducees seem in fact to have known and applied a method of passing such binding laws, which were at least temporarily valid. During the Hellenistic period they seem to have established a book dealing with authoritative judgements and decrees, and to have deposited this book in the Temple archives.[4] According to the ancient calendar of festivals, Megillat Taanit, Rabbinic Judaism celebrated on the 4th Tammuz the memory of the abolition of a ספר גזרתא.[5] The rabbinic scholiast says, in his commentary on this, that the Sadducees had a written and deposited "book of *gezerot*" (היה כתוב ומונח לצדוקים ספר גזרות) which was read when passing judgement, or on similar occasions.[6] This codex was removed by the Pharisees, presumably during the time of Alexandra Salome. In this context the

---

[1] *Ant.* 18.1.4. Cf. the warning given in Matt. 16.2 for the teaching of the Pharisees *and* the Sadducees! See also T Yoma I.9, b Yoma 19b, T Nid. V.1.

[2] The material is collected by BILLERBECK, *Comm.* IV, pp. 344 ff. Cf. Joach. JEREMIAS, *Jerusalem zur Zeit Jesu* (2nd ed. 1959) II: B, pp. 98 ff. — It is interesting to note L. A. ROSENTHAL's thesis concerning anti-Sadducaic tendencies in many of the ancient *halakot* in the Mishnah, *Über den Zusammenhang der Mischna* I (2nd ed. 1909), pp. 49–79.

[3] The Sadducees and Pharisees. A Study of their Respective Attitudes towards the Law, in *Rabbinic Essays* (1951), pp. 27 ff. Other views are to be found e.g. in SCHÜRER, *Geschichte* II, pp. 475 ff.

[4] For the publication technique which lies behind the expression "written and deposited" (כתוב ומונח) see S. LIEBERMAN, *Hellenism in Jewish Palestine* (1950), pp. 85 ff. Cf. V. BURR, Editionstechnik, in *Reallex. f. Ant. u. Christ.* IV (1959), col. 597 ff. See also F. FR. VON SCHWIND, *Zur Frage der Publikation im römischen Recht* (1940).

[5] See ed. H. LICHTENSTEIN in *Hebr. Un. Coll. Ann.* 8–9 (1931–32), p. 331 (separate, p. 75).

[6] For a commentary on this passage, see the discussion *ibid.*, pp. 295 ff. (35 ff.).

scholiast also notes the principle observed in Pharisaism (Rabbinic Judaism) that oral Torah must remain *oral*: אין כותבין הלכות בספר.

The scholiast, who appears on this point to have had access to a good tradition, gives us an interesting hint that the Pharisees' attack on the Sadducees' codex was not limited merely to its contents, but also had to do with the fact of its being *written*.[1] The Pharisees' attitude here seems to be both clear and consistent. They advocated faith in the Torah, down to the smallest detail, and considered themselves bound by the *whole* of God's teaching to the fathers of the people (האבות), and not only by that which had been written and deposited. What was written in this codex was no more binding than the remainder of the traditional complements to the Law of Moses. Furthermore, it is certain that the Sadducees' book contained a number of *gezerot* which the Pharisees did not recognize.

The Pharisees thus stand out in the struggle with the Sadducees—if we have interpreted the sources correctly—as energetic advocates of the principle that oral Torah is, and must remain, *oral* Torah. It is probable that the Pharisees are here conserving a more ancient practice. It is in fact likely that in the third and second centuries B.C., writing had still not come into such widespread use in the non-priestly circles from which the Pharisaic scholars came, as it was to do in the Hellenized priestly circles in Jerusalem. But it is also probable that the Pharisees were driven, in the struggle with the Sadducees, to strengthen their own position and adopt a more negative attitude toward scrolls containing oral Torah: notes of *halakot*, or of midrashic or targumic material. We shall return to this topic later.[2]

Another phenomenon which we must bear in mind is that it is evidently during this period that a more highly organised school system—in its essentials—began to develop in Palestine.[3] The very fact that the methodical study of the oral law (ἡ παράδοσις τῶν πρεσβυτέρων), as a definite *corpus*, distinct from the Scriptures,[4] was begun, provides the conditions for the conscious distinction we have mentioned.

Finally, such a distinction would seem to have been desirable and useful in connection with the encounter between Judaism and the sur-

---

[1] Correctly emphasized by J. S. BLOCH, *Einblicke in die Geschichte der Entstehung der talmudischen Literatur* (1884), pp. 14 ff.

[2] Below, Ch. 11 E.

[3] For the development of the school system, see below, Ch. 4 and 8.

[4] See below, Ch. 7 A and 11 D.

rounding Gentile world, not least in the recruiting of proselytes. Proselytism does not, however, seem to have played such an important role for the Jews' leading doctrinal authorities that we can agree with Blau, when he maintains that the distinction *originated* in this context.[1]

Taking such factors into consideration, it is probable that the distinction was, as it were, "in the air" for Judaism, surrounded as it was by Hellenism during the centuries immediately before Christ. We must nevertheless stress that there is an essential difference—both in terminology and in fact—between the Hellenistic rhetor's distinction between νόμοι ἔγγραφοι (*ius scriptum*) and νόμοι ἄγραφοι (*ius non scriptum*) and the Jewish distinction between תורה שבכתב and תורה שבעל פה. It is true that certain νόμοι ἄγραφοι can be of the same type as certain elements in תורה שבעל פה, but this should not be allowed to obscure the essential difference which is there in principle. The rhetors distinguished between two laws *of different nature, of different essence*: νόμος ἔγγραφος is an officially promulgated and hence a fixed, "written", law. Νόμος ἄγραφος again is a law, which is in itself an unwritten law, whether it be a matter of "the natural law" or of traditional customs, customary law.[2] The Rabbis distinguish between two laws *which are transmitted in different ways*: תורה שבכתב is evidently an abbreviation of תורה שנאמרה בכתב or possibly תורה שנתנה בכתב.[3] This is distinguished from תורה שבעל פה, i.e. תורה שנתנה בעל פה or תורה שנאמרה בעל פה.[4] The distinction here is not between, on the one hand, an "outer" law, fixed by some kind of legislation, and, on the other, one which is in itself unwritten. On the contrary, in both cases, it is primarily a matter of commandments, decrees, fixed authoritative laws. Instead, a distinction is drawn between that part of the law which is transmitted in writing and delivered officially (in connection with jurisdiction, teaching, public worship, etc.) as a reading from a book,[5] and that part which, though its essential

---

[1] *Ursprung und Geschichte*, pp. xxii ff., emphasizes that the oldest support for the distinction is to be found in traditions concerning the confrontation with representatives of the Greco-Roman world. — Further to the problem, see the works quoted by F. Maass, Von den Ursprüngen der rabbinischen Schriftauslegung, in *Zeitschr. f. Theol. u. Kirche* 52 (1955), pp. 156 ff.

[2] For the Hellenistic ἄγραφος νόμος-concept, see Hirzel, ΑΓΡΑΦΟΣ ΝΟΜΟΣ. Cf. also the other references given above, p. 21, n. 4.

[3] Bacher, *Terminologie* I, p. 89.

[4] Cf. *ibid.*

[5] See also below, Ch. 4–5.

passages are officially determined and its wording is fixed, is transmitted orally and in official contexts is delivered from memory.[1]

We might mention in passing that this is quite typical. During the centuries after Alexander, Hellenism evidently made its presence very much felt in Palestine.[2] These influences were not limited to those circles whose attitude to Hellenism was more or less open, but also reached those who opposed it—though in that case the influence is more indirect. We see in the Jewish educational system, for example, many interesting resemblances to corresponding phenomena in the Hellenistic schools. It is, however, seldom a matter of direct correspondence, and thus seldom a question of direct borrowing, or direct taking over. As a rule it is a matter of indirect influence—as in the above-mentioned example—or what appears to be direct contradiction. The higher "rabbinic" schools were by their very nature a great and effective counter to Hellenism. At the same time, though, their growth and formation was undoubtedly stimulated by the Hellenistic schools of rhetoric.[3]

The rabbinic distinction is thus drawn from precisely that point of view in which we are interested: that of how the material is transmitted and studied, and how it is used in official contexts. This impression is strengthened if we turn our attention to another pair of concepts in the rabbinic world of ideas.

The distinction in principle and practice between written and oral Torah is seen with striking clarity in the basic *terminology of study*. As BACHER, with his usual astuteness, has shown, the Tannaitic Rabbis consistently use different terms to denote the study of the two disciplines.[4] This consistent terminology is an eloquent witness to the clarity with which the distinction between written and oral Torah was maintained within Rabbinic Judaism. Thus "to study the written Torah" is קרא or, more fully, קרא את המקרא, whereas "to study the oral Torah" is שנה or, more fully, שנה את המשנה.[5]

---

[1] See also below, Ch. 7 and 11 E.

[2] See TCHERIKOVER, *Hellenistic Civilization*.

[3] For the way in which the Jewish schools were a powerful bulwark against Hellenism, but at the same time were influenced by Hellenism, see W. BOYD, *The History of Western Education* (6th ed. 1954), pp. 56 ff., and N. MORRIS, *The Jewish School* (1937), pp. 11 f., 37 ff. Hellenistic influence on the Jewish school system has been pointed out by many, e.g. K. H. RENGSTORF, art. διδάσκω κτλ., in *Theol. Wörterb.*, ed. G. KITTEL, II (1935), pp. 138 ff.

[4] See *Terminologie* I, pp. 34, 117 f., 174 f.; 122 f. and 194 f., cf. IDEM, Das altjüdische Schulwesen, in *Jahrb. f. jüd. Gesch. u. Lit.* 6 (1903), pp. 74 f.

[5] Cf. BLAU, *Ursprung und Geschichte*, pp. xviii ff.

The written Torah, as an object of study, is thus called מקרא, "reading", "that which is read": the term can denote both the act of reading and the object of reading.[1] To study the written Torah is, as we have mentioned, קרא, "to read", since this study is in principle reading—reading from the written scroll. It is, however, worth pointing out that the term קרא often—though not always—has a very narrow meaning: by this word is meant nothing but the actual *reading* of the text in question. And elementary instruction in מקרא as a rule included little more than teaching the children to read the written text fluently and correctly, and to translate it.[2]

We have pointed out that the oral Torah, as an object of study, is called משנה, "repetition", "that which is repeated", which term—being a typical so-called *ma*-nomen—refers both to the act of repetition and the object of repetition. And to study this discipline is שנה, since this study is in principle oral repetition: the teacher's instruction, the pupil's learning—in fact all study and maintenance of knowledge within this discipline—rests on the principle of oral repetition.[3] It is therefore not mere chance that we find a collective term, שנה, for the whole of the mighty and many-faceted activity implied by an occupation with the sacred oral tradition, and a collective term, משנה, for the entire tradition with all its branches.[4] The Aramaic equivalent of משנה is מתניתא and that of שנה is תני, תנא. The Church Fathers often rendered שנה by the Greek δευτεροῦν, and משנה by δευτέρωσις.[5]

We have now given an account of the wider meaning which the terms משנה and שנה often have. The terms may, however, also have a narrower meaning, referring to a definite *part* of the mighty oral tradition, or its study. We shall give an account of this in due course, in our section on the oral Torah.[6]

The distinction between written and oral Torah, when transmitting and studying the Torah, is thus seen programatically by Rabbinic

---

[1] E. KUTSCH, מקרא, in *Zeitschr. f. d. Alttest. Wiss.* 65 (1953), pp. 247 ff., deals only with the meaning of the term before it had the technical meaning which is most usual in Tannaitic and Amoraic usage.

[2] See further below, Ch. 4.

[3] SCHÜRER, *Geschichte* I (3rd and 4th ed. 1901), pp. 113 f., BACHER, *Terminologie* I, p. 194, and below, Ch. 6–12.

[4] For terminology, cf. also LIEBERMAN, *Hellenism*, pp. 83 f., and R. BLOCH, Écriture et Tradition dans le Judaisme, in *Cahiers Sioniens* 8 (1954), pp. 19 ff.

[5] For proof, see *inter alia* SCHÜRER, *op. cit., ibid.*

[6] Below, Ch. 7 B.

Judaism. We must, however, point out that this is by no means as simple as it appears to be.

The written Torah, when studied, is carefully committed to memory, learned by heart.[1] Written Torah therefore *functions* in the memories of those learned in the Scriptures as memorized texts, being quoted from memory and used, for example in debates, from memory, although in decisive contexts—the transmission of the text, the teaching of the Scriptures and the readings in public worship—it must be read from a book.[2]

On the other hand, when we consider the oral Torah, it is evident that written notes (ὑπομνήματα etc.) did in fact exist.[3] They were used in order to facilitate private repetition and the maintenance of knowledge, although the oral Torah in its decisive, public, contexts—the teaching of the oral Torah, legal proceedings, preaching, etc.—had to be repeated from memory.[4]

The distinction is therefore this: the one part of the Torah is in principle Scripture, Scripture which is read, whilst the other is oral tradition, tradition which is repeated. In the former case, the written text is official and plays a primary role; in the other, such notes as may exist are of private nature and play a subsidiary role. We shall deal with this in more detail in the course of our investigation.[5]

The distinction between written and oral Torah is thus far from simple. But since the distinction was drawn within Rabbinic Judaism, particularly when dealing with the Torah from the point of view of transmission and study, we must accept it and make it the foundation on which the arrangement of our investigation of rabbinic techniques of transmission rests.

These brief remarks on some details of rabbinic terminology must suffice here. A more detailed analysis will be found in BACHER's works on the terminology of transmission and interpretation used by the Rabbis.[6]

---

[1] Below, Ch. 4.

[2] Cf. below, Ch. 2–5.

[3] See below, Ch. 11 E.

[4] See further below, Ch. 6–12.

[5] Below, particularly Ch. 11 E.

[6] *Terminologie* I and II (see also *Tradition*, pp. 1 ff.). It is essential that the German edition of this excellent work, which is so vital to the present hermeneutical debate, should be reprinted.

We can now define the task which we have set ourselves in the first part of our investigation (Ch. 2–12). We shall concentrate on Judaism in the Tannaitic (i.e. from ca. 10 A.D.) and Amoraic periods. Our task is to attempt to give a concrete picture of how, *from the purely technical point of view*, the sacred Torah was transmitted during these centuries. Our major interest will be concentrated on the transmission of the oral Torah, but we must also devote a relatively detailed section to the written Torah.

We are here limiting ourselves to that main current within Judaism which was dominated by the Pharisaic scholars, that section which is usually called *Rabbinic Judaism*.[1] (We shall use this designation despite the fact that it is not strictly applicable to that part of the Tannaitic period prior to the fall of the Temple. Similarly, we shall use the term "the Rabbis" to denote the scholars *en bloc* within the Pharisaic-Rabbinic tradition, although the title is inadequate when applied to those earlier than Rabban Joḥanan ben Zakkai.) Our concentration upon Rabbinic Judaism is due to the fact of its being the leading, and the most influential, current within Judaism at the beginning of the Christian era, and to the fact of its position of dominance becoming definitive during the centuries immediately following; but it is also due to the fact that within this group the oral Torah was held to be sacred and authoritative, and was therefore transmitted with reverence, with care, and by means of a method which was so conscious that it is described in the source material.

The remaining representatives of the more important groups within Judaism during the period mentioned above (Sadducees, Essenes, Apocalyptic circles) will be dealt with only incidentally. A superficial check has revealed no evidence that a technique of transmission substantially different from that of the Pharisees was applied within these groups. It is, however, probable that written transmission played a more prominent role within these groups than in Rabbinic Judaism, and that they used written texts to a greater extent in the course of teaching. We have already attempted to determine the Sadducees' attitude: they had complementary laws written in a book which was deposited in the Temple archives, and this book—or copies of it—could be used officially, and thus also in teaching.

---

[1] For the concept "normative Judaism", see the remarks in MOORE, *Judaism* III (1930), pp. v ff. and I, pp. 254 ff. Cf. H. ODEBERG, Normativ judendom, in *Norsk Teol. Tidsskrift* 30 (1929), pp. 88 ff.

The attitude of the Essenes is not entirely clear. In that form of Essenism which we encounter in Qumran we find scrolls with written halakah: the Manual of Discipline and the Sect Rule. We understand that no less than twelve examples of the former have been hereto discovered: a complete scroll in Cave One, and fragments of ten scrolls in Cave Four and of one in Cave Five.[1] We must now ask whether this is a question of a written, authorized document, deposited in the archives of the sect: a document of which several other examples existed and were used, *inter alia* in the course of teaching and jurisdiction. Or is it a matter of a more unofficial copy of passages from the sect's halakah, i.e. a "scroll of secrets", מגילת סתרים,[2] of which several examples existed? If the former alternative is correct, then on this point the sect had an attitude similar to that of the Sadducees; if the latter, then their attitude resembled that of the Pharisees.

Also within Apocalyptic circles—if we are justified in isolating these as special groups—there seems to have existed the practice of writing down, with a candidness foreign to Pharisaism, their own specific revelations and doctrines. It is true that these books are "scrolls of secrets", in the sense that they are intended for a limited, initiated circle,[3] but they are *written works* in a sense different from the Pharisees' notes of oral Torah, which retains its character of being *oral* traditional material. It is, however, difficult to make a comparison, since we know so little about the Rabbis' "scrolls of secrets". The Apocalyptic groups' study of their secret books[4] seems to have been carried on following roughly the same principles as the study of the written Torah, though there would seem to have been no reason why, in these circles, such texts could not

---

[1] M. Burrows, *More Light on the Dead Sea Scrolls* (1958), p. 408; cf. J. T. Milik, rec. of P. Wernberg-Møller, The Manual of Discipline (1957), in *Rev. Bibl.* 67 (1960), pp. 411 ff., with a list of variant readings in the different mss.

[2] Concerning these, see further below, Ch. 11 E.

[3] For the general tendency to treat sacred sayings and texts as "secret" in this meaning, see J. Leipoldt, S. Morenz, *Heilige Schriften* (1953), pp. 88 ff.; cf. O. Perler, Arkandisziplin, in *Reallex. f. Ant. u. Christ.* I (1950), col. 667 ff.

[4] On the different categories of "holy Books", see G. Widengren, *The Ascension of the Apostle and the Heavenly Book* (1950), I. Engnell, Livets bok, in *Sv. Bibl. Uppslagsverk* II (1952), col. 105 ff., L. Koep, *Das himmlische Buch* (1952), idem, Buch IV, in *Reallex. f. Ant. u. Christ.* II (1954), col. 725 ff., Leipoldt, Morenz, *op. cit.*, F. Nötscher, Himmlische Bücher und Schicksalsglaube in Qumran, in *Rev. de Qumr.* 1 (1958–59), pp. 405 ff.

be learned from the lips of the teacher.[1] Furthermore, the transmission of unwritten sacred words evidently followed the same simple basic principles as the transmission of the oral Torah. We shall therefore not concentrate any particular attention upon it in the course of this investigation.

---

[1] Cf. however our remarks below, pp. 123, 157 and 196 f., on the general scepticism towards the written word in Antiquity.

THE TRANSMISSION OF THE WRITTEN TORAH

CHAPTER 2

The Attitude to the Text

THE SCHOLAR who works with rabbinic literature is liable repeatedly to be faced with a remarkable synthesis of circumstances—circumstances which he previously thought to be irreconcileable. This applies not least to the one who investigates the attitude of the Rabbis to the written Biblical text.

We have already suggested that Jewish scribes attributed an immeasurable and inexhaustible wealth of content to the Divine Word.[1] This is particularly true of the word of Scripture. The task of the people of God, from the scribes' point of view, is by means of a right attitude of listening to (שמע), and seeking in (דרש) the Scriptures, to find out all their Divine gifts: their joy and consolation, their warning and punishment, their instruction and teaching, their directives and laws for every situation of life. It is thus not merely a matter of taking note of the obvious pronouncements of Scripture, but also of distinguishing the more or less obscure hints and suggestions to be found there. The modern observer must take account of the way in which the Biblical text is used, as though it had a whole series of meanings—and even several wordings![2]

The written *midrashim* provide plentiful examples of this process. It is easy to find early examples in the LXX; some LXX translations in particular have applied midrash exegesis of the kind we have mentioned.[3] The principles upon which the Scriptures were used are seen

---

[1] Above, p. 19.

[2] For the way in which midrash exegesis functions, see *The Jew. Enc.* VIII (1904), pp. 548 ff., art. Midrash (S. HOROVITZ), Midrash Haggadah (J. THEODOR) and Midrash Halakah (J. Z. LAUTERBACH); I. L. SEELIGMANN, Voraussetzungen der Midraschexegese, in *Suppl. to Vet. Test.* 1 (1953), pp. 150 ff., and R. BLOCH, Midrash, in *Dict. de la Bible*, Suppl. V (1957), col. 1263 ff.

[3] See A. KAMINKA, *Studien zur Septuaginta an der Hand der zwölf kleinen Prophetenbücher* (1928), IDEM, Septuaginta und Targum zu Proverbia, in *Hebr. Un. Coll. Ann.* 8–9 (1931–32), pp. 169 ff., and I. L. SEELIGMANN, *The Septuagint Version of Isaiah* (1948).

with particular clarity in the commentaries (פשרים) from the Dead Sea caves, in particular the so-called Habakkuk Commentary.[1]

There we see how the text is presented little by little, after which follows the exposition. In this exposition (פשר) we find how use is made of the various possibilities of understanding the words of the text. One word in the text may arouse associations with other words of similar spelling and similar sound. The text is read as though it were multiform: as though each word had several different meanings and as though the text had more than one wording.[2] An important principle of interpretation is provided by such a "play on words".[3] This can to some extent be explained by saying that the expositor knew of, and used, *variae lectiones* from other editions of the same text.[4] But this explanation is inadequate.[5] The expositor's possibilities have obviously by no means been exhausted with the existing *variae lectiones*.

The technique which has been used might perhaps be formulated in this way: careful attention is paid to the sound of the sacred text, its writing is thoroughly examined, and its secrets uncovered; the expositor makes use of every possibility of interpretation and every useful association awakened by the text. It goes without saying that the expositor,

---

[1] From the comprehensive literature, see *inter alia* W. H. BROWNLEE, Biblical Interpretation among the Sectaries of the Dead Sea Scrolls, in *The Bibl. Archaeol.* 4 (1951), pp. 54 ff., K. ELLIGER, *Studien zum Habakuk-Kommentar vom Toten Meer* (1953), pp. 118 ff., B. J. ROBERTS, The Dead Sea Scrolls and the O. T. Scriptures, in *Bull. of the J. Ryl. Libr.* 36 (1953–54), pp. 75 ff., K. STENDAHL, *The School of St. Matthew* (1954), pp. 183 ff., and O. BETZ, *Offenbarung und Schriftforschung in der Qumransekte* (1960).

[2] The best known examples are from 1QpH, col. IV.9. (Hab. 1.11), where the text has וישם though the commentary also uses the variant ואשם, and in col. XI.9 (Hab. 2.16), where the text's הרעל is complemented in the commentary by the variant והערל. For further examples, see W. H. BROWNLEE, *The Text of Habakkuk in the Ancient Commentary from Qumran* (1959), pp. 118 ff. The occurrence of such "dual readings" has been remarked upon by several scholars.

[3] This is emphasized by SEELIGMANN, *Voraussetzungen*, pp. 157 ff., and after him by B. GÄRTNER, The Habakkuk Commentary (DSH) and the Gospel of Matthew, in *Studia Theol.* 8 (1955), pp. 2 ff.

[4] STENDAHL, *op. cit.*, pp. 185 ff., stresses, with BROWNLEE (*Biblical Interpretation of Habakkuk*, p. 73; cf. IDEM, *The Text of Habakkuk*, pp. 114 ff.), that the commentary in 1QpH often makes use of readings which are known from other recensions and versions.

[5] Cf. GÄRTNER, *op. cit., ibid.* For the way in which different scholars have treated the occurrence of dual readings in 1QpH, see BROWNLEE, *The Text of Habakkuk, ibid.*

to the extent to which he is familiar with the traditions, can take advantage of the long and rich tradition of readings and interpretations of the text which previous commentators have left him; he can make use of the midrashic and targumic tradition. If he is a teacher of the Scriptures, he is familiar, thanks to the textual examination (διόρθωσις) of the scrolls out of which he teaches, with textual variants of different kinds.[1] If he is one of those whose profession it is to copy or correct the sacred Scriptures (סופרים ,ספרים סופרים מגיהי), he may in addition draw from the text-critical *masorah* with which he is familiar.[2] Such knowledge is applied, consciously or unconsciously, here. It is also worth emphasizing that from our point of view, it is impossible to draw any *sharp* distinction between spontaneous, inspired exposition and a consciously practised, methodical commentary on the text.[3] In either case the Biblical text is an awakener of associations, and in either case the traditional material known to the expositor comes in one way or another into the exposition.

The Habakkuk Commentary from Qumran is, as far as its basic technique of exposition goes, by no means unique. Had that been the case, we should have been unable to use it here, since we are concentrating first and foremost on Rabbinic Judaism. We have already pointed out that similar principles were applied by the translators of the LXX.[4] The technique of midrash exegesis, the basis of which is in fact extremely ancient and has interesting non-Jewish parallels,[5] thus oc-

---

[1] For διόρθωσις as an element in teaching, see below, pp. 51 and 124 f.

[2] On this subject, see below, pp. 45 ff.

[3] As Roberts correctly points out, *The Dead Sea Scrolls and the O.T.*, pp. 76 ff.

[4] A good example is to be found in Hab. 3.2b בקרב שנים חייהו בקרב שנים תודיע ברגז רחם תזכור reproduced in the LXX by ἐν μέσῳ δύο ζῴων γνωσθήσῃ, ἐν τῷ ἐγγίζειν τὰ ἔτη ἐπιγνωσθήσῃ, ἐν τῷ παρεῖναι τὸν καιρὸν ἀναδειχθήσῃ, ἐν τῷ ταραχθῆναι τὴν ψυχήν μου ἐν ὀργῇ ἐλέους μνησθήσῃ. On the relation between TM and LXX at this point, see B. Gerhardsson, Djuren vid Jesu krubba, in *Från bygd och vildmark* 47 (1960), pp. 28 ff. — See further the works given above, p. 33, n. 3.

[5] Attention has been drawn, and correctly so, to the importance of ambiguous sayings in the interpretation of riddles and oracles in the Near East and in Hellenism. Cf. Lieberman, *Hellenism*, pp. 71 ff., Seeligmann, *Voraussetzungen*, pp. 152 ff., F. Maass, Von den Ursprüngen der rabbinischen Schriftauslegung, in *Zeitschr. f. Theol. u. Kirche* 52 (1955), pp. 141 ff. Cf. from our point of view S. Schott, *Die Deutung der Geheimnisse des Rituals für die Abwehr des Bösen* (1954), pp. 26 f. (168 f.). — Both the noun and the verb from the root פשר (פתר) are used, typically enough, in connection with the interpretation of dreams, signs, oracles, and sacred scriptures. Cf. Elliger, *Studien zum Habakuk-Kommentar*, pp. 156 f.

curs centuries before the beginning of our period. BROWNLEE[1] has justifiably pointed to the connection between the midrash technique in the Habakkuk Commentary from Qumran and those hermeneutic principles (מדות)[2] formulated by the Tannaitic and Amoraic Rabbis. The points of agreement, though relative,[3] are convincing enough. It is evident that the *middot* of the Tannaim are no radical innovation. The Scriptures had for centuries been expounded in ways essentially similar to those current in Tannaitic and Amoraic times. Hillel, R. Ishmael and R. Eliezer are innovators only in so far as they attempt to determine, logically and conceptually, the traditional, dynamic expository method.[4] The attempt to determine the complicated methods of midrash exegesis still further was to continue for some time.[5]

Thus the Tannaitic and Amoraic Rabbis saw the Biblical text—as did the author of the Habakkuk Commentary—as having rich possibilities of interpretation. They had access to a tradition of variant readings and interpretations,[6] a tradition on which they drew when teaching the Torah, and they were also responsible for the creation of new readings and new interpretations. This is most evident on those many occasions when they use the formula אל תקרי ... אלא to denote that at that partic-

---

[1] *Biblical Interpretation*, pp. 54 ff.

[2] In connection with these, see H. L. STRACK, *Einleitung in Talmud und Midraš* (5th ed. 1930), pp. 95 ff. (Eng. ed. 1959, pp. 93 ff.), J. BONSIRVEN, *Exégèse rabbinique et exégèse paulinienne* (1939), LIEBERMAN, *op. cit.*, pp. 47 ff., E. STARFELT, *Studier i rabbinsk och nytestamentlig skrifttolkning* (1959).

[3] When ELLIGER, *op. cit.*, pp. 159 ff., criticises BROWNLEE's comparison between the hermeneutical principles of Qumran and those of the Rabbis he seems to have been thinking when making his comparison mainly of the Rabbis' *halakic* exegesis, which was faithful to the text. The exegesis we find in 1QpH must however be compared with the Rabbis' haggadic exegesis, in which they allowed themselves a quite imaginative treatment of the text.

[4] SCHÜRER, *Geschichte* II, p. 397, calls Hillel's *middot*, very aptly, "eine Art rabbinischer Logik". Cf. the pioneer works of D. DAUBE, Rabbinic Methods of Interpretation and Hellenistic Rhetoric, in *Hebr. Un. Coll. Ann.* 22 (1949), pp. 239 ff., and Alexandrian Methods of Interpretation and the Rabbis, in *Festschrift* H. LEWALD (1953), pp. 27 ff., and of LIEBERMAN, *Hellenism*, pp. 47 ff., which attempt to determine the relationship on concrete points between Hellenistic and rabbinic ways of arguing.

[5] D. HOFFMANN, *Zur Einleitung in die halachischen Midraschim* (1887), p. 5, points out that Malbim (d. 1879) reckoned up no less than 613 rules of exposition in his commentary on Sifra!

[6] See e.g. the rich collection of readings of the texts of Sam., Josh. and Judg. which V. APTOWITZER has assembled from rabbinic literature in his work *Das Schriftwort in der rabbinischen Literatur* I–V (1906–15).

ular moment they have ceased to read the text in the traditional way, and are now using a new method.[1]

One might expect, considering this attitude to the Biblical text, in many ways liberal and imaginative, that the O.T. text would have been subject to constant alteration during the centuries which separate the dawn of the Christian era from the final written version of the Masoretes. One might expect the text, during these centuries, to have been a fluid entity, which was not stabilized and made permanent before the time of the post-Talmudic Masoretes.[2] This idea, however, has been thoroughly refuted by the continued research and discoveries of the 20th century. It has been established, beyond any shadow of a doubt, that alterations to the text of the O.T. during the period in question are remarkably few in number.[3]

The large number of texts discovered at Qumran has provided us with new material which we have to take into account when discussing the history of the text of the O.T. Examination of these texts, and the scholarly debate which has surrounded them, has not yet reached the stage at which it is possible to come to a considered opinion on the whole complex of problems involved;[4] for our purposes, a few comments will suffice.

---

[1] See A. ROSENZWEIG, Die Al-tikri-Deutungen, in *Festschrift* I. LEWY (1911), pp. 204 ff.

[2] C. RABIN, The Dead Sea Scrolls and the History of the O.T. Text, in *Journ. of Theol. Stud.* 6 (1955), pp. 180 f., compares the way in which the Qumran sect makes use of several different recensions of the same text with the recognition by expositors of the Koran of several parallel versions of the text; he produces the thesis that a "limited variability" of the text was recognized in Qumran. A similar theory was advanced by O. H. BOSTRÖM (*Alternative Readings in the Hebrew of the Books of Samuel*, 1918) and G. GERLEMAN (*Synoptic Studies in the O.T.*, 1948, espec. pp. 24 ff.) in connection with the pre-masoretic text. This solution does not seem to be feasible, at least for Rabbinic Judaism during the period with which we are dealing in the present investigation.

[3] See B. J. ROBERTS, *The O.T. Text and Versions* (1951), pp. 1 ff.; cf. H. S. NYBERG, Das textkritische Problem des A. T:s am Hoseabuche demonstriert, in *Zeitschr. f. d. Alttest. Wiss.* 52 (1934), pp. 241 ff., and I. ENGNELL, lately in *Grammatik i gammaltestamentlig hebreiska* (1960), pp. 10 f. See also the following note.

[4] From the masses of contributions to the debate with which we are concerned here we may select: M. H. SEGAL, The Promulgation of the Authoritative Text of the Hebrew Bible, in *Journ. of Bibl. Lit.* 72 (1953), pp. 35 ff., RABIN, *op. cit.*, pp. 174 ff., M. GREENBERG, The Stabilization of the Text of the Hebrew Bible, in *Journ. of the Amer. Orient. Soc.* 76 (1956), pp. 157 ff., H. M. ORLINSKY, Notes on the Present State of the Textual Criticism of the Judean Biblical Cave Scrolls, in

In the first place, the discoveries show that no fixed standard text had been effectively spread over the whole of Israel at that time. There were without doubt a number of popular versions (*vulgata*) of the sacred texts.[1]

But secondly, we now know that at that time, that recension which we call "masoretic" was already in existence; this is true of at least some of the books of the O.T.[2] One of the Isaiah scrolls (1QIs[b]), together with some fragments of the Psalter (4QPs), show a very close resemblance to the masoretic text.[3] It is also significant that the correctors of the text whose work can be traced in all manuscripts,[4] have on this occasion not introduced readings from any other version, as has happened when other manuscripts have been corrected. Readings from this text (1QIs[b]) have been introduced into the other Isaiah scroll (1QIs[a]), but never vice versa.[5] This would seem to indicate that this version was treated in these circles as being in a class by itself.[6] That is a moot point, however.

The discovery of these two texts (1QIs[b], 4QPs) has thus made it

---

A Stubborn Faith, Papers ... Presented to Honor W. A. IRWIN (1956), pp. 117 ff., J. PH. HYATT, The Dead Sea Discoveries: Retrospect and Challenge, in *Journ. of Bibl. Lit.* 76 (1957), pp. 1 ff., P. W. SKEHAN, The Qumran Manuscripts and Textual Criticism, in *Suppl. to Vet. Test.* 4 (1957), pp. 148 ff., IDEM, The Period of the Biblical Texts from Khirbet Qumrân, in *Cath. Bibl. Quart.* 19 (1957), pp. 435 ff., F. M. CROSS, *The Ancient Library of Qumrân and Modern Biblical Studies* (1958), pp. 120 ff., G. W. AHLSTRÖM, *Psalm 89* (1959), P. E. KAHLE, *The Cairo Geniza* (2nd ed. 1959), B. J. ROBERTS, The Second Isaiah Scroll from Qumrân (IQIsb), in *Bull. of the J. Ryl. Libr.* 42 (1959), pp. 132 ff.

[1] For those manuscripts which may be called *vulgata*-manuscripts, see LIEBER-MAN, *Hellenism*, pp. 20 ff., and below, p. 43, n. 3.

[2] Since the Pentateuch was considered to be incomparably the most important of the Biblical writings it must have been fixed first. The Prophetic writings must have come second, and the other writings third. The Psalter has perhaps been in an exceptional position. S. B. HOENIG, *The Great Sanhedrin* (1953), p. 90, considers that the Great Sanhedrin exercised strict control over the books of the Pentateuch, since these formed the basis of all legislation. This point of view has much to recommend it. — Thus we must reckon with the fact that the Pentateuch was fixed before the text of the Book of Isaiah.

[3] A detailed presentation of the material is given by S. LOEWINGER, The Variants of DSI II, in *Vet. Test.* 4 (1954), pp. 155 ff. For classification and critical evaluation of the variants, see M. MARTIN, *The Scribal Character of the Dead Sea Scrolls* I–II (1958), I, pp. 339 ff., and ROBERTS, *The Second Isaiah Scroll*.

[4] See MARTIN, *op. cit.* I, part 2. Cf. below.

[5] See *ibid.*, pp. 279 ff., II, p. 695.

[6] So ROBERTS, *The Dead Sea Scrolls*, pp. 95 f., and MARTIN, *op. cit.* II, p. 695.

clear that the masoretic recension of the text was in existence at the beginning of the Christian era and—as far as certain books at least are concerned—is not a later creation of the Masoretes.

We must ask, thirdly, *how far* the determination of the standard text had advanced. If a heretical sect had among its texts one which to all intents and purposes agreed with that which the post-Talmudic Masoretes were later to fix graphically with such precision, what did the texts look like which were to be found in the temple archives of the time,[1] and which were used by the leading scholars of "official" Judaism in their services, their legal affairs and their teaching?[2] MARTIN and B. J. ROBERTS, in their analysis of 1QIs[b], have shown that this was *per se* far from being an irreproachable example of the version it represents.[3] It cannot have been the best example of this version to be found in Israel at that time.

ROBERTS points out, correctly, that it is unreasonable to suppose that the Rabbis or the "orthodox" Masoretes should at some later stage—or at any stage, for that matter—have adopted a sectarian text, and records the conclusion to which 1QIs[b] compels us: that the so-called masoretic version (and here it might be prudent to limit this to certain of the books)[4] is not the result of R. Aqiba's work of standardization, but existed before the Christian era began.[5] We must also take into account the fact that the texts discovered at Murabbaat, which obviously originate with orthodox Jews, correspond exactly to the masoretic text.[6] This can hardly be interpreted to mean that the O.T. texts were cor-

---

[1] For the Temple archives, see below, pp. 53 f.

[2] HYATT, *The Dead Sea Discoveries*, p. 6, points out that "we cannot be sure that Jerusalem was as free in such matters as was Qumran". Similar views are expressed by ROBERTS, *The Dead Sea Scrolls*, pp. 95 f., and GREENBERG, *The Stabilization of the Text*, pp. 165 f.

[3] MARTIN, *op. cit.* I, pp. 339 ff., and ROBERTS, *The Second Isaiah Scroll*, pp. 143 f., show that 1QIs[b] cannot have been the direct prototype of the text later used by the post-Talmudic Masoretes. ROBERTS, *ibid.*, also points out that the division into paragraphs in 1QIs[b] diverges from the tradition taken over by the Masoretes in no less than 22 cases. 1QIs[b] is thus not the work of a scribe who had access to the "orthodox" Jerusalem *masorah*.

[4] See above, p. 38, n. 2.

[5] ROBERTS, *ibid.*, argues that this recension of the text has existed at least since the Maccabean period.

[6] See R. DE VAUX, Les grottes de Murabba'at et leurs documents, in *Rev. Bibl.* 60 (1953), p. 264, and J. T. MILIK, Le travail d'édition des manuscrits du Désert de Juda, in *Suppl. to Vet. Test.* 4 (1957), p. 17.

rected and fixed between the period at which the Qumran texts were written and that of the Murabbaat texts (ca. 100 A.D.). It is scarcely likely that any "stabilization" of the text can have taken place during these hectic centuries.[1]

We can leave this question, however. For our purposes, it is sufficient to point to such an imperfect scroll as 1QIs[a], and to see how little even this deviates from the masoretic text.[2] Thus the text of the written Torah has, during the period with which we are concerned here, i.e. from the beginning of the Christian era, been preserved with remarkable precision. This is so, despite the fact that exposition was at this time carried on in the most diverse and imaginative ways, and despite the fact that changing religious, social and political circumstances caused the text to be understood in different ways. It is an eloquent picture we get if we compare the preserved—i.e. the finally fixed—masoretic text with the preserved *targumim*, even the Targum of Onkelos,[3] not to mention the *midrashim*. Side by side with a general tendency towards diverse, dynamic adaptation of the content of the text, there has continually been a tendency to detailed, static reproduction of its wording.

It is not possible to interpret this in such a way as to say that some Rabbis—or some groups—understood the Divine Word as being flexible

---

[1] GREENBERG, *The Stabilization of the Text*, p. 161, considers that "only after the consolidation of Rabbinic Judaism between the two revolts (70–132) did a more thorough supervision of the text on the basis of the standard become possible". As against this we must quote ROBERTS' assertion that there is no reason to draw a line of development from 1QIs[b] to the masoretic text, *The Dead Sea Scrolls*, pp. 95 f. Cf. above, p. 39, n. 3. — We ought also to remember that the rabbinic literature says nothing about such a new methodical attempt to stabilize the text; see below.

[2] C. KUHL, Schreibereigentümlichkeiten. Bemerkungen zur Jesajarolle (DSIa), in *Vet. Test.* 2 (1952), pp. 307 ff., describes this scroll and its variants in detail. — We may mention in this context that the carelessness which many have pointed out in the writing of the Qumran texts (see e.g. ELLIGER, *Studien zum Habakuk-Kommentar*, p. 58, and ORLINSKY, e.g. *Notes on Textual Criticism*, p. 124), is not confirmed by MARTIN's careful analysis. After his palaeographical examination of the textual material he concludes that the copying and correction of the texts cannot be characterized as careless, I, pp. 406 ff.

[3] Despite the "fast peinliche Wörtlichkeit" (SCHÜRER) by which it is partly characterized in the form in which it has been preserved for us. See A. BERLINER, *Targum Onkelos* I–II (1884), II, pp. 101 ff., and A. SPERBER's new edition *The Bible in Aramaic* I (1959). A similar picture would seem to be given by the announced publication by A. DIEZ MACHO of the recently discovered entire Palestinian Targum (see *Suppl. to Vet. Test.* 7, 1960, pp. 222 ff.).

and dynamic, while others saw it as being static. It is true that some were mainly interested in the faithful preservation of the text and others in using it in all its spiritual potential,[1] but seen overall, we find the two tendencies side by side within the same rabbinic tradition, and even in the work of a single Rabbi.[2] And the two tendencies are held together in one and the same attitude to the Divine Word, one and the same "view of Scripture", if we may be allowed the expression. It is just because it is the Sacred Word, the source of endless riches, which is found in the Scriptures, that each and every syllable must be both preserved and used.[3] These two tendencies are also psychologically associated: the perception of the text as sacred leads partly to a desire to preserve the text without corruption, and partly to a desire to appropriate all its incomparable riches. Furthermore, certainty that the sacred words of the text have in fact been preserved without distortion adds to the frankness with which the very letter of the text is drawn upon for teaching purposes.

We must ask instead: In what context has the dynamic tendency been dominant, and in what context the static? Which situations have led to the adaptation of the text, and which to its reproduction?

One of these need not detain us. The tendency toward liberal (which is by no means the same as disrespectful) treatment of the Divine Word is to be found—more or less thoroughgoing in form—in most situations of the life of the Jewish people. To generalize and exaggerate a little, we might say that all practical "use of the text" is adaptation of the text. It would therefore seem to be more fruitful, methodologically speaking, to try to determine and stress the most important situations in which the text was *reproduced*. The question might thus be formulated: *where was the dominant attitude one of reproducing the text in its untouched, traditional state?*

---

[1] See below for the Scripture specialists.

[2] There is naturally a certain difference of degree in the concepts of different Rabbis, different groups, different tendencies—and during different epochs; this does not alter the overall picture. See L. DOBSCHÜTZ, *Die einfache Bibelexegese der Tannaim* (1893), and W. BACHER, *Abraham Ibn Esra's Einleitung zu seinem Pentateuch-Commentar* (1876), pp. 361 ff.; for a more detailed treatment, the same author's work on the haggadah material of the Tannaitic and Amoraic Rabbis.

[3] See H. S. HIRSCHFELD's early but stimulating book *Der Geist der talmudischen Auslegung der Bibel I. Halachische Exegese* (1840), pp. 103 ff., for the Rabbis' view of the sacred character of the text of Scripture, and the consequences of this view for their exposition.

When the question is put in this way, there appear to be three contexts which stand out as the most important, though on different levels.

We must first take into consideration the deliberately cultivated professional reproduction of the text. Even before the beginning of the Christian era, it is clear that in Israel the importance of preserving the text of the written Torah was appreciated; measures were being taken to ensure its preservation, and its reproduction free from the least distortion. Detailed reproduction of the text had thus become a function *per se*, with its own intrinsic value. It is significant that the correction of a corrupt passage in the Torah was regarded as being a meritorious action from the religious point of view. We shall here summarize the various measures taken in order to ensure the careful transmission of the text into one function and one context, under the title of *the deliberate and methodical preservation of the text*. What is happening here is nothing less than a form of text-transmission, the primary object of which is to preserve the text. This is incomparably the most important context for the reproduction of the text.

The other context in which the text was reproduced is on rather a different level. Here, the preservation of the Torah text is not the main purpose of the activity; the Torah is instead being *passed on to the people*—if we may express it in this way. But this is also a kind of transmission: transmission in the service of education. We refer here to elementary instruction given in the Scripture school or in private, in which great importance is placed upon the accuracy of the text; thus we have here a most significant "conserving" situation, even if the preservation of the text is not the primary objective.

The third context which we must consider is the reading of the Scriptures in public worship. The primary intention here is not at all to preserve the text of the Torah, nor is it to pass on the text to the people by means of some act of transmission, but *to read* (קרא) *the sacred text as a sacred rite*, before God and the worshipping congregation. Great importance is attached to the correct reproduction of the text; the ambition is to read the text as traditionally given, as an unaltered and unassailable entity, sharply distinguished from the many-faceted, liberal usage, and the adaptation inseparable from all exposition. Since the correct reproduction of the text was considered so important, and since Scripture reading took place regularly in all synagogues, we are here dealing with a situation which must have meant a great deal for the preservation of the Torah in Israel.

We shall now devote a chapter to each of these three contexts in turn.

CHAPTER 3

Deliberate and Methodical Preservation of the Text

THE WRITTEN Torah (תורה שבכתב) was passed on in writing. We must begin by considering that copying of the text carried out by Scripture copyists, in whose work we find most striking signs of respect for the proper wording of the text, linked with an ambition to reproduce it correctly. We shall then widen our perspective to consider other measures expressly intended to preserve (שמר) the purity of the Torah text in Israel.

Certain of the newly-discovered texts convince us, as we have already pointed out,[1] that some at least of the books of the so-called masoretic recension of the text were in existence before the beginning of our era. This means that the text must have been preserved with remarkable care during the centuries prior to their graphic fixing by the post-Talmudic Masoretes. But how did this come about? Rabbinic material[2] gives us quite clear information on that point. It is true that it is generally difficult to trace the various preservative measures back any further than to R. Aqiba, or perhaps a little earlier; but the careful transmission, which—as the new discoveries suggest—has been carried on at some previous stage, can scarcely have followed entirely different lines.

It is conceivable that private copying of the sacred Scriptures may have taken place at the beginning of our era, but such copying is not likely to have been extensive.[3] In any case, the scrolls which were used

---

[1] Above, p. 38.

[2] Apart from the references spread throughout the talmudic and midrashic material, see מסכת סופרים: *Masechet Sopherim*, ed. J. MÜLLER (1878). Parts of this tractate are translated by H. BARDTKE, Der Traktat der Schreiber (Sopherim), in *Wissensch. Zeitschr. d. Karl Marx-Univ. Leipzig* 3 (1953–54), pp. 31 ff. The material has been critically worked through by L. BLAU in his comprehensive *Studien zum althebräischen Buchwesen* (1902). Cf. also S. KRAUSS, *Talmudische Archäologie* III (1912), pp. 131 ff., and O. PROCKSCH, Der hebräische Schreiber und sein Buch, in *Von Büchern und Bibliotheken, ...* E. KUHNERT *dargebracht* (1928), pp. 1 ff.

[3] For the distribution of the text of Scripture in Tannaitic and Amoraic times, see BLAU, *Studien*, pp. 84 ff., cf. A. SPIRO, Samaritans, Tobiads, and Judahites in Pseudo-Philo, in *Proceed. of the Amer. Acad. for Jew. Research* 20 (1951), pp. 283 ff. The ideal that each person should have his own copy of the Torah (BLAU, *op. cit.*,

in connection with public worship, with instruction, and with the administration of justice—so important for Judaism as a whole—have not been written by amateurs. Those responsible for the official copying of the texts were specialists. Such a professional copyist is called סוֹפֵר (Aram. סָפְרָא) or occasionally לִבְלָר (from Lat. *libellarius*).[1]

This concept is, however, flexible, and consequently difficult to define exactly.[2] *Sofer* means "Scripture specialist", and has two main aspects. The leading emphasis may rest partly in the fact that the person in question "knows his letters", and is a skilled writer; in which case the word often means "writer", "copyist", "notary", etc. On the other hand, it can imply that he "knows the Scriptures", and in the old Jewish milieu that means the sacred Scriptures; the word then means "one who is schooled in the Scriptures". The concept of *sofer* thus has to do with both these poles of meaning.

pp. 86 ff.) was certainly long belonging to the category of *pia desideria*, as emphasized correctly by L. Löw, *Graphische Requisiten* II (1871), pp. 1 ff. LIEBERMAN, *Hellenism*, pp. 25 ff., has pointed out the striking likeness between the different forms of the text of the Greek classics then in circulation and the different types of Biblical manuscripts. The exact recensions, ἠκριβωμένα, of the Hellenistic grammarians (cf. below, p. 55) did not crowd out the *vulgata* recensions, κοινά (cf. T. W. ALLEN, *Homer*, 1924, pp. 302 ff.). In connection with the latter, it is important to remember that they were not necessarily inaccurately written in every case, but simply represented a form of text which scholars had not cared for and corrected. — According to M. MARTIN, *The Scribal Character of the Dead Sea Scrolls* I–II (1958), II, p. 714, the Scripture texts from Qumran do not give the impression of having been written by a single school of scribes (in Qumran); they appear rather to have been gathered up from various quarters. If that were the case these discoveries would provide a fine example of the Biblical texts of the categories κοινά and φαυλότερα, originally private and in any case not owned by the synagogue congregation, which were to be found within Judaism at that time. It is however not possible to say, in the present state of research, whether this conclusion can reasonably be drawn.

[1] See on this subject Löw, *op. cit.*, pp. 9 ff., BLAU, *Studien*, pp. 180 ff., KRAUSS, *Talmudische Archäologie* III, pp. 166 ff. The latest work on the problem of whether in the term and the fact of סָפְרָא (סוֹפֵר) we must reckon with Egyptian or Babylonian influence, is J. LEWY, The Problems Inherent in Section 70 of the Bisutun Inscription, in *Hebr. Un. Coll. Ann.* 25 (1954), pp. 188 ff. For the terminology, see further BACHER, *Terminologie* I, pp. 135 f., and J. LEVY, *Wörterbuch über die Talmudim und Midraschim* I–IV (2nd ed. 1924), sub vocibus. It is worth noting that the Qumran texts show signs of having been written by men who were well acquainted with their work; see MARTIN, *op. cit.* I, pp. 97 ff., on the subject of the use of lines and other technical details which reveal whether or not the writer was unskilled.

[2] BACHER, *op. cit.*, *ibid.*

The meaning of the term seems to have "degenerated" during the centuries between the Exile and the fall of the Temple, a development which can be paralleled elsewhere.[1] During the earlier period the word *sofer* can be used to denote the great masters, the leading wise men of Israel. Ezra and the leading "scribes" who followed him were so called, and the title continued to be applied to the scholars of that period, but after the fall of the Temple the term was no longer used to denote a leading master of erudition, a Rabbi, a חכם.[2] (The interesting development in the nature of learning which is obviously reflected in this shift in terminology lies outside the scope of this work.)

We can nevertheless still discern a certain logic in the use of the term. After the fall of the Temple, *sofer* still meant a specialist in the written Torah, one who worked either as a writer of the Scriptures, a teacher of the Scriptures, or, often, as both. Thus specialists in the written Torah, whether of a simpler or a more qualified type,[3] are referred to by the same term. A fully qualified Rabbi, on the other hand, was not called *sofer*. The Hellenistic equivalent of Rabbi is the fully trained rhetor (σοφιστής) but the teaching carried on by the *sofer* was rather the equivalent of that entrusted to the grammarian (γραμματικός).[4]

We might mention in passing that even Rabbis of the highest class undertook professional writing for economic reasons, by the side of their unpaid teaching posts as Rabbis. The best known of these is R. Meir, who was *sofer* (לבלר) by profession. But this should not be allowed to confuse the issue. R. Meir was not a *sofer* in his capacity of Rabbi, but as a professionally trained copyist and Scripture specialist;[5] this applies equally to those like him. We shall soon return to this topic.[6]

Those responsible for the normal and normative copying of the

---

[1] E.g. in Babylonia. On the Babylonian schools, see below, p. 57, n. 3.

[2] Cf. M Sot. IX.15 (b Sot. 49ab) and see BILLERBECK, *Comm.* I (1922), pp. 79 f., and Joach. JEREMIAS, γραμματεύς, in *Theol. Wörterb.*, ed. KITTEL, I (1933), pp. 740 ff.

[3] Cf. below, pp. 50 ff.

[4] Cf. below, pp. 59 ff., 124 f.

[5] Meir already had the "divine" work of a Torah copyist when he came to R. Ishmael: לבלר אני b Sot. 20a. I b Git. 67a (bar.) we read: רבי מאיר חכם וסופר. Cf. also b Erub. 13a. See further W. BACHER, *Die Agada der Tannaiten* I–II (1884–90), II, p. 10.

[6] See below, pp. 50 ff. N. B. the נחום הלבלר, which is mentioned in M Peah II.6. In b Sanh. 11b (bar.) and elsewhere is mentioned a יוחנן סופר הלז together with Gamaliel I. (Cf. BERLINER, *Targum Onkelos* II, p. 90.) See further BACHER, *op. cit., ibid.*

sacred texts often knew their words off by heart,[1] thanks to their basic Scripture knowledge, their activity in school or "college",[2] or at least to the frequent copying of the same book—a limited number, since not all had, like R. Huna, copied the entire Torah seventy times,[3] or like R. Ishmael ben Jose or R. Ḥiyya, knew the text so well that they could write out the whole of the Scriptures (scil. with correct ketib) from memory.[4] But despite this capacity for memorizing—a capacity which to us is nothing short of incredible[5]—Rabbinic Judaism had an emphatically repeated rule that the written Torah was not to be copied out from memory (כתב מלב, כתב מפה). The written Torah was to be passed on in written form, and must therefore without question be copied from a written Vorlage (כתב מן הכתב).[6] According to R. Joḥanan, not a single letter might be copied without having the text before one's eyes![7] The Rabbis experienced a certain amount of difficulty with the tradition that on one occasion in Ephesus the leading scribe R. Meir, on finding that a Hebrew scroll of Esther was missing, had been compelled to write one out from memory in order to be able to read from a book at the festival.[8] In the Talmud this is explained by stating that this was an emergency[9] (the missing text had to be obtained from somewhere) and that R. Meir had an incomparable visual accuracy.[10] The rule that copies

---

[1] Pointed out by BLAU, Studien, p. 169, cf. p. 3 and pp. 80 f., and IDEM, Zur Einleitung, pp. 85 f.

[2] On this subject, see below, Ch. 4, 8–9.

[3] b Bab. Batr. 14a. Presumably by Torah is meant the Pentateuch. Ibid. R. Ami is said to have written 400 Torah scrolls, which R. Hamnuna however doubts.

[4] R. Ishmael b. Jose says: "I can write out the whole Scripture from my memory" (יכיל אנא כתב כל קריא מן פומי) p Meg. IV.1; cf. b Meg. 18b. — See further BLAU, Zur Einleitung, pp. 85 f., and Studien, p. 30. R. Ḥanael (b Meg. 18b) ought also to be mentioned.

[5] In this thesis we shall quote a great deal of material which shows how the art of memorization flourished in this milieu. In a case like this, historians must be on their guard against a priori doubts based on the present state of our own culture.

[6] See b Meg. 18b, p Meg. IV.1; see further BLAU, Studien, pp. 184 ff. and KRAUSS, Talmudische Archäologie III, pp. 163 and 318. — The preservative measures applied to the text of Megillah must a fortiori have been applied to the other parts of the Holy Scriptures.

[7] b Meg. 18b. אמר רבי יוחנן אסור לכתוב אות אחת שלא מן הכתב

[8] T Meg. II.4; cf. b Meg. 18b (bar.) ולא מצא שם מגילה עברית כתובה כתבה מפיו וקראה מתוכה and p Meg. IV.1.

[9] b Meg 18b; cf. par. in p Meg. IV.1. הא רבי מאיר כתב שעת הדחק שאני

[10] The words from Prov. 4.25 were (b Meg 18b) applied to Meir: שאני רבי מאיר מדקיים. Cf. Eccl. R. 2.18: רבי מאיר הוה כתבן טב מובחר ביה ועפעפיך יישרו נגדך ("a good copyist of

must be made from a written text made it possible effectively to avoid turning *ketib* gradually into *qere*. And the distinction between *ketib* and *qere*, finally determined by the post-Talmudic Masoretes, is still eloquent witness to the success with which the copyists were prevented from turning their memorized versions into scripture.[1]

The copyist who wanted to transmit the written Torah according to the "orthodox" halakah thus had to have a written edition before him.[2] In other words, he had to have access to a *ketib* tradition. But the copying of the text could not normally be undertaken by a person equipped with nothing but eyes, with which to see the text, and an ability to write down letters. It was not merely a question of silent, graphic reproduction of the written consonants. As DAIN has shown, the writer reads to himself the text he is engaged in committing to parchment.[3] This observation should be complemented by the reminder that reading aloud was the custom in Antiquity;[4] this evidently also took place when texts were being copied.[5] Anyhow, this seems to have been the case within Judaism.[6] We can see in the rabbinic texts how it is assumed that the copyist will read aloud when writing.[7] It is a debateable point, whether or not the Torah could be written to another's dictation, when the second person is reading from a written *Vorlage*.[8] The orthodox

---

the very best", LIEBERMAN, *Hellenism*, p. 25.) For the variants in Meir's mss., see SEGAL, *The Promulgation of the Authoritative Text*, pp. 45 f.

[1] For different ways of treating the *qere-ketib* problem, see R. GORDIS, *The Biblical Text in the Making: A Study of the Kethib-Qere* (1937), H. M. ORLINSKY, Problems of Kethib-Qere, in *Journ. of the Amer. Orient. Soc.* 60 (1940), pp. 30 ff., and IDEM, The Origin of the Kethib-Qere System: A New Approach, in *Suppl. to Vet. Test.* 7 (1960), pp. 184 ff. Cf. also below, p. 49, n. 2.

[2] Cf. concerning the scroll of Esther, mentioned in b Meg. 18b: דמנחה מגילה קמיה וקרי לה מינה פסוקא פסוקא וכתיב לה.

[3] *Les manuscrits* (1949), pp. 37 ff., partic. pp. 41 f.

[4] On the subject of reading aloud in Antiquity see below, Ch. 11 F.

[5] See particularly J. BALOGH, „Voces Paginarum". Beiträge zur Geschichte des lauten Lesens und Schreibens, in *Philologus* 82 (1926–27), pp. 84 ff., 202 ff.

[6] See BLAU, *Studien*, pp. 185 f. Cf. also E. HAMMERSHAIMB, On the Method, Applied in the Copying of Manuscripts in Qumran, in *Vet. Test.* 9 (1959), pp. 415 ff.

[7] This is clear from M Meg. II.2. The writer meets, if he has the intention (אם כון לבו), the remarkably strict ritual demand for a valid reading: היה כותבה ... יצא (cf. below, pp. 67 ff.). See BLAU, *op. cit.*, *ibid.* Cf. also the words of Rabbi, b Ber. 13a.

[8] The thesis, so long held by scholars, that in the Greco-Roman world books were produced by dictating them to a staff of scribes, seems to have unsufficient foundation in the sources. See T. C. SKEAT, The Use of Dictation in Ancient Book-

Rabbis seem to have prohibited this practice.[1] But in any case, *qere* is also seen to function when the text is passed on in written form; the copying of the Scripture is thus one situation in which a *qere* tradition was compelled to be kept alive.

As we know, the Rabbis occasionally referred to something which they called מקרא סופרים, "the reading of the scribes (or Scripture specialists)",[2] and which was regarded as being conclusive in doubtful cases. It is the same thing which is referred to when the traditional reading is defended—evidently before the time of R. Aqiba—by the words יש אם למקרא, i.e. "the (traditional) reading has a genealogy"[3] which must derive, according to the typical form of thought, from the giving of the Law on Sinai. It is rather difficult to decide whether the term סופרים, as used here, refers to the great leaders during the centuries after Ezra, or to the Scripture specialists (copyists and Scripture teachers) of a later

---

production, in *Proceed. of the Brit. Acad.* 42 (1956), pp. 179 ff., and L. KOEP, Buch I, in *Reallex. f. Ant. u. Christ.* II (1954), col. 664 ff.

Many scholars consider that 1QIs[a] is very carelessly written (cf. above, p. 40, n. 2) and bears distinct traces of having been written to dictation or simply from memory. It is naturally possible that this may have been done in *certain circles* in Israel (cf. IV Ezr. 14). In this case, however, the facts seem to be far from straightforward. MARTIN, for example, after a careful palaeographical analysis of 1QIs[a], is not prepared to call it carelessly written. On this point see also HAMMERSHAIMB, *op. cit.* Some idea as to the way in which scriptures were produced has also been obtained from the reconstruction of the Qumran scriptorium. It seems, however, to be still not clear how this scriptorium was used. Did the scribes sit and write at the long tables, as most scholars think? Or did the scribes sit *on* the tables, as B. M. METZGER believes (The Furniture in the Scriptorium at Qumran, in *Rev. de Qumr.* 1 (1958–59), pp. 509 ff.)? Or did the scribes sit on benches and rest their books on their knees, with the *Vorlage* on the table before them? This last possibility seems to be the most likely.

BLAU, *Studien*, pp. 184 ff., considers that Torah scrolls could be written to dictation even in Rabbinic Judaism; cf. KRAUSS, *Talmudische Archäologie* III, p. 163. It is however not possible to draw this conclusion—as BLAU does—from the haggadah in b Bab. Batr. 15a (bar.), which tells how Moses received the Torah on Sinai, by writing to God's dictation: משה אומר וכותב (cf. b Men. 30a). Here we have the compulsive thought that the Torah—according to the doctrine—must proceed from the mouth of God.

[1] p Meg. IV.1, b Meg. 18b with par. With reference to these passages LIEBERMAN considers it out of the question—with good reason—that Torah scrolls could be written to dictation within Rabbinic Judaism: *Hellenism*, p. 85.

[2] b Ned. 37b etc. See BACHER, *Terminologie* I, pp. 134 and 120 f.

[3] Sifra ad Lev. 12.5, b Sanh. 4ab etc. BACHER, *ibid.*, pp. 119 f. N.B. according to BACHER, R. Judah ben Roes is probably earlier than R. Aqiba.

date. It is probable that it is the first group which is meant primarily, but that does not exclude the latter, since in Tannaitic and Amoraic times it was the latter group which was professionally responsible for the written Torah text.[1]

The copyists were thus the bearers both of a *ketib* tradition and a *qere* tradition. But there is one further element in their equipment. They had a more or less full tradition, מסורת (later called מסורה),[2] having to do with the correct writing and reading of certain doubtful points in the text and with a number of other textual questions: *tiqqune soferim*, *itture soferim*, *puncta extraordinaria*, the marking of pericope divisions, etc. This tradition of the checking of the text obviously dates from a period long before the birth of Christ, although it has naturally grown, developed—and changed—during the centuries before the final fixing of the text.[3] This must have existed in principle as long as the copying of the sacred texts has been cultivated among the Jews.[4] It is interesting to note that the Qumran texts appear to reveal the existence of a form of *masorah*,[5] even in those manuscripts, whose writers have not followed the halakah, formed at the nucleus of Judaism. This is no more than we might have expected: all writers needed a *masorah*, but we can scarcely expect to find the same *masorah* in use everywhere.

To be sure, we cannot judge all the *soferim* en bloc. It is evident that there have existed different schools of copyists within Judaism: different copyists have been professionally trained by different masters. Furthermore, different copyists have been able to represent different

---

[1] Cf. BACHER, *op. cit.*, p. 134. For the *qere-ketib* problem, see above, p. 47, n. 1.

[2] On this subject, see W. BACHER, Die Massora, in his work *Die Hebräische Sprachwissenschaft* (1892), P. KAHLE, Die masoretische Überlieferung des hebräischen Bibeltextes, in H. BAUER, P. LEANDER, *Grammatik* I (1922), LIEBERMAN, *Hellenism*, pp. 28 ff., 38 ff., B. J. ROBERTS, *The O.T. Text*, pp. 40 ff., and most recently M. GERTNER, The Masorah and the Levites, in *Vet. Test.* 10 (1960), pp. 241 ff. The latter gives an account of the thirteen different proposals for the vocalization of this term which have so far been given (p. 242); he himself vocalizes it מְסֹרָה.

[3] See the works referred to in the previous note, particularly LIEBERMAN, *ibid*.

[4] Characteristic of the rabbinic point of view is b Ned. 37b–38a: *miqra soferim*, *itture soferim* and *qere-ketib* belong to the revelation received by Moses on Sinai (הלכה למשה מסיני).

[5] This is how we must understand certain of the "para-textual elements", of which MARTIN gives an account, *The Scribal Character* I, p. 144. 1QIs[b] contains no such elements. It can be seen *inter alia* from the division of the liturgical readings that this ms. was not written in the "leading" section of Judaism. See ROBERTS, *The Second Isaiah Scroll*, pp. 143 f.

religious groups: thus they have been able in some measure to appropriate different rules, covering such topics as the division of the liturgical lessons. The Qumran texts provide ample proof of the existence of such varying groups.

We may take it for granted that a school of copyists, or several schools, were connected with the centre of post-Exilic Judaism, the Jerusalem Temple.[1] The priests and Levites had from time immemorial had the task of preserving the Torah;[2] and the limited but quite reliable witness, provided by the rabbinic tradition, suggests e.g. that correctors of books (מגיהי ספרים), paid out of Temple funds, were connected with the Temple.[3] However, we know very little about the way in which these priestly and levitical schools functioned during the period of the Temple. It is possible that the Qumran scriptorium can be taken as a smaller version of the comparative phenomenon in the Jerusalem Temple.

If we turn our attention to the material from the Tannaitic and Amoraic periods, we find there details of various families and schools of copyists. Some of these *soferim*, *liblarin*, carried on a business of copying texts professionally: a more or less direct analogy to the practice of Hellenistic booksellers.[4] In this context we can safely ignore them. From our point of view it is more interesting to look at those *soferim* who, by virtue of their position as Scripture specialists, undertook professional copying of the sacred texts by the side of their teaching. Some of these *soferim*—for the most part those of inferior qualifications—taught children in the various synagogue congregations; we shall have more to say about these in the next chapter. But others—though the boundaries between the groups are indistinct—seem to have cultivated a quite advanced form of textual criticism, and were sometimes connected in other ways to the leading centres of learning. We must say a little about these.

From the Hellenistic world we know that in various towns there were men having a literary education, γραμματικοί, *grammatici*,[5] who taught

---

[1] Cf. Jer. 36.10, 20 f., Josephus, *Ant.* 11.5.1: γραμματεῖς τοῦ ἱεροῦ.

[2] See below, p. 86, n. 5.

[3] b Ket. 106a: מגיהי ספרים שבירושלם היו נוטלין שכרן מתרומת הלשכה. In p Sheq. IV.3, Num. R. 11.3, they are called מגיהי ספר העזרה. See BLAU, *Studien*, p. 107.

[4] See BLAU, *op. cit.*, pp. 188 ff. For Greco-Roman booksellers, cf. e.g. W. SCHUBART, *Das Buch bei den Griechen und Römern* (2nd ed. 1921), pp. 146 ff., and H. L. PINNER, *The World of Books in Classical Antiquity* (1948), pp. 22 ff. See however above, p. 47, n. 8.

[5] See below, Ch. 11 A.

the classical texts, both copying them and teaching children to read
them. These professional grammarians carried on a certain amount of
text-critical work. Διόρθωσις, *emendatio*, was a vital element in the
teaching of written texts in the ancient world; the state of the manuscripts compelled it.[1] But in a number of cultural centres—first and
foremost Alexandria—this work of textual criticism was soon impelled
to a high level of qualification.[2] The work of the Alexandrian grammarians (γραμματικοί, κριτικοί) in relation to the classical texts is well
known, and we shall not waste words describing it.

Somewhat similar circumstances are to be seen within Judaism,
though we must be content with a few suggestions, since the situation
does not as yet seem to have been analysed. There it is evident that
certain *soferim* specialized so effectively in the problems (*ketib, qere,
masorah*) of the Biblical texts themselves that they became, in some
sense, qualified γραμματικοί. And in that case, we here appear to be
dealing with the predecessors of the post-Talmudic Masoretes.

The first of these text specialists whose names are given to us in the
rabbinic tradition are Naqqai the Scribe (נקאי ספרא),[3] from the time of
the persecutions of Hadrian, and one of his disciples, R. Hamnuna the
Scribe (רב המנונא ספרא).[4] A disciple of the latter, Ḥanina ben Ḥama, was
able to correct even the Patriarch himself, R. Judah, over the reading
of Ezek. 7. 16.[5] Thus these *soferim* accepted and trained disciples. The
rabbinic tradition mentions a number of such specialists in the reading
and writing of the Scriptural text: men who were to be consulted in case

---

[1] On this subject, see H.-I. MARROU, *Saint Augustin et la fin de la culture antique*
(1938), pp. 20 ff., IDEM, *Histoire de l'éducation dans l'antiquité* (4th ed. 1958), p.
230, and below, Ch. 11 A.

[2] See further O. SCHULTHESS, Γραμματεῖς, in PAULY–WISSOWA–KROLL's *Real-
Encyclopädie* VII (1912), col. 1708 ff., and A. GUDEMAN, Grammatik, *ibid.*, col.
1780 ff., and IDEM, Κριτικός, *ibid.*, XI:2 (1922), col. 1912 ff., J. E. SANDYS, *A
History of Classical Scholarship* I (3rd ed. 1921), pp. 6 ff., J. W. H. ATKINS, *Literary
Criticism in Antiquity* I–II (1934), G. MURRAY, The Beginnings of Grammar, in
Greek Studies (1946), pp. 171 ff. Cf. also E. A. PARSONS, *The Alexandrinian Library*
(1952).

[3] p Maas. Shen. V.2, Eka R. 3.7, and elsewhere; see W. BACHER, Ein Räthsel
in der Litteratur weniger, in *Mag. f. d. Wiss. d. Judent.* 17 (1890), pp. 169 ff., and
ibid. 18 (1891), pp. 50 f., IDEM, *Terminologie* I, p. 135.

[4] p Taan. IV.2, Eccl. R. 7.7, W. BACHER, *Die Agada der Palästinensischen
Amoräer* I (1892), pp. 1 f., and *Terminologie* I, *ibid.*

[5] The same evidence as in the previous note. For his knowledge of the Scriptures, see also Rashi ad b Taan. 27b.

of doubt.[1] It is clear that these, by virtue of their position as Scripture specialists, were often both Scripture teachers and Scripture writers simultaneously. Some of them seem to have been connected in one way or another with the leading colleges.[2]

These specialists have as a rule the professional title ספרא (Heb. *sofer*), or the normally synonymous title קרא.[3] This is clear evidence that their special knowledge is not due to their position as leading Rabbis, *hakamim*, but rather to their being specialists in the Scriptural text, *soferim*.[4] We should not be confused by the fact that some of them could become leading Rabbis.

Scripture specialists, "orthodox" in their views, and with a positive relationship to the leading colleges—or simply occupying seats there— were guided by the Rabbis' rules regarding such matters as the division and marking of pericopes. In the colleges they were also able to learn a great deal about the meaning of the words of the text: here they find supplementary material to their *masorah*.[5] It can hardly be wrong to suppose that the post-Talmudic schools of Masoretes carried on the tradition from such Scriptural γραμματικοί.

Be that as it may. It is clear that certain more or less advanced specialists, *soferim* of varying schooling and skill, worked particularly in order to preserve faithfully the unimpaired text of Scripture. But it is also clear that the Rabbis were generally in sympathy with this endea-

---

[1] See e.g. how Samuel ben Naḥman is consulted in the evidence brought forward by BACHER, *Die Agada der Paläst. Am.* I, pp. 480 f., n. 4–7 and n. 1 resp.

[2] So e.g. R. Huna is consulted in his capacity of ספרא דסדרא in p Kil. III.1, p Shab. IX.2. To the meaning of the term סדרא, see WIESNER, *Die Jugendlehrer der talmudischen Zeit* (1914), p. 36.

[3] It would be of great interest to students of the question as to how, and by whom, the early *masorah* was carried to examine in greater detail the traditions concerning those men who in the talmudic and midrashic material have the title ספרא or קרא. A great deal of the preparatory work has been done by W. BACHER in his works on the haggadah of the Amoraic and Tannaitic Rabbis. Cf. also WIESNER, *Die Jugendlehrer der talmudischen Zeit.* — P. KAHLE, in his famous works on the (post-Talmudic) Masoretes in East and West considers that these were responsible for extensive creative contributions; see e.g. *Masoreten des Ostens* (1913), *Masoreten des Westens* I–II (1927–30), *The Cairo Geniza*, pp. 57 ff. It is difficult to agree with this judgement.

[4] See above, p. 45.

[5] A certain amount of work was also devoted in the colleges to an attempt to determine the simple meaning of the text; see e.g. DOBSCHÜTZ, *Die einfache Bibelexegese der Tannaim*, BONSIRVEN, *Exégèse rabbinique et exégèse paulinienne*, pp. 38 ff., STARFELT, *Studier i rabbinsk och nytestamentlig skrifttolkning*, pp. 48 ff.

vour and—though with varying intensity—worked to preserve the true text of the Torah in Israel. We see this in their knowledge of and reverence for *ketib, qere* and *masorah*, as well as in their general interest in the fixing of the simple meaning of the transmitted text; not least do we observe the same thing in their attempts to establish a *textus receptus*, to oppose popular editions, and to approve the standard edition[1]—preserved in detail and "critically assured"—which was later to be called the masoretic text.

It is evident that this endeavour is well under way in Rabbinic Judaism early in the second century A.D. But did it suddenly begin at that time?

SEGAL, on a basis of indications in Aristeas, Josephus, Philo and the Dead Sea Scrolls, has maintained that these attempts to establish a *textus receptus* began soon after the Maccabean wars;[2] B. J. ROBERTS seems to want to antedate this even farther.[3] In point of fact, there is a great deal to be said for the theory that these attempts began in the pre-Tannaitic period. Had they been *set in motion* in Tannaitic times, the rabbinic tradition ought to have preserved some mention of it; were it a question of rabbinic innovation, it is unlikely that our sources would have been silent on the question. The rabbinic tradition assumes, however, that the corrections to the *ketib* of the standard text (*tiqqune soferim, itture soferim*, etc.) were undertaken by the great leaders and scholars of pre-Tannaitic times: the old *soferim*. During the Tannaitic and Amoraic periods the Rabbis were responsible only for certain corrections to the *qere*.[4] According to reliable tradition, standard copies were deposited in the Temple (as was later the case with the synagogues), and it was against these that the other Torah versions could be corrected.[5] Correctors (מגיהי ספרים) were to be found in the Temple.[6] In

---

[1] Cf. BLAU, *Studien*, pp. 186 ff.

[2] *The Promulgation of the Authoritative Text*; cf. GREENBERG, *The Stabilization of the Text of the Hebrew Bible*, pp. 157 ff.

[3] ROBERTS, *The Second Isaiah Scroll*, particularly pp. 143 f.

[4] See LIEBERMAN, *Hellenism*, pp. 28 ff., 38 ff. — Cf. also A. GEIGER, *Urschrift und Übersetzungen der Bibel*, pp. 308 ff.

[5] For evidence and discussion, see BLAU, *Studien*, pp. 99 ff. As to ספר העזרה, a debated problem in this context, see BLAU, *op. cit.*, pp. 107 ff.. and SEGAL, *op. cit.*, pp. 42 f. Cf. KRAUSS, *Talmudische Archäologie* III, p. 163.

[6] See above, p. 50, n. 3. Illustrative of the Rabbis' way of thinking is the haggadah in Pesiqta (ed. S. BUBER, 1868) 197b, Deut. R. 9.9, that Moses wrote a copy of the Torah for each tribe, with an archive copy to the tribe of Levi. — For

line with this is the fact which the author of the Letter of Aristeas presupposes, that the High Priest of the Jerusalem Temple had at his disposal the unquestioned standard copy of the Torah (the Pentateuch).[1] Josephus, who was the son of a priest, born and brought up in Jerusalem,[2] appeals to the books in the Temple archives (τὰ ἀνακείμενα ἐν τῷ ἱερῷ γράμματα) when writing on the history of Israel;[3] he also vouches for the Jews' century-old respect for the text of the sacred Scriptures, saying that no one has ever dared to add to them, take away from them, or alter anything in them.[4]

All Rabbis sympathized with these attempts in Israel to establish a standard text correct in every detail (ἠκριβωμένα);[5] all took part more or less actively, even those who devoted the bulk of their energies to the deep and many-faceted midrash exegesis. There are preserved many rabbinic sayings which stress the importance and the value of careful and accurate copying and correction of the sacred scrolls.[6] As we mentioned earlier, they were well able to combine respect for an accurate text with the certainty of the inexhaustible possibilities of the text as expounded.[7] Of course it goes without saying that it took some time before the corrected standard text won complete approval in the whole

---

the correction process, see BLAU, op. cit., pp. 186 ff.; cf. KRAUSS, op. cit., pp. 161 ff., 170 f. For the corresponding phenomena in the Greco-Roman world, see e.g. T. BIRT, Das antike Buchwesen (1913), pp. 283 ff.; cf. L. HAVET, Manuel de critique verbale appliquée aux textes latins (1911), pp. 331 ff. For διόρθωσις as an element in teaching, see below, pp. 124 f. For the methodical correction which the Dead Sea Scrolls have undergone, see MARTIN, The Scribal Character II.

[1] Aristeas 176; cf. Josephus, Ant. 12.2.6. For the problem, see BLAU, Studien, pp. 100 ff. E. J. BICKERMAN, The Colophon of the Greek Book of Esther, in Journ. of Bibl. Lit. 63 (1944), pp. 339 ff., also deals with the depositing of books in archives in the Hellenistic world. For the synagoge archives in the Judaism of the Diaspora, see J. JUSTER, Les Juifs dans l'Empire romain I (1914), pp. 474 f. For the problem in general, see further K. GROSS, Archiv, in Reallex. f. Ant. u. Christ. I (1950), col. 614 ff.

[2] Vita 1–2.

[3] Ant. 5.1.17, referring to the exact examples of the Pentateuch, and Ant. 3.1.7 ἐν τῷ ἱερῷ ἀνακειμένη γραφή on the Book of Joshua. Josephus' argument is naturally tendentious (for the type, see E. PETERSON, ΕΙΣ ΘΕΟΣ, 1926, pp. 217 ff.); it is nevertheless unlikely that it lacks all basic reality.

[4] Cont. Ap. 1.8. The saying is delivered in traditional style, see LEIPOLDT, MORENZ, Heilige Schriften, pp. 53 ff.

[5] See above, p. 43, n. 3.

[6] See BLAU, Studien, pp. 186 ff.

[7] Above, p. 41.

of Hebrew-speaking Judaism. It is evident that *variae lectiones* were long preserved, even in some Biblical manuscripts, such as those which LIEBERMAN, using the terminology of the Alexandrian grammarians, calls κοινά or even φαυλότερα;[1] this is true particularly of those synagogue congregations situated at some distance from the leading academic centres. The Rabbis knew of many *variae lectiones*.[2] It is, however, difficult to know whether a Rabbi, when using a *varia lectio*, has taken it from the actual text of some manuscript (possibly the one he learned off by heart in school) or from the rich midrash tradition, indirectly from the targum tradition, or whether he is using traditional masoretic records (possibly marginal notes).[3]

We have now said enough to show that in Tannaitic and Amoraic times, the transmission of the written Torah implies rather more than the mere satisfaction of a practical need for books, whether for services, teaching, or any other purpose. The preservation of the text of the written Torah has become a function *per se*, and its importance is appreciated. Thus the centuries of care lavished on the sacred text by learned copyists and Scripture teachers has spread, and become an overall effort, approved of by all Rabbis, to give all Israel copies, correct in the most minute detail, of those sacred Scriptures in which not even the smallest point was without its importance.

---

[1] *Hellenism*, pp. 25 ff., comparing with ALLEN, *Homer*, pp. 302 ff., which presents the various recensions of the Homeric text (cf. above, p. 43, n. 3). APTOWITZER, *Das Schriftwort in der rabbinischen Literatur* I, p. 3, points out that *vulgata* texts were still in existence within Rabbinic Judaism in the 8th–9th centuries, and even as late as the 12th century.

[2] APTOWITZER, *op. cit.* I–V; cf. above, p. 36.

[3] Did the famous readings which have been found in R. Meir's copy of the Torah (see above, p. 46, n. 10) stand in the actual text or in the margin? The latter possibility is preferred by BACHER, *Die Agada der Tannaiten* II, p. 10. Cf. below, p. 161.

CHAPTER 4

The Importance of Elementary Teaching for the Preservation of the Text

IN THE PREVIOUS chapter we dealt with those measures, the primary object of which was to preserve the sacred text of the written Torah. We shall now proceed to consider two other contexts which were of importance for the preservation of the text, although this was not the primary object of the activities in question. First, we have to consider elementary Scripture teaching.

The Jewish educational system of Tannaitic and Amoraic times has been the object of many specialist studies.[1] In spite of this, many points still have not been cleared up, owing *inter alia* to the nature of our sources. One of these is the important question of the relationship between Hellenistic[2] and Jewish schools.[3] It is evident that there were striking resemblances between the two, but it is equally evident that

---

[1] The older, usually uncritical literature on the Jewish educational system is listed in SCHÜRER, *Geschichte* II, pp. 491 f. A great deal of material is to be found in the chapter "Schule" in KRAUSS, *Talmudische Archäologie* III, pp. 199 ff., but it must be read critically, since the author's desire to create a synthesis causes him to bring together into *one* picture material belonging to different milieus and periods. Such a method is far from being impossible in a milieu so bound by tradition as is the rabbinic, but is not valid in the extent to which KRAUSS applies it. — Among critical works published subsequent to this we may note T. PERLOW, *L'éducation et l'enseignement chez les Juifs à l'époque talmudique* (1931), N. MORRIS, *The Jewish School* (1937), N. DRAZIN, *History of Jewish Education from 515 B.C.E. to 220 C.E.* (1940), and E. EBNER, *Elementary Education in Ancient Israel* (1956). In the two latter works is given a comprehensive survey of the general literature on Jewish education during the Tannaitic and Amoraic Periods. For further literature, see the Bibliography below, pp. 337 ff.

[2] For education in the Greco-Roman world, see two recent and excellent works, H.-I. MARROU, *Histoire de l'éducation dans l'antiquité* and M. P. NILSSON, *Die hellenistische Schule* (1955). Among older works may be mentioned P. BEUDEL, *Qua ratione Graeci liberos docuerint* (1911), E. ZIEBARTH, *Aus dem griechischen Schulwesen* (2nd ed. 1914), K. J. FREEMAN, *Schools of Hellas* (3rd ed. 1922). For a broader presentation of the cultural and spiritual background of the Hellenistic school, see W. JAEGER, *Paideia* I–III (Eng. trans. 1939–45). Further literature will be named in due course. See below, Ch. 11 A and the Bibliography.

[3] For this relationship, see my remarks above, p. 27, and below, pp. 88 f.

they differed on many vital points.[1] It is not a question of a simple equation: nothing but a profound and detailed comparison is capable of giving us an accurate picture of this interesting relationship. But this is outside the scope of this present work; we shall therefore do no more than note in passing some of the more interesting correspondences.[2]

At the beginning of the Christian era there were two types of Torah school in Judaism. In the first, בית ספר or בית סופר, was given elementary instruction in the written Torah; in the other, בית המדרש, a more advanced study of the oral and written Torah was carried on. It is not easy to say how these schools originated.[3] We consider it likely that they originated independently, and that it was only gradually that they became organized into a systematic unity. It may not be out of place here to devote a few words to the origin of the *bet sefer* before carrying on to consider methods of instruction. We shall return to the *bet hammidrash* in our section on the oral Torah.[4]

The *bet sefer* evidently began as a private concern.[5] According to the Law (Deut. 6. 7 ff.) a father was in duty bound to teach his son the Torah. But it was some time before the art of writing penetrated to the mass of the people. Consequently, during the centuries immediately following the Exile, the number of fathers who were able to teach their sons to *read* the Torah was small. The impressive institution into which the *bet sefer* was later to develop probably began in these circumstances. Men (priests and Levites)[6] schooled in the Scriptures, *soferim*, undertook to teach not only their own sons, but the sons of others as well. They

---

[1] The most important difference is that physical culture, which played such a decisive role in the Hellenistic school, scarcely occurs at all in the Jewish. Almost the same is true of room for the teaching of music.

[2] For relationship with schools in Egypt and the rest of the Near East, see L. DÜRR, *Das Erziehungswesen im A. T. und im antiken Orient* (1932), and the short notes and bibliography in MARROU, *Histoire de l'éducation*, pp. 18 ff., 467 ff. See also the following note.

[3] For a comparison with Babylonian schools, see (apart from S. LANDERSDOR-FER, Schule und Unterricht im alten Babylonien, in *Blätter f. d. Gymnasial-Schulwesen* 45, 1909, pp. 577 ff., and B. MEISSNER, *Babylonien und Assyrien* II, 1925, partic. pp. 324 ff.) S. N. KRAMER, *Schooldays: a Sumerian composition relating to the education of a scribe* (1949), A. FALKENSTEIN, Die babylonische Schule, in *Saeculum* 4 (1953), pp. 125 ff., C. J. GADD, *Teachers and Students in the Oldest Schools* (1956).

[4] Below, Ch. 8.

[5] Cf. Babylonian schools; FALKENSTEIN, *op. cit.*, pp. 126 f., GADD, *op. cit.*, p. 25.

[6] For the standing of the priests and the Levites as the original bearers and guardians of the Torah, see below, p. 86, n. 5.

exploited their own professional skill and set up small schools. Stimulated by the Hellenistic milieu,[1] these enterprises flourished on Palestinian soil, and a degree of public control and public organization came to be applied, though not to any great extent before the fall of the Temple. The school system was later developed even further, and the schools became democratized. During the second century A.D., they more and more assumed the character of publicly organized and controlled establishments, connected with the synagogue.[2]

Since in the first century the schools were private concerns, it is difficult to decide how numerous they were. It is hard to know how many teachers, skilled in the Scriptures, were at that time engaged in teaching the reading of the Torah in their homes, in the open air or in connection with some synagogue; *permanent* connection with the synagogue did not become general until the second century A.D.[3] Scripture knowledge seems however to have been extensive among the Jews of this period—at least in the classes of society and the circles illuminated by our sources. Josephus and Philo bear witness, though with a certain amount of that exaggeration inseparable from apologetics and propaganda, to the sterling and the widespread quality of Torah knowledge among the Jews of their time.[4] The Dead Sea Scrolls add new proof-material to what we already know of this solid Torah-study.[5] But neither Philo, Josephus nor the Dead Sea Scrolls give us any further information as to how elementary instruction in the Torah was carried on; the *bet sefer* is never mentioned.[6] Our witness to this comes from the rabbinic tradition,

---

[1] Cf. above, p. 27, for the way in which Jewish schools are simultaneously influenced by Hellenism and offer powerful resistance to Hellenism.

[2] For a sound and balanced estimation of the growth of the school system, see MORRIS, *The Jewish School*, pp. 3 ff. Cf. also MOORE, *Judaism* I, pp. 308 ff., and EBNER, *Elementary Education*, pp. 38 ff.

[3] See MORRIS, *op. cit.*, pp. 48 ff.

[4] Philo, *Leg. ad Cai.* 31, Josephus, *Cont. Ap.* 2.17 f. Cf. *ibid.* 2.25 and *Vita* 2; *Ant.* 15.10.5.

[5] The sect desired to "seek God" (דרש אלהים) especially in the meaning of "seek God in the Torah" (דרש בתורה): 1QS I.1 ff., V.7 ff.; see further VI.6 ff., VIII.11 ff. For the importance of the study of the Torah for the people, see also 1QS II.3, IV.2, V.11, 21, 23. The sect's own Scriptures also witness on every page to the extent of the people's knowledge of the Scriptures, and how easily Scriptural words and ideas are used. Cf. BETZ, *Offenbarung und Schriftforschung*. See also below, 234 ff.

[6] As far as Qumran is concerned, the lack of a special term for the Torah school may be due simply to the fact that they had no special house or room (בית) for school-teaching, and had to use the sect's big assembly-room. Cf. W. H. BROWNLEE,

according to which there existed large numbers of elementary schools in Israel before the fall of the Temple.[1] According to one tradition,[2] Simeon ben Shetaḥ (ca. 100 B.C.) arranged for children to attend a *bet sefer*; according to another,[3] elementary schools were originally started in Jerusalem, and then in the provinces, after which the High Priest Joshua ben Gamala (ca. 60–70 A.D.) arranged for the establishment of schools in every province and every town. Although this information leaves a great deal to be desired with regard to thoroughness and accuracy, it is by no means improbable.[4] We may be quite sure that at the time of the fall of the Temple there were private elementary schools in all the Jewish towns of Palestine, and that the larger villages of Judaea also had such schools. This does not mean that school attendance was general at that time, though. The frequent mention of ignorant *amme-haares* is a fact which must be taken into consideration.[5] It is quite evident that only people of certain circles sent their children to the *bet sefer*; the propertied classes and the representatives of Torah piety would, for different reasons, seem to have taken the lead here.[6] But toward the end of the Amoraic period, school attendance was, to judge from the evidence, quite general, although not compulsory, among the Jews.

The sources give us no direct information as to how instruction in these Scripture schools was carried on during the first century A.D. But remembering the character of teaching in Antiquity—conservative and utterly bound by tradition—we have every reason to suppose that it was carried on in much the same way as during subsequent centuries. The picture which we have from this time is as follows:

The *bet sefer*,[7] as its name implies, is a school of Scripture. The teacher

---

Biblical Interpretation, in *The Bibl. Archaeol.* 14 (1951), p. 58. The ten year instruction mentioned in 1QSa I.1 ff. (7 f.) must refer to a form of organized teaching process, probably taken over from priestly circles in Jerusalem. Cf. Ab. V.21.

[1] p Meg. III.1, b Ket. 105a, b Git. 58a; Eka R. proem. 12, *ibid.* 2.4, Cant. R. 5.12. This evidence was put together so long ago as in W. BACHER's study Das altjüdische Schulwesen, in *Jahrb. f. Jüd. Gesch. u. Lit.* 6 (1903), p. 61.

[2] p Ket. VIII.11.

[3] b Bab. Batr. 21a.

[4] We have no reason to enter into a renewed discussion of this problem here. On this subject, see BACHER, *op. cit.*, *ibid.*, MORRIS, *The Jewish School*, pp. 14 ff., EBNER, *Elementary Education*, pp. 38 ff.

[5] For these see BILLERBECK, *Comm.* II (1924), pp. 494 ff., R. MEYER, Der 'Am hā-'Āreṣ, in *Judaica* 3 (1947), pp. 169 ff.

[6] Cf. MORRIS, *op. cit.*, *ibid.*

[7] To the name, cf. Sumerian *é-dub-ba*, "tablet-house", KRAMER, *Schooldays*, p. 5.

is usually called סוֹפֵר (Aram. סָפְרָא);[1] he is the one who is familiar with the art of writing, with books, and with the holy books in particular. We have already had occasion to mention that the meaning of the word *sofer* had "degenerated" between the Exile and the fall of the Temple, and that in Tannaitic and Amoraic times the title normally denoted a scholar of lower rank, a Scripture specialist who, by virtue of his knowledge of Scripture, worked either as a copyist, a Scripture teacher, or both.[2] As a type, he was clearly inferior to a Rabbi.[3] The difference between them is about the same as between a mediocre γραμματικός[4] and a fully qualified σοφιστής, in Hellenistic terms. The skill and learning of the *soferim* was, naturally enough, variable, and we have already pointed out that some *soferim* were evidently expert text critics, and may even have been connected in some way with the leading colleges.[5] It is therefore certain that some individual *soferim* were able to pass on solid and many-sided teaching in the Torah.[6] But it is also clear from our source material that regular elementary teachers (*soferim*) normally were of limited competence—as were many regular Hellenistic school-teachers. Seemingly, the only thing taken for granted was that they should be able to read and write the Torah with an acceptable degree of accuracy and skill, and give the transmitted translation (תרגום). In any case there is no indication that such a teacher was required to carry on instruction in the interpretation and exposition of Scripture (מדרש). This was clearly outside the normal scope of the *bet sefer*.

The teaching in a *bet sefer* thus concentrated on the written Torah (תורה שבכתב). If we ignore the most elementary instruction in the alpha-

---

[1] Also מקרי ינוקי, מקרי דרדקי, מלמד תינוקות. For the term סוֹפֵר (סָפְרָא) see BACHER, *Terminologie* I, pp. 135 f., and LEVY and JASTROW *Lexica*, sub vocibus. For the matter, cf. L. WIESNER, *Die Jugendlehrer der talmudischen Zeit* (1914) and M. ARZT, The Teacher in Talmud and Midrash, in M. M. KAPLAN *Jubilee Volume* (1953), pp. 35 ff.

[2] Above, pp. 44 ff.

[3] See e.g. the famous saying of R. Eliezer ben Hyrkanos, M Sot. IX.15 (b Sot. 49ab), p Meg. IV.5, and Rashi ad b Sot. 49ab.

[4] For σοφισταί and γραμματικοί see above, pp. 51, n. 2, and below, pp. 124 f.

[5] Above, pp. 50 ff.

[6] This applied particularly to teachers, who were responsible, not only for Scripture teaching, but also for other didactic and legal tasks in the congregation; see e.g. the demands made on Levi bar Sisi, Pesiqta (BUBER) 165b. Cf. also such as R. Ḥiyya bar Abba, b Taan. 9a, and those many cases where a leading Rabbi gave private instruction to his son or to other private pupils. See MORRIS, *The Jewish School*, p. 249, n. 17.

bet, and the learning of such things as certain prayers, benedictions and hymns,[1] there seems really to have been only one subject on the curriculum of the *bet sefer*, to wit מקרא, the reading of the sacred Scriptures.[2] We might possibly speak of two subjects, depending on how narrowly we define the term *miqra*; for in all probability the children also learned the translation of the text of Scripture (תרגום).[3] The dominant programme for the *bet sefer* was thus to teach the children to *read* (קרא) the sacred text of the written Torah, with correct vocalization, accentuation and cantillation, fluently (and from memory). In this way they were trained for the sacred act known as מקרא, ἀνάγνωσις, i.e. the reading of the lesson, as carried out in public worship[4] and in other, more private situations.

We must not forget here the extremely important role played in Antiquity by reading and recitation, among Greeks, Romans and the surrounding peoples, both in cultic and non-cultic contexts.[5] Literary teaching in Hellenistic "primary" and "secondary" schools was intended first and foremost to cultivate beautiful and accurate recitation of the classical works (ἀνάγνωσις ἐντριβὴς κατὰ προσωδίαν);[6] and in the advanced schools, expressive and aesthetic rhetorical delivery was practised intensively.[7]

---

[1] For the curriculum, see MORRIS, *op. cit.*, pp. 71 ff. and cf. EBNER, *Elementary Education*, pp. 74 ff.

[2] The programme for *bet sefer* and *bet hammidrash* is given concisely in R. Hoshaia's famous saying concerning schools in Jerusalem before the fall of the Temple: בית ספר למקרא ובית תלמוד למשנה p Meg. III.1, p Ket. VIII.11. — For the limited objectives of teaching in the *bet sefer*, see SCHÜRER, *Geschichte* II, pp. 494 f., BACHER, *Schulwesen*, pp. 75 ff., KRAUSS, *Talmudische Archäologie* III, pp. 230 f.

[3] Younger boys were in fact allowed to read (the text) and translate (give the targum) during the service, according to M Meg. IV.5 f., etc.; on this point, see BACHER, *op. cit.*, p. 76, KRAUSS, *op. cit.*, p. 232, MORRIS, *op. cit.*, pp. 159 ff., EBNER, *op. cit.*, p. 80. It is on the other hand possible to draw the conclusion that children were not normally taught the targum from the fact that the teacher *in his normal way* had to teach (מלמד כדרכו) those texts which could not be translated during the service, M Meg. *ibid*. This conclusion seems however to be untenable. — A Sifre passage (quoted by EBNER, *op. cit.*, p. 115, n. 33; I have not been able to locate it) gives the impression that the study of the targum followed the learning of the text of Scripture: "(The study of) *miqra* leads to *targum*, *targum* to *mishnah*, *mishnah* to *talmud*, *talmud* to practice and practice to the (rightous) work." (מקרא מביא לידי תרגום תרגום מביא לידי משנה משנה מביא לידי תלמוד תלמוד מביא לידי מעשה.)

[4] See the next chapter. Cf. Test. Lev. XIII.2 f.

[5] See e.g. LEIPOLDT, MORENZ, *Heilige Schriften*, pp. 88 ff., and below, Ch. 11 F.

[6] See MARROU, *Histoire de l'éducation*, pp. 215, 230 f., and below, Ch. 11 A. The Greek formula from Dionys. Thrax, see GUDEMAN, *Grammatik*, col. 1809.

[7] Concerning the rhetor-schools, see below, p. 125, n. 1.

The term קרא in the majority of cases means nothing else than *to read the text* of the written Torah;[1] we emphasize once more that instruction in the *bet sefer* was concentrated mainly on the learning of a correctly cantillated reading of the sacred text, and probably also the learning of the relatively simple translation given in the *targum*. The Jews obviously wished their children to understand what they read, but a deeper understanding and more thorough study of the meaning of the text belonged necessarily to the higher studies carried on in the *bet hammidrash*.[2] If we remember that the *bet sefer* was normally a school for children (boys)[3]—who began between the ages of five and seven[4]—that the children's knowledge of Biblical Hebrew was sure to be extremely deficient, and that as a rule the first book to be taught was Leviticus,[5] we understand that "mechanical" learning was the only possibility. Anyone who wanted to count himself educated had to proceed from the *bet sefer* to the *bet hammidrash* in order to deepen and complement his rather mechanical knowledge. The Rabbis criticized bitterly those who were satisfied with the deficient knowledge they had obtained at the elementary stage.[6]

Just as children in Hellenistic schools had to get to grips with Homer, ὁ τοῦ παντὸς προφήτης,[7] at a very early stage,[8] so the Jewish school-

---

[1] This observation has been stressed by L. Löw, in his article Die Tradition, in *Gesammelte Schriften* I (1889), p. 252: "Unter Mikra verstand man in der talmudischen Zeit das mechanische Lesen, ohne Rücksicht auf das Verständnis (Ned. 37b)". Cf. DOBSCHÜTZ, *Die einfache Bibelexegese der Tannaïm*, pp. 8 f., BLAU, *Studien*, p. 81, KRAUSS, *Talmudische Archäologie* III, p. 232, ARZT, *The Teacher in Talmud and Midrash*, pp. 36 ff., EBNER, *Elementary Education*, p. 80.

[2] For the programme for *bet hammidrash* see above, p. 61, n. 2, and further, below, Ch. 8–10.

[3] For the teaching of girls, see MOORE, *Judaism* II, pp. 128 ff., MORRIS, *The Jewish School*, pp. 24 ff., DRAZIN, *History of Jewish Education*, pp. 119 ff.

[4] Ab. V.21, b Bab. Batr. 21a, b Ket. 50a. Cf. further BACHER, *Schulwesen*, p. 64, KRAUSS, *op. cit.*, pp. 220 ff., EBNER, *op. cit.*, pp. 69 ff.

[5] This arrangement would seem to be original (thus BACHER, *Schulwesen*, p. 67, and KRAUSS, *op. cit.*, p. 235). *Bet sefer* originated in priestly and Levitical circles, where Leviticus must have been a suitable text for learning first. This practice was tenaciously maintained, even when in certain circles a start had been made with Genesis as beginners' book. — For another view of the matter, see MORRIS, *op. cit.*, pp. 89 ff., and EBNER, *op. cit.*, pp. 77 ff.

[6] See e.g. b Sot. 22a and further, below, Ch. 9.

[7] Aristides Quint., De mus. III (ed. M. MEIBOMIUS, 1652, p. 162). Cf. Xenophon, *Symp.* 4.6: Ὅμηρος ὁ σοφώτατος πεποίηκε σχεδὸν περὶ πάντων τῶν ἀνθρωπίνων.

[8] BEUDEL, *Qua ratione*, pp. 29 ff., ZIEBARTH, *Aus dem griechischen Schulwesen*, pp. 130 ff., FREEMAN, *Schools of Hellas*, pp. 93 ff., 227 ff., 247 ff. Cf. JAEGER, *Paideia* I, pp. 35 ff.

child had to begin with the most important of all books, the Torah (Pentateuch). In both cases the text had to be learned off by heart: memorizing, as we shall see in due course, played a basic educational role in Antiquity.[1] But according to rabbinic doctrine,[2] the learning of the text of the written Torah might not take place by one method: that one by which the teacher read the text aloud over and over again until the children knew it off by heart; this method (ἀποστοματίζειν, *praelegere*, *dictare*) was evidently common among Hellenistic teachers,[3] and was used in Judaism in connection with the study of the *oral* Torah.[4] The written Torah could not be learned from the teacher's mouth (מתוך הפה): it had to be learned from the book (בכתב).[5] The aim was to teach the child to *read* (קרא) the text, fluently and accurately (which in practice meant off by heart).[6] The teacher had therefore to place the text in his pupils' hands; he had to copy Scriptural passages for their use—a practice which the Rabbis treated with open disapproval[7]—and even entire books, before he could begin to teach.[8] One common procedure seems to have been for the teacher to give his pupils short passages written on writing boards (פינקסיות, πίνακες), then texts written on small scrolls (מגילות), and finally complete books (ספרים).[9] The Pentateuch was the first concern of these studies; then came the Prophets; the "Writings" were last in importance.[10] The programme provided for the learning

---

[1] See further below, Ch. 11 A.

[2] See below, Ch. 11 E.

[3] See T. KLAUSER, Auswendiglernen, in *Reallex. f. Ant. u. Christ.* I (1950), col. 1030 ff., cf. also BEUDEL, *op. cit.*, pp. 38 ff., ZIEBARTH, *op. cit.*, pp. 123 ff., FREEMAN, pp. 92 ff.

[4] See below, the chapters on the oral Torah. The method was naturally used in the home as well, when a father taught his son the first important key-sayings and texts from the written Torah. It is not impossible that the rabbinic rules are directed against an ancient *popular* practice, that of teaching the Torah only by *Vorsprechen*.

[5] See the passages quoted as evidence below, pp. 157 ff.

[6] See further below. To read a text of Scripture is therefore always קרא (never שנה), even when it is done from memory. When misunderstanding is to be avoided it can be referred to e.g. as קרא על פה, M Sot. VII.7. To deliver a passage from the oral Torah, on the other hand, is never קרא, but always שנה. See BACHER, *Terminologie* I, pp. 174 f. and 194, and cf. above, pp. 27 ff.

[7] See BLAU, *Studien*, pp. 66 ff., KRAUSS, *Talmudische Archäologie* III, pp. 208 f.; cf. EBNER, *Elementary Education*, pp. 67 ff.

[8] See previous note. — For similar methods in Hellenism, see MARROU, *Histoire de l'éducation*, pp. 214 ff.

[9] Cf. below, pp. 161 f. and 201 f.

[10] E.g. Deut. R. 8.3.

of the entire body of Scripture, though we may suppose that many teachers were compelled to make considerable cuts when it came to the "Writings" and even the Prophets.

The method current in Hellenistic schools was for the pupils to learn their study texts off by heart (ἐκμανθάνειν, *ediscere*).[1] This method of study was practised, if possible, even more generally and more energetically in Jewish schools. The Talmudic literature makes it plain in many ways that the children had to learn Scripture texts by heart. It is often mentioned there how children learn their *pensa* (פסוקין)[2] aloud and memorize them.[3] We hear of teachers and others testing the children's capabilities by asking them to read out (from memory) their *pensum*.[4] Here, too, we encounter the custom, widespread in Antiquity, of asking the schoolchild to read his *pensum*, and then treating it as something of an oracle[5]—a kind of *rhapsodomantia*.[6] The texts memorized in the *bet sefer* were to be kept as a lifelong attainment. Hieronymus stated that the Palestinian Jews of his day knew Moses and the Prophets off by heart:[7] even the children demonstrated a remarkable capacity for memorizing.[8] And if we turn to the Rabbis, the Talmudic literature bears witness to their unequalled memory-knowledge of the written texts. When a Rabbi quoted some word of Scripture, he had no need to give any reference, since every teacher and pupil had to know where the text in question was to be found.[9] A scholar who shows indecision when dealing with the

---

[1] Above, p. 63, n. 3, and below, Ch. 11 A.

[2] Also פרשה and דף (column); cf. Hieron., *Ep.* 54.11 (MPL XXII, 555), *fixus versuum numerus*, see BLAU, *Studien*, p. 122.

[3] KRAUSS, *Talmudische Archäologie* III, pp. 227 ff.

[4] E.g. T Hor. II.5 f., b Git. 56a, 68a, b Ḥag. 15ab, etc. See further KRAUSS, *op. cit.*, p. 228 (with notes, pp. 352 f.).

[5] KRAUSS, *op. cit.*, p. 228, and LIEBERMAN, *Hellenism*, p. 195.

[6] For such phenomena outside Judaism, see P. COURCELLE, Source Chrétienne et Allusions Païennes de l'épisode du "Tolle, Lege", in *Rev. d'Hist. et de Philos. Rel.* 32 (1952), pp. 171 ff., particularly pp. 180 ff., and LIEBERMAN, *op. cit.*, pp. 195 ff.

[7] *Libros Prophetarum ac Moysi memoriter revolventes, Comm. in Is.* 58.2 (MPL XXIV, 561). See KRAUSS, *op. cit.*, p. 231 (with notes), and LIEBERMAN, *op. cit.*, p. 52.

[8] *Comm. in Ep. ad Tit.* 3.9 (MPL XXVI, 594 ff.). Cf. Eus., *Praep. Ev.* XI.5 (MPG XXI, 852); LIEBERMAN, *ibid.*, KRAUSS, *ibid.* — Cf. what Eusebius says about certain Christians, *Mart. pal.* XIII (MPG XX, 1516).

[9] BLAU, *Studien*, p. 81, points out correctly the extraordinary knowledge of the Scriptures presupposed by their practice of seldom or never naming the place of a verse quoted by them. For them it is sufficient to use a formula such as דכתיב, שנאמר, etc.

written Torah is ironically recommended to return to the elementary school![1]

The children, then, had to learn the text "mechanically" (and memorize it) from a written book. It goes without saying that we here have a context in which the wording of the text is preserved. It is clear that this was recognized in Tannaitic and Amoraic times. Attention had been paid to the part played by Scripture teachers in the accurate maintenance of the Torah. The elementary instructions given by the teachers on such points as vocalization, the distinction between *ketib* and *qere*, and accentuation, were considered important. Those who wished to preserve the text without alteration considered it essential that the teacher should be accurate (דייק).[2] R. Aqiba stressed the importance of a man teaching his son the (written) Torah from a copy which had undergone careful correction (διόρθωσις), ספר מוגה.[3] And these words handed down from R. Aqiba are later explained by R. Mesharsheya as implying that a mistake which creeps in the beginning (i.e. when first learned) is not easily eradicated.[4]

Thanks to the careful learning of the Scriptural text in elementary school, where the teacher was not primarily concerned with different possibilities of textual interpretation and reading, deeper meaning and usage, but with teaching the children to read the cantillated text accurately from memory, it is the traditional wording of the text which forms the basis of all further Scripture study. When the boy or the man is later faced with the task of *reading* the text, he is not faced with the choice of several equally possible readings, one of which he may choose according to taste. The text has an obvious traditional reading (מקרא). We must now once again call attention to what the Rabbis called מקרא סופרים, the reading of the *soferim* (the old scholars and Scripture specialists —and also the copyists and the Scripture teachers).[5] The basis of the sacred text is provided by one traditional reading, though it is possible to read and interpret individual words in varying ways.

---

[1] A well known saying is זיל קרי בי רב הוא b Sanh. 33b, b Hor. 4a; from this point of view cf. b Ber. 5a, 61a, b Git. 29a, b Ḥul. 81b.

[2] b Pes. 112a. On the requirements for a teacher, see further KRAUSS, *op. cit.*, pp. 217 ff., EBNER, *Elementary Education*, pp. 51 ff.

[3] וכשאתה מלמד את בנך למדהו בספר מוגה b Pes. 112a. — For the care shown by the Hellenistic teachers of literature, see MARROU, *Histoire de l'éducation*, p. 375. For διόρθωσις as a permanent element in teaching, see also below, pp. 124 f.

[4] b Pes., *ibid.*, with the commentary of KRAUSS, *op. cit.*, p. 209. — Cf. the illustrative haggadah in b Bab. Batr. 21a.

[5] Above, p. 48.

It is an interesting fact that neither the Tannaitic nor the Amoraic Rabbis regarded all readings and interpretations as being of equal value. "The simple meaning of the text" for them stands over against all the various reinterpretations and new readings (דרשות and אל תקרי readings, whether using the available *variae lectiones* or not). The many and varied usages and interpretations of the text must not be allowed to lead to the abandonment of the simple meaning of Scripture. Among the Amoraic Rabbis a well known sentence circulated: "The Scripture never departs from its simple meaning" (אין מקרא יוצא מידי פשוטו).[1] And it is typical that *among the Tannaites*, the most usual designation of the simple meaning of Scripture is כמשמעו (or כשמועו), i.e. the text as "heard" according to tradition, the way in which the text is traditionally read and understood.[2] We also see the way in which the transmitted form of the text is here retained, despite all dynamic and flexible interpretations. A traditional *miqra* always forms the keynote of the symphony which the Scriptures play to a learned "orthodox" Rabbi.

We have now said enough to show the important role which elementary teaching must have played in the conservation of the text of the written Torah. Those men we know as *soferim* have also in their capacity of elementary teachers done a vital piece of work. BACHER's eloquence is quite justified, when he describes their contribution to the preservation of the Torah in Israel.[3]

---

[1] b Shab. 63a, b Yeb. 11b, 24a. The device was probably formulated by R. Josef, according to DOBSCHÜTZ, *Die einfache Bibelexegese der Tannaïm*, pp. 11 ff.

[2] For the term, see BACHER, *Terminologie* I, pp. 190 ff., though this does not emphasize sufficiently strongly the primary meaning of the term, that it denotes the *transmitted* wording and meaning of the text: משמע (שמוע)! Other Tannaitic designations for the simple meaning of the text are דברים ככתבם and ודאי; see BACHER, *ibid.*, pp. 89 and 49. I hope in another context to be able to return to the question of the interesting difference in meaning between the Tannaitic designations כמשמעו etc., and the Amoraic term פשט (פשוט).

[3] *Schulwesen*, pp. 75 f.

CHAPTER 5

The Importance of Public Worship for the Preservation of the Text

WE HAVE TOUCHED upon a third context in which the text has been preserved: the reading of the Scriptures (מקרא, ἀνάγνωσις), as carried out above all in public worship. We shall be content here with a consideration of worship in the synagogue, since this was the only form to survive the catastrophe of A.D. 70, and since from a technical point of view the Scripture readings in the Temple did certainly not differ from those occurring in the synagogue. The private reading of the Scriptures will not be considered in this chapter.

As is well known, readings from the Torah and the Prophets had at the dawn of our era long been fixed points in the ritual of public worship.[1] We need not here concern ourselves with the problem of how far advanced was the process of establishing fixed and uniform pericopes for the festivals and the normal Sabbaths; nor need we discuss the difference between the Babylonian one-year cycle and the Palestinian three-year cycle or the differences between the pericope system in use in Rabbinic Judaism and those used by various sects.[2]

We have already indicated that one of the main objectives of the *bet sefer* teaching of the written Torah was that of equipping growing boys to read the text in the synagogue services.[3] Furthermore, we have stressed that Scripture reading (מקרא, ἀνάγνωσις) was a well-defined holy rite, carried out in a cantillated style. Recitation in worship was

---

[1] On this subject, see further Maseket Soferim Ch. 10 ff. (ed. MÜLLER, pp. xvii ff., with commentary, pp. 143 ff.), L. ZUNZ, *Die gottesdienstlichen Vorträge der Juden* (2nd ed. 1892), pp. 1 ff., 342 ff., P. GLAUE, *Die Vorlesung heiliger Schriften im Gottesdienste* I (1907), pp. 1 ff., I. ELBOGEN, *Der jüdische Gottesdienst in seiner geschichtlichen Entwicklung* (1913), pp. 155 ff., 245 ff., BILLERBECK, *Comm.* IV, pp. 154 ff. Cf. also H. St. J. THACKERAY, *The Septuagint and Jewish Worship* (1923).

[2] Apart from the works named in the previous note, see J. MANN's unfortunately unfinished work *The Bible as Read and Preached in the Old Synagogue* I (1940) and N. WIEDER, The Old Palestinian Ritual—New Sources, in *Journ. of Jew. Stud.* 4 (1953), pp. 30 ff., 65 ff.

[3] Above, p. 61.

not undertaken less carefully among the Jews than among the surrounding peoples.[1]

Scripture reading was thus a distinct entity, sharply distinguished from explanatory translation (תרגום) and the expository or practically applied sermon (מדרש, דרשה), which also had its place in worship. Scripture reading did not, then, merely form a basis for instructional translation and preaching, but had its own intrinsic value.

The Rabbis did much to prevent the boundary between Scripture reading and application from becoming obliterated. We need only point out that according to their teaching, in the service the sacred texts were to be read from the book (בכתב), despite the fact that the reader usually knew the texts in question off by heart; the targum, on the other hand, must not be delivered from the book, but from memory (על פה), although notes of targumic material certainly existed, and although complete targum scrolls probably were available for non-official use.[2] Seen from one point of view, the targum belonged to תורה שבעל פה, and in public (i.e. services, teaching, etc.) must be repeated from memory. Furthermore, we encounter rules which lay down that the Torah reader (הקורא) and the targum "reader" (מתורגמן) must not be one and the same person;[3] that the former might not help the latter with the translation;[4] and that the targum reader might not begin before the Torah reader had finished.[5] We need not go into the question of the degree to which these Tannaitic and Amoraic precautions were observed during the first century A.D.[6] It is sufficient to state that Scripture reading had long been a fixed element in the ritual of worship, and thus a well-defined entity,

---

[1] Concerning the recitation of holy Scriptures in worship in other parts of the ancient world, see the references given below, Ch. 11 F, and above, p. 31, n. 4.

[2] For this problem, see the estimate of principle above, Ch. 1, and below, Ch. 11 E. Cf. in addition ZUNZ, op. cit., p. 9 ff., BERLINER, Targum Onkelos II, pp. 80 ff., BILLERBECK, Comm. IV, pp. 157, 160, 162, 164, and cf. J. KAPLAN, The Redaction of the Babylonian Talmud (1933), pp. 261 ff., partic. pp. 283 ff. — For the existence of written targums, see ZUNZ, op. cit., pp. 65 ff., BERLINER, op. cit., pp. 88 ff. New indices can evidently be based on the newly-discovered entire Palestinian targum; see DIEZ MACHO, The recently discovered Palestinian Targum, in Suppl. to Vet. Test. 7 (1960), pp. 222 ff.

[3] T Meg. IV.20, p Meg. IV.1.

[4] b Meg. 32a (bar.).

[5] b Sot. 39b. — N.B. that the precautions apply primarily to the reading from the Torah (Pentateuch).

[6] Cf. Luke 4.20: Jesus rolls up the book (πτύξας τὸ βιβλίον ...) before beginning to preach in the synagogue. Cf. below, pp. 226 f.

not to be confused with translation and commentary; further, that it is quite certain that at that time a clear distinction was observed between the written Torah and the various forms of the oral Torah.[1]

The importance of the actual cantillation for the preservation of the wording should be mentioned.[2] We ought also to remember that the Rabbis stressed the importance of the reader having read the text in advance several times in order to carry out his task properly.[3] School teachers or the synagogue servant seem often to have been given the task of preparing in advance the presumptive readers of the Sabbath day's *lectiones*.[4]

We need scarcely point out that the clear distinction between Scripture reading on the one hand, and translation and commentary on the other, had an effect both on the congregation and the reader. The congregation could not confuse what was cantillated as *miqra* (i.e. the actual text) with the translation (targum).[5] Nor was the reader tempted to allow his reading of the text to be affected by considerations of translation and commentary.[6] Nor need consideration for the congregation have affected him to any great extent: the use and application of the text was

---

[1] Cf. above, pp. 21 ff. — It is clear that the targum was originally *oral* translation (and interpretation) of the written sacred text. The development which we see during the centuries about the beginning of the Christian era is that the targum begins to be stabilized and copied down. We see Gamaliel and other Pharisaic doctrinal authorities opposing these copies of the targum as *Scripture*, and opposing their use *inter alia* in public worship. (See below, pp. 157 ff.) We have however no evidence to show that written Aramaic targums were in fact used in worship before the end of the Amoraic period. — On this question, see further BERLINER, *op. cit.*, pp. 88 ff.; cf. STRACK, *Einleitung*, pp. 9 ff. (Eng. ed., pp. 12 ff.), and KAPLAN, *op. cit., ibid.*

[2] See further below, Ch. 11 F.

[3] See the exemplary *maaseh* on R. Aqiba in Tanch. יתרו 90a. Cf. Ex. R. c. 40 beginning. Dr. R. EDELMANN, Copenhagen, who has been kind enough to read my ms. and has given me much valuable advice and many suggestions, has drawn my attention to the principle we find in b Ber. 8b: "twice *miqra* and once *targum*" (שנים מקרא ואחד תרגום) which is probably to be placed in this context. Cf. T Bab. Mes. II.21.

[4] M Shab. I.3, T Shab. I.12.

[5] b Meg. 32a (bar.); BERLINER, *op. cit.*, p. 84, refers also to Tanch. וירא and כי תשא (from the old Jelamdenu) and Pesiqta. R. c. 5. — The targum was also delivered with a resonant, cantillated voice (cf. below, Ch. 11 F).

[6] This "temptation" must have been much more obtrusive in earlier times, when the meaning of the Hebrew text was better understood by the people. Cf. GERTNER, *The Masorah and the Levites*.

after all dealt with in the targum and sermon. Objectionable passages could be avoided by deliberate reinterpretation in the targum, and those texts which were considered altogether unsuitable for the people were read without any translation at all![1]

It might in fact be said that from one point of view, the Scriptures were presented to the Rabbis in both a fixed and a flexible form: *miqra* and *targum*. The targum is a mediator between the fixed and uncompromising holy word of Scripture and the shifting reality which the same word addresses at various times. The targum gives—and invites—a smooth, dynamic and flexible use of the text of Scripture. But at the same time it shields the actual text against the danger of successive alterations in word and form. In order to understand the Rabbis' attitude to the word of Scripture, their "view of Scripture" and their hermeneutics, it is vital that we bear in mind the fact that when they preached to and taught the people, the Scriptures might be said to have two forms.

The targum[2] and its exponents thus played an important, though indirect, role in the conservation of the text. There was no need to alter the text itself; the Scripture readings could be carried out in accordance with tradition, and left unaltered. It would seem to be obvious, therefore, that the reading of the Scriptures in public worship came to be one of the most important contexts for the preservation of the traditional wording of the text, *qere*. We must take into account the fact that a number of minor variations occurred in the readings of different synagogue congregations and different readers: not all scrolls belonged in the ἠκριβωμένα category. Similarly, it was unavoidable that, despite all precautions, a number of minor alterations were incorporated into the text during the course of the centuries. But these are trivial and quite unimportant in this context. Seen as a whole, the Scripture readings (מקרא, ἀνάγνωσις) in the synagogue services must have exercised a decided influence in favour of the conservation of the text.

---

[1] M Meg. IV.10, T Meg. IV.31 ff. and the gemara ad loc. in both Talmuds, Maseket Soferim 9.8 ff. (ed. MÜLLER, pp. xvi f., with commentaries on pp. 137 ff.). — It is probable that other passages were also delivered without translation in different places and at different times; cf. ELBOGEN, *Der jüdische Gottesdienst*, pp. 187 ff.

[2] The phenomenon which we know as the targums should be seen in connection with the nature of translation and interpretation (*Dolmetschen*) in Antiquity as a whole. For this problem, see A. HERMANN, Dolmetschen im Altertum, in K. THIEME, A. HERMANN, E. GLÄSSER, *Beiträge zur Geschichte des Dolmetschens* (1956), pp. 25 ff., A. HERMANN, W. VON SODEN, Dolmetscher, in *Reallex. f. Ant. u. Christ.* IV (1959), col. 24 ff. — Cf. also E. J. BICKERMAN, The Septuagint as a Translation, in *Proceed. of the Amer. Acad. for Jew. Research* 28 (1959), pp. 1 ff.

CHAPTER 6

The Task and its Limitations

A MODERN WESTERNER who, by way of rapid and effective communications, is constantly receiving new impulses and impressions from practically the whole world, has difficulty in adequately appreciating the role played by *tradition*—in its widest meaning—in a comparatively closed cultural milieu, where new impulses coming from without are relatively unimportant, and the cultural heritage is all the more comprehensive. Here are parents, relations and families; here are the various actions and pronouncements of home and society; here is practically everything which the growing individual encounters—*transmitting*.

This comprehensive heritage from the forefathers is thus received by the growing person and accepted, step by step. He gradually assimilates a traditional way of life: experiences and forms the patterns of his own existence. Transmission takes place, in a sense, at all times and in all places. It is however important to maintain that the transmission process is particularly concentrated on certain foci, such as the home, the place of work and the cult centres, and on certain persons, such as the father, the masters of the different trades, and the priesthood at the cult centres. This applies both to the *oral* tradition, i.e. that tradition which is passed on by word of mouth, and the *practical* tradition, i.e. behaviour-patterns, customs, institutions.

As far as religious tradition is concerned, it is well known that such tradition has as a rule a very broad basis among a people, and is known and maintained—though to a varying extent—by everyone. The people as a whole are to some extent the bearers of tradition. Without minimizing the role played by the people as preservers of tradition, we must, however, be quite clear as to the special role—the fundamental role—played here by certain specialists who, more or less professionally, carry on the traditions vital to the religious group.

This applies not least to *oral* tradition of religious character. The importance of oral tradition in the ancient Near East, and in Israel and post-Exilic Judaism in particular, has been stressed by a number of modern scholars, not least in Scandinavia.[1] These scholars have also emphasized the role which must have been played by certain specialists (traditionists and traditionalist circles) when it came to the preservation of the sacred oral tradition which had been handed down from the fathers.[2] It is easy, too, to find examples within other cultural groups of the way in which the transmission of the sacred oral tradition was taken in hand by distinct specialists, who often functioned rather like living books.[3]

From these general considerations, we shall now proceed to the task of trying to give a concrete picture of the way in which—from the technical point of view—the oral Torah (תורה שבעל פה)[4] was transmitted within Rabbinic Judaism during the first centuries A.D.

That faith in the future, in the coming salvation and restoration, in the Messiah and the Kingdom of heaven, which so markedly characterized certain Apocalyptic groups at this time, was also essential to

---

[1] Among Scandinavian works on the subject may be mentioned: H. S. NYBERG, Das textkritische Problem des A.T:s, in *Zeitschr. f. d. Alttest. Wiss.* 52 (1934), pp. 241 ff., IDEM, *Studien zum Hoseabuche* (1935), H. BIRKELAND, *Zum hebräischen Traditionswesen* (1938), S. MOWINCKEL, Oppkomsten av profetlitteraturen, in *Norsk Teol. Tidsskrift* 43 (1942), pp. 65 ff., I. ENGNELL, *Gamla Testamentet. En traditionshistorisk inledning* I (1945), IDEM, Profetia och tradition, in *Sv. Exeg. Årsbok* 12 (1947), pp. 110 ff., Art. Gamla Testamentet, Litterärkritik, Profeter, Traditionshistorisk metod, etc., in I. ENGNELL, A. FRIDRICHSEN, *Sv. Bibl. Uppslagsverk* I–II (1948–52), IDEM, Methodological Aspects of O.T. Study, in *Suppl. to Vet. Test.* 7 (1960), pp. 13 ff., H. RINGGREN, Oral and written transmission in the O.T., in *Studia Theol.* 3 (1949), pp. 34 ff., E. NIELSEN, *Oral Tradition* (1954), IDEM, *Shechem* (1955), G. W. AHLSTRÖM, *Psalm 89* (1959). — A more limited role is assigned to oral tradition by G. WIDENGREN, *Literary and Psychological Aspects of the Hebrew Prophets* (1948), and IDEM, Oral Tradition and Written Literature among the Hebrews, in *Acta Orient.* 23 (1959), pp. 201 ff. — A positive introduction to the Scandinavian debate is NIELSEN's work *Oral Tradition*. Also instructive, though written more from a negative point of view, is A. H. J. GUNNEWEG, *Mündliche und schriftliche Tradition der vorexilischen Prophetenbücher* (1959), in which further literature, including non-Scandinavian, is quoted. — For the latter work, see my review in *Sv. Exeg. Årsbok* 25 (1960), pp. 175 ff.

[2] See e.g. ENGNELL, *Gamla Testamentet*, pp. 39 ff., and IDEM, Gamla Testamentet, in *Sv. Bibl. Uppslagsverk* I, col. 659 ff., and Traditionshistorisk metod, *ibid.* II, col. 1429 ff., NIELSEN, *Oral Tradition*, pp. 18 ff., 39 ff.

[3] See the material gathered by H. M. and N. K. CHADWICK, *The Growth of Literature* I–III (1932–40), and S. GANDZ, The Dawn of Literature, in *Osiris* 7 (1939), pp. 261 ff.; cf. also NIELSEN, *op. cit.*, pp. 18 ff.

[4] For the meaning of the term, see above, Ch. 1.

Rabbinic Judaism. But even when this fact is recognized, we must also point out that the past—or, to be more precise, God's work on behalf of Israel, and his gifts to Israel—played a vital role in Rabbinic Judaism. On this subject, MORRIS writes,[1] quite correctly:

"... The chief content of Jewish culture as well as of Jewish education was tradition, the memories of the past, with the departure from Egypt as its central fact. These memories were kept alive by a system of ritual and ceremonial which in Talmudic times had already achieved an extraordinary richness and variety, hardly paralleled in the history of any other people. Throughout his life, from birth to death, the Jew was surrounded by an endless succession of sign and symbol, ceaselessly exhorting him 'to remember'."

If we now proceed to enquire after the most important *centres* for the preservation and maintenance of this sacred tradition, i.e. the Torah, we are compelled to the following conclusion (though no degrees of relative importance are here implied):

1. The home, with its habits and customs of worship, and the character of its teaching.

2. The synagogue and the Temple, with their public worship on feast-days, Sabbaths and, possibly, on certain ordinary weekdays.

3. The places in which school teaching was carried on: בית ספר, בית המדרש.

4. Those places in which the courts, בית ישיבה), בית דין, סנהדרין, (המדרש),[2] held their sessions.

The three latter centres cannot be sharply distinguished. Public worship had a distinct teaching character, and also aimed at stressing the sacred laws; teaching participated in the character of worship, and concentrated to a great extent on the law; the courts did not aim merely at lawmaking and the administration of justice, but also at the maintenance of faith in, reverence for, and knowledge of, God's Torah.

The foundations of the knowledge of, and familiarity with, the Torah, were laid at home. The child grew up in a milieu in which religious, ethical and social behaviour-patterns were stamped and permeated by the Torah.[3] In addition, they had to learn important passages (κεφάλαια)

---

[1] *The Jewish School*, p. 117.

[2] For the courts of justice, see lately S. B. HOENIG, *The Great Sanhedrin* (1953). On the terms בית המדרש and ישיבה (properly "session"), see below, Ch. 8.

[3] Cf. Josephus, *Cont. Ap.* 2.16 ff. — It is significant that in those cases where the halakah is open to doubt, the Rabbis can exhort an inquirer to go out and see what

from the Torah by heart.[1] The extent and effectiveness of this teaching must, however, have varied considerably from case to case, depending upon the degree of faith in, and knowledge of, the Torah exhibited by the individual paterfamilias—not to mention other factors.

We know, *inter alia* from the Greco-Roman world, the extent of the part played by participation in the various functions of public life in the upbringing of the young person.[2] The same applies, *mutatis mutandis*, among the Jews. In contact with the ceremonies of social life, with the Sabbath services (and services on certain other weekdays) in the synagogues, and with the feast days in the Temple, the growing generation was constantly having its knowledge of the Torah enriched. Worship in the synagogue, with its interplay of fixed ritual elements and flexible, dynamic instruction was tremendously important in familiarizing the Jewish people with the contents of the Torah. This applies equally to the part which must be classified under the category of written Torah, as to that belonging to the oral Torah: the boundaries, as we have already mentioned, are not easily drawn.[3] To draw attention to the important practical role played by the synagogue services in the maintenance of faith in, and knowledge of, the Torah, is merely to repeat a truism.

But if this be granted, the fact remains that of the centres of transmission which we have noted, the *schools* are in a class by themselves. Here, the transmission of the oral Torah takes place to a degree quite different from that practised in the other centres we have mentioned— programmatically and methodically. In order to avoid misunderstanding it might be as well to point out that by "schools"—and in this case the qualified schools (בתי מדרשות)—we do not mean the school buildings, but the *activity*: the qualified work on, and teaching of, the Torah, the importance of which we shall consider later.[4] In pre-Tannaitic and Tannaitic times, and particularly in poor congregations, it seems likely that

---

the people do, "for although the Israelites are not prophets they are the sons of prophets" who carry—though to a varying extent—the sacred Torah tradition and allow it to characterize all they do. See e.g. b Pes. 66a, p Shab. XIX.1; cf. p Peah VII.6, p Maas. Shen. V.2, p Yeb. VII.3.

[1] Cf. Josephus, *Ant.* 4.8.12. For teaching at home, see further above, pp. 57 f.

[2] See e.g. NILSSON, *Die hellenistische Schule*, espec. pp. 60–75, and MARROU, *Histoire de l'éducation*, passim.

[3] Above, pp. 28 f.

[4] Ch. 7–12.

this teaching often took place in the synagogue. In such cases, the *bet hammidrash* is the synagogue, used as a locale for qualified studies.

Thus we have various centres—which may be within the synagogue, in some other locale, or may be situated in the open air[1]—where school teaching is carried out, and where the oral Torah is passed on: these are the *bate midrashot*. It is on these we shall focus our attention in this part of our examination.[2]

This also means that specialists, the Rabbis and their disciples, come into the foreground when we enquire after the *persons* who do the transmitting. The methodical school study of the oral Torah did not concern all and sundry. This took place, as we have seen, in schools of the *bet hammidrash* type, and transmission was in the hands of more or less learned specialists. It was naturally possible for scholarly fathers (חכמים) to teach their sons the oral Torah;[3] it was also presumably possible for some fathers, conscious of their responsibility,[4] to have received defensible views, without having undergone formal rabbinic training, by taking part in services and listening to the discussions of the learned specialists. But we have no evidence that the average father was able directly to transmit the *texts* of the oral Torah to his sons, if he had not himself been methodically taught by someone familiar with the traditions.[5]

If we now consider the actual *object* of oral transmission, תורה שבעל פה, we find ourselves faced by a particularly diverse and indefinite entity. Anyone who has been concerned with "the sea of the Talmud" knows how highly diversified is the material written there.[6] Furthermore, the

---

[1] For outdoor teaching, see A. Büchler, Learning and Teaching in the Open Air in Palestine, in *Jew. Quart. Rev.* 4 (1913–14), pp. 485 ff., S. Krauss, Outdoor Teaching in Talmudic Times, in *Journ. of Jew. Stud.* 1 (1948–49), pp. 82 ff.

[2] For these, see further below, pp. 85 ff.

[3] For the learned Rabbis' teaching of their own sons, see e.g. b Ab. Zar. 52b, b Qid. 30a (bar.), 48b, b Bek. 33b.

[4] For a father's duty to teach his son the Torah (Deut. 6.7, 11), see e.g. T Ḥag. I.2, T Qid. I.11, b Qid. 29a: וללמדו תורה ... האב חייב בבנו למולו. Cf. b Qid. 29b, 30a, b Suk. 42a. For the care actually shown by fathers on this point, see e.g. Josephus, *Cont. Ap.* 2.16 ff. Cf. Philo, *Leg. ad Cai.* 16; 31.

[5] It is stated in b Qid. 30a that a father is not in duty bound to teach his son the Mishnah.

[6] Jastrow gives a good description of the contents of the Talmud, in the Preface (p. v) to his *Dictionary*: "The subjects of this literature are as unlimited as are the interests of the human mind. Religion and ethics, exegesis and homiletics, jurisprudence and ceremonial laws, ritual and liturgy, philosophy and science, medicine

rich oral interpretative tradition which complements this textual material[1] is also included in the concept "the oral Torah". If our task were that of describing, exhaustively and with the correct nuances, the way in which all this material was transmitted, this book would be endless. Our task must be defined, and we propose to do so in the following way:

As far as the *material* is concerned, we shall concentrate mainly on the question of how the *basic* material of the oral Torah was transmitted— thus that material upon which the Rabbis themselves laid particular emphasis. This means *in concreto* that we must concentrate, first, on the transmission of that material which was fixed in the Mishnah; secondly, on that in Tosefta and the Tannaitic *midrash* collections (Mekilta, Sifra, Sifre) or which exists as dispersed *baraitot*.[2] We shall, however, continually give due consideration also to the more peripheral material in the oral Torah.

When dealing with the *transmission*, we shall concentrate on educational transmission, i.e. that methodical transmission which took place more or less regularly within the framework of organized teaching. Due attention will also be paid to qualified professional transmission, directly aimed at the preservation of the text, which became something of an independent function as from that time when an (orally) published mishnah[3] was in existence. The extent to which it was possible, outside scholarly circles, to practise any method of transmission other than the educational, is difficult to determine. It is not probable that any such alternative method existed. The rabbinic technique of transmission is, on the whole, *basically* so primitive and "popular" that it is difficult to think that it should vary substantially from that transmission technique which could be applied outside the schools. We shall devote one section to a brief account of that form of transmission which consisted in the pupils' imitation of the exemplary behaviour of their teacher.[4]

Further, we shall limit ourselves to an attempt to determine the es-

and magics, astronomy and astrology, history and geography, commerce and trade, politics and social problems, all are represented there, and reflect the mental condition of the Jewish world in its seclusion from the outer world, as well as in its contact with the same whether in agreement or in opposition."

[1] On this subject, see below, pp. 79 ff.

[2] For the term, see references below, p. 84, n. 1.

[3] On the publication of the Mishnah, see LIEBERMAN, *Hellenism*, pp. 83 ff., and below, pp. 119 ff.

[4] Below, pp. 182 ff.

sentials of the rabbinic method of transmission. By paying too much attention to details we run the risk of generalizing on some point, when the point in question is really more the speciality of an individual Rabbi or of a particular school.

By determining the essentials[1] of transmission technique, we should reach far enough back in time to make a comparison with the comparative phenomena in early Christianity relevant. Education in Antiquity was really not characterized by rapid changes. Least of all in such an utterly conservative milieu as that of Rabbinic Judaism, bound to tradition and devoted to ritual, is it conceivable that any radical innovations could be carried out in the course of a few decades. A radically new teaching method does not win universal approval in the Babylonian and Palestinian colleges in a generation—not even in an age of revolution. The fact that the basic principles of transmission were for the most part identical everywhere—though there were variations, as we shall see—in second century Tannaitic colleges, and later in the Amoraic colleges, must mean that on this point, nothing radically new was introduced by R. Aqiba; he must basically have adopted the traditional teaching method, and only developed and improved it.

It seems to be indisputable that R. Aqiba made important contributions in connection with the re-editing of the traditional material in the oral Torah, and that he was the first to create a mishnah which could strictly be called published (though orally published)[2]—and furthermore, other collections[3] of traditional material in mishnaic or midrashic form.[4] But it is significant that such collections established themselves so rapidly and so generally, and that other, older collections continued to be used by the side of them.[5] This shows that R. Aqiba's mishnah does not represent a total innovation in method for transmission, learning and study. We must suppose that the older midrash and mishnah collections, which existed prior to R. Aqiba,[6] were transmitted and studied in

---

[1] What is meant by "the essentials of transmission technique" will be clear from the following chapters.

[2] LIEBERMAN, *ibid.* Cf. A. GUTTMANN, Akiba, "Rescuer of the Torah", in *Hebr. Un. Coll. Ann.* 17 (1942–43), 395 ff.

[3] LIEBERMAN, *op. cit.*, pp. 90 ff.

[4] For these form-categories, see below, Ch. 7 B.

[5] See on this subject I. LEWY, *Über einige Fragmente aus der Mischna des Abba Saul* (1876), pp. 1 f.

[6] For such collections, see D. HOFFMANN, *Die erste Mischna und die Controversen der Tannaim* (1882), L. A. ROSENTHAL, *Über den Zusammenhang, die Quellen und*

a similar way, technically speaking. The opposite point of view is in any case nothing but a rather vague guess. We say this, fully aware that the catastrophes of A.D. 70 and A.D. 135 brought with them certain changes in the Rabbis' views and actions.[1]

Finally, a word about the way in which the results of this investigation are presented. Our presentation is synthetic, not analytic; we have thus chosen to begin by sketching certain main outlines: these will be found in the chapter on the way in which the oral Torah is carried (9). In the next chapter (10) we limit the field to the more special question as to how the oral Torah was directly passed on. Finally, individual points are taken up one at a time in the long chapter on the pedagogics and technique of oral transmission (11). The chapter on the origin of the oral texts (12) should be treated as an appendix, which takes up one side of the problem from a different point of view.

---

die Entstehung der Mishna I–III (1918; I–II comprise the 2nd ed. of Über den Zusammenhang der Mischna I–II).

[1] On the subject of the continuity of the rabbinic tradition, see MOORE, Judaism III, pp. 17 ff. — U. WILCKENS, Die Bekehrung des Paulus als religionsgeschichtliches Problem, in Zeitschr. f. Theol. u. Kirche 56 (1959), pp. 273 ff., follows RÖSSLER (see above, p. 20) and maintains that the conception of Law was entirely different in the Apocalyptic groups than in the Pharisaic.

CHAPTER 7

The Character and Divisions of the Oral Torah

A. *Character: Texts with Complementary Interpretation*

IN THE SECTION on the written Torah, we remarked upon the simple, but very important, distinction which the Rabbis drew between text and interpretation: מקרא and מדרש. We mentioned in addition that this distinction was so basic that the organized school system was itself based upon it: the elementary school (בית ספר) had, as its primary objective, to teach the children the text of the written Torah (מקרא), while the interpretation (מדרש) of the text belonged to the more advanced school.[1]

In point of fact it seems to have been common linguistic practice in pre-Tannaitic times simply to designate the sacred, authoritative tradition as מדרש, i.e. as Torah interpretation.[2] This practice continues into Tannaitic and Amoraic times, though at this stage the term is usually limited to a definite *part* of the oral Torah, as we shall soon see.[3]

If we now concentrate our attention on the oral tradition which, seen from one point of view, fulfils the function of being an complementary interpretation of the written Torah, we find that it is also possible within this category to draw a distinction—though not a clear distinction—between text and interpretation. The most important material in the oral Torah is in fact formulated in quite a fixed way. It consists of nothing less than a chain of short, *oral passages of text*: midrashic focal texts, assembled on the guiding principle of the continuous text of Scripture; and further, halakah statements and haggadah passages,[4] put together on different principles of arrangement into collections of oral textual material (which is of interpretative character, though this may not always be clear from the form). These collections of sacred texts are, however, only part of the sacred authoritative oral tradition. They also have a complement of interpretative material. With each oral text,

---

[1] Above, pp. 59 ff.

[2] See L. BLAU, Ursprung und Geschichte des technischen Ausdrucks „Mündliche Lehre" in *Mechiltha*, trans. by J. WINTER, A. WÜNSCHE (1909), pp. xviii ff.

[3] Below, p. 83.

[4] For these words as form-critical terms, see below, pp. 83 f.

which is usually extremely condensed and abbreviated (e.g. a הלכה, a chapter or a tractate of הלכות), there is to be found a complementary interpretative exposition (תלמוד).[1] It is thus possible from one point of view to call the fixed part of the oral Torah the oral text tradition; the more dynamic and flexible part can be called the interpretative tradition. This is very much over-simplified, as we shall shortly see, but is not without reason.

The distinction between text tradition and interpretative tradition within the oral Torah is particularly clear from the Tannaitic and Amoraic Rabbis' methodical study of the fundamental collections of traditional material in the oral Torah. This study normally takes place in two main stages: partly that authoritative text material (the collection as a whole, or a greater or lesser part thereof) is "mechanically" impressed on the individual's mind, and partly that this traditional text is interpreted and expounded.[2]

However, it is not only the basic material in the oral Torah which should be treated as oral text material. This term must also be used to denote important elements in the interpretative tradition which accompanies the basic collections. The collections of traditional texts in fact gather around these new collections: continual interpretation gives constant rise to newly concentrated text material. We need only remind ourselves of the way in which a *talmud* text grows out, in the different schools, around the *mishnah*: a new concentrated text which is itself in need of interpretation![3]

If we would understand this remarkable process we must study the educational theory, and the teaching and study techniques, applied by the Rabbis. In the pictures which we have from Tannaitic and Amoraic texts of the activities of teachers and pupils, we see how they have access by memory to enormous quantities of oral traditional material: their teachers' sayings, stories about their teachers and the like, form a body of material which must be classified as oral text material, even if it is not always formulated so definitely and carefully as the *basic* text material. It is comparatively seldom that we are given the impression that the Rabbis and their disciples in general are giving account in their own words of their teachers' positions and approximate views. Occasionally, when dealing with halakic problems, the teaching of some au-

---

[1] For this term, see references below, p. 104, n. 3.

[2] Below, Ch. 10.

[3] For the origin of *gemara*, see below, pp. 104, 118 f., 129, 132.

thority can be compressed into odd words: "forbids", "declares unclean", and so on;[1] it is, however, normally a question of the quotation from memory of a portion of oral text (a statement or a story). Knowledge is carried in the form of sayings and stories which have been memorized; material is kept in mind—from the point of view of study technique—in such a form: the memory actually functions in such categories. It is interesting to remark that these principles were not even abandoned when the Talmud underwent its final redaction and written formulation. It is well known, how eager the men behind this edition were to save space. Nevertheless, it does not normally occur to them to use their own abstract generalizations and summaries when giving account of the traditional differences of opinion between various authorities. Instead, they present the traditional discussions and decisions by repeating the words of the different Rabbis, or by quoting stories about the way in which the Rabbis acted. And they did this in spite of the fact that they were using valuable space by repeating a tradition in one single context several times—word for word.[2]

The explanation, as we have already indicated, is to be found in rabbinic study technique. The material which must be known is *memorized*. It is imprinted on the memory ready formulated, and is kept alive by constant repetition. It is carried on the lips, על פה.[3] The study of the Torah is, according to a typical rabbinic mode of expression, "a work of the *mouth*", and they call the *mouth* blessed for having been created as a receptacle for the Torah.[4] Transmission therefore means, in the first place, the process of faithful repetition (שנה) of a saying or a narrative by which the receiver is enabled faithfully to reproduce it himself: "putting the words into his mouth".[5] To this is added—if the transmission is to be thorough—the commentaries and interpretation which the statement requires. This complement can, however, be left out; it may for various reasons be postponed to a higher educational level;[6] it may be omitted, if the one who is passing on the material as-

---

[1] See also below, pp. 171 ff.

[2] Dr. R. EDELMANN has drawn my attention to the relevance of this fact in this context. — For principles of abbreviation, see below, Ch. 11 C.

[3] Cf. Greek διὰ στόματος ἔχειν (Eunap., *Vit. soph.* 473).

[4] b Sanh. 99 b.

[5] As to the phenomenon *in ancient Israel*, such expressions as "put the words in someone's mouth" or "on someone's heart", הדברים בפי (על לבב) פלוני, שים (נתן), Deut. 11.18, 18.18, 31.19, 2 Sam. 14.3, Job 22.22, Is. 51.16, 59.21, Ezr. 8.17, give us a picture of the way in which oral texts were transmitted. Cf. below, p. 135.

[6] See below, pp. 102 ff. and 113 ff.

sumes that the one receiving it understands the saying without commentary; or it may simply be missing, because the one passing on the saying does not know how it is to be understood.[1]

In order to understand how the oral Torah is transmitted, we consider it to be of fundamental importance that attention be paid to the interplay of more or less fixed text transmission and a more flexible commentary (which takes place, however, in traditional style and often makes use of a number of quite fixed elements).[2] This is incidentally also of considerable importance for the overall understanding of the way in which the Rabbis formed their concepts. We shall deal with the question in more detail in the following chapters.

We pointed out earlier that the term משנה can be used by the Rabbis as a collective term for the sacred, authoritative oral Torah, viz. when this is seen as an object of study.[3] All this material is in fact learned by means of a study technique based on the principle of repetition. We have now remarked that the term מדרש may also be used as a collective term for the oral Torah, when seen as Torah interpretation. In order to avoid misunderstanding, we must make it quite clear that not the whole of the oral Torah *originated* as Scripture interpretation. The oral Torah does not only contain such as has been derived from the written Torah by direct interpretation, but also contains decrees and decisions made by the leaders of Judaism and by the leading corporations in post-Exilic times—the so-called *gezerot* and *taqqanot*—and also regulations which originated, for example, in custom and customary law.[4] But these are the statements of modern scholarship, working on the historical method. The Rabbis were to some extent conscious of the varying sources and origins of the material,[5] but that did not stop them from seeing—in principle—the oral Torah as a whole as the interpretation of the written Torah—an interpretation given by God on Sinai![6]

---

[1] See below, pp. 132 f.

[2] See below, pp. 118 f.

[3] Above, p. 28.

[4] M. GUTTMANN, *Zur Einleitung in die Halacha* I–II (1909–13) and cf. also S. ZEITLIN, The Halaka, in *Jew. Quart. Rev.* 39 (1948–49), pp. 1 ff., partic. pp. 21 ff., and H. A. WOLFSON, *Philo* I (1948), pp. 186 ff.

[5] BACHER, *Tradition*, pp. 33 ff.; cf. further S. KATZ, *Die mündliche Lehre und ihr Dogma* I (1922), pp. 19 ff., B. J. BAMBERGER, Revelations of Torah after Sinai, in *Hebr. Un. Coll. Ann.* 16 (1941), pp. 97 ff.

[6] We quote—as an example—a basic doctrinal statement, current in the school of R. Aqiba: כל התורה הלכה למשה מסיני (b Nid. 45a). Cf. BACHER, *op. cit.*, p. 35. See also below, Ch. 12 A.

We ought perhaps also to point out here that it is not entirely satis-
factory, from a historical point of view, to say that the oral Torah
merely had an interpretative *function*. It is nearer to the truth to say
that the oral Torah, when compared with the written, had an interpretative, particularizing, complementary and sometimes modifying[1]
function.[2]

B. *The Divisions of the Oral Text-material*

How the text-material of the oral Torah can best be divided up, is
always a debateable point. The Rabbis themselves, as early as in Tannaitic times, often used a practical division into three, and it is this
which we shall adopt here, though it is not made on the strictly form-
critical basis which a modern scholar might wish. As BACHER has
shown,[3] the Rabbis often divided the oral Torah (i.e. משנה in the broadest
meaning of the term) into three branches or disciplines: הלכות, מדרש(ים)
and הגדות.

In this connection, מדרש means the exposition of the text of Scripture
which was transmitted in a definite[4] (or in a freer) form; it is either a
question of presenting the contents of the text or of giving exegetical
consideration to some item of doctrine.[5] In the latter case, the term
תלמוד may also be used. מדרש denotes both the actual exegetical operation and its result. In the singular, the term can denote both the individual Scripture exposition and its result, though the plural may also be
used in connection with the latter.

By הלכות is meant in this context the normative, oral doctrinal statements (*Satzungen*), transmitted in definite form and freed from their
midrashic elements, i.e. without indication of their relation to the

---

[1] See S. ZUCROW, *Adjustment of Law to Life in Rabbinic Literature* (1928).

[2] For these matters, cf. further F. WEBER, *Jüdische Theologie* (2nd ed. 1897),
pp. 91 ff., MOORE, *Judaism* I, pp. 251 ff., J. BONSIRVEN, *Le judaisme palestinien* I
(1934), pp. 263 ff., W. G. KÜMMEL, Jesus und der jüdische Traditionsgedanke, in
Zeitschr. f. d. Neutest. Wiss. 33 (1934), pp. 107 ff., R. BLOCH, Écriture et Tradition
dans le Judaisme, in *Cahiers Sioniens* 8 (1954), pp. 9 ff. Expected soon: G. VERMÈS,
Scripture and Tradition in Judaism (1961).

[3] Les trois branches de la vieille tradition Juive, in *Rev. des Ét. Juives* 38 (1899),
pp. 211 ff., expanded in *Die Agada der Tannaiten* I (2nd ed. 1903), pp. 475 ff. See
also under appropriate words in *Terminologie* I.

[4] See BLAU's correct criticism of BACHER, *Ursprung und Geschichte*, p. xviii.

[5] Cf. J. Z. LAUTERBACH, Midrash and Mishnah, in *Rabbinic Essays* (1951),
pp. 163 ff. For the way in which midrash exegesis functions, see above, pp. 33 ff.

Scriptures. הלכות can be exchanged for the collective term הלכה or—and this is important—for the term משנה, which thus also has this restricted meaning, referring to a collection of fixed, orally transmitted points of doctrine—mainly הלכות, whether it be a question of משנה κατ' ἐξοχήν, or any similar collection (ברייתות).[1] We might mention in passing that משנה may also refer to an individual point of doctrine, i.e. be synonymous with הלכה.

A halakic midrash (מדרש הלכה) is thus a statement of halakah, together with its exegetical consideration or motivation.[2]

Finally, by הגדות we understand the non-halakic statements of doctrine, whether non-legalistic Scripture interpretations or didactic points of doctrine of a different kind. A statement of halakah (הלכה) is easily distinguished from a halakic midrash (מדרש הלכה), but a haggadah is often a haggadic midrash (מדרש הגדה). The distinction is rough, and is drawn for practical reasons. When a haggadah is called a haggadic midrash, it tells us explicitly that the haggadah in question has the character of Scripture exposition.[3]

The terminology is, as we can see, fluid, despite the fact that we have been able to simplify the terminological problem by ignoring the fact of the terms being used in other ways. For our purposes, we have no cause to set aside this ancient division of the oral Torah.

---

[1] On the term *baraita*, ברייתא, or מתניתא ברייתא, denoting a Tannaitic doctrinal statement which failed to find a place in the Mishnah κατ' ἐξοχήν, and is left "outside", see STRACK, *Einleitung*, p. 2 (Eng. ed. pp. 4 f.).

[2] See D. HOFFMANN, *Zur Einleitung in die halachischen Midraschim* (1887), pp. 1 ff.

[3] For the terminology, see further GUTTMANN, *Zur Einleitung* I–II, and *Lexica* by LEVY and JASTROW, sub vocibus.

CHAPTER 8

Schools for the Study of Oral Torah

As WE SHALL deal in the following sections with the methodical study of the *oral Torah*, we must first make some introductory remarks about those schools in which this study was carried on, the schools which have the name בית המדרש. We have already considered the elementary Scripture school, בית ספר.[1]

בית המדרש (with the plur. בתי מדרשות)[2] is a very comprehensive designation, which in reality covers a complex variety of schools: from the quite elementary "mishnah schools" to the most highly qualified rabbinic academies (ישיבות, etc.) in Palestine and Babylon.[3] We therefore prefer to render this word (בית המדרש) by a term which is similarly elastic: college.

At the beginning of our era there were thus more or less privately governed[4] colleges of this kind within Judaism. The most famous were the educational institutions founded by Hillel and Shammai, בית הלל, בית שמאי. (This is undoubtedly a case of two different school foundations connected with two prominent teachers, and not merely two tendencies within Pharisaism or within the Great Jerusalem Sanhedrin.)[5] The

---

[1] Above, pp. 56 ff.

[2] Synonyms: בית תלמוד, בית ועד, ישיבה (and sometimes בית דין). The designations are as a rule used interchangeably. For the terminology, see LEVY's and JASTROW's *Lexica*, sub vocibus. On the fact that the *bet hammidrash* and the *bet din* fulfil similar functions, note that the verb דרש and the noun מדרש are used to denote not only the searching in, and interpretation of, the Scriptures, but also the examining of a person (e.g. 1QS VI.14) or a legal case (e.g. CD XX.6). On the different meanings of the term דין, see lexica. Cf. C. RABIN, *Qumran Studies* (1957), pp. 103 f.

[3] For an elementary introduction, see W. BACHER, Academies in Babylonia, and, Academies in Palestine, in *The Jew. Enc.* I (1901), pp. 145 ff., B. HELLER, Bet ha-Midrasch, in *Enc. Jud.* IV (1929), col. 410 ff., S. KLEIN, S. BIALOBLOCKI, Akademien, talmudische, *ibid.* I (1928), col. 1171 ff., R. GORDIS, Academies, in *The Univ. Jew. Enc.* I (1948), pp. 63 ff. Additional literature will be quoted subsequently.

[4] The leading colleges, and particularly that in Jabneh, are accorded more official recognition as from the fall of the Great Sanhedrin in the catastrophe of A.D. 70.

[5] This is correctly pointed out by GUTTMANN, *Zur Einleitung* I, pp. 37 ff., and E. BIKERMAN, La chaîne de la tradition pharisienne, in *Rev. Bibl.* 59 (1952), p. 49.

origins of such colleges[1] are, however, obscure.[2] The information given
by the rabbinic tradition about בתי דינין and בתי מדרשות in Jerusalem
before the fall of the second Temple seems to a considerable extent to be
coloured by the situation in late Tannaitic and Amoraic times, though
too much scepticism in face of this information is unwarranted.[3] We
are in any case compelled to the conclusion that a purposeful work on
the Torah must have been carried on in connection with the Temple
in Jerusalem during the centuries between the Exile and the fall of the
second Temple. The government of the country,[4] the administration of
justice, and religious instruction demanded interpretation, application
and the complementing of the Law.[5] Qualified study and a purposeful
transmission must have taken place.[6]

During the Hellenistic centuries, however, important political, ad-
ministrative and legal changes took place among the Jews of Palestine,
changes which the scarcity of the source material makes it difficult

---

[1] Josephus also mentions other schools around outstanding teachers; see e.g.
Bell. 1.33.2, *Ant.* 17.6.2.

[2] BIKERMAN, *op. cit.*, p. 49, understands *bet Hillel* and *bet Shammai* to be Hellenistic school foundations: "Ces 'Maisons' étaient des Écoles, et des Écoles hellé-
nistiques." He makes a comparison with the language of Horat. C. I, 29.14, "*Socra-
ticam ... domum*". The use of בית in such a context is however quite natural.

[3] The real crux of the matter lies in the difficulty in reconciling rabbinic information with Josephus' account. On this, see SCHÜRER, *Geschichte* II, pp. 237 ff.,
which exaggerates the view that the rabbinic tradition projects the rabbinic academy backward in time to a period before the fall of the Temple, and HOENIG, *The
Great Sanhedrin*, which goes too far in the opposite direction. Cf. W. BACHER,
Sanhedrin, in HASTINGS' *Dictionary of the Bible* IV (1902), pp. 397 ff.

[4] Particularly during the Hellenistic period.

[5] On the original role of the priests and Levites as bearers and preservers of the
Torah, see Deut. 17.8 ff., 19.16 ff., 2 Chron. 19.8 ff., Jer. 2.8, 18.18, Hagg. 2.12 ff.,
Mal. 2.1 f., Sir. 45.6 ff.; Josephus, *Cont. Ap.* 2.21, 23, *Bell.* 3.8.3, Philo, *Quod deter.*
19.1; Test. Lev. XIII, 1QS V.2 f., 8 f., IX.7, CD XIII.2 ff.; M Sanh. I.3, M Ket. I.5;
XIII.1, M Ohal. XVII.5, M Rosh Hash. I.7 and elsewhere. Cf. G. ÖSTBORN, *Tōrā
in the O.T.* (1945), pp. 89 ff., J. BONSIRVEN, *Le judaïsme palestinien* II (1935),
pp. 130 f., SCHÜRER, *Geschichte* II, pp. 240 ff., M. GERTNER, The Masorah and the
Levites, in *Vet. Test.* 10 (1960), pp. 241 ff. — For a comparison illustrative of the
priests' position as expounders of the law in the Greek tradition, see P. EHRMANN,
De iuris sacri interpretibus Atticis (1908), A. W. PERSSON, *Die Exegeten und Delphi*
(1918), J. H. OLIVER, *The Athenian Expounders of the Sacred and Ancestral Law*
(1950).

[6] Note the way in which certain *zeqenim* prefer two older precedents (concerning
outspoken prophets of judgement) in the council mentioned in Jer. 26.17 ff.

adequately to evaluate.[1] During this period the non-priestly Torah scholars gained increasing influence. The priestly and non-priestly traditions in Israel had met at the highest level and had been compelled to form a unity, although a far from harmonious unity. In the controversy between the Sadducees and Pharisees we definitely encounter a many-faceted conflict between groups coming from different traditional backgrounds: different religious attitudes, different social and economic positions, different attitudes to the Hellenistic environment, different attitudes to the question of administration, jurisdiction and study. But we are scarcely justified in resolving the conflict in some simple formula, in which the Sadducees are placed on one side and the Pharisees on the other; the situation is evidently much more complicated than that.[2] But we must take all this into account when we consider the growth of colleges in the leading circles in Jerusalem.

If we leave these Jerusalem circles for a moment we find, for example in Qumran, another group within which was carried on a form of Scripture study which penetrated deeper than to the elementary learning (reading) and translation of the written Torah. The Qumran texts show that within this sect an intensive midrashic study of the Scriptures (מדרש התורה) was carried on; this was evidently of apocalyptic-mystical nature.[3] Furthermore, the sect had its own strict interpretation of the Law and its fixed halakah,[4] which was partly laid down in writing.[5] We may take it that the members of the sect were compelled to know this halakah off by heart.[6] It is, however, possible that it could be learned from a book,[7] in contrast to the Pharisees' halakah, which had to be learned from the lips of the teacher.[8] Unfortunately, the documents give us no clear picture of how this complementary Torah material was studied. We have, on the other hand, some interesting glimpses of the

[1] Until the present Qumran material has been worked through, see—apart from SCHÜRER, Geschichte II, pp. 57 ff.—V. TCHERIKOVER, Hellenistic Civilization and the Jews (1959).

[2] For a detailed bibliography on these problems, see W. BEILNER, Christus und die Pharisäer (1959), pp. 249 ff.

[3] See references above, p. 58, n. 5, and below, pp. 234 ff., and further, the works referred to above, p. 34, n. 1.

[4] 1QS, 1QSa and CD. Variant readings seem to be traceable in different copies; see above, p. 31, n. 1.

[5] Cf. notes above, p. 31.

[6] Cf. e.g. 1QS V.21, 23, VI. 18.

[7] Above, pp. 31 f.

[8] Above, pp. 27 ff., and below, Ch. 9–12.

way in which the sect's halakah was developed: by new laws being "uncovered" (נגלה), discovered, "found" (נמצא), in the course of the midrashic study of the Scriptures, by the determining of halakic decisions
at the "sessions of the many", and the like.[1] The term *bet hammidrash*
does not occur in the Qumran scriptures—the sect has on the whole a
different terminology than that of the Rabbis[2]—but the sect's מושב,
"session", seems to correspond closely to the Rabbis' ישיבה.[3]

Similar midrashic Scripture study was also carried on in other circles
of Jewish Torah piety.[4] Nor must we forget the different schools which
various kinds of wisdom teachers (מושלים, חכמים), faithful to the Torah,
gathered around them. The Book of Sirach gives us an interesting picture of such a "school", in which the Torah, the Covenant, and the
Temple with its priests, are respected and loved,[5] but where the pupils
are at the same time exhorted to go to other lands in order to share
their wisdom.[6] Here we see an openness to the Oriental and Hellenistic
environment which deserves our attention. And in the Hebrew version
of the Book of Sirach[7]—if this is not a later translation from the Greek![8]
—we find the oldest written support for the term בית המדרש.[9]

The rabbinic colleges are doubtless a further development of an
institution which for many centuries had existed in Israel: professional

---

[1] See RABIN, *Qumran Studies*, pp. 95 ff. Cf. objections below, p. 246.

[2] RABIN, *op. cit.*, pp. 108 ff.

[3] RABIN, *op. cit.*, pp. 108 ff., 102 ff. On the sessions, see further below, pp. 245 f.
— The expression בית התורה in CD XX. 10, 13 does not seem to refer to any earthly
institution, see C. RABIN, *The Zadokite Documents* (2nd ed. 1958), p. 39. The expression בית המשפט, 1QpH VIII.2, X.3, is also eschatological. But there is a possibility
in both cases that the language is based on the sect's name for the house which
they used for study and law-making. Cf. the Rabbis' בית דין (respectively ישיבה)
and their ideas concerning בית דין (ישיבה) של מעלה.

[4] Cf. also below, Ch. 14 D.

[5] On the attitude to the Torah and the Covenant, see proem. and passim, for the
attitude to Temple and priests, see 7.29 ff. (cf. 35.1 ff.). In Ch. 24 the Divine Wisdom
says that God has fixed its permanent dwelling on Zion (οὕτως ἐν Σιὼν ἐστηρίχθην·
ἐν πόλει ἠγαπημένῃ ὁμοίως με κατέπαυσεν, v. 10 f.). Wisdom is the Torah (v. 23).

[6] 39.1 ff., cf. 34.9 ff. For Sirach's ideas of wisdom, see further partic. 38.24–34. —
Cf. MOORE, *Judaism* I, pp. 37 ff.

[7] For the international character of the Wisdom Literature, see e.g. O. EISS-
FELDT, *Einleitung in das A.T.* (2nd ed. 1956), pp. 740, 743 f.

[8] Thus C. C. TORREY, The Hebrew of the Geniza Sirach, in A. MARX *Jubilee
Volume, Engl. Sect.* (1950), pp. 585 ff.

[9] 51.23. Already pointed out by BACHER, *Terminologie* I, p. 207. — Cf. Sir.
38.24–39.11.

work on the Torah, its interpretation, explanation, application and complement. But before the development reached the schools of Hillel and Shammai or the academies in Jabneh and elsewhere—with their double character of school and court—a number of lines had without doubt converged. The development which led to the rabbinic colleges was certainly stimulated by different forms of educational foundation in Palestine and the surrounding territories. One problem which has been investigated very little concerns the relations between the rabbinic colleges and the "higher" schools in the Oriental and Hellenistic environment.[1] When Josephus can refer to the Jewish חכמים as σοφισταί,[2] it is not merely due to his general tendency of presenting his material in Hellenistic categories. The resemblance between Jewish ḥakamim and certain Hellenistic rhetors is not so remote as we are inclined to believe.[3] The conclusion seems unavoidable that communication and influence in fact took place.[4] On the other hand, it is possible for similar institutions to grow up in one and the same cultural area, relatively independent of one another. We ought therefore to avoid too superficial talk about borrowing and influences. This complex of problems demands a wide and thoroughgoing examination, but we cannot go further into the question here. We shall only—as in the previous section—note in passing some of the more striking parallels.

In the Scripture school (בית ספר) the pupil learned, as we have already pointed out, to read the text of the written Torah (מקרא) and probably the translation of the text (תרגום) as well. There does not seem to have been any real interpretation (מדרש) at this educational stage. Interpretation was learned in the higher schools.[5]

This interpretation, midrash, was however extremely conservative and traditional. The teacher's main task was to familiarize his pupils

---

[1] MORRIS correctly emphasizes (*The Jewish School*, p. 12) that a purely Greek gymnasium-school for young people had been established in Jerusalem before the Maccabean Wars (1 Macc. 1.14, 2 Macc. 4.9, 12).

[2] *Bell.* 1.33.2, 2.17.8. Other designations to be noticed are ἐξηγηταί (τῶν νόμων) *Ant.* 17.6.2, 17.9.3. Cf. above, p. 86, n. 1.

[3] See further below, pp. 103 ff.

[4] Cf. also the evidence concerning Jewish and Oriental influence on the Greek tradition of scholarship, H. LEWY, Aristotle and the Jewish Sage, in *The Harv. Theol. Rev.* 31 (1938), pp. 205 ff.; A.-J. FESTUGIÈRE, Grecs et sages orientaux, in *Rev. de l'Hist. des Rel.* 130 (1945), pp. 29 ff.

[5] Above, pp. 59 ff.

with the traditional interpretative and complementary material, which is called oral Torah (מדרש, משנה). In point of fact, the learning of the most important *texts* of the oral Torah was one of the main elements in the study carried out in Rabbinic Judaism's institutions of the *bet hammidrash* type. The other was training in the technique of interpretation, application and dialectics.[1]

The Rabbis distinguished between two ways in which the oral Torah might methodically be learned. The first was the midrashic method. The traditional material in the oral Torah was studied in such a way that it was learned in connection with the consecutive text of Scripture. The text of Scripture was the principle of arrangement. The material was grouped in relation to the texts.

The other method was the mishnaic, in which the material in the oral Torah was studied as an independent entity, disconnected from the text of Scripture, and grouped on other principles of arrangement. The relation to the Scripture text, and the principles of derivation from the text, or connection with the text, are not indicated until the time comes to expound the oral text which has been learned.[2]

The first of these methods of study seems to have been the more ancient, but both occurred side by side in the first centuries A.D.[3] In the long run, it was the mishnaic which became the more usual: the normal school system was organized in accordance with it.[4] But the midrashic method of study continued to be cultivated, especially in some schools.

In both cases, however, the basic traditional, fixed material, which interprets and complements the written Torah, is learned by heart and interpreted. In the following chapters we shall attempt to show how this takes place.[5]

We do not know how schools of the *bet hammidrash* type were organized during the century before Jabneh. Presumably the pupil had even then to pass through a more elementary school, in which the most important passages of the oral Torah were learned (on either the mishnaic or the midrashic principle) before he could be an effective disciple

---

[1] Below, Ch. 9.

[2] Below, pp. 151 ff.

[3] See e.g. J. Z. LAUTERBACH, Midrash and Mishnah, in *Rabbinic Essays* (1951), pp. 163 ff. Cf. the fact that the *halakot* of 1QS have a mishnaic, not a midrashic form.

[4] LAUTERBACH, *ibid.*

[5] Below, pp. 93–189.

of one of the great masters of the oral Torah. At all events, the school system was later generally organized more and more on this principle—which is quite natural *per se*—in Tannaitic and Amoraic times. There we must distinguish between the lowest schools of the *bet hammidrash* type, which were so simple that many scholars refuse to call them by that name. In these the text of the halakah collections (the received Mishnah in the Amoraic period) was learned.[1] These primary schools for the study of the oral Torah, the first superstructure of the *bet sefer*, are known to scholars as mishnah schools.[2] It is, though, better to use the more relative designation of "the mishnah stage". It is unquestionably a matter of an intermediate stage between the *bet sefer* and more qualified study (תלמוד). On the other hand, it is not always possible to define an independent, concrete case of a mishnah school.[3]

From the mishnah stage, the pupil proceeded to the talmud stage, the aim of which was to complement and deepen those insights hitherto obtained—though quite mechanically—into the oral Torah (and at the same time, the written Torah as well), and also to practise the techniques of interpretation and dialectics.[4] Within this advanced stage there were several forms of the rabbinic college. Periodical assemblies of the leading Rabbis were also to be found at this level. Here, however, we are entering an area of study which has not as yet been the object of adequate research. We are still waiting for one of the leading experts in Rabbinic Judaism to give us a comprehensive description of the way in which these various rabbinic colleges, assemblies and "sessions" were organized, the functions of the various officials, the different "classes" and levels of study to be distinguished there, and the different activities carried on in them.[5] We might mention in passing that the material which

[1] On this subject, see below, pp. 113 ff.

[2] Thus e.g. S. KRAUSS, *Talmudische Archäologie* III (1912), pp. 231 f.

[3] It is typical that there is no special designation for such mishnah schools (e.g. בית משנה); instead they are called בית תלמוד or בית המדרש, BLAU, *Ursprung und Geschichte*, pp. xviii f. KRAUSS points out that the terms בית תלמוד and בית המדרש are used interchangeably, *op. cit.*, pp. 201 (and n. 14, p. 337) and 204; see further BACHER, *Terminologie* I, pp. 103 ff. and 199 f.

[4] On this subject see below, pp. 101 ff.

[5] The following special studies may be mentioned: A. SCHWARZ, Die Hochschulen in Palästina und Babylon, in *Jahrb. f. jüd. Gesch. u. Lit.* 2 (1899), pp. 83 ff., W. BACHER, Zur Geschichte der Schulen Palästinas im 3. und 4. Jahrhundert, in *Monatsschr. f. Gesch. u. Wiss. d. Judent.* 43 (1899), pp. 345 ff., IDEM, Die Gelehrten von Caesarea (רבנן דקיסרין), *ibid.* 45 (1901), pp. 298 ff., H. T. DE GRAAF, *De Joodsche Wetgeleerden in Tiberias van 70–400 n. C.* (1902), H. KOTTEK, Die Hoch-

has been brought forward concerning the activity in Hellenistic schools of philosophy, rhetorics and law is intended to illuminate a number of hitherto obscure points.[1]

It is beyond the scope of this present study to deal with these points in more detail, and we shall limit ourselves to the making of certain comments and the drawing of certain distinctions necessary to our theme, as we attempt to sketch the main features of the rabbinic technique of transmission. In order to avoid misunderstanding, it might be as well to say that we are here concentrating on a definite *part* of the activity which took place in the rabbinic colleges: the transmission.

---

schulen in Palästina und Babylonien, in *Jahrb. der Jüd.-Lit. Gesellsch.* 3 (1905), pp. 131 ff., S. KRAUSS, Die Versammlungsstätten der Talmudgelehrten, in *Festschrift* I. LEWY (1911), pp. 17 ff., IDEM, Outdoor Teaching in Talmudic Times, in *Journ. of Jew. Stud.* 1 (1948–49), pp. 82 ff., A. MARMORSTEIN, La réorganisation du doctorat en Palestine au troisième siècle, in *Rev. des Ét. Juives* 66 (1913), pp. 44 ff., J. Z. LAUTERBACH, The Name of the Rabbinical Schools and Assemblies in Babylon, in *Hebr. Un. Coll. Jubilee Volume* (1925), pp. 211 ff., S. K. MIRSKY, Types of Lectures in the Babylonian Academies, in *Essays ... in Honor of* S. W. BARON (1959), pp. 371 ff. See also the works named above, p. 56, n. 1.

[1] For literature on this topic, see below, p. 124, n. 2–p. 126, n. 3.

CHAPTER 9

How Oral Torah is Carried

To DESCRIBE the way in which oral Torah is transmitted is to describe a complicated interplay between basic solidity and complementary flexibility. We shall begin by considering the fixed element, showing at once as clearly as possible how the fixed material in the oral Torah is carried. We fix our attention first on the traditionists *par excellence*: those men who, in Tannaitic and Amoraic colleges, were the principle of careful oral transmission incarnate, and who were succinctly called "traditionists", שונים or תנאים,[1] though they should be distinguished from the great Tannaitic teachers who went by the later title. Here we can see particularly clearly how an oral text is carried. It is a pity that these phenomena, who are so interesting from an exegetical point of view, and from the point of view of the history of religion, literature and culture as a whole, have never been the subject of a thorough monograph in any of the more important languages. They appear only to have been dealt with in short essays or, in passing, when various talmudic problems have been under consideration.[2] We shall here attempt to

---

[1] For terminology, see BACHER, *Terminologie* I, pp. 194 f., II, pp. 238 ff., and IDEM, *Tradition*, p. 20, J. N. EPSTEIN, Zur Babylonisch-Aramäischen Lexikographie, in *Festschrift* A. SCHWARZ (1917), pp. 319 ff. Cf. also J. LEWY, *Interpretation des I. Abschnittes des paläst. Talmud-Traktats Nesikin* (1895), pp. 3 ff., and LEVY's and JASTROW's *Lexica*, sub vocibus.

[2] The material for these is listed and grouped by BACHER in his work *Tradition* (1914). Unfortunately, all commentaries in this work are written *derek qesarah*, and most chapters in this large book resemble concordances. For a complementary grouping of the Tosefta material, see C. ALBECK, Die Herkunft des Toseftamaterials, in *Monatsschr. f. Gesch. u. Wiss. d. Judent.* 69 (1925), pp. 326 f.

The professional *tannaim* are considered, more or less briefly, in the following works: J. N. EPSTEIN, *Der gaonäische Kommentar zur Ordnung Tohoroth* (1915), pp. 48 ff., M. GUTTMANN, Zur Entstehung des Talmuds, in *Entwicklungsstufen der jüdischen Religion* (1927), pp. 43 ff., J. KAPLAN, *The Redaction of the Babylonian Talmud* (1933), pp. 206 ff., S. GANDZ, The Rōbeh רוֹבֵה or the Official Memorizer of the Palestinian Schools, in *Proceed. of the Amer. Acad. for Jew. Research* 7 (1935–36), pp. 5 ff., LIEBERMAN, The Publication of the Mishnah, in *Hellenism*, pp. 83 ff. Of earlier works may be mentioned: L. Löw, *Graphische Requisiten* II (1871),

give a relatively thorough picture of the way in which these ideal traditionists carried their texts. Attention will then be concentrated on the
other figures (teachers and pupils) in the rabbinic colleges, who carried
their material in substantially the same way, though in this case we
can also see how the flexible element of the tradition is passed on.

It is quite natural that a need should have been felt in the colleges for
most of the given textual material in the Jewish tradition.[1] A considerable part of this material could not however be publicly transmitted
in writing,[2] and so the collections of scrolls had to be complemented by
living books: the masters needed, as *adiutores*, traditionists who had
learned correctly the various oral collections of texts. A number of such
traditionists, *tannaim*, naturally formed part of the necessary resources
of a college.

The task of these *tannaim* was thus not that of having at their disposal the spirit and contents of a given general tradition, and of being
able to teach it. Their task was that of being able, on demand, to reproduce orally, or recite (שנה) the oral text material needed by a Rabbi
or by a college.[3] We may join R. Naḥman in calling such a traditionist
"a basket full of books" (צנא דמלי סיפרי)[4] or, to use a more modern
metaphor, a living book or a living library.[5] The way in which the un-
sympathetic observer regarded the precise, "mechanical" reproduction
of the text material achieved by the *tannaim* is best seen from a popular
proverb quoted in the Talmud:

pp. 128 ff., J. S. BLOCH, *Einblicke in die Geschichte der Entstehung der talmudischen Literatur* (1884), particularly pp. 68 ff. These are also dealt with in many works published in Hebrew.

[1] The problem of college archives has not yet been thoroughly investigated.
Cf. J. GUTMANN, Archive und Archivwesen, in *Enc. Jud.* III (1929), col. 236 ff.
For the situation in the surrounding areas, see K. GROSS, Archiv, and C. WENDEL,
Bibliothek, in *Reallex. f. Ant. u. Christ.* I (1950), col. 614 ff. and II (1954), col.
231 ff. Cf. also above, p. 53, n. 5.

[2] See above, Ch. 1, and below, Ch. 11 E.

[3] See further, below.

[4] b Meg. 28b (see also below, p. 107); cf. b Moed Qat. 24b. In order to understand
the picture we must remember that among the Jews, as in the Hellenistic world,
books were often carried and kept in baskets. — On the living "baskets of books",
see further W. BACHER, Ein bisher nicht erkanntes persisches Lehnwort im babylonischen Talmud, in *Zeitschr. d. Deutsch. Morgenl. Ges.* 67 (1913), p. 270, and IDEM,
Tradition, pp. 239 f. and 618 ff.

[5] Cf. Eunapios' opinion of Longinus (*Vit. soph.* 456), that he was "a living
library and a walking museum" (βιβλιοθήκη τις ἦν ἔμψυχος καὶ περιπατοῦν
μουσεῖον); J. W. H. WALDEN, *The Universities of Ancient Greece* (1910), p. 344.

רטין מגושא ולא ידע   "The magian mumbles and does
מאי אמר תני תנא   not understand what he is saying.
ולא ידע מאי אמר.   In the same way[1] the *tanna* recites and does not understand
what he is saying." (b Sot. 22a)

The literal reproduction of the oral text material by these *tannaim* was so "mechanical" as to require no deeper knowledge of the meaning of the texts. An unintelligent pupil was quite capable of becoming a good *tanna*, if he had a good memory.[2] This naturally does not mean to say that no *tanna* had any insight into the meaning, motivation and use of the material. On the contrary, the best of the *tannaim* seem even to have had a part of the text-critical *masorah* at their disposal for their oral text material.[3]

We have a natural and close parallel in the Homeric rhapsodists. Xenophon says of some of them, that they were very particular about the exact words of Homer, but very foolish themselves.[4] There were, however, others who were able, not only to recite, but also to interpret their texts.[5]

The Rabbis were in any case conscious of the variable accuracy and reliability of the different traditionists. Some became famous for their extreme precision, and could become the teacher's reference book, if we may be allowed the expression. We need only remember R. Isaac ben Abdimi, whom R. Judah Hannasi made his chief *tanna*—revised and proof-read.[6] LIEBERMAN draws a striking parallel between such precise

---

[1] When translating quotations, we have set complementary phrases within parentheses only when they are relevant to the factual meaning of the text.

[2] Cf. LIEBERMAN, *Hellenism*, p. 88.

[3] EPSTEIN, *Der gaonäische Kommentar*, p. 50; cf. LIEBERMAN, *op. cit.*, p. 97.

[4] Xenophon, *Mem.* 4.2.10 (τὰ μὲν ἔπη ἀκριβοῦντας, αὐτοὺς δὲ πάνυ ἠλιθίους ὄντας); *Symp.* 3.6.

[5] See J. E. SANDYS, *A History of Classical Scholarship* I (3rd ed. 1921), pp. 30 f., and W. SCHADEWALDT, Die Gestalt des homerischen Sängers, in *Von Homers Welt und Werk* (2nd ed. 1951), pp. 54 ff.

[6] Cf. the words of R. Judah: פקון שאלון לרבי יצחק רובא דבחנת ליה כל מתניתא p Maas. Shen. V.1; cf. b Bab. Batr. 87a, b Ḥul. 110a. For his role in the redaction of the Mishnah, see J. LEWY, in *Jahresber. d. Jüd.-Theol. Semin. zu Breslau* (1905), p. 25, and A. MARX, Strack's Introduction to the Talmud and Midrash, in *Jew. Quart. Rev.* 13 (1922–23), p. 353, GANDZ, *The Rōbeh*, pp. 8 ff., who reads רבי יצחק רוֹבֶה. The latter term corresponds to Arab. *rāwī* (cf. below, p. 121, n. 3). For the process of redaction, see below, p. 119 ff.

traditionists, דוּוקני, and the accurate copies of the books of classical
literature, ἠκριβωμένα.[1] Some traditionists, on the other hand, were
regarded as being less reliable. In b Ber. 38 b (b Ḥul. 86 b, b Ker. 27 a) for
example, R. Benjamin ben Jefet is placed well beneath R. Ḥiyya ben
Abba as a traditionist, since the latter gave careful consideration to the
passages from the tradition, and repeated them every month before
his teacher, R. Joḥanan.[2]

The amount of text known by these *tannaim* must also have varied
considerably. It is certain that some had only a few collections of texts
at their disposal, while others had many more. In b Qid. 49 b we have a
well-known statement defining the exacting standard demanded from
the one who in Amoraic times would be counted a fully-qualified *tanna*.
Such a one must know (repeat) all the most important collections of
tradition (in the form in which they existed at that time): Mishnah,
Sifra, Sifre and Tosefta,[3] in the same way as a Scripture specialist (קרא)
must know (read) the whole of Scripture accurately (certainly also from
memory)—the Law, the Prophets and the Writings.[4]

Not all text material was regarded as being of equal importance, and
there was therefore some variation in the care with which it was transmitted. It is thus a well-known fact that the received Mishnah was transmitted more carefully than the *baraita* collections.[5] This does not mean,
however, from the purely technical point of view that they were transmitted differently *in principle*. Furthermore, it is also well-known that
not all haggadic sayings were transmitted with the same painstaking
care for their wording as were the halakic statements; in the former case,
the margin of variation or abbreviation was greater than in the latter.
But this does not mean that a Rabbi's important haggadic sayings—

---

[1] *Hellenism*, p. 97. LIEBERMAN parallels the designation for the examples revised
by the Alexandrian grammarians, ἐξητασμένα, with the term בחנת, used for the
"revised" Mishnah. R. Judah says of R. Isaac ben Abdimi: דבחנת ליה כל מתניתא
p Maas. Shen. V.1 (see above, p. 95, n. 6).

[2] b Ber. 38 b: רבי חייא בר אבא דייק וגמיר שמעתה מרבי יוחנן ... ועוד רחב״א כל תלתין יומין
מהדר תלמודיה קמיה דר״י. Cf. b Ber. 33 a, b Pes. 52 b. See also below, pp. 169 f.

[3] b Qid. 49 b: אמר לה תנא אנא עד דתני הילכתא ספרא וסיפרי ותוספתא על מנת. (The Munich
ms. omits וסיפרי.) Cf. b Meg. 28 b. See also HOFFMANN, *Zur Einleitung*, pp. 12 f., and
BACHER, *Tradition*, p. 240.

[4] b Qid. 49 a: אמר לה קרא אנא עד דקרי אורייתא נביאי וכתובי בדיוקא. On these Scripture
specialists, see above, pp. 50 ff.

[5] See on this subject S. HOROVITZ, review of BACHER, Tradition, in *Monatsschr.
f. Gesch. u. Wiss. d. Judent.* 60 (1916), pp. 153 ff.

for nothing could be more mistaken than to judge all haggadic sayings en masse—were transmitted on the principle of some method other than the halakic. We need only remind ourselves of the plain fact that haggadic passages, and even a whole tractate (Abot), are incorporated into the Mishnah; and even more extensively into the Talmud.[1] The same is true of the midrashic sayings.[2]

In the talmudic material we gain some extremely interesting insights into the attitude taken in the Amoraic colleges to the text which a *tanna* recites before his teacher.[3] The oral text is there made the object of critical examination, a form of διόρθωσις.[4] Negative criticism of the received text of the Mishnah is never advanced by the earlier Amoraic Rabbis, and seldom by the later, despite the fact that they frequently argue over its interpretation.[5] The traditionists' text is accepted as being perfectly correct. When it is a matter of texts from other collections (*baraita* collections, *midrash* collections) the traditionist's text is usually accepted as being correct, and is only interpreted.[6] But occasionally the traditionist's text attracts particular attention, often depending, however, on the fact that its *contents* conflict with the received Mishnah. The text then becomes the object of negative criticism. In exceptional cases it may come about that the passage in question is declared invalid, and rejected.[7] As a rule, though, it is not rejected; nor is the wording

---

[1] Cf. below, pp. 145 ff. and 177 ff. KAPLAN is justified in emphasizing (*The Redaction*, pp. 199 f.) that in the Talmud the contents of a haggadic lecture (or a topic in such a lecture), can be referred to as briefly and on the same key-word principle as a halakah verse. Cf. below, p. 146.

[2] On the transmission of the midrash collections, see below, pp. 116 ff.

[3] See BACHER's list of the material in *Tradition*, pp. 255 ff., and cf. ALBECK, *Herkunft*, pp. 325 f. — The set phrase is: תנא פלוני קמיה דרבי פלוני.

[4] For διόρθωσις as a permanent element in literary teaching in the Hellenistic schools, see H.-I. MARROU, *Saint Augustin et la fin de la culture antique* (1938), pp. 21 ff., and IDEM, *Histoire de l'éducation*, p. 230. Cf. also below, pp. 124 f.

[5] On the way in which the different "readings" in the Talmud are given in the Mishnah, see BACHER, *Terminologie* II, p. 238. The first Amoraic Rabbi to criticize the text of the Mishnah is Resh Laqish, as LIEBERMAN points out, *Hellenism*, pp. 97 ff.

[6] See evidence in BACHER, *Tradition*, pp. 255 ff.

[7] See e.g. b Shab. 106a, b Erub. 9a, b Yoma 43b. Here the teacher says to the traditionist: פוק תני לברא. BACHER has in *Tradition*, pp. 255 and 257, corrected the interpretation of this remark which he gives in *Terminologie* II, p. 239. — The verb for "to cancel" is often סמי; sometimes the *tanna* asks: איסמייה, "Shall I cancel it (the *baraita*)?", e.g. b Bab. Batr. 77b. See further BACHER, *Terminologie* II, p. 142 with passages quoted in evidence.

willingly altered. The text is instead given an interpretation which does not conflict with the received tradition.[1] If, however, such an interpretation should prove impossible, the text may then be altered. The wording of the elements in the tradition is corrected by a process of retouching by the master,[2] by removing an incorrect formula from the doctrinal passage,[3] or by the addition of some complementary formula.[4]

Here we have an extremely interesting picture of the way in which the mass of text material is sifted, purified and corrected, and of the way in which the college's own recognized text collections came into being.[5] We are shown *one* of the factors explaining the characteristic relationship between different parallel traditions: how in one passage of traditional material we may have a strange combination of extensive literal agreement and sudden additions, omissions or revision of certain sections. This does by no means always—or only—depend on the material having been altered in the memories of the traditionists or in transmission; nor does it always depend on the material having been transmitted in collections, the functions of which varied. It is thus sometimes due to conscious sifting, planing down, correcting, complementing—and redaction—in some prominent college. However, in this context we shall not devote more time to this aspect. What has been said above is intended to show, first, that the traditionist's reading is not to be considered as a general reproduction of some dynamic and fluid tradition, but as the repetition of an oral text (which is later authorized in certain cases—with or without correction—within a college, where it is later transmitted and used with authorized wording); and secondly, that the traditionist, *tanna*, is a living book, a "recorded text".

Who were these traditionists *par excellence*? The fact of a master (whether prophet, teacher or poet) having some chosen pupil who was

---

[1] See e.g. p Ab. Zar. II.7, b Bab. Qam. 91b, b Bab. Mes. 27a, *ibid.* 58a and 58b.

[2] See e.g. b Ber. 57a, b Git. 52b, b Yeb. 40a, b Ker. 11a, *ibid.* 11b, b Pes. 68a, b Men. 17a. The traditionist may also correct himself, e.g. p Bab. Qam. VIII.9.

[3] See e.g. b Ab. Zar. 26a, *ibid.* 26b.

[4] See e.g. b Ber. 57a, b Nid. 24b. — For further material in connection with the problem which is dealt with in n. 7, p. 97–n. 4, p. 98, see BACHER, *Tradition, ibid.*, and cf. HOROVITZ, review of BACHER, *op. cit.*

[5] Cf. HOFFMANN, *Zur Einleitung*, pp. 12 ff., and LIEBERMAN, *Hellenism*, pp. 88 ff., which shows that in the colleges there existed a sort of oral act of publication and authorization. The term לחברה (ה)נכנס, "enter the college", corresponds *mutatis mutandis* to the expression εἰσφέρειν εἰς τὴν βιβλιοθήκην, *ibid.* On the forms for oral publication, see also below, pp. 119 ff.

particularly responsible for the transmission of his work, certainly originated in the mists of Antiquity;[1] but we are concerned here with one special form of this phenomenon: the *tannaim*. The designation *tanna*, referring to a special recitator in a college, appears to date from the time of R. Aqiba, i.e. it appears to be as old as the oldest (orally) published mishnah.[2] The use of special *tannaim* was developed in Amoraic times into something of an institution. From contemporary—and also from late[3]—references, we gain the impression that these *tannaim* were sometimes not reckoned as belonging to the college's company of teachers and pupils in general; instead they seem to have been counted as being a form of official, connected with the college for the purpose of maintaining the necessary oral texts and text collections. They were purely and simply living *books*: textbooks and concordances. They might possibly be counted as a sort of ὑποδιδάσκαλος,[4] since they were evidently also responsible for simple teaching consisting of the bare transmission of the oral text material. We might speculate and suggest that it was often a matter of pupils who demonstrated outstanding powers of memory or receptive pupils who lacked the capacity for developing into mature and independent scholars. It is in any case so, that it was with the aid of an élite of such skilled professional traditionists that the masters in the leading colleges preserved the oral Torah in an authorized form until written copies began to be of official importance.[5] They still play an important role in the rabbinic colleges during the Gaonic period.[6] Such *tannaim*, under the supervision of the masters, were therefore responsible for the authorized transmission. When the text of the oral Torah is committed to such a *tanna*, it is justifiable to talk about a transmission, the main purpose of which is the preservation of the text.[7]

---

[1] See H. M. and N. K. CHADWICK, *The Growth of Literature*, GANDZ, *The Dawn of Literature*, D. B. MACDONALD, *The Hebrew Literary Genius* (1933), p. 89. — For a comparison with the situation in the Arabic world, see J. PEDERSEN, *Den arabiske bog* (1946), pp. 5 ff.

[2] Thus LIEBERMAN, *op. cit.*, p. 88, who associates himself with J. N. EPSTEIN. — Cf. KAPLAN, *The Redaction*, pp. 214 ff.

[3] For the institution of *tanna* under the Gaonic period, see EPSTEIN, *Der gaonäische Kommentar*, pp. 48 ff.

[4] For ὑποδιδάσκαλοι in Hellenistic schools, see e.g. L. GRASBERGER, *Erziehung und Unterricht im klassischen Alterthum* II (1866), pp. 145 f.

[5] For the unofficial role played by notebooks and "scrolls of secrets", see below, Ch. 11 E.

[6] EPSTEIN, *op. cit.*, *ibid*.

[7] Cf. above, p. 42, and see further below, pp. 119 ff.

We must however complement the picture at once by pointing out that it was not only these eminent specialists who carried the text of the oral Torah in a carefully learned state. It is a most significant fact that it is impossible to draw a clear distinction between these *tannaim* and other teachers and pupils in the colleges. This is particularly true of the Tannaitic period. At that time, normal teachers and pupils functioned as transmitters of the oral text collections which they had learned, and therefore had at their disposal.[1] It is sufficient from this point of view to remember the way in which the Amoraic Rabbis, in retrospect, refer to the teachers of tradition in general during this period, as *tannaim*. All those who concern themselves with the methodical study of the traditional source material in the oral Torah learn this material in the form of oral texts, intended to be repeated from memory. This seems simply to have been the current method of learning important texts—whether written or not—in Antiquity. Evidence can be found in the Hellenistic schools of different types: in the instruction given by "teachers of letters" (γραμματισταί), grammarians, rhetoricians, lawyers and popular philosophers.[2] On this point, therefore, the distinction between a professional traditionist and an ordinary teacher or pupil is at the very most a question of the extent to which the texts were known, and the accuracy with which they were known, and is not a distinction in principle between different methods of learning.

This fact, that in the early Tannaitic period—the century prior to R. Aqiba—we are unable to distinguish between special professional traditionists and other teachers and pupils, also means that *during this epoch* we do not need to distinguish any special form of transmission aimed primarily at conserving the text. During this early epoch, the methodical transmission of the oral Torah is subject to the requirements of instruction: it is in fact part of that instruction. And as we know, instruction means essentially the education of "lawyers". Thus the text of the oral Torah is for the most part sustained by teachers and pupils.

The teachers and their pupils must also continue to know by heart the basic sections of the oral Torah. Here the Mishnah occupied a special position. The other oral text collections were never granted the same central position as was the Mishnah, and they were therefore not so

---

[1] This can easily be assured by studying BACHER's list (*Tradition*, pp. 72 ff.) of those who delivered the traditions in Tannaitic colleges. Cf. also GANDZ, *The Rōbeh*, pp. 6 f.

[2] See below, pp. 124 ff. and cf. p. 193, n. 2.

widely studied; their distribution varied. In addition, different teachers often specialized in different subjects.

It is however clear that the Tosefta[1] and the most important midrash collections were relatively widely distributed in the colleges quite early in the Amoraic period. And the number of those able to function as traditionists grew in proportion to the distribution of the collections. Certain collections were transmitted by a limited number of men. Those of the school of R. Ishmael professionally responsible for the carrying of the midrash collections[2] cannot have been too few in number, nor can those responsible for R. Ḥiyya's and R. Hoshaia's mishnah collections (תנאי דבי רבי חייא ודבי רבי הושעיא).[3] But those collections which we might call the *differentia specifica* of certain teachers,[4] could not originally be transmitted by any but their own disciples and their followers. This is why we occasionally hear of an enquirer undertaking a long pilgrimage in order to receive the traditions of some definite teacher, i.e. the traditions from a more specific collection.[5] There was a degree of interplay between the different colleges, thanks to the custom, widespread among the Jews (and in Antiquity generally) by which a pupil, after a period of residence with a teacher or in a college, proceeded to another master or another college[6] in which he was able, if called upon to do so, to transmit items of doctrine from his former teachers.[7]

Knowing the basic text material in the oral Torah by heart is an elementary accomplishment, presupposed of every teacher and pupil at the more advanced stage.[8] Those Jewish boys who were privileged to follow the paths of organized study had no alternative to the careful

---

[1] We have no reason here to go into the special problem of the relation between Tosefta and Mishnah (on this, see A. GUTTMANN, *Das redaktionelle und sachliche Verhältnis zwischen Mišna und Tosephta*, 1928) or such questions as the date at which Tosefta was written down. See the most recent review of various proposals for a solution, B. DE VRIES, The Problem of the Relationship of the Two Talmuds to the Tosefta, in *Tarbiz* 28 (1959), pp. 158 ff. (Hebr.; Eng. summary pp. III f.).

[2] See on this subject BACHER, *Tradition*, pp. 227 ff., and cf. HOFFMANN, *Zur Einleitung*, p. 18.

[3] See BACHER, *Tradition*, pp. 222 ff.

[4] E.g. the mishnah of Eliezer ben Jacob the Elder (1. cent.), Ab. IV.11.

[5] As e.g. when a pupil of R. Eleazar ben Shammua is consulted by R. Judah Hannasi, b Men. 18a, T Zeb. II.17. — See also b Bes. 27a, b Moed Qat. 22a, b Nid. 48a, etc.

[6] b Ber. 63b, b Ab. Zar. 19a (quoted below, p. 132), and passim.

[7] See the material in BACHER, *Tradition*.

[8] Cf. BACHER, *Terminologie* II, pp. 240 f., and see further, below.

memorizing of the most important basic material of the oral Torah. In the most usual course of studies,[1] after the elementary Scripture school (*bet sefer*) the boy had to proceed to the study of the Mishnah, whether for some private teacher, in a separate school ("mishnah school"), in a school linked with the *bet sefer*, or in some subdivision of the *bet hammidrash*.[2] When first learning this received Mishnah, it was evidently not the practice to go into the meaning and use of this transmitted material in detail. The object of this stage of education was just to memorize the brief mishnah text.[3] More detailed explanation of the mishnah (תלמוד) was reserved for a later educational stage. Nor does the mishnah teacher (מַשְׁנֶה) seem to have had any higher competence, or to have been in particularly high regard among the Rabbis.[4] (We are not concerned here with those cases in which the great scholars gave private mishnah instruction to chosen pupils; such cases are exceptional.) The competence of a normal mishnah teacher evidently did not have, *mutatis mutandis*, to exceed that of a Scripture teacher; in the sphere of the oral Torah he had to know and to be able to teach the received text, and give those *elementary* explanations which were necessary to the

---

[1] For the normal course of studies, see SCHÜRER, *Geschichte* II, pp. 494 ff., KRAUSS, *Talmudische Archäologie* III, pp. 220 ff.; cf. L. BLAU, *Zur Einleitung in die Heilige Schrift* (1894), pp. 10 f., and IDEM, *Studien zum althebräischen Buchwesen* (1902), pp. 67 f. The clearest picture of the course of studies is provided by the constantly recurring accounts of the branches of the written and oral Torah, see BACHER, *Terminologie* I, pp. 33 ff., 42 f., 89 ff., 103 ff., 117 ff., 197 f., 199 ff. — We are not concerned here to examine in detail the somewhat differently orientated course of study followed in the relatively few schools in which an attempt was made to conserve the midrashic method of study, as opposed to the mishnaic. This does not materially alter the overall picture which we have attempted to draw. Cf. notes on the midrashic way of studying the oral Torah, above, p. 90, and below, pp. 116 ff.

[2] KRAUSS, *op. cit.*, imposes uniformity in an illegitimate way; see above, p. 56, n. 1.

[3] The limited objectives of teaching on the mishnah level have often been pointed out; see L. Löw, Die Tradition, in *Gesammelte Schriften* I (1889), p. 252, J. LEWIT, *Darstellung der theoretischen und praktischen Pädagogik im jüdischen Altertume* (1895), pp. 48 ff., SCHÜRER, *op. cit.*, *ibid.*, KRAUSS, *op. cit.*, pp. 218 ff. For variations in meaning of the verb שנה and noun משנה, see above, pp. 27 f.

[4] For a more detailed study of משנים and סופרים, see the evidence quoted by BACHER, *Terminologie* I, p. 135. See further L. WIESNER, *Die Jugendlehrer der talmudischen Zeit* (1914) and M. ARZT, The Teacher in Talmud and Midrash, in M. M. KAPLAN *Jubilee Volume* (1953), pp. 35 ff. — For the Rabbis' criticism of these teachers, see below.

correct learning of the text. These two teachers, סוֹפֵר and מַשְׁנֶה, as we have already remarked, were about as far beneath a fully qualified Rabbi as was a mediocre γραμματικός[1] below a fully qualified σοφιστής (*rhetor*) in the Hellenistic world.[2] We might mention in passing that it was evidently not unusual for one and the same man to function as both *sofer* and *mashneh*.[3]

Elementary mishnah teaching and knowledge is often mentioned in the Talmud in a rather derogatory way.[4] This does not mean that the Rabbis dismissed the "canonical" Mishnah—such an idea is so unreasonable as to be quite out of the question[5]—but that they opposed the notion that the mastery of the text of the Mishnah should be education enough.[6] Real interpretation of the Mishnah text was not undertaken until a more advanced type of teaching was reached: that carried on at that level which we have called "the talmud stage". At that level no pains were spared to penetrate the meaning of the Mishnah; the object was to bring learning and insight to bear on the analysis and exposition of the Mishnah.[7] "Mechanical" knowledge of the text was here complemented by the mature interpretative tradition. The leading masters' presentation was listened to, in the form of a commentary on the text,[8] a lecture[9] or a definitive statement as an answer to a question or a final

[1] To teach מקרא and משנה is different from teaching חכמה, M Sot. IX.15 (b Sot. 49 a), b Bab. Mes. 33 a. Cf. the difference between a teacher of children and a חכם in b Pes. 29 b.

[2] Cf. above, p. 60, and below, p. 124 f.

[3] ARZT, *op. cit., ibid.*

[4] See e.g. b Bab. Batr. 145 b, b Sanh. 100 b; cf. b Bab. Mes. 33 a.

[5] A typical statement is to be found in b Bab. Mes. 33 a. — On the Mishnah's "canonical" position, see e.g. I. LEWY, *Über einige Fragmente aus der Mischna des Abba Saul*, pp. 1 ff., J. Z. LAUTERBACH, Mishnah, in *The Jew. Enc.* VIII (1904), p. 610. — For the phenomenon, see BACHER, *Die Agada der palästinensischen Amoräer* I (1892), p. 241, and cf. WEBER, *Jüdische Theologie*, pp. 100 ff.

[6] See further, below.

[7] On the technique used in debate and exposition at this stage, see M. ESCHELBACHER, Probleme der talmudischen Dialektik, in *Monatsschr. f. Gesch. u. Wiss. d. Judent.* 68 (1924), pp. 47 ff., 126 ff.; cf. also A. HAHN, ספר עוקרי הרים *The Rabbinical Dialectics* (1879). — The nature of the learned work on this level is clear from the precise technical terminology which is there developed; see M. MIELZINER, *Introduction to the Talmud* (3rd ed. 1925), pp. 198 ff., and BACHER, *Terminologie* I–II.

[8] Cf. below, pp. 118 f.

[9] The different kinds of rabbinic doctrinal lecture have not as yet been fully examined. An attempt to distinguish the different types has been made by MIRSKY, *Types of Lectures in the Babylonian Academies.*

decisive word, rounding off a discussion.[1] Under the masters' direction, and in mutual discussion, the pupils had to examine the lapidary doctrinal statements and to enter more deeply into their secrets: their meaning, motivation, usage and area of application.[2] Actual or hypothetical problems of doctrine were here considered, seriously or for the sake of practice. The material had to be mastered to perfection; the leading thought and intention (שיטה) of the transmitted sayings had to be laid bare; real or apparent contradictions had to be resolved; each item of doctrine had to be delimited and determined, both with regard to meaning and to scope.

In other words, at the talmud stage the student had, on the one hand, to absorb complementary knowledge (גמרא and תלמוד)[3] and, on the other, to train his capacity for intellectual mastery and dialectical use of the material (סברא,[4] פלפול[5]). Comparison with the activity in Hellenistic schools for lawyers and rhetors (σοφισταί) reveals many instructive resemblances.[6]

We must point out a further important fact. As we have seen in our previous examination, the pupil on the lower educational level is mainly *receptive*. He makes a positive contribution to the teaching with his questions and answers, but since at this stage instruction consists mainly of the learning of existing textual material, and leaves little scope for interpretation and discussion, the positive role of the pupil is extremely restricted. The situation at the talmud stage is different. Here, the pupil contributes to the teaching with his questions and his remarks. We

---

[1] Cf. below, p. 140; cf. p. 119.

[2] See also below, Ch. 12.

[3] The two terms are not synonymous. On the term גמרא, see W. BACHER, Gemara, in *Hebr. Un. Coll. Ann.* 1904, pp. 26 ff. (Cf. C. LEVIAS, Word Studies, *ibid.*, p. 152), and *Terminologie* II, pp. 28 ff., and further, KAPLAN's account of the different ways in which the origin and meaning of the term can be understood, *The Redaction*, pp. 195 ff. He seems to be partly correct in his observations, but the term גמרא cannot be interpreted in *all* passages as he would have it. Cf. also below, pp. 118 f. In p Talmud יליף (אלף) is used instead of גמר; see BACHER, *Gemara*, p. 29. For the term תלמוד, see IDEM, *Terminologie* I, pp. 199 ff.

[4] For the term סברא, see BACHER, *Terminologie* II, pp. 129 ff. Cf. also below, p. 132. On gemara and sebara as different strata in the Talmud, see H. KLEIN, Gemara and Sebara, in *Jew. Quart. Rev.* 38 (1947–48), pp. 67 ff., Gemara Quotations in Sebara, *ibid.* 43 (1952–53), pp. 341 ff., Some Methods of Sebara, *ibid.* 50 (1959–60), pp. 124 ff.

[5] For the term פלפול, see BACHER, *op. cit.*, II, p. 157. See also below.

[6] For bibliography, see below, p. 124, n. 2–p. 126, n. 3.

might say that at the talmud stage there is not the same distinction
between teaching and learning, between teacher and pupil, as there is
on the lower levels of education. Here they *work* together on the Torah.[1]
Another relevant factor is that they here *create* authoritative text
material. Doctrinal questions are taken up for decision in the leading
colleges. *Halakot*, and other doctrinal statements and texts, are fixed.
What takes place in the advanced college is thus not only teaching,
training in interpretation and application, but also lawmaking and
jurisdiction.[2] The boundary between בית המדרש and בית דין is not easy
to draw.[3]

The school system during the Tannaitic and early Amoraic periods
was not uniformly constructed in such a way as to enable the pupil first
to go through a special mishnah section before entering the talmudic
college. But it is none the less the rule at the "sessions" of the Amoraic
colleges that work proceeded without the written Mishnah text,[4] and
that it was assumed that every teacher and pupil at this stage knew the
oral Mishnah—or at least four orders of it—off by heart.[5] It was assumed that this knowledge had in some way been acquired earlier. (It
is certain that written notes, ὑπομνήματα, were used to some extent in
private.)[6] A typical saying is recorded in b Taan. 7b–8a as having been
spoken by Resh Laqish: "If you see a pupil for whom the study of the
talmud appears to be heavy as iron, that is because his knowledge of the
mishnah is not fluent."[7] One piece of advice which he offers to such a
person is that he ought to be careful to know his mishnah (i.e. that
portion to be dealt with on the occasion in question) in advance.[8] Resh
Laqish was himself in the habit of repeating his mishnah paragraph
"forty times" before presenting himself to R. Joḥanan;[9] R. Adda bar

[1] Cf. below, Ch. 14 D.
[2] Cf. below, Ch. 12 A, 14 E and 15 E.
[3] Cf. above, p. 85, n. 2.
[4] See HOROVITZ, review of BACHER, Tradition, pp. 68 f. — Löw, *Graphische Requisiten* II, pp. 122 ff. and BLOCH, *Einblicke*, pp. 76 ff., are right in remarking upon the notable fact that not a single written copy of the Mishnah is mentioned in the Talmud, although other written documents are often mentioned there. Cf. below, pp. 159 f.
[5] See above, p. 101, n. 8.
[6] See below, pp. 157 ff.
[7] b Taan. 7b–8a: אם ראית ת' שתלמודו קשה עליו כברזל בשביל משנתו שאינה סדורה עליו.
[8] *Ibid.* 8a: אם משנתו סדורה לו מעיקרא ...
[9] *Ibid.*: הוה מסדר מתניתיה ארבעין זמנין. On "forty" as a round and symbolic number, see J. BERGMANN, Die runden und hyperbolischen Zahlen in der Agada,

Ahabah used to repeat his work "twenty-four times" before coming to Raba.[1] In b Hor. 12a we hear R. Mesharsheya impressing upon his sons the importance of revising the mishnah which is to be discussed before going to their teacher.[2] (An extra piece of advice in this connection is that they are to revise by the side of a stream, so that their revision will flow like running water!)[3]

We shall soon return to the subject of the methods used for transmission and learning. All we wish to point out here is that it is not only the traditionists *par excellence*, the *tannaim*, who carry the texts in a form, the wording of which is fixed. This is done, with a varying degree of precision and scope, by all the teachers and pupils in the colleges. It was, naturally enough, principally the mature teachers who had access to collections of oral text material of impressive size. It is expressly said, referring to some of them—e.g. R. Naḥman ben Jacob, R. Sheshet and R. Menashia ben Taḥlifa—that they were able to reproduce the Mishnah, Sifra, Sifre and Tosefta.[4] But a mature teacher must know even more.

To have the wording of the most important collections of texts at one's disposal is in fact regarded by the Rabbis as being nothing more than *elementary knowledge*. This accomplishment is essential to a man's studies, in the same way that access to a Torah scroll and mastery of *miqra* is basic to the deeper study of Scripture. But it is not enough. We have earlier touched upon the fact that the advanced Rabbis did not overestimate the knowledge passed on in the process of transmitting an oral text collection. The rabbinic traditional material contains in many places criticism directed against that type of traditionist or scholar who is only able to repeat the traditional text material—in this case mainly *halakot*—without penetrating its meaning and becoming practised in its use. They are called שונרי הלכות, שונים (תנאים) or משנים. The type seem to recur frequently in both Tannaitic and Amoraic times, and its occurrence builds on just that situation with which we are here dealing: that the oral traditional material—mainly the halakic, the nucleus of the oral Torah—is transmitted as blocks of definitely formulated, con-

in *Monatsschr. f. Gesch. u. Wiss. d. Judent.* 82 (1938), pp. 370 ff., and the context in Talmud.

[1] *Ibid.* On "twenty-four" as a round and symbolic number, see BERGMANN, *op. cit.*, pp. 367 f.

[2] b Hor. 12a: אמר להו רב משרשיא לבריה כי בעיתו מיעל ומיגמרי קמי רבייכו גרסו מתניתא ועלו לקמי רבייכו.

[3] *Ibid.*: וכי גרסיתו גרסו על נהרא דמיא דכי היכי דמשכן מיא משכן שמעתתייכו.

[4] b Shebu. 41b, b Ber. 47b; cf. BACHER, *Tradition*, p. 240.

centrated oral text, which were memorized without needing to give detailed consideration to the meaning and use of the material.

Criticism is thus directed against the living books about whom we have spoken: שונים (תנאים). But we must notice that criticism was not directed against the fact of their mechanically repeating the text of the traditional halakah collections, but against the fact that their knowledge went no farther than this mechanical learning process. It was their *limitations* which were condemned.[1] When R. Naḥman ben Isaac was requested to give a funeral oration for one scholar who was able to repeat Sifra, Sifre and Mishnah (which may also have included Tosefta)[2], he answered that the most he could say would be to praise him for being a basket filled with books (צנא דמלי ספרי)![3]

The implications of this criticism appear more clearly in a number of sayings collected in b Sot. 22a, which refer to such *shonim/tannaim*. We read that the one who has learned the Scriptures and the Mishnah, but has not "served the Rabbis"[4] (זה שקרא ושנה ולא שימש תלמידי חכמים), i.e. who has not completed his studies in a more advanced college,[5] is given various nicknames, bestowed by various Rabbis: he is called an *am haares*, a fool, a Samaritan and a magian (מגוש, כותי, בור, עם הארץ). The last of these comes from R. Aḥa bar Jacob, who connects it with a popular proverb which we have already had occasion to quote: "The magian mumbles and does not understand what he is saying. In the same way the *tanna* recites and does not understand what he is saying."[6] R. Isaac applied to this type of scholar (שונין הלכות) the words of Prov. 24. 21,

עם שונים אל תתערב.   "Enter not into relations with *shonim*" (b Sot. 22a).[7]

---

[1] Since we are concerned here only to sketch the main trends, we have simplified somewhat. Different Rabbis evaluated those who reproduced the texts somewhat differently; see b Meg. 26b, 28b, b Qid. 49a, p Moed Qat. III.7, and cf. below.

[2] Thus BACHER, *Tradition*, p. 240.

[3] b Meg. 28b; cf. above, p. 94.

[4] The expression deserves closer investigation. It has evidently undergone a far from unimportant development in meaning. Have we in the שמוש תלמידי חכמים a remnant of an older type of teaching, comparable with the ancient Roman methods of legal education? On this point, see F. SCHULZ, *History of Roman Legal Science* (1946), pp. 55 ff.

[5] Cf. above, pp. 89 ff., and below, pp. 181 ff.

[6] The text is given above, p. 95.

[7] An *al-tiqre* reading.

And a warning was issued against such persons:

התנאים מבלי עולם.   "The *tannaim* judge the world into
corruption" (*ibid.*).

This saying was applied by Rabina to those who teach halakah direct
from their mishnah (שמורין הלכה מתוך משנתן, *ibid.*), i.e. without that
complementary knowledge and deeper insight provided by more advanced studies.

The person who was able only to repeat *halakot* was thus inexorably
stamped by the majority of Rabbis as being only half-educated. He is not
treated as a worthy תלמיד חכם,[1] b Meg. 26 b,[2] since a worthy *talmid
ḥakam* must be one who is able to explain his mishnah (שיודע לבאר
משנתו)[3]—to quote a fully representative saying of R. Abba ben Memel.
He must have entered the circle of disciples of one or more Rabbis, or a
college, in order to complement, by listening and imitation, his knowledge of the interpretative tradition belonging to the Scriptures and
the Mishnah; and also to sharpen, in general study and analysis of the
traditional material of the oral Torah, the edge of his intellect,[4] and increase his ability to use and apply the Torah in jurisdiction, teaching and
exposition. If the terms may be used in their more original meaning, it
might be said that the ideal *talmid ḥakam* ought to have mastered
(apart from the Scriptures) the *mishnah* and *gemara* material, and to be

---

[1] The opinion advanced by WEBER (*Jüdische Theologie*, pp. 131 ff.), BILLER-
BECK (*Comm.* I, 1922, pp. 496 f.) and K. H. RENGSTORF (μαθητής, in *Theol. Wörterb.*, ed. G. KITTEL, IV, 1942, pp. 434 ff.) that חכם denotes an ordained Rabbi and
תלמיד חכם a fully qualified but unordained rabbinic pupil is an over-simplification.
Linguistic practice here is variable. See the material listed in I. GOLDBERGER, Der
Talmid Chacham, in *Monatsschr. f. Gesch. u. Wiss. d. Judent.* 68 (1924), pp. 211 ff.,
291 ff., and cf. MARMORSTEIN, *La réorganisation du doctorat*.

[2] Cf. b Meg. 28 b and the debate in p Moed Qat. III.7, as well as b Qid. 49 a. See
also GUTTMANN, *Zur Einleitung*, pp. 20 and 30, and LAUTERBACH, *Midrash and
Mishnah*, pp. 165 f., where the problem is also related to the fact that certain teachers
held fast to the old midrashic method of study. See also GOLDBERGER and MARMOR-
STEIN, *op. cit.*

[3] p Moed Qat. *ibid.* Cf. Eccl. R. 6.9. Cf. also Josephus, *Ant.* 20.11.2: μόνοις δὲ
σοφίαν μαρτυροῦσι τοῖς τὰ νόμιμα σαφῶς ἐπισταμένοις καὶ τὴν τῶν ἱερῶν γραμμάτων
δύναμιν ἑρμηνεῦσαι δυναμένοις.

[4] Many passages emphasize the way in which a Rabbi consciously poses problems,
etc., in order to "sharpen" (חדד) the intellect of his pupils: לא אמר רבי פלוני
אלא לחדד בה התלמידים. Thus: R. Joshua, b Naz. 59 b; R. Aqiba, b Erub. 13 a, b Nid. 45 a;
R. Huna, b Zeb. 13 a; and others. See also GOLDBERGER, *Der Talmid Chacham*,
pp. 215 f., and KAPLAN, *The Redaction*, p. 226.

skilled in *sebara*. This includes the learning of the material of the traditional halakic midrash collections,[1] together with the technique of
midrashic exegesis. He ought also to be a good haggadist. It goes without
saying that few men even approached this ideal: only men of the stature
of Rabban Joḥanan ben Zakkai[2] and R. Aqiba.[3] The masters concentrated, as a rule, on certain special areas of study.

The Rabbis' criticism of the *shonim* must in practice have been
directed against the most one-sided *tannaim* in the colleges;[4] but its
main object must have been the majority of mishnah teachers (*mashnim*)
out in the synagogue congregations. It would seem evident that this
criticism of the *shonim* is due to the fact that the Rabbis represented a
higher standard of knowledge and advocated a higher—and perhaps to
some extent differently characterized—educational ideal. As we have
already mentioned, the mature Rabbi could look down on the mediocre
mishnah teacher in the same way that a fully qualified and well trained
Hellenistic rhetor looked down on the type of grammarian who could
teach his pupils the correct reading (ἀνάγνωσις) of the classical texts, but
could not give any deeper interpretation (ἐξήγησις), and was in any case
unable to master the rhetorician's highly valued art (τέχνη ῥητορική).[5]

It is conceivable that the Rabbis' criticism of the mishnah teachers
also reflects a more ancient conflict between somewhat different educational methods. It is true that the fully developed rabbinic school system
is—on the whole—a fairly organic whole, but it comprises different
elements (the study of *miqra*, *mishnah* and *talmud*) which may have had
rather different histories. The Rabbis' criticism of *shonim* may perhaps
be understood from one point of view as being a sign that the attempt to
impose uniformity on the course of education was not an unqualified
success.[6] This problem is, however, difficult to solve, owing to the nature
of the source material.

Be that as it may, we have already noted that the equipment of a
learned Rabbi has various constituents. We can draw a rough distinction between two main elements: (i) knowledge of the traditions, and

---

[1] For the way in which the traditional midrash material was learned in the
course of systematic study, see below, pp. 116 ff. Furthermore, isolated elements
were also learned in connection with talmudic discussions; see below, pp. 175 ff.

[2] b Suk. 28a. On him, see BACHER, *Die Agada der Tannaiten* I, pp. 25 ff.

[3] *Ibid.*, pp. 271 ff.

[4] On the best *tannaim*, see above, pp. 95 f.

[5] See also above, p. 60 and 103.

[6] Cf. above, p. 107.

(ii) skill in the technique of exposition, dialectics and the art of presentation in general. For natural reasons, these different elements were of varying import for different Rabbis, and were evaluated differently.[1] Some valued the filled "basket of books" more highly than the incontrovertible, sophisticated "pilpulist" (בעל פלפול)[2]; others vice versa. The ideal for some was "the caulked cistern which never loses a drop",[3] considering it an honour never to say anything (i.e. to teach a doctrine) which they had not heard from their teacher. The great example for teachers of this type was R. Eliezer ben Hyrkanos[4]—although the principle was older.[5] For others, the ideal was that of the intractably powerful and astute dialectician "who tears up mountains by the roots".[6] They related with admiration the case of the scholar in Jabneh who could produce 150 arguments to prove that certain reptiles were clean, although according to the written Torah (Lev. 11. 29 ff., 41 ff.) they were and are unclean.[7] Admiration of sophistic τέχνη was, as we know, widespread in Antiquity, and we should not be surprised to find it occurring in certain rabbinic circles. It would be unjust to blame the rabbinic sophists for τὸν ἥττω λόγον κρείττω ποιεῖν, but an example such as that of the anonymous teacher from Jabneh, which we have just quoted, shows the direction in which admiration of thoroughgoing dialectic technique was capable of leading.

However the two elements we have discussed may have been evaluated by the Rabbis, no Rabbi was willing to forsake either of them. The traditionist, bursting with solid tradition, had to be able to use his text material; the acute pilpulist had to have text material from which

---

[1] This has been pointed out by many scholars, e.g. I. LEWY, *Über einige Fragmente*, pp. 1 f., and ESCHELBACHER, *Probleme der talmudischen Dialektik*, pp. 47 ff.

[2] Cf. b Bab. Batr. 145 b.

[3] Ab. II.8: בור סוד שאינו מאבד טפה.

[4] לא אמרתי דבר שלא שמעתי מפי רבי מעולם (the Munich ms. reads רבותי), b Suk. 28 a (cf. 27 b), b Yoma 66 b, and elsewhere.

[5] L. A. ROSENTHAL is right when he points out that the careful distinction drawn between words which have been heard and those which have not been heard characterizes the whole school of Rabban Joḥanan ben Zakkai: *Über den Zusammenhang* III, pp. 56 ff. See e.g. M Par. I.1, M Ker. III.7, p Pes. IX.6, p Yeb. VIII.4, b Suk. 28 a (Rabban Joḥanan b. Z. himself).

[6] b Hor. 14 a: עוקר הרים.

[7] b Erub. 13 b. — Cf. what R. Judah says in Rab's name, b Sanh. 17 a: אין מושיבין בסנהדרין אלא מי שיודע לטהר את השרץ מן התורה. Cf. also R. Judah's words on R. Meir's pupils, b Qid. 52 b, b Naz. 49 b.

to begin and on which to work.[1] Valid sacred law and respected authoritative texts were the necessary objects of study. Everyone therefore maintained—though with varying emphases—the need of both knowledge of the tradition and of technical skill; they therefore sought both to memorize the basic text material and, as we have seen, to cultivate their ability to use it.

We have been mainly occupied here with the Amoraic period, but we have also been back into the Tannaitic period. From the point of view of the sources, however, most of what we have said cannot be traced farther back than to R. Aqiba. What is then to be said about the time before Aqiba? How were the משנה ראשונה, about which we hear before Aqiba,[2] and the tractates and other collections which existed before Aqiba,[3] carried? How did they transmit the *halakot* which had been valid for centuries, and which were edited by R. Aqiba and his followers in such a way as to enable us to check them in their written form? How was the great παράδοσις τῶν πρεσβυτέρων carried? We have already considered this question.[4] It seems extremely improbable that transmission before Aqiba can have taken place following entirely different principles from those later observed, though there may have been certain differences. The balance of probability is that the basic material in the oral Torah was transmitted and learned in a fixed form as early as during the last century of the Temple; this material was arranged in blocks, grouped on midrashic and mishnaic principles.[5] Even if it is not always easy for us to penetrate the re-editing later carried out by such men as R. Aqiba, R. Judah and others, it has been successfully shown that older collections, with older priciples of arrangement, lie behind the collections which have been preserved to us.[6] It is furthermore a significant fact that the older Tannaites occasionally learned their

---

[1] Cf. the Roman rhetors' ingenious way of referring to the teaching of the law: *hastas ministrare*, "to provide ammunition"; see SCHULZ, *History of Roman Legal Science*, p. 55.

[2] M Sanh. III.4, M Ed. VII.2, M Git. V.6, M Naz. VI.1. On this, see HOFFMANN, *Die erste Mischna und die Controversen der Tannaim*, and LAUTERBACH, *Mishnah*, p. 610.

[3] On these, see STRACK, *Einleitung*, pp. 16 ff. (Eng. ed. pp. 20 ff.).

[4] Above, pp. 77 f.

[5] Cf. BACHER, *Tradition*, p. 70.

[6] See HOFFMANN, *op. cit.*, L. A. ROSENTHAL, *Über den Zusammenhang der Mischna* I (2nd ed. 1909), and also STRACK, *Einleitung*, p. 22 (Eng. ed. p. 25), H. DANBY, *The Mishnah* (1933), pp. xxiv f.

halakah from their teachers without being able to convey any further explanation of them.[1] This is one of the signs which show that even at this early period learning and interpretation were two different elements in instruction,[2] i.e. that even at this time the oral Torah was carried in virtually the same way as in that period which we have mainly discussed here.

---

[1] See below, p. 132 f.
[2] See below, Ch. 11 A.

CHAPTER 10

How Oral Torah is Passed On

IN THE PREVIOUS chapter we observed the interplay between solidity and flexibility in the transmission of the oral Torah. We have seen how the basic material is carried as formulated oral texts, recorded in the memories of teachers, pupils and professional traditionists, ready to be quoted or otherwise used when required. In this chapter we are going to concentrate on the actual act of transmission in its real meaning: the act by which such an oral text is passed on to a receiver. In order to try and give a concrete picture of the way in which this takes place, we shall quote a number of examples from various levels of education, and from different situations. The object of this chapter is modest: to draw a rough outline of the act of transmission. The next chapter will be devoted to the details of the theory and practice of transmission.

We have already made the acquaintance of the Rabbis' criticism of mishnah teachers and the study of the mishnah.[1] We saw that the criticism was based on the fact that mishnah teaching gave no detailed information as to the meaning of the condensed mishnah text. Knowledge was therefore quite superficial. We must now ask how this relatively "mechanical" mishnah teaching was carried out. How was the oral Torah passed on at this educational level?

In the circles in which we are moving, bound as they are by tradition, we need not expect any radical variations or educational innovations. The mishnah teacher (מַשְׁנֶה) and the Scripture teacher (סוֹפֵר) worked side by side. Occasionally, one and the same person would combine the activities of *sofer* and *mashneh*.[2] Every *mashneh* had in any case been through the Scripture school (*bet sefer*). It is therefore not surprising that we find a striking resemblance between the simple pedagogics in the two schools. In both cases it was the teachers' task to teach their pupils, faithfully and accurately, an accepted, authoritative and respected collection of texts. The only important difference was that in one case the text is a *written text* and must be learned as a *reading* (מִקְרָא) from a book

---

[1] Above, pp. 103 ff.
[2] Above, p. 103.

114

(בְּסֵפֶר);[1] in the other it is an *oral text* which has to be learned by repetition (מִשְׁנָה) from the lips of the teacher (עַל פֶּה, מִתּוֹךְ הַפֶּה).[2] It is possible that there was a further important difference. It is extremely doubtful whether mishnah teachers in general gave their pupils anything corresponding to the targum—i.e. any "explanatory translation" (see below)—while this most probably took place, as we have seen, in the *bet sefer*.[3]

In both cases the authoritative text was learned passage by passage. It is significant that according to a haggadah in Eka R. 1.31, a man hungering for the wisdom of the Torah on the streets of Jerusalem asks his fellow, "Teach me to read a column (הַקְרִינִי דַּף אֶחָד), teach me to repeat a section (הַשִּׁינִי פֶּרֶק אֶחָד)!"[4]

A well-known tradition[5] tells of R. Ḥiyya the elder that if the Torah should be forgotten in Israel he would proceed in the following way: he would buy seeds of flax, plant them, reap the flax, and make ropes, with which he would capture some hinds; from their skins he would then make scrolls on which he would write (from memory) the Torah (Pentateuch). Then he would go to a town where there was no teacher, and there teach five boys to read (מִקְרִינָא) a book each from the Pentateuch, and teach six other boys to repeat (מַתְנִינָא)[6] a mishnah order each. The boys would then be able to teach one another.

If we overlook the unique elements in this speculation, we see that R. Ḥiyya's plan is intended to create a situation in which he can carry out regular instruction in *miqra* and *mishnah*. He wishes to be able to teach as a *sofer* and a *mashneh*. He must teach the children to read the written Torah from a book,[7] despite the emphasis which he places upon the fact that he knows it so perfectly that he is able to write it out from memory.[8] As far as we know, there is nothing to indicate the extent to which Scripture teachers used clever pupils to assist them in their teaching. It is not

---

[1] Above, pp. 27 ff. and 62 ff.

[2] Above, pp. 27 ff., and below, pp. 157 ff.

[3] Above, pp. 60 ff.

[4] Cf. Lev. R. 25.1.

[5] b Ket. 103b, b Bab. Mes. 85b.

[6] Note the different terms for teaching written and oral Torah. See above, pp. 27 f.

[7] See above, pp. 62 f.

[8] That he was compelled to write from memory, which was also forbidden, is due to the conditions on which the hypothesis is based: "If the Torah were to be forgotten in Israel ..."

improbable *per se*.[1] Again, the oral Torah must be learned by oral repetition, and this is precisely what R. Ḥiyya does. It is by no means improbable that mishnah teachers allowed gifted pupils to specialize in different orders and function as a sort of ὑποδιδάσκαλος. It is in any case usual at *higher* levels of study, in the colleges, for various teachers, and pupils (and *tannaim*) to be particularly responsible for different collections of texts. As late as the 12th century, one Rabbi (R. Isaac ben Samuel) had between 60 and 70 pupils who memorized the various parts of the Babylonian Talmud, and together comprised a living copy of the Talmud.[2]

It is scarcely possible to reconstruct in detail the method used by the mishnah teachers. But on a basis of the diverse items of information in the Talmud we receive the impression that these teachers spelled out the oral texts time and time again (at least four times) for their pupils, with expressive articulation, careful pronunciation and faithful traditional cantillation, and that the pupils had to repeat it several times, in chorus and individually, upon which the teacher corrected mistakes and gave that measure of elementary commentary which was necessary for the correct learning of the text.[3] It is possible that skilled mishnah teachers could add an explanatory commentary to the difficult text: a sort of

---

[1] The Bell-Lancaster system of pedagogics had its forerunners, as LEWIT points out, quite correctly, *Darstellung der theoretischen und praktischen Pädagogik im jüdischen Altertume*, p. 19. It also has its forerunners in the ancient ὑποδιδάσκαλοι on various educational levels. See above, p. 99, n. 4.

[2] See GUTTMANN, *Zur Entstehung des Talmuds*, pp. 47 ff. There were on the other hand individual teachers who had enormous reserves of memorized knowledge. A famous example is the exiliarch Natronai b. Ḥabibai (8th century), who emigrated to Spain, where he is reputed to have written a complete Talmud from memory; see N. BRÜLL, Die Entstehungsgeschichte des babylonischen Talmuds als Schriftwerkes, in *Jahrb. f. Jüd. Gesch. u. Lit.* 2 (1876), p. 51.

[3] See the items we present in the next chapter. Cf. Ex. R. 41.5. LEWIT, *op. cit.*, p. 48, describes the methods of the mishnah-teachers in these words: "In der Mischnahabteilung war das Hauptpensum: die tradierten Mischnahsätze wörtlich auswendig zu lernen. Der Schüler musste die ganze Mischnah auswendig lernen allein durch den Vortrag des Lehrers. Der Lehrer trug die Mischnahsätze nach einer ihm überkommenen, zweckmässig scheinenden Reihenfolge vor, ohne sich auf die Erklärung und Motivierung der vorgetragenen Sätze einzulassen. Die mitgeteilten Sätze wiederholte die ganze Klasse singend, bis sie ein jeder auswendig wusste (Meg. 32a)." — Cf. Löw, *Graphische Requisiten* II, p. 129, whose formulations are followed closely by LEWIT. — For a comparison with methods in the Hellenistic schools, see MARROU, *Histoire de l'éducation*, pp. 215 and 366, and further, below, pp. 124 ff.

targum or simply a sort of elementary talmud;[1] that part of the process
of instruction was however either missing or most rudimentary in the
teaching of the average mishnah teacher: so much is clear. We have already noted that their competence was as a rule rather limited.[2] But
they also had a valid reason for not going deeper into the exposition of
the mishnah text: the more advanced studies on the talmud level were
devoted to this branch of learning.

The oral Torah seems also to have been passed on at the higher level
of the rabbinic colleges—in other words, at the talmud stage—on the
basis of much the same method as that used at the mishnah stage. We
see, for example, that when the midrash collections were systematically
worked through, these were learned section (פרק) by section.[3] The only
differences here seem to be that the teacher adds a deeper and wider
commentary to the text which is to be learned, and that the text can be
the subject of discussion. A concrete picture is provided by a saying of
R. Ḥiyya, preserved in b Ber. 11 b:

"I often stood before (i.e. was a disciple of) Rab in order to learn passages of Sifra de be Rab (לתנויי פרקים בספרא דבי רב). He used first to
wash his hands, recite a berakah and then teach us our section
(הוה מקדים וקא משי ידיה ובריך ומתני לן פרקין)."

It is worth noticing in passing that instruction in the oral Torah is a
sacred action, surrounded by certain ritual stipulations[4] which varied
somewhat according to the sacredness and authority of the object of
study.[5]

We may take a further example from advanced instruction; this has
to do with the teaching of another collection which the pupils did not
have the opportunity of learning in their earlier studies: a collection of

---

[1] This is clear from such examples as b Taan. 9a, b Shab. 68b, b Yeb. 9a, b Hor.
8a, etc. and from the fact that a distinction was drawn, in some places at least,
between merely repeating (and learning to repeat) a mishnah text, and teaching
such a text with complementary interpretation. See the words of Ulla in b Meg.
28b: תני ארבעה and מתני ארבעה. Alfasi understands this as being a distinction between מי שגמר תלמוד and מי ששונה ארבעה סדרי משנה. For the utterly differentiated
terminology, see BACHER, Terminologie II, pp. 238 ff., and cf. J. LEWY, Interpretation, pp. 3 ff.

[2] Above, pp. 102 f.

[3] b Ber. 11b, 14b, b Erub. 36b.

[4] On this, see context in the gemara, b Ber. 11b.

[5] For the ritual laws for the passing on of esoteric doctrines, see below, p. 166.

halakot in the category of *Derek Eres*.[1] It is thus a question of a tractate belonging to the periphery of the oral Torah; as we know, it was not taken into the Mishnah. A *baraita* in b Ber. 22a tells how the patriarch R. Judah happened on one occasion to be going with his disciples by the side of a river when they addressed to him the "ritual" prayer for instruction: "Our master, teach us a section of the halakot of *Derek Eres* (רבינו שנה לנו פרק אחד בהלכות דרך ארץ)." R. Judah then stepped into the river and took a bath of purification, for he had incurred pollution, before passing on to them the desired passage (ירד וטבל ושנה להם).[2] To judge from the context, it concerns scarcely more than the passing on of the actual text.[3] It is possible, but not probable, that the complementary commentary is included.[4] We can also note in passing that R. Judah wished to appear before his disciples in a state of ritual cleanliness when transmitting a passage, although it is a question of a subject such as *Derek Eres*.[5]

There was however a somewhat different way of learning an oral text collection. It was first learned *as a whole*; analysis and interpretation were undertaken later. The study of the collection in question was organized in two stages: we might call them a *mishnah stage* and a *talmud stage*. In the following example, which we have taken from b Yeb. 72b, we are concerned with a midrash collection: Torat Kohanim, i.e. an earlier equivalent of Sifra. In this tradition the story is told of Resh Laqish, that he hears that the son of Pedat (Eleazar) knows Torat Kohanim. He goes to him and learns to repeat the traditional collection in *three days*, after which he spends *three months* penetrating the meaning and usage of the material he has learned.[6] It seems in this case as though the learned and astute Resh Laqish were traditionally supposed to be able to interpret this material on his own.[7] Less outstanding men must,

---

[1] On *halakot* of this type, see Guttmann, *Zur Einleitung* I, pp. 3 f. and 21. — It is difficult to say what relation this early collection of *halakot* in the *Derek Eres* genre, named also in p Shab. VI.2, can have to the later compilations *Derek Eres Rabba* and *Derek Eres Zutta* (see Mielziner, *Introduction*, p. 64).

[2] The Munich ms. reads ועלה ואח״כ שנה.

[3] See the context in Talmud.

[4] The verb would seem to have the meaning "to repeat", "to pass on by repetition".

[5] R. Judah here subjects himself to a stricter halakic practice than that which he teaches. Cf. below, pp. 186 and 317 ff.

[6] נפק תנייה בתלתא יומי וסברה בתלתא ירחי.

[7] For the common rabbinic idea that an astute and gifted scholar is able, by his

however, receive instruction in the interpretation of the text if they are to avoid becoming mechanical reproducers of the texts, "baskets full of books". They must participate in some Rabbi's methodical study of such collections of texts, as we saw earlier in the case of R. Ḥiyya and his study of Sifra de be Rab.

The previous example might be said to move on the highest level. In this way a learned Rabbi might in early Amoraic times complement his knowledge by learning a previously unknown text collection. We have yet another example of the way in which a leading Rabbi was able to complement his knowledge of the oral Torah. This example is from the Tannaitic period. A *baraita* in b Hor. 13b tells how on one occasion R. Meir and R. Natan wanted to humiliate Rabban Simeon ben Gamaliel by challenging him in the college to expound the admittedly difficult[1] tractate Uqsin,[2] which he did not know. But Jacob ben Qodshi prevented the patriarch's humiliation by sitting in his upper room (עלייה)[3] and working through the tractate in question. The formulation is in these words: "He expounded, gave the text and repeated it, gave the text and repeated it (פשט גרס ותנא גרס ותנא)."[4] R. Simeon's suspicions were aroused, he concentrated his attention and familiarized himself with the text which Jacob had read. On the following day he was able to expound the tractate when called upon to do so. (In order to understand this narrative we must remember that in connection with the methodical study of the mishnah text, the text of a fixed commentary (גמרא) was developing in the various schools, as a basis for deeper intellectual application.)[5] The formulation of this *baraita* is rather obscure, and the scene

---

interpretation or his dialectic skill, to rediscover and reconstruct hidden or lost wisdom, see below, p. 173.

[1] b Ber. 20a.

[2] For the later fate of this early tractate, see b Taan. 24a, 24b, b Sanh. 106b.

[3] On עלייה (ὑπερῷον), see KRAUSS, *Die Versammlungsstätten der Talmudgelehrten*, pp. 30 ff., and BILLERBECK, *Comm.* II, p. 594.

[4] For the terms, see LEVY's and JASTROW's *Lexica*, sub vocibus. For the term גרס see further L. GINZBERG, Beiträge zur Lexikographie des Aramäischen, in *Festschrift* SCHWARZ (1917), p. 341, and LEVIAS, Word Studies, in *Hebr. Un. Coll. Ann.* 1904, p. 152. — My thanks are due to Dr. R. EDELMANN, for correcting my translation of the above quotation.

[5] For the term גמרא, see above, p. 104, n. 3. On the development of the relatively fixed *gemara* text in the different schools, see J. LEWY, *Interpretation*, pp. 3 ff., W. BACHER, Talmud, in *The Jew. Enc.* XII (1906), pp. 1 ff., KAPLAN, *The Redaction*. The term denoting the taking up of a tradition into the fixed *gemara* text is קבע; b Erub. 32b (with par.): אמרי ליה קבעיתו ליה בגמרא. Cf. b Bek. 36b. See BACHER,

it depicts is so unique that we ought not to press its details too far. But without doing so, we can nevertheless see in this example how *traditional* this instruction is, even at the highest college level. Even the principal, delivering a lecture on a tractate, passes on for the most part traditional material. In order to be able to hold such a lecture, the presiding Rabbi must have been instructed both in the text and in the interpretation of the tractate: both the tractate's *mishnah* and its *talmud*.[1] R. Simeon had not earlier undergone this instruction, but his omission was remedied at the last minute.

In the examples which we have dealt with so far, oral Torah has been passed on in the form of text collections or sections (פרקים) from such collections. We ought perhaps to notice that the same method was used when individual doctrinal statements (הלכות and the like) were passed on. There are several passages in the Talmud where a student, or a teacher, consults a Rabbi or a traditionist either on some doctrinal question or on the wording of some tradition. Thus we read:

תנא מיניה ארבעין	"He learned it from him "forty
זימנין ודמי ליה כמאן	times", and it became for him as
דמנח בכיסיה.	though it lay in his purse."[2]

"Forty" is a round number.[3] What is being said is that the doctrinal statement in question was passed on through being repeated several times, until the receiver knew the text by heart.[4]

These examples have shown that the methodical transmission of oral Torah took place on all school levels in such a way that the teacher/ traditionist equips his receivers with the oral text by repeating it several times, and that a further element—the interpretation of the text in question—is required before knowledge can be reckoned as complete. This interpretation seems on the lowest educational level to be extremely rudimentary, if it exists at all, but it is accorded more and more importance, the higher up in the school system we go.

We shall finally consider the perfectly formed act of transmission by which a finally-redacted oral text collection is *published*—by being

Terminologie II, pp. 185 f. KAPLAN points out that תני is also used with the same meaning, *op. cit.*, pp. 206 ff. See further, LEWY, *op. cit.*, *ibid.* Cf. also below, p. 129, n. 1, and p. 132.

[1] We use these terms here for forms of delivery, not concrete literary products.
[2] b Meg. 7b; see further, b Ket. 50a, b Ber. 28a, b Ket. 22b and elsewhere.
[3] BERGMANN, *Die runden und hyperbolischen Zahlen in der Agada*, pp. 370 ff.
[4] See further below, pp. 133 ff.

passed, with solemn ritual, to professional traditionists and others (teachers, pupils and hearers). Here we have something which we might regard as an equivalent of that transmission, the primary object of which is the conservation of the text, which we considered in our description of the transmission of the written Torah.[1]

A *baraita* in b Erub. 54b[2] shows how the Rabbis imagined Moses—the arch-Rabbi—to have set about passing on the finally-redacted oral Torah (משנה) to Israel. As we know, the Rabbis considered that the mishnah was given by God to Moses on Sinai.[3]

"Our masters learned: In what way was mishnah published (i.e. passed on to the traditionists in finally-redacted form: כיצד סדר משנה)?[4] Moses learned (למד) from the mouth of the Almighty. Then Aaron entered and Moses repeated (שנה) to him his chapter (פירקו). Then Aaron moved and sat down on Moses' left. Thereupon Aaron's sons entered and Moses repeated to them their chapter. Thereupon his sons moved and Eleazar sat down on Moses' right and Itamar on Aaron's left. (R. Judah said: Aaron was always on Moses' right.)[5] Thereupon the elders entered and Moses repeated to them their chapter, and when the elders had moved to one side all the people entered and Moses repeated to them their chapter. Aaron had thus heard what was transmitted four times, his sons three times, the elders twice and all the people once. Moses now left them and Aaron repeated his chapter to them. Then Aaron went out and his sons repeated their chapter to them. Then his sons went out and the elders repeated their chapter to them. Thus everyone had heard (every) chapter four times. From this R. Eliezer drew the conclusion that a man is bound to repeat (every tradition) four times for his pupil.[6] This final conclusion is drawn *a maiore ad minus*: Aaron, who learned from Moses, who had learned from the Almighty, must (be taught) in this way; how much more must then an ordinary pupil, who learns from an ordinary teacher."

It is evident that this picture is a copy of procedure in the rabbinic colleges. Moses is presented—as he so often is in rabbinic literature—as

---

[1] Above, pp. 42 ff.

[2] Cf. Sifra, c. 3, beginning.

[3] Above, p. 82.

[4] For the term סדר, see LIEBERMAN, *Hellenism*, pp. 90 ff., and cf. BACHER, *Terminologie* I, p. 130, II, p. 133.

[5] An interpolation, which we set within parentheses.

[6] See more on this subject, below, pp. 133 ff.

the real arch-Rabbi: משה רבינו.[1] The comparison between Moses' method
of working and that of the Rabbis is, as the above quotation shows,
made by the Rabbis themselves. It is however doubtful whether R.
Eliezer ben Hyrkanos would have made this comparison.[2] In that case
he had an entirely different concrete idea of the meaning of the term
mishnah in this context from that held by the Rabbis of the Amoraic
period. It is more probable that R. Eliezer's rule was subsequently connected with this haggadah.

Be that as it may. LIEBERMAN has good grounds for supposing that
it is possible, from this *baraita*, to deduce the procedure followed when
R. Aqiba (in different stages) arranged and published (סדר, תקן)[3] his
Mishnah. We quote:[4]

"The procedure adopted by the master was probably something like
the following. He taught the new *Mishnah* to the first *Tanna*; afterwards
he taught it to the second *Tanna* (in the presence of the first), then to the
third etc. Subsequently the first *Tanna* repeated the *Mishnah* to the
second, to the third etc. Then the second *Tanna* recited it to the third,
to the fourth etc. ... After the *Mishnah* was systematized, (סדורה) and
the *Tannaim* knew it thoroughly by heart, they repeated it in the college in the presence of the master who supervised its recitation, corrected it and gave it its final form.—Thus, the old *Mishnah* was augmented by a new stratum formed of the later interpretations. The new
material was incorporated in the old version, the compilation was
systematized and edited, committed to the memory of a group of *Tannaim*, and finally 'entered the college'.[5] The new *Mishnah* was thus
published in a number of 'copies' (ἴσα) in the form of living books, which
subsequently spread and multiplied."[6]

---

[1] R. BLOCH, Quelques aspects de la figure de Moïse dans la tradition rabbinique,
in *Cahiers Sioniens* 8 (1954), pp. 211 ff.

[2] Thus BACHER, *Die Agada der Tannaiten* I (2nd ed.), p. 102.

[3] Cf. p. 120, n. 4. For the term תקן, see LIEBERMAN, *op. cit.*, *ibid.*, and BACHER,
Terminologie I, p. 204. Cf. the technique of edition in the Arabic world, PEDERSEN,
Den arabiske bog, p. 21. See further, above, p. 95, n. 6.

[4] LIEBERMAN, *op. cit.*, p. 93.

[5] For the expression, see above, p. 98, n. 5.

[6] Cf. J. LEWY in *Jahresber. d. Jüd.-Theol. Semin. zu Breslau* (1905), pp. 25 f.

CHAPTER 11

Some Details of the Theory and Practice of Transmission

WE HAVE ATTEMPTED in the two previous chapters to sketch the rough outlines of the way in which the oral Torah is carried and passed on. In this chapter we shall go into the theory and practice of transmission in more detail. We shall separate and consider more closely a number of characteristics which give us an insight into the process which was carried on, and help us to understand how the Rabbis were able to transmit and preserve these enormous quantities of oral material during the centuries.

We must first of all take note of two basic pedagogical principles: (a) that the material is memorized, and (b) that the learning of the wording of the text as a rule precedes the study of the meaning of the text (section A). We shall then see the way in which teachers and pupils make a conscious effort to preserve the exact wording of the transmitted authoritative texts (B). This attitude implies a general attempt to present the doctrinal material in a form which is as brief—and schematic—as possible. We shall therefore devote one section to a consideration of this tendency to condense the material into brief texts and sayings (C); this brings us to the various methods by which memorization was facilitated: in other words, the rabbinic technique of mnemonics (D). A section is also devoted to the unofficial role played by notes, note-books and secret scrolls (E). Further, we shall take note of the importance which a couple of elements in the actual technique of repetition must have had for the facilitation of transmission (F). We shall finally look at the Rabbis' measures for maintaining the masses of oral text material which they had received and learned (G).

We shall in general illustrate each point which we take up, partly by quoting the pedagogical rule which the Rabbis themselves formulated, partly by exemplifying the way in which the principle worked in practice, and partly by pointing out certain signs in the written traditional material, signs which indicate that the principle in question was actually applied. We shall for the sake of clarity first quote the rule, although from the historical point of view it would seem not to have been formulated until long after the practice had arisen and been established.

A. *Two Basic Pedagogical Principles*

Long before any human hand had formed the signs which make up the art of writing, there existed an oral tradition. Long before any literary work had been committed to writing, there existed "oral literature": formulated *geistiges Gut*, delivered from memory and transmitted orally.[1]

So much can be supposed. But what we can state is even more important, something which we can see with our own eyes in historical times: that the introduction of the art of writing into a culture implies, at least to begin with, very little alteration in the standing of the oral tradition. First, it takes a long time for the art of writing to be practised and developed to such an extent as to be capable of functioning as an effective vehicle for spiritual products. Secondly, it takes a long time for the art of writing to spread to such an extent as to be mastered adequately in all those circles within which *geistiges Gut* is transmitted. Thirdly, it takes a long time to make such a clean break with the hereditary tradition, that writing can come into use all along the line for the various purposes which have long been dealt with orally. We know from many cultures what a strong opposition can be awakened by the introduction of writing, particularly when it is a matter of the writing down of various kinds of oral text material; this opposition can, however, vary in strength in different circles.[2] And fourthly, it takes time for the book to become an independent form of expression, and not merely an aid to memory. It takes time to desert the principle that the material of knowledge and texts are dead things if they are not imprinted on the memory and function there. In the tradition of western culture it is only in our own day that the memory has been *effectively* unloaded into books. Not until our own day have we learned to accept a form of education which to a great extent consists of being able to find the material which is required in the right books, without needing to carry it all in the memory. Not until our day has the pedagogical revolution taken place which has been called "the dethronement of memory".[3]

Memorization is thus an original and elementary method of study, the origins of which are lost in prehistory. It played an essential role in ancient educational theory within the cultural areas in which we are

---

[1] See works of GANDZ and CHADWICK quoted above, p. 72, n. 3.

[2] See further, below, sec. E.

[3] MORRIS, *The Jewish School*, p. 114.

interested. The general attitude was that words and items of knowledge must be memorized: *tantum scimus, quantum memoria tenemus!*

A closer look at Hellenistic practice is instructive. In the elementary schools the children were first taught the alphabet, but were later taught to recite from memory,[1] with the correct melodic accentuation, chosen passages out of the classical texts, principally the all-wise Homer. Such commentary to the text as was offered by the "teacher of letters" (γραμματιστής)—if comments were made at all—was extremely elementary.[2] When literature was taught on the next school level by the grammarian (γραμματικός) the children continued to learn classical texts— still primarily Homer—by heart. But at this level the teacher added direct interpretation to this education in recitation, though the interpretation was naturally of variable scope and depth.[3] The grammarian's method of instruction seems on the whole to have been very consistent and to have remained essentially unaltered from the centuries before Christ to the end of Antiquity (and even longer). At about the beginning of the Christian era there even appears a fairly definite *theory* concerning the grammarian's task and his teaching method. We quote Marrou: "C'est ... aux alentours de notre ère, après Denys et avant Quintilien, qu'apparaît la définition classique à laquelle s'arrêtera la tradition antique : le travail du grammairien sur un auteur se divise en quatre opérations : la critique du texte, la lecture, l'explication, le jugement : διόρθωσις, ἀνάγνωσις, ἐξήγησις, κρίσις." After having described the laborious work upon the text which is implied in διόρθωσις and ἀνάγνωσις, Marrou goes on to say: "Une étude aussi minutieuse du texte rendait facile la mémorisation : tout semble indiquer que chez le grammairien, comme à l'école primaire, la récitation du texte appris par cœur succédait à la lecture."[4]

---

[1] See above, pp. 62 ff.

[2] See P. Beudel, *Qua ratione Graeci liberos docuerint* (1911), pp. 6 ff., Marrou, *Histoire de l'éducation*, pp. 210 ff., 359 ff. See also E. Ziebarth, *Aus dem griechischen Schulwesen* (1914), pp. 123 ff., K. J. Freeman, *Schools of Hellas* (3rd ed. 1922), pp. 93 ff. Cf. further A. Burk, *Die Pädagogik des Isokrates* (1923), pp. 22 ff., 117 ff., and T. Klauser, Auswendiglernen, in *Reallex. f. Ant. u. Christ.* I (1950), col. 1030 ff.

[3] Beudel, *op. cit.*, pp. 29 ff., Marrou, *op. cit.*, pp. 223 ff., 369 ff., and the other works mentioned in the previous note, *ibid.* For more detail on the grammarians, see the works cited p. 51, n. 2.

[4] *Ibid.*, pp. 230 f. Cf. idem, *Saint Augustin*, p. 20, on the Latin grammarians: "Il était classique depuis Varron de distinguer dans cette étude quatre phases : *lectio,*

If we take a further step upward, i.e. to the highest schools, the rhetor- (σοφιστής-)schools, we find that here too, the practice of learning by heart plays a vital role. The pupils received basic instruction in the complicated τέχνη ῥητορική which consisted of learning to memorize the precise definitions, the elaborate classifications and subclassifications formulated in the precepts of rhetoric, as well as a number of κοινοὶ τόποι (loci communes); further, they had to learn by heart great portions from the works of the authors, a number of model compositions (προγυμνάσματα) etc.[1]

In the schools of philosophy were read the writings of the philosophers, and explanations were given of incomprehensible expressions (ἐξήγησις τῆς λέξεως). Here, too, the method was practised by which the pupils had to learn the contents of the most important texts so thoroughly that they were able to repeat them from memory. Epictetus compares the method he used for reading and text commentary with that used by the grammarians, and says that the only difference is that these have Homer as the object of study, while he himself studies Chrysippus.[2] Just as the grammarian teaches his pupils to read Homer from memory, so the philosopher teaches his pupils definitions, conclusions and important basic premises.[3] It is however impossible at this stage to say how general this form of teaching was in the various schools of philosophy.[4] The question would be worth detailed investigation.

It seems to be rather difficult to reach any definite conclusions con-

---

emendatio, enarratio, judicium. Lectio : lecture expressive à haute voix ...; à la lecture se rattache la recitatio : le jeune élève ... apprenait par cœur les meilleurs passages des auteurs ..."

[1] See H. VON ARNIM, Leben und Werke des Dio von Prusa (1898), pp. 4–222, F. SCHEMMEL, Der Sophist Libanios als Schüler und Lehrer, in Neue Jahrb. f. d. klass. Altert. 20 (1907), pp. 52 ff.; cf. also IDEM, Die Hochschule von Konstantinopel im IV. Jahrhundert p. Ch. n., ibid. 22 (1908), pp. 147 ff., WALDEN, The Universities of Ancient Greece, pp. 195 ff., K. ALEWELL, Über das rhetorische ΠΑΡΑΔΕΙΓΜΑ (1913), BURK, op. cit., ibid., W. KROLL, Rhetorik, in PAULY-WISSOWA–KROLL–MITTELHAUS, Real-Encyclopädie, Suppl. VII (1940), col. 1043 ff., D. L. CLARK, Rhetoric in Greco-Roman Education (1957), p. 65, MARROU, Histoire de l'éducation, pp. 268 ff., 380 ff.

[2] Ench. 49.3.

[3] SCHEMMEL, Die Hochschule, pp. 164 f.

[4] How were the so-called λόγοι Σωκρατικοί transmitted within certain schools of philosophy? On these, cf. A.-H. CHROUST, Socrates: Man and Myth (1957), index, p. 330, sub voce. On transmission within schools of philosophy, see further, below, p. 193, n. 2.

cerning the form of legal instruction in the oldest period of the Greco-Roman world.[1] But we can see, at least in later Antiquity, the role played in law schools by memorization. The technical expression for the study of law was "to memorize the laws" (ἐκμανθάνειν νόμους).[2] "Der Lehrer diktierte den Schülern den Text und gab dazu Erläuterungen. Die tägliche Aufgabe bestand in dem Auswendiglernen des Diktats", writes SCHEMMEL,[3] referring to the methods used in the famous Berytos law school.

These examples should suffice to show the general and basic role played by memorization in Classical Antiquity. The part played by the same phenomenon in Judaism has been considered at length in Chapters 4, 9 and 10 of this work.[4] *The material was memorized.* This is the first of the two basic pedagogical principles which must be observed in order to understand the rabbinic technique of transmission.

We can go one step further. It is clear from the examples we have advanced from the Hellenistic schools how general was the practice, when it came to the study of important texts, of first learning the text in question (whether from a book or only from the lips of the teacher) and then passing on to analysis and interpretation, whether this took place at once or not until a higher school level was reached. *The material is first committed to memory, and then an attempt at understanding is undertaken.* The principle is *per se* quite natural in a milieu in which books are clumsy or valuable or both, and in which no one is satisfied when the material is to be found on the book-shelves, but wishes to have it in the memory.

This educational principle, of "learn first, and then understand" was

---

[1] Cf. what Lucianus says about the learning of the laws in the time of Solon, *Anach.* 22; see also Plato, *Prot.* 326 D. Cf. WALDEN, *op. cit.*, p. 11.

[2] F. SCHEMMEL, Die Schule von Berytos, in *Philol. Wochenschr.* 43 (1923), col. 238. Cf. the words of Josephus in *Cont. Ap.* 2.17 on Moses' commandment that the law should not be heard once for all or twice or on several occasions, but that it should be carefully learned by heart, τοῦτον (sc. τὸν νόμον) ἀκριβῶς ἐκμανθάνειν. See also *ibid.* 2.18: αὐτοὺς (sc. τοὺς νόμους) ἐκμανθάνοντες ἔχομεν ἐν ταῖς ψυχαῖς ὥσπερ ἐγκεχαραγμένους.

[3] *Ibid.* — On the education of lawyers in ancient Rome, see further, B. KÜBLER, Rechtsschulen, in PAULY-WISSOWA–KROLL–WITTE, *Real-Encyclopädie* R–Z: 1 (1914), col. 380 ff., and IDEM, Rechtsunterricht, *ibid.*, col. 394 ff., SCHULZ, *History of Roman Legal Science*, particularly pp. 55 ff., 119 ff., W. KUNKEL, *Herkunft und soziale Stellung der römischen Juristen* (1952), pp. 334 ff., L. WENGER, *Die Quellen des römischen Rechts* (1953), pp. 611 ff.

[4] Above, pp. 56 ff., 93 ff.

generally practised within Rabbinic Judaism, in connection with both the study of the written and the oral Torah.[1] It was particularly natural when studying the oral Torah. The pupils had to have texts, but when these could not be laid before them in written form, they had to be passed on to them orally, as the teacher, by constant repetition, "recorded" them on the memories of his pupils.

The Rabbis, as we shall soon see, worked along such "natural" pedagogical lines. They even went so far as to formulate rules for this procedure. Clearest of all are perhaps two ancient sayings which Raba motivates from the Scriptures.[2] Thus in b Ab. Zar. 19a (b Ber. 63b) we find:

לעולם ילמד אדם תורה ואחר כך יהגה.	"One should always study the Torah (first) and meditate[3] on it afterwards."

In this saying, Torah is used in its widest meaning, denoting both the oral and the written Torah. Here, too, is justified the method of first learning the Torah and then making it the object of interpretation and commentary. The same is also true of the second saying (b Ab. Zar. *ibid.*) although in this case the emphasis differs somewhat:

לעולם ליגריס איניש (ואף על גב דמשכח) ואף על גב דלא ידע מאי קאמר.	"One should always recite,[4] (although one forgets and) although one does not understand what one is saying."

Here is justified a recitation (of the oral Torah) which takes place without understanding the meaning of the passage of text which has been

---

[1] The fact that this principle was followed by the Rabbis has often been pointed out; the consequences of this procedure have not however been considered in detail. Cf. however R. WOHLBERG, *Grundlinien einer talmudischen Psychologie* (1902), p. 41, which makes a hazardous attempt to combine the talmudic thought-forms with modern (1902) psychological categories. — Löw, *Die Tradition*, p. 252, speaks accurately and pregnantly of "die Methode des talmudischen Alterthums, nach welcher der Wortlaut des zu erlernenden Objectes zuerst dem Gedächtnisse mechanisch eingeprägt wurde, bevor man an das Verständnis und die begriffliche Auffassung desselben ging", and hints also at the consequences. See also MORRIS, *The Jewish School*, pp. 125 ff.

[2] See the context in b Ab. Zar. 19a.

[3] For an alternative interpretation of the verb הגה in this saying, see LEVY, *Wörterbuch*, sub voce.

[4] On גרס as a term for "mechanical" repetition, see above, p. 118, n. 4.

learned. The one who is reciting is here placed on the same level as the half-educated recitator, of whom it was said:

רטין מגושא ולא ידע   "The magian mumbles and does
מאי אמר תני תנא   not understand what he is saying.
ולא ידע מאי אמר.   In the same way the *tanna* recites
  and does not understand what he
  is saying" (b Sot. 22a).[1]

The principle with which we are here dealing applies to all teaching, but in practice applies particularly to the *basic* teaching of Scripture and of the Mishnah. We may also quote a saying—which is unfortunately not unambiguous—of the dying R. Eliezer ben Hyrkanos, who said, referring to the teaching of children:

מנעו בניכם מן ההגיון   "Keep your sons away from
והושיבום בין ברכי   (premature) meditation, and place
תלמידי חכמים.   them (first) in the care of the
  learned" (b Ber. 28b, bar.).

Though this leaves us in some doubt,[2] Samuel ben Naḥman speaks very plainly (p Ab. Zar. II.7):

בשעה שתלמידין   "As long as your pupils are not of
קטנים כבוש לפניהן   age, hide from them the words of
דברי תורה הגדילו   the Torah (i.e. the meaning, for
ונעשו כעתודים גלה   which they are still immature) but
להם רזי תורה.   when they have grown up and become like rams, then reveal to
  them the secrets of the Torah".[3]

---

[1] Cf. above, p. 95.

[2] For the interpretation of this saying, see BACHER, *Die Agada der Tannaiten* I (2nd ed.), pp. 97 f., in which various possibilities are discussed. Cf. also L. GINZBERG, *Eine unbekannte jüdische Sekte* (1922), ad CD X.6 (which discussed the term הגיון in connection with the Damascus Sect's enigmatic ספר ההגו), and GANDZ, *The Dawn of Literature*, p. 433. It is not impossible that this word is a warning, referring to dangerous Gnostic, Theosophic or Christian interpretations. It is however quite out of the question that the rabbinic principle we are discussing here ("first learn and then understand") could have originated in such considerations. There is no doubt that we are dealing with an ancient, "primitive" technique of teaching, fixed in faithful conformity to tradition. It is only natural that practical motivations of different kinds should be brought forward in different contexts.

[3] Cf. Cant. R. 1.2. On R. Samuel's pedagogics, see BACHER, *Die Agada der Paläst. Am.* I, pp. 490 f.; cf. also KRAUSS, *Talmudische Archäologie* III, p. 224 and my remarks in the previous note.

Referring to the highest level of teaching, we may quote a late, but most representative, maxim, a Saboraic (?) commentary to a saying of R. Kahana (b Shab. 63a)[1]:

ליגמר איניש   "Let a man first learn and then
והדר ליסבר.   penetrate (that which he has
                    learned)."

The way in which this pedagogical principle *functions*, has been dealt with at sufficient length above, particularly in Ch. 9–10. We consider it unnecessary to repeat what we have already said on this subject.

This pedagogical method distinguishes the learning of the wording of the text from the learning of its meaning. (It might be said in passing that, psychologically speaking, learning to repeat a text is one thing: understanding it is another.) As a consequence of this procedure we find, *inter alia*, that the preservation of the meaning of the text does not always succeed in keeping pace with the preservation of its wording. This is in point of fact an observation which is often made in connection with traditional material: critical examination of the wording of a traditional text often proves it originally to have had a different meaning from that which it had for its most recent traditionist, or for the one who copied down or edited a traditional collection.[2] (We have also pointed out that the Rabbis were in principle unwilling to correct the wording of either the written or the oral Torah; instead they gave the old sayings a new interpretation, differing from that which the wording apparently required.)[3]

Similarly, this pedagogical procedure has meant that statements whose meaning has been forgotten, whose wording has despite all precautions been damaged, or which have in one way or another become incomprehensible, nevertheless continue to be transmitted. This is a fact which the student of the Talmud often encounters, and which is not

---

[1] Cf. Deut. R. 8.3 (ad 30.11), Ex. R. 41. 2. — See in addition b Suk. 29a on how Rabba ben Ḥama and R. Ḥisda first acquainted themselves with the *gemara* text before proceeding to the intellectual application, *sebara* (on the terms, see above, p. 104, n. 3–4); cf. b Sot. 20a, b Sanh. 68a.

[2] On the sayings (parables) of Jesus T.W. MANSON has correctly pointed out, that "the early Church remembered better than it understood" (review of Joach. JEREMIAS, Die Gleichnisse Jesu, in *New Test. Stud.* 1, 1954–55, p. 58.) This fact is a hint that the principle "learn first, and then understand" was applied in the early Church too.

[3] Above, pp. 97 f.

altogether unknown to the textual critic working on the Old Testament. The words were sacred and the tradition authoritative.[1] This in its way witnesses to the fact that the ancient pedagogical principles linked with the name of Raba, were actually followed. One should learn the Torah first and meditate on it later, and one should continually read and repeat the Torah, even though it may not be understood.

B. *Conservation of the Authentic Wording*

The art of reproducing another person's statements in one's own words, and of abstracting points of view and ideas from someone's words, has been carried to considerable lengths in the Hellenized West. But the art was not practised in ancient Israel. A person's views were conveyed in his own words. Authentic statements contained the authority and power of the one who uttered them; this we know from the Old Testament.[2]

This also applies to Rabbinic Judaism, though certain developments and changes have come about.[3] We can distinguish tendencies towards a more abstract mode of thought.[4] We see above all the method—which was taken to extreme lengths—of subjecting authoritative sayings to thorough penetration and exegesis.[5] But reverence and care for the

---

[1] GUNNEWEG, *Mündliche und schriftliche Tradition*, p. 73, characterizes the oral tradition *inter alia* with these words: "Richtig tradieren kann man nur, was man verstanden hat oder meint verstanden zu haben." This does not apply in a milieu in which the principle—and a very ancient principle, doubtless—is followed, of reciting the sacred traditional texts faithfully in accordance with the wording, "even if one does not understand what one is saying". It has often been reported from other cultures, and not least from the so-called "primitive" cultures, that the traditionists recite long, melodious traditional texts without understanding a word. On this subject, see L. LEVY-BRÜHL, *Das Denken der Naturvölker* (1921), pp. 87 f., and M. JOUSSE, *Le style oral rythmique et mnémotechnique chez les verbo-moteurs* (1925), partic. pp. 155 ff. — On the archaic hymns of the Arval brethren and the Saliares, it is said that not even the singers who transmitted them understood them (Quintilianus, *Instit. orat.* 1.6.40).

[2] See J. PEDERSEN, *Israel* I–II (1926), pp. 167 ff., P. HEINISCH, *Das „Wort" im A.T. und im alten Orient* (1922), L. DÜRR, *Die Wertung des göttlichen Wortes im A.T. und im antiken Orient* (1938), pp. 92 ff.; for the wider religio-historical perspective, see G. MENSCHING, *Das heilige Wort* (1937), and the works quoted above, p. 31, n. 4.

[3] Cf. J. Z. LAUTERBACH, The Belief in the Power of the Word, in *Hebr. Un. Coll. Ann.* 14 (1939), pp. 287 ff.

[4] See e.g. below, sec. C.

[5] See further, above, Ch. 9, and below, Ch. 12 A.

ipsissima verba of each authority remains unaltered. In the colleges no attempt was made to give a synopsis of the views of the old masters; their words were quoted—together with the name of the one who had uttered them.[1]

An ancient rule for the Rabbis' pupils was formulated in this way:

אדם חייב לומר   "It is a man's duty to state (a
בלשון רבו.   tradition) in his teacher's words."

This rule is to be found first in M Ed. I.3, as a commentary to the fact that Hillel here quotes a halakah dealing with the bath of purification, using in the process a unit of measurement (הין) which has passed out of common use. The same tradition, with the same commentary, is again to be found in b Shab. 15a; this educational rule recurs elsewhere in the Talmud, as a commentary on the awkwardness of the traditional formulation of certain sayings.[2] The question of the period at which this rule originated in the form in which we have cited it, is open to discussion;[3] but that it corresponds exactly to the practice followed by Hillel in the above example is undeniable. It would scarcely be going too far to maintain that this practice is extremely ancient in Judaism.

We see that the rule is formulated in general terms, but it goes without saying that the principle was mainly applied in connection with decisive doctrinal statements and basic textual material; the teacher's

---

[1] The duty of delivering a saying in the name of its originator (אמר דבר בשם אומרו; Ab. VI.6, bar., ed. MARTI, BEER, cf. b Meg. 15a, b Ḥul. 104b, b Nid. 19b, etc.) is stressed, directly and indirectly, in innumerable passages of the Talmud. The naming of the originator is intended partly as a guarantee of authenticity (see A. PERLS, Das Plagium, in *Monatsschr. f. Gesch. u. Wiss. d. Judent.* 58 (1914), pp. 311 ff., who overstates this point of view) and partly as a proof of its authority (see M. GUTTMANN, *Zur Einleitung* II, p. 57, who is correct in emphasizing the Rabbis' interest in naming the authors of the traditions, in order to make clear the authority and "legislative" competence which lay behind the respective sayings). — The fact that the halakah verses from the time of the Temple are mainly anonymous is due to the simple fact that at that time, Judaism had a unified doctrinal centre, from which halakah was issued (cf. ממנו יוצאת תורה לכל ישראל M Sanh. XI.2); see further, below, Ch. 14E. — Many scholars have justifiably compared the Rabbis' chains of tradition with the *isnād* in the Islamic tradition; on this subject, see J. HOROVITZ, Alter und Ursprung des Isnād, in *Der Islam* 8 (1918), pp. 39 ff., J. ROBSON, The Isnād in Muslim Tradition, in *Transactions from Glasgow Univ. Orient. Soc.* 15 (1955), pp. 15 ff.

[2] b Bek. 5a, b Ber. 47a; cf. b Erub. 53a, etc.

[3] N. BRÜLL considers the sentence to be a gloss in the Mishnah text, review of WEISS, דור דור ודורשיו, in *Jahrb. f. Jüd. Gesch. u. Lit.* 4 (1879), p. 64.

complementary sayings and his commentary, on the other hand, were presumably not impressed upon the memory with the same care for the exact wording.

Another tradition is of interest in this context. In b Ab. Zar. 19a we read that R. Ḥisda reads out to his pupils the traditional doctrinal statements, current in the school of R. Jannai, that the man who learns the Torah from only one teacher never sees any sign of blessing.[1] His pupils thereupon take his teaching *ad notam* and seek another teacher, Raba, who explains, however, that the rule in question applies only to *sebara* (סברא), i.e. the intellectual appreciation of doctrinal content; it would, however, be better for them to learn *gemara* (גמרא), i.e. the fixed complementary and interpretative commentary to the mishnah,[2] from a single teacher, in order to avoid dealing with different modes of expression (לריפלוג לישני).

This tradition is interesting from our point of view because it has to do with advanced studies. It is not mishnah and talmud which are here distinguished from each other, but *gemara* and *sebara*: the traditional mishnah commentary which a teacher teaches in a fixed form, and its less rigidly formulated interpretation and intellectual acquisition. We see that the objective is to learn the *gemara* literally by heart; different formulations are treated as tending to lead the pupil astray.[3] At the same time, we see that different teachers (and colleges) are assumed to have different *gemara*.

The principle of literal repetition and memorization of a teacher's words can also be seen *in function* in a number of passages in the Tannaitic and Amoraic material. We have just seen it functioning with Hillel and have noted a number of other passages in which it is directly pointed out. We may further draw attention to those cases in which a teacher or traditionist can transmit a traditional doctrinal statement (i.e. its exact wording) without being able to explain its meaning. In M Par. I. 1 we find, for example,[4] that no less than the first century R. Joshua on three occasions reads out traditional doctrinal statements, but says that he is unable to explain them.

[1] כל הלומד תורה מרב אחד אינו רואה סימן ברכה לעולם.

[2] For the terms, see above, p. 104, n. 3–4. On the relationship between *gemara* and *sebara* see particularly the illustrative passages in b Sot. 20a (bar.), b Sanh. 68a (bar.), b Suk. 29a; cf. also b Yoma 33a.

[3] That the *gemara* was cantillated is clear from b Bes. 24a with par.; J. Lewy, *Interpretation*, p. 4. See further, below, pp. 163 ff.

[4] Other examples referring to R. Joshua: M Pes. IX.6, M Yeb. VIII.4: ... שמעתי ואין לי לפרש.

כך שמעתי סתם.   "Thus have I heard (as authoritative tradition)[1] purely and simply
(i.e. without explanation or complement)."[2]

He has at his disposal only the bare wording of the traditional halakah, without knowing any complementary interpretation. We also see
his younger contemporary, R. Tarfon, transmitting doctrinal statements without being able to pass on any explanation or scriptural consideration.

אני שמעתי ולא היה לי   "I have heard so (as valid tradi-
לפרש.   tion) but I have no explanation."[3]

The formula "I have heard" (שמעתי) shows that we are not here
dealing with statements which the Rabbi has found in some written
text;[4] he has heard them as tradition from his teachers.

A further indication of the same tendency is to be seen in the fact that
even in the early part of the Tannaitic period the Rabbis discussed the
interpretation of certain formulae in the traditional doctrinal statements.[5]

The pupil is thus in duty bound to maintain his teacher's exact words.
But the teacher is also responsible for seeing that the exact wording is
preserved. The oral material which the teacher really wishes to teach
his pupils—whether his own doctrinal statements or passages of transmitted doctrine—is not merely to be read out quite generally in the
course of preaching or teaching. He must repeat it over and over again,
until he has actually passed it on to his pupil or pupils: i.e. until they
know the passage in question by heart.

---

[1] On שמע in the meaning of "to hear as authoritative tradition", see BACHER,
Tradition, pp. 9 ff.

[2] For the term סתם, see BACHER, *Terminologie* I, p. 138, cf. *ibid*, p. 157; for the
matter, see further A. GUTTMANN, The Problem of the Anonymous Mishna, in
Hebr. Un. Coll. Ann. 16 (1941), pp. 137 ff.

[3] T Zeb. I.8; b Zeb. 13a (bar.), Sifra ad Lev. 1.5: שמעתי ... ואין לי לפרש. For
further examples of the same matter, see BACHER, *op. cit.* I, p. 157, II, p. 166.

[4] The possibility that what is comprised under this quotation formula may exist
partly in private note-books (see below, sec. E) is naturally not excluded.

[5] On this subject, see I. LEWY, *Über einige Fragmente*, pp. 26 ff., HOFFMANN,
Die erste Mischna und die Controversen der Tannaim, pp. 37 ff., and IDEM, *Zur Einleitung*, p. 5; cf. ROSENTHAL, *Über den Zusammenhang der Mischna* I–II (2nd ed.),
passim.

The Rabbis themselves formulated pedagogical rules on this point, too. In b Erub. 54b (bar.)[1] the rule of R. Eliezer ben Hyrkanos is said to have been that the teacher had to repeat a doctrinal passage to his pupil four times:

חייב אדם לשנות "A man's duty is to repeat (a
לתלמידדו ארבעה פעמים. passage) to his pupil[2] four times."

In the same section are reproduced R. Aqiba's principles which seem, to judge by their formulation, to be older pedagogical rules,[3] merely given Scriptural support by R. Aqiba.

מניין שחייב אדם לשנות "From whence (do we have the
לתלמידו עד שילמדנו... rule) that *a man's duty is to repeat
ומניין עד שתהא סודרה to his pupil until he has learned?*...
בפיהם... From whence (do we have the rule
ומניין שחייב להראות that *a man must repeat) until it is
לו פנים... well arranged* (i.e. flows easily) *in
their mouths?* ...
From whence (do we have the
rule) that *a man's duty is to explain clearly for him?*"

(We here omit the passages of Scripture which support the various pedagogical rules. The parallel in Mek. ad 21.1 will be dealt with in due course.)

It goes without saying that R. Aqiba's rule was the natural rule, the one which the teachers must often have had to follow—mishnah teachers in particular! In this milieu there was no objection to frequent repetition. A well-known saying of Hillel is reproduced in b Ḥag. 9b (bar.): "The man who repeats his chapter (שונה פרקו) one hundred times is not to be compared with the man who repeats it one hundred and one times."[4] And when the question of the Rabbis' repetition for their pupils is taken up, it is the tireless Rabbi who is praised. Thus R. Perida is treated as exemplary; he used to repeat every passage "four hundred

---

[1] The saying is quoted in its context, above, p. 120.

[2] The Munich ms. reads תלמודו.

[3] That we are here dealing with an exegetical consideration of older pedagogical rules is clear *inter alia* from the awkward transition from sing. to plur.: תלמידו but פיהם. The tradition in Mek. ad 21.1 (see below) is more unified in its construction.

[4] On continuous repetition, see further, below, sec. G.

times" for a dull pupil, and once when the pupil in question had still not absorbed the passage, R. Perida proceeded to repeat it "four hundred times" more.[1] This hyperbolical description gives us a most eloquent picture of the simple, yet effective, methods used by teachers when they wished to pass on doctrinal passages to their pupils.

A further illustration of the teachers' tireless repetition is provided by the above-mentioned description of how a Rabbi was consulted on a point of doctrine, and is said to have repeated his answer, as a doctrinal statement, "forty times", until the pupil had it "in his purse".[2]

Thus we see how the care exercised by the teacher for the exact wording of the oral text functions.

In conclusion we shall widen our horizon somewhat to consider a text from Mek. ad Ex. 21.1, which has not hitherto been given the recognition it deserves:[3]

"R. Aqiba says: *And These Are the Ordinances*, etc. Why is this said? Since it says: 'Speak unto the children of Israel and say unto them' (Lev. 1.2), I know only that he was to *tell them once*.[4] How do we know that he was to *repeat* (שנה) it to them a second, a third and a fourth time until they *learned* (ילמדו) it? Scripture says: 'And teach thou it the children of Israel' (Deut. 31.19). This might mean that they need only *learn* (למדין) it but not *repeat* (שונין) it. But Scripture says: 'Put it in their mouths' (*ibid.*). Still this might mean that they need only *repeat* (שונים) it but need not *understand*[5] (יודעין) it. Therefore it says: 'And these are the ordinances which thou shalt set before them.' Arrange them (ערכם)[6] in proper order before them like a set table, just as it is said: 'Unto thee it was shown that thou mightest know' (*ibid.* 4.35)."

Here, in fact, we have the rabbinic pedagogical system in a nutshell.[7]

---

[1] b Erub. 54b. "Four hundred" is a round number (cf. above, p. 105, n. 9).

[2] See above, p. 119.

[3] I am following J. Z. LAUTERBACH's ed. (III, 1935, p. 1) and translation (however, cf. below, n. 5). The italics are mine.

[4] The verb is here omitted: אין לי אלא פעם אחת.

[5] LAUTERBACH translates "fully understand", but in so doing obscures the meaning of the saying.

[6] Strictly speaking, no new element is introduced here; all that is done is to explain the previous words: אשר תשים לפניהם. It is however possible that the sentence "arrange ... set table" refers to the fact that the teacher is to arrange the sayings in an order suitable for memorization; ערך is occasionally used as a synonym for סדר.

[7] Note the resemblances to, and differences from, the methods of the Greco-Roman grammarians, which we have dealt with briefly above, sec. A.

The teacher is not merely to state the doctrinal passages, but is to repeat them until his pupils know them. The pupils must themselves be able to repeat them. And this is not enough. Teaching must be consummated by interpretation and exposition, so that the pupils understand what they have learned to repeat.

We ought to be able to see the consequences of this respect for the teacher's authentic words and methodical concern for the exact wording of doctrinal material in the oral traditional texts. It is true that we must take into account what may have taken place in the process of final redaction, where restyling, reshaping and re-editing were probably carried out to some extent. But it is interesting to be able to state that not even then was there any extensive break with the rule of adherance to the teacher's mode of expression. Not even linguistic variations in the traditional passages have been evened out. Elements of the tradition in Hebrew alternate with elements in Aramaic, even within the same passage: the narrative framework may be in Hebrew, with the dialogue in Aramaic, or vice versa.[1] (This was of course possible, since the Rabbis and their pupils mastered both languages.) But more than that: it is possible in these compound traditional collections to distinguish—even in their final form—the modes of expression used by different teachers and different schools.[2] We need only call to mind the typical technical terminology of the Ishmaelite school, or the peculiar oaths favoured by R. Tarfon.[3]

C. *Condensation and Abridgement*

When a teacher's words are accorded considerable authority and when an attempt is made carefully to preserve them—and when instruction is concentrated generally on memorization—brevity and conciseness are important virtues. We see this very clearly in ancient

---

[1] See e.g. H. ODEBERG, *The Aramaic Portions of Bereshit Rabba* I (1939), passim. — M. H. SEGAL, *Grammar of Mishnaic Hebrew* (1927), has seen and emphasizes the connection between the Rabbis' rule of transmitting in the teacher's terms and the mixture of languages in the written traditional texts.

[2] BACHER, *Terminologie*, passim. The most flagrant example is the well known difference between the technical terms used by the different schools, e.g. between the schools of R. Ishmael and R. Aqiba.

[3] אקפח את בני, "may I bury my children", M Ohal. XVI.1, Sifra ad Lev. 1.5, b Shab. 116a, etc. On the subject, see further BACHER, *Die Agada der Tannaiten* I (2nd ed.), pp. 342 ff.

Judaism, from the wise men (מושלים, חכמים) of the Old Testament and through the whole of Rabbinism. The tendency to concentrate teachings and texts, expressing them with the utmost brevity, is general. There was a very active consciousness of the importance of such concentration, of condensing material into concise, pregnant—and if possible also striking, pithy and succinct—sayings. An ancient proverb says that "a sharp peppercorn is better than a basket of gourds".[1]

This pedagogical rule is expressed in b Pes. 3b (bar.)[2] in this way:

לעולם ישנה אדם   "A man should always teach his
לתלמידו דרך קצרה.   pupil (orally) in the shortest way."[3]

This rule itself expresses "in the shortest way", *derek qesarah*, a very common pedagogical tendency in Rabbinic Judaism. For the sake of simplicity we shall concentrate here on two main aspects which are not easily distinguished: (a) the attempt to summarize teachings epigrammatically, in synthetic summaries and inclusive fundamental statements; (b) the attempt to express oneself concisely and elliptically.

If we begin with the first of these aspects, we may recall the general striving we find at an earlier date within Judaism—embryonic even in the written laws in the Pentateuch[4] but occurring in a developed form later, in pre-Tannaitic, Tannaitic and Amoraic times—the attempt to discover summary statements and generalizations inclusive of a number of separate details. (This is indubitably a case of genuine development within the Jewish tradition itself. The natural presuppositions for this development in fact existed, as we shall soon see, though it appears likely that it was stimulated by Hellenistic influence.)[5] For example, the Torah is searched for one super-commandment which summarizes in itself a number of individual commandments. Such a commandment is pointed out as being "father" or "ancestor" (אב), with every separate commandment dependent upon it as a "descendant" (תולדא). A search

---

[1] b Meg. 7a (b Ḥag. 10a, b Yoma 85b, etc.): טבא חדא פילפלתא חריפתא ממלי צני קרי. On this saying, see further LEVY, *Wörterbuch*, sub voce פלפלתא.

[2] Also b Ḥul. 63b. The actual rule is stated as having been formulated by R. Meir, but the phenomenon is certainly—as we have already pointed out—very ancient.

[3] Further on the matter, see R. Sherira's Epistle (ed. B. LEWIN, 1921, pp. 28 f.).

[4] Random examples are Lev. 21.17, 25.2: a summing-up verse precedes the details; in Num. 30.17 the opposite is the case. See further, notes 3 and 6, p. 139.

[5] D. DAUBE, Precept and Example, in *The N.T. and Rabbinic Judaism* (1956), pp. 86 ff.; cf. IDEM, Principle and Cases, *ibid.*, pp. 63 ff.

is made for a universal statement (כלל)[1] which contains every detailed rule (פרט).[2] A search is even made for a summary for the entire Torah. R. Aqiba thus calls Lev. 19.18 "the great *kelal* in the Torah" (כלל גדול בתורה).[3] Hillel says of his negatively formulated "golden rule":

זו היא כל התורה כולה	"This is the whole Torah. The rest
ואידך פירושה הוא.	is only commentary."[4]

And R. Simeon ben Azzai calls the doctrine of man's likeness to God, as expressed in Gen. 5.1, "the great *kelal*" (כלל גדול).[5] — We also find this tendency in the N. T. According to Matt. (22.34 ff.) a Pharisaic scholar (νομικός) asked Jesus about the great(est) commandment (ἐντολὴ μεγάλη) in the Torah; Jesus answered that Deut. 6.5 is the greatest and first commandment and Lev. 19.18 the second[6] and that all the Law and the Prophets "hang" (κρέμαται, תלה) on these two, i.e. are derivable from them.[7] According to Paul, who on this occasion argues in remarkable conformity with *bet Hillel*, all the commandments in the Torah are comprehended (ἀνακεφαλαιοῦσθαι) in the "word" (λόγος) on love for one's neighbour (Lev. 19.18), Rom. 13.8 ff.

We find this striving functioning to an even greater extent in connection with the teaching of the oral Torah. It is well known that the Mishnah often has a basic statement, a *kelal*, as a heading for a number of separate halakah statements: כלל אמרו וגו'. Or a series of separate statements in the Mishnah may be concluded by a summarizing overall rule: זה (ה)כלל וגו'.[8]

It is evident that interpretation of the law—and similar forms of

---

[1] Also גוף.

[2] For the terms and their use, see BACHER, *Terminologie* I–II, sub vocibus. For the matter, see further the two essays of DAUBE quoted above, p. 137, n. 5, together with the works on rabbinic hermeneutics mentioned above, p. 36, n. 2.

[3] Sifra ad Lev. 19.18 and elsewhere.

[4] b Shab. 31a (bar.).

[5] Sifra, *ibid.*

[6] The two commandments are put together according to a rabbinic method of combination; see B. GERHARDSSON, *The Good Samaritan — the Good Shepherd?* (1958), p. 6.

[7] Cf. D. DAUBE, Basic Commandments, in *The N. T. and Rabbinic Judaism*, pp. 247 ff.

[8] E.g. M Peah I.4, M Shebi. VII.1, *ibid.* VII.2; M Maas. I.1, M Shab. VII.1. For the matter, see MIELZINER, *Introduction*, p. 194, and A. SCHWARZ, *Die hermeneutische Quantitätsrelation in der talmudischen Literatur* (1916), pp. 163 ff., ignoring the author's basic thesis on the Rabbis' logic.

legal activity—provided a context in which this striving could function. Basic summarizing rules and abstract generalizations were necessary to jurisprudence. We recognize this same need in legal activity elsewhere, e.g. in Roman law.[1] But it would be wrong to treat this attempt as mainly a striving after basic legal principles. There is no doubt that the attempt is first and foremost *pedagogical*: an attempt is made to hold together a massive complex of sacred, traditional, authoritative teaching material: to facilitate transmission, learning, memorization, understanding and usage. This is clear from the fact that the tendency in question is just as strong outside the legal field, outside the halakic discipline.

Kelal (כלל, כללא) does not as a rule mean primarily a basic legal or logical principle, but just a summarizing, inclusive, condensed statement, irrespective of the field with which it deals.[2] Thus *kelal* denotes not only a concentrated basic statement, a generalization which introduces (or concludes) a series of commandments in the written or oral law, but also the concentrated summary or heading of a haggadic exposition.[3] The Rabbis themselves were aware that the Scriptures often begin by giving a general condensed summary of what is to be presented before explaining it in detail; or vice versa: יש פרשיות שהוא כולל בתחלה ופורט בסוף פורט בתחלה וכולל בסוף.[4] This insight, which could occasionally be misused for the harmonization of contradictory traditions,[5] builds on an indisputably correct observation—one which the Rabbis were able to make because they applied similar pedagogical principles themselves. The old traditionists whose recitation is reproduced in certain of the books of the Old Testament seem actually to have made use of such traditio-technical finesse, first indicating, in a concentrated summary the contents of the recitation, then proceeding to particularize.[6] We shall return to this topic in the next section.

---

[1] See F. SCHULZ, *Prinzipien des römischen Rechts* (1934), particularly pp. 35 ff.

[2] See BACHER, *Terminologie* I, pp. 79 ff., II, pp. 83 ff.

[3] The term כלל is used e.g. in the following way:

אלה הדברים אשר תדבר אל בני ישראל (Ex. 19.6) כלל.

זאת חקת התורה (Num. 19.2) כלל...

זאת חקת הפסח (Ex. 12.43) כלל.

Mek. ad 12.43 (ed. LAUTERBACH, I, p. 117). — Cf. Sifre Deut. ad 13.2: *kelal* verses are to be found in the prophets as well as in the Pentateuch.

[4] Mek., *ibid.*

[5] E.g. of the two creation narratives—a partially motivated harmonization!

[6] E.g. Gen. 1.1, 5.1, 18.1, 22.1, etc. In this case the Rabbis' point of view is worthy of our attention. Such summaries ought not to be automatically treated as

Further, it is clear from the above-mentioned examples from the lips of Hillel, R. Aqiba and R. Simeon that the use of *kelal* summaries also occurred in haggadic teaching. In each case we are dealing with *kelal* statements which are not strictly halakic. Other examples are abundant.

In Ab. II.9 we find a tradition from the teaching of Rabban Johanan ben Zakkai. The problem which is being considered (in this case posed by the teacher himself) is, first, what is the good way (דרך טובה) for a man to follow and, secondly, what is the evil way (דרך רעה). In each case four of Johanan's most outstanding pupils are allowed to give their answers before the master himself decides the question:

רואה אני את דברי אב״ע מדבריכם שבכלל דבריו דבריכם.	"I give Eleazar ben Arak's saying precedence over your sayings, since your sayings are included in his saying."

We may consider in passing the ritual of teaching: a question, contributions from the pupils and finally a decisive word from the master himself. But what is important here from our point of view is that Eleazar's saying is given precedence because it provides a *kelal* summary of what the others have said. Here we have a clear demonstration of the ideal of condensation, and the example is taken from the haggadic field.[1]

We may take a further example from Mek. ad 13.2,[2] which relates how certain pupils came to R. Joshua ben Hananiah after having heard a Sabbath lecture given by R. Eleazar ben Azariah. R. Joshua asks what new teaching Eleazar had given them on this occasion (... חידש דבר), whereupon the pupils answer that "he read this *kelal* (כלל זה דרש)", and proceed to repeat a concentrated doctrinal statement— a haggadic midrash—consisting of a text of Scripture (Deut. 29.9), a question of haggadic type and an answer supported by Scripture. Later in the conversation the pupils say: "He also read this *kelal* (עוד כלל זה דרש)", after which they repeat a Scripture verse (Jer. 23.7-8) and a parable. Here we see how those pupils who have come from Eleazar ben Azariah's Sabbath lecture carry in their memories a number of highly

being part of the framework imposed at the time of the final written redaction. — It is of great interest from our point of view that *kelal* statements occur in such works as Ecclesiastes; 1.2: *kelal* verse for the whole book; 3.1 etc.: *kelal* verse for shorter passages.

[1] See also below, pp. 173 ff.
[2] Ed. LAUTERBACH, I, pp. 131 ff. — Cf. T Sot. VII.9 ff., b Ḥag. 3 ab, p Ḥag. I.1.

concentrated repetition-texts, each containing a main point or an important topic from the doctrinal lecture, and that these have a special name, *kelalot*. We do not know very much about the way in which the Rabbis held their Sabbath lectures,[1] but it seems to be clear from such examples as this that they considered it important to emphasize the main elements (τόποι) in the form of highly concentrated repetition-texts, *kelalot* — which were either halakah statements, short midrash passages or haggadic sayings of some kind: parables, key-words, catch-words (*Stichworte*), and the like.[2] Another possibility is that the *pupils* sought to summarize the Rabbis' words in such concise memory-passages.[3] However, the former possibility seems, in the light of teaching method generally, to be the more likely.

Nevertheless, what we have here referred to as a tendency to condensation or abridgement ought not to be limited to the term *kelal*, which has several meanings.[4] It would be better to speak about *condensed memory-texts*. Practically the whole of the material which is to be found in the Jewish traditional literature consists of such texts, but it would not be in the best interests of terminological clarity if all this material were to be judged from one point of view and given the term *kelalot*.

The way in which this tendency functions may be further illustrated by means of a reference to the extreme concentration of halakah verses (הלכות),[5] both in the Mishnah and the Talmud. They are there freed from all unnecessary detail, all explanations and comments, and are presented in a highly concentrated form. This was evidently already practised during the Temple period in the Sanhedrin, when a legal action had to be decided;[6] the Rabbis did so at the college "sessions" when concluding a discussion on the law by fixing, with or without a vote, a halakah; likewise the Amoraic Rabbis, when they summarized their

---

[1] See however the essay by MIRSKY mentioned above, p. 91, n. 5.

[2] Cf. b Sanh. 38b on R. Meir's principle of letting his public discourses consist of one-third halakah, one-third haggadah and one-third parable.

[3] Cf. below, Ch. 12A. — A third possibility which must be taken into consideration is that stylization and abbreviation are to some extent the work of editors and copyists. Cf. the proverb quoted as a mnemonic in b Ab. Zar. 9a and 9b: "The copyist is sparing, the *tanna* is redundant (ספרא בעירא תנא תוספאה)." This viewpoint, remembering rabbinic teaching principles, cannot however be accorded a degree of importance sufficient to affect what we have said above.

[4] P. 138, n. 2.

[5] We use the term here of the concisely fixed halakah statement: above, Ch. 7B.

[6] Cf. below, Ch. 14E.

142

doctrinal lectures or debates in a brief, precisely formulated decision (הוראה).[1]

It would be interesting here to cast a glance at the role accorded by Hellenistic teachers to summary doctrinal statements of various kinds: κεφάλαια, περιοχαί, ἐπιτομαί etc.[2]

We can now proceed to the second aspect, (b). Verbosity was not regarded as a praiseworthy quality in Rabbinism.[3] Conciseness was a highly prized virtue: the Rabbis' terseness is legendary. The well thought-out, brief, pregnant statement was their ideal. But the rule enjoining a teacher to teach "in the shortest way" was not primarily intended as a general recommendation to brevity; it was intended to stress the importance of a teacher formulating as concisely as possible *the important doctrinal statements*: those which were intended for faithful memorization and transmission; in other words, condensed memory-texts. The rule is expressed thus: לעולם ישנה אדם לתלמידו דרך קצרה. The verb shows that the rule has to do with oral teaching; it is very probable that in this case the verb שנה has its stricter meaning of "repeat", "transmit". The object is to *transmit*, to teach the pupil to *repeat* concisely. After all, there was no particular need for such brevity in all the teacher's commentaries and explanations; it was, however, of the greatest importance that necessary brevity should be observed in connection with that which was to be repeated as tradition.

The rule of brevity in transmission has been an important complement to the rule which states that the teacher's own words are to be preserved. Teachers were compelled to condense their lessons into brief statements, summarizing all they had to say on the subject. But it is evident that if a teacher failed to express himself with the required brevity, his sayings could be abbreviated by teachers and pupils at a later stage in the transmission process. It is thus certain that the two above-mentioned

[1] For the term, see M. GUTTMANN, *Zur Einleitung* I, pp. 13 ff.

[2] We catch a glimpse of the same phenomenon in those circles in which the Hermetic writings originated. A. J. FESTUGIÈRE, who stresses the resemblances between the methods used in the Hellenistic schools and those of the Hermetic circles, quotes an interesting example from *Stob., Herm.* XI.3: "Si tu gardes en mémoire ces sentences, tu te rappelleras aussi, sans difficulté, les choses que j'ai développées (διεξῆλθον) devant toi en de multiples *logoi*; car ces sentences sont les sommaires (περιοχαί) de mes enseignements précédents", *La révélation d'Hermès Trismégiste* II (1949), p. 40.

[3] A number of rabbinic statements are quoted by BILLERBECK, *Comm.* I, pp. 639 f.

rules—of brevity and authenticity—from one point of view came into conflict on an occasion.[1]

We must however proceed one step further in our examination of the process of condensation. It is not enough that a long doctrinal exposition may be summarized in a condensed memory-text, and transmitted in the form of a concise statement which takes its place among the other oral texts "recorded" in the memory. The condensation process goes a step further. These concise memory-texts gradually become more numerous, and it becomes necessary to have a brief reference system for many of them, when they are to be alluded to, named, referred to, or kept in their appropriate place in the block of tradition. A convenient verbal system for them is needed; they are therefore given a name, a title, a heading—or whatever it may be called. This may be said, from the point of view of the psychology of memory, to be a further summary of what is already a concise summary, in the form of key-words or catch-words. (In the next section we shall consider the Rabbis' term for these: סימנים.)

These condensations, these "names" for passages of tradition, correspond directly to the names given to the pericopes (parashot and haftarot) in the written Torah. These, as is well known, consisted either of the introductory word (incipit) to the pericope in question or—more usually—of some decisive word from the pericope itself, a word which was sometimes a quite adequate indication of its contents but which occasionally was little more than a catch-word.[2] The pericope Ex. 3.1 ff. is—for instance—called "the thorn-bush" (cf. Luke 20.37).[3] With the

[1] This is clearest in those cases where a brief and concise halakah verse is produced out of a transmitted saying. On this problem, see e.g. A. GUTTMANN, Das redaktionelle und sachliche Verhältnis zwischen Mišna und Tosephta. See also below, Ch. 12 A.

[2] Concerning the way in which literary products were named in Antiquity, cf. E. NACHMANSON, Der griechische Buchtitel (1941) and C. WENDEL, Die griechisch-römische Buchbeschreibung verglichen mit der des Vorderen Orients (1949). — W. F. ALBRIGHT counts Ps. 68 as a catalogue of psalms, in which the first two or three lines of each (incipits) are quoted, A Catalogue of Early Hebrew Lyric Poems (Psalm LXVIII), in Hebr. Un. Coll. Ann. 23: 1 (1950–51), pp. 1 ff. See also IDEM, Notes on Psalms 68 and 134, in Norsk Teol. Tidsskrift 56 (1955), pp. 1 ff., in which he answers the criticisms of MOWINCKEL. For Akkadian parallels to this method of giving brief names to various texts, see ALBRIGHT's references in A Catalogue, p. 8 and Notes, pp. 9 f., n. 5.

[3] For a convenient collection of some names of Scriptural pericopes, see G. AICHER, Das A. T. in der Mischna (1906), pp. 17 ff., and cf. B. M. METZGER, The Formulas Introducing Quotations of Scripture in the NT and the Mishnah, in Journ. of Bibl. Lit. 70 (1951), pp. 303 ff.

help of this "name" for the passage in question, this association-word, a learned man is able to hit upon the text which is referred to and—if required—repeat it. He may then proceed to an explanation, giving a commentary which more or less faithfully reconstructs and sets forth the teachings which were earlier concentrated in this text.

An example. In b Bab. Batr. 174a[1] we read that Rabba bar (bar) Ḥana said, in R. Joḥanan's name:

<table>
<tr>
<td>כל מקום ששנה רבן
שב״ג במשנתנו הלכה
כמותו חוץ מערב
וצידן וראיה אחרונה.</td>
<td>"Wherever Rabban Simeon ben Gamaliel teaches anything in our Mishnah, the halakah follows him, except in the case of the Guarantor, Sidon, and Latter Proof."</td>
</tr>
</table>

Mention is here made of three halakic sayings of Rabban Simeon ben Gamaliel, three sayings found in different parts of the Mishnah, merely by producing a catch-word for each.

The passages in question are:

a. M Bab. Batr. X.7

<table>
<tr>
<td>רבן שב״ג אומר אם יש
נכסים ללוה בין כך
ובין כך לא יפרע
מן הערב ...</td>
<td>"Rabban Simeon ben Gamaliel says: If the borrower had property, in neither case would he exact payment from the guarantor ..."</td>
</tr>
</table>

b. M Git. VII.5

<table>
<tr>
<td>אמר רבן שב״ג מעשה
בצידן באחד שאמר
לאשתו ...</td>
<td>"Rabban Simeon ben Gamaliel said: A man in Sidon once said to his wife ..."</td>
</tr>
</table>

c. M Sanh. III.8

<table>
<tr>
<td>אמר רבן שב״ג מה
יעשה זה שלא היה
יודע שיש לו עדים
ומצא עדים לא היה
יודע שיש לו ראיה
ומצא ראיה ...</td>
<td>"Rabban Simeon ben Gamaliel said: What should he do, that did not know that he had witnesses, then found witnesses, or that did not know that he had proof, then found proof ..."</td>
</tr>
</table>

---

[1] The example is analysed by BRÜLL, <i>Die Entstehungsgeschichte des babylonischen Talmuds als Schriftwerkes</i>, p. 59.

Here we see, quite apart from the absolute mastery of the Mishnah which this method presupposes,[1] the way in which the condensation process has gone one step further. The passage of doctrine has been given a name which can be used on those occasions when it is unnecessary to repeat the entire passage of oral text. We see, too, that in the second of the above examples the name given is a quite mechanical catch-word, while the other two convey something of the contents of the passage of tradition which is referred to.[2]

That Sidon stands as the name of one of these traditional texts leads us to emphasize an important fact. The narrative framework of a saying (or certain details of it) often fills a definite mnemonic function. So e.g. hints as to the time, the place or the situation in which a statement was made. Thus the need for a framework with characteristic details is felt from the beginning of the process of transmission, not only at the final redaction!

If we may be allowed to simplify matters and schematize, we find that a teacher's instruction or a doctrinal discussion may later take three different forms for the pupil or traditionist.[3]

(i) The lecture, interpretation or doctrinal discussion as a whole (תלמוד), to the extent to which it has been retained in the pupil's memory.

(ii) One or more condensed memory-texts (משנה):[4] a halakah verse, a midrash, a haggadah or some such form, i.e. important material which it is intended that the pupil should be able to *repeat*. And possibly:

(iii) A designation in the form of a heading, a catch-word (סימן)[5] to which the pupil may have devoted particular attention, or which he may simply have written down in his notebook.[6]

With the assistance of iii the pupil or traditionist is able to call to mind and repeat ii; with ii as a basis of association he can attempt to reconstruct i. The mention of *Sidon* prompts the Mishnah-filled Rabbi to repeat the passage of M Git. VII.5 about Rabban Simeon ben Gama-

---

[1] Cf. also b Nid. 7 b.

[2] For further examples, cf. BRÜLL, *op. cit.*, *ibid.*

[3] Cf. in the synoptic tradition Matt. 13: v. 3 ff. a parable (a "passage of repetition", *mishnah*), v. 19 ff. the interpretation (*talmud*), v. 18 the heading or catchword (*siman*). See also *ibid.* v. 24 ff. (*mishnah*), v. 36 (*siman*), v. 37 ff. (*talmud*).

[4] In the meaning of a "passage of repetition".

[5] On this subject, see the following section.

[6] See below, sec. E. — On the schematic division cf. L. FINKELSTEIN, The Transmission of the Early Rabbinic Traditions, in *Hebr. Un. Coll. Ann.* 16 (1941), pp. 115 ff.

liel; then, on a basis of this passage, he can provide—on demand—a more or less detailed explanation: a commentary containing complementary traditional material, *gemara, talmud*.

However, the picture may have a rather different appearance. FIN-KELSTEIN has shown[1] that the wording of certain haggadic traditions, written down in different places, can vary except when it comes to the decisive catch-word or catch-words. One example concerns a haggadah of Abraham as גדול העולם. This is copied down in four places,[2] and the wording of each varies from all the others, except in the matter of the actual key-word גדול העולם. FINKELSTEIN is justified in drawing the conclusion that we are here dealing with a type of tradition which was not transmitted as a text with fixed wording, but was instead freely formulated; only the actual key-word, the name of the haggadah, the decisive catch-word, was fixed and carefully memorized or written down.[3] In that case we are dealing here—referring back to our previous schema—with a tradition in which no definitely formulated recitation text (ii) was needed between the exposition (i) and the catch-word (iii).

Such a freely worded haggadah was often linked with key-words in the text of Scripture, without the necessity of its direct incorporation in a midrash collection. M. GUTTMANN has pointed out that of the 300 "fox fables" told by R. Meir according to b Sanh. 38b–39a, and of which all but three are lost, the three remaining in the Talmud (*ibid.*) are only alluded to by verses of Scripture—Ezek. 18.12, Lev. 19.36 and Prov. 11.8—but are not there written down; these three examples were first copied down by Rashi.[4] The verses of Scripture functioned as catch-words, and with their help it was possible to actualize the haggadah in question. A good deal of haggadah material similarly "accompanied" the Scriptural text for centuries.

[1] *Op. cit.*, pp. 122 ff. For further examples, see *ibid.*, pp. 115 ff. — Dr. EDELMANN draws my attention to the fact that in certain cases, one of the great fathers may have been given a permanent epithet, by which he is known in many different haggadah traditions. This must be taken into account when traditions of this type are to be estimated. The above example cannot however be explained in this way.

[2] Sifre Deut. 38, b Qid. 32b, Mek. ad 18.12 (ed. LAUTERBACH, II, pp. 177 f.). — In Mek. de R. Simeon ad 18.12 the catch-word is גדול הדור, which FINKELSTEIN is right to interpret as an *oral* variant (*op. cit.*, p. 125).

[3] Cf. L. FINKELSTEIN, Introductory Study to Pirke Abot, in *Journ. of Bibl. Lit.* 57 (1938), pp. 13 ff.

[4] M. GUTTMANN, *Zur Entstehung des Talmuds*, pp. 53 f. — Cf. KAPLAN's correct observation that in the Talmud a haggadah can be cited in a couple of words, *The Redaction*, pp. 199 f.

But this brings us to the technique of mnemonics in its stricter meaning, which we shall consider in our next section. We shall at this point merely add a few words on the type of haggadic material to which this last example has introduced us.

It is a known fact that for the process of memorization a great part of the haggadic material had an advantage, as compared with the halakic; the haggadic material remained in the memory much more easily, on account of the nature of its contents, often dramatic-epic in character, and its poetic-didactic form. The poetic-didactic refinements (assonance, *paranomasia, parallelismus membrorum*, etc.) of the non-halakic material in the Old Testament and in rabbinic literature have often been remarked upon,[1] and rightly so. We should like in this context to draw particular attention to R. PAUTREL's analysis, in which he has succeeded in showing that haggadic doctrinal passages (parables, narrative traditions, etc.) are often very symmetrically constructed;[2] this facilitated their reconstruction in the memory if only the beginning—or catch-word— were clear.

Associated with a catch-word in the text of Scripture, or linked in some other way with a preserved catch-word, such haggadic traditions were able to continue in existence through the centuries, and could be reconstructed in a form which varied very little, thanks to their schematic construction and the preservation of the decisive catch-word.

When we turn our attention to the written traditional material we find an overwhelming illustration of how carefully and how generally the rule of teaching and transmitting דרך קצרה was applied. The lapidary style of rabbinic traditional literature is so well known that we need not comment further on that fact. As has often been pointed out, all this material has been formulated and grouped with a view to memorization. This took place at the oral stage. (We must also take into account the fact that also copyists occasionally abbreviated texts which were familiar to them, but this does not affect what has already been said.) But, as is clear from the above, and as we shall attempt to demonstrate further in

---

[1] E.g. G. B. GRAY, *The Forms of Hebrew Poetry* (1915), É. DHORME, *La Poésie Biblique* (1931), T. H. ROBINSON, *The Poetry of the O.T.* (1947); cf. also C. F. BURNEY, *The Poetry of Our Lord* (1925). On the Rabbis' poetry, see also the note following.

[2] *Les canons du mashal rabbinique*, in *Rech. de Science Rel.* 26 (1936), pp. 5 ff.; cf. IDEM, *Des abréviations subies par quelques sentences de Jésus dans la rédaction synoptique*, *ibid.* 24 (1934), pp. 344 ff. — Cf. also M. JOUSSE, *Études sur la psychologie du geste. Les Rabbis d'Israel. Les Récitatifs rythmiques parallèles* I (1930).

the next chapter[1], this concise form of expression, *derek qesarah*, was not due to the traditionists alone. It is also obvious that the teachers were themselves in favour of giving the essence of their teaching in pregnant key-words and key-texts.

If we overlook the somewhat freer treatment which the haggadic material receives in principle, what we have said applies to halakic, midrashic and haggadic material.[2] It is dealt with in the form of concise and elliptical texts, which in this form contain only the most essential elements of teaching, whether the brief key-word be understood as a condensed memory-text, needing only explanation and commentary, or as a heading or an extreme abridgement of a somewhat more detailed doctrinal passage. From our point of view, however, this is of minor importance, since this abbreviated text material is in any case in need of analysis, explanation, exposition and commentary. The Rabbis were fully justified in criticizing[3] those whose knowledge of the tradition reached no further than the repetition of these highly compressed memory-texts, those who had not sat at the feet of those Rabbis who were able to expound these texts, and pass on all the riches of knowledge which earlier teachers had bound fast to these catch-words.

D. *Mnemonic Techniques*

A problem which has not, to our knowledge, attracted the attention it deserves, is that of the mnemonic helps which may consciously have been used during the most ancient period of Israel's history in those circles in which oral traditional material was transmitted.[4] It would be strange if, in a milieu in which a mass of oral material was passed on from generation to generation, no observations were made from experience in the field of mnemonics: experience obtained by the fathers and elder traditionists and passed on to their pupils.

The material in the Old Testament which may reasonably be supposed to have been passed on as oral tradition before being written down is, as is well known, often collected on a catch-word principle or, to use a better term, on a principle of association. We are quite right in

---

[1] Below, pp. 173 ff.

[2] On the fact that the methodical study of important haggadah texts and *midrashim* proceeded in principle in the same way as the study of halakah texts, see above, pp. 96 f., and also below, pp. 177 ff.

[3] See above, Ch. 9.

[4] Cf. however S. GANDZ, The Knot in Hebrew Literature, in *Isis* 14 (1930), pp. 189 ff., which draws rapid and superficial conclusions.

understanding this as being an elementary psychological law in operation: memorized material is grouped on the basis of associations of
similarity and connection. But is this the whole truth? The question is
whether or not we are guilty of romanticism, of treating the ancient
bearers of tradition as being totally ignorant and unsophisticated, if we
understand the process as being one of *unconscious* principles of grouping. Did they really fail to notice that all material is not equally easily
memorized, irrespective of the way in which it is grouped? Did they not
discover principles of grouping, mark these and use them consciously as
helps in transmission?

We may take as an example the collection of prophetic words in
Deutero-Isaiah (Is. 40–55). Here we find that the material is dealt with
on a remarkably strict *factual* basis of composition; but at the same time
it is grouped on a catch-word principle.[1] The individual elements, the
sayings, are not put together at random. We must therefore ask whether
the one who gave this collection its final form was aware of his simple
but effective method of composition. It would scarcely be going too far
to say that this principle of association is an ancient conscious method
of arranging oral traditional collections in such a way as to make them
easier the memorize and recite. For it is clear that this principle of association fills its real function in the process of memorization and
delivery from memory.[2] If it is also used in the editing of written texts,
this is partly a relic of an ancient oral principle of arrangement, but
mainly a measure to facilitate memorization and delivery from memory.
As we have already pointed out, in this milieu the act of copying down
did not mean that the process of memorization was discontinued.[3] It is
well known that in the written examples of the Talmud we see how
mnemonics of various kinds are introduced as a help to continued oral
transmission.[4]

---

[1] My thanks are due to Professor I. ENGNELL for pointing out this fact. On the
problem of composition, see IDEM, Jesajas bok, in *Sv. Bibl. Uppslagsverk* I (1948),
col. 1032 f., and cf. EISSFELDT, *Einleitung in das A. T.*, pp. 399 ff.

[2] The sharp distinction between written and oral Torah naturally does not belong in this period.

[3] Cf. Deut. 31.24 ff.: The Law is written in a book, which is laid by the Ark of the
Covenant *for a witness* (והיה שם בך לעד); Ex. 17.14 f.: A description of a battle
against the Amalekites is written down by Moses *as a reminder* (כתב זאת זכרון בספר)
and is taught to Joshua (ושים באזני יהשוע). These passages give interesting indications of the role played by written copies (at least in some cases) during the
older period. Cf. above, p. 81, n. 5.

[4] On this subject, see BRÜLL, *Die Entstehungsgeschichte*, pp. 61 ff.

Another example is to be seen in the alphabetic psalms: these psalms which have been arranged in the form of an acrostic, the first letter of each going to make up the alphabet.[1] Is it not likely that this principle of composition was used, *inter alia*, to facilitate the oral delivery and transmission of the psalms, as was later the case with the alphabetic Mishnah collections?[2]

We can, however, leave on one side the question of the role played by mnemonics in Old Testament times; we wish merely to indicate the existence of the problem.[3] Our interest is limited to the time between the beginning of the Christian era and the close of the Amoraic period. Here the situation is quite clear; the Rabbis were well aware that memorization could be facilitated by a technique: sometimes simple, sometimes advanced. The experience and observation of centuries has produced results; when we come to the end of the Amoraic period we find a technique of mnemonics which had developed enormously. We shall shortly consider this question.

The technique of mnemonics was applied several centuries before Christ in the rhetoric schools of the Hellenistic world; we do not however know very much about the forms taken by this phenomenon.[4] We shall not stop to discuss the extent to which Hellenistic influence in this matter may have been absorbed by Judaism. As we have already said, it is only to be expected *prima facie* that certain mnemonic observations are made in every milieu in which large quantities of oral material are transmitted. We need not presume that everybody has received impulses from Simonides of Keos!

Some Rabbis receive special mention from this point of view. R. Judah ben Ilai is particularly noted among the Tannaites; R. Naḥman bar Isaac, the great גמרנא וסדרנא,[5] and R. Judah ben Ḥanina among the

[1] Ps. 9–10, 25, 34, 37, 111, 112, 119, 145. Cf. Nahum 1, Prov. 31.10 ff., Sir. 51.13 ff.; see M. Löhr, Alphabetische und alphabetisierende Lieder im A.T., in *Zeitschr. f. d. Alttest. Wiss.* 25 (1905), pp. 173 ff., and idem, Psalm 7, 9, 10, *ibid.* 36 (1916), pp. 230 ff. See further Bacher, *Terminologie* II, p. 7, and A. Kurfess, T. Klauser, Akrostichis, in *Reallex. f. Ant. u. Christ.* I (1950), col. 235 ff.

[2] On this, see Rosenthal, *Über den Zusammenhang der Mischna* I (2nd ed.), §§ 78 f.

[3] A. Carlson, in a coming dissertation on the Ark traditions, will deal with the problem of composition of 2 Sam. from the point of view of *inter alia* association technique.

[4] E. Wüst, Mnemonik, in Pauly-Wissowa–Kroll, *Real-Encyclopädie* XV: 2 (1932), col. 2264 f.

[5] b Pes. 105 b.

Amoraic Rabbis.[1] This is not to say that these were the only ones who were conscious of the refinements of mnemonic technique. That they are singled out for special mention is evidently due to the fact that they distinguished themselves by laying particular emphasis on this aspect; the more elementary technique of mnemonics was practised by every Rabbi.

We may quote some statements of principle. In b Erub. 54b R. Ḥisda supports, with an *al-tiqre* interpretation of Deut. 31.19, the statement that "the Torah is acquired only by (mnemonic) signs (אין תורה ניקנית אלא בסימנין)". This appears to be a transmitted verse, to which R. Ḥisda merely gives Scriptural support. Such a supposition is strengthened by the following passage in which we read that R. Taḥlifa made that statement before R. Abahu, who replied, "You deduce it from that passage; we take it from the following: 'Set up marks for yourself ...' (הציבי לך ציונים, Jer. 31.21)."[2] R. Eliezer is said to have derived Scriptural support from Prov. 7.4, "'Say to Wisdom, you are my sister, and call Insight faithful (מדע)', (which means) make signs (מודעים) for the Torah."[3] From these quotations[4] we see that the technique of mnemonics was not only *applied*; there was also a general doctrinal statement which laid it down that it should be used, and efforts were made to find its Scriptural warrant. Before we consider the meaning of the term סימן[5] in more detail, we shall deal with a more elementary technique of mnemonics, used by the Rabbis generally.

Jewish tradition is strongly of the opinion that in the earliest period the oral Torah was studied *midrashically*, i.e. in connection with the continuous text of Scripture.[6] However, during the centuries before our era another way of studying the oral Torah had begun to develop: the *mishnaic*, i.e. without connection with the continuous text of Scripture.[7]

---

[1] See J. BRÜLL, *Die Mnemotechnik des Talmuds* (1884, in Hebrew), pp. 24 and 21 respectively, and N. BRÜLL, *Die Entstehungsgeschichte*, p. 59.

[2] *Al-tiqre* interpretation.

[3] רבי א׳ אמר מהכא אמר לחכמה אחתי את ומדע לבינה תקרא עשה מודעים לתורה.

[4] See also b Shab. 104a, b Erub. 21b, *ibid.* 53a.

[5] See below, p. 153, n. 6.

[6] For this problem, see LAUTERBACH, *Midrash and Mishnah*, pp. 163 ff. For further literature to the debate on the problem, see F. MAASS, Von den Ursprüngen der rabbinischen Schriftauslegung, in *Zeitschr. f. Theol. u. Kirche* 52 (1955). p. 153, n. 1–6.

[7] For an exemplification of the difference between a doctrinal statement in mishnaic and midrashic form, see HOFFMANN, *Zur Einleitung in die halachischen Midraschim*, pp. 1 ff.

The detached mishnaic statements were studied as independent entities, put together in blocks of varying extent and composition. The question has often been asked and discussed, when the change from the midrashic to the mishnaic method took place.[1] The answers given have varied. The question seems however—in this extreme form—to be merely academic (see below).

If we consider the midrashic method of studying the oral Torah, we can see how the continuous text of Scripture functions as a principle of arrangement—a mnemonic help. Sayings in the Scriptural text attract those halakic and haggadic doctrinal statements which belong to the texts in question. In this situation the text attracts not only those doctrinal statements which are directly deduced from the Scriptural passage, but also those which only have some other association—occasionally very loose—with the text. The words and phrases of the text of Scripture function as a chain of mnemonic catch-words, pointing to one oral doctrinal statement after another, giving a wave (זכר)[2] here, a hint (רמז)[3] there. This is the way in which the midrashic text collections were arranged (סדר מקרא). The learned, who knew the written text of Scripture with extraordinary virtuosity, were able to keep in mind their oral passages of tradition, thanks to the continuous support provided by the Scriptural text with its unvarying chain of key-words: its mnemonics.

It could often happen that a mass of traditions were linked with a definite passage of Scripture. We may take as an example the case of Eliezer ben Hyrkanos, who is said to have delivered 300 halakot to a single verse of Scripture (Ex. 23.17).[4] We can see from such an example how indistinct the boundary between material grouped (and formulated) on midrashic and mishnaic principles could be. But how was such a collection of halakot grouped? Or, leaving this particular case and widening the question to its proper compass, how was the mishnaically arranged and studied material grouped in the period before R. Aqiba?

---

[1] It is perhaps better to say: when the mishnaic method began to be used more widely. Both methods continued to be used side by side.

[2] That this term means "Erinnerungszeichen", "Mnemonikon", and the way in which the phenomenon it describes functions, has been clearly shown by W. BACHER in Ein alter Kunstausdruck der jüdischen Bibelexegese, in Zeitschr. f. d. Alttest. Wiss. 18 (1898), pp. 83 ff., and Zum Verständnisse des Ausdruckes זכר לדבר ibid. 19 (1899), pp. 166 ff., together with Terminologie I, pp. 51 ff.

[3] For the term, see BACHER, Terminologie I, pp. 182 f.

[4] T Sanh. XI.5.

There need be little doubt over this matter. It is a well known fact that in the finally fixed Mishnah certain special passages are known to have been put together before R. Judah, and even before both R. Meir and R. Aqiba.[1] The grouping after factual connection which these men sought is often broken into by an older grouping, arranged according to somewhat different principles. These older blocks of material were in fact not held together to any great extent on a basis of factual congruence, but of other principles of composition. For example, sayings are put together because they originate from one and the same author or were delivered on one and the same occasion or because they have a catch-word—a figure or some other characteristic word or expression—in common (or because they often belong to the same Scripture pericope).[2] The contents and principle of composition of the block is thus often indicated at the beginning of the saying: "In five cases is a *perutah* prescribed ..."[3] "In these matters *bet Shammai* judged more leniently and *bet Hillel* more strictly ..."[4] and so on. Here we see an original elementary technique of mnemonics in function. Elements of the tradition are grouped together with the help of a conscious mental connection, such as a definite catch-word. If the traditionist is sure of his catch-words he is able to call to mind entire blocks of material. Notebooks and the "scrolls of secrets" were able to fulfil a function here, but we shall consider this in our next section.

We can now proceed to consider the more advanced technique of mnemonics, which we have hitherto left on one side. The facts which we must briefly summarize here are well known to rabbinic scholars[5]; it is however necessary to our context that they be dealt with at this point. The term זכר is not used, but instead the designation סימן (Gk. σημεῖον),[6] "mnemonic sign", which is often synonymous.[7] These "signs" have

---

[1] Cf. HOFFMANN, *Die erste Mischna und die Controversen der Tannaim*, and ROSENTHAL, *Über den Zusammenhang der Mischna* I (2nd ed.), and see also STRACK, *Einleitung*, p. 22 (Eng. ed., p. 25), and DANBY, *The Mishnah*, pp. xxiv f.

[2] See STRACK and DANBY, *op. cit., ibid.*

[3] חמש פרוטות הן M Bab. Mes. IV.7.

[4] אלא דברים מקולי בית שמאי ומחומרי בית הלל M Ed. IV.1.

[5] See J. Z. LAUTERBACH, Mnemonics, in *The Jew. Enc.* VIII (1904), pp. 631 f., and KAPLAN, *The Redaction*, pp. 230 ff.

[6] See S. KRAUSS, *Griechische und lateinische Lehnwörter im Talmud, Midrasch und Targum* II (1899), sub voce, IDEM, *Talmudische Archäologie* III, pp. 174, 231, BACHER, *Terminologie* I, p. 131, and II, pp. 139 f.

[7] In many contexts (לדבר) זכר is the equivalent of (לדבר) סימן.

quite correctly been divided into two groups.[1] The first fulfils a function similar in some respects to that of the Scripture texts in the midrash collections. Known phenomena of one sort or another are allowed to lead the thoughts to a doctrinal statement or a particular crucial point in it: one which needs special attention and emphasis. These *simanim* thus help the traditionist both to remember and to remember correctly. How do they function?

In order to mark a fact, impress it clearly on the memory and prevent faulty memorization, the Rabbis often provide it with a *siman*.[2] They use a text of Scripture[3] as that *siman* which leads the thoughts. They can take a known doctrinal statement,[4] a figure of speech or a proverb;[5] they may take a familiar situation in human life[6] or in nature,[7] and use it to call to mind a doctrinal statement or the problematical point in it. These *simanim* often serve to prevent mistakes in respect of authors, figures or other facts which are easily confused in the memory.

For example, in M Ab. Zar. I.3 the pagan festivals Calendae and Saturnalia are reckoned in reverse chronological order. In order to emphasize this and to avoid confusion, R. Ḥanan bar Raba takes Ps. 139.5 as a mnemonic:

וסימניך אחור וקדם   "Your mnemonic shall be: Thou
צרתני.   hast set me behind and before."[8]

In b Ḥul. 46a (b Men. 86a) is mentioned that R. Ḥiyya used to throw away the sap of olives (אנפקטן); R. Simeon ben Rabbi, on the other hand, dipped his food in it. In order to avoid confusion between the two on this point, an Amoraic Rabbi refers to a known proverb:

וסימניך עשירין   "Your mnemonic shall be: The
מקמצין.   rich are parsimonious."

---

[1] LAUTERBACH, *op. cit., ibid.*

[2] J. BRÜLL, *Die Mnemotechnik des Talmuds*, contains a comprehensive list of *simanim* in the Talmud. See also the list in E. M. PINNER's edition of Berakot (1842), Einleitung, pp. 22a–b.

[3] E.g. b Ab. Zar. 8a., b Pes. 114a.

[4] E.g. p Meg. III.5.

[5] E.g. b Men. 43a.

[6] E.g. b Shab. 66b.

[7] E.g. b Ber. 3a (bar.).

[8] b Ab. Zar. 8a. This and the next example are taken from LAUTERBACH, *op. cit., ibid.*

(R. Simeon ben Rabbi was famed for his riches.) In b Ber. 3a is quoted a haggadah linked with Jer. 25.30, a passage which reads:

> "The Lord shall roar from on high,
> and utter his voice from his holy habitation;
> he shall mightily roar upon his habitation ..."

From the threefold repetition R. Eliezer draws the conclusion that the Lord roars during all three watches of the night. And as a support for the memory he provides a mnemonic sign (סימן לדבר): "The ass brays during the first watch of the night, the dogs bark during the second, and during the third the child sucks from its mother's breast, and the woman talks with her husband."

These three examples have been chosen at random from the many to be found in the Talmud.[1] These *simanim* often follow passages for which the memory needs a lead and a support. They are presumably to be considered as remnants of a larger body, a larger didactic *masorah*. They occur in any case more profusely in older text-witnesses than in younger.[2]

The second group of *simanim* comprises memory-words or memory-sentences: words or sentences formed by taking characteristic letters or decisive key-words from a longer doctrinal passage or from a group of such doctrinal passages which it is desired should be kept together. It is often a matter of meaningless words or nonsense verses.

Such *simanim* are thus formed by making up a word, using letters taken from the names of the authors and/or characteristic letters taken from the sayings. Or a nonsense verse may be created out of a long halakah or a group of halakah verses.

This is best illustrated by quoting a number of examples.

In M Men. XI.4 we read that "The loaves for the wave offering were *seven* (hand-breadths) long and *four* wide and their horns were *four* finger-breadths (high). The loaves of shewbread were *ten* (hand-breadths) long and *five* wide and their horns were *seven* finger-breadths (high). Rabbi Judah (ben Ilai) says: So that you may not make a mistake (remember the mnemonic): ZaDaD YaHaZ (רבי יהודה אומר שלא תטעה זד"ד יה"ז)." These letters of course denote the figures 7, 4, 4, 10, 5 and 7.

This is a relatively early example of the way in which the decisive

---

[1] For further examples, see the works quoted p. 154, n. 2; cf. also J. S. BLOCH, *Einblicke*, pp. 74 ff.

[2] See N. BRÜLL, *Die Entstehungsgeschichte*, pp. 61 ff.

elements—and in this case also the easily-confused words in a difficult
doctrinal statement—are isolated in the briefest possible form and made
into a mnemonic, to which the pupil or traditionist must pay particular attention, and which he must learn or perhaps write down.

Another example, chosen quite at random, is provided by b Ber. 57b,
in which a group of four sayings is preceded by the decisive key-word
from each: "Body, body, summary, restore and exalt. Mnemonic sign
(הגו״ף הגו״ף מעי״ן משיבי״ן ומרחיבי״ן סימן).״¹

We can take a third example, since we have touched upon it earlier in
a different context:² b Bab. Batr. 174a, where Rabba bar bar Hana says,
in the name of R. Joḥanan:

"Wherever Rabban Simeon ben Gamaliel teaches anything in our
Mishnah, the halakah follows him, except in the case of the Guarantor,
Sidon and Latter Proof (חוץ מערב וצידן וראיה אחרונה).״

We thus see that these *simanim* are often expressions of a system of
abbreviations which has with some justification been compared to
shorthand.³ In both cases the object is to find short and convenient
symbols for words and sentences. The words, sentences and doctrinal
passages can later, with the help of these abbreviations, be reconstructed
in their entirety. By means of such memory-words and memory-phrases
a Rabbi or a *tanna* was able to summarize the oral Torah to a considerable degree: transforming it into short formulae and figures, and, *sit
venia verbo*, stenograms and cyphers. With the help of these specially
learned or specially written abbreviations, the traditionists—by which
term we mean principally the most advanced professional traditionists—
were able to reproduce the mighty blocks of oral text which were there
summarized. N. BRÜLL is right when he emphasizes the role which these
simanim must have played at a time when the talmudic text-material
was not written down, and also at a time when written texts played
little part in the study of the oral Torah.⁴

However, in Amoraic times a considerable—though unofficial—role
was played by written notes, though these varied in extent. We must
now briefly consider this aspect.

¹ *Simanim* of this type may vary in the mss. (see e.g. N. BRÜLL, *op. cit., ibid.*).
So the Munich ms. omits this one.

² See above, sec. C.

³ On this subject, cf. KRAUSS, *Talmudische Archäologie* III, pp. 173 f. and 231,
who follows M. STEINSCHNEIDER. Greco-Roman shorthand seems however to be
still an obscure chapter; see A. MENTZ, *Geschichte der Kurzschrift* (1949).

⁴ *Op. cit.*, pp. 58 ff., even though he carries his conclusions too far.

E. *Use of Written Notes*

We have earlier had occasion to point out the way in which within Rabbinic Judaism the oral Torah was distinguished from the written, and the evident energy which went to maintain the principle that the latter should be publicly taught and delivered from the written page, while the former was to be delivered from memory.[1] A classical problem in Talmud research is that of the meaning, motives and consequences of the Rabbis' struggle against the written transmission of the oral Torah.[2] We have no reason to take up this well-worn subject for renewed discussion here;[3] it is in fact far from easy to produce any essentially new viewpoints at all. We shall deal only with some points which are relevant to our subject.

The problem must be placed in a wide context. We are familiar with the opposition to letters and writing which manifested itself in many cultures at the time when the art of writing was introduced and which lives on, in various ways and various forms, long afterward.[4] This would seem to be very much a matter of unwillingness to break with ancient usages and customs which often owed their preeminence to religious authority. But there were other contributory factors as well. Such unwillingness may occasionally be more in the nature of superstition: we know that writing was often originally a magical process.[5] Sometimes it may be of a more rational nature: doubt is expressed as to the ability of letters and written words to reproduce the full life, power and meaning of the spoken word. This latter form was by no means the least common expression of opposition to the written word in the ancient Near East and in Classical Antiquity.[6]

---

[1] See above, pp. 23 ff.

[2] On this subject, see STRACK, *Einleitung*, pp. 9 ff. (Eng. ed., pp. 12 ff.), MIELZINER, *Introduction*, p. 281, KAPLAN, *The Redaction*, pp. 261 ff., LIEBERMAN, *Hellenism*, pp. 83 ff.

[3] The most important among the relevant texts are conveniently reproduced in KAPLAN, *op. cit., ibid.*

[4] See GANDZ, *The Dawn of Literature*, pp. 440 ff., who has correctly placed the classical Talmud problem in this wider perspective, although his solution is rather superficial. Cf. also above, p. 123.

[5] See e.g. G. VAN DER LEEUW, *Phänomenologie der Religion* (2nd ed. 1956), pp. 494 f.

[6] On the more rational criticism of the written word, see e.g. Plato, *Phaedr.*, 275 ff.; cf. *Prot.* 329A and 347E, *Theait.* 164, Quint., *Instit. orat.* 2.2.8. For an exposition of Plato's ideas on the subject, see W. JAEGER, *Paideia* III (1945), pp. 194 ff. See also Aristeas 127, Papias in Eusebius, *Hist. Eccl.* III. 39 and below, pp. 196 f.

The learned Pharisees were hardly opposed to writing in principle, but it is possible that with their faithfulness to tradition, which they considered to be a religious duty, they preserved an archaic practice on this point, the transmission of the oral Torah. And as we have earlier remarked, it is also probable that they were compelled to strengthen their own position in their conflict with the Sadducees.[1]

Furthermore, the problem must be seen in connection with the common reluctance to make public certain "esoteric" texts, which for various reasons were restricted to a limited group. As an argument against the writing of texts the Amoraic Rabbis claimed, *inter alia*, that the oral Torah was Israel's secret (מסטירין) which God wished to be revealed only to the righteous.[2] A close parallel is provided by the way in which the mystery-texts were handled in certain Hellenistic religious groups.[3] We stress that this applies only to *certain* groups, for secret *written* texts seem to have played a remarkable role in the mystery religions of Classical Antiquity.[4] From one point of view, an even more adequate parallel would seem to be provided by the reluctance of the lawyers of ancient Greece and Rome to produce a generally available legal code.[5]

Again, the written Torah was already fixed and recognized as Scripture —even as incomparable Holy Scripture—long before the Pharisaic scholars began to gain a dominant influence in Judaism. It was treated as having been taken over in its written form from the venerable fathers— and even from God Himself. We may perhaps go so far as to say that the Pharisee's reverence for the sacred written Torah was a contributory cause of his opposition to the written fixing of the oral Torah, though there seem to be other factors behind the struggle of Pharisaism and the colleges of Rabbis over this point.[6]

It appears however to be the case that this classical Talmud problem

---

[1] Above, pp. 23 ff.

[2] *Tanch.* (Verona 1595) וירא 9 a. For other, similar sayings, see STRACK, *op. cit.*, p. 14 (Eng. ed., pp. 17 f.). — Further instances of the term מסטירין (μυστήριον) will be found in KRAUSS, *Lehnwörter* II, p. 346.

[3] On this subject, see O. PERLER, Arkandisziplin, in *Reallex, f. Ant. u. Christ.* I (1950), col. 667 ff. (with bibl.).

[4] See e.g. H.-I. MARROU, ΜΟΥΣΙΚΟΣ ΑΝΗΡ (1937), pp. 259 ff., FESTUGIÈRE, *La révélation d'Hermès Trismégiste* II, pp. 34 ff., who stresses the striking formal resemblance between the *traditio mystica* and the methods used in Greco-Roman schools. Cf. also IDEM, *L'idéal religieux des Grecs et l'évangile* (1932), pp. 120 ff.

[5] See SCHULZ, *History of Roman Legal Science*, p. 25.

[6] Cf. above, Ch. 1.

has advanced a step nearer solution since LIEBERMAN worked out[1]—
on rather new lines—the difference between authorized published editions and private notes, making a comparison with the Hellenistic categories of ἐκδόσεις and written ὑπομνήματα,[2] and clarifying the forms
of the *oral* publication which the Rabbis evidently practised. We have
already considered this topic more than once.[3]

The actual rule, that the oral Torah should not be transmitted in
written form, is not to be found explicitly quoted until b Git. 60 b (b Tem.
14 b):

דברים שבכתב אי אתה	"You shall not deliver/transmit
רשאי לאומרן על פה	sayings (transmitted) in writing
דברים שבעל פה אי	orally; you shall not deliver/
אתה רשאי לאומרן	transmit sayings (transmitted)
בכתב.	orally in writing."[4]

The practice seems however to be established before the beginning of
the Christian era. The Rabbis attribute such a practice to Gamaliel
the Elder and,[5] as we have seen, it seems to have been given its accentuated form a century earlier, in the controversy between the Sadducees
and Pharisees.

תורה שׁ(נאמרה) בעל פה,[6] "the Torah which is transmitted on the
lips", must, according to the Rabbis, be transmitted and delivered orally.
In Tannaitic and Amoraic times it seems clear—*mirabile dictu*—that
there was no written Mishnah available. If the Mishnah existed in
written form, then the written examples were not in official use. Not a
single written copy of the Mishnah is referred to in the Talmud,[7] where

---

[1] *Op. cit.*

[2] On this distinction, see the summary provided by V. BURR, Editionstechnik,
in *Reallex. f. Ant. u. Christ.* IV (1959), col. 597 ff., L. KOEP, Buch I, *ibid.* II (1954),
col. 664 ff., and the comprehensive art. by C. H. ROBERTS, The Codex, in *Proceed.
of the Brit. Acad.* 40 (1954), pp. 169 ff. See further the works listed in n. 3, p. 162.

[3] Above, pp. 120 f. and elsewhere.

[4] The author here is R. Judah bar Naḥmani, the *meturgeman* of R. Simeon ben
Laqish. Cf. p Peah II.6 with par., p Meg. IV.1, Tanch. וירא 5, *ibid.* כי תשא 34.

[5] b Shab. 115 a (bar.).

[6] See above, p. 26.

[7] The worth of this circumstance as an indication is correctly stressed by Löw,
Graphische Requisiten II, pp. 122 ff., and LIEBERMAN, *Hellenism*, p. 87. Cf. Löw,
ibid., and BLOCH, *Einblicke*, p. 88, who also stress the importance of the fact that
Mishnah quotations are never introduced by a formula for quotation from a written
work.

books and written documents of all kinds are often mentioned, and where we hear of practically everything belonging to the sphere of college and of study. Oral Torah is delivered from memory in the course of instruction and debates. And when it becomes necessary to check up on some point, it is not a published book, nor a document in the college archives, which is consulted; instead one must "go out and consider and find"[1] or consult a teacher or a *tanna*.[2] The story is told of no less a person than the Patriarch R. Judah himself, that he was consulted on the wording of a passage in his Mishnah, and advised his questioners to consult, not a deposited Mishnah book, but his authorized head *tanna*.[3] And when certain Amoraic Rabbis began to break with the old rule that oral Torah must be transmitted orally, and sought some precedent, they were unable to find any support for the writing down of text material from the Mishnah; instead they had to refer to a number of rather vague cases of an older doctrinal authority copying down certain *halakot*.[4]

But in spite of this attitude of principle to the oral Torah, teachers and pupils, practised in the art of writing, were naturally unable to avoid enlisting the help of the pen in their efforts to master the rapidly expanding oral doctrinal material which was so important to them. STRACK has, with a number of examples, proved that this in fact took place.[5] Not that official books existed—μὴ γένοιτο—but private notes and copies did so. We hear that teachers and pupils have writing tablets and notebooks (פינקסירות, πίνακες)[6] or "scrolls of secrets" (מיגלות סתרים)[7] at their disposal, or that a teacher or a pupil makes notes in a haggadah

---

[1] נפק דק ואשכח b Ber. 19a etc. For further examples, see STRACK, *Einleitung*, p. 13 (Eng. ed., p. 16 and notes, p. 245), and BACHER, *Terminologie* II, p. 147, sub voce עין, and p. 217, sub voce שכח.

[2] E.g. b Bab. Mes. 34a, b Nid. 43b and passim.

[3] p Maas. Shen. V.1: אמר לון פוקון שאלון לרבי יצחק רובא דבהנת ליה כל מתניתא. Cf. also p Ket. IV.11 — For the matter, see further GANDZ, *The Rōbeh*, pp. 8 ff.

[4] This viewpoint is brought forward by KAPLAN, *The Redaction*, p. 264.

[5] *Op. cit., ibid.*

[6] E.g. p Maas. II. 4, b Men. 70a, b Shab. 156a. For the term and the matter, see KRAUSS, *Lehnwörter* II, pp. 466 f., IDEM, *Talmudische Archäologie* III, pp. 144 f., where other types of notebook are also described. — See also LIEBERMAN, *Hellenism*, pp. 203 f., who stresses that a *pinax* often had several pages. Cf. ROBERTS, *The Codex*, pp. 169 ff.

[7] E.g. b Shab. 6b, 96b, b Bab. Mes. 92a. Cf. Origen, *In Matth. Comm. Ser.* § 28 (MPG XIII, 1636): *ex libris secretioribus qui apud Judaeos feruntur*, STRACK, *Einleitung*, p. 11 (Eng. ed., p. 244, n. 23). J. Z. LAUTERBACH's interpretation in Megillat Setarim, in *The Jew. Enc.* VIII (1904), p. 427, is untenable.

book (ספר אגדתא).[1] We even find the resourceful pupil making notes on the college wall![2] There is clear witness to the character and purpose of such notes: it is evidently a matter of private notes (written ὑπομνήματα etc.)[3] intended to facilitate learning and continued memorization, practice and future repetition. Books served as "reminder-books" (ספרי זכרון).[4] The most relevant comparative material is to be found in the more advanced Hellenistic schools.[5]

We may suppose that the notebooks belonging to the Rabbis' pupils contained in general such key-words and catch-words (סימנים) and also summarizing memory-texts of the kind discussed in the previous section. Nor is it impossible that such catch-words were written in the margins of personal copies of the Torah.[6] But there were also "scrolls of secrets" with more comprehensive summaries of text-material from the oral Torah. Haggadah texts in particular seem to have been copied out in this simple and unofficial way: we catch several glimpses of the "haggadah book" in the talmudic material.[7]

It is however generally true to say that these private notes and scrolls are only *glimpsed* in the source material, due naturally to the fact that they were illegitimate in principle and therefore formally suppressed. In any case we seek in vain for a general rule—of the same type as the pedagogical rules we have quoted above—laying down that such notes *are* to be taken.[8]

The use of notebooks and the like seems to have been more usual in Palestine than in Babylon; opposition to the act of writing seems to have

---

[1] E.g. b Ḥul. 60b, b Shab. 89a.

[2] p Kil. I.1.

[3] LIEBERMAN, *op. cit.*, pp. 87 f.; cf. pp. 203 ff.

[4] For the ספר זכרון and ספר הזכרנות, cf. Est. 6.1; Mal. 3.16 (cf. Ezr. 4.15, 6.2); CD XX.19, b Ber. 6a and elsewhere. The heavenly "reminder books" must have some earthly equivalent (cf. above, p. 88, n. 3).

[5] See below, p. 162, n. 3.

[6] E.g. *al-tiqre* readings as catch-words for midrashic exposition. Some of the variants in "R. Meir's copy" (see above, p. 46, n. 10, and p. 55, n. 3) may conceivably have been of this type. See *inter alia* STRACK, *op. cit.* p. 11; cf. MARX, review of this work, p. 353, and the alteration (approved by STRACK himself?) in the English translation, p. 14.

[7] Of particular interest here is "the haggadah book of the school of Rab" (ספר אגדתא דבי רב), b Sanh. 57b, which was evidently a more comprehensive collection of written *haggadot*. See further STRACK, *op. cit.*, *ibid.*

[8] R. Joḥanan however gives a recommendation: ברית כרותה היא הלומד אגדה מתוך הספר לא במהרה הוא משכח (p Ket. V.1).

162

been weaker in the Palestinian colleges than in the Babylonian.[1] Influence from the Hellenistic schools of rhetoric and philosophy was presumably stronger in *Eres Jisrael* than in Mesopotamia,[2] and it is known that pupils in Hellenistic schools made good use of their skill in writing, copying down their ὑπομνήματα, ὑποσημειώσεις, σχολαί, χρεῖαι, προγυμνάσματα etc.[3]

It is interesting to note in this context the way in which the Mishnah describes the sessions of the Great Sanhedrin prior to the fall of the Temple. According to M Sanh. IV.3 there stood before the judges two scribes of the judges (סופרי הדיינין) who "wrote down the words of them that favoured acquittal and the words of them that favoured conviction (כותבין דברי המזכין ודברי המחייבין),"[4] though whether or not they also wrote down the verdict is not clear. It is common knowledge that the sessions in the rabbinic colleges, to judge by all appearances, very largely followed a more ancient form of legal procedure. It is tempting to imagine[5] that two scribes were also present in the rabbinic sessions, writing down "the words of them that favoured acquittal and the words of them that favoured conviction", or in other words, that a sort of minute-book was kept. But such official minutes are not mentioned; even less can we expect to find that such were referred to, consulted or brought into use in public teaching. The hypothesis must therefore be abandoned.

---

[1] Pointed out by N. Brüll, *Die Entstehungsgeschichte*, pp. 5 ff.

[2] The fact that in Palestinian sources the learned can be called "scholastics", "philosophers", "sophists" (סופיסטין, פילוסופין, אסכולסטיקין) also supports this view; see Krauss, *Lehnwörter* II, pp. 87, 446, 377.

[3] On the difference between, on the one hand συγγράμματα, ἐκδόσεις etc., and on the other written ὑπομνήματα, ὑποσημειώσεις etc., and on the use of notes in schools and as a subsidiary support for the school tradition, see von Arnim, *Leben und Werke des Dio von Prusa*, pp. 175 ff., W. Jaeger, *Studien zur Entstehungsgeschichte der Metaphysik des Aristoteles* (1912), pp. 135 ff., K. Gronau, *Poseidonios und die jüdische-christliche Genesisexegese* (1914), pp. 294 ff., W. Bousset, *Jüdisch-Christlicher Schulbetrieb in Alexandria und Rom* (1915). Cf. also the articles above, p. 159, n. 2.

[4] See also b Sanh. 34a, 35a, 36b, and below, pp. 246 ff. Cf. the ancient idea of the "tablet of grace" and "the tablet of sin", L. Koep, Buch IV, in *Reallex. f. Ant. u. Christ.* II (1954), col. 725 f., idem, *Das himmlische Buch in Antike und Christentum* (1952), pp. 3 ff. Cf. also I. Engnell, Livets bok, in *Sv. Bibl. Uppslagsverk* II (1952), col. 105 ff. — On the role of writing in Oriental and Hellenistic jurisdiction, see the references in Koep, *Das himmlische Buch*, pp. 17 f.

[5] Thus Kaplan, *The Redaction*, pp. 266 f., who does not however point out *the hypothetical character* of this suggestion.

In the sessions of the Rabbis the *tannaim* had taken the place of the *soferim*.[1]

The copies of oral Torah which we encounter in rabbinic literature up to the end of the Amoraic period are thus mainly private and unofficial written ὑπομνήματα. It is a matter of secret, subsidiary helps to a form of learning which is to function in all important situations and function, moreover, as memorized knowledge. That is why we are able to cast no more than a quick glance in the direction of these written notes in the course of our description of the way in which the oral Torah—technically speaking—was transmitted.

F. *Techniques of Repetition*

In our day, when a never-ending stream of printed material is continually passing before our eyes, we are far too apt to forget that the literary works of Antiquity were not intended for readers sitting in quiet seclusion and leafing through rapidly produced and rapidly obsolete publications. In the first place, the greater part of the ancient literature is intended for the ears as much as, if not more than, the eyes. The normal method of reading was reading *aloud*.[2] Words were meant to *sound*; authors wrote works which were meant to be read aloud. And when considering such writings as those which comprise secondary copies of oral tradition or alternative forms of oral presentation, we must pay particular attention to the fact that we are here dealing with the *spoken* word.[3]

Secondly, this reading—reading aloud or public oral delivery—was not carried out in the relaxed, neutral tones of everyday speech, but

---

[1] On these, see above, pp. 93 ff.

[2] A famous case is provided by Augustine's undisguised astonishment over the fact that Ambrosius read silently, and his attempt to explain the phenomenon, *Conf.* 6.3. On reading aloud in Antiquity, see J. BALOGH, "Voces paginarum". Beiträge zur Geschichte des lauten Lesens und Schreibens, in *Philologus* 82 (1926–27), pp. 84 ff., 202 ff., and further references in KRAUSS, *Talmudische Archäologie* III, p. 352, n. 221, and MARROU, *Saint Augustin*, p. 89, and IDEM, *Histoire de l'éducation*, pp. 214 f., and 516, n. 4.

[3] See previous section. On the scepticism toward the written word which was common in Antiquity, see *ibid.*, n. 6. On the way in which written works (συγγράμματα) often also function to a great extent as memory-texts, delivered from memory, see above, sec. A.

with solemn, cultivated and practised cantillation (of varying types, which we cannot consider here).[1]

And thirdly, most literary products were not intended to be heard with half one's mind or to be skimmed through, but were to be read and listened to, time and time again, with attention and reflection.

This latter point, applying particularly to the condensed memory-material of the type which is to be found in the rabbinic tradition, has been dealt with elsewhere in this investigation. The two former points will be taken into consideration in this section, as they have undoubtedly both played an important role in the transmission and maintenance of the rabbinic tradition.

We frequently see in the Tannaitic and Amoraic traditional literature the importance which is attached to the fact that repetition should be carried out in a sonorous and distinct voice. We may take note of a linguistic contraposition, which places the term "transmit/repeat" (שנה = שנא) over against the term "whisper" (לחש);[2] the actual term transmit/repeat thus includes the idea that the words are to *sound*. The principle is here self-evident, as formulated so strikingly by Rabbi in b Ber. 13a:

השמע לאזניך	"Let your ears hear what you
מה שאתה מוציא מפיך.	allow to cross your lips."[3]

In b Ber. 22a we read that R. Judah ben Batyra saw a pupil mumbling (שהיה מגמגם)[4] and said to him:

בני פתח פיך ויאירו	"My son, open your mouth, and
דבריך.	let your words *shine* forth."[5]

The story was also told, as a general example, of the way in which one of R. Eliezer's[6] pupils repeated in a whisper (שונה בלחש) as a result of

---

[1] See e.g. E. NORDEN, *Die antike Kunstprosa* I (3rd ed. 1915), pp. 55 ff., MARROU, *Histoire de l'éducation*, pp. 215, 230 f. On the situation in the Jewish tradition, see below.

[2] b Ber. 22a.

[3] The quotation has to do with the reading of *Shema*, and is really an exegesis of the introductary imperative שמע; we have cited it here only because it illustrates how the Rabbis emphasize the importance of reading *aloud*. — Cf. Sifre Deut. ad 6.7.

[4] The reason for his mumbling was that he was ritually impure (cf. M Ber. III.4). For the laws concerning ritual purity and different forms of occupation with the Torah, see the context of b Ber. 22a.

[5] The Munich ms. reads והאיר.

[6] ben Hyrkanos? ben Jacob?

which he forgot everything in three years (b Erub. 54a).[1] And in the same context is reproduced a tradition concerning Beruriah, R. Meir's learned wife,[2] that she corrected a pupil who repeated in a low voice, saying to him that learning is assured only if it is fixed in all 248 members of the body.[3] Samuel's words to R. Judah are also quoted:

שירנא פתח פומיך קרי
פתח פומיך תני כי
היכי דתקיים ביך
ותוריך חיי.

"O keen scholar, open your mouth and read (the written Torah); open your mouth and repeat (the oral Torah), so that (your knowledge) may be maintained in you and that which you have learned may live" (*ibid.*).[4]

It is not easy to say what were the origins of the practice of reading both oral and written Torah *aloud*. We are evidently dealing with an ancient original practice, supported by all manner of ideas on the power, effectiveness and riches of content of the spoken words—in contrast to what the earliest scribes had succeeded in committing to writing. What is perhaps most interesting for our purposes is that the Rabbis directly opposed incipient tendencies towards silent reading and silent repetition.[5] This would seem to be due, partly to general faithfulness to the practice of the old masters, and partly to various more or less obscure ideas. One motive which we can grasp, and which was important, was that distinct pronunciation facilitated memorization and maintenance of the tradition, and obviated its being forgotten or distorted into inarticulate nonsense, or an incomprehensible mumble.[6]

---

[1] Cf. Sifre Deut. ad 6.7 and Deut. R. 8.4.

[2] On her, see R. GORDIS, Beruriah, in *The Univ. Jew. Enc.* II (1948), p. 243.

[3] For the understanding of this saying, cf. Elisha ben Abuya's words in Abot de R. Natan I, 24. MORRIS, *The Jewish School*, p. 139, connects her statement with the fact that recitation was supported with certain bodily movements; it is however uncertain whether this is meant by the statement in question.

[4] Instead of תני וגו׳ the Munich ms. reads: שני כ״ה דתר׳ חיי ותקיים בידך.

[5] This does not however mean that silent thought or silent reading were concepts, foreign to their way of thinking. N.B. the expression זכר בלב in contrast to זכר בפה in b Meg. 18a and הרהור (meditation) opposite to דבור (loud recitation), b Ber. 20b, b Shab. 150a; cf. also M Ber. III.4. Even the deeper study referred to by the verb עין seems occasionally to have been thought out in silence.

[6] Cf. b Qid. 30ab, on the ideal that the words of the Torah shall be sharpened in one's mouth (דברי תורה מחודדים בפיך), and Ab. VI.6 (ed. MARTI, BEER) on the importance of determining exactly the tradition which is received; המכון את שמועתו is prefigura-

If we remember that it was normal both in Classical Antiquity and in the ancient Near East to read and repeat aloud, not only in public but—with certain modifications—when one "sat in one's house or walked along the road",[1] then the practice of transmitting *secret* doctrines *in a whisper* (בלחש, בלחישה) stands in its correct perspective. This whispering was often due to reverence for the Holy One, for the sacred matters with which the words dealt, and for the powers of the spirit-world who were thought to be present in the place where such matters were brought up.[2] But it was also due to a desire to prevent such highly sacred teachings—or any other teachings which were for other reasons to be kept secret—from spreading to an immature human public,[3] to the common people, that transmission took place in a whisper. This stands out with exemplary clarity in the famous second chapter of M Ḥag. (and in both the Babylonian and Palestinian *gemara* on the chapter, as well as in Tosefta, *ibid.*).

Intimately connected with the custom of reading and repeating aloud was the practice of reading the written Torah and repeating the oral with a rhythmical melody (נגון, נעימה). In ancient Judaism the sacred texts were recited with cantillation,[4] as is still done today in Jewish synagogues and among the Samaritans—not to mention other, more distant parallels. This cantillation was learned in the schools—cf. reading, recitation and the art of oral delivery in Hellenistic schools[5]—and we know that it was this which the post-Talmudic Masoretes attempted, in the case of the written Torah, to fix graphically by means of their vowel-signs and accents.[6]

We may quote a couple of illustrative sayings. When R. Aqiba wished to stress the importance of the daily study of the Torah, he said:

tive. In both cases it would seem that the material must be read/repeated distinctly, even though this fact does not perhaps lie in the foreground of these two sayings. Cf. also the ideal, Ab., *ibid.*, of עריכת שפתים.

[1] N.B. also that traditions can be *stolen* through the overhearing of recitation, T Bab. Qam. VII.8 ff.

[2] M Ḥag. II.1, T Ḥag. II.1, b Ḥag. 14a, p Ḥag. II.1.

[3] b Ber. 22a.

[4] See e.g. E. WERNER, The Origins of Psalmody, in *Hebr. Un. Coll. Ann.* 25 (1954), pp. 327 ff., S. ROSSOWSKY, *The Cantillation of the Bible* (1957), A. W. BINDER, *Biblical Chant* (1959). Apart from earlier evidence, see now 1QS X.8. Cf. BILLERBECK, *Comm.* I, p. 516, and A. Z. IDELSOHN, *Hebräisch-orientalischer Melodienschatz* I–III (1914–22).

[5] See above, p. 164, n. 1.

[6] See e.g. P. KAHLE, *Masoreten des Westens* II (1930), pp. 42 ff., and most recently A. DíEZ MACHO, La cantilación protomasorética del Pentateuco, in *Estudios Bíblicos* 18 (1959), pp. 223 ff.

זמר בכל יום זמר בכל   *"Sing* every day, *sing* every day"
יום.   (b Sanh. 99 b).[1]

And a well known saying of R. Joḥanan reads:

כל הקורא בלא נעימה   "He who reads (the Scriptures)
ושונה בלא זמרה   without melody and repeats (the
עליו הכתוב אומר וגם   oral Torah) without song,[2] con-
אני נתתי להם חקים   cerning him the Scripture says:
לא טובים וגו'.   Therefore I also gave them statutes which were not to their
advantage (Ezek. 20.25)" (b Meg.
32 a).[3]

This is noteworthy from our point of view. Rhythm and cantillation certainly did not originate for pedagogical reasons, but they fulfil *de facto* a pedagogical function: the texts which are learned in this way are memorized and transmitted more faithfully and more exactly than those learned in other ways.[4] Folk-lore provides many examples of the tenacity with which archaic wording lives on in cantillated traditional texts, long after the meaning of the texts has been forgotten.[5]

It is rather an odd thought that the rough textual material of the Mishnah was recited in this cantillated fashion, but the sources provide —as we have seen—quite clear evidence that this in fact took place. The situation is much more clearly appreciated in connection with symmetrical and poetical material of the haggadic type. For further development of this theme, we may refer to M. JOUSSE's analysis of rhythm in rabbinic oral texts.[6]

It would have been interesting to have considered in this context

---

[1] Haplographie in the Munich ms. — Cf. T Ohal. XVI.8, T Par. IV.7. BACHER's reading, *Der Agada der Tannaiten* I (2nd ed.), p. 296, can hardly be correct.

[2] The Munich ms. reads אמירה.

[3] Mas. Soferim 3. 10. Cf. also b Ned. 38a. On the cantillation of the *gemara* text, see b Bes. 24a, with par. — b Sanh. 101a seems to be directed against the use of the texts of Scripture as profane songs. For an alternative judgement, see M. GERTNER, The Masorah and the Levites, in *Vet. Test.* 10 (1960), p. 265.

[4] Cf. BLOCH, *Einblicke*, p. 74, MORRIS, *The Jewish School*, pp. 140 ff. The latter points out that awareness of this existed in Antiquity (Platon, Quintilianus).

[5] See above, p. 130, n. 1.

[6] *Le style oral rythmique et mnémotechnique chez les verbo-moteurs* (1925), IDEM, *Études sur la psychologie du geste. Les Rabbis d'Israel* I.

other pedagogical details, such as the didactic facial expressions which were evidently used,[1] as well as the use of gestures and bodily movements to impart dramatic shape to the doctrinal material.[2] We cannot however go into these details here.

G. *Measures to Counteract Forgetfulness*

The Rabbis waged a conscious and energetic war against forgetfulness. The traditional literature contains many words of warning and many sayings which stress the importance of keeping alive one's knowledge of the sacred Torah, written as well as oral.[3] We shall quote only one such saying, the words of R. Meir in Ab. III.9:

כל השוכח דבר אחד
ממשנתו מעלה עליו
הכתוב כאלו מתחיב בנפשו.

"Every man who forgets a single word of his mishnah (i.e. what he has learned), Scripture accounts it unto him as if he had forfeited his soul!"[4]

The Rabbis pass on various rules for the strengthening of the memory,[5] but stress above all the great universal principle of continual repetition. Cicero's saying was applied to its fullest extent in Rabbinic Judaism: *repetitio est mater studiorum*. Knowledge is gained by repetition, passed on by repetition, kept alive by repetition.[6] A Rabbi's life is one continual repetition. The traditional literature contains countless hyperbolical sayings, stressing that the words of the Torah should constantly be on one's lips, that they are to be studied day and night, and so on;[7] many pictures are also drawn of the conscientious Rabbi. We need only call to mind the wandering Rabbi of Ab. III.8, repeating the oral Torah as

---

[1] Pesiqta R. c. 20, Mas. Soferim 16.2 and elsewhere, pointed out by W. BACHER, Das alt-jüdische Schulwesen, in *Jahrb. f. jüd. Gesch. u. Lit.* 6 (1903), p. 74.

[2] Cf. JOUSSE, *Le style oral*, pp. 20 ff., and above, p. 165, n. 3.

[3] See e.g. T Ohal. XVI.8, b Sanh. 99a (bar.), Sifre Deut. ad 1.13, 6.7, 11.22 and 32.2, Abot de R. Natan I, 24, Ab., passim, and see further BLOCH, *Einblicke*, pp. 86 f., and BONSIRVEN, *Le judaïsme palestinien* I, pp. 287 f., 292.

[4] Ed. MARTI, BEER. — Cf. b Men. 99b.

[5] b Hor. 13b. Cf. b. Ab. Zar. 19a b. — b Bab. Mes. 85a: R. Zeira fasted for 100 days in order to *forget* the Babylonian Talmud! His intention was to learn the Palestinian Talmud instead.

[6] See e.g. the words of Hillel, above, p. 134.

[7] On the role played by such Biblical texts as Josh. 1.8 and Ps. 1.2, see below, Ch. 14 D. See also the works named in n. 3 above.

he walked, or the exemplary Rabban Joḥanan ben Zakkai, who is said never to have been idle, but to have sat and repeated his texts without pause.[1] Even when lying in a dark Roman prison, he knew the time of day from his recitation (מפשטריה; Eka R. 1.31).

The Tannaitic and Amoraic traditions are nevertheless able to relate how even the high Rabbis could forget what they had once known—even the collections they had taught to others. The Talmudic literature is usually sufficiently sympathetic to say that their forgetfulness was a result of ill health. In such a situation a teacher must contact his own former pupils in order to have his knowledge restored.

The story is told of no less a personage than the Patriarch R. Judah, that he had been ill and had forgotten the thirteen mishnah orders he had himself edited and taught; he was therefore forced to re-learn the lost orders, of which R. Ḥiyya could repeat seven and a fuller who had attended his lessons the other six.[2] Similarly, R. Abdimi is said to have taught R. Ḥisda about burnt offerings, and then to have forgotten that particular tractate, whereupon he had to go back to R. Ḥisda to have his knowledge restored.[3] And R. Joseph, who had been Abaye's teacher but who—on account of illness—had forgotten everything, was taught again by Abaye.[4] This was the procedure in connection with the oral Torah; such copies as may have existed were obviously not used as reference books.[5]

In this context we ought also to pay attention to repetition in a different meaning, as it is occasionally mentioned: from time to time, the scholar would retrace his footsteps and revise, going through the material he had learned earlier. R. Ḥiyya bar Abba is said to have had a general *viva voce* for his teacher R. Joḥanan every month.[6] R. Sheshet in Shilhi was in the habit of repeating everything he had learned every thirtieth day,[7] after which he would lean against a door-bolt and say, "Rejoice, my soul, rejoice, my soul! To you I have read (the Scriptures); for you I have repeated (the oral Torah)."[8] And of other Rabbis it is said that

---

[1] b Suk. 28a: ולא מצאו אדם יושב ודומם אלא יושב ושונה. Cf. also the words of Rab, b Bes. 24b.

[2] b Ned. 41a. Cf. b Bab. Mes. 43b, 44a, b Ab. Zar. 52b.

[3] b Men. 7a.

[4] b Ned. 41a.

[5] See above, sec. E. Cf. also examples given in BLOCH, *Einblicke*, pp. 77 ff.

[6] b Ber. 38b with par., see above, p. 96.

[7] b Pes. 68b.

[8] חדאי נפשאי חדאי נפשאי לך קראי לך תנאי.

when the Angel of Death stood at their threshold, they bade for a respite, during which time they could repeat all they knew of the sacred Torah. The verse: "Blessed is he who comes thither (to the other world) with his knowledge in his hand (fresh)", is quoted several times in the Talmud.[1] The story is told in b Ket. 77b of R. Ḥanina ben Papa, and in b Moed Qat. 28a of R. Ashi,[2] that, lest he should enter the other world unprepared and unequipped, he requested the Angel of Death to grant him thirty days in which to revise all the sacred texts he had learned[3] during a long life of study.

---

[1] b Bab. Batr. 10b, b Pes. 50a, b Moed Qat. 28a, b Ket. 77b.

[2] On his diligence in study, see b Bab. Mes. 75b.

[3] ואהדרי לתלמודאי.

CHAPTER 12

The Origins of Oral Torah

OUR OBJECT in the previous chapters has been mainly to consider the process of transmission in action. We shall now by way of conclusion bring forward a number of observations and reflections on the complicated question of the way in which doctrinal material, in the form of oral texts, is *introduced* into the more rigid process of transmission, and becomes an object of formal transmission of the kind we have attempted to describe. For the more factual and legalistic aspects of the question of the origins of the various categories of the oral Torah, we may recommend M. GUTTMANN's excellent *Zur Einleitung in die Halacha*.[1]

For the limited purposes of this chapter, we must be content with a very rough form-critical division of the material, into a sayings-tradition (דברים) and a narrative tradition (מעשים).[2] In the latter case it is a definite type of traditional element which we are considering: narratives concerning a Rabbi's actions, retold with the object of gaining from them halakic—or haggadic—teachings.

A. *The Sayings-tradition* (דברים)

The Rabbis transmitted the texts of the written Torah, subjecting them to interpretation, thorough examination and penetration (מדרש, תלמוד, דקדוק, פלפול etc.). A similar procedure was observed with the traditional texts in the oral Torah. They transmitted them as passages for repetition and subjected them to a pilpulistic examination, explanation and many-sided usage.[3] In this way they could obtain a great deal of knowledge and wisdom from the authoritative texts given in the tradition.

---

[1] I–II (1909–13).

[2] For the difficult question of how the rabbinic traditional material is to be form-critically divided up, see P. FIEBIG, *Der Erzählungsstil der Evangelien* (1925), IDEM, *Rabbinische Formgeschichte und Geschichtlichkeit Jesu* (1931), M. DIBELIUS, Rabbinische und evangelische Erzählungen, in *Theol. Blätt.* 11 (1932), col. 1 ff., and IDEM, *Die Formgeschichte des Evangeliums* (3rd ed. 1959), pp. 131 ff.

[3] See above, particularly pp. 103 ff. As an example we may mention that R. Ḥama bar Ḥanina gives six different interpretations of Gen. 29.2 in Gen. R. 70.8, and eight interpretations of Ex. 13.17 in Pesiqta 84b. R. Isaac uses one and the same parable in four different ways in p Ber. IX.1—and so on. See also BACHER, *Terminologie* II, p. 214.

A modern critical observer is often led to suspect overinterpretation when he sees how much the Rabbis were able to extract from a traditional text, handed down from the venerable and authoritative fathers; behind the text they were always able to discern the after-glow of Sinai. He often feels himself to be dealing with model examples of a not uncommon error: that of taking the text and asking of it questions which belong to a later epoch, and of reading into the words of the old masters facts and opinions which must have lain far beyond their horizon.

The Rabbis themselves would however be most unwilling to admit that their spiritual interpretation implied that they were reading into the ancient texts ideas which were not there—despite the fact that they were not unacquainted with the concept of "reading in".[1] They were quite sure on one point, that the ancient, sacred and authoritative sayings—of all categories—in fact contained a mass of deep and rich knowledge.[2] All that was required was to draw out the content of these sayings, of carrying out an adequate and a spiritual exegesis. The sayings were therefore subjected to this comprehensive and penetrating examination.

An illustration of their attitude to the transmitted texts is given by the haggadah tradition of what happened to the saying of Antigonos of Soko (Ab. I.3), that one should serve God without a thought of reward.

"Antigonos of Soko had two pupils who studied his sayings (שהיו היו שונין בדבריו) and transmitted them to their pupils (והיו שונין לתלמידים) and their pupils to their pupils. But these (latter) stood up and penetrated into the meaning of the sayings (עמדו ודקדקו אחריהם) and said, 'Why did our fathers say this? Is it possible for workers to work all day without being paid in the evening? If our fathers had believed (known) that there is another world and that there is a resurrection they would not have said this.' (Thus they believed neither in another world nor in a resurrection!) They then stood up and broke with the Torah, and two sects arose from them, the Sadducees and the Boetusians."[3]

The factual contents of this text pose a separate problem,[4] which we

---

[1] Thus e.g. R. Ishmael directs the following critical words against R. Eliezer ben Hyrkanos: "You say to the Scripture: 'Silence, while I interpret!' " (הרי את אומר לכתוב שתוק עד שאדרוש), Sifra ad 13.49, ed. WEISS 68b.

[2] On the idea that the authoritative oral Torah was given by God on Sinai, see above, p. 82, n. 5–6.

[3] Abot de R. Natan I.5, ed. S. SCHECHTER, p. 26.

[4] The Rabbis naturally denied that the Sadducees' disciples had on this occasion interpreted the ancient words of Antigonos correctly.

cannot go into here. We mention this saying only because it gives us what we might term a cross-section of the process of tradition. The rabbinic methods of argument are also shown clearly. They are perfectly aware that pilpulistic examination of the ancient texts produces results which are not immediately evident from the bare wording of the text. But they are none the less convinced that the results of such acute exegesis are actually *drawn* from the sayings. They wish to *reconstruct* and *rediscover* the wisdom of the ancients.[1]

It would scarcely be an over-simplification to say that the typical Rabbi had in general no wish to be creative in his teaching. He wanted to seek out (דרש) what God had already given in the sacred Torah tradition handed down from the fathers; he worked in the desire that God might reveal (גלה) to him what was already there—though more or less hidden—in the words he had taken over. The most common idea was that of reconstructing what the ancients themselves meant.[2] But we also encounter the idea that God allows the favoured Rabbi to rediscover more than the ancients themselves found in their own sayings:[3] a most interesting idea, but one which we cannot stop to consider.

The Rabbis thus held the transmitted texts to be extremely rich in content.[4] And there can be no doubt that to characterize the Rabbis' exegesis of these texts superficially by the word "over-interpretation" is to jump to conclusions. Pilpulistic examination and depth-interpretation is in fact by no means an isolated phenomenon in this milieu. It has to be seen in connection with old Jewish pedagogics as a whole, and it proves to be dependent upon a further important pedagogical phenomenon.

We must at this point give a further reminder of what we have referred to as the "condensing tendency": the effort to reproduce the essence of

[1] Cf. ESCHELBACHER, *Probleme der talmudischen Dialektik*, pp. 53 ff., who is correct in stressing the role played by the category of *renaissance* in rabbinic thought. The new is considered to be rediscovery. See also BACHER, *Tradition*, pp. 41 ff.

[2] Even the words delivered by an astute pupil before his teacher are given on Sinai, p Peah II. 6, p Meg. IV.1, b Meg. 19b, etc. For the way in which lost or forgotten teachings are rediscovered, see e.g. b Suk. 44a, b Shab. 104a, b Tem. 16a, etc. The pilpulist dives into the mighty deeps (in order to bring up pearls) (b Bab. Qam. 91a).

[3] E.g. the haggadah in b Men. 29b on Moses' amazement over what R. Aqiba derives from the Torah. See also Ex. R. 41.6: Moses was given only *kelalim*, their development being left to coming generations.—Cf. 1QpH VII.1 ff., 1QS VIII.15, etc.

[4] Cf. also above, p. 62, n. 7.

teaching in highly concentrated texts and key-words.[1] The teacher's procedure when instructing, and when formulating and passing on tradition might be said to be a reverse image of the procedure for interpretation of the traditional texts. In one case the words are to be filled to the brim; in the other, emptied to the bottom. In one case the teacher's material must be condensed into a few pregnant words, rich in associations; in the other, the meaning of the concentrated statements is to be explained. In one case we see an attempt at extreme synthesis; in the other, a tendency towards extreme analysis. It is not easy to see which of these two currents in pedagogical procedure should be given historical priority.

The fact that such a richness of content is attributed to the sayings which have been handed down in the tradition is therefore not solely due to reverence for the sacred authoritative tradition which came down from the immortal fathers[2]—and for Him who was seen behind the fathers; it is also due to the consciousness that the transmitted texts were intended by their originators to be packed, despite their brevity, with content.

Such general observations must be made before going into the question of how "sayings" became the object of systematic transmission, since this question is extremely complicated.

We can begin with the self-evident fact that no learned rabbinic discussion or procedure has been preserved for history *in its entirety* and that no Jewish Rabbi has had *all* his sayings handed down to posterity. That which remains, that which has become recited "tradition" in the meaning of the word which we have used here, is always a *selection*. The question is, where is this selection made?

The question cannot be answered in general terms. We shall therefore concentrate our attention upon three main possibilities which must always be taken into consideration.

We must first of all take note of the important selection which is made by the teacher himself; at this early stage certain sayings are stressed as being of particular importance. (We use the word "teacher", for the sake of simplicity, to apply to every originator of an authoritative saying which becomes an object of transmission.)

---

[1] Above, Ch. 11 C.

[2] Cf. Philo, *Spec. leg.* I.4.8, and the concepts of *opiniones quas a maioribus accepimus de dis immortalibus* (Cicero, *De nat. deor.* 3.2), GANDZ, *The Dawn of Literature*, RANFT, *Der Ursprung des katholischen Traditionsprinzips*, pp. 179 ff., BIKERMAN, *La chaîne de la tradition pharisienne*, p. 52.

We noticed earlier in our investigation the simple pedagogical technique, consisting of a distinction between text and interpretation, and we have seen how generally this technique was applied in the course of systematic instruction in both the oral and the written Torah. This technique was however not only brought into use in connection with the written or oral texts which were already in existence, but also when an authoritative teacher delivered his own teachings, or when a learned college (בית דין, ישיבה) fixed an item of doctrine.

This is particularly striking in the halakic field. We may call to mind the way in which a halakah statement[1] was formed. When a leading doctrinal authority deals with a halakic question in a doctrinal lecture, or when a learned college discusses such a question at one of its "sessions", a great deal is said illustrative of the different aspects of the question: reasons for and against are produced, relevant Scriptural texts are quoted, and relevant traditions are repeated in the course of the debate.[2] No teacher or pupil treats all the traditional and the new words of wisdom which are offered as being unimportant or unnecessary. But they are all nevertheless excluded when the actual halakic doctrinal statement (a *halakah*, a *horaah*, a *din* etc.) is determined upon, as concisely as possible. The halakic statement is formulated without ornament, without interpretation, without explanation and without motives; it is in this form that it is fixed and memorized.

Thus the formation of the brief halakah statement is perhaps the clearest case of a text being condensed by its originator or in its original situation and set aside as being particularly important and particularly brief in extent but rich in content.

But this does not mean that the pupil or the one participating in the discussion is to remain ignorant of the interpretation, motivation, consideration and use of the statement, thus forgetting everything but the bare halakah rule. A good pupil, his ears open and his mind alert, who had followed his teacher's lessons or had listened to a learned debate during a college session, would keep in mind many of the concentrated and wise traditions and new "sayings" which were brought forward (and repeated) in the course of exposition or discussion. If we may be allowed to use certain rabbinic terms which are usually limited to strictly literary use, we might describe the situation in this way: a good pupil fixes and holds in his memory not only the bare halakah statement, but also

---

[1] On the halakah verse as a form-element, see above, Ch. 7 B.

[2] See the *gemara*.

necessary additions (a sort of *tosefta*), an exposition (a sort of *talmud*), an indication of its relation to Scripture (a sort of *midrash*) and other additional associations, intended to explain and illustrate the statement in question.

It is therefore extremely typical that one and the same tradition is often carried forward in different broad forms: as a *mishnah* verse (*halakah*), as a verse in *tosefta* form, as a text with additional midrashic element—a halakic *midrash*—or as a verse with complementary *gemara* and *talmud*. Sometimes, or perhaps it would be better to say often, this fixing of a doctrinal statement in different broad forms took place at different stages of the process of transmission; at all events, the material has a general tendency to expand. But this ought not to divert our attention from the fact that when the halakic statement was formulated in its shorter form a great deal which had been said, repeated and impressed in the process was only implied, and was not taken explicitly into the brief halakah statement. This had the form of an abridgement, a condensation of a wider explanation or of a more or less extensive discussion. It sometimes had the form of a statement *extracted from* a larger transmitted "saying" of, or story about, an older doctrinal authority.[1] The Rabbis were therefore in principle fully justified in treating the explanation of a transmitted statement given by the teachers as an attempt to reconstruct what had been implicitly incorporated into the statement. They were equally justified in maintaining that more than the bare halakah statement was memorized and transmitted from that situation in which the statement in question was formulated: thus that the oral interpretative tradition goes in principle back to its originator or to the original doctrinal discussion. The fact that they are in practice often guilty of over-interpretation and of making secondary additions does not alter the situation.

In this connection, too, we have come across the fact that concentrated halakic memory-texts of other types were also formulated in this way by the originator, being intended for memorization: a broader form of halakah statement; a concentrated and essential commentary upon it; a summary of a midrashic operation, the purpose of which is to indicate the basis of a doctrinal statement; or a decisive answer to a question—to

---

[1] See C. ALBECK, *Untersuchungen über die Redaktion der Mischna* (1923), pp. 5 f., and M. GUTTMANN's review of the same in *Monatsschr. f. Gesch. u. Wiss. d. Judent.* 69 (1925), pp. 388 ff. Cf. BACHER, *Tradition*, p. 603, and see also below, sec. B.

name only some of the possibilities. We have however dealt with these in an earlier chapter.[1]

A similar situation is to be found in the haggadic field. Here, too, certain sayings are stressed by the teacher himself as being particularly important and rich in content. The teacher did not formulate all his sayings with the same care, nor did he repeat each one four, twenty-four, forty or four hundred times—according to the time it took his pupils to learn them.[2] But this was just what he did with his important key-words, his concise and pregnant words of wisdom.[3]

The same applies to *kelal* verses, which are to be regarded either as the contents or decisive theme of a doctrinal lecture, or part of one; we have earlier had occasion to quote examples.[4] Some parables—though not all—also seem to have fulfilled a similar function: viz. that type of parable which is not limited to one main point but has several main elements, all of which are intended to be used in exposition.[5] (Since the time of A. JÜLICHER,[6] such parables have been known by the somewhat misleading term of allegories.)

Other condensed memory-texts prove by their symmetrical or poetical construction[7] to have been more than chance replies, produced in connection with teaching or preaching. The teacher, whether deliberately or not, was himself concerned, when delivering such well-formulated—and certainly oft-repeated—sayings, to give them a place among the other repeated texts which his pupils had in mind; they were thus from the very first the objects of careful memorization.

In this context we must also take account of a further phenomenon, one which is however extremely difficult to define: the experience of inspiration. In his great work on the psychology of inspiration[8]—un-

---

[1] Above, Ch. 11 B.

[2] Above, *ibid.*

[3] See above, Ch. 11 C–D.

[4] Above, pp. 140 f.

[5] For examples of such parables, see P. FIEBIG, *Altjüdische Gleichnisse und die Gleichnisse Jesu* (1904), pp. 77 ff., and M. HERMANIUK, *La Parabole Evangélique* (1947), pp. 163 ff.

[6] *Die Gleichnisreden Jesu* I (2nd ed. 1899).

[7] In each individual case we must also consider the possibility that stylization and improvement in formulation has taken place during the process of transmission. It is not always possible to assume—as so often happens—that the best constructed and most aesthetically formulated variant of a transmitted saying is the most original.

[8] *Mystikens psykologi. Besatthet och inspiration* (1926), 665 pp.

fortunately available only in Swedish—Tor ANDRÆ produces evidence to prove that those persons who experience religious or artistic inspiration regard the "visions" they "see" or the "words" they are "given" as invaluable. The "words" they "receive" in the moment of inspiration have an enormous subjective value, and are accorded a richer and more important content than the words they themselves formulate by means of conscious intellectual activity.[1] They therefore regard it as particularly essential that these words should be heeded and preserved; they take steps to ensure this, impressing them on the memories of their disciples or writing them down. Typical for the inspired person is a *Drang* to "didactic" or "literary" activity; the *Drang* concentrates particularly on the preservation and passing on of the incomparable treasures he or she has "received".[2]

The unprejudiced historian who studies the rabbinic material cannot in one sweep deny to more than two thousand named pious doctrinal authorities the ability to experience religious or artistic inspiration. On the contrary, we must take into account that at least some teachers—and haggadists in particular—placed special emphasis on certain of their sayings, delivering them with particular care just because they considered them to be particularly "wise" words which they had "received" in moments of inspiration. The critical attitude of the Tannaitic and Amoraic Rabbis to new prophetic revelation and the like[3] ought not to be allowed to obscure this phenomenon. Their scepticism is directed particularly against those revelations which do not agree with the Torah. But on the other hand, that which is revealed, uncovered (נגלה) during the course of work on the Torah is regarded as being from God, words given in principle on Sinai.[4] It is very probable that within this framework certain "sayings" were regarded in a special way as having been "received".

We must thus pay attention, in both the haggadic and halakic disciplines, to the fact that the teacher himself gave a number of pregnant

---

[1] *Op. cit.*, pp. 176 ff. and passim.

[2] *Ibid.*

[3] On this problem, see I. HEINEMANN, Die Kontroverse über das Wunder im Judentum der hellenistischen Zeit, in *Jubilee Volume in Hon. of...* B. HELLER (1941), pp. 170 ff., A. GUTTMANN, The Significance of Miracles for Talmudic Judaism, in *Hebr. Un. Coll. Ann.* 20 (1947), pp. 363 ff., J. W. BOWMAN, Prophets and Prophecy in Talmud and Midrash, in *Evang. Quart.* 22 (1950), pp. 107 ff., 203 ff., 255 ff.

[4] See above, p. 82, n. 5–6. On the way in which new secrets of the Torah were "uncovered" in Qumran, see also above, p. 87 f., and below, pp. 234 ff.

sayings as repetition-texts, which he impressed on his pupils' memories
by means of frequent repetition; furthermore, he gave commentaries,
expositions and explanations. In this way selection took place in the
various forms of the teacher's own instruction.

Secondly, we must take note of the selection which took place through
the teacher's own personal pupils. Here were taken and preserved, not
only those sayings which the teacher's frequent repetition marked out as
being particularly important, but also many of his other sayings, which
also became the objects of repetition, conscious memorization and systematic transmission.

Reverence for the main doctrinal authority, the bearer of the Sinai
tradition[1]—and the ideal of absorbing all his wisdom, paying attention
to all his teaching and carefully preserving his every word—lead quite
naturally to the preservation in the pupils' memories—and in their
notebooks—of many sayings spoken by the teacher on only one occasion:
passages from his doctrinal lectures and his lessons, words spoken in the
course of doctrinal discussion and in everyday intercourse with his pupils
and others—and the like.[2] In these cases it is the pupil who lays hold of
certain sayings from his teacher's mouth and makes them into tradition.
In this way they were—in the pupils' memories—incorporated into that
collection of important *debarim* which was handed down to posterity in
the form of a preserved tradition.

These sayings cannot be said to be intended by the teacher as condensed memory-texts. They are rich in meaning only to the extent that
every pronouncement of a wise, pious and laconic teacher is deep and
rich in content.

One type of traditional passage which is interesting from our point of
view is in a class by itself. The Talmud relates in some cases[3] how an
Amoraic traditionist is asked by the Rabbis whether he has heard a
statement from its stated author expressly, בפירוש, or whether he had
taken it מכללא, i.e. inferred it from the author's basic postulates, his
teachings on similar questions or from his practical conduct or his actions on some definite occasion (see below, pp. 182 ff.).[4] In all these cases

---

[1] On reverence for the teacher, see below, p. 182, n. 5.

[2] Cf. the saying of Rab, b Ab. Zar. 19b, that one should learn even the profane
talk (שיחת חולין) of the *talmide chakamim*!

[3] b Shab. 39b, 40a, b Erub. 46a (par.!), b Yeb. 60b, b Git. 39b.

[4] On this problem, see BACHER, *Terminologie* II, p. 169, and M. GUTTMANN's
review of ALBECK, pp. 388 ff.

the traditionist answers that he has heard the statement in question expressly delivered by the teacher: ‏בפירוש שמיע לי‎ (‏אנא‎). We see from these cases that halakah sayings transmitted in a teacher's name can on an occasion be *formulated* by a pupil/traditionist according to the teacher's own basic postulates or his conduct. The Amoraic Rabbis at all events consider it feasible. This deductive formulation can naturally take place also at a later stage in the process of transmission, as we shall see in due course.[1]

Thirdly, we must take into account the continued selection—or rather the continued *choice* of textual passages—which takes place in later generations of teachers and pupils. Sayings which were not earlier regarded as being particularly important but which belonged on the relatively free, less definitely formulated periphery of the oral Torah may, for various reasons, be later incorporated into the corpus of carefully transmitted texts; this may for example be due to the fact that they have connections with a doctrinal question of halakic, haggadic or midrashic nature which is not brought up for debate until later. If such a question be brought up, and someone quotes a hitherto neglected saying of some ancient doctrinal authority, this saying can come into the systematic process of transmission we have described.

We obtain a lively picture of the way in which this could happen in the many Talmudic descriptions of doctrinal discussions at the "sessions" of the rabbinic colleges. The questions for discussion are illustrated by various speakers, who produce sayings of older authorities (and narrative traditions concerning them). One and the same "saying" may be brought up in different contexts, being relevant to the discussion on more than one point of doctrine. Here we have a typical situation in which a hitherto neglected tradition can suddenly gain great authority because it gives some indication as to how an ancient doctrinal authority would have decided the current question.

Seen from one point of view, every rabbinic doctrinal discussion of a distinct question may be said to be an inventory of what is given, explicitly or implicitly, in Scripture and in the oral tradition. An examination is made to see whether or not the problem has already been decided—and if not, on what traditional lines it must be decided.[2] Occa-

---

[1] Cf. the text-critical note which often appears in the *gemara*: ‏והא דפלוני לאו‎ ‏בפירוש איתמר אלא מכללא איתמר‎ b Ber. 9 a (par.!).

[2] On this, see further below, pp. 254 ff. and 312 f.

sionally another form of inventory is drawn up: for instance, when the editing of a tradition-collection calls for the deliberate gathering in of all the existing traditions concerning one complex of problems[1] or derived from one particular teacher.[2] Here, too, we have the conditions on which hitherto relatively unknown sayings of an older teacher can be drawn into the central nucleus of transmitted texts.

B. *The Narrative Tradition* (מעשים)

When the Amoraic Rabbis worked out the detailed halakah in the course of sessions in the leading Babylonian colleges, they put forward the basic thesis that it is not possible without more ado to extract halakah מפי תלמוד, i.e. from the pronouncements and discussions of the learned, nor מפי מעשה, i.e. from a narrative tradition of a Rabbi's actions or his decisions in individual cases, but only from that which is clearly given as הלכה למעשה, i.e. halakah for practical guidance.[3]

There can be no doubt that this is a sharper and more precise form of the earlier principles upon which halakah was constructed. The earlier Rabbis drew their halakah—evidently with a quite different candour— from a מעשה רב, i.e. from a narrative tradition concerning a teacher.[4] We occasionally find in the Mishnah that a halakah is deduced in this way from a narrative tradition, and we often see a halakah verse and an ancient narrative tradition side by side; one must as a rule suppose that the formulated halakah verse has been derived from the latter.[5]

It is in general a striking fact that narrative traditions in the basic part of the oral Torah are subjected to the same pilpulistic examination and penetrative interpretation as are the sayings-traditions (even when the binding halakah has not been directly derived from them). The Talmud bears eloquent witness to this.

---

[1] As e.g. when the summons was sent out to the great council in Usha, according to Cant. R. 2.5: "They sent to the elders of Galilee and said: Whoever has learned, let him come and teach, and whoever has not learned, let him come and learn." On the way in which older *halakot* were gathered and fixed in Jabneh, see H. KLÜGER, *Über Genesis und Composition der Halachasammlung Edujot* (1895).

[2] See e.g. b Bab. Batr. 87 a; cf. b Ḥul. 110 a.

[3] תנו רבנן אין למדין הלכה לא מפי תלמוד ולא מפי מעשה עד שיאמרו לו הלכה למעשה b Bab. Batr. 130 b(b Nid. 7 b); cf. b Bab. Batr. 83 a (N.B. var. lect.).

[4] On the category מעשה רב, see e.g. b Shab. 21 a, 126 b, b Nid. 65 b; cf. b Bab. Batr. 83 a. — JASTROW, sub voce מעשה, translates incorrectly: "a practical decision is a teacher".

[5] See ALBECK, *Untersuchungen*, pp. 5 f., 102 f. Cf. above, pp. 83 f., and below.

Here, too, we tend to suspect over-interpretation; but we must place the Rabbis' procedure in its correct context.

Disinterested historiography is a late concept in history. In Antiquity, what was narrated concerning the fathers had a practical purpose: that of providing examples to be emulated, warnings, or other definite lessons. Jewish, Hellenistic and Christian traditions in the sources are all *tendentious*, whether edifying or otherwise didactic.[1] Those who formed the narrative traditions of Rabbinic Judaism did so with the basic intention of preserving and spreading, in one way or another, the many-faceted wisdom of the Torah in face of all the situations of life. The inherited custom of the chosen people was regarded as authoritative;[2] consequently its main bearers—the teachers, the wise men, the great doctrinal authorities—were in a class apart. These men did not only bear that part of the oral Torah which was called "custom" (מנהג)[3] and which had a limited normative standing, but also the fixed halakah (הלכה) which rested on the foundations of valid law and order. Furthermore, they had the right—within certain limits—to make authoritative pronouncements, decisions (דינין) on how the Torah was to be observed in various existential situations.[4] The most mature teachers thus incarnated the perfect tradition from the fathers, from Sinai and from God.[5] That is why their words and deeds were of such interest. The pupil

---

[1] Correctly emphasized by BIKERMAN, *La chaîne de la tradition*, pp. 44 ff. Cf. DAUBE, *Precept and Example*, pp. 86 f. M. DIBELIUS' statement, *Formgeschichte*, pp. 10, 12, 28, 241, that the authorities of early Christianity did not formulate the Jesus tradition in order to preserve it for posterity, but merely in order to proclaim the message of salvation, is a false alternative. Early Christianity had its own basic tendency (that of presenting its overwhelming message of Christ, in its various aspects), as had Jewish and Hellenistic teachers. And in all these cases there lay a more or less powerful historical foundation in the authoritative traditional material which was dealt with. Sometimes the worth of these sayings was entirely dependent upon their historicity; cf. below, Ch. 14.

[2] Cf. above, Ch. 6.

[3] See M. GUTTMANN, *Zur Einleitung* II, pp. 74 ff., and A. PERLS, Der Minhag im Talmud, in *Festschrift* I. LEWY (1911), pp. 66 ff.

[4] On the different types of halakah, see GUTTMANN, *op. cit.*

[5] Concerning the authoritative position of the teacher, which is presented in rabbinic literature on innumerable occasions and in innumerable ways, see e.g. M Bab. Mes. II.11, M Ker. VI.9, T Bab. Mes. II.29, Ab. IV.12, Mekilta ad 17.9, 18.12 (ed. LAUTERBACH II, pp. 140 and 177 f. respectively), Sifre Deut. ad 6.9 and passim. For a wider religio-historical judgement, see L. DÜRR, Heilige Vaterschaft im antiken Orient, in *Heilige Überlieferung* (1938), pp. 1 ff., and A. J. FESTUGIÈRE, *La révélation d'Hermès Trismégiste* I (1944), pp. 332 ff. (with older literature). For a

had to absorb all the traditional wisdom with "eyes, ears and every member" by seeking the company of a Rabbi, by serving him (שימש), following him and imitating him (הלך אחרי), and not only by listening to him. The task of the pupil is therefore not only to hear (שמע) but also to see (ראה). The pupil is a witness (עד) to his teacher's words; he is a witness to his actions as well.[1] He does not only say, "I heard from my teacher ..." (שמעתי מרבי פלוני וגו'),[2] but also, "I saw my teacher do this or that ..." (ראיתי את רבי פלוני וגו').[3]

This terminology has as a rule a distinctly legal character. The pupil/traditionist tells what he has seen and heard.[4] The "eyewitness" character of certain sayings is occasionally directly stressed with terms as עד, עדות, העיד.[5] So for example in Jabneh, when the halakah is fixed after various traditionists have come forward as witnesses (עדים) and borne witness to (העיד) the way in which the older halakah functioned or how it was worded.[6] Many of these accentuated eyewitness accounts (עדיות) are collected in the early Mishnah tractate Eduyot.[7] The value of such sayings—for the Rabbis—is entirely dependent upon their historicity.[8]

---

comparison between the Rabbis' conception of the relationship between the laws and their bearers and the corresponding Hellenistic phenomena, see further the works mentioned above, p. 21, n. 4., and DAUBE, *Precept and Example*, pp. 86 ff. On Philo's somewhat Hellenistic ideas on this point, see particularly H. A. WOLFSON, *Philo* I–II (2nd ed. 1948), II, pp. 180 f.; cf. *ibid.* I, pp. 188 ff.

[1] On the problem which arose when a revered teacher did not live as he taught, see e.g. b Ḥag. 15ab.

[2] E.g. M Erub. II.6; M Orlah II.5.

[3] E.g. b Ber. 24ab, 38b, cf. *ibid.* 39b. — Cf. the typical conception expressed in Dio Chrysost., *Orat.* LV, *De Hom. et Socr.* (ed. G. DE BUDÉ II, 1919, p. 148): Socrates was a pupil of Homer because he was an imitator of his works and words, μιμούμενος τὰ ἔργα καὶ τοὺς λόγους [αὐτοῦ]. See also the context. Cf. K. H. RENGS-TORF, μανϑάνω κτλ., in *Theol. Wörterb.*, ed. G. KITTEL, IV (1942), pp. 393 ff., 418 ff.

[4] On the legal principle that only the eyewitness can validly give evidence, see e.g. T Nid. I.5; cf. b Nid. 7b (bar.), p Nid. I.3.

[5] BACHER, *Tradition*, pp. 15 ff.

[6] See KLÜGER, *Über Genesis und Composition der Halachasammlung Edujot.*

[7] Sayings of this accentuated witness-character in the two *Talmudim*, but outside the tractate Ed., are collected in KLÜGER, *op. cit.*, pp. 112 ff.

[8] R. BULTMANN, operating with the same alternative as DIBELIUS (see p. 182, n. 1), writes, referring to *die Rabbinengeschichten*: "Sie wollen ihrer Bedeutung nach, die sie für die Diskussion haben, gar keine historischen Berichte sein, sondern Illustrationen eines Satzes. Gleichwohl können sie historische Elemente enthalten, nicht nur, indem sie die historische Sphäre wirklicher Diskussionen richtig wider-

The pupil is a witness of the words and actions of his teacher, and when a question is brought up during a college session, the various teachers and pupils who participate in the discussion are able to illustrate the question by repeating or applying a narrative tradition concerning the procedure of an earlier teacher, in order to actualize with this *maaseh* the way in which such a doctrinal authority would have settled the question.

We quote a number of random examples.

In M Suk. III.9 the question is asked: "At what point should they wave the *lulab*?" Rules are produced from the schools of Shammai and Hillel, after which these words follow: "R. Aqiba said, I was once in attendance upon Rabban Gamaliel and R. Joshua (צופה הייתי ברבן וגו') and while all the people waved their *lulabin,* they shook them only at the words, 'Save now, we beseech thee, O Lord' (Ps. 118.25)."

In b Ber. 24a we hear how R. Ḥanina says, in a discussion of the question as to whether it is lawful to hang up *tefillin* (in the closet): "I saw Rabbi (אני ראיתי וגו') hang up his *tefillin*."

In b Ber. 38b R. Ḥiyya bar Abba answers a question on the benedictions in these words: "I saw R. Joḥanan (אני ראיתי וגו') eat a salted olive, reading a benediction both before and after ..."

We ought perhaps to point out that it is not normal to say *explicitly* that one saw. As a rule this element is omitted, and the actual happening alone is narrated; the narrative is often introduced by some set formula: פעם, כבר, אחת, מעשה.

To quote a further random example: in M Suk. II.5 we have these words, answering the question of whether one might eat outside the booth (*sukkah*) during the Feast of Tabernacles:

"Once when they brought cooked food to Rabban Joḥanan ben Zakkai to taste and two dates and a pail of water to Rabban Gamaliel, they said, 'Bring them up to the booth'."

In this way the alert pupil by studying his teacher's behaviour can learn his wisdom, even on those points on which he does not give verbal

spiegeln, sondern auch, indem sie Erinnerungen an wirkliche Begebenheiten bewahren", *Die Geschichte der synoptischen Tradition* (4th ed. 1958), p. 52. This may be correct when it is a matter of certain imaginative haggadic narratives, e.g. about the O. T. Patriarchs, but when dealing with rabbinic narratives of the kind we have been considering in this chapter, his judgement is in direct conflict with the actual facts of the case. BULTMANN, *ibid.*, says, about the way in which Jesus in Mark 10.2–9 contraposes two Scripture passages: "bei den Rabbinen ist das m. W. unerhört". This is a misunderstanding.

instruction. The paths of the Torah are also taught in this way—the way of *imitatio magistri*. The rabbinic tradition preserves examples of pupils (e.g. the young Aqiba) who followed the conduct of their teachers in the most private situations, giving as their motive, "This has to do with the Torah and I must learn" (תורה היא וללמוד אני צריך).[1]

There is however no reason to stop at the *pupils'* attitude in this context; the *teachers*, too, knew that the Torah is learned by imitation. They were conscious of their position as authorities, conscious that their lives provided visible instruction. It would seem, incidentally, that this is one of the most ancient of all pedagogical principles.[2]

Teachers wished to instruct not only in word, but also in deed. Phenomena which would be worthy of close attention are what we might term the Rabbis' *didactic symbolical actions*:[3] these concrete, visible measures whereby they capture the attention of their pupils,[4] after which they either explain what they have done or leave it to the pupils to work it out for themselves.

As an example we may quote a tradition preserved in b Shab. 31 a (and in more detail in Abot de R. Natan I,15). A Gentile who was not willing to believe in the oral Torah was being instructed by Hillel in the written Torah. On the first day Hillel repeated to him the Hebrew alphabet in its correct order; on the following day he repeated it backwards. The Gentile wondered what this all meant, and so Hillel interpreted his didactic symbolic action. He had wanted to point out and stress that

[1] b Ber. 62a (bar.). For some other examples, see BILLERBECK, *Comm.* I, pp. 528 ff.

[2] See GANDZ, *The Dawn of Literature*, pp. 271 f. Cf. the reflections of G. TARDE, *Les lois de l'imitation* (2nd ed. 1895), which are still worthy of consideration. For a modern examination of the psychology of imitation, see N. E. MILLER and J. DOLLARD, *Social Learning and Imitation* (4th print. 1948).

[3] These can however be distinguished from the so-called prophetic symbolic actions only roughly. On the latter, see G. FOHRER, *Die symbolischen Handlungen der Propheten* (1953), and IDEM, Die Gattung der Berichte über symbolische Handlungen der Propheten, in *Zeitschr. f. d. Alttest. Wiss.* 64 (1952), pp. 101 ff. Cf. also G. STÄHLIN, Die Gleichnishandlungen Jesu, in *Kosmos und Ekklesia* (1953), pp. 7 ff. In the work of Jesus we find both prophetic (or more correctly: messianic) and didactic symbolic actions. The latter type is represented e.g. by Mark 9.36 f., the former by Mark 11.12 ff. (with par.) and, from one point of view, by all Jesus' miracles. The boundaries are—as we have said—flexible.

[4] Cf. b Men. 43b: "Seeing leads to thinking" (ראיה מביאה לידי זכירה), referring to the function of *zizit*.

confidence in the written Torah rested on the same basis as confidence in the oral Torah: the acceptance of tradition, represented by the teacher.

But it is not only the conscious didactic symbolic actions which go to make up the Torah's visual teaching. *There is no distinct boundary between these deliberate pedagogical measures and the teacher's way of life as a whole.* We shall take a number of examples to illustrate the conscious effort made by the teacher to conduct his life with respect to his pupils' imitation and their interpretation of their teacher's actions.

In T Ber. I.1 (with par.) there is related a *maaseh* about the actions of the Hillelite Eleazar ben Azariah one day when it was time for the *Shema* to be read. According to the school of Shammai the *Shema* must be read lying down;[1] the school of Hillel leaves the choice of position free. Eleazar happened to be lying down at the time, and as a Hillelite he had every right to read the *Shema* in this position. He nevertheless stood up and read standing. In the Tosefta[2] his course of action was motivated— and rightly so—by the traditional sentence: שלא יראו התלמידים ויעשו קבע כדבריך ("Lest the pupils should see it and establish a fixed halakah after your words"—or in this case "after your actions").[3]

Another very illustrative tradition is to be found in T Dem. V.24 which tells a *maaseh* concerning a visit of R. Aqiba to a Samaritan village. When vegetables were placed before him, he first set aside a tenth, and then ate. Rabban Gamaliel, who was with him, reprimanded him for this, since he had acted against the general rule (דברי חביריך). R. Aqiba thereupon answered that he had only set aside a tenth on his own account, and had not declared this to be a halakah in Israel; Rabban Gamaliel then drew his attention to the fact of his setting aside a tenth here constituted a halakah in this place.[4] (Here there is no learned majority to show, on a basis of their differently orientated practice, that R. Aqiba was acting only on his own account when he deliberately applied this stricter halakic practice.)[5]

---

[1] A hyper-literal interpretation of Deut. 6.7.

[2] T Ber. I.6; cf. b Ber. 11a and p Ber. I.6.

[3] This statement is a traditional sentence (cf. par.) referring not only to a teacher's actions, but also to his words. דבר denotes also elsewhere (cf. Biblical Hebrew) an action or the account of an action, e.g. M Shab. XXIV.5.

[4] תדע שבקעתה הלכה בישראל שעישרתה ירק שלך.

[5] On the possibility of a Rabbi voluntarily adopting a personal code which was stricter than the valid halakah, see e.g. b Ber. 22a and p Erub. IV.1. Cf. M. GUTT-MANN, *Zur Einleitung* II, pp. 78 f., 92. Cf. also Paul's argument in 1 Cor. 9.14 f., below, pp. 317 ff.

In b Erub. 93b, 94a there is a *maaseh* which tells how a dividing wall between two houses collapsed on the Sabbath. R. Samuel, in whose "area"[1] this happened, commanded it to be replaced by a stretched cloth, whereupon Rab turned away his head. Rab was in fact a guest of R. Samuel and was therefore compelled by custom to respect his "legislative" authority in that place. But his pupils (and others) could on the other hand gain the impression on such an occasion as this that he also allowed the above-mentioned work to be carried out on the Sabbath. He therefore turned away his head to avoid giving rise to a wrong interpretation of his tactful silence.

Such examples, which are far from being outstanding, show that the teacher was, and had to be, conscious of his actions. His behaviour is taken as an example, as teaching. The teacher knows that his pupils will deduce his halakic opinions from his conduct; the conclusions which they draw must be the correct ones. He must therefore be prepared to behave in such a way as to help his pupils to interpret his conduct correctly.

It therefore does not conflict in principle with the intentions of the old doctrinal authorities when their actions are taken as paradigms in the colleges, as manifestations of insight into the Torah and of the "legislative" authority they bear within themselves—which they in their turn have taken from the fathers, from Sinai and from God. It is not without reason that the later teachers deduce teachings from their practice; what is important is that these deductions should be correct. And the Rabbis were well aware of this fact.[2]

Critical scholarship must therefore ask in every individual case whether later Rabbis have over-interpreted a narrative tradition or not. It is impossible to answer the question by means of a generalization.

We have now considered some important factors which must be taken into consideration when asking how the narrative tradition originated. (In this context we must ignore narrative traditions of the imaginative, legendary haggadah type; we are concerned only with narrative traditions about a teacher's actions and events drawn from his life.)[3]

[1] On the areas within which the different Rabbis and rabbinic colleges had "legislative" authority, see GUTTMANN, *op. cit.* II, pp. 55 ff.

[2] Apart from the examples just mentioned, we may refer to some others; see e.g. b Meg. 28b, b Shab. 21a, b Bab. Batr. 130b.

[3] DIBELIUS, *Formgeschichte*, pp. 131 ff., describes a number of different types of rabbinic stories, but his principles of division and selection differ from ours. Cf. also BULTMANN, *Geschichte*, pp. 42 ff., 181, 247 ff.

The teachers, conscious that their lives provided a form of visual teaching, were thus from one point of view themselves the prime movers of all narrative tradition concerning themselves. The question however remains: When were such traditions *formulated*?

Here, too, we must consider the various possibilities. First and foremost there is the possibility that a teacher was personally responsible for formulating the traditions concerning himself, viz. in those cases where he made his conduct or behaviour an object of interpretation or the basis of teaching; or when he illustrated, by means of such a narrative, his own attitude to some question. Such cases would however seem to be few in number.

The other main possibility is that a narrative tradition is formulated within the pupils' circle. When a teacher acts in a conspicuous manner it must be reckoned that the entire circle would observe it; but when it is a matter of everyday events it is more due to the observation and interest of the individual that the event in question is noticed. Such a tradition would not seem to have been *formulated* by the witness until later, in connection with jurisdiction, doctrinal discussion, teaching or preaching, i.e. when the teacher's conduct can be used to illustrate a posed question, as was the case in the examples we have just quoted.[1] If it concerns the conduct of some great doctrinal authority or has to do with important matters, the narrative can thereupon be incorporated in its traditional stylized form into the oral texts which are memorized and repeated in the way we have described.

A special case arises if the narrative tradition is not only memorized as a complementary teaching, but is taken up into the authoritative text-collection which happens to be in the course of redaction at that time: as happened for instance when eyewitness accounts were incorporated into the Mishnah at the time of its first redaction,[2] or when the *debarim* and *maasim* were taken into the text of the finally-redacted commentary on the Mishnah (*Gemara*).[3]

---

[1] A typical case is found in b Ber. 24 a. In the course of an Amoraic discussion on whether or not *tefillin* might be laid beneath the pillow in the bed of a married couple, the practice of various Rabbis is quoted. R. Hamnuna says: "I once stood before (i.e. was a pupil of) Raba, and he said to me: 'Go and bring me my *tefillin*.' I found them between the bolster and the pillow, not under his head, and I knew that it was a bath day (in connection with sexual intercourse). He had done this in order to teach us a halakah for practical guidance."

[2] E.g. the material in M Ed., see above, p. 183.

[3] See above, p. 118, n. 5.

Finally it is quite natural for a narrative from the relatively free periphery of the oral Torah to be accorded more interest at a later date, and be made the object of systematic transmission; this can be due to the problem with which it deals being first drawn into deliberate halakic discussion at a later stage in the transmission process, or to a desire to legitimate altered halakic practice by producing the practice of an earlier doctrinal authority by way of a precedent. It is well known that halakah was never entirely uniform in Talmudic times in different areas within Judaism;[1] in addition it was to some extent variable.[2]

It goes without saying that there are many possible variations within these three areas, and that the origin of each separate narrative tradition must be judged on its own merits. Here we have merely aimed at bringing forward a number of observations and reflections on the problem as a whole.

Another extremely interesting question concerns the way in which authoritative oral material for one reason or another occasionally comes to *lose* its authoritative position and disappears, depreciates or is retained only after correction. From one point of view this process is the direct opposite of that with which we have been dealing, but we are unable to go into the question here.

---

[1] On this subject, see M. GUTTMANN, *Zur Einleitung* II, pp. 55 ff.

[2] *Ibid.*, pp. 74 ff., 82 ff.

PART TWO

The Delivery of the Gospel Tradition
in Early Christianity

Introductory Remarks

A FAMILIAR ELEMENT in the reasoning of the Church Fathers is the appeal
to the undistorted tradition from the Apostles (Christ). It has often
been said that we are here dealing with a Jewish heritage, or with the
result of incidental Jewish influence. This may be so. But the question
is not solved so easily. During the centuries around the beginning of the
Christian era it was not only among the Jews that the appeal to tradition
was made. This also took place in various groups in the Hellenistic
world: in the mystery religions and similar currents, in schools for
philosophers, rhetoricians, lawyers, and even doctors![1]

The technique of transmission in these groups would be worth in-
vestigating.[2] However, we shall here concentrate on the young Church,
asking how its members transmitted the tradition from, and about,
Christ, i.e. the gospel tradition. We shall pay special attention to the
evidence of the early Fathers, of the author of the Acts of the Apostles
and, finally, of Paul. Our investigation will terminate at this point;
in a final chapter we shall sketch the outlines which have already begun
to appear.

During the course of the investigation it has proved to be the case
that we cannot use the same clear-cut formulation of the problem in
this part as that we employed in Part One. The question of the technique
of transmission must be placed in a wider context. In the following,
we shall therefore also consider some other aspects of the complicated
question of tradition, without however losing sight of our main problem.

---

[1] Pointed out by E. BIKERMAN, La chaîne de la tradition pharisienne, in *Rev.
Bibl.* 59 (1952), pp. 44 ff. Cf. T. W. MANSON, *The Servant-Messiah* (1953), pp. 2 f.

[2] For the transmission in the various schools, cf. the references in BIKERMAN,
op. cit., *ibid.*, MANSON, *op. cit.*, *ibid.*, and the works, mentioned above, pp. 124 ff.
For a comparison with the technique of transmission in the schools of philosophy
and in the mystery religions, cf. P. BOYANCÉ, *Le culte des Muses chez les philosophes grecs* (1937), partic. pp. 48 ff., and the works, mentioned above, p. 158, n. 4.
For the transmission among the new-Pythagoreans, see F. BOEHM, *De symbolis
Pythagoreis* (1905), and A. DELATTE, *Études sur la littérature Pythagoricienne*
(1915), pp. 271 ff. — Very comprehensive is J. RANFT, *Der Ursprung des katholischen
Traditionsprinzips* (1931); cf. also A. DENEFFE, *Der Traditionsbegriff* (1931).

CHAPTER 13

The Testimony of the Post-Apostolic Church

THERE EXISTED in the early Church a *traditional* conception of the origin of the Gospels. This conception was expressed in certain passages in Papias and Irenaeus, and in the anti-Marcionite gospel prologues; it was thus well able to influence the views of the later Church Fathers. It is therefore not surprising that the items of information given in the early Church's statements on the origins of the Gospels—which have been so carefully investigated and quoted—agree to such an extent.

To simplify somewhat, we may say that for the authors of the early Church, the question of how the Gospels originated is part of the greater question of the authenticity and reliability of the Christian tradition. The evidence agrees on this point. There is general agreement that all four Gospels derive from well known, reliable traditionists who stand at one or two removes from Jesus Christ. It is either a question of the Master's own disciples (Matthew, John) or the Apostles' disciples (Mark, Luke).

The traditionist categories are unmistakeable: they concern someone who has been a personal disciple (μαθητής, cf. also "interpreter", ἑρμηνευτής); someone who followed as a disciple (ἀκολουθεῖν, παρακολουθεῖν; cf. ἀκόλουθος) his master and personally heard (ἀκούειν; cf. ἀκουστής) him, and was therefore guaranteed to be familiar with his proclamation and teaching (εὐαγγέλιον, διδασκαλία, λόγοι; κηρύσσειν, λέγειν etc.). Emphasis is occasionally placed on the fact that the person in question was an eyewitness (αὐτόπτης) or that he bears witness (μαρτυρεῖν) to what he has heard.[1]

It is natural that the early Church authors found it difficult to assign the Gospels to a definite literary category (*Gattung*). We are still aware of that difficulty today.[2] But it is not difficult to see from whence they

---

[1] The well known passages are conveniently brought together in E. PREUSCHEN, *Antilegomena* (2nd ed. 1905), pp. 91 ff., A. HUCK, H. LIETZMANN, *Synopse der drei ersten Evangelien* (9th ed. 1936), pp. vii ff., D. J. THERON, *Evidence of Tradition* (1957), pp. 24 ff., 40 ff.

[2] See K. L. SCHMIDT, Die Stellung der Evangelien in der allgemeinen Literaturgeschichte, in ΕΥΧΑΡΙΣΤΗΡΙΟΝ, *Studien ... H.* GUNKEL *... dargebracht* (1923),

derived the categories which they use when describing the Gospels.
We shall return in due course to the question of the Gospels and the
category of "Holy Scriptures"; for the moment, however, we are most
interested in the formal *Gattung* to which the Gospels were assigned. The
nearest of such categories proves to be the ὑπομνήματα notes which
occurred in the school tradition.[1] Eusebius speaks, in connection with the
traditional view, of τῶν τοῦ κυρίου διατριβῶν ὑπομνήματα which were first
copied down by Matthew and John in an emergency.[2] The other references describe the way in which the evangelists copied down and/or
edited their work on the basis of material which had long been in use in
the work of preaching and teaching, and which had therefore been
memorized or—one might suppose—existed in private notebooks.[3]
When Justin characterizes the Gospels as the Apostles' ἀπομνημονεύματα,
he is using a literary category which is well known to his readers;[4] but
typically enough, that which might be said to stand closest to the private
notes of the school tradition.[5]

Concerning Mark, Papias[6] says that he copied down carefully what
he remembered of Peter's teaching (ὅσα ἐμνημόνευσεν, ἀκριβῶς ἔγραψεν).
This is not a complete edition, but a selection (ἔνια γράψας ὡς ἀπεμνη-
μόνευσεν).[7] There is no question of this being a well-edited edition, but
a collection of memorized material of *loci* character (οὐ μέντοι τάξει).[8]
Irenaeus uses the expression: τὰ ὑπὸ Πέτρου κηρυσσόμενα ἐγγράφως
ἡμῖν παραδέδωκεν,[9] while Clement of Alexandria says that Peter's hearers exhorted Mark, as one who had long been a follower of Peter and

---

pp. 51 ff., and H. RIESENFELD, The Gospel Tradition and its Beginnings, in *Texte
u. Unters.* 73 (1959), pp. 43 ff. (in the separate ed., 1957, pp. 1 ff.).

[1] See above, pp. 158 ff.

[2] *Hist. Eccl.* III. 24.

[3] Cf. below, pp. 201 f.

[4] See SCHMIDT, *op. cit.*, pp. 55 ff.

[5] SCHMIDT has not seen this, and his judgement is therefore unbalanced in the
work mentioned.

[6] In Eus., *Hist. Eccl.* III.39. — J. KÜRZINGER, Das Papiaszeugnis und die Erstgestalt des Matthäusevangeliums, in *Bibl. Zeitschr.* N.F. 4 (1960), pp. 19 ff., is
justified in his basic thesis, that the terminology of this passage must be seen in the
light of the language of the rhetor schools.

[7] Cf. T. Y. MULLINS, Papias on Mark's Gospel, in *Vig. Christ.* 14 (1960), pp. 219 ff.

[8] For the terminology, see KÜRZINGER, *op. cit.*, pp. 30 ff. The phrase ὃς πρὸς
τὰς χρείας ἐποιεῖτο τὰς διδασκαλίας is translated by KÜRZINGER: "Dieser machte
seine Unterweisungen nach Art der Chreiai".

[9] *Adv. Haer.* III.1, in Eus., *Hist. Eccl.* V.8 (MPG XX, 449).

had memorized his teaching, to write down what Peter had said (ὡς ἄν ἀκολουθήσαντα αὐτῷ πόρρωθεν καὶ μεμνημένον τῶν λεχθέντων, ἀναγράψαι τὰ εἰρημένα).[1] Clement also has something to say on Peter's attitude to his disciple's measures. Here we see in sharp outline the way in which the Alexandrian's thoughts worked. We know from Hellenism how the pupils of a philosopher or a rhetor occasionally published written works, consisting of *hypomnemata*: material which they had memorized or had copied into their notebooks from their teacher's lessons. Such measures did not always win the approval of the teacher, and he sometimes went so far as to produce a revised edition or simply a new version of the work in question.[2] It is this which impels Clement to state—in two different contexts[3]—what was Peter's attitude to his pupil's action.

Luke's Gospel, which from the literary point of view has more of the character of a publication, ἔκδοσις (see the prologue!), is none the less said by Irenaeus to be a definitive written version of the gospel proclaimed by Paul (τὸ ὑπ' ἐκείνου [sc. Παύλου] κηρυσσόμενον εὐαγγέλιον ἐν βίβλῳ κατέθετο).[4]

Matthew is said, after a long period of teaching, to have assembled and edited the holy words "in the Hebrew manner of delivery" ('Εβραΐδι διαλέκτῳ τὰ λόγια συνετάξατο).[5] And John, who is said constantly to have made use of the method of oral proclamation,[6] published his spiritual Gospel at the end of his life, at the request of his friends.[7]

In these items of information we find time and time again that the writing down of the Gospels was really an emergency measure adopted for various reasons.[8] This is by no means—as later theologians have so

[1] *Hypot.*, in Eus., *Hist. Eccl.* VI.14 (MPG XX, 552).

[2] Quint., *Instit. orat.* 1, praef. 7–8, Arrianos, *Epict.*, *Diatrib.*, praef. 7–8, Galenos, *De libris propriis*, praef. See to the matter H. VON ARNIM, *Leben und Werke des Dio von Prusa* (1898), pp. 175 ff., and S. LIEBERMAN, *Hellenism in Jewish Palestine* (1950), pp. 87 ff.

[3] Eus., *Hist. Eccl.* II.15, VI.14.

[4] *Adv. Haer.* III.1.1, in Eus., *Hist. Eccl.* V.8.

[5] Papias, in Eus., *Hist. Eccl.* III.39. KÜRZINGER, *Das Papiaszeugnis*, pp. 32 ff., points out that in the language of the rhetor schools, διάλεκτος often means "form of style and delivery".

[6] Eus., *Hist. Eccl.* III.24.

[7] *Ibid.* VI.14; cf. III.24 and Canon Muratori, lines 9 ff.

[8] E.g. Eus., *Hist. Eccl.* III.24, III.39, VI.14, Clem. Alex., *Strom.* I.9.1 f., 14.4. — Cf. E. F. OSBORN, Teaching and Writing in the First Chapter of the Stromateis of Clement of Alexandria, in *Journ. of Theol. Stud.* N.S. 10 (1959), pp. 335 ff.

often maintained—due to any ideas concerning the unique character
of the gospel, but is a commonplace which we recognize from elsewhere
in Antiquity: an attitude of scepticism to the written word. The idea is
stressed—not least in the school tradition—that what can be learned
from the written page cannot be compared with that which may be
learned from the lips of a living person. The consummate knowledge is
to be found in oral teaching, in which the pupil receives not only texts,
but also interpretation.[1]

The verbs μιμνήσκεσθαι and μνημονεύειν, with their compounds,
play an interesting role, both in the passages we have mentioned and
elsewhere in the oldest Christian literature.[2] Certainly it would be a
rewarding task to examine all these passages in the light of linguistic
practice and educational technique, particularly in the Hellenistic rhetor
tradition.

These early Church passages on gospel origins harmonize well with
their authors' way of *using* the gospel material. We limit ourselves
here to the post-apostolic age up to the middle of the 2nd century. The
way in which the Apostolic Fathers used the gospel material gives us a
somewhat confusing picture;[3] it is, however, far from being incomprehensible.

There are many difficulties. These appear first and foremost when we
examine the formulae of quotation. On a couple of occasions, sayings of
Jesus are produced as Scripture quotations (ὡς γέγραπται, ἑτέρα δὲ
γραφὴ λέγει)[4] but in these cases, special circumstances may have had
their effect;[5] in any case, they are exceptional. For the most part, use
is made of quotation formulae such as: λέγει ὁ κύριος, εἶπεν ὁ κύριος,

---

[1] See above, p. 157.

[2] Cf. O. MICHEL, μιμνήσκομαι κτλ., in *Theol. Wörterb.*, ed. KITTEL, IV (1942),
pp. 678 ff., N. A. DAHL, Anamnesis, in *Studia Theol.* 1 (1947), pp. 69 ff. — R.
HEARD, The Ἀπομνημονεύματα in Papias, Justin and Irenaeus, in *New Test. Stud.*
1 (1954–55), pp. 122 ff., too sharply isolates the phraseology of the early Church
passages from the language of the contemporary milieu.

[3] On this topic, see the most recent works, É. MASSAUX, *Influence de l'Évangile
de saint Matthieu sur la littérature chrétienne avant saint Irénée* (1950), L. E. WRIGHT,
Alterations of the Words of Jesus as Quoted in the Literature of the Second Century
(1952), and H. KÖSTER, *Synoptische Überlieferung bei den apostolischen Vätern*
(1957). Cf. also O. ANDRÉN, *Rättfärdighet och frid* (1960), pp. 81 ff.

[4] Barn. 4.14, 2 Clem. 2.4.

[5] See the discussion in KÖSTER, *op. cit.*, pp. 125 ff., 70 ff.

ἐκέλευσεν ὁ κύριος.[1] These formulae do not reveal without more ado
whether the quotation in question is taken from a written or an oral
tradition. In fact, the Apostolic Fathers can use the same formulae
when introducing quotations from the written O.T.: εἶπεν ὁ θεός, φησὶν
ὁ θεός, φησὶν ὁ ἐκλεκτὸς Δαυίδ.[2]

Further difficulty arises when we examine the source references. Τὸ
εὐαγγέλιον is an ambiguous word. When we read: ὡς ἐκέλευσεν ὁ κύριος
ἐν τῷ εὐαγγελίῳ αὐτοῦ, λέγει ὁ κύριος ἐν τῷ εὐαγγελίῳ, ὡς ἔχετε ἐν τῷ
εὐαγγελίῳ[3] etc., it is impossible from the source reference to tell with
any degree of certainty whether the author is thinking about a written
or an oral gospel. An additional fact in connection with this problem
is that a book or a literary product was often referred to by the name
of its originator. The writings of the prophets can be called οἱ προφῆται;
the Book of Isaiah may be known as (ὁ) Ἡσαΐας and—by analogy—
the Apostles' writings may be called οἱ ἀπόστολοι and "the words of
the Lord" simply ὁ κύριος.[4]

A final difficulty is found when examining the wording of the so-
called quotations. Here there is no question of direct quotations in the
strict meaning of the word, but of sayings of Jesus, reproduced freely
or adapted in some way to the context. In no case can we say that the
author intends directly to *transmit* a saying of Jesus; in each case he
uses sayings of Jesus—if we may apply the distinction which we drew
previously. We must therefore be extremely careful when attempting
to draw conclusions from sayings of Jesus used in this way, as to which
version of the text the author knew, or the extent to which the gospel
tradition was fixed at this time.[5] A fact worth our consideration is that
the Apostolic Fathers also use the N. T. Epistles freely,[6] although
on this occasion there is no question of the text being "fluid". Even
when using short quotations from the O.T. they adapt—though not to
any great extent. Only in long O.T. quotations does careful reproduction

---

[1] 2 Clem. 5.2, 4.5, Did. 8.2 and elsewhere.

[2] 1 Clem. 10.4, 33.5, 52.2 and elsewhere.

[3] Did. 8.2, 2 Clem. 8.5, Did. 15.3; cf. Did. 11.3, 15.4, Ign. Smyrn. 5.1, 7.2, Phil.
5.1, 8.2, 9.2.

[4] Cf. e.g. Hegesippus (in Eus., *Hist. Eccl.* IV.22): ὡς ὁ νόμος κηρύσσει καὶ οἱ
προφῆται καὶ ὁ κύριος.

[5] Köster's book is full of premature conclusions drawn from the quotations
adapted in the texts.

[6] Cf. the material in *The N.T. in the Apostolic Fathers*, by a Committee of the
Oxford Society of Historical Theology (1905).

or faithful repetition from memory become natural. The reasons for this are easily explained.

The problem of the Apostolic Fathers' attitude to the gospel material is thus not easily solved. So much seems however to be perfectly clear, that the gospel (τὸ εὐαγγέλιον) was not at this time regarded as being *written* in the same way as the O.T. word of God.

This cannot be explained by some idea such as that Christ and his Word might have been regarded as being less authoritative than the O.T. The absolute divine authority of Christ according to the Apostolic Fathers is too well known for there to be any need to consider such a question.

Nor is the explanation to be found in the idea that the nature of the gospel was a preached kerygma which was unable to stand the process of fixing and writing down. As we have just pointed out, the scepticism of the authors of the early Church toward the written word is a commonplace, recurring elsewhere in ancient school traditions.[1]

At all events, we have here touched upon the explanation. We must first of all be quite clear as to what a *book* was, strictly speaking, in Antiquity. A book had to be published (ἐκδίδοσθαι) and spread on the open market. Notes taken in a limited circle were not normally called συγγράμματα.[2]

Furthermore, we must reckon with another fact when dealing with written versions of living tradition. Such versions find it difficult, in those circles within which the tradition lives on, to compete with the tradition itself. It appears unnatural to regard living traditional material as something written, simply because written versions have come into being. It is an illuminating fact that quotations from the school tradition and the like are not introduced by such words as γέγραπται. We may recall the way in which Philo quotes the school tradition.[3]

We must also consider what it is that characterizes the category "Holy Scriptures" (ἱεραὶ γραφαί). To their nature normally belongs the

---

[1] Above, p. 197.

[2] L. KOEP, Buch I, in *Reallex. f. Ant. u. Christ.* II (1954), col. 676 f., V. BURR, Editionstechnik, *ibid.* IV (1959), col. 597 ff., and above, p. 162, n. 3. Cf. KOEP, *op. cit.*, col. 679 ff., on writing material and the like mentioned in the N.T. and in the early Church texts.

[3] See W. BOUSSET, *Jüdisch-Christlicher Schulbetrieb in Alexandria und Rom* (1915), pp. 43 ff. (which underestimates the role of memorization and places too much emphasis on written notes); cf. A. J. FESTUGIÈRE, *La révélation d'Hermès Trismégiste* II (1949), pp. 521 ff.

fact either that their real or supposed origin is lost in the mists of Antiquity, with the immortal Fathers who stood close to the heavenly world; or that they were expressly claimed to be divine books, revealed to, passed on to, or copied by, some gifted person; or that they were God-given Scriptures, written as a result of divine inspiration or to divine dictation.[1] The fact that no evangelist expressly presented his work in this way was certainly a contributory factor to the unequal position which the Gospels occupied from the first in relation to the traditional holy books of the LXX. During the first period of the Church the Gospels do not seem to have been regarded without question as "Holy Scriptures", but rather as "Holy Word" (ἱερὸς λόγος) or oral (messianic) Torah.[2]

Finally, we must take a further fact into consideration. The 2nd century seems to have been well advanced before the four Gospels gained anything like a *general* distribution to *all* of the more important congregations in the rapidly expanding Christian Church. For a number of decades many were evidently satisfied with one or two of the Gospels, conscious that other congregations had other versions of the gospel. If the indications are to be believed, the gospel material functioned to a great extent orally. We shall soon return to this topic.

After this look at the information provided by the early Church on the Gospels, and the way in which the gospel material was quoted and used at this time, we turn now to the history of the text. There, too, we have a number of interesting indications.

As is well known, we are able for the most part to trace the history of the N.T. text back to about A.D. 200; we find even at that time that we can distinguish four recensions. A work of edition evidently took place in different provinces of the Church towards the end of the 2nd century. Christian γραμματικοί and κριτικοί have been at work.[3] But before this time it is clear that the N.T. text was not copied with the same minute precision as later. This is not to say that it was not copied —to all appearances—with both care and respect,[4] but it was evidently not copied in a way which could compete in precision with the Jewish

---

[1] See the works referred to above, p. 31, n. 4.

[2] On the way in which the tradition from and about "the Lord" takes the place of the oral Torah in early Christianity, see below, Ch. 14 C–E and 15 D–E.

[3] Cf. also R. M. GRANT, *The Letter and the Spirit* (1957), pp. 143 ff.

[4] See C. H. ROBERTS, The Christian Book and the Greek Papyri, in *Journ. of Theol. Stud.* 50 (1949), pp. 167 f.

Scripture specialists' copying of the text of the written Torah, or with
the best Hellenistic grammarians' and copyists' transmission of the text
of the Greek classics (the category ἠκριβωμένα).[1]

This is explained principally by the fact that during this period the
text of the Gospels was clearly copied for the most part by private copyists.[2] The majority of the examples belonged to the category κοινά. But
certain types of textual variants—assimilations and harmonizations—can
scarcely be explained other than by the fact that the text of the Gospels
was at this time still not regarded as being fixed *in the smallest detail*.

Another indication is to be found in the history of the text or, to be
more precise, in N.T. palaeography. It is a known fact that in the
Christian Church we find the Holy Scriptures in codex form at an un-
expectedly early date. This is all the more remarkable[3] when we consider
the Hellenistic and Jewish milieus. In the Greco-Roman world the scroll
enjoyed almost undisputed supremacy as the repository of literary
work: a book *was* a scroll.[4] In Judaism, too, the scroll was unchallenged
as the vehicle of the written divine Word.[5] With this in mind, it is all
the more remarkable that as early as the beginning of the 2nd century
—and presumably even earlier—the codex was used in the Church.
Some scholars have connected this with the possibility that the gospel
literature was derived from *notebooks*, which were often in codex form.[6]

From our point of view, this explanation is very striking and deserves
serious consideration.

There is a good deal of evidence that the majority of Jesus' disciples
came, not from some Jewish sect, but from the main stream of Judaism:
from that section of the people which looked to the learned Pharisees
as its teachers and spiritual leaders.[7] If what we have said earlier in this
work is correct, Pharisaic Judaism stressed energetically the distinction
between written and oral Torah, and opposed tendencies, towards both
the written transmission of the oral Torah, and the recognition of possible

---

[1] Cf. above, p. 43, n. 4, and pp. 49 ff.

[2] Cf. e.g. ROBERTS, *ibid*.

[3] F. KENYON, *Books and Readers in Ancient Greece and Rome* (1932), pp. 94 ff.

[4] See C. H. ROBERTS, The Codex, in *Proceed. of the Brit. Acad.* 40 (1954), pp. 169 ff.

[5] See L. BLAU, *Studien zum althebräischen Buchwesen* (1902).

[6] ROBERTS, *The Christian Book*, pp. 160 ff., LIEBERMAN, *Hellenism*, pp. 203 ff.,
H. RIESENFELD, in G. LINDESKOG, A. FRIDRICHSEN, H. RIESENFELD, *Inledning till
N.T.* (1951), pp. 300 ff.

[7] See below, Ch. 14 and 15.

copies of such material as official books.[1] It is against such a background that we must see the fact that for several decades the tradition concerning Christ appears to have been carried orally. This was normal traditional procedure in this section of Judaism.[2] But just as the Rabbis' pupils had their own private notes, their written *hypomnemata*, written on tablets, in notebooks of various kinds, in haggadah books and scrolls of secrets,[3] so they began within the Church to write down parts of the tradition concerning Christ in the same way.[4] With the help of such notes, but naturally on a basis of oral tradition, a beginning was then made to put together more extensive collections in the style of the Gospel of Mark—both oral and written. Since notebooks in codex form contained notes of gospel material at an early stage in the history of the Church, a way was opened for the continued use of the codex.[5] Practical factors also came into the picture.[6] Because the codex began to be used for the Gospels, it also became permissible to use it for the other N.T. and O.T. Scriptures.[7] The development appears to have followed these lines.

By the middle of the 2nd century, the four Gospels had reached a position in which it began to be natural to quote them as Holy Scripture: a development which later spread very rapidly and which became accepted in different parts of the Church.[8] But up to this time the Gospels are *holy tradition* rather than Scripture, and function to all appearances mainly orally. Can we now bring forward any concrete ideas as to the methods which were used in the Church at this time when the gospel texts—from the purely technical point of view—were to be orally transmitted?

Information in the sources seems to be practically non-existent, and we are thus compelled to work for the most part by analogy. Certain observations appear, however, to lie within the bounds of reason and probability.

[1] See above, pp. 23 ff. and 157 ff.

[2] LIEBERMAN says, *op. cit.*, p. 205, that Jesus' disciples would have *transgressed the Law* if they had written down the gospel in form of a book to be published, but this is going a little too far.

[3] See above, pp. 160 ff.

[4] Cf. LIEBERMAN, *ibid.*, RIESENFELD, *ibid.*, ROBERTS, *The Codex*, pp. 187 ff.

[5] ROBERTS, *op. cit., ibid.*

[6] RIESENFELD, *op. cit., ibid.*

[7] ROBERTS, *op. cit.*, p. 189, LIEBERMAN, *Hellenism*, p. 208.

[8] Cf. T. ZAHN, *Geschichte des neutestamentlichen Kanons* I (1888), pp. 60 ff.

How were catechumens taught in the Church at this time? It is probable, at least in some cases, that teaching was based on the Scriptures;[1] in the second century it may also have been based on some Gospel document.[2] Remembering the natural and essential role played by the practice of memorization, both in Judaism and in Hellenism, it is also reasonable to suppose that the catechumen had to learn by heart a number of formulae, sayings, important texts (κεφάλαια) and summaries (ἐπιτομαί), and that the sacred words were also interpreted for him.[3] Another element in the instruction of catechumens comprised—evidently very early in the history of the Church's development—the *traditio symboli* and *traditio orationis dominicae*; in these cases there is no doubt that it was a question of memorization: the teacher taught his pupil to read the sacred text from memory (*reddere*).[4]

What level of instruction and what knowledge can we assume the leading men in the Church to have possessed at that time: οἱ ἐπίσκοποι, πρεσβύτεροι, διάκονοι, διδάσκαλοι etc.? To what extent were they compelled to bear the apostolic tradition concerning Christ written on their hearts, i.e. learned by heart? The many occasions on which the Church's authors (Irenaeus in particular) mention that those who held office in the Church were the bearers of the genuine apostolic tradition[5] can scarcely be due to nothing more than apologetic motives.

As early as the 2nd century a highly qualified learned work was in progress in certain Church centres on Christian doctrine. The Alexandrian scholastic tradition is the best known, but similar scholarly foundations were in existence elsewhere, and in these a rich and noteworthy Christian doctrinal tradition was in process of formation.[6] The roots which this

[1] Cf. Acts 8.26 ff., and below, pp. 233 f.

[2] Iren., *Adv. Haer.* IV.32.1 (MPG VII, 1071), Hippol., *The Apostolic tradition* IV.2 (35), trans. by B. S. EASTON (1934), p. 54; see K. STENDAHL, *The School of St. Matthew* (1954), p. 17.

[3] On the problem, cf. D. VAN DEN EYNDE, *Les Normes de l'Enseignement Chrétien dans la littérature patristique des trois premiers siècles* (1933).

[4] T. KLAUSER, Auswendiglernen, in *Reallex. f. Ant. u. Christ.* I (1950), col. 1034ff.

[5] D. B. REYNDERS, Paradosis. Le progrès de l'idée de tradition jusqu'à saint Irénée, in *Rech. de Théol. Anc. et Médiév.* 5 (1933), pp. 155 ff., H. HOLSTEIN, La tradition des Apôtres chez saint Irénée, in *Rech. de Science Rel.* 36 (1949), pp. 229 ff., E. MOLLAND, Irenaeus of Lugdunum and the Apostolic Succession, in *The Journ. of Eccl. Hist.* 1 (1950), pp. 12 ff., R. P. C. HANSON, *Origen's Doctrine of Tradition* (1954), A. BENOIT, Écriture et Tradition chez saint Irénée, in *Rev. d'Hist. et de Philos. Rel.* 40 (1960), pp. 32 ff.

[6] See BOUSSET, *Jüdisch-Christlicher Schulbetrieb*, A. VON HARNACK, *Die Mission und Ausbreitung des Christentums* I (4th ed. 1924), pp. 332 ff., F. V. FILSON, The

work of scholarship may have had in the work of the earliest period of
Christendom on the logos is a most interesting question:[1] one which is
not easily answered, however. The same applies to the problem of how
the first Christian doctrinal tradition was transmitted, technically
speaking.[2]

A couple of items of information may however be of interest in this
context, since they give us two concrete pictures of the way in which
transmission could take place in the 2nd century Church.

In the first, a famous passage from Irenaeus,[3] we are dealing with a
regular teaching situation. Irenaeus relates that he carries in his memory
many traditions which he received in his childhood from Polycarp:

"I can even name the place where the blessed Polycarp sat and taught
(καθεζόμενος διελέγετο), where he went out and in. I remember his way
of life (τὸν χαρακτῆρα τοῦ βίου), what he looked like, the addresses
(τὰς διαλέξεις) he delivered to the people, how he told (ἀπήγγελλε) of
his intercourse with John and with the others who had seen the Lord,
how he remembered their words (ἀπεμνημόνευε τοὺς λόγους αὐτῶν) and
what he had heard from them about the Lord, about his miracles, and
about his teaching (τῆς διδασκαλίας). As one who had received this
from eyewitnesses of the word of life (ὡς παρὰ αὐτοπτῶν τῆς ζωῆς τοῦ
Λόγου παρειληφώς) Polycarp retold everything in accordance with the
Scriptures (σύμφωνα ταῖς Γραφαῖς).[4] I listened to this then, because
of the grace of God which was given me, carefully, copying it down,
not on paper, but in my heart (ὑπομνηματιζόμενος αὐτὰ οὐκ ἐν χάρτῃ
ἀλλ' ἐν τῇ ἐμῇ καρδίᾳ). And I repeat it (ἀναμαρυκῶμαι) constantly in
genuine form by the grace of God."

First of all, we may note that the tradition is linked with authoritative
spokesmen. This is an extremely characteristic factor in a milieu in which

---

Christian Teacher in the First Century, in *Journ. of Bibl. Lit.* 60 (1941), pp. 317 ff.,
H. FR. VON CAMPENHAUSEN, *Kirchliches Amt und geistliche Vollmacht in den ersten
Jahrhunderten* (1953), pp. 65 ff., 195 ff., R. HOLTE, *Beatitudo och Sapientia* (1959),
pp. 112 ff.

[1] BOUSSET, *op. cit.*, pp. 308 ff., STENDAHL, *op. cit.*, pp. 17 ff.

[2] On this subject, see below, partic. Ch. 15 D–E.

[3] In Eus., *Hist. Eccl.* V.20 (MPG XX, 485).

[4] Note the way in which the message is supported on the one hand by the evidence
of eyewitnesses, and on the other by the Scriptures, just as in the Lucan and Pauline
writings and in the logos from the Jerusalem church which is delivered in 1 Cor.
15.3 ff. On this subject, see below, Ch. 14–15. This provides a fine example of
continuity between apostolic and post-apostolic tradition.

tradition and authority play an important part. At all events, this is extremely marked in Rabbinism,[1] and in the early Church as far back as the sources take us.[2] Who it is that communicates a tradition is of vital importance, as is the question: from whom did he derive it? When Irenaeus quotes a tradition, he often gives a chain of reliable traditionists: he heard it from the elders who in their turn had been disciples of the Apostles (οἱ πρεσβύτεροι τῶν ἀποστόλων μαθηταί; *presbyteri apostolorum discipuli*)—one of his typical formulations.[3]

Secondly, we see that Irenaeus claims to have learned the tradition by heart. He had no need to write down his *hypomnemata*. By the grace of God he was enabled to retain it in exact form. We can see from this the great value placed upon faithful and exact memorization. We can at the same time, in accordance with his formulation, reckon with the fact that it was not unusual to support the memory by the taking of written notes.

Irenaeus' lively portrait of Polycarp's life and conduct must be seen in the light of what we have said in an earlier chapter on the subject of *imitatio magistri*.[4]

The second example—an item of information from the early Church which has been even more widely used—is taken from Papias, and gives us an interesting picture of the way in which a teacher consults reliable and knowledgeable spokesmen and collects traditions from them.

According to Eusebius, Papias,[5] in the introduction to the five books in which he expounds the words of the Lord, expressed his reverence for those who speak of "the commandments which are given *by the Lord* for faith, and which derive *from the very truth*." (It is thus a matter of finding the right traditionists in order to come into contact with the pure stream flowing from the source of divine revelation *in Christ*. This concept—common among the Church Fathers[6]—is a close parallel

---

[1] See above, partic. p. 131, n. 1, and Ch. 12.

[2] See below, Ch. 14–15. On the great importance attached to tradition in Islam, see above, p. 131, n. 1.

[3] The presbyteros traditions in Irenaeus are reprinted e.g. in PREUSCHEN, *Antilegomena*, pp. 99 ff.; cf. the discussion in J. DANIÉLOU, *Théologie du Judéo-Christianisme* (1958), pp. 55 ff., and J. MUNCK, Presbyters and Disciples of the Lord in Papias, in *The Harv. Theol. Rev.* 52 (1959), pp. 223 ff.

[4] Above, Ch. 12 B; cf. below, Ch. 15 D–E.

[5] *Hist. Eccl.* III.39 (MPG XX, 297).

[6] See e.g. Irenaeus, *Adv. Haer.* III.5.1 (MPG VII, 857); cf. HOLTE, *Beatitudo*, p. 184.

to the Rabbis' wish to come into contact with the Sinai revelation by
way of the genuine tradition.) The passage of Papias continues:

"And then whenever someone came who (as a disciple) had accompanied the elders (εἰ δέ που καὶ παρηκολουθηκώς τις τοῖς πρεσβυτέροις ἔλθοι) I used to search for (ἀνέκρινον) the words of the elders:
what Andrew or what Peter had said (εἶπεν) or what Philip or what
Thomas or what James or what John or what Matthew or any other
disciple of the Lord, or what Aristion or what John the Elder, the disciples of the Lord, say (λέγουσιν)."

This is the witness of an early Church authority, who says in the next
sentence that he relied less in principle upon the written word (τὰ ἐκ τῶν
βιβλίων) than upon that which came from the living and abiding (human)
voice (τὰ παρὰ ζώσης φωνῆς καὶ μενούσης). He has thus not copied down
the traditions concerning Christ which these men were able to pass on
to him on these occasions, but has learned them carefully, impressed
them upon his memory (καλῶς ἔμαθον καὶ καλῶς ἐμνημόνευσα). The
fact that in later life he becomes responsible for five books is another
matter.

A well known crux in this saying is precisely what is meant by οἱ
πρεσβύτεροι.[1] Does this word refer to bearers of authority from the
generation after the Apostles? In that case this passage states that the
tradition from the Lord reached Papias *via* the Apostles, the "presbyters"
and the "presbyters'" disciples. But another possibility is that the term
πρεσβύτεροι includes.the Apostles,[2] in which case the chain of tradition
is one link shorter. In this context we can leave the question open.[3]

It is important to be able to state that in this passage the Apostles
do not stand as traditionists *en bloc*, but individually. Nor does the
method of expression used here seem to have been due to mere chance.
Eusebius mentions, a little later in his description,[4] that Papias often
expressly mentions Aristion and John the Elder by name in his books
and quotes their traditions: ὀνομαστὶ γοῦν πολλάκις αὐτῶν μνημονεύσας,
ἐν τοῖς αὐτοῦ συγγράμμασι τίθησιν αὐτῶν παραδόσεις. Here we may

---

[1] On this old problem, see lately MUNCK, *op. cit.*

[2] Thus MUNCK, *op. cit.*

[3] From one point of view the problem is purely syntactical: does the τί-clause
define what Papias inquired about or does it define what the elders said? In the
first case "the elders" denotes the apostolic generation; in the second, the generation after the Apostles.

[4] III.39 (MPG XX, 297).

glimpse a terminology—and method—of transmission of the same type as that used by the Rabbis: "Rabbi A. said in Rabbi B.'s name."[1]

Finally, we shall consider an extremely interesting passage from the pseudo-Clementine *Recognitiones*, a work which is unfortunately very difficult to date and to place.

In the first chapter of the second book,[2] the author causes Peter to speak of the power of habit, and to quote examples from his own life. He has adopted the habit of forcing himself to awaken after midnight. "I have adopted the habit of recalling in my memory (*revocare ad memoriam*) the words of my Lord which I heard from himself, and because of my longing for them I force my mind and my thoughts to be roused, so that, awaking to them, and recalling and repeating each one of them, I may keep them in memory (*ut evigilans ad ea et singula quaeque recolens ac retexens possim memoriter retinere*)".

The continuation of the argument is irrelevant in this context. We cannot draw any extensive conclusions from this passage, either. The nature of the source does not permit it. It is however worthy of our attention, since it counteracts our too-modern—though spontaneous and unconscious—ideas on the measures taken by a pupil in Antiquity to keep fresh the sayings and the knowledge he had obtained from his teacher. It shows the way in which the circles in which this part of the pseudo-Clementine tradition came into being[3] imagined Peter to have set about familiarizing himself with, and mastering, the sayings of Jesus. The closest parallel would seem to be the haggadah on Rabban Joḥanan ben Zakkai who, sitting in the pitch darkness of a Roman prison, measured the passage of time with the help of his recitation of the Mishnah.[4]

---

[1] Cf. above, p. 131, n. 1. Cf. also the quotation from Irenaeus above, p. 204.

[2] II.1 (MPG I, 1249).

[3] On the difficulty of estimating the origins of the material of the pseudo-Clementine writings, see the review of the present state of research, in G. STRECKER, *Das Judenchristentum in den Pseudoklementinen* (1958), pp. 1 ff.

[4] See above, p. 169.

CHAPTER 14

The Witness of Luke

WE MUST NOW leave the early Fathers, and proceed to a consideration of the writings of Luke[1]—particularly the Acts of the Apostles; our object will be an evaluation of the information provided by the *auctor ad Theophilum*. We shall not concern ourselves with questions of dating and authorship: for our purposes it is sufficient to recognize that we are here dealing with a source which derives from an early Christian authority of the second half of the first century.

The question of the reliability of Luke's information about the early Church is still being debated as energetically as ever. Opinions differ sharply. This is particularly evident from HAENCHEN's recent commentary on Acts,[2] and from the debate occasioned by the publication of this work.[3]

To what extent did Luke have access to reliable tradition and authentic sources? To what extent did he reshape his material? Or did he compose the narrative himself? It is obvious that Luke is extremely purposeful, both as an author (historian) and as a theologian. His overall view of the history of salvation, as demonstrated most recently by CONZELMANN[4] and HAENCHEN,[5] shows a striking degree of completeness. His description of the ministry of Jesus and the history of the Church up to the 60's is also very well thought out, and is developed remarkably logically in his two-part history.[6]

---

[1] I believe that Λουκᾶς ὁ ἰατρός wrote both Luke and Acts, but the term "Luke" is used in this book only to denote the *auctor ad Theophilum*, whoever he may be.

[2] E. HAENCHEN, *Die Apostelgeschichte* (1956, 3rd ed., which we use here, 1959); cf. IDEM, Tradition und Komposition in der Apostelgeschichte, in *Zeitschr. f. Theol. u. Kirche* 52 (1955), pp. 205 ff.

[3] See, apart from reviews, e.g. R. BULTMANN, Zur Frage nach den Quellen der Apostelgeschichte, in *N.T. Essays ... in memory of* T. W. MANSON (1959), pp. 68 ff., and J. JERVELL, Til spørsmålet om tradisjonsgrunnlaget for Apostlenes gjerninger, in *Norsk Teol. Tidsskrift* 61 (1960), pp. 160 ff. — For an earlier analysis of modern works on Acts, see J. DUPONT, *Les problemes du Livre des Actes d'après les travaux récents* (1950).

[4] H. CONZELMANN, *Die Mitte der Zeit* (3rd ed. 1960).

[5] In his commentary.

[6] See further, below, A–E.

This fact often gives rise to illegitimate conclusions. It seems to be an extremely tenaciously-held misapprehension among exegetes that an early Christian author must *either* be a purposeful theologian and writer *or* a fairly reliable historian. This misapprehension is applied to the author of Acts, to the Evangelists, and to those who preceded the Evangelists in forming the various elements of the gospel tradition. The pioneer form-critics DIBELIUS and BULTMANN have contributed materially to the perpetuation of this error. They work on a basis of an over-simplified alternative, maintaining that the men who shaped the gospel tradition had no wish to preserve memories for posterity, but *instead* wished by their proclamation to arouse faith in Christ.[1] This is a false alternative. To present the problem in this way fails to do justice to the deep-rooted respect for divine revelation which was felt in Antiquity (and elsewhere): to that profound reverence associated with the words which were "heard" and the things which were "seen", i.e. those events which were understood and interpreted in religious categories. Nor does it do justice even to the reverence commanded by the authoritative teacher or a received authoritative tradition. The fact of the early Christian Apostles, teachers and Evangelists having presented their material with a religious end in view does not necessarily mean *per se* that their memories ceased to function, or that their respect for historical facts vanished.[2]

Luke is, as we have said, an extremely purposeful theologian and writer. But this does not exclude the possibility that he may be faithful to the tradition he has received. In certain parts of his account we are able to check his attitude to his sources. For example, we can see how he edits and retouches the Markan material; but it cannot be said that he makes any very extensive alterations.[3] Even the language is subjected to comparatively little correction.[4] The writer of the prologue to Luke's

---

[1] M. DIBELIUS, *Die Formgeschichte des Evangeliums* (3rd ed. 1959), e.g. pp. 10, 12, 28, 241. Cf. R. BULTMANN, *Die Formgeschichte des Evangeliums* (4th ed. 1958), p. 52.

[2] Cf. above, p. 182, on the fact that the preaching and teaching of early Christianity, from the formal point of view, had a *tendency* which resembled in principle all other teaching of religious or educational character in Antiquity.

[3] In his answer to the criticism of BULTMANN, in Quellenanalyse und Kompositionsanalyse in Act 15, in *Zeitschr. f. d. Neutest. Wiss.*, *Beih.* 26 (1960), HAENCHEN says (p. 157): "Wir könnten den Markustext nicht aus Lukas rekonstruieren." This may possibly be true of the *wording* of the text.

[4] This has been demonstrated most recently in an as yet unpublished investigation by L. HARTMAN.

Gospel had a different personal style from that he uses when reproducing the gospel traditions. When working on Acts, Luke can hardly have had access to such extensive and well-established source material as that which he used when shaping his Gospel.[1] There can however be no doubt that he used a number of sources when working on Acts.[2] We thus have good reason to suppose that he had every respect for the material of the tradition, and for the happenings described in the tradition, which he regarded as decisive, sacred tradition. We must stress that Luke's view of the messianic events, and of the role of Jesus and the Apostles as mediators of ὁ λόγος τοῦ κυρίου, must have limited his freedom to reshape the material he had received, material which purported to have been spoken by them, or to describe what God accomplished through them.[3]

Opinions may differ on this point. One thing ought, however, to be self-evident. The question of the reliability of Luke's account is not to be decided by referring to the fact of his being a purposeful theologian and author. What we know as Lucan theology may have been common creed in early Christianity, or in parts thereof. And the material from which Luke constructs his exposé of the history of early Christianity *may* be derived from reliable spokesmen or reliable sources; it may, at least in some cases, be a source of reliable information.

In this chapter we shall attempt to gather up the information which Luke gives us on the origins of the synoptic tradition, and on its transmission and use in the earliest period of the Church. In order to shorten and simplify the account, and in order to make the results of this examination relatively independent of our own attitude to the problem of the sources of Acts, we shall not base our argument on Luke's sources, but on his own account. We shall attempt to determine what Luke himself says and what he means. In our presentation we shall not, at first, draw any distinctions between probable and improbable, or even between historical and super-historical, but shall attempt quite simply to decide what is the meaning of Luke's witness on the relevant questions.[4]

---

[1] Cf. DIBELIUS, *Formgeschichte*, p. 3, and IDEM, Stilkritisches zur Apostelgeschichte, in *Aufsätze zur Apostelgeschichte* (3rd ed. 1957), pp. 12 ff.

[2] See B. REICKE, *Glaube und Leben der Urgemeinde* (1957); cf. L. CERFAUX, the section: Les Actes des Apôtres et le Christianisme primitif, in *Recueil* L. CERFAUX II (1954), pp. 61 ff., B. GÄRTNER, *The Areopagus Speech and Natural Revelation* (1955), pp. 26 ff., BULTMANN, *Zur Frage*, and below.

[3] See below, particularly sec. B–E.

[4] Cf. the way in which CONZELMANN determines his task, *Die Mitte*, pp. 1 ff.

This does not mean that we shall detach the witness of Luke from the historical context in which Luke himself places it. On the contrary: we shall bring together at certain important points the Lucan description of the faith and life of the Jerusalem church, and ideas and concepts from contemporary Palestinian Judaism. This is intended to show the categories with which Luke is working, and the way in which his evidence is to be understood. (In fact Luke is very much dependent upon Palestinian tradition.) In the two last sections, on a basis of Luke's account, we shall comment on certain aspects of the historical situation of early Christianity.

We have called this chapter, in accordance with Luke's own ambitions, "The Witness of Luke". The *auctor ad Theophilum*, according to his famous prologue, wishes to give an orderly account of the events connected with the history of Jesus and the Church; in this way Theophilus (and those like him) will recognize the reliability (ἵνα ἐπιγνῷς ... τὴν ἀσφάλειαν) of the *logoi* he has been taught, or those things of which he has heard[1] (both translations are possible).

Luke's work is apologetic in its purpose.[2] He wishes to demonstrate the reliability (ἡ ἀσφάλεια) of the matters he relates, and to bring forward proof of them. When producing proof he makes extensive use of a traditional Jewish principle of argument and proof. In Deut. 19.15 (cf. 17.6 and Num. 35.30) it was laid down that a case should be decided on the evidence of two or three witnesses. This principle of argument and proof came into more widespread use during the centuries immediately before the Christian era, not least in torah-centric groups.[3] It was a definite principle of Rabbinic Judaism in the Tannaitic and Amoraic periods — and not only in the context of jurisprudence. The distinctive role played by this traditional method of proof for Jesus[4] and the early

---

[1] On this translation, see H. J. CADBURY, in *The Beginnings of Christianity* I, vol. II (1920), pp. 509 f.

[2] On the Lucan writings as apology, see H. J. CADBURY, The Purpose Expressed in Luke's Preface, in *The Expos.* 21 (1921), pp. 431 ff., and H. SAHLIN, *Der Messias und das Gottesvolk* (1945), pp. 30 ff. Both emphasize the fact that in his prologue Luke uses terms which at the end of Acts are used in specifically legal contexts. On the meaning of the prologue, see also P. SCHUBERT, The Structure and Significance of Luke 24, in *Zeitschr. f. d. Neutest. Wiss., Beih.* 21 (1954), pp. 165 ff.

[3] See H. VAN VLIET, *No Single Testimony* (1958), pp. 43 ff.

[4] The information that during his Galilean ministry Jesus sent out his disciples, and sent them out two by two, Mk. 6.7 with par., is certainly historical. (N.B. that in the list of the Apostles which is included in the apostolic tractate Matt. 10.1 ff.,

Church has recently been pointed out by VAN VLIET.[1] The thoroughness with which Luke uses it—with a number of variations—had earlier been demonstrated by MORGENTHALER.[2] We shall later consider this factor in various contexts.

One might imagine this concern for definite proof when presenting the gospel to be a secondary characteristic of the early Christian tradition. It might be due either to the fact that the author was writing with a particular apologetic end in view, to the fact that he was writing at a period when the "original enthusiasm" had begun to wane, or to the fact that the development known to some scholars as "Frühkatholizismus" was already well advanced. To sketch the history of early Christianity on such lines as these is however to over-simplify. Investigation of "pneumatic" movements the world over has shown the extent to which rational and irrational elements are inextricably interwoven, and how spontaneity and legalism, charismatic and institutional elements are to be found, inseparably side by side.[3] A recent example is to be seen in the Qumran sect, a group having powerful eschatological expectations and an equally powerful "pneumatic" character, but which at the same time was very strictly and narrowly organized, observing a strict law and definite doctrinal axioms, down to the smallest detail of everyday life. The sect had its law and its logic (see 1QS, 1QSa, CD). When we encounter similar phenomena in early Christianity we are not able to classify them as later or secondary. They may be original.[4]

In the proof brought forward by Luke, prophetic sayings, divine inspiration and miracles play a considerable role. The chain of messianic events of which the Annunciation of John the Baptist was the first, is seen by Luke as a series of examples of acts and words of divine power. This seems, however, to be characteristic of the whole of early Christianity, though its forms may vary.[5] The young Church was conscious of the Apostles are grouped two and two.) Cf. Joach. JEREMIAS, Paarweise Sendung im N.T., in *N.T. Essays ... in memory of* T. W. MANSON, pp. 136 ff. For other examples of the two-witness principle in the work of Jesus, see VAN VLIET, *op. cit.*, pp. 87 ff.

[1] *Op. cit.*

[2] *Die lukanische Geschichtsschreibung als Zeugnis* I–II (1949), which is perhaps guilty of a certain exaggeration.

[3] T. ANDRÆ, *Mystikens psykologi* (1926). — Cf. VON CAMPENHAUSEN, *Kirchliches Amt und geistliche Vollmacht*.

[4] Cf. O. LINTON, *Das Problem der Urkirche in der neueren Forschung* (1932), particularly pp. 206 ff.

[5] On the view of Luke, see E. SCHWEIZER, πνεῦμα κτλ., in *Theol. Wörterb.* VI (1957), pp. 401 ff.

being "the eschatological body of election" (*die eschatologische Heils-gemeinde*), richly endowed with Spirit and power, sophia and gnosis; in their preaching and teaching its members constantly based their arguments on prophecy, and on miracles and signs.[1]

We obtain a different picture when we turn our attention to Rabbinic Judaism. But we must not exaggerate the difference. They, too, believed in divine miracles and signs; it was heresy to deny them! They recognized "Biblical" miracles, but believed that miracles—minor miracles, at least —were still possible.[2] As A. GUTTMAN has pointed out, during the period of the Temple a revelation (בת קול) could even settle a halakic controversy.[3] *Bet Hillel* was less sceptical on this point than *bet Shammai*.[4] A development took place, however, parallel with the growth of Christianity. It is probable that it was the latter factor which caused the Rabbis to adopt a stricter attitude to miracles and signs, at least in connection with the settling of legal and doctrinal questions.[5] We find R. Joshua in Jabneh (after A.D. 70) ignoring a voice from heaven (בת קול), saying that the Torah is not in heaven (Deut. 30.12).[6] And by the third Tannaitic generation[7] matters had gone so far that a rule was formulated, to the effect that "one should not (when deciding halakic questions) mention miracles" (אין מזכירין מעשה נסים).[8] However, this was not what was believed at the time of the Temple. Then, מעשה נסים played a certain—though not a very prominent—role in Pharisaic doctrinal discussions as a whole, and in *bet Hillel* in particular.[9]

---

[1] Cf. T. W. MANSON, The Argument from Prophecy, in *Journ. of Theol. Stud.* 46 (1945), pp. 129 ff.

[2] See A. GUTTMANN, The Significance of Miracles for Talmudic Judaism, in *Hebr. Un. Coll. Ann.* 20 (1947), pp. 363 ff.

[3] *Op. cit.*, pp. 367 ff. Cf. Acts 10.9 ff. and below, p. 315.

[4] E.g. T Nezir. I.1 (with par.): "*Bet Shammai* says that no testimony based on the *bat Qol* be admitted, *bet Hillel* admits it" (בית שמאי אומ' אין מעידין על בת קול ובית הלל אומ' מעידין על בת קול). See further GUTTMANN, *op. cit., ibid.*

[5] So GUTTMANN, *op. cit.*

[6] אמר רבי יהושע לא בשמים היא p Moed Qat. III.1, b Bab. Mes. 58b–59a; see the analysis made by GUTTMANN, *op. cit.*, pp. 374 ff.

[7] *Op. cit.*, pp. 391 ff.

[8] E.g. b Ḥul. 43a, b Ber. 60a, b Yeb. 121b.

[9] From this point of view, N.B. Matt. 12.38 ff. with par. and 16.1 ff. with par. See also below, p. 283.

A. *Jerusalem and* ὁ λόγος τοῦ κυρίου

Jerusalem had been an obvious focus for the Jewish people ever since
the time of the Kings of Israel. Powerful traditional religious concepts
were connected to the town itself, to Zion, the holy mountain on which
it was built, and to the Temple at its "centre". Here was "the centre of
the earth", "the navel of the world", etc.—concepts which we recognize
from the thoughts and beliefs of other peoples concerning their temple
and their capital.[1]

It is particularly important from our point of view to take note of the
connection which exists between Jerusalem and the Torah or, to use
another formulation, between Jerusalem and the word of the Lord
(דבר יהוה, ὁ λόγος τοῦ κυρίου). As an ancient national sanctuary the
town had for centuries been the place where the Torah had its dwelling;
in ancient times oracles were received here, the oracles were interpreted
here; it was here that the prophets appeared, it was here that oracular
and prophetic sayings were transmitted and interpreted.[2] It was thus
here that the sacred oral and written texts had their most important home;
here they were cultivated, here work was carried out on these manifestations of divine revelation. In the words of Sirach (24.10, 23), the
wisdom of God, in the form of the Torah, had a permanent dwelling on
Zion. The Jews' highest doctrinal court, the Great Sanhedrin, held its
sessions within the actual Temple area, in a room which was called
"the Chamber of *Gazit*";[3] it was from this place that the Torah proceeded
to the whole of Israel (תורה לכל ישראל ששממנו יוצאת, M Sanh. XI.2;
cf. Is. 2.3).[4]

Jerusalem's position as a centre for the Torah was codified in the Holy
Scriptures. In Deut. (17.8 ff.)[5] it was laid down that those disputes which
could not be decided in the local courts—the Masoretic text reads
"within thy gates" (בשעריך), LXX, "in your towns" (ἐν ταῖς πόλεσιν

---

[1] See Joach. JEREMIAS, *Golgotha* (1926), pp. 43 ff., B. SUNDKLER, *Jésus et les
païens* (1937), pp. 21 ff., Å. V. STRÖM, *Vetekornet* (1944), pp. 159 ff., M. ELIADE,
Ewige Bilder und Sinnbilder (1958), pp. 44 ff.

[2] For a review of the present debate on the connection between the prophets and
the Temple, see A. H. J. GUNNEWEG, *Mündliche und schriftliche Tradition* (1959),
pp. 81 ff.

[3] לשכת הגזית. The meaning of this name is uncertain. See e.g. E. SCHÜRER,
Geschichte II (4th ed. 1907), pp. 263 f., and S. B. HOENIG, *The Great Sanhedrin*
(1953), p. 81.

[4] See below, sec. E.

[5] Cf. also 2 Chron. 19.8 ff.

ὑμῶν)—should be referred for decision to "that place which the Lord thy God chooses" (המקום אשר יבחר יהוה אלהיך בו). There "the Word" (הדבר) and the law (התורה) were to be conveyed to the people. Since "that place which the Lord thy God chooses" became one of the Jews' names for Jerusalem, the position of the town as a centre for the Torah was laid down in that text; it was a fact to which the pious Jew was to pay attention even when the town lay in ruins.

There was also a general expectation that Jerusalem was to keep its central position in the period of the coming salvation. At that time —according to the prophecies—the springs of salvation were to be opened in Jerusalem, on the very site of the Temple, and their strength was to proceed from the holy city (Ezek. 47.1 ff., Joel 4.18, cf. Is. 12.3 ff., Zech. 13.1, 14.8). The prophecy of Isaiah (2.3) says, concerning the salvation of the peoples "at the end of days" (TM: באחרית הימים, LXX: ἐν ταῖς ἐσχάταις ἡμέραις):

כי מציון תצא תורה	ἐκ γὰρ Σιὼν ἐξελεύσεται νόμος
ודבר יהוה מירושלם.	καὶ λόγος κυρίου ἐξ Ἰερουσαλήμ.

"For from Zion shall the law proceed,
And the word of the Lord from Jerusalem." (Cf. Micah 4.2.)

When faced with these powerful traditional[1] Jewish concepts, it is not surprising that Jerusalem played the role for Jesus and the early Church that it in fact played. We must be satisfied here with an extremely brief sketch of the way in which *Luke* presents this fact.[2] Luke thus relates how the birth of the forerunner was announced at the altar of incense in the Jerusalem Temple (1.8 ff.), how the child Jesus was taken to Jerusalem, to the Temple (τὸ ἱερόν), in order to be circumcised (2.22 ff.), how the twelve-year-old Jesus leaves his parents and remains in the Temple (N.B. *sitting in the midst of the scholars*, καθεζόμενον ἐν μέσῳ τῶν διδασκάλων!)[3] in order to be ἐν τοῖς τοῦ πατρός μου (2.41 ff.), how Jesus talks on the Mount of Transfiguration with Moses and Elijah about

---

[1] On the power of these ideas among the Rabbis, see BILLERBECK, *Comm.* IV, p. 1239, sub voce Jerusalem (1–3).

[2] For the problem in general, see W. SCHMAUCH, *Orte der Offenbarung und der Offenbarungsort im N.T.* (1956). N.B. *ibid.*, pp. 82 ff., on the tendency to use the form Ἰερουσαλήμ in *positive* statements. CONZELMANN, *Die Mitte*, pp. 66 ff., 124 ff., pays little attention to the problem of the theological role of Jerusalem.

[3] Here we already have Luke's stress on the Temple as a place where *work with the "word of God"* was carried on. Cf. below.

the destiny which he was to fulfil in Jerusalem (τὴν ἔξοδον αὐτοῦ, ἣν ἤμελλεν πληροῦν ἐν Ἰ., 9.30 f.), how Jesus consciously turns his steps toward Jerusalem and the decisive events he had clearly forseen (9.43 ff., 51 ff.),[1] how the drama of suffering, death and resurrection is played out in Jerusalem (19.28 ff.), and how the Risen Lord directs that the Apostles' activity is to begin in Jerusalem. Reference is also made in this connection (24.46 f.) to the Scriptures: "It is written that ... repentance unto remission of sins should be preached in his name unto all the nations, beginning from Jerusalem" (οὕτως γέγραπται ... κηρυχθῆναι ... ἀρξάμενοι ἀπὸ Ἰ.).[2] It is probable that it is the prophecy of Isaiah which we have just mentioned, which is here principally referred to. Further, the Apostles are commanded to remain in Jerusalem (ὑμεῖς δὲ καθίσατε ἐν τῇ πόλει) until they have been "clothed with power from on high" (24.49). The commandment of the Risen Lord to the Apostles, that they are not to leave Jerusalem (ἀπὸ Ἰ. μὴ χωρίζεσθαι) until they have received that which the Father had promised and Jesus had conveyed to them, is repeated in the introductory chapter of the Acts of the Apostles (1.4). Here the Risen Lord also says that the Apostles are to be his witnesses both *in Jerusalem* and in all Judaea and in Samaria, and unto the uttermost part of the earth (1.8). These sayings on the way in which the word of God proceeds, are made explicit in what follows. According to Luke, the Apostles do not go out as missionaries during the Church's first period; they remain in Jerusalem.[3] This is described with striking emphasis by Luke. They stay in Jerusalem, they teach—remarkably enough—in the area of the Temple (not of course in the Chamber of *Gazit* but in the Porch of Solomon) and in private houses.[4] They fill Jerusalem with their teaching (5.28). The congregation grows around them—in Jerusalem.[5] People come to Jerusalem from the nearby towns in order to obtain a share of the powers which are in motion around the Apostles (5.15 f.). And Luke emphasizes in 8.1 ff., when describing the persecution which struck the first congregation and which began the effective spread of the gospel, that all *with the exception of the Apostles* were scattered. We lose sight of the

---

[1] Cf. CONZELMANN, *op. cit.*, pp. 48 ff.

[2] On the question of Luke's use of the participle ἀρχόμενος, cf. J. W. HUNKIN, „Pleonastic" ἄρχομαι in the N.T., in *Journ. of Theol. Stud.* 25 (1924), pp. 390 ff.

[3] N.B. that Luke omits the traditions about the appearances in Galilee.

[4] E.g. 2.46; 3–4; 5.12, 20 f., 25, 42.

[5] 1.13 ff.; 2.41, 47; 5.12 ff.; 6.7, etc.

apostolic circle in the description of the victorious progress of the gospel which follows. To be sure, Peter's journeys to the various churches are mentioned,[1] but we hear nothing of the work of the other Apostles. It seems likely from the description of the Council of Apostles in Ch. 15, where we obtain new evidence of Jerusalem's undisputed position as the centre from which the word of God proceeds,[2] that the Apostles— except Peter—as a body are still in Jerusalem. (Peter's presence in Jerusalem was probably no more than temporary.)[3] When Paul visits Jerusalem (Ch. 21 ff.) it is James the brother of the Lord and "the elders" who are at the head of the original congregation (21.18). The twelve are not mentioned. They have left Jerusalem.

Jerusalem thus plays a strongly emphasized, positive role—we shall touch on the *negative* role played by the town only in passing[4]—in the account of the history of salvation as described by Luke. This positive role does not however depend upon such representative groups as the Great Sanhedrin or the priests; nor is it dependent upon the doctrinal authority of the Pharisees or the Sadducees, or upon the Essenes, who are not named. It depends upon Jesus, as the Christ, the Apostles and those who have joined them. Luke is also concerned to emphasize that "all the people" in Jerusalem are favourably inclined, both to Jesus and to the young Church.[5] We must therefore say a few words on the way in which the Apostles and the original congregation around them are presented as—shall we say—"the true Jerusalem".

Lk. 19.28–21.38 is built on an older collection of traditions concerning Jesus. On a basis of the evidence it appears that we have here a collection of traditions, the main elements of which had been brought together into one block before the time of Mark. The clarity with which these traditions deal with the *concrete* problems of the early Church in Jerusalem[6] gives us good reason for supposing that what we are here dealing with

---

[1] 8.14 ff.; 9.32 ff.; 10–13.

[2] See below, sec. E and Ch. 15.

[3] O. CULLMANN, *Petrus* (1952), pp. 41 ff.

[4] See further, SCHMAUCH, *Orte*, pp. 82 ff.

[5] E.g. Lk. 19.48, 20.19, 21.38, 22.2, Acts 2.47, 5.13 f. There is thus no question of "anti-semitism": the thought is that "the true Israel" is made up of those Jews who receive the Messiah, those who let themselves be saved from an untoward generation. The Gentiles may also gain access to this corpus, "as many as the Lord our God calls", Acts 2.38 ff. — Note how the killing of Jesus is said to have taken place in ignorance (Lk. 23.34, Acts 3.17; cf. 1 Cor. 2.8).

[6] E.g. the question of the right to localize their teaching to the site of the Temple; cf. Lk. 20.1 ff. with par. with Acts 4.7, 5.12 ff.

is an revised and expanded form of a very ancient Jerusalem tractate of traditions concerning Jesus. We must however in our argument keep to the Lucan presentation of these things. It is evident that he is perfectly well aware of the function filled by these passages of tradition.

This passage, full as it is of Scriptural allusions, begins (19.28–48) by describing how Jesus as the Messiah makes his entry into the holy city and comes into the area of the Temple (καὶ εἰσελθὼν εἰς τὸ ἱερόν ...). He drives out the merchants from the Temple in a messianic symbolic action: he *purifies* the Temple in order to proclaim instead[1]—with a quotation of Scripture—its character of *a house of prayer* (οἶκος προσευχῆς). *He then makes the area of the Temple the scene of his teaching.* In v. 47 we read that he teaches in the Temple every day (καὶ ἦν διδάσκων τὸ καθ᾿ ἡμέραν ἐν τῷ ἱερῷ).[2] It would seem to be clear that Luke connected this with the prophecies on how the springs of salvation were to be opened on the site of the Temple[3] and how the word of God should proceed from Jerusalem.

Luke notes that "all the people" support him. The high priests, the scribes and the elders of the people do not do so, however, nor do the Pharisees and Sadducees. In v. 39 ff. Luke has already described the way in which a number of Pharisees attempted to silence the messianic greetings directed toward Jesus. The Evangelist also describes in this context the tears of Jesus the Messiah over the city which ignores its time of visitation. There[4] begins at this point a negative theme which later runs beside the positive theme. In 20.1–8, an account is given of the way in which Jesus is questioned by the high priests, the scribes and elders concerning his authority for teaching in the Temple (ἐν ποίᾳ ἐξουσίᾳ ταῦτα ποιεῖς). His evasive answer seems to imply that he, like John the Baptist, had his commission "from above". 20.9–19 comprises a parable on how the *vineyard* (a traditional metaphor for the chosen people Israel)[5] is to be taken from the husbandmen and given to

---

[1] On the meaning of the messianic symbolic action which the cleansing of the Temple comprises, see R. H. LIGHTFOOT, *The Gospel Message of St. Mark* (1950), pp. 60 ff.

[2] Cf. the fact that the Temple is already said in 2.41 ff. to be the place where the "teachers of Israel" are active. On the meaning of the periphrastic construction, see G. BJÖRCK, ΗΝ ΔΙΔΑΣΚΩΝ (1940), and D. TABACHOWITZ, *Die Septuaginta und das N.T.* (1956), pp. 41 ff.

[3] Cf. John 7.37 ff.

[4] Cf. however 13.13 ff.

[5] See Joach. JEREMIAS, *Die Gleichnisse Jesu* (4th ed. 1956), pp. 59 ff.

others. In the interpretation given by Luke, we read that the scribes and Pharisees understand that "the husbandmen" in the parable refers to them. The pericopes 20.20–26 and 20.27–40 present Jesus in doctrinal debate with the Pharisees and the Sadducees respectively. He is attacked but succeeds in silencing his opponents; cf. also v. 41–44. V. 45–47 is a saying of Jesus which accuses the scribes of devouring widows' houses, and 21.1–4 is a *maaseh* in which Jesus teaches his disciples on the correct evaluation of poor widows. 21.5–36 contains the Lucan version of the eschatological discourse. Emphasis is here placed upon the judgement which is soon to strike Jerusalem "κατὰ σάρκα", the Jerusalem which refuses to receive him, and the destruction and the eschatological trials which are imminent. The negative theme of judgement over those who refuse to take account of their time of visitation, which began in the narrative of the entry into Jerusalem, here takes the upper hand.

Finally, Luke notes once more, in v. 37–38, that Jesus teaches in the Temple every day, and that all the people come in order to hear him. (Then follows the passion narrative: Jesus is rejected by the Great Sanhedrin[1] and by Herod, and is condemned—as a concession to the pressure brought to bear by the high priests and the scribes—by Pilate, the Roman procurator.)

In this material, Jesus of Nazareth has thus been presented as the Messiah and true shepherd of Israel,[2] who comes to his people and to the holy city. The other shepherds of the people demonstrate their apostasy and reject him. As the shepherd of Israel, he has the Temple (τὸ ἱερόν) as the focus of his activity. It is here that he passes on his logos. The traditions which Luke has quoted concerning Jesus should be compared with the situation of the original congregation as described in Acts. The congregation does not stand in an attitude of opposition to the Temple. On the contrary: *the area of the Temple is the most important centre for the teaching of the Apostles*. It is also here that the Christians come together to pray. The Apostles are questioned by the Great Sanhedrin on their authority for carrying on this activity, and in whose name they do so (see below sec. B).

The view of the history of salvation which Luke expresses in this way undoubtedly has to do with the early Christian concept of "the new

---

[1] We shall not deal with the debate on the question of which court it was that judged Jesus. Luke is concerned with the Great Sanhedrin.

[2] On this theme, see B. GERHARDSSON, *The Good Samaritan — the Good Shepherd?* (1958).

Temple". The Qumran texts reveal that in the period before the dawn of the Christian era it was expected in certain Jewish groups that in the last days, God would build a new Temple, a spiritual Temple not made with hands.[1] These ideas played an important role for Jesus and early Christianity[2] and certainly for Luke also, but we cannot take up such a complicated problem in this context.[3]

These brief indications should suffice as a demonstration of the way in which Luke's thoughts function. The prophecies and expectations concerning the holy city and its "centre", the Temple, must be fulfilled. It is in Jerusalem that the act of atonement must take place, and it is from Jerusalem that the logos of God must proceed in the age of salvation. But the Messiah has as the servants of his logos, not the high priests, the scribes and the elders, nor the Pharisees, nor the Sadducees, but the Apostles and the other disciples of Jesus, to whom "all the people" are sympathetically inclined. These Apostles are — according to a saying of Jesus — designated to sit on thrones judging (κρίνοντες, שופטים!) the twelve tribes of Israel (Lk. 22.29 f.). We must therefore proceed in our investigation in order to see how Luke describes the role of the Apostles as bearers and preservers of ὁ λόγος τοῦ κυρίου.

B. *The Apostles and* ὁ λόγος τοῦ κυρίου

It is a well-known fact that Luke is quite consistent in his use of the term ἀπόστολος.[4] If we ignore Acts 14.4, 14, where the linguistic practice of some source is presumably reproduced, Luke never uses this term to denote any persons other than the twelve. In Lk. 6.13 we read, typically enough: προσεφώνησεν τοὺς μαθητὰς αὐτοῦ, καὶ ἐκλεξάμενος ἀπ' αὐτῶν δώδεκα, οὓς καὶ ἀποστόλους ὠνόμασεν.[5]

[1] See Y. YADIN, A Midrash on 2 Sam. vii and Ps. i–ii (4Q Florilegium), in *Isr. Explor. Journ.* 9 (1959), pp. 95 ff., and D. FLUSSER, Two Notes on the Midrash on 2 Sam. vii, *ibid.*, pp. 99 ff.

[2] See e.g. Mk. 14.58 with par., 15.29 with par., John 2.19, Acts 6.13 f. and A. COLE, *The New Temple* (1950).

[3] Cf. below, pp. 270 and 278.

[4] On the problem of the various uses of the term ἀπόστολος, see K. H. RENGSTORF, ἀπόστολος, in *Theol. Wörterb.* I (1933), pp. 406 ff., E. M. KREDEL, Der Apostelbegriff in der neueren Exegese, in *Zeitschr. f. Kath. Theol.* 78 (1956), pp. 169 ff., 257 ff., and H. RIESENFELD, Apostel, in *Die Rel. in Gesch. u. Gegenw.* I (3rd ed. 1957), col. 497 ff.

[5] Cf. H. FR. VON CAMPENHAUSEN, Der urchristliche Apostelbegriff, in *Studia Theol.* 1 (1947), pp. 104 f., 115 ff.

The designation "the twelve" (οἱ δώδεκα), which Luke often uses in his Gospel, occurs only once in Acts (6.2). However, "the eleven" are mentioned twice at the beginning of Acts (1.26, 2.14)[1] and twice in the last chapter of the Gospel (24.9, 33).

In his description of the way in which the circle of Apostles was complemented after the apostasy of Judas (Acts 1.15 ff.), Luke gives us what practically amounts to a definition of the qualifications ascribed to the twelve Apostles. First, they "companied with us all the time that the Lord Jesus went in and went out among us, beginning from the baptism of John, unto the day that he was received up from us"; secondly, they were specially chosen (ἐκλέγεσθαι) and commissioned to witness concerning Jesus and the resurrection. The fact that they are chosen by Jesus himself is stressed in Acts 1.2 as in Lk. 6.13.[2] Even the one who was brought into the circle of the twelve as a replacement for Judas was considered to have been chosen by the Lord himself. The casting of lots, after prayer for the intervention of God, is understood as being a process of election from above (Acts 1.24).

The main view of the Apostles which we find in Acts is that they are Christ's *witnesses* (μάρτυρες), who are to bear witness (μαρτύριον) of all that he said and did and everything which had to do with him, particularly his resurrection.[3] They also bear witness of all that is written about him. In Lk. 24.36 ff., to which we shall return in due course, there is reproduced a very concrete tradition concerning the way in which the Apostles were made witnesses of the resurrection. And in Acts 4.20 (cf. 26.16) we read—in the terms of a legal commonplace[4]— that the Apostles, as reliable witnesses, bear witness only to what they

---

[1] N.B. the readings of Codex Bezae in locis.

[2] The information that Jesus himself chose the twelve is certainly historical; see B. RIGAUX, Die „Zwölf" in Geschichte und Kerygma, in *Der historische Jesus und der kerygmatische Christus* (1960), pp. 468 ff. From the information that at the time when Matthias was chosen, the Jerusalem church numbered 120 members (Acts 1.15), one might guess that the college of the twelve was originally chosen by the congregation on the principle of "chiefs of ten" (on this principle in Qumran, see C. RABIN, *Qumran Studies*, 1957, pp. 107 f.), but this would be free speculation, built only on Luke's editorial comment in Acts 1.15. It is difficult to understand the later history of the college of the twelve if it originated in this way. It is also difficult to explain away the role played by the twelve in the synoptic tradition.

[3] See the most recent work, PH.-H. MENOUD, Jésus et ses témoins, in *Église et Théologie* 23 (1960), pp. 7 ff. See also L. CERFAUX, Témoins du Christ d'après le Livre des Actes, in *Recueil* L. CERFAUX II (1954), pp. 157 ff.

[4] Cf. the notes of S. KRAUSS, in his edition of *Sanhedrin, Makkōt* (1933), pp. 303 f.

themselves have seen and heard. As in the linguistic practice of late Judaism, the terms μάρτυς and μαρτύριον (עֵד, עֵדוּת) have a distinctly legal sound.[1] It is worth remembering that these terms are used not only in connection with witness of events but also of sayings and teachings.[2]

The twelve, together with their apostolic commission (διακονία καὶ ἀποστολή 1.25; cf. 1.17 and 6.4), have been equipped with Holy Spirit and power,[3] which is manifest in their varying activities: as they confront men in powerful and effective language with the need of making a decision for or against Christ[4]; as they call them to faith, conversion and baptism;[5] as they teach all that has to do with the Kingdom of God; as they administer Church discipline;[6] as they heal the sick and perform other mighty works, miracles and signs[7]—which are understood to be the seal of divine approval on their authority from Jesus.[8]

According to Luke, one of the most important sides of the Apostles' activity is that they teach and witness to Jesus Christ. The missionary term εὐαγγελίζειν is used in this connection only exceptionally of the Apostles' activity during this period.[9] A more usual term is διδάσκειν, "teach".[10] Teaching takes place—following the practice of Jesus—in the area of the Temple on the one hand, and in private houses on the other.[11] Just as the scribes often held their learned meetings in some upper room (עֲלִיָּה, ὑπερῷον),[12] so an upper room was the first *private* meeting-place for the Apostles and other adherents of Christ during the earliest period of the Church (Acts 1.13).

It may be worth observing that according to Luke the Jewish leaders

---

[1] Cf. above, pp. 182 ff.

[2] See BACHER, *Tradition*, pp. 15 ff. Cf. also R. ASTING, *Die Verkündigung des Wortes im Urchristentum* (1939), pp. 595 ff.

[3] E.g. Lk. 24.49; Acts 1.4 f., 8; 2.1 ff.; 4.8, 31; 8.15 ff.

[4] Acts 2.37 f.; 4.29, 33; 10.44, etc.

[5] 2.38 ff.

[6] 5.1 ff.

[7] 2.43, 3.1 ff.; 4.29 f., 5.12, etc.

[8] 2.22; 14.3; cf. 2 Cor. 12.12, Rom. 15.19.

[9] 5.42; cf. later 8.25 and 10.36. N.B. καταγγέλλειν 4.2; cf. 13.5, 38; 15.36, 16.17, etc.

[10] 4.2, 18; 5.21, 25, 28, 42. On the διδαχή of the Apostles, cf. 2.42, 5.28. On the different terms for preaching and teaching, see ASTING, *Die Verkündigung*, pp. 120 ff., and CONZELMANN, *Die Mitte*, pp. 204 ff. See also K. H. RENGSTORF, διδάσκω κτλ., in *Theol. Wörterb.* II (1935), pp. 141 ff.

[11] 3.1, 4.1 ff.; 5.21, 25, 42; cf. Lk. 24.53, Acts 2.46, 5.12 ff.

[12] See S. KRAUSS, Die Versammlungsstätten der Talmudgelehrten, in *Festschrift* I. LEWY (1911), pp. 27 ff., and BILLERBECK, *Comm.* II, p. 594.

consider the activity of the Apostles as a kind of new (pneumatic) school
or sect-foundation.[1] The question asked by the Great Sanhedrin of the
Apostles is a factual parallel to that they asked of Jesus, according to
Lk. 20.1 ff.: "By what power,[2] or in what name, have you done this
(ἐν ποίᾳ δυνάμει ἢ ἐν ποίῳ ὀνόματι ἐποιήσατε τοῦτο ὑμεῖς; 4.7)?" We
then read that the Sanhedrin forbids them to speak or to teach *in the
name of Jesus* (μὴ φθέγγεσθαι μηδὲ διδάσκειν ἐπὶ τῷ ὀνόματι τοῦ Ἰησοῦ;
4.18). This terminology is not difficult to identify. The disciples of other
doctrinal authorities in Judaism are also said to have spoken in the
name of their teacher (אמר בשם (משום) רבי פלוני)[3] or received power,
authority (רשות)[4] to teach, to judge, etc. To be sure, the Apostles'
speech in the name of Jesus and their actions carried out on his authority
are thought to be much more *pneumatic*, but this should not be allowed
to obscure the structural and terminological similarity with parallel
cases in that milieu in which the early Church took shape.

An additional relevant fact is that Luke uses the term "disciples"
(μαθηταί) as a designation for Christians.[5]

We must emphasize that Luke's main term for the "Word" of which
the Apostles are servants is not εὐαγγέλιον[6] and even less κήρυγμα,[7] but
"the word of God" (ὁ λόγος τοῦ θεοῦ, דבר יהוה) or "the word of the
Lord" (ὁ λόγος τοῦ κυρίου);[8] it is often difficult in this connection to
decide whether "the Lord" denotes God or Christ: both are given the

---

[1] Cf. 24.14: κατὰ τὴν ὁδὸν ἣν λέγουσιν αἵρεσιν ...; 24.5, 28.22.

[2] It seems as though in this connection, δύναμις is practically synonymous with
ἐξουσία, meaning not only "power" but "authority". It is certain that behind the
Greek is to be found the Hebrew רשות, Aramaic רשותא.

[3] H. BIETENHARD, ὄνομα, in *Theol. Wörterb.* V (1954), pp. 242 ff., fails to give
sufficient consideration to the connection between the rabbinic formulae and their
N.T. equivalents. However, cf. his argument, pp. 267 and 270. Cf. also F. BLASS,
A. DEBRUNNER, *Grammatik des neutestamentlichen Griechisch* (9th ed. 1954),
§ 206, 2*.

[4] Cf. n. 2, above.

[5] 6.1 f., 7; 9.1, 10, 19, etc. Cf. on the language K. H. RENGSTORF, μανθάνω κτλ.,
in *Theol. Wörterb.* IV, pp. 462 ff.

[6] The word occurs only twice in the Lucan writings, Acts 15.7, 20.24.

[7] The word occurs only once: Lk. 11.32 (on the preaching of Jonah).

[8] ὁ λόγος τ. θ.: Lk. 5.1, 8.11, 21, Acts 4.31, 6.2, 6; 11.1, 13. 5, etc. ὁ λόγος τ. κ.:
Acts 8.25, 12.24 (B vg), 13.49, 15.35 f., etc. Cf. RIESENFELD, *The Gospel Tradition
and its Beginnings*, p. 58 (22).

title of *Kurios*.[1] It can also be called "the Word" (ὁ λόγος, הדבר).[2] That
which is proclaimed can sometimes be called simply "Christ" or "the
Christ Jesus".[3] The content of the proclamation is sometimes referred
to as a definite part of the messianic events, most usually its climax:
the resurrection.[4]

Naturally, there are a number of variations in meaning, when in
various contexts Luke uses the concept ὁ λόγος (ὁ λ. τοῦ θεοῦ, ὁ λ. τοῦ
κυρίου), but the author of the Acts of the Apostles seems on the whole
to have a quite consistent and relatively straightforward concept of the
word of God. The divine logos appears to the author of Acts to be almost
an independent and personified entity, like the Jewish concept of the
Torah.[5] Referring to the success achieved by the Apostles' proclamation, Luke says—to quote a typical formulation—that the word
of God "grew" (ηὔξανεν, 6.7, 12.24, 19.20).

As we have seen, the author of Acts does not leave us in ignorance
of the essential content of that which he calls *the word of the Lord* or
the Word. This is dealt with in rather more detail in those summaries of
the Apostles' speeches given by the author in 2.22 ff., 3.12 ff., 4.8 ff.,
5.29 ff. and 10.34 ff. The latter passage has justifiably aroused the
attention of scholars.[6] Luke here expressly gives a short resumé of that
logos which the Apostles serve and which they spread. Here he presents
"the word which he (God) sent unto the children of Israel, preaching
good tidings of peace by Jesus Christ" (τὸν λόγον ὃν ἀπέστειλεν τοῖς
υἱοῖς Ἰσραὴλ εὐαγγελιζόμενος εἰρήνην διὰ Ἰησοῦ Χριστοῦ); this takes
the form of a resumé of the facts of Christ's ministry, from his baptism by John to the resurrection, a summary concluded with the emphasis on the fact that the Apostles have to witness (διαμαρτύρεσθαι) and
that the prophets also bear witness (μαρτυρεῖν) to these things.

"The word of the Lord", as it has been entrusted in the first place to
the Apostles, thus encompasses not only the cardinal points in the history

---

[1] ὁ Κύριος: Lk. 1.6, 9, 11; 5.17 (God). 7.13, 19; 10.1, 12.42 (Christ). Acts 2.39,
3.19, 5.19 (God). 1.21, 5.14, 7.59 (Christ), etc.

[2] ὁ λόγος: Lk. 1.2, Acts 4.4, 6.4, 8.4, 10.44, 11.19, etc.

[3] E.g. κηρύσσειν τὸν Χριστόν, Acts 8.5, εὐαγγελίζεσθαι Χριστὸν Ἰησοῦν, 5.42.

[4] Acts 1.22, 2.31, 4.33; cf. 4.2, 17.18.

[5] Cf. ASTING, *Die Verkündigung*, pp. 108 ff.

[6] See the pioneer essay by C. H. DODD, The Framework of the Gospel Narrative
(1932), reprinted in *N. T. Studies* (1953), pp. 1 ff., and IDEM, *The Apostolic Preaching and its Developments* (1936), pp. 48 ff., from which the lively debate proceeded.
Cf. DIBELIUS, *Formgeschichte*, pp. 14 ff.

of salvation (the suffering, death and resurrection of Christ), but in fact everything which Christ both did and taught, and everything which happened to him, from the beginning of his public ministry: everything of which the Apostles are eyewitnesses. This is indirectly shown by the passage 1.21 ff. also, where emphasis is placed on the fact that an Apostle must have followed Jesus from that day on which he was baptized by John.[1] "The word of the Lord" is thus not only the *kerygma* but also the *didache*.

This word of the Lord which in the last days "has been sent to the sons of Israel" is however—according to Luke—not radically new, but only a fulfilment of that to which Moses and all (the other) prophets bore witness. There is thus a basic connection between the witness of the Apostles and that of the prophets or, as it is sometimes called, between the witness of the Apostles and that of the *Scriptures*. We must therefore pay attention to the way in which Luke presents the relationship between the tradition concerning Christ and the Holy Scriptures.

C. *The Ministry of Christ and the Holy Scriptures (O.T.)*

Early Christianity was not torah-centric: it was Christo-centric. This stands out in sharp relief to anyone who compares the early Christian documents with documents and traditions from the various torah-centric groups of contemporary Judaism. There can be no mistaking the point at which early Christianity had its religious *centre of experience*.

It is however easy to ignore the fact of the role which the Holy Scriptures nonetheless played for early Christianity, since this role is not always directly pointed out or described in the sources.[2] The traditional Holy Scriptures, handed down from the fathers, possessed an authority and a degree of sacredness which was never questioned, either by Jesus

---

[1] Cf. H. RIESENFELD, Tradition und Redaktion im Markusevangelium, in *Zeitschr. f.d. Neutest. Wiss.*, Beih. 21 (1954), pp. 158 ff., who emphasizes that the missionary preaching and teaching of the early Church did not merely give traditional material of *loci* character, but also an overall picture of Jesus and a rough outline of his ministry. Cf. below, pp. 299 f., on the possibility that the λόγος τοῦ εὐαγγελίου which we find in 1 Cor. 15.3 ff. is a passage from a more extensive logos.

[2] Cf. e.g. the words of LEIPOLDT on the situation in the earliest Church: "Es scheint zunächst unnötig, christl. Bücher zu verfassen. Eine Weisung Jesu in dieser Richtung liegt nicht vor. Die Erinnerung an den Herrn ist lebendig. Der Geist ergänzt sie. Das Ende scheint nahe. *Im Notfalle hat man das A.T. das man durch allegorische Deutung verwendbar macht*" (Buch II, in *Reallex. f. Ant. u. Christ.* II, 1954, col. 711; the italics are mine). Im Notfalle!

or by early Christianity. This does not mean to say that early Christianity *decided* to submit to the authority of the Scriptures and to accept these Scriptures. They were *taken over*; this was self-evident, as self-evident as the "taking over" of God and of sacred history. Nor did they see any opposition or rivalry between the Scriptures and Christ; on the contrary: it was in Christ that the Scriptures found their fulfilment, their completion, their consummation. Early Christianity was never faced with the problem of whether or not to accept a "canon". Their problem—if it was a problem—was to find the correct interpretation of an existing collection of Scriptures whose holiness and authority were undisputed.

We can study this situation to advantage in the writings of Luke. Here we have a basic thought, that the Apostles are able to build their proclamation on two reliable divine "witnesses": on the one hand, the words and works of Christ (and his suffering, death and resurrection above all) together with their continuation in the deeds of the Apostles, inspired to work wonders by the Spirit; and on the other, the witness of the Scriptures. The Apostles are witnesses to the words and works of Jesus, and they are also entrusted with the capacity for the correct interpretation and exposition of the Scriptures. We do not need to consider Luke's *variation* of this "two witness theme" in more detail at this point.[1]

According to Luke, Jesus began to expound the Scriptures during the period of his earthly ministry. He gives us a description of this work of exposition—a description which is evidently intended to be both a programme and a paradigm—in 4.16 ff. Jesus enters the synagogue at Nazareth on the Sabbath day, in accordance with his custom. He is there called upon to read the Scripture lesson (ἀνάγνωσις, מקרא), from the prophets.[2] Certain parts of the ritual stand out clearly. Jesus stands up in order to read aloud (ἀνέστη ἀναγνῶναι)[3] and unrolls (ἀνοίξας, פתח) the scroll himself. When the lesson is completed, he rolls up (πτύξας, גלל) the scroll again, gives it to the synagogue servant and sits down (ἐκά-

---

[1] See above, pp. 211 ff., and MORGENTHALER, *Die lukanische Geschichtsschreibung als Zeugnis* I–II.

[2] Reading from the Law is not mentioned here. Is this to be understood to mean that in the Church in which this tradition obtained its final form, only the Prophets were read in public worship, and that this is reflected in the narrative? This appears to be improbable, in view of the role played by the Law — Christologically interpreted — in the Lucan writings. The fact that the reading of the Torah is not mentioned would seem to be due only to the technique of narration.

[3] In the synagogue they stood up to read: עמד לקרות.

θισεν) in order to teach.[1] His teaching begins with a programmatical statement: "Today this Biblical text[2] is fulfilled in your ears" (σήμερον πεπλήρωται ἡ γραφὴ αὕτη ἐν τοῖς ὠσὶν ὑμῶν).[3] Then follows a "sermon" with its words of messianic authority in relatively free relation to the text.[4]

Concerning the relationship which stands out at this point between the actual messianic events and the Scriptures, we must be content to note two things: (i) The word of Scripture is used as an authoritative witness to Christ. It is made to strengthen and support the actual messianic events, and to bear powerful divine witness. At the same time, it illustrates, interprets and clarifies the Christ-event. If we may be allowed to simplify a little we might say that the Scriptures are here used as an interpretation and as a witness. (ii) This use of the word of Scripture, however, has consequences for the word itself. The Scriptures, because of their application to the actual Christ-event, are given a definite interpretation. In this exposition the disciples have been given a Christ-midrash. The foundations are laid for the *Christian* exposition of Scripture; the early Christian midrash tradition has begun to develop. We shall consider this in a little more detail in due course.

According to Luke, the disciples did not gain complete knowledge of the meaning of the ministry of Christ and at the same time complete insight into the way in which the Scriptures should be interpreted and used until after the resurrection of Christ. It is an important principle to state that in the Lucan writings there is no question of a "dumb" historical event being given the gift of speech by means of a later interpretation. Instead, it is a matter of a mysterious divine act of revelation, which has hitherto been only *partly* understood, having its meaning *fully* revealed and interpreted. In the words and works of Christ—and particularly in his suffering, death and resurrection—is realized the divine plan of salvation. This can be understood to some extent during the time of Jesus' earthly ministry, but its complete meaning is not revealed until after the resurrection.[5]

---

[1] In the synagogue, the one who held the didactic sermon sat down: יושב ודורש.

[2] Like כתוב and מקרא, γραφή means both "Scripture" and "Passage of Scripture" (see *Lexica*). It is the latter meaning which applies in this case.

[3] On the meaning of the term πληροῦν, see H. LJUNGMAN, *Das Gesetz erfüllen* (1954).

[4] Further, cf. above, Ch. 5.

[5] As the most adequate parallel we might consider the two stages in teaching. The text is first learned, and a certain—though as a rule very incomplete—under-

In Luke 24¹ is described, first of all, the experience of the women at the tomb. As they stand wondering at the fact of the empty tomb they are exhorted by two white-clad men to remember what Jesus had said during his earthly ministry (μνήσθητε ὡς ἐλάλησεν ὑμῖν ἔτι ὢν ἐν τῇ Γαλιλαίᾳ): that he should suffer and arise. Prophetic sayings² of Jesus are thus called into play in order to reveal the secret of the empty tomb. When the women remember³ the words of Jesus (ἐμνήσ-θησαν τῶν ῥημάτων αὐτοῦ) they understand what has happened.

Luke then describes the experience of two disciples on the road to Emmaus. Just as Jews, faithful to the Torah, when they sat in their houses and walked on the road "always" talked about the manifold wisdom of the Torah,⁴ so the disciples of Jesus talk about "the things concerning Jesus of Nazareth" (τὰ περὶ Ἰησοῦ τοῦ Ναζαρηνοῦ, v. 19, cf. 14). They are described as being unable to understand the meaning of the suffering and death of Christ and the message of the empty tomb, and are therefore also unable to *believe* the fact of salvation. The Risen Lord, who thereupon comes to them, rebukes them for being foolish and slow of heart to believe in all *that the prophets have spoken* (ὦ ἀνό-ητοι καὶ βραδεῖς τῇ καρδίᾳ τοῦ πιστεύειν ἐπὶ πᾶσιν οἷς ἐλάλησαν οἱ προφῆται). The Messiah, in accordance with the will of God, must (ἔδει)⁵ suffer and arise, and we then read that he began⁶ with Moses

standing is reached; then follows the next stage: interpretation, the "uncovering" of the secrets of the text which has been learned (see above, Ch. 11A). The same applies to the pedagogical symbolic actions: first the action is carried out, and it conveys—at least to those having insight—a certain preliminary understanding. Then follows the interpretative activity through which the full implications are laid bare (see above, Ch. 12B).

¹ For a more detailed analysis of the chapter, see SCHUBERT, *The Structure and Significance of Luke 24*, pp. 165 ff.

² On the role accorded by Luke to prophecy, see SCHUBERT, *op. cit.*

³ Luke here grants the women access to the sayings spoken secretly by Jesus to his disciples on the subject of his coming passion (9.22, 43 ff., 18.31 ff.). In this and similar texts, to "remember" can hardly mean to recall something which had been forgotten, but rather to *repeat* sayings to oneself, and to allow them once more to have their effect on the soul. Cf. DAHL, *Anamnesis*, pp. 70 ff.

⁴ See above, Ch. 11 G, and BILLERBECK, *Comm.* II, p. 273.

⁵ See E. FASCHER, Theologische Beobachtungen zu δεῖ, in *Zeitschr. f. d. Neutest. Wiss.*, Beih. 21 (1954), pp. 228 ff.

⁶ The Lucan phrase ἀρξάμενος ἀπὸ Μωϋσέως (or the like), Lk. 24.27, Acts 8.35, seems to be taken from the educational terminology of the Greek-speaking synagogue. Cf. A. WIFSTRAND, Stylistic Problems in the Epistles of James and Peter, in *Studia Theol.* 1 (1947), p. 180, and HUNKIN, „*Pleonastic*" ἄρχομαι, pp. (395 ff.) 401 f.

and all the prophets and fully explained to them in all the Scriptures the things concerning himself (καὶ ἀρξάμενος ἀπὸ Μωϋσέως καὶ ἀπὸ πάντων τῶν προφητῶν διηρμήνευσεν αὐτοῖς ἐν πάσαις ταῖς γραφαῖς τὰ περὶ ἑαυτοῦ). Presumably the meaning here is that the Risen Lord takes representative passages from the different groups of Scripture, or from each of the different books, and applies or expounds them.[1] In other words, he gives them a Christological midrash exegesis, an exegesis which is also understood as being spiritual illumination ("Was not our heart burning[2] within us", v. 32). He opens the Scriptures for the disciples (διήνοιγεν ἡμῖν τὰς γραφάς), as we read in v. 32. This also fills another function: it allows the witness of the Holy Scriptures to support and interpret the messianic events, and thus it arouses faith.

In the following pericope, 24.35 ff., Luke narrates how the Risen Lord appears to the twelve,[3] together with a number of other disciples. In this pericope it is said on the one hand, that the Apostles have their qualifications as eyewitnesses completed by being allowed to witness the actual fact of Christ's resurrection, and on the other, that they gain the final and definitive ability to understand the meaning of Scripture correctly.

In v. 36–43, a description is given of the way in which the Apostles are allowed to see and touch the Risen Lord, and how he eats in their sight. They are therefore able to witness that he is bodily and literally risen (cf. Acts 1.3). They are able to function as witnesses of the resurrection, μάρτυρες τῆς ἀναστάσεως.[4]

In v. 44–45, there follows a description of how the Apostles are enabled to understand the Scriptures:

εἶπεν δὲ πρὸς αὐτούς· οὗτοι οἱ λόγοι μου οὓς ἐλάλησα πρὸς ὑμᾶς ἔτι ὢν σὺν ὑμῖν, ὅτι δεῖ πληρωθῆναι πάντα τὰ γεγραμμένα ἐν τῷ νόμῳ Μωϋσέως καὶ τοῖς προφήταις καὶ ψαλ-

"And he said unto them, These are my words which I spoke unto you, while I was yet with you, how that all things must be fulfilled which are written in the law

---

[1] For the meaning of this passage in principle, see H. ODEBERG, *Kristus och Skriften* (3rd ed. 1950), pp. 3 ff., and E. STARFELT, *Studier i rabbinsk och nytestamentlig skrifttolkning* (1959), pp. 254 ff.

[2] D reads "veiled".

[3] On the relation between this pericope and the Emmaus pericope, see SCHUBERT, *The Structure*, pp. 169 ff.

[4] The Apostles are characterized in this way in Acts 1.22: a programmatical formulation! Cf. 1 Cor. 15.15.

μοῖς περὶ ἐμοῦ. τότε διήνοιξεν αὐτῶν τὸν νοῦν τοῦ συνιέναι τὰς γραφάς.

of Moses, and the prophets, and
the psalms, concerning me. Then
opened he their mind to understand the Scriptures."

It is important to note that what Jesus said in his earthly teaching
also plays a role here. *Sayings of Jesus are repeated* and are "used".
But more important is the question of content. We are concerned to
investigate Luke's accunt of the relationship between the messianic events and the Scriptures. During his earthly ministry (ἔτι ὢν σὺν ὑμῖν)
Jesus taught his disciples that the messianic prophecies of the Scriptures
applied to him. But this preliminary teaching did not convey complete
understanding to the Apostles. Luke strongly emphasized earlier (9.45,
18.34) their inability to comprehend Jesus' predictions, his suffering
and his resurrection. He now describes the way in which Christ, after
his resurrection, not only allows the Apostles to see with their own eyes
that he is indeed risen, but at the same time opens their minds in such
a way that they are completely enabled to understand the witness of the
Scriptures concerning him. This latter gift seems scarcely to be conceived
as merely a spiritual bestowal of the charisma of Scripture interpretation. It seems rather to be intended—as in the previous pericope—as a
Spirit-filled teaching in pneumatic exegesis.

The way in which Luke understands the events recorded in v. 36–45
is perfectly clear. The divine logos has been passed on to the Apostles
on the basis of two witnesses. The twelve can testify, not only to what they
saw and heard, as eyewitnesses of the words and works of Christ—the
climax of which is the passion and resurrection—but also to what the
Scriptures say about him. *They are bearers, not only of the tradition concerning Christ, but also of the correct interpretation of the Scriptures.* We
read in the next verse:

"And he said unto them, *Thus it is written,* that the Christ should
suffer, and rise again from the dead on the third day; and that repentance unto remission of sins should be preached in his name unto all
the nations, beginning from Jerusalem. *Ye are witnesses of these things*
(ὑμεῖς μάρτυρες τούτων)."

In the introduction to Acts, Luke refers back to what he described
in his previous work, although on that occasion one has the impression
that the ascension took place immediately after the Risen Lord's appearance to the twelve (24.50 ff.). We read here that the Lord showed

himself to his disciples for "forty days" and spoke with them about the Kingdom of God (λέγων τὰ περὶ τῆς βασιλείας τοῦ θεοῦ). Just as Moses received the holy Torah in the course of forty days' fellowship with God on the mountain according to the Jewish tradition,[1] so on this occasion the twelve receive the principle of eschatological logos in all its fulness during forty days.[2]

It is interesting to note in this connection that the coming outpouring of the Spirit is spoken of as "the promise of the *Father* which ye heard from *me*: John indeed baptized you with water ..." It is thus partly *Scripture* (the prophecies on the pouring out of the Spirit, and in particular Joel 2.28 ff.), partly *the tradition of Christ* (a prophetic saying of Jesus, Lk. 3.16 with par.), which also is brought into use here.

We can also mention here, parenthetically, that the same saying of Jesus is repeated and used in Acts 11.16. There (11.2 ff.) Peter is taken to task for having visited uncircumcized and eaten with them. He defends himself by referring, first, to a revelation he had had (an argument from a בת קול), and secondly, to the fact that the Gentiles were allowed, through a miracle of God, to receive the Spirit (an argument from מעשה נסים), and thirdly, by quoting and using the saying of Jesus concerning the outpouring of the Spirit over "the disciples" (ἐμνήσθην δὲ τοῦ ῥήματος τοῦ κυρίου, ὡς ἔλεγεν ...).

It is unnecessary to consider in more detail the way in which the Apostles refer, in those speeches which are reported in Acts, on the one hand to that which they themselves have seen and heard, and on the other to the witness of the Scriptures. The fulfilled messianic events and their continuation in the remarkable events of the first period of the Church form one element (the first "witness") in the Apostles' evidence; the words of the prophets the other. The Apostles refer either to the messianic events as a whole or to parts thereof; either to the witness of the prophets (Scriptures) as a whole or to individual passages of Scrip-

---

[1] Ex. 24.18, Deut. 9.9, 18.

[2] Cf. A. WIKENHAUSER, Die Belehrung der Apostel durch den Auferstandenen, in *Vom Wort des Lebens*, *Festschrift f.* M. MEINERTZ (1951), pp. 105 ff. It is not improbable that Luke is acquainted with traditions about the conversations of the Risen Lord with his disciples, similar to those which we find in the later apocryphal literature. — A question of particular interest is that of the relation which can have existed between the traditions used by Luke in Lk. 24.44 ff. and Acts 1.2 ff., and the early Christian midrash used by Paul in 2 Cor. 3.12 ff.; see below, pp. 285 f. (N.B. that D in v. 32 reads καρδία ... κεκαλυμμένη.)

ture.[1] The unity between the actual messianic events and the prophecies of the Scriptures is stressed most emphatically. "I believe *all* that is written in the Law and the prophets," says Paul before Felix (24.14); "I say *nothing other than* that which the prophets and Moses have foretold," he says before Festus (26.22).[2]

In the speeches of the Apostles which Luke introduces into his presentation in Acts, he uses a certain amount of material from the early Christian midrash tradition.[3] We have several examples of the way in which the early Church interpreted and used the Scriptures. This early Christian midrash exegesis thus has—according to Luke—its origin, in principle, in Jesus' teaching of his disciples, both during his earthly ministry and above all after his resurrection.

The author of Acts also gives us a number of concrete pictures of how the Scriptures were used, technically speaking, in the teaching of early Christianity. His method of describing the way in which the early Christian doctrinal authorities take part in the synagogue services agrees remarkably well with the narrative of Jesus' appearance in the synagogue at Nazareth. After the Scriptures have been read in accordance with the regular order of service, there follows a hortatory exposition. Thus if some early Christian teacher is called to read, he presents the Christian message on a basis of the text which has been read. A description is given of such a case in Acts 13.13 ff. After readings from the Law and the Prophets, Paul is called upon to speak, whereupon he delivers a synagogue sermon, rich in Scriptural proofs concerning Christ.

In Acts 17.1 ff. we are given a new example of early Christian teaching in the synagogues. Here, too, the word concerning Christ is delivered with the Scriptures as the point of departure and the basis of argument. Paul speaks (or discusses) for three Sabbaths in the Thessalonica syna-

---

[1] For an analysis of the speeches in Acts, see DODD, *The Apostolic Preaching*, B. GÄRTNER, Missionspredikan i Apostlagärningarna, in *Sv. Exeg. Årsbok* 15 (1950), pp. 34 ff., IDEM, *The Areopagus Speech and Natural Revelation*, B. REICKE, A Synopsis of Early Christian Preaching, in A. FRIDRICHSEN and others, *The Root of the Vine* (1953), pp. 128 ff. See also J. DUPONT, L'utilisation apologétique de l'A.T. dans les Discours des Actes, in *Ephem. Theol. Lovan.* 29 (1953), pp. 289 ff.

[2] The intimate relation between the apostolic preaching and the Scriptures is emphasized very strongly by H. ODEBERG, e.g. *Kristus och Skriften*, and *Skriftens studium, inspiration och auktoritet* (1954), passim.

[3] For a detailed analysis of the early Christian midrash material in Acts 1.16–20, 2.17–21, 2.25–28 (with 13.34 f.), 3.22 f., see STARFELT, *Studier*, pp. 129–225. See further C. H. DODD, *According to the Scriptures* (1953).

gogue on a basis of the Scriptures, expounding and proving (διελέξατο αὐτοῖς ἀπὸ τῶν γραφῶν, διανοίγων καὶ παρατιθέμενος ὅτι...), on the one hand, that it was necessary for the Messiah to suffer and to rise from the dead, and on the other, that this Messiah is identical with the Jesus whom Paul proclaimed. It is not altogether certain that what Luke is here describing is a period of teaching which took place within the actual service. It is possible that we are here dealing with midrash teaching, or with doctrinal discussion of the Torah, within the synagogue, but extra to the services.[1]

In the same chapter (v. 10 f.) we hear how the people willingly received the word (ἐδέξαντο τὸν λόγον) in the Jewish synagogue congregation in Beroea, and how they "examined the Scriptures daily, whether these things were so" (καθ᾽ ἡμέραν ἀνακρίνοντες τὰς γραφὰς εἰ ἔχοι ταῦτα οὕτως). It was necessary for the Apostles to parallel the *Christ-logos* and the witness of the *Scriptures*.[2] Therefore midrash exegesis was undertaken. This type of Scripture research, which was common not only in Qumran but also in other torah-centric groups, is also mentioned in John 7.52: one must "seek, examine" (ζητεῖν, ἐρευνᾶν, דרש) in order to "find" (εὑρίσκειν, מצא) whether or not a doctrinal statement is justified.[3]

We must finally consider the narrative of the Ethiopian courtier in Acts 8.26 ff. Here Luke gives a case in which an individual, a *sebomenos*, or a proselyte was taught. A courtier, sitting in his chariot and reading —aloud, naturally—from his scroll of Isaiah (LXX) is asked by the evangelist Philip: "Do you understand what you are reading (ἆρά γε γινώσκεις ἃ ἀναγινώσκεις)?"[4] He answers: "How shall I (understand), if no one directs me (πῶς γὰρ ἂν δυναίμην ἐὰν μή τις ὁδηγήσει με)?" A relatively advanced education was required in Antiquity in order to learn to read and understand a book by oneself. The direction and help of someone who had himself learned to read and understand the matter was needed. In this case, however, a further crux developed: here it was also a matter of the difficulty of correctly understanding the *prophecies*. We read that Philip then opened his mouth and "beginning from this

---

[1] Cf. below on ἡ διδαχὴ τῶν ἀποστόλων, pp. 240 ff.

[2] The rabbinic expression for proving, with the help of exegesis, the validity of what one teaches, is קיים תלמודו. Cf. further, below, pp. 264 and 287 f.

[3] "That which is found" (הנמצא) is often identical with "that which is revealed" (הנגלה). Cf. RABIN, *Qumran Studies*, p. 100. Cf. those cases in which one "goes out, thinks about, and finds" confirmation in the *oral* Torah (see above, Ch. 11 E).

[4] It is not impossible that this is a normal "ritual" question of teaching.

passage,[1] proclaimed to him the gospel concerning Jesus" (ἀρξάμενος ἀπὸ τῆς γραφῆς ταύτης εὐηγγελίσατο αὐτῷ τὸν Ἰησοῦν). Proclamation led rapidly to baptism. The unique elements in this episode should not turn our attention away from the valuable information contained in this narrative on early Christian teaching methods. Is. 53 seems to have played a prominent role in early Christian proclamation and teaching,[2] but so, too, did other O.T. pericopes.

To sum up: The examples which we have quoted here show that Luke finds it typical for the early Christian proclamation to *proceed from*[3] *texts in the Holy Scriptures*, to interpret and use these Christologically, or to present the Christian message more freely, but still in connection with the text. Another way is to *proceed from the message of Christ* (the tradition concerning Christ) and to examine the Scriptures in order to see whether the new logos agrees with the words of the Holy Writ or to prove the validity of what one teaches. The Scriptures are continually being quoted in the early Christian proclamation and teaching concerning Christ. A common method of argument is to appeal, on the one hand, to the tradition of Christ and, on the other, to the Scriptures. The connection between the tradition of Christ and the Holy Scriptures was thus according to Luke not merely an idea or a concept, but a reality which determined the entire method of the early Church when presenting its logos. And the Apostles were considered to be the bearers, both of the tradition of Christ, and of the correct interpretation of the Scriptures.

D. Διακονία τοῦ λόγου

In the first chapter of this book we dealt briefly with the role played by the Torah in post-Exilic Jewish piety.[4] Its position as mediator of the divine revelation in all its forms became more and more central and dominating. This development is illustrated by the fact that the ancient expression "to seek God", דרש את יהוה,[5] in late Judaism often meant simply "to seek God in the Torah",[6] or is replaced by the expression

---

[1] Cf. above, p. 228 f., on Lk. 24.27.

[2] Cf. H. W. WOLFF, *Jesaja 53 im Urchristentum* (3rd ed. 1952).

[3] N.B. the role played by the preposition ἀπό in the texts we have quoted above.

[4] Above, pp. 19 f.

[5] E.g. Gen. 25.22, 2 Kings 22.18. In such contexts "to seek" is also בקש and the name of God varies. On this matter, see I. ENGNELL, Söka Gud, in *Sv. Bibl. Uppslagsverk* II (1952), col. 1322 f.

[6] In order to understand the process of development in this case, note the expression דרש את דבר יהוה, e.g. 1 Kings 22.5, 2 Chron. 18.4.

"to seek (i.e. to explore) the Torah", דרש (ב)תורה, a development which is noticeable in the most recent books of the O.T., and particularly clearly in the Qumran texts.[1]

The Torah had for the Jews an incomparable intrinsic value as bearer of the divine revelation—even as the divine revelation itself. The most important of all tasks is thus to "seek", i.e. "explore" (דרש) the Torah, to "work" (עסק) with the Torah, to "strive" (עמל) with the Torah, to "preserve" (שמר)[2] the Torah, to "learn" (למד) the Torah, to "teach" the Torah and "perform" (עשה) the precepts of the Torah—to name only some of the more common expressions. Devotion to, and intercourse with, the divine revelation in the Torah had thus a high and absolute *intrinsic* value for those faithful to the Torah.

A typical characteristic of the torah-centric groups is their endeavour to be completely and absolutely obedient to the Torah. The *whole* of the Torah is to be kept, it is to be kept *in the smallest detail*, and with all one's heart and all one's soul.[3]

The attempt at *complete* subjection to the might of the Torah could be linked with a number of concrete sayings in the Holy Scriptures, and two in particular:

(i) Joshua 1.8

TM:

לא ימוש ספר התורה הזה	"This book of the Torah shall not
מפיך והגית בו יומם	depart out of thy mouth, but thou
ולילה למען תשמר לעשות	shalt mediatate upon it day and
ככל הכתוב בו.	night, that thou mayest observe
	to do according to all that is
	written therein."

LXX:

οὐκ ἀποστήσεται ἡ βίβλος τοῦ νόμου τούτου ἐκ τοῦ στόματός σου, καὶ μελετήσεις ἐν αὐτῷ ἡμέρας καὶ νυκτός, ἵνα συνῇς[4] ποιεῖν πάντα τὰ γεγραμμένα.

---

[1] Ezr. 7.10. On the terminology of the Qumran writings, see above, p. 58, n. 5, and O. Betz, *Offenbarung und Schriftforschung in der Qumransekte* (1960).

[2] Note that שמר is not (always) the same as "*to do*" (עשה) what the Torah commands.

[3] Cf. the way in which Josephus uses such words as ἀκριβείᾳ, μετ' ἀκριβείας, ἐπ' ἐξακριβώσει, *Vita* 38, *Bell.* 2.8.14, *Ant.* 17.2.4, when he wishes to characterize the Pharisees' study of the Law. See also Acts 22.3, 26.5, Phil. 3.5; Schürer, *Geschichte* II, pp. 456 ff. See further H. Braun, *Spätjüdisch-häretischer und frühchristlicher Radikalismus* I–II (1957).

[4] B reads εἰδῇς.

236

(ii) Psalm 1.1 f.

TM:

אשרי האיש אשר...   "Blessed is the man that ... has
בתורת יהוה חפצו   his delight in the Torah of the
ובתורתו יהגה יומם   Lord; and meditates in his Torah
ולילה.   day and night."

LXX:

μακάριος ἀνήρ ... ἐν τῷ νόμῳ κυρίου τὸ θέλημα αὐτοῦ, καὶ ἐν τῷ νόμῳ
αὐτοῦ μελετήσει ἡμέρας καὶ νυκτός.

There is no doubt that it is in obedience to such passages of Scripture
that an intensive study of the Scriptures was carried out by the Dead
Sea sect. In 1QS VI. 6 ff. we read that: "And in (every) place where
there are ten (men), there shall not lack one[1] who continually, both day
and night,[2] searches in (or works on) the Torah (ואל ימש במקום אשר
יהיו שם העשרה איש דורש בתורה יומם ולילה תמיד) concerning that which
is proper in fellowship with one's neighbour. And the many shall watch
together[3] (והרבים ישקודו ביחד) the third part (watch)[4] of every night
during the year in order to read in the book and explore the commandments and to pray together (לקרוא בספר ולדרוש משפט ולברך ביחד)."

WERNBERG-MØLLER has advanced the hypothesis that in this text an
ע has been exchanged for a ח; in that case the first sentence in this quotation would read that the work on the Torah was carried on in shifts (חליפות
א״לר instead of על יפות א״לר).[5] This is an attractive hypothesis, but it
would seem to be better to retain the present wording of the text, at least
until the readings of the other copies of the Manual of Discipline have
been published.[6] We shall return to the meaning of the verb שקד
which we translated above by "watch".

Our sources are insufficient for us to know in detail how other torah-
centric groups organized their study of the Scriptures at this time.

---

[1] This man is presumably a priest; see BETZ, *Offenbarung*, pp. 19 ff.

[2] For the expression, see further below.

[3] On the term יחד, see J. MAIER, Zum Begriff יחד in den Texten von Qumran,
in *Zeitschr. f. d. Alttest. Wiss.* 72 (1960), pp. 148 ff.

[4] See G. VERMÈS, *Les manuscrits du Désert de Juda* (1953), p. 145. It is possible
to translate "a third of the nights of the year", but this interpretation causes great
difficulties.

[5] Observations on the Interchange of ע and ח in the Manual of Discipline (DSD),
in *Vet. Test.* 3 (1953), pp. 104 ff.

[6] Cf. above, p. 31.

We do however know that an intensive work on the Torah was carried on. It was a Pharisaic ideal to be the first to arrive at college in the morning, and to be the last to leave in the evening: an ideal among others embraced by Rabban Joḥanan ben Zakkai.[1] Interesting traditions also narrate that deliberations took place in colleges *by night*. A haggadah tradition[2] concerning the experiences of Hillel when he was a pupil in the college of Shemaiah and Abtalion, reveals that deliberations were still in progress at daybreak. Another tradition tells how Rabban Gamaliel II and the elders lay at table in the house of Boetos ben Zonin in Lydda, and that they discussed the *halakot* on the Passover the whole of that night until cock-crow.[3] The study of the Torah by night, both by groups and individuals, is also mentioned elsewhere in rabbinic sources.[4]

With this striving after the fullest possible intercourse with the word of God, those in torah-centric groups experienced the extreme tension between work on the Torah and earthly duties. This is not a new problem. We can see glimpses of it in the O.T. texts, and it is clearly expressed in the famous passage Sir. 38.24–39.11.[5] The sayings in Josh. 1.8 and Ps. 1.2, however, expressing the ideal that one should study the Torah day and night, became the objects of special attention during the centuries around the beginning of the Christian era. In Test. Lev. XIII,[6] the priestly paterfamilias exhorts his sons to teach their children, in order that they may be able to read the Torah *constantly* (ἀναγινώσκοντες ἀδιαλείπτως τὸν νόμον τοῦ θεοῦ), though this seems to be a hyperbolical expression for *persevering* Torah study. We have seen that the problem was solved in Qumran; they took the study of the Torah to be a collective responsibility and appointed one particular person, primarily a priest, who was to carry on uninterrupted study of the Torah.[7] The expression must also be regarded as metaphorical in this case: that he was to devote all his time from morning to night to work on the Torah. Or, if the text

---

[1] E.g. b Suk. 28a.

[2] b Yoma 35b.

[3] T Pes. X.12.

[4] See BILLERBECK, *Comm.* II, pp. 419 f., 617.

[5] For the negative attitude to work in the O.T. texts, see I. ENGNELL, art. Arbete, in *Sv. Bibl. Uppslagsverk* I (2nd ed. 1961), sub voce. The author shows that the view of Sir. (38.24 ff.) is only a development of the genuine O.T. attitude to work.

[6] Ed. R. H. CHARLES (1908), p. 53.

[7] BETZ, *Offenbarung*, pp. 19 ff.

is damaged and WERNBERG-MØLLER's hypothesis is correct, they took the commandment of Scripture literally, and solved the problem by carrying on research *in shifts*.[1] From the Rabbis we can quote the tradition that Eliezer ben Hyrkanos asks R. Joshua how the saying in Ps. 1.2 is to be kept, and receives the reply that this refers to the recitation of *Shema*: if a man reads *Shema* morning and evening, God *imputes* it to him as though he were occupied with the Torah day and night.[2] R. Ishmael's solution is only to be expected. With his concept that "the Torah speaks in the language of men"[3] he is able to interpret this passage of Scripture as a hyperbole, and is thus able to admit the existence of the study of the Torah and worldly affairs side by side.[4] (This solution was very common in rabbinic circles. Normally a Torah scholar had a craft beside his learned work.)[5] Another possibility is suggested by R. Simeon ben Yoḥai: If Israel (i.e. the faithful in Israel) devote themselves completely to the Torah, it is certain that others will take care of the worldly duties which need to be carried out.[6]

The study of the Torah is thus regarded as being the most important of all tasks.[7] A document which is worth our attention in this context is an ancient benediction to be used when entering (or leaving)[8] the college. According to rabbinic tradition, it was used by Neḥonia ben Haqqanah (a contemporary of the Apostles). There is however nothing to prevent

---

[1] Cf. P. WERNBERG-MØLLER, *The Manual of Discipline* (1957), p. 104.

[2] Midr. Ps. § 17, 18b; cf. b Men. 99b.

[3] דברה תורה כלשון בני אדם, e.g. b Ber. 31b; Sifre Deut. ad 11.14. Cf. BACHER, *Terminologie* I, p. 98.

[4] b Ber. 35b. Cf. Sifre Deut., *ibid.*

[5] E.g. the words of Rabban Gamaliel ben R. Judah: "The study of the Torah is good (when it is carried on) together with a worldly occupation", Ab. II.2. Cf. the commentary of K. MARTI, G. BEER (1927), ad Ab. I.10b, p. 23, and Joach. JEREMIAS, *Jerusalem zur Zeit Jesu* (2nd ed. 1958), II B, pp. 101 ff.

[6] b Ber. 35b (bar.). *Ibid.* (bar.) we find the words of R. Judah ben Ilai, that former generations made the study of the Torah their regular task (קבע), and their worldly tasks to incidentals (עראי): later generations do the opposite. — For the different views held by the Rabbis, see also M. GUTTMANN, Hantwerk, in *Enc. Jud.* VII (1931), col. 949 ff.

[7] See BILLERBECK II, pp. 185 f.; cf. III (1926), pp. 85 ff., on the Rabbis' discussions on the subject of what is the more important, to study or to act in accordance with what one has learned. The Dead Sea texts show that the tendency to set the study of the Torah as the highest duty was stronger in pre-Tannaitic and early Tannaitic times than BILLERBECK thought.

[8] In b Ber. 28b (bar.) it is said that the benediction was used when entering college; in p Ber. IV.2 (bar.) that it was used when leaving. Cf. T Ber. VII.2.

it being older. According to the version preserved in the Babylonian tradition (b Ber. 28 b, bar.; cf. p Ber. IV.2, bar.), it is worded so:

"I thank thee, the Eternal One, my God, that thou hast cast my lot among those who sit in the college (ששמת חלקי מיושבי בית המדרש), and not among those who sit at the corners of the streets. For I arise early, and they arise early. I arise early to the words of the Torah (אני משכים לדברי תורה), and they arise early to works of vanity. I strive (עמל) and they strive. I strive and am repaid, they strive and are not repaid. I run and they run. I run toward eternal life. They run toward the well of destruction."

We can now proceed direct to early Christianity. It is most striking that we find that the same problem—*mutatis mutandis*—is also dealt with there: it is clearly expressed and clearly answered. Luke in his Gospel (10.38 ff.) reproduces a tradition on Jesus' visit to the sisters Martha and Mary. Martha opens her house for the Master and his disciples. Her actions are best illustrated by the ancient words of wisdom transmitted from the lips of Jose ben Joezer (2nd cent. B.C.): "May your house be a place of assembly (בית ועד) for the wise; make yourself dusty with the dust of their feet and drink their words with thirst" (Ab. I.4).[1] In the teaching scene which is then described, Martha is made to represent service, mundane work: she is distracted by much work (περιεσπᾶτο περὶ πολλὴν διακονίαν), we read in the text. It is presumably "table-service" which is meant, but this is not quite certain. But Mary, "also sits (like the other disciples)[2] at the feet of Jesus and listens to his words" (ἣ καὶ παρακαθεσθεῖσα πρὸς τοὺς πόδας τοῦ κυρίου ἤκουεν τὸν λόγον αὐτοῦ). Martha calls Jesus' attention to Mary's neglect of mundane duties, but the Master decides the question. Mary "has chosen the good part (τὴν ἀγαθὴν μερίδα ἐξελέξατο), which shall not be taken away from her". A number of the mss. also have the saying that only *one thing* is necessary, but we can leave the unusually complicated textual question on one side when dealing with this part of the answer.[3] (The variant readings bear witness to the various ways in which an attempt was made within the Church to solve this particular problem.)

[1] Cf. W. MANSON, *Comm.* (6th impr. 1948), ad loc.

[2] Prof. RIESENFELD has drawn the attention to the formula ἣ καί in this context. Cf. Å. V. STRÖM, Bibelns syn på arbetet, in *Ny Kyrklig Tidskrift* 25 (1956), pp. 46 f., E. LALAND, Die Marta-Maria-Perikope Lukas 10.38–42, in *Studia Theol.* 13 (1959), pp. 70 ff.

[3] For an analysis of the different readings in v. 41 f., see M.-J. LAGRANGE, *Comm.*, ad loc.

There can be no question of the parallel to the problems and the material we have just quoted. It is clear that the ancient college benediction reproduces thoughts and a phraseology which were typical in Palestinian colleges at the beginning of the Christian era. In the benediction, we hear how comparison is made between the lot (חלק) of one who sits in college, arises early to the words (דברים) of the Torah, strives with the Torah and receives an eternal reward (שכר) and the lot of one who sits at the corner of the street, who is constantly active, but with mundane things: the one who strives, but receives no reward. In the tradition of Martha and Mary we hear how the one who sits at the feet of the Lord and listens to his word (λόγοι) has chosen the good lot (μερίς) which shall not be taken away from her (by God), and on the other hand, of the one who is distracted by much service, whose lot is deprecated. The most important difference is that Martha is busy with important and good tasks, and not with works of vanity. But this stresses even more strongly how clearly the occupation with the word of God is placed on a higher level than mundane duties.

In Acts 6, the same problem appears, though in a different form. There, Luke describes a conflict in the early Church. The conflict has to do with the daily common meals. The matter is taken up by the Apostles, evidently in the course of some general session in the early congregation (see below, section E). We read that the Apostles call (προσκαλεσάμενοι) the *multitude* of the disciples (τὸ πλῆθος τῶν μαθητῶν), which indicates the members of the congregation apart from the Apostles. We might compare the כל העם (or רוב) of the Qumran congregation.[1] The Apostles state before the multitude that it is not fitting that they should leave the service of the word of God in order to serve at tables (καταλείψαντας τὸν λόγον τοῦ θεοῦ διακονεῖν τραπέζαις). A group of seven ought therefore to be nominated to take these tasks in hand. The Apostles are to devote themselves steadfastly to prayer and the service of the Word (ἡμεῖς δὲ τῇ προσευχῇ καὶ τῇ διακονίᾳ τοῦ λόγου προσκαρτερήσομεν).[2] The proposal is approved.

In the pericope on Martha and Mary, Jesus approves of the fact that Mary has left (κατέλειπεν) service (διακονεῖν) to Martha in order to listen to the word of the Lord (τὸν λόγον αὐτοῦ [sc. τοῦ κυρίου]). In Acts, the Apostles reject a situation in which they must (occasionally)

---

[1] Cf. S. E. JOHNSON, The Dead Sea Manual of Discipline and the Jerusalem Church of Acts, in *The Scrolls and the N.T.* (1957), p. 135, and BETZ, *Offenbarung*, p. 4.

[2] D has the periphr. conjug.: ἐσόμεθα προσκαρτεροῦντες.

leave (καταλείψαντας) the word of God (τὸν λόγον τοῦ θεοῦ) in order to serve (διακονεῖν) at tables. It is the same problem which we meet in both texts. Devoted attention to the word of God is in both cases accorded an incomparable first-hand value. The difference between the two pericopes is also worth our notice. The former is a doctrinal passage which fills the function of showing the task which, according to Jesus, must be the most important for his followers, that of listening to the word of the Lord. In the latter pericope the Apostles take a stand which —at least according to Luke—seems to be in part based on the tradition of Jesus' saying concerning Martha and Mary. It is because occupation with the word of the Lord is the most important of all that it is unsuitable for the Apostles to leave (even occasionally) their service of the Word in order to serve at tables. The college of Apostles is therefore freed from even the important diaconal work in order to be able entirely to devote themselves to prayer and the service of the Word. Similarly the Dead Sea sect set aside one man in every place where there were to be found ten for full-time occupation with the Torah. He is there called דורש התורה.[1]

It may be worth our while to refer to further material from the torah-centric circles as a commentary to the formulations in Acts 6.4.

The verb προσκαρτερεῖν means "to persist obstinately", "to devote oneself (to an occupation or an office)". The nearest Hebrew equivalent would seem to be שקד.[2] This verb, which in Biblical Hebrew commonly carries the meaning "to be on the alert", "to watch", in mishnaic Hebrew usually means "to be industrious", "to persist". The word is used *inter alia* precisely to refer to concentrated, persistent occupation with the study of the Torah. An industrious Rabbi was called שקוד[3] or שקדן.[4] R. Eleazar ben Arak (1st cent. A. D.) says in Ab. II.14: "Be assiduous in learning (הוה שקוד ללמוד)".[5] In the version of the above-mentioned college benediction which is to be found in the Palestinian Talmud, we read: אני שוקד, "I am industrious"; this may perhaps mean "I arise early". At this point the Babylonian version has: אני משכים, "I arise early"; this may possibly mean "I am industrious". The verb שקד appears

[1] BETZ, *op. cit.*, pp. 19 ff.

[2] Rather than חיל.

[3] b Ket. 43b, p Ned. VIII.3.

[4] M Sot. IX. 15, T Sot. XV.4 and elsewhere.

[5] Readings: some mss. read "Be assiduous in learning the Torah (and know) ..." Others however leave out (ודע) תורה (cf. the ed. of MARTI, BEER, ad loc.). In either case it is a matter of learning from the Torah.

only once in the Dead Sea texts, in the quotation from 1QS (VI.7), which we have already quoted. It is most natural to translate with the word "watch", but the meaning "to address oneself in a concentrated and persevering manner (to)" is not too remote.

When προσκαρτερεῖν is used in Acts 6.4 to refer to the Apostles, it does not however mean "watch", but "to address oneself in a concentrated and persevering manner"—from morning to night—(to prayer and the service of the Word).

What, then, is meant by διακονία τοῦ λόγου? BILLERBECK has brought forward the expression שמושה של תורה, "service at the Torah" (b Ber. 7 b, bar.), as an equivalent of this expression.[1] If we exchange תורה in this phrase for the synonym הדבר, we have the formula שמושו של דבר, i.e. "service at the Word". שמושה של תורה in b Ber. 7 b is approximately synonymous with שמוש (תלמידי) חכמים.[2] By this expression is meant the comprehensive and deepened study of the Torah which is carried on by means of personal fellowship with notable scholars, by serving them and in their company penetrating the living and comprehensive learning contained in the Torah. When, as for example in b Ber. 7 b, a distinction is drawn, שמוש can be distinguished from למוד: i.e. the actual service (of the scholars) can be distinguished from the obtaining of knowledge of the Torah; this is, however, a subtle distinction. In other cases, it is clear that the object of serving the Rabbis was not to render them service, but to study—and also to keep alive—the Torah. שמוש חכמים is even a term applied to the qualified study of the Torah on the highest level. It is important to note that this study was not understood as being merely a process of *learning*, as the *receiving* of knowledge. The disciple himself takes part, and is active with questions and contributions to the discussion. At this stage the boundary between teaching and learning is extremely flexible.[3]

Having stated this, one is nevertheless left wondering whether שמושה של תורה is the correct Hebrew equivalent of διακονία τοῦ λόγου. We can equally well expect an expression in the construct: שמוש הדבר,[4] שירות הדבר, or something of the sort. The Greek Genetive is probably a gen. obi. and the correct translation "service *of* the Word". We do not intend at this

---

[1] *Comm.* II, p. 647.

[2] BILLERBECK, *ibid.*; cf. I, pp. 527 ff.

[3] See above, pp. 104 f. Cf. also RENGSTORF, μανθάνω κτλ., in *Theol. Wörterb.* IV, pp. 403 ff.

[4] F. DELITSCH translates in this way, ספרי הברית החדשה (7th ed. 1886), in loc.

stage to indulge in speculations concerning the possible existence of an original Aramaic expression behind this text.[1]

In order to understand what is meant by διακονία τοῦ λόγου, we are however not recommended to such terminological suggestions. Luke's own presentation gives us quite clear information, both on the nature of ὁ λόγος and the position held by the Apostles. We need only summarize briefly what we have already said in order to have certain fixed points on which to base our estimate of the expression διακονία τοῦ λόγου.

By ὁ λόγος (6.4), i.e. ὁ λόγος τοῦ θεοῦ (6.2), Luke means *that word of God which, in the last days, proceeds from Jerusalem*. From the point of view of content, this logos has its focus in the suffering, death and resurrection of Christ, but nevertheless comprehends—as Luke expresses clearly and decisively—all that Jesus did and taught from his baptism by John to the ascension. An important factor with regard to this logos is that it is particularly entrusted to the *Apostles*, that it is served by them and witnessed to by them. In the prologue to his twin volumes, Luke says that "those matters which have been fulfilled among us" have been transmitted to us by those who became from the beginning eyewitnesses and servants of the Word (καθὼς παρέδοσαν ἡμῖν οἱ ἀπ'ἀρχῆς αὐτόπται καὶ ὑπηρέται γενόμενοι τοῦ λόγου). There can be no question that he is thinking primarily of the Apostles, i.e. the twelve;[2] this is, as we have seen, clear from his language on the one hand, and his method of drawing the Apostles' qualifications and activity on the other. According to Acts 1.21 ff., one of the qualifications of an Apostle was to have been with Jesus from the beginning of his public ministry to the ascension. The Apostles were taught both during his earthly ministry and after his resurrection on the subject both of the meaning of his work of salvation and the way in which the Scriptures were to be interpreted. They are specially chosen; according to Acts 1.25 they have been entrusted with ἡ διακονία καὶ ἀποστολή, based on the fact that they are the witnesses (μάρτυρες) of Christ. And here, in Acts 6.1 ff., is now narrated how they

---

[1] If this is a question of a *technical term* from the Palestinian school-language, it is to be expected that it will be Hebrew, and not Aramaic.

[2] STENDAHL, *The School*, pp. 32 ff., and P. BALDUCELLI, Professor Riesenfeld on Synoptic Tradition, in *Cath. Bibl. Quart.* 22 (1960), pp. 416 ff., want to distinguish in the prologue of Luke between αὐτόπται and ὑπηρέται τοῦ λόγου. It is intrinsically possible, probable even, that Luke could have drawn such a distinction, but he seems as a matter of fact not to have done so, either in his prologue or in continuation. "Those who from the beginning were eyewitnesses and ministers of the Word" are for him primarily the Apostles.

are set free from other tasks in order to devote all their time to prayer and to διακονία τοῦ λόγου.

That the Apostles are ὑπηρέται τοῦ λόγου thus means that they have charge of and serve "that word which God (in the latter days) sent to the sons of Israel, preaching peace through Jesus" (10.36 ff.), in the same way as Moses and Joshua and their followers (the "disciples of Moses")[1] had the charge of and served the Divine Word from Sinai.

As an analogy to this, διακονία τοῦ λόγου stands as a designation for the Apostles' service of the Word. This activity BILLERBECK calls *die Verkündigung des Evangeliums*.[2] This is not correct, at least not if the word *die Verkündigung* be given the purely proclamatory meaning which it normally bears in modern exegesis and theology. Luke docs not present the twelve Apostles as heralds, travelling around and proclaiming the message. During the first period of the Church they are a *collegium*, active in Jerusalem, acting as *witnesses* (μάρτυρες) to Christ, and *teaching* (διδάσκειν) in the name of Jesus. Their witness has, as we have seen, a strikingly didactic character, based as it is upon the actual messianic events and on the Scriptures. Teaching is carried out partly in public (in the Temple), partly in private (at home in houses). One of the main elements around which, according to the famous passage Acts 2.42, the early congregation gathered, and by which it was held together, is the teaching of the Apostles: ἦσαν δὲ προσκαρτεροῦντες τῇ διδαχῇ τῶν ἀποστόλων[3] καὶ τῇ κοινωνίᾳ, τῇ κλάσει τοῦ ἄρτου καὶ ταῖς προσευχαῖς.

In this quotation, in which each and every word contains its own difficult problems,[4] we must pay attention to the verb προσκαρτερεῖν as a designation for the persistent and concentrated devotion to one matter. Furthermore, we notice the periphrastic conjugation which is used in order to describe a permanent, continuous condition;[5] the Apostles' teaching is thus one of the important pieces of work *carried on* in the early Church. And there is no doubt that it is principally this which is meant by διακονία τοῦ λόγου.

---

[1] תלמידיו של משה b Yoma 4a (bar.).

[2] *Comm.* II, p. 647.

[3] D adds "in Jerusalem".

[4] Cf. the parallel in 1QS VI. 2 ff. For an analysis of this passage and the parallels 4.32–35, 5.11–16, see most recently H. ZIMMERMANN, Die Sammelberichte der Apostelgeschichte, in *Bibl. Zeitschr.* N.F. 5 (1961), pp. 73 ff., where an account is also given of the various proposals for the solution of the problem of the sources Luke may have used when writing his summaries.

[5] See BJÖRCK, ΗΝ ΔΙΔΑΣΚΩΝ, p. 47; cf. BLASS, DEBRUNNER, *Grammatik*, § 353.

It is worth stressing in connection with this διδαχή of the Apostles that it is not to be understood as merely a case of "passing on teaching", or "delivering addresses". There is no doubt that their work on the logos is to a large extent a matter of "doctrinal discussion", based on the reading of a text of Scripture and perhaps the reciting of the tradition of Christ as well, or on concrete problems which have been posed and discussed during the process of "taking stock" of that which is given in the Scriptures and the tradition of Christ,[1] and that which was "revealed" in the as yet unfinished miraculous course of salvation. We shall attempt in the next section (E) to illustrate this in more detail.

We thus interpret the witness of Luke in Acts 6.1 ff. in the following way: The principal tasks of the Apostles were to pray and to serve the Word. The latter task, διακονία τοῦ λόγου, seems to be practically identical with what Luke calls διδαχὴ τῶν ἀποστόλων. By this is meant, not mere proclamation, but *teaching*: a doctrinal work based on the Scriptures and the tradition of Christ. This work with the logos was regarded by the early Church as being of such vital importance, and has such scope, that on one definite occasion the Apostles were solemnly exempted from certain other tasks, important in themselves, in order that they might be able to concentrate uninterruptedly—"night and day", metaphorically speaking—on that task and on prayer.

E. *An Early Christian "General Session"*

The Qumran congregation had its own general session (מושב הרבים) in which questions of various kinds were considered and resolutions were passed.[2] For the sake of simplicity,[3] we shall here keep to the description of this session which is to be found in the Manual of Discipline VI.8 ff. We see from this description that the participants were divided into three categories: the priests (הכוהנים), the elders (הזקנים) and all the people (כול העם), who occupied their appropriate places in a fixed order of

---

[1] The form-critics speak about the gospel tradition being formed on a basis of *certain needs* which made their presence felt in the congregations. If the situation in the early Christian milieu has anything to teach us about the comparative phenomena in the young Church, it would seem to be more realistic to say that certain elements in the synoptic tradition (e.g. the narrative traditions) were formulated in the course of the discussion of definite, clearly posed problems. Cf. below, Ch. 16.

[2] E.g. 1QS VI.13 ff., VII.21, CD XIV.12 ff. See RABIN, *Qumran Studies*, pp. 102 ff.

[3] We shall not here consider the question of the alterations which can have taken place during the two centuries or more in which the sect flourished.

seniority. Careful rules, again based on order of seniority, applied to the
questioning and utterance of those present: for instance, one person is not
to begin to speak until the previous speaker has finished. Deliberations
led to decisions, although it is not clear from the terminology whether
such decisions were reached by a general vote or by acclamation. In
this assembly it is, however, hardly likely that resolutions were passed
by a general vote, or as a result of a majority decision.[1] The sect's
hierarchical organization was so strict, and the leaders—particularly
the priests—commanded such respect and wielded such authority,[2] that
resolutions can scarcely have been passed in this way. It is more likely
here, as in the early Church, that decisions were made when the leaders
agreed upon a proposal, to which the assembly as a whole gave its
approval.[3]

RABIN is justified in comparing the session, מושב, of the Qumran
congregation with a rabbinic session, ישיבה.[4] But there is no reason
why the comparison should be confined to *rabbinic* sessions. It is evident
that the Rabbis carried on, by and large, an order of procedure for such
meetings which already existed during the period when the Sadducees
also formed a powerful element in Jewish administration, lawmaking
and jurisdiction.

A number of passages in M Sanh. bear witness to the way in which the
ancient Sanhedrin was organized and to the procedure followed in its
sessions.[5] According to these, the judges sat in a semicircle (כחצי גורן
עגולה).[6] It is not improbable that during the period of the Temple this
semicircle was arranged in the old order of precedence: priests, Levites,
(other) Israelites, though this is not clear from the scanty sources. At
all events, a definite order of precedence was observed in the matter of

---

[1] RABIN, *op. cit.*, pp. 105 f., considers that decisions were made in accordance
with the opinion of the majority. יזקפו (mishnaic niphal) should mean "they stand up
to vote" (1QS VII.10 ff.).

[2] On the role and position of the priests, see e.g. CD XIII.2–4, 1QS IX.7; cf. V.2 ff.

[3] Thus B. REICKE, The Constitution of the Primitive Church in the Light of
Jewish Documents, in *The Scrolls and the N.T.*, pp. 146 ff., following LINTON's
account of the way in which doctrinal questions were decided in the early Church,
in *Das Problem der Urkirche*, pp. 189 ff. Cf. below.

[4] *Qumran Studies*, pp. 103 ff.

[5] On this subject, see I. JELSKI-GOLDIN, *Die innere Einrichtung des grossen Synedrions zu Jerusalem* (1893), pp. 81 ff., SCHÜRER, *Geschichte* II, pp. 266 f., and most
recently HOENIG, *The Great Sanhedrin*, pp. 85–108.

[6] IV. 3.

seating, however this precedence may have been estimated.[1] Senior members sat in the middle,[2] and in front of the semicircle of judges stood two scribes of the judges (סופרי הדיינין), one to the right and one to the left, who wrote down the words of them that favoured acquittal and the words of them that favoured conviction.[3] (We have earlier had occasion to point out that these scribes seem to be replaced by *tannaim* in the later rabbinic sessions.)[4] In front of these there sat three rows of Rabbis' disciples, each in his appropriate place.[5] The people took up positions outside these circles.[6] In the course of such sessions, members were questioned and made their statements in order: in certain cases the senior representative (הגדול) was allowed to speak first;[7] and in others a start was made with the junior representative, or "from the side" (מן הצד) as it was called.[8] The Rabbis' disciples were allowed, in some questions at least, to contribute to the debate,[9] but had no vote in the passing of resolutions. The general public had no say in these matters. Judgement was passed by means of a vote of the actual college of judges, within which, according to the Mishnah, a majority decision was valid.[10] The judges *stood up* to vote (עומדין למינין).[11]

In the "sessions" of the rabbinic colleges, the procedure was for the most part identical.[12] A number of modern scholars even go so far as to maintain that the description in the Mishnah of the Sanhedrin sessions is nothing more than a large-scale anticipation of sessions in the later rabbinic academies, in Jabneh and elsewhere. This seems however to be a case of exaggerated scepticism.[13] Deliberations in rabbinic sessions also

---

[1] On the problem, see SCHÜRER, *op. cit.* II, pp. 248 ff., and HOENIG, *op. cit.*, pp. 53 ff.

[2] See KRAUSS, *Sanhedrin*, pp. 155 f.

[3] M Sanh. IV.3.

[4] Above, p. 162. The notaries in the Sanhedrin were presumably established by the Sadducees.

[5] M Sanh. IV.4.

[6] See KRAUSS, *op. cit.*, pp. 156 ff.

[7] M Sanh. IV.2. Cf. Josephus, *Ant.* 16.11.3.

[8] *Ibid.*

[9] M Sanh. IV.1, IV.4, b Git. 58b, 59a; cf. on Rabbi's rule about always beginning from the side, b Sanh. 36a, b Git. 59a.

[10] E.g. M Sanh. IV.1, V.5. The same applied to the fixing of halakah in the colleges; see below.

[11] M Sanh. V.5, T Ohal. IV.2.

[12] See JELSKI-GOLDIN, *Die innere Einrichtung*, pp. 81 ff.

[13] Cf. above, pp. 85 f.

followed a quite strict ritual and an order of seniority was again observed. Senior members (זקנים) sat in the middle.[1] Legal cases, whether actual or purely theoretical, were similarly considered. Words of Scripture and oral traditions were brought forward, as were arguments pro and contra. When a question proved not to have been definitively decided by the Scriptures, or by some previous decision on the part of a doctrinal authority, it was discussed[2] and formally decided by a vote. The same applied to those cases in which the halakah varied, i.e. when different districts, schools or doctrinal authorities had hitherto observed different practices.[3] This majority decision must not be understood too democratically. The opinions of prominent scholars carried a great deal of weight, and in reality often decided the question. We thus read that during the time of Rabban Gamaliel II, for example, that halakah was fixed in accordance with his opinions.[4] We shall return to this question later.

In the eleventh chapter of M Sanh. (XI.2 ff.) we have an extremely interesting description of the measures taken during the period of the Temple to deal with a rebellious elder (זקן ממרא).[5] This tradition has traces of the Rabbis' wishful thinking and capacity for anticipating the event, but it is quite certain that its basic features are historically reliable.[6]

In Jerusalem there were three courts of justice (בתי דינין) at the time of the Temple: the first "used to sit" (יושב), i.e. held its sessions at the gate of the Temple Mount, the second at the gate of the Temple Court, and the third in the Chamber of *Gazit*. Deputations from courts held in local congregations used at that time to come first to the court which assembled at the gate of the Temple Mount and say: In this way have I expounded (כך דרשתי) and in this way have my fellows expounded;

---

[1] KRAUSS, *Sanhedrin*, pp. 155 ff. Note that the early schools also had their "senior members": e.g. M Suk. II.7, זקני בית שמאי וזקני בית הלל. — The term "elders" is used in several different ways. In Acts 15 the term is not used to refer to the inner circle, which in Gal. 2 is called οἱ στῦλοι. See below, p. 278.

[2] Cf. above, pp. 103 ff., and 175 ff.

[3] Cf. H. KLÜGER, *Über Genesis und Composition der Halachasammlung Edujot* (1895), pp. 109 ff., on the fixing of the undecided *halakot* (הלכות תלויות) in Jabneh. On variations in halakah between different districts, see M. GUTTMANN, *Zur Einleitung in der Halacha* II (1913), pp. 55 ff.

[4] b Erub. 41a.

[5] On the meaning of the phrase זקן ממרא על פי בית דין, see KRAUSS, *Sanhedrin*, pp. 287 ff.

[6] Deut. 17.8 ff. was *valid law* in post-Exilic times!

thus have I taught (כך לימדתי) and thus have my fellows taught. If the court had heard an authoritative tradition (אם שמעו), applicable to the doctrine in question,[1] it was pronounced. Otherwise the deputation proceeded to the court which sat at the gate of the Temple Court, where they stated their case in the same way. If the second court had heard no relevant authoritative tradition which could decide the matter in dispute, the deputation, by now augmented, went to "the Great Sanhedrin that was in the Chamber of Gazit, *whence the Law proceeds* unto all Israel (בית דין הגדול שבלשכת הגזית שממנו יוצאת תורה לכל ישראל), as it is written, *from that place which the Lord shall choose* (Deut. 17.10)". Here the matter was decided. Should it be the case that even the Great Sanhedrin had no tradition, the question was discussed, and an authoritative and valid decision was given. This passage continues by quoting a tradition from R. Judah ben Ilai (M Sanh. XI.4) to the effect that when judgement had been passed on a rebellious elder, they had to "write and send messengers (apostles) to every place" (וכותבין ושולחין שלוחים בכל המקומות)[2] in order to relate what had happened.

The two passages of Scripture concerning Jerusalem as a centre for the Torah, which we quoted above (sec. A) are also applied in this mishnah tradition. From the first (Deut. 17.10) a formula is expressly quoted; echoes of the other (Is. 2.3) can also be detected: שממנו יוצאת תורה.

We can now proceed to consider the 15th chapter of the Acts of the Apostles, in which Luke describes a doctrinal conflict between, on the one hand, a number of Jerusalem Christians, previously members of the *Pharisaic* party (presumably of *bet Shammai*),[3] and, on the other, the Antiochene teachers Paul and Barnabas, of whom the former, at least, was a former *Pharisee*—and even a former pupil of *bet Hillel*.[4] We thus have every reason for comparing the course of this conflict with the corresponding phenomena in Rabbinic Judaism—at this early stage called Pharisaic Judaism—or, to be more accurate, with rabbinic traditions of Jewish doctrinal controversies during the period of the Temple.

---

[1] On the distinction between doctrinal questions which have, and have not, been decided, see further, below, pp. 312 f.

[2] KRAUSS in his edition follows those mss. which omit שלוחים.

[3] Thus H. J. SCHOEPS, *Theologie und Geschichte des Juden-Christentums* (1949), p. 259.

[4] Cf. below, p. 289.

Luke describes,[1] by way of introduction, how a number of members
from the first Christian congregation in Jerusalem arrive in Antioch.
According to Codex Ψ (and presumably also Codex Bezae), these formerly
belonged to the party of the Pharisees; this seems to be what Luke
means (cf. v. 5). Be that as it may; they learn in Antioch that circumcision according to the Law of Moses (which carries with it the duty of
observing the Law) is necessary for salvation. Luke conveys this doctrinal
statement with a brevity and precision worthy of the best rabbinic
traditionists: a significant factor when we come to make an estimate of
the type of source-material[2] he has used: καί τινες κατελθόντες ἀ. τ. 'Ι.
ἐδίδασκον τοὺς ἀδελφοὺς ὅτι ἐὰν μὴ περιτμηθῆτε τῷ ἔθει τῷ Μωϋσέως, οὐ
δύνασθε σωθῆναι.[3]

This gives rise to a not inconsiderable discord and debate (στάσις καὶ
ζήτησις)[4] between the teachers on one side, and the Antiochene teachers[5]
Paul and Barnabas on the other. According to Codex Bezae, Paul holds
fast to the principle that everyone, as far as circumcision is concerned,
should remain in the condition in which he happened to be at the time
of his conversion to Christ (ἔλεγεν γὰρ ὁ Π. μένειν οὕτως καθὼς ἐπίσ-
τευσαν διισχυριζόμενος); he stresses this as a permanent doctrinal
principle in his epistles.[6] Such a detailed definition of the conflict does
not occur in any other group of texts. The result of the controversy, according to Codex Bezae, is that the men from Jerusalem command

---

[1] On the question of the basis in the sources, see E. HAENCHEN, *Comm.* ad
loc., and IDEM, *Quellenanalyse und Kompositionsanalyse*, pp. 153 ff., and cf. R.
BULTMANN, *Zur Frage nach den Quellen*, pp. 68 ff.

[2] Can Luke be thought to build on oral traditional passages of rabbinic type,
which present with great brevity a dialogue containing the respective participants'
doctrinal statements on the question under discussion? For examples, see BACHER,
Tradition, pp. 142 ff.

[3] Codex Bezae reads: ἐὰν μὴ περιτμνηθῆτε καὶ τῷ ἔθει Μωϋσέως περιπατῆτε.

[4] To be sure, in the language of the N.T. ζήτησις often has the negative meaning
of "strife", "dispute", but this must not obscure the fundamental meaning
of the term: "legal or doctrinal examination", "doctrinal debate", etc. Cf. W. BAUER,
Wörterbuch (4th ed. 1952), sub voce. In Jewish Greek, ζήτησις is rendered by מדרש
(see H. A. WOLFSON, *Philo* I, 2nd ed. 1948, pp. 193 f.); this Hebrew term is used
to refer to the examination of the Scriptures, the examination of a person, the
examination of a legal case or a doctrinal question (cf. above, p. 85, n. 2).

[5] On the position held by Paul and Barnabas according to Acts 13.1 f., see
E. PETERSON, Zu Apostelgeschichte 13.1 f., in *Nuntius* 2 (1949), p. 1: "Barnabas
und Paulus gelten in Antiochia als christliche Rabbinen." The term Rabbi is not
quite suitable, but the observation is important; it is confirmed in 15.1 ff.

[6] 1 Cor. 7.17 ff.; cf. Rom. 2.25 ff., Gal. 5.6, 6.15.

(παραγγέλλειν) that Paul and Barnabas with some others should go up to Jerusalem in order to have the doctrinal question (ζήτημα) settled (κρίνεσθαι) by the Apostles and presbyters there. This version of the course of events makes the men from Jerusalem treat Paul and Barnabas practically as "rebellious elders".[1] The other groups of texts express the matter in such a way as to place Paul and Barnabas in a less dependent position. Ἔταξαν can mean that an unanimous decision to send a deputation up to Jerusalem was taken in order to have the dispute settled. There is however no doubt that what Luke is here describing is the way in which *an important doctrinal question is referred to the Church's highest doctrinal authority* in Jerusalem. The meaning of Luke's terminology is clear from his use of ζήτημα[2] and κρίνεσθαι in 25.19 f.

If the information given by Luke in Acts 15.1 ff. be correct, the young Church has, though in its own way,[3] followed the regulations in Deut. 17.8 ff. Its highest college of judges (שופטים) had its headquarters in Jerusalem. The Twelve Apostles have already begun to judge the twelve tribes of the new Israel (cf. Lk. 22.29 f.).

Acts 15.4 ff. describes how the Antiochene deputation is received (παραδέχεσθαι) by the Apostles and presbyters in Jerusalem.[4] What follows—whether it originally belonged together with Luke's narrative in v. 1–4 or not—is a description of a regular early Christian general session (מושב הרבים). Here we see the three groups: the Apostles, the elders and the multitude (οἱ ἀπόστολοι, οἱ πρεσβύτεροι, ἡ ἐκκλησία). The resemblance to the grouping of the Qumran congregation's sessions—the priests, the elders and all the people (כול העם, הזקנים, הכוהנים)—is striking.[5] But it is probable that the closest resemblance would be to the grouping of contemporary Sanhedrin sessions, if only we knew more of the exact details of such assemblies.[6]

---

[1] Cf. M Sanh. XI.3, quoted above. Codex Bezae is not against Paul on this point (N.B. v. 24), but expresses itself in such a way as to place Paul in a more definite position of inferiority to the twelve than the other texts express. This may be worth our attention in connection with the question of how this recension of the text is to be estimated. Cf. also on v. 2 of D the commentary of KRAUSS, *Sanhedrin*, pp. 299 and 303, on those who accompanied the rebellious elder to the higher court.

[2] Cf. also 18.15, 23.29, 25.19, 26.3.

[3] The Qumran community followed these regulations in another way.

[4] Note the curious reading of D!

[5] Cf. JOHNSON, *The Dead Sea Manual of Discipline*, pp. 134 f.

[6] There is still the difference that at the meetings of the Sanhedrin the "multitude" were not counted among those who made the decisions. This difference—which was not large in practice—that in the early Church the "multitude" only *agrees*,

The dispute is then taken up for consideration. After representatives of the Antioch congregation have given an account of their missionary work among the Gentiles, a number of Christians, previously members of the Pharisaic party, stand up (ἐξανέστησαν), claiming that Gentiles won for Christ must be circumcized and must observe the Law of Moses (λέγοντες ὅτι δεῖ περιτέμνειν αὐτοὺς παραγγέλλειν τε τηρεῖν τὸν νόμον Μωϋσέως).[1] There follows a consultation between the Apostles and the elders, as active participants; the multitude naturally takes no part in the proceedings: συνήχθησαν δὲ οἱ ἀπόστολοι καὶ οἱ πρεσβύτεροι ἰδεῖν περὶ τοῦ λόγου τούτου. Whether the Apostles and the elders withdraw κατ' ἰδίαν in order to negotiate is not clear; it is however improbable. The multitude is again present in v. 22.[2]

After a heated debate (πολλῆς δὲ ζητήσεως γενομένης),[3] Peter stands up and makes a statement. He recalls his own apostolic experience and states that, in his opinion, since God has bestowed the Spirit upon un-circumcized as well as upon circumcized Christians, and has thereby borne witness to them (θεὸς ἐμαρτύρησεν αὐτοῖς), there is no reason to lay the yoke of the Law upon converted Gentiles.[4] According to Luke, Paul and Barnabas make a similar statement.

James then addresses the assembly in support of Peter. "The words of the Prophets"—here represented by Amos 9.11 ff.—agree (συμφωνοῦσιν) with the witness of God Himself, according to what Peter has said. James therefore solemnly pronounces his decision: διὸ ἐγὼ κρίνω; cf. the rab-binic הרי אני דן.[5]

We might mention in passing that proceedings seem to have begun "from the side" and to have culminated with the contributions of the most senior, Peter and James, of whom the latter evidently presided over the session.[6] Paul and Barnabas, as the accused, or as temporary guest participants, have no place in the permanent order of seniority.

So, continues Luke, the Apostles and the elders, with the whole

---

as was probably the case in Qumran as well, has nevertheless a symbolic meaning in principle.

[1] Note the brief and pregnant doctrinal statement which expresses their halakic point of view. Tradition of rabbinic type, oral—or copied down oral—tradition!

[2] On Paul's version of the council of Apostles in Jerusalem, see below, pp. 276 ff.

[3] Cf. our commentary to v. 2 above.

[4] N.B. the version of Bezae: Peter speaks in the Spirit (v. 7) and the multitude keeps silence after the elders have given their assent to what he has said (v. 12).

[5] For the expression, see BACHER, *Terminologie* I, pp. 20 f.

[6] Cf. the order of Gal. 2.9 and below, p. 278.

ecclesia determine (ἔδοξε τοῖς ἀποστόλοις καὶ τοῖς πρεσβυτέροις σὺν ὅλῃ τῇ ἐκκλησίᾳ) to send chosen men, Barnabas and Silas, to the congregations in Antioch, Syria and Cilicia. They are to communicate the decision[1] orally, but the Jerusalem congregation through them also writes a letter (γράψαντες διὰ χειρὸς αὐτῶν) which is to be read aloud in the churches. Barnabas and Silas thus become the Jerusalem congregation's "apostles" (שלוחים) for this purpose.[2]

Luke is not interested in describing all the details of the debate or of the procedure followed when a verdict is reached. We are given no clear information as to the way in which the decision is made, from the purely technical point of view. But as LINTON has shown, everything points to the fact that the verdict is reached as a result, not of a majority decision, but of a decision made by *the leaders* and adopted by the assembly as a whole. A hierarchical assembly, as on this occasion, comes to a decision when the leaders' judgement receives the acclamation of the rest of the congregation.[3]

Luke does not mention whether or not notaries were present at the session; it is not expressly stated that the decision was written down. On the other hand, however, the decision includes the provision that the congregations in question are to be *informed* not only orally, but also in writing. A striking parallel is to be seen in the case of Rabban Gamaliel II, who had the Babylonian congregations informed in writing of a decision reached by him and his colleagues,[4] a concrete case in which we see how the law proceeds from Jerusalem! We may also recall the above-mentioned passage from M Sanh. XI.4, in which it was stated, in the matter of rebellious elders, that oral and written notification of the verdict was to be sent to the various districts.[5]

Nor does Luke mention whether or not interpreters were present at the session, or how the decision acquired its Greek form. Information of this kind, which might possibly have been of use in mastering the

---

[1] Luke calls the decretal: τὰ δόγματα τὰ κεκριμένα ὑπὸ τῶν ἀποστόλων (D: τὰς ἐντολὰς ἀποστόλων!), 16.4.

[2] On the expression, see S. KRAUSS, Apostel, in *Enc. Jud.* III (1929), col. 1 ff.

[3] *Das Problem der Urkirche*, pp. 189 ff.

[4] b Sanh. 11 b with par. Cf. HAENCHEN, *Comm.*, ad loc. — Gamaliel was not the first to send out written notification of decisions reached in Jerusalem; see KRAUSS, *Apostel*.

[5] This regulation is ascribed to R. Judah ben Ilai, and is thus not from the first century. It shows however what lay within the bounds of possibility, and derives its importance from the information recorded in the previous note.

difficulties connected with the *text* of the Apostolic decretal,[1] and which would have given us valuable assistance when estimating the languages used in the early Church, is unfortunately unavailable.

We must now make some observations on the doctrinal situation in early Christianity. The worth of such observations as these is dependent, not upon the accuracy or otherwise of *the individual details* of Luke's picture of the history of early Christianity—some details are obviously *not* in order![2]—but upon whether Luke is well-informed *in general* on the way in which the early Church, in preaching and teaching, presented its logos; and, further, on the methods of argument used by the Church in preaching, teaching, school discussions, doctrinal decisions, polemics and apologetics. We are now able, on a basis of our previous investigations, to come to certain conclusions on these points. It is obvious that Luke is very well acquainted with the mental processes, methods of argument, and practical measures connected with preaching and teaching in the early Church's Palestinian milieu; his witness cannot lightly be dismissed on a basis of such *a priori* concepts as that of "Frühkatholizismus". The historian must pay careful attention to the information given by so *early* a witness as Luke on the ideological and practical situation of early Christianity.

We are now going to give a brief account of the methods of argument used by torah-centric Jewish groups—principally Rabbinic Judaism—in the course of debates similar to that recorded in Acts 15. This should illuminate the doctrinal situation of early Christianity with particular clarity. How were doctrinal (*halakic*) questions dealt with in Tannaitic debates? What course did the discussion take?

Some questions are decided beyond any shadow of a doubt in the written Torah or, to be more precise, in the *miqra*. The literal meaning (כמשמעו) of the text[3] of Scripture settles the matter, the Rabbis accepting its judgement without question. (A commandment contained in the Scriptures is abrogated only in extreme cases.)[4] Such questions are scarcely discussed, even in the rabbinic colleges. Anyone who is unfamiliar with the *miqra* is recommended to return to the infants' school![5]

---

[1] In contrast to most scholars, HAENCHEN, *Comm.*, ad loc., considers that not even the apostolic decretal was a source for Luke. Cf. BULTMANN's criticism in his essay *Zur Frage nach den Quellen*, pp. 71 ff., and HAENCHEN's answer, *Quellenanalyse und Kompositionsanalyse*, pp. 160 ff.

[2] To this problem, see DUPONT, *Les problemes*, pp. 50 ff.; cf. below, pp. 276 ff., 307.

[3] Cf. above, p. 66.

[4] Cf. above, p. 83.

[5] See above, pp. 64 f.

Other questions are decided by referring to the oral Torah. The traditional halakah on most fundamental questions is so ancient as to be practically identical throughout the whole of Rabbinic Judaism, though local variations are not unknown. But since the fall of the Temple deprived Judaism of its legislative centre, the halakah became in many respects different from place to place, largely because the various colleges had "legislative" authority within their respective districts. There thus existed a number of local traditions apart from the common basic tradition.[1]

When a question was debated in college, it might, as we have seen, prove to be straightforward and clearly decided in the *miqra*, in which case further debate was superfluous. It might be equally straightforward and equally clearly decided in the *mishnah* or, to be more precise, in a former "legislative" act or in an authoritative statement made by some recognized doctrinal authority of the past. In the normal course of events, discussion in these cases is again superfluous. If the members of the court have heard an authoritative tradition they produce it, אם שמעו אמרו, as M Sanh. XI.3 so succinctly puts it. It is an important rule in this connection that a clear distinction is to be drawn between those questions which have, and those which have not, been decided. In the former case, the person asked is to say: שמעתי, "I have heard as an authoritative tradition"; in the latter, he must say: לא שמעתי, "I have heard no authoritative tradition on this matter".[2]

Debate on an undecided question, as we have earlier pointed out,[3] largely takes the form of a review of what has been given in the written and oral Torah: (a) the Scriptures are either *interpreted* (דרש), i.e. an attempt is made, using some method approved by those present, to reach a decision from the Holy Scriptures, or skilfully to use and apply verses of Scripture. This Scripture-based argument may sometimes appear (from our point of view) to be a quite rational operation (דין) following fixed hermeneutical principles (מדות); or it may occasionally be a more irrational midrash.[4] (b) Or the material of the oral Torah may be *interpreted*; i.e. sayings of older teachers, and narratives concerning them, may be repeated, as being more or less directly relevant to the matter

---

[1] Cf. above, p. 131, n. 1.

[2] See further, BACHER, *Tradition*, pp. 9 ff. Cf. also RANFT, *Der Ursprung des katholischen Traditionsprinzips*, pp. 148 f.

[3] Above, pp. 179 ff.

[4] See the works mentioned above, p. 34, n. 1.

under discussion. They are then *applied* to the question or *used* in order to decide it—the whole by means of a more or less acute interpretation.[1]

Finally comes the argument from reason (סברא)[2]—i.e. reason directed by the Wisdom of the Torah—from which it is possible, in practice rather than in principle, to set apart the argument from the processes of nature and of life (דרך ארץ).[3] Such arguments as these carry very little weight in comparison with arguments drawn from the Holy Scriptures and authoritative tradition.

Should questions prove not to have been decided in the past, they are as a rule decided—at the end of the debate—by means of a vote, if the court in question has the authority to make such decisions. If we look beneath the surface, however, the decision has already been made. The relevance of the arguments advanced, the convincing nature of the evidence,[4] and the position and authority of the speakers, have in effect already decided the question; the vote is thus as a rule little more than a formality. This is all the more natural when we remember that the vote was not designed to place the seal of approval upon the personal wishes and thoughts of those present, but to determine the sacred, authoritative Torah's answer to the question under discussion.

The doctrinal debate described by Luke in Acts 15 must be seen against this background. What we have said above is particularly relevant, since the main figures in the controversy are former Pharisees. We must nevertheless beware of exaggerating this fact unduly. Even had the protagonists come from some other Jewish background, the alternative methods of argument which we have described might still be expected to have been applied. The only difference would have been that the Sadducees—and to some extent the Qumran congregation—did not argue on the unquestioned basis of an *oral* Torah, but of a complementary body of Torah material, the most important parts of which were written down.[5] This does not however alter the overall picture of the possible ways of conducting an argument to any great extent.

The doctrinal controversy in Antioch has to do with the circumcision

---

[1] See above, Ch. 12.

[2] E.g. b Sanh. 88b, p Ber. IX.3. On the term, cf. BACHER, *Terminologie* II, pp. 131 f., and above, p. 104.

[3] E.g. b Sanh. 88b.

[4] The development in Tannaitic and Amoraic times tends in the direction of according learned argument a greater and greater importance; the majority decision thus becomes more and more a formality. Cf. RABIN, *Qumran Studies*, p. 106.

[5] Cf. above, pp. 21 ff., and 157 ff.

of Gentiles who have been converted to Christ. On this point the literal text of Scripture, i.e. the *miqra*, has nothing to say. Had there been a text of Scripture which laid down whether or not Gentiles won for the Lord in the coming age of salvation[1] were to be circumcized, no controversy could have arisen. The members of the early Church had no hesitation in subjecting themselves to the plain word of Scripture on matters concerning the coming Messianic age.[2] We must however point out that most of the prophetic material on the coming age of salvation is of such a nature that it must be *interpreted*, or at least *given a definite application* on a basis of certain presuppositions. Early Christianity had therefore to cultivate the *interpretation* of Scripture: *midrash* (of a certain type).[3]

Early Christianity also had its own counterpart to the oral Torah (mishnah in its widest meaning). We are not now thinking of the halakah tradition which those converted to Christ brought with them from their various backgrounds, whether Pharisaic, Sadducean, Essene or Apocalyptic. It is certain that a considerable period of time must have elapsed before they discovered and came to terms with ways of thought and norms of behaviour which had a more or less evident origin in "the tradition of the elders" (ἡ παράδοσις τῶν πρεσβυτέρων). "The leaven of the Scribes and the Pharisees"[4] could not be removed overnight, even though a number of sayings of Jesus attacking "the tradition of the elders" had been preserved.[5] However, it is clear that these converts were in a state of conscious doctrinal conflict, principally with the scribes of the Pharisees, but also with the Sadducees; this opposition must thus have been quite conscious from the very first. Another relevant factor is that the early Christian congregations appear to have had an effective common life, in which ways of thought and norms of behaviour which conflicted with *the sayings of Jesus and the narratives of the works of Jesus* were certainly eliminated and corrected relatively quickly and relatively

---

[1] In order to estimate the use of Scripture in early Christianity it is necessary to take account of the belief of the early Church that a new epoch in the history of salvation had been inaugurated.

[2] On the question of the position of the Torah in the coming age of salvation, according to the Jewish view, see W. D. DAVIES, *Torah in the Messianic Age and/or the Age to Come* (1952).

[3] Cf. above, sec. C.

[4] Matt. 16.6 with par., 11.

[5] E.g. Mk. 7.1 ff. with par., Matt. 23. 1 ff. with par.

effectively. It is in fact at this point that we must seek early Christianity's equivalent of the oral Torah.[1]

Had there been some saying of Jesus (λόγος κυρίου) dealing clearly with this matter, the doctrinal controversy would again have been avoided. Or if one of the protagonists had been ignorant of the existence of such a saying, and someone had been able to say, in the words of the Rabbis, שמעתי (ἤκουσα) or מקבלני (ἐγὼ παρέλαβον),[2] and had been able to repeat a saying of Jesus on the circumcision of the Gentiles, a saying which he had received as a tradition, then the matter would have been cleared up and the controversy settled. In the next chapter we shall see how Paul subjects himself to the plain meaning of the sayings of Jesus.[3] There is no reason to suspect any early Christian teacher of having had any other attitude to the authority of the sayings of Jesus. All historical probability is in favour of Jesus' disciples, and the whole of early Christianity, having accorded the sayings of the one whom they believed to be the Messiah at least the same degree of respect as the pupils of a Rabbi accorded the words of *their* master!

There were thus—in principle—three possibilities remaining for the settlement of the controversy:

(i) To interpret or "use" a text of Scripture in such a way as to present a proof which was acceptable to the conflicting parties. We shall see in the next chapter how at a later stage Paul is able to defend his own attitude on this very question with a sort of *gezera shawa*.[4] If Paul had been able, in the course of the Antioch debate, to produce a similar interpretation of Scripture, which was at the same time acceptable to his opponents, the debate could scarcely have ended in deadlock.

(ii) A similar possibility would have existed, had someone been able to interpret or use a saying of Jesus in such a way as to convince those present that the question had been decided by the Lord himself. In the next chapter we shall also consider the way in which Paul argued on the basis of the tradition concerning Christ.[5]

(iii) A question of this kind could never have been settled by purely rational arguments.[6]

---

[1] See in more detail below, Ch. 15 D–E.
[2] See below, pp. 312 ff.
[3] Pp. 309 ff.
[4] Pp. 286 ff.
[5] Pp. 311 ff.
[6] Cf. below. pp. 317 f. and 320.

Had the controversy been over a less vital question, and had Paul been regarded by these Jerusalem Christians, not merely as a "prophet and teacher" (Acts 13.1),[1] but as an Apostle of Christ, on a par with the other Apostles and sent to a particular district,[2] the controversy could also have been settled in a different way. Different districts could have been allowed to observe different practices in certain questions.[3] But on this occasion the matter at issue was particularly important, and the Church could not be permitted to split into two radically differing camps. Furthermore, there is evidence, not least from the Pauline epistles, that the early Church was surprisingly insistent on having unified doctrine and halakic practice.[4]

We shall not attempt to discuss the question of which version of the doctrinal controversy in Antioch—Bezae's sharper or the other text-groups' milder account—is the more original. It is sufficient to note that the matter is taken up at a general session, though we are not given much information as to the actual course of the debate. Luke merely hints (in v. 7) at the long and heated discussion (πολλῆς δὲ ζητήσεως γενομένης), and confines himself to a statement of the two final and decisive utterances. Whether or not Luke has had access to reliable tradition, these two speeches are worthy of our attention.[5] Peter has no text of Scripture to point to, nor has he a saying of, or a narrative about, the Lord. He therefore argues from what we might call an *apostolic maaseh*, referring to something with which his listeners were familiar, viz. his own experience as an Apostle: that Gentiles have received the gift of the Holy Spirit. His hearers have previously heard an account of this: ὑμεῖς ἐπίστασθε ὅτι ... (v. 7).[6] This event is taken to be the witness of God: θεὸς ἐμαρτύρησεν αὐτοῖς ... We thus see how an argument can proceed, not only from the words and works of Jesus, but from (miraculous) events (מעשה נסים) in the experience of the Apostles. Another example of an apostolic *maaseh*, preserved and transmitted as a source of example, encouragement and doctrine, is reproduced by Luke no less than three times in Acts (9.3 ff., 22.6 ff., 26.12 ff.): the

[1] See above, p. 250, n. 5.
[2] As Paul himself later estimates his position; see below, Ch 15 E.
[3] N.B. that on certain points the Jewish Christian and Gentile Christian congregations had different halakah.
[4] Cf. below, pp. 291 ff.
[5] On the speeches in Acts, see above, p. 232, n. 1.
[6] Peter (and Luke!) assume that their hearers (readers) are acquainted with what he experienced in Joppa and Caesarea, 10.1 ff., 11.1 ff.

tradition of Paul's conversion. This passage of tradition, this logos, was certainly transmitted as part of Paul's apostolic credentials,[1] although it could be used in other ways as well, e.g. in order to show how "persecutors and men of violence" could be received by the Lord. It is a well-known fact that traditions about the Apostles are also to be found in the synoptic Gospels. LINTON has pointed out that the "example" (τύπος-) motive is prominent in these traditions;[2] we have noted another above: the "credential" motive.

The statement of James is also of interest, since he argues from a text of Scripture. Although the dividing line between *miqra* and *midrash* is often hard to define, we must on this occasion say that we are dealing with a midrash. The nature of the text quoted by James is not such that its literal meaning decides the matter without further question. When applied to this case, and used in order to throw light upon this particular problem, it is however given a definite interpretation *through which* it assumes relevance.[3] At the same time, the early Christian midrash tradition became augmented.

In conclusion, we must point out that the final decision, the logos which is formulated, is not presented as "a saying of the Lord", λόγος

---

[1] Cf. below, Ch. 15 A on the tradition of the authorization of Peter.

[2] *Das Problem der Urkirche*, pp. 96 ff. HAENCHEN, *Comm.*, p. 87, maintains that there were no "Apostelgeschichten" in the early Church. This statement, which BULTMANN also accepts, *Zur Frage nach den Quellen*, p. 74, is justifiably contradicted by JERVELL, *Til spørsmålet om tradisjonsgrunnlaget for Apostlenes gjerninger*, pp. 160 ff. Cf. LINTON, *Das Problem der Urkirche, ibid.*, and see below, Ch. 15 C–E.

[3] HAENCHEN, *Quellenanalyse und Kompositionsanalyse*, p. 157, says, referring to "die Jakobusrede": "ihr Schriftbeweis (ist) keine alte Tradition: der hier benutzte LXX-Text missversteht den hebräischen Konsonanttext an zwei Stellen und verkehrt dabei dessen Sinn ins Gegenteil. (אדם wird als 'Adam', statt als 'Edom' verstanden, und יִרְשׁוּ in יִדְרְשׁוּ verlesen.) Will man im Ernst behaupten, Jakobus habe die Heidenmission ausgerechnet in Jerusalem mit einem sinnwidrigen LXX-Zitat gerechtfertigt? Nein, hier spricht der Schriftsteller Lukas selbst."

It is possible that Luke is here speaking himself. But his way of using the Scriptures is exactly that used in Jerusalem at the beginning of the Christian era. What HAENCHEN here calls "Verlesungen", "Missverständnisse", "sinnwidrige Zitate" were called *midrash* in the Jewish circles in which Jesus appeared and in which the primitive Church developed. The one who could interpret the Scriptures, and uncover their secrets through new readings, and new interpretations, with or without minor adaptations of the text, with or without the use of existing *variae lectiones*, was considered to be in possession of wisdom bestowed by God (חכמה). Cf. above, Ch. 2.

κυρίου,[1] "received from the Lord"[2] nor as a decision pronounced "in the name of Jesus", ἐν τῷ ὀνόματι τοῦ Ἰησοῦ; instead, the solemn pronouncement is made: "The Holy Spirit and we have decided ...", ἔδοξεν γὰρ τῷ πνεύματι τῷ ἁγίῳ καὶ ἡμῖν ... This phraseology is evidence of a well-developed spiritual self-consciousness.[3] The rabbinic tradition knew only three courts on which the *Shekinah* rested, and all were placed in O.T. times.[4] This form of words is also evidence of a sharp distinction drawn, according to Luke, between what was "heard" as a saying of Jesus and what the Church itself formulated. On this point the Pauline and Lucan evidence agrees remarkably well (see below, Ch. 15 E).

---

[1] Cf. 1 Thess. 4.15.
[2] Cf. e.g. 1 Cor. 11.23 and below, pp. 311 ff.
[3] Cf. JOHNSON, *The Dead Sea Manual of Discipline*, pp. 130 ff.
[4] See M. GUTTMANN, *Zur Einleitung in die Halacha* I, p. 36.

CHAPTER 15

The Evidence of Paul

A. *The Apostolates of Peter and Paul*

After their Master's departure, those who had been Jesus' nearest disciples took over the leadership of his *ecclesia*. When seen against the background of the situation we have described in Chapters 6–12, this development appears quite natural; indeed, obvious. In the group around Jesus of Nazareth, a long personal discipleship must have weighed heavily in favour of anyone who claimed to speak in his Master's name. In addition, the sources inform us that from among his disciples Jesus himself chose an inner circle of twelve chief disciples; this information is certainly historically reliable.[1] This special election and authorization, coming from the Master himself, must have given the twelve a decisive authority among the followers of Christ, particularly when it was a matter of carrying on his work: of functioning as the eschatological "judges", of leading his *ecclesia*, transmitting, interpreting and spreading his teaching, instructing and doing mighty works "in his name". Finally, the twelve were able to refer to the confirmatory authorization they had received, according to certain emphatically expressed passages, in connection with the appearances of the Risen Lord. They thus had an outstanding position as Jesus' disciples, his eschatological *synedrion*[2] and his original Apostles.[3]

---

[1] Cf. above, p. 221, n. 2, and below.

[2] See above, Ch. 14. Cf. E. SCHWEIZER, *Gemeinde und Gemeindeordnung im N.T.* (1959), pp. 22 ff. and 41 f. See also M. WEISE, Mt 5.21 f., in *Zeitschr. f.d. Neutest. Wiss.* 49 (1958), pp. 116 ff. — Ignatius calls the twelve *synedrion*, Magn. 6.1, Trall. 3.1; cf. Trall. 2.2, Philad. 5.1, 8.1, Smyrn. 8.1 (*ibid.*, p. 119).

[3] The thesis which is sometimes advanced, that the twelve are not to be counted as being in the category of "Apostles" seems to be somewhat strange. According to both Paul and Luke, the Apostles are "witnesses of the resurrection" above all (see above, Ch. 14 C, and below, Ch. 15 C), and according to the particularly important logos quoted in 1 Cor. 15.3 ff., Peter was the first to meet the Risen Lord, followed by the twelve collectively. The twelve must therefore have been regarded as being *Urapostel*. The question which is of real importance is: of what did the peculiar position of the twelve consist, and on what was it based? — On this problem cf.,

Paul of Tarsus had never been a personal disciple of Jesus of Nazareth, and thus had no such relationship to fall back upon; for that reason he found it difficult in some circles to win a hearing for his claim to be an Apostle of Jesus Christ. This is easily understood against the background of the situation we have described in Chapters 6–12. The struggle for the recognition of his apostolate is indirect evidence of the authoritative position of the original Apostles, the personal disciples of Jesus, in the young Church.

The Pauline apologia in Gal. 1–2 has been subjected to the most minute scrutiny;[1] and rightly so. Here we have a very early and unimpeachably genuine piece of evidence, dealing with certain factors basic to the history of early Christianity, and with a complex of doctrinal problems; this evidence is provided by one of the leading figures of the early Church. To be sure, the description given here is not distinguished by its dispassionate objectivity, but on the other hand, its author takes God to witness that he is telling the truth (1.20). This must at least mean that he makes no deliberately false statements.[2]

When this apologia has been critically examined, great attention has been paid to such questions as: the accusations which the Apostle is here answering, the doctrines his opponents set up against the Pauline gospel, and the identity of these adversaries *in concreto*. But on the other hand, insufficient attention has been paid to a question which we might express as follows: What are the positive aspects of the apostolate and the origins of the gospel which Paul *presupposes*, takes up in his argument, and relates himself and his gospel to? We shall proceed on the basis of this question.

It is clear from Paul's account in Galatians (1.6 ff.) that the Galatian

---

apart from the above-mentioned works, p. 220, n. 4, E. KÄSEMANN, Die Legitimität des Apostels, in *Zeitschr. f. d. Neutest. Wiss.* 41 (1942), pp. 33 ff. (and the opposite point of view, R. BULTMANN, *Exegetische Probleme des zweiten Korintherbriefs*, 1947, pp. 20 ff.) It is difficult in this context to follow the view of G. KLEIN, Galater 2,6–9 und die Geschichte der Jerusalemer Urgemeinde, in *Zeitschr. f. Theol. u. Kirche* 57 (1960), pp. 275 ff.

[1] See, apart from commentaries ad loc., e.g. A. FRIDRICHSEN, Die Apologie des Paulus Gal. 1, in *Norsk Teol. Tidsskrift, Bihefte*, 21 (1920), pp. 53 ff., KÄSEMANN, *op. cit.*, O. LINTON, The Third Aspect, in *Studia Theol.* 3 (1949), pp. 79 ff., and E. KLOSTERMANN, Zur Apologie des Paulus Galater 1,10–2,21, in *Gottes ist der Orient, Festschrift f.* O. EISSFELDT (1959), pp. 84 ff.

[2] Cf. the judgement of E. MEYER, *Ursprung und Anfänge des Christentums* III (1923), p. 179.

church had "begun to turn to a different gospel" which "is not a gospel". They had begun to demand the circumcision of Gentile Christians, which implied their subjection at least to certain parts of the Law (5.1 ff.). This meant according to Paul that they had rejected the Pauline gospel. For the main point of the message which Paul calls "my gospel"[1] is that the Gentiles, without circumcision and without being made subject to the Law of Moses, can now be incorporated into the people of God, and can obtain a share in salvation through faith in Christ's atonement alone.[2] To deny the validity (the divine truth) of the specifically Pauline gospel must go hand in hand with the denial of Paul's apostolate and apostolic authority. To judge from Paul's account, his adversaries had dismissed him as a mere teacher, a transmitter of *human* doctrine, an apostle (ἀπόστολος, שליח) *sent by men*. Furthermore, they had evidently placed particular emphasis on his inferior standing in relation to the original Apostles and the leading figures in the Jerusalem congregation. It is scarcely to be expected, however, that we shall be able to correlate all the accusations met by Paul in Gal. into a systematic whole.[3]

In this situation, Paul has to prove the validity of his gospel (cf. the Rabbis' קיים תלמודו);[4] this can only be done by proving the validity of his apostolate. However, when he does this, he must proceed from a current, accepted concept of what constitutes an Apostle or, to be more precise, from those ideas current in early Christianity as to what enables a person to claim to be an Apostle of Jesus Christ.

Early Christianity's concept of the apostolate seems to have two main roots.[5] On the one hand, they built on a basis of those ideas, shaped and determined with legal precision, as to what constitutes a human apostle (שליח).[6] Such a one must be authorized and sent by the originator of the commission in person, and not through some other intermediary or some other apostle.[7] On the other hand, they built on traditional ideas of the distinction between what God brings about direct, unmediated,

---

[1] Rom. 2.16, 16.25, 2 Tim. 2.8; 2 Cor. 4.3, 1 Thess. 1.5, 2 Thess. 2.14; 1 Cor. 15.1, Gal. 1.11, 2.2.

[2] See A. FRIDRICHSEN, *The Apostle and his Message* (1947).

[3] On the question of the nature of the accusations faced here by Paul, see the works quoted above, p. 263, n. 1. Cf. also W. SCHMITHALS, Die Häretiker in Galatien, in *Zeitschr. f. d. Neutest. Wiss.* 47 (1956), pp. 25 ff.

[4] Cf. below, p. 287.

[5] See RIESENFELD, *Apostel*, col. 497 f.

[6] See KRAUSS, *Apostel*.

[7] M Git. III.6; cf. T. W. MANSON, *The Church's Ministry* (1948), pp. 36 f.

and what he does through an intermediary (a mediator, angel or man),[1] and the distinction which was also observed between the prophet, charismatically endowed, called and provided with his message direct from heaven, and the one who may only transmit what has previously been revealed. Both the prophet and the teacher are considered to have been equipped with the word of God, but the prophet has a different standing from the teacher, since he has been *sent* by God direct, and hence is an "Apostle of God".[2]

The early Church's concept of the apostolate was, however, not limited to these general presuppositions. They were primarily based on the teaching and actions of Jesus, and on those events, so difficult for the historian to estimate, which are described as being direct meetings with the Risen Lord. As we shall now see, this is clear, not least from Paul's argument in Gal. 1–2.

At the very beginning of the letter to the Galatians, Paul introduces himself solemnly as "an Apostle, not from men, nor through man, but through Jesus Christ, and God the Father ..." He then attacks (v. 6 ff.) the Galatians' apostasy to another gospel and pronounces a solemn curse on those who preach a message contradictory to that which he has passed on to the congregation. We notice here that Paul's gospel is a quite well-defined entity: the congregation is expressly said to have "received" (παραλαμβάνειν) it from the Apostle. A similar use of terms is to be observed elsewhere in the Pauline *corpus*: in 1 Cor. 15.1 it is τὸ εὐαγγέλιον, and in 1 Thess. 2.13, λόγος ἀκοῆς, which are said to have been "received" (παραλαμβάνειν) by the congregations as a result of Paul's preaching.[3] The gospel is thus on such a level that it *can* be made the object of teaching and transmission. This important fact is also substantiated in another way in the course of Paul's argument: were the gospel an entity which *could not* be transmitted and taught, then Paul would have had no cause to deny that he had received it in such a way.[4] We notice in addition that there is no question of Paul having authority

---

[1] E.g. the Passover Haggadah ad Ex. 12.12. See D. DAUBE, The 'I am' of the Messianic Presence, in *The N.T. and Rabbinic Judaism* (1956), pp. 325 ff.

[2] The Rabbis called certain of the O.T. prophets שלוחים, i.e. the ones who worked miracles; see the evidence in BILLERBECK, *Comm.* III, pp. 3 f.

[3] Cf. below, pp. 295 ff.

[4] See FRIDRICHSEN's objections against H. SCHLIER (*Comm.* ad loc.), *The Apostle*, pp. 20 f.

over the gospel. He is himself bound by it. He formulates his curse in such a way that it would recoil upon himself, should he preach in opposition to the gospel: ἀλλὰ καὶ ἐὰν ἡμεῖς (v. 8). Paul thus treats the gospel as an "objective" entity, received from the Lord, and himself as its "servant" (cf. διάκονος τοῦ εὐαγγελίου, Eph. 3.7 f., Col. 1.23).[1] Continuing, Paul attempts to show that his gospel is of immediate divine origin; he has not received it from man, but direct from the Lord. He also clarifies his relationship to the original Apostles in Jerusalem (v. 15 ff.), and goes on to explain the meaning of the gospel (2.11 ff.).

In this connection it is extremely important to take note of the way in which Paul conducts his argument. He proceeds from Peter's apostolate as a given and accepted fact, the legitimacy of which he has no need to demonstrate. Nor does he attack it. But he sets himself up as a parallel to Peter, his Gentile apostolate as a parallel to Peter's Jewish apostolate, his gospel for the Gentiles as a parallel to Peter's gospel for the Jews.[2]

Peter has been entrusted with the gospel of circumcision (τὸ εὐαγγέλιον τῆς περιτομῆς); in the same way Paul has been entrusted with the gospel of non-circumcision (τ. εὐ. τῆς ἀκροβυστίας). The one who has worked for (ἐνεργήσας) Peter in his apostolate of circumcision (ἀποστολὴ τῆς περιτομῆς), has likewise worked for Paul in his apostolate to the Gentiles ([ἀ.] εἰς τὰ ἔθνη). The Apostles in Jerusalem had decided that Paul's mission field was to be among the Gentiles, and Peter's among the circumcized (ἡμεῖς εἰς τὰ ἔθνη, αὐτοὶ δὲ εἰς τὴν περιτομήν), 2.7 ff.[3]

Paul, when describing these matter, refers to Peter now as Πέτρος, now as Κηφᾶς (כיפא). Is this pure chance? Does he accept this title, "the Rock", only as a name, the meaning of which he has no need to consider closely?[4] Or is he familiar with the early Christian tradition giving Peter his authorization as the bed-rock of the Church, as the prince

---

[1] Cf. 1 Cor. 3.5, 2 Cor. 3.6, 6.4, 11.23, Col. 1.25.

[2] Cf. W. L. KNOX, *St Paul and the Church of Jerusalem* (1925), pp. 363 ff.

[3] See FRIDRICHSEN, *The Apostle*.

[4] That Peter and Cephas are the same person ought to be perfectly evident. On this problem, see CULLMANN, *Petrus*, pp. 11 ff., IDEM, πέτρα, Πέτρος, Κηφᾶς, in *Theol. Wörterb.* VI, pp. 94 ff., H. CLAVIER, Πέτρος καὶ πέτρα, in *Zeitschr. f. d. Neutest. Wiss.*, Beih. 21 (1954), pp. 94 ff. On the concepts of Peter as "the rock" and the early Christian ecclesia as a building, see the comparative material from Qumran presented by O. BETZ, Felsenmann und Felsengemeinde, in *Zeitschr. f. d. Neutest. Wiss.* 48 (1957), pp. 49 ff. See also above, pp. 220 and 270.

of Apostles (Matt. 16.17–19)?[1] The latter alternative is extremely probable, since in this context Paul refers to Simon bar Jona by the name of "the rock" both in its Greek and in its Aramaic form. Probability approaches the bounds of certainty when we examine Paul's argument in more detail, since he bases his argument on precisely the same leading motives as those which appear in the tradition of Peter's primacy.

In Matt. 16.13 ff. we have preserved a logos containing Peter's authorization as "the Rock".[2] We have good reason to suppose that we are here dealing with a compound of two separate traditions, and that the second of these, v. (16) 17–19, is taken from a lost tradition of how Peter became the first to meet the Risen Lord.[3] This conclusion is however disputed. At all events, it is clear that what we have here is the tradition of Peter's authorization. In its written form it is in these words:

"He said to them, 'But who do you say that I am?' Simon Peter replied, 'You are the Christ, the Son of the living God (σὺ εἶ ὁ χριστὸς ὁ υἱὸς τοῦ θεοῦ τοῦ ζῶντος).' And Jesus answered him, 'Blessed are you, Simon bar Jona! For flesh and blood (σάρξ καὶ αἷμα) has not revealed (ἀπεκάλυψεν) this to you, but my Father who is in heaven. And I tell you, you are Peter (Πέτρος) and on this rock (πέτρα) I will build my Church, and the gates of Hades shall not prevail against it. I will give you the keys of the Kingdom of heaven, and whatever you bind on earth shall be bound in heaven, and whatever you loose on earth shall be loosed in heaven.'"

From the point of view of terminology and motif, we are here moving within a specific part of the synoptic area: the sphere of the messianic secret. According to the synoptic writers' accounts the title of *Son of God* is one of the μυστήρια which are not granted to this world. If we exclude the introductory narratives in Matthew (1.1–4.11) and Luke (1.1–4.13), and the passion narrative, the title of "Son of God" is used in the synop-

---

[1] The Matthaean tradition that Simon bar Jona received his name כיפא (Πέτρος) in connection with his commission to be the foundation stone of the new ecclesia seems to be probable. Cf. however CULLMANN, *Petrus*, pp. 15 f.—That Simon's name *bar Jona* meant "outcast" or "bandit" is possible, but extremely unlikely.

[2] Cf. the tradition of the authorization of Paul, Acts 9.1 ff., 22.3 ff., 26.9 ff.

[3] 1 Cor. 15.4, Lk. 24.34; cf. John 21.15 ff. Thus BULTMANN, *Theologie des N.T:s*, p. 46, and many others.—For an analysis of Matt. 16.13–23, see A. VÖGTLE, Messiasbekenntnis und Petrusverheissung, in *Bibl. Zeitschr.* N. F. 1 (1957), pp. 252 ff., 2 (1958), pp. 85 ff. (with comprehensive bibliography). According to VÖGTLE not even v. 17–19 are an original unity.

tics only on those occasions when Jesus' appearance is in the nature of a theophany (the walking on the water, the transfiguration), and when Jesus is addressed by the clairvoyant demons.

The compound expression *"flesh and blood"* (σάρξ καὶ αἷμα, בשר ודם)[1] occurs nowhere else in the synoptic material.

In the same way, the concept of *revelation*, the "uncovering" (ἀποκα-λύπτειν, גלה) of certain divine secrets, plays a definite role in the synoptic tradition. The motif is central and limited at one and the same time. Referring to Jesus' secrets, we read in Matt. 11.25 ff. (with par.) that the Father has hidden these things from the wise and understanding, but "revealed" (ἀπεκάλυψας) them to the simple, and that no one knows the Father except the Son and any one to whom the Son chooses to "reveal" him.[2] The motif recurs in our passage of tradition on Peter's gnosis that Jesus is the Son of God. In Lk. 17.30 the parousia is referred to as the day on which the Son of man is (definitively) "revealed". The secrets of the Kingdom of heaven (τὰ μυστήρια[3] τῆς βασιλείας τῶν οὐρανῶν) are said in Matt. 13.11 (with par.) to be hidden in Jesus' parables, or perhaps in his teaching as a whole;[4] the disciples are said to have been given the understanding of these secrets (ὑμῖν δέδοται γνῶναι τὰ μ. κτλ.), but not οἱ ἔξω.[5] Further, we read in a saying of Jesus in Matt. 10.26 ff. (with par.) that nothing is hidden except in order to be "revealed"; the saying is interpreted as being a prophecy that the esoteric teaching of Jesus is to be proclaimed openly and publicly. The motif thus plays a limited, but extremely central role in the material which we have from the synoptic writers. The history of early Christianity is hardly made easier to understand by claiming, as some scholars do, that these motives are secondary in the gospel tradition.[6]

We are thus dealing with a definite part of the gospel tradition and a definite group of motives.

---

[1] There does not appear to be any evidence for a corresponding *Aramaic* phrase.

[2] Cf. the interpretation of this word given by E. NORDEN in his famous book *Agnostos Theos* (1913), pp. 277 ff.

[3] Mark reads singular.

[4] So JEREMIAS, *Die Gleichnisse Jesu*, pp. 7 ff.

[5] This term is not used by Matt. in this context. Cf. Mk.

[6] See W. MANSON, The ΕΓΩ ΕΙΜΙ of the Messianic Presence in the N.T., in *Journ. of Theol. Stud.* 48 (1947), pp. 137 ff., and DAUBE's particularly important article, *The 'I am' of the Messianic Presence.* — Cf. below, p. 280, on the way in which the revelation is often thought to take place in an earthly substratum: events, words, writings.

When Paul seeks in Gal. 1–2 to show that he is not Peter's inferior, and is not dependent upon him, but is his *apostolic equal*, how does he conduct his argument?

"For I would have you know, brethren, that the gospel which was preached by me is not man's gospel (κατὰ ἄνθρωπον).[1] For I did not receive it from man (παρὰ ἀνθρώπου), nor was I taught it (ἐδιδάχθην), but it came through a revelation of Jesus Christ (ἀλλὰ δι᾽ ἀποκαλύψεως Ἰησοῦ Χριστοῦ)," 1.11 f.

Paul goes on to say, in v. 15 ff.: "But when he who had set me apart before I was born, and had called me through his grace, was pleased to reveal (ἀποκαλύψαι) his Son (τὸν υἱὸν αὐτοῦ) to me,[2] in order that I might preach him among the Gentiles, I did not confer with flesh and blood (σαρκὶ καὶ αἵματι), nor did I go up to Jerusalem to those who were Apostles before me, but I went away into Arabia ..."

Here, too, we can observe the three elements which we emphasized in the tradition of how the head figure in the group of those whom Paul calls οἱ πρὸ ἐμοῦ ἀπόστολοι was proclaimed as "the rock": (i) The decisive point is the revelation of the fact that Jesus is the *Son of God* (cf. Rom. 1.4). (ii) Paul received this gnosis, not from man (v. 11), nor by conferring with *flesh and blood* (v. 15). (iii) It is the heavenly Father who has *revealed* it (v. 15), which can evidently be varied to say that the risen Jesus Christ revealed it (v. 12).

If we now make a rapid survey of Pauline terminology, we find that the phrase "flesh and blood" is far from being common in the Apostle's vocabulary. Apart from this passage, it is used only twice in the *corpus paulinum* (1 Cor. 15.50, Eph. 6.12), and is thus practically as striking here as it is in the synoptic material.

A "Son of God"-Christology is fundamental for the whole of Pauline teaching (a situation clarified not least by the text we are at present considering). It is thus impossible to draw any conclusions from the occurrence of this motif in this context.

The concept of the "revelation" of divine secrets is also a central theme in Pauline teaching. Of particular importance in this connection are the sayings on the divine mystery (τὸ μυστήριον, τὰ μυστήρια)[3] which in

---

[1] P. GAECHTER, *Petrus und seine Zeit* (1958), p. 373, paraphrases "um menschlicher Schwäche zu schmeicheln" — GAECHTER's good work is unfortunately strikingly tendentious.

[2] ἐν ἐμοί is the same as ἐμοί, BLASS, DEBRUNNER, *Grammatik*, § 220.

[3] We do not need to stop to consider the differences in meaning between singular and plural, not unimportant in themselves.

the latter days has been revealed to "us", ἡμῖν (*the Apostles*), 1 Cor. 2.10
to "the holy *Apostles* and prophets by the Spirit", Eph. 3.5. Without
obscuring the fact that revelations are also granted to others apart from
the Apostles (Col. 1.26; cf. also 1 Cor. 2.6 ff.), it is important to note the
way in which they have been entrusted in a special manner with the
revealed mystery: they are to be regarded as stewards of the mysteries
of God (οἰκονόμοι μυστηρίων θεοῦ), 1 Cor. 4.1.[1]

From what has already been said, we must regard it as extremely
probable that Paul was familiar with the logos of Peter's authorization,
and that Paul in addition assumes his readers to be familiar with the
reasons for Peter's primacy which can be derived from this tradition.
The decisive argument for this view is that Paul expresses himself in
this way *when he wishes to show his own apostolate to be a parallel to Peter's
accepted apostolate.*

Another resemblance is worth our attention. In the tradition of Peter's
authorization we read, "on this rock I will build (οἰκοδομήσω) my
Church," Matt. 16.18. In 2 Cor. 10.8 and 13.10, Paul refers to his apostolic
authority as "an authority for building up" (ἐξουσία εἰς οἰκοδομήν),
given by the Lord;[2] the Church is here conceived of as being a temple,
built out of "living stones".[3] We shall return later, in section E, to
Peter's and Paul's authority to "bind and loose" (δέειν καὶ λύειν),
which refers principally to doctrinal authority.

According to Paul's account in Gal. 1–2, there are thus two apostolates[4]
in early Christianity. Or, to be more precise, those who are called οἱ
ἀπόστολοι Ἰησοῦ Χριστοῦ may be divided into two groups. The first group,
led by Peter,[5] has "the apostolate of circumcision" (ἡ ἀποστολὴ τῆς

---

[1] Cf. below, sec. C.

[2] The connection between Luke and Paul on this point has been noted by C. H.
Dodd, ΕΝΝΟΜΟΣ ΧΡΙΣΤΟΥ, in *Studia Paulina in honorem* J. de Zwaan (1953),
p. 109.

[3] Apart from the already known comparative material from Rabbinic Judaism
(teachers are builders), we must now take account of extremely important new
material from Qumran: the concept of how God is to build a house for thee (David)
in the last days (בית יבנה לכה), i.e. a new spiritual temple, 4 QFlor. X (published
by J. M. Allegro, Fragments of a Qumran Scroll of Eschatological Midrāšîm, in
Journ. of Bibl. Lit. 77, 1958, pp. 351 ff.). See above, pp. 220 and 266.

[4] Fridrichsen has the honour of being the first — among modern scholars —
to note this. See his little book *The Apostle.*

[5] Klein, *Galater 2,6–9*, pp. 284 f., has not noticed the role played by the category
of הראשון (the first one, which is the representative of his group) in the thought of
early Christianity and Judaism; he therefore finds it problematical that the thought

περιτομῆς); the other, led by Paul, has "the apostolate of non-circumcision" (ἡ ἀποστολὴ τῆς ἀκροβυστίας). The first is sent to the circumcised; the second to the uncircumcised. This division of the mission field was confirmed at the proceedings of the Apostles in Jerusalem. It appears probable that this order encountered certain difficulties in practice, and could only become a provisory arrangement. But we have no reason to doubt Paul's statement, given under oath, that such an agreement was in fact reached at the negotiations in Jerusalem.

Further, according to Paul's account the original Christian message of salvation, τὸ εὐαγγέλιον, has been revealed in two forms, "the gospel of circumcision" and "the gospel of non-circumcision" (τὸ εὐ. τῆς περιτομῆς, τὸ εὐ. τῆς ἀκροβυστίας). These two have all their basic components in common (1 Cor. 15.2 ff.; cf. 1.10 ff.), but give rise to two somewhat different messages. One, the meaning of which was revealed to Peter, proclaims what the work of Christ means to the circumcised; the other, the meaning of which was revealed to Paul, proclaims what the work of Christ means to the uncircumcised. The term τὸ εὐαγγέλιον can be used in an absolute sense to refer to the message of salvation preached by all Christ's Apostles. But when in certain contexts Paul defines what he calls "my gospel" or "the gospel which I preach", he is not referring to a message common to all the Apostles, but to that special form of the message with which he has been entrusted. The Gentiles, thanks to the work of Christ, in the new period in the history of salvation which that work has created, can now, without circumcision and submission to the Law of Moses, be incorporated into the people of God and be granted a share in the gifts of salvation. The account given by Paul in Gal. 2 would be meaningless if "Paul's gospel" and "Peter's gospel" were *completely* identical.[1]

It is clear from Paul's account that he does not oppose circumcision *per se*, as far as it concerns men of Jewish birth (cf. Rom. 2.25 ff., 3.1 ff.). These may continue to practise it, provided they do not place their trust in it; their trust must rest on the new creation brought about by Christ (Gal. 6.15; cf. 5.6, 1 Cor. 7.19; Rom. 2.25 ff.; Col. 3.11), and pro-

in Paul's account oscillates between Peter and the other Apostles of his category. This is in reality no problem.

[1] L. CERFAUX, La tradition selon saint Paul, in *Recueil* L. CERFAUX II (1954), p. 256, rejects FRIDRICHSEN's idea that the gospel is revealed in two forms. The differences in their points of view are mainly a matter of terminology, but it is difficult to see how Paul's formulations can be interpreted in a way essentially different to FRIDRICHSEN's.

vided that they draw the right consequences from the gospel, "walk on the right road toward the truth of the gospel" (ὀρθοποδεῖν πρὸς τὴν ἀλήθειαν τοῦ εὐαγγελίου, Gal. 2.14; cf. 2.5).[1] But when circumcision is demanded of Christians of Gentile birth, men who have never been subject to the Torah, then Paul regards his entire gospel as having been denied (Gal. 5.1 ff.).

To return to Peter: it is also clear that he does not insist on circumcision. We can see from the accounts both of Luke and of Paul (Acts 15, Gal. 2) that Peter and Paul hold similar theological views[2]—a fact which is worth emphasizing in face of repeated attempts to create a gulf between Paul and the original Apostles. What divides Peter and Paul is little more than that while the latter looks upon doctrinal problems as clear matters of principle, Peter seems rather to proceed by taking up practical attitudes to individual situations, and appears to have been less consistent in drawing the consequences of the gospel.[3] We have no reason to exaggerate this situation, however. The fact that Paul's extra-legal Gentile gospel was recognized by the original Apostles in Jerusalem, led by James and Peter, is remarkably powerful evidence for the Apostles' regard for the consequences of the gospel. The decision to exempt Gentile Christians from circumcision and conformity to the Law must certainly be regarded as one of the most radical and revolutionary doctrinal decisions ever reached in Jerusalem.

This brings us to the questions of the unity of the gospel, the unity of the young Church and the relations between the original Apostles and Paul.

As we have seen, Paul denies in Gal. 1 that he received his gospel from man or by human mediation, i.e. through teaching or tradition. This statement, which recurs in other contexts as well (Rom. 1.1 ff., 16.25 ff., Eph. 3.2 ff.) is made with the greatest emphasis. It is not uttered on the spur of the moment; it expresses a certainty which for Paul was of fundamental importance. If we are to understand his concept of the gospel or his attitude to the early Christian tradition, we must accept this statement as being in principle of primary importance. This does not of course mean that these words of Paul are to be over-interpreted. This particular by-path has been actively populated ever since the days

---

[1] For the translation, see G. D. KILPATRICK, Gal. 2.14 ὀρθοποδοῦσιν, in *Zeitschr. f. d. Neutest. Wiss.*, *Beih.* 21 (1954), pp. 269 ff.

[2] This is correctly stressed by e.g. FRIDRICHSEN, *op. cit.*, p. 13, and CULLMANN, *Petrus*, pp. 67 ff.

[3] Cf. G. DIX, *Jew and Greek* (1953), pp. 35 ff.

of the Tübingen school: it is none the less a by-path.[1] Paul's account in Gal. 1 must be placed together with, and judged in connection with, all the other relevant passages in the Apostle's letters.

We can see from Paul's account in the various letters that he considers the Church of Christ to be a unity, having its centre in Jerusalem. Here, too, is the Church's highest doctrinal authority, represented by "those of repute" (οἱ δοκοῦντες) in the congregation, i.e. principally the circle of the twelve. It is from here that the word of God (ὁ λόγος τοῦ κυρίου) proceeds. Paul recognizes this, and makes use of traditions originating from this Jerusalem doctrinal centre.

How are these statements, which we shall further substantiate in due course, to be equated with what Paul says in Gal. 1, that he did not receive his gospel from, or through, man? The solution is to be found in the simple fact that "the gospel" (τὸ εὐαγγέλιον) in its meaning of "message of salvation" does not include everything that is called "the word of God" (ὁ λόγος τοῦ θεοῦ). Or, if we may be allowed to use another pair of terms, which are also somewhat ambiguous: the *kerygma* (κήρυγμα, in its meaning of "the elementary missionary message as it is proclaimed")[2] and the *didache* do not coincide. Paul claimed to have received the former from the Risen Lord direct. (But he does not seem to have been aware that his attitude on that occasion must have been conditioned by what he already knew about Jesus' execution.) He could make no such claim for the *didache*. On the contrary: Paul's arguments when teaching are drawn not so much from his revelations as from the Scriptures and the authoritative "tradition from the Lord".[3] Therefore we cannot cut all the lines of communication between the original Apostles and Paul on the strength of Paul's statement that he did not receive "his gospel" through any human agency.

We shall consider these theses in more detail in the following sections.

---

[1] On the way in which the views of the Tübingen school have persisted, despite the fact that their philosophical foundations have been abandoned, see J. MUNCK, *Paulus und die Heilsgeschichte* (1954), pp. 61 ff.

[2] On the terminological and factual obscurity in the use of this concept, see K. STENDAHL, Kerygma und kerygmatisch, in *Theol. Literaturzeit.* 77 (1952), col. 715 ff., and W. BAIRD, What is the Kerygma?, in *Journ. of Bibl. Lit.* 76 (1957), pp. 181 ff.

[3] See below, sec. E.

B. *Jerusalem and* ὁ λόγος τοῦ θεοῦ

Paul did not look upon Jerusalem as a city among other cities. He too saw Jerusalem as the holy city, which had played—and would continue to play—a central role in the unfolding of the drama of salvation. He too recognized the principle that the word of God would proceed from Jerusalem in the last days. He too accepted the twelve Apostles and the first Christian congregation as guardians of that logos which proceeded from Jerusalem.[1] His account, which confirms, complements and corrects Luke's version, is thus of particular value.

We have earlier touched upon the fact that Paul's opponents had attempted to turn the Apostles and the Jerusalem congregation against him.[2] It is therefore natural for Paul to be very much concerned to stress his equality with the other Apostles, and his *relative* independence of the Jerusalem congregation. But we none the less find that he recognizes the principle that it is from Jerusalem that the word of God proceeds.

Paul even goes so far as to say that Jerusalem is the point of departure for his own mission. In Rom. 15.18 ff.[3] he gives a rapid survey of his work as an Apostle, saying that "from Jerusalem and as far round as Illyria I have fully preached the gospel of Christ (ὥστε με ἀπὸ Ἰερουσαλὴμ καὶ κύκλῳ μέχρι τοῦ Ἰ. πεπληρωκέναι τὸ εὐ. τοῦ Χ.)." We see from this formulation how self-evident it was for Paul to place Jerusalem at the centre of the word of God, that word which in the latter days was to go out even to the Gentiles.

Paul treats the Gentile Christian congregations as imitators (μιμηταί) of the churches in Jerusalem and the rest of Judaea. This implies that they must be prepared to share the difficulties and persecution which the early Church believed to be the lot of Christ and the messianic congregation (1 Thess. 2.14). But it implies above all that they are deliberately to receive from them the word of God, and they are to imitate their halakic practice.[4] What Paul says in Rom. 15.26 ff. is most enlightening on this point. The collection which the Gentile Christian congregations contributed to "the saints at Jerusalem", i.e. the Jerusalem congregation, was motivated by an argument to the effect that, since the Gentile Christians have been made partakers of the

---

[1] We shall attempt to demonstrate this in the following pages.

[2] Above, p. 264.

[3] The arguments against the Pauline origin of Chapters 15 and 16 do not seem to me to be tenable.

[4] See below, pp. 291 ff.

spiritual things of the Jerusalem church, they are obliged to minister unto them out of their material resources. This is a simple application of the rule expressed by Paul in Gal. 6.6 (cf. 1 Cor. 9.11): "Let him who is taught the word communicate unto him who teaches in all good things."[1] In this case the Jerusalem church is the teacher of the other churches.

Paul's insistence on taking up collections in the Gentile Christian congregations to the Christians in Jerusalem is powerful evidence, not only that he considered the Church to be a unity, but that he accorded the Jerusalem congregation precedence over other congregations (cf. below).

In 1 Cor. 14.36, Paul speaks a language which is easily understood, bearing in mind what we said in the last chapter.[2] The Corinthian church was showing a tendency to take the shaping of public worship and teaching into its own hands; Paul therefore asks them, a little ironically:

ἢ ἀφ' ὑμῶν ὁ λόγος τοῦ θεοῦ ἐξῆλθεν, ἢ εἰς ὑμᾶς μόνους κατήντησεν;	"What! Did the word of God proceed from you, or are you the only ones it has reached?"

These arguments, which are easily recognizeable from the sayings of the Rabbis, are built on two basic principles: that the chosen people of God are to have *one* common "law" (Lev. 24.22),[3] and that the law is to proceed from Jerusalem (Deut. 17.8 ff., Is. 2.3).[4] We may quote a close parallel from rabbinic sources. R. Hananiah (ca. 110), in the Babylonian town of Nehar-Paqod, had taken the liberty of making some decisions which, according to the tradition, a local authority had no right to do; R. Natan's scornful comment was: "Does the Torah proceed from Babel, and the word of God from Nehar-Paqod?"[5]

As far as Paul is concerned, we shall return (in section E) to the fact that he strives energetically after common halakah in "all the congregations of the saints". His questions in 1 Cor. 14.36 indicate what his normative standards are likely to have been. Early Christianity has its

---

[1] The principle is older than Paul. Cf. Rom. 15.27.

[2] Particularly pp. 214 ff.

[3] משפט אחד יהיה לכם, quoted e.g. M Sanh. IV.1, b Sanh. 28a.

[4] Quoted above, p. 215.

[5] p Ned. VI.13, p Sanh. I.3; cf. b Ber. 63a. BILLERBECK corrects the name (to Nehar Paqor), *Comm.* III, p. 469.

centre in the Jerusalem church, whence the word of God has proceeded and whence it proceeds. In 1 Cor. 14.36 there can be no question of another place, another congregation, another *collegium*, another doctrinal authority; this is evident, not only from the fact that Paul here builds on the words of Scripture, referring to the role of Jerusalem, but also that he suggests in other contexts where the doctrinal centre of early Christianity is to be found.

We find in Gal. 1.17 that at the time of Paul's conversion, the original Apostles (οἱ πρὸ ἐμοῦ ἀπόστολοι) were in Jerusalem. This is of particular importance to the historian, since the information comes from a man who had previously, on his own admission, carried out an intensive campaign of persecution against the Christian congregation (Gal. 1.13 f., 23, Phil. 3.6).[1] He must in the circumstances have gathered a good deal of information about the centre of Christianity, and the whereabouts of its leaders, even though *detailed* information was perhaps not readily available. There can be little doubt that he added to this information after his conversion.

Three years later, when Paul sought to make the acquaintance of Peter, the leader of the Apostles,[2] the latter proved similarly to be in Jerusalem. So was James, the brother of the Lord (1.18 f.). That Paul met just these two on that particular occasion is hardly likely to have been a mere coincidence.[3] One might speculate as to why Paul met none of the other Apostles.[4] Was it due to a deliberate wish on the part of Paul—or the others—that he met only these two of the leaders? Or were the remainder of the twelve temporarily absent from Jerusalem? Or did chance play its part in the drama? It is virtually impossible to decide one way or the other from the evidence.

In Gal. 2.1 ff. Paul gives us a noteworthy piece of evidence, to the effect that the Church has a supreme doctrinal centre, consisting of the leaders of the Jerusalem congregation. He confesses that, fourteen years after his conversion, he travelled up to Jerusalem and presented his gospel for the approval of the highest doctrinal court; he did not present

---

[1] LINTON, *The Third Aspect*, pp. 81 ff., shows that there is a connection between what Paul in Gal. 1.13, 23, says that the Galatians "have heard" about him and the traditions which Luke takes up in Acts. (LINTON seems however to drive his thesis too far.) Luke has not created a freehand drawing of Paul in Acts!

[2] On the purpose of this visit, see below, pp. 297 ff.

[3] See FRIDRICHSEN, *The Apostle*, p. 17.

[4] I think that οἱ ἀπόστολοι in Gal. 1.19 is synonymous with οἱ δώδεκα.

some definite logos or a particular point of halakah, but the gospel which he claimed to have received as a revelation direct from the Lord. He submitted to them[1] the message he used to proclaim among the Gentiles, fearful that in his work as an Apostle he was running, or had run, in vain (ἀνεθέμην αὐτοῖς τὸ εὐαγγέλιον ὃ κηρύσσω ἐν τοῖς ἔθνεσιν, ... μή πως εἰς κενὸν τρέχω ἢ ἔδραμον). That Paul confesses this fact in this context—in the midst of an apologia for his high apostolate and his *relative* independence—is eloquent evidence of the role played by the leaders of the Jerusalem church (οἱ δοκοῦντες) in the affairs of the young Church, as its highest doctrinal authority.

In his epistles, Paul is not interested in describing the organization of the Jerusalem congregation, its orders of public worship, or the procedure it followed in teaching, in doctrinal and in judicial sessions. Nevertheless we do catch a glimpse now and again of certain outlines.

If we combine the evidence of Gal. 2 with Acts 15, there would seem to be a possibility that Paul refers first to a session with the entire congregation (ἀνεθέμην αὐτοῖς), and then to private deliberations with "those of repute" (κατ᾽ ἰδίαν δὲ τοῖς δοκοῦσιν). If this was the procedure one might ask whether a decision was reached at this point, or in the course of a subsequent general session.

However, it is not advisable to read Gal. 2 in the light of Acts 15. In the account of Paul nothing is expressly said about the "elders" or "the multitude". Only "those of repute" and Paul are mentioned as active participants in the negotiations.

The meaning of the phrase "those of repute" (οἱ δοκοῦντες)[2] is not clear. Paul appears to have adopted an existing designation comparable with the Qumran congregation's "renowned men" (אנשי השם).[3] There can be little doubt, however, that this group consisted primarily of the twelve,[4] remembering the self-evident role as first-hand witnesses

---

[1] "᾽Ανατίθεσθαι τινι τι (med.) heisst jemandem etwas darlegen, genauer: jemandem etwas zur Begutachtung oder auch Entscheidung vorlegen," SCHLIER, *Comm.*, ad loc.

[2] V. 2 and 6c; cf. the formulations in v. 6a and 9. For the discussion of the term οἱ δοκοῦντες, see W. FOERSTER, Die δοκοῦντες in Gal. 2, in *Zeitschr. f. d. Neutest. Wiss.* 36 (1937), pp. 286 ff., C. K. BARRETT, Paul and the "Pillar" Apostles, in *Studia Paulina in honorem* J. DE ZWAAN (1953), pp. 1 ff., KLEIN, *Galater 2,6–9 und die Geschichte der Jerusalemer Urgemeinde.* For a new interpretation of v. 6, see KLOSTERMANN, *Zur Apologie des Paulus Galater 1,10–2,21*, pp. 86 f.

[3] 1 QSa II.2, 8, 11, 13; cf. 1 QM II.7, III.3 f. The resemblance is only formal.

[4] Is the designation οἱ δοκοῦντες also a pun on οἱ δώδεκα?

ascribed to them by Pauline and other documents.[1] But does the term "those of repute" also include a group of "elders"? This point is not clarified. Within the group, however, we catch a glimpse of a smaller body,[2] the three "pillars" (οἱ στῦλοι),[3] James, Cephas and John. The fact that the name of James (the Brother of the Lord) comes first certainly means that he was the leader of the congregation, and that he presided at its various sessions. The same situation is mentioned in Acts 15. James presumably replaced Peter as leader of the Jerusalem congregation after the latter had been compelled to flee from Jerusalem (Acts 12.17).[4] Peter's presence in Jerusalem at the council of Apostles was probably no more than temporary.[5]

According to Paul's account, "those of repute" in the Jerusalem congregation had recognized both his gospel and his apostolate, and had given him the right hand of fellowship:

"When they saw that I had been entrusted (πεπίστευμαι)[6] with the gospel to the uncircumcised, just as Peter had been entrusted with the gospel to the circumcised—for he who worked (ἐνεργήσας) through Peter for the mission to the circumcised worked through me also for the Gentiles—and when they perceived the grace that was given to me,[7] James and Cephas and John, who were reputed to be pillars, gave to me and Barnabas the right hand of fellowship (κοινωνία), that we should go to the (lands of the) Gentiles and they to the circumcised (Palestine)."

---

[1] 1 Cor. 15.3 ff., a fundamental logos, recognized by *all* Apostles (v. 11); see below, pp. 280 ff. and 296 ff.; see further above, Ch. 14.

[2] See SCHLIER, *Comm.*, ad loc. Cf. BARRETT, *op. cit.*, pp. 1 ff.

[3] New material for the understanding of the image and the term is now to be found in the Qumran literature. See H. N. RICHARDSON, Some notes on 1QSa, in *Journ. of Bibl. Lit.* 76 (1957), pp. 111 and 121 (1QSa I.12 f. יסודות עדת הקודש), and BETZ, *Felsenmann und Felsengemeinde*, pp. 49 f.

[4] We catch a glimpse of a strange development in the documents. The original group of three στῦλοι seems to have consisted of Peter and the two sons of Zebedee (Mk. 5.37 with par., 14.33 with par., Lk. 8.51). The factors which seem to have contributed to this alteration were that Peter was forced to leave Jerusalem (Acts 12.17), on which James the brother of the Lord took over the leadership (*ibid.*; Acts 15.13, 21.18 ff., etc.). James the son of Zebedee was early martyred, Acts 12.2. Peter kept his position as στῦλος even during the time when he was mainly a missionary (in Palestine).

[5] Cf. above, p. 217.

[6] On the term, cf. e.g. Rom. 3.2, 1 Cor. 9.17, 1 Thess. 2.4, 1 Tim. 1.11, Tit. 1.3.

[7] They recognized his call (πεπίστευμαι) and his equipment (ἐνήργησεν) when they saw these confirmed by the results achieved (the apostolic signs!): τὴν χάριν. Cf. FRIDRICHSEN, *The Apostle*, p. 12.

This decision did not mean that two churches had been set up side by side: such was not the object. The Church, the apostolate and the gospel were regarded as being one. In support, we need only recall the vital importance of Paul's conviction that Christ is not "divided", and that the Church is undivided in essence, and must therefore stand as a unity, though inclusive of diversity (1 Cor. 1.11 ff., 12.12 ff., Gal. 3.28, Eph. 2.11 ff., Col. 3.11). The decision only gave rise to the drawing up of practical boundaries: between a Jewish and a Gentile area (geographically speaking),[1] between a mission directed to the Jews and a mission directed to the Gentiles, between a message intended for the Jews and one intended for the Gentiles. In section E we shall deal in greater detail with the implications of the Apostles' decision to grant Paul his apostolate to the "area" of the Gentiles, without subjecting him to any particular demands. Here we shall draw attention only to Paul's recognition —in principle—of the position of the *collegium* of Apostles (οἱ δοκοῦντες) in Jerusalem as the Church's highest doctrinal authority. His own relation to this *collegium* of the Apostles is rather like the relation between the single Rabbi and his colleagues (חברים). The *collegium* has authority over against the single Apostle.[2] This is implied in Paul's words (2.6): "As to me, those who were of repute *imposed* nothing upon me" (ἐμοὶ γὰρ οἱ δοκοῦντες οὐδὲν προσανέθεντο).[3] This form of expression could only refer to a superior authority.

The unity of the young Church is likewise seen in the fact that "those of repute" in the Jerusalem church, led by James, exercised oversight over all the local congregations, including those which lay beyond the frontiers of Palestine. In Gal. 2.12 Paul mentions "certain men from James" (τινὲς ἀπὸ Ἰακώβου) who had been sent to the Antioch congregation. This expression can hardly be interpreted as referring to a chance visit; it must refer to men *sent* by James. Paul in no way suggests that

---

[1] "The geographical character of the division is proved by the fact that Paul regarded himself as sent not only to the Gentiles, but also to the Jews among them (Rom. 1.13 f.; 1 Cor. 9.20, Acts passim). From this we may draw a couple of important inferences. Firstly, in the opinion of Paul the Jewish Church was bound to the Holy Land and had no existence *as a Church* outside of its boundaries ...", FRIDRICHSEN, *op. cit., ibid.*

[2] Cf. L. CERFAUX, L'unité du Corps apostolique dans le N.T., in *Recueil* L. CERFAUX II, pp. 227 ff. I hope later to have the opportunity of returning to the question of the relation between the *collegium* and the single member.

[3] On the verb, see SCHLIER, *Comm.*, ad. loc.; cf. BAUER, *Wörterbuch*, sub voce.

this inspection was illegitimate. It is the fact of Peter's having been guilty of hypocrisy[1] on that occasion which aroused Paul's anger.

The collection for "the saints in Jerusalem", though it scarcely provides a parallel to the Temple tax,[2] must also be understood as being a tangible expression of the unity of the Church under the leadership of the Jerusalem congregation. We have already discussed the way in which Paul motivated this collection.

C. *The Apostles as "Eyewitnesses" and Expounders of the Scriptures*

It seems to have been generally accepted in early Christianity that the deepest secrets in the Christian message were received as revelation (ἀποκάλυψις). This revelation was not however regarded as being an isolated entity which came down from heaven, but as the uncovering of secrets, granted in a visible, audible or seizable substrate. We have just seen the way in which Luke presents this: the message of the Apostles is delivered "in Spirit and power", but also in the form of an eyewitness account of what they themselves had seen and heard, and of what is to be found in the Holy Scriptures.[3] Luke was not the first to adopt this attitude. The same scheme, though with certain variations, recurs in Paul. Nor was he the first. In 1 Cor. 15.3 ff. he quotes a logos which he had received as authoritative tradition, undoubtedly from Jerusalem.[4] Here we encounter precisely the same technique of proof: Christ died for our sins *according to the Scriptures*, arose on the third day *according to the Scriptures*, and showed himself *to Cephas, to the twelve, to more than five hundred brethren, to James, to all the Apostles, and to Paul.*

This logos is not one among many. It is the very λόγος τοῦ εὐαγγελίου, i.e. a summary of the basic elements in the gospel itself. Paul emphasizes —a statement that cannot readily be doubted—that he and the other Apostles preach in accordance with this logos (v. 11). We are here dealing with an early source, and a source, moreover, which is emphasized as being particularly important and particularly reliable.

In this ancient logos, which we shall consider in more detail in due

---

[1] N.B. that Peter is only *visiting* Antioch, in Paul's "district" (cf. above, p. 187, and below, Sec. E). See also FRIDRICHSEN, *The Apostle*, pp. 12 ff.

[2] H. LIETZMANN, *Geschichte der Alten Kirche* I (1932), pp. 65 ff.

[3] Above, Ch. 14, partic. sec. C.

[4] See above, pp. 274 ff., and below, pp. 296 ff.

course,[1] and which is representative of the preaching both of the twelve and of Paul, we shall take note of two important things. The essential bases of the actual message contain two elements: (i) that Christ's Apostles, in the widest meaning of the term, are eyewitnesses, and (ii) that the Scriptures confirm the "truth" (reliability) of the course of events as described.

(i) In the concept of "apostle" (*shaliah*) was included, as we have seen,[2] the fact that the person sent must have been personally authorized by the one delivering the commission, and not by some intermediary. It is not therefore surprising to find that in the thought of early Christianity, an Apostle of Christ must be sent by Christ himself. According to the view of Paul it is sufficient that he has met the Risen Lord and received his message (that Christ is risen and that atonement has taken place) from him direct. For Paul, an Apostle is a "witness of the resurrection" above all. This seems also to have been the belief in Jerusalem Christianity: they considered those who were "witnesses of the resurrection" to be Apostles.[3] But it is evident that the concept of the *disciple* bulked larger in the thought of the Jerusalem church than in Paul. It was doubtless a great merit in the Jerusalem church to have "accompanied Jesus from his baptism by John to his ascension".[4] It is therefore probable that in these circles the concepts of Apostle and *disciple* were not so clearly distinguished as in Paul; Paul's reasons for doing so are easily explained.

Be that as it may. It is clear that an Apostle—in the widest meaning of the word—of Christ had, in the eyes of early Christianity, a distinctive position in relation to the other early Christian doctrinal authorities. For an Apostle was an *eyewitness*. A permanent element of the actual missionary message was that its facts were based on the evidence of reliable witnesses. In the previous chapter we saw the way in which Luke presents this fact, and we have remarked above on the way in which it is presented in the logos quoted in 1 Cor. 15.3 ff. *The Apostles, when proclaiming the gospel, claim to be eyewitnesses.* One wonders whether the fact that they—or Paul at least—were accused of preaching "themselves" is a reflection of this.[5] Paul does not deny it altogether when

---

[1] Below, pp. 299 ff.
[2] Above, pp. 264 f.
[3] See above, Ch. 14 B–C.
[4] Above, *ibid.*
[5] Cf. also below, sec. E.

answering his accusers, but he does present the matter in its correct proportions: "For what we preach (κηρύσσομεν) is not ourselves, but Jesus Christ as Lord, *with ourselves as your servants* for Jesus' sake" 2 Cor. 4.5.

However, the original Apostles were not considered to be merely "eyewitnesses of the resurrection". They had accompanied Jesus of Nazareth during his ministry in Galilee and Judaea, and were able, by virtue of their discipleship, to bear witness to the words and works of the Master—just as other disciples bore witness (העיד, μαρτυρεῖν) to what they had heard (שמע, ἀκούειν) from their master, and to what they had seen (ראה, ὁρᾶν) him do.[1] Historical probability is on the side of the Lucan information that the first Apostles claimed to be witnesses of what Jesus had done and taught. They were witnesses, not only when proclaiming the message of the resurrection, but also in their teaching (cf. e.g. Acts 10.39).

Paul considered himself to be a witness of the resurrection (N.B. particularly 1 Cor. 15.16), but was unable to make any claim to be an eyewitness of what Jesus did and taught. On such points he turns instead to received tradition. Such a terminology as ἐγὼ παρέλαβον ὃ καὶ παρέδωκα is quite unambiguous, if we assume Paul to have had anything in common with his historical milieu. He must be referring in these words to what he had received as *authoritative* tradition: tradition derived from some authoritative teacher or *collegium*, or coming through reliable channels, i.e. direct or via reliable traditionists.[2] In sections D and E we shall consider in more detail the way in which Paul's argument in his *didache* is based on traditions from, and about, Jesus, where a direct disciple of Jesus would have been able to argue on a basis of what he had heard from Jesus, or seen Jesus do.

But this fact, that the early Christian message claimed to be the eyewitness account of definite persons who were able to vouch for the "truth" of their information, had a number of definite consequences. The witnesses took up an important intermediate position between the actual messianic event and the early Christian evangelists and teachers. When the Apostles' disciples—or other early Christian teachers—were to preach or teach the message, they had to fall back upon the witness

---

[1] See above, pp. 182 ff.

[2] On the fact that an appeal to tradition is an appeal to *authoritative* tradition, see BACHER, *Tradition*, pp. 1 ff.

of the Apostles. *They mentioned the Apostles in their preaching and their teaching.*

This is no deviation from the original method of presenting the message of early Christianity. It is a simple consequence of the fact that the message was presented as an eyewitness account. In the first phase the object was to produce witnesses; in the second, to find witnesses to what the witnesses had said. This is the way in which transmission functioned among the Rabbis, and evidently also in early Christianity. There is a direct organic development from the apostolic claim that the Risen Lord had been seen by Peter and the others, to the post-apostolic concern to prove that one's information came from "Mark, who was the interpreter of Peter", from "Polycarp, who was a disciple of John", or from "the elders, the disciples of the Apostles".[1]

The information of the sources, that the Apostles presented their preaching and teaching in the form of an eyewitness account, is definitely not a concession to *secondary* rationalistic and apologetic needs. These needs were there from the beginning. In the milieu in which the early Christian message was first delivered, there must have been a reaction which called for credentials and proof. That must have been the reaction to the message of the resurrection, and to numerous narratives about what Jesus said and did.[2] Jesus was himself often faced with the task of proving the genuineness of his mission, his "doctrine" and his actions:[3] the historicity of these statements cannot be doubted. The Apostles must have been faced by the same demand, which could be partially, but never entirely, ignored. Furthermore, it is likely that the need for "definite proof" (cf. Acts 1.3) was also felt in the ranks of the Church.

(ii) Paul claimed, according to Luke: "I believe everything laid down by the Torah or written in the Prophets", Acts 24.14. In the Apostle's own writings this belief is expressed with unmistakeable confidence: "Whatever was written in former days (in the Holy Scriptures) was written for our instruction" (ὅσα γὰρ προεγράφη, εἰς τὴν ἡμετέραν διδασκαλίαν ἐγράφη), Rom. 15.4; cf. 1 Cor. 9.10, 10.11. According to Luke, Paul also confessed, "I say nothing but what the Prophets and Moses said would come to pass", Acts 26.22. It seems to be the same principle with which Paul identifies himself in 1 Cor. 4.6, when he quotes the

---

[1] See above, Ch. 13.
[2] Cf. above, pp. 212 f.
[3] Matt. 12.38 ff., 16.1 ff., Mk. 8.11 ff., Lk. 11.29 ff., John 2.18 ff., 6.30 ff.

doctrinal statement, compressed almost to the limits of intelligibility: "not beyond the things which are written" (τὸ μὴ ὑπὲρ ἃ γέγραπται).[1] For Paul, the Scriptures are the words of God (τὰ λόγια τοῦ θεοῦ, Rom. 3.2).[2] He is entirely in agreement with the opinion that they provide an inexhaustible source of revelation, comfort, teaching, instruction and discipline. It is unthinkable for him that the Scriptures should be dispensed with.

But the position and function of the Scriptures have *altered*, thanks to the work of Christ. The most important alteration is that Law, or rather νόμος, in the Scriptures, has been brought to an end in Christ, Rom. 10.4. The Law has had its day, as it were a parenthesis between the age of promise and the age of grace, but the day of the Law has now come to an end.[3] But the day of the Scriptures is not ended. It is extremely characteristic that when Paul wants to prove that the Law has come to an end in Christ, he argues with great energy from the Law. One might go so far as to say that Paul's dependence on the Scriptures is never so much in evidence as when he is proving that the Law has been superseded.[4] We shall return to this theme, however.

According to Paul, the old has come to an end and something new has come about in Christ, 2 Cor. 5.17. But this newness is predicted in the Scriptures, Rom. 1.1 ff., 3.21, and now, when the hitherto hidden mystery is finally revealed, it is announced on a basis of the prophetic writings: μυστηρίου... σεσιγημένου... φανερωθέντος δὲ νῦν διά τε γραφῶν προφητικῶν... γνωρισθέντος, Rom. 16.25 f.,[5] cf. Eph. 3.1 ff. It was always there, though hidden; but now it is revealed.[6]

We encounter similar concepts in Rabbinic Judaism,[7] but the most relevant comparative material is to be found in the Qumran documents.

---

[1] To this saying, cf. besides the commentaries ad loc. O. LINTON, "Nicht über das hinaus was geschrieben steht", in *Theol. Stud. u. Krit.* 102 (1930), pp. 425 ff., and P. WALLIS, Ein neuer Auslegungsversuch der Stelle I Kor. 4,6, in *Theol. Literaturzeit.* 75 (1950), col. 506 ff.

[2] See ad loc. J. W. DOEVE, Some Notes with Reference to ΤΑ ΛΟΓΙΑ ΤΟΥ ΘΕΟΥ in Romans III 2, in *Studia Paulina in honorem* J. DE ZWAAN, pp. 111 ff.

[3] O. LINTON, Lag 2., in *Sv. Bibl. Uppslagsverk* II (1952), col. 10 ff. (13 ff.).

[4] See O. LINTON, Paulus och juridiken, in *Sv. Teol. Kvartalskrift* 21 (1945), pp. 182 ff.

[5] This actual formula is perhaps deutero-Pauline, but the idea Pauline. — Cf. Col. 1.24 ff., 2.2 f.

[6] N.B. Rom. 9–11. Paul exposes a mystery (11.25), which has been revealed to him in the Scriptures!

[7] Cf. above, p. 173.

The new "revelations" which were so important to this sect, are presented as having been revealed *in* the Scriptures. Since the Law was given and the words of the prophets were spoken, secrets have been hidden in the sacred words;[1] but they have now been "uncovered" (נגלה) for the teacher of righteousness, for the student of the Torah, for the whole sect; they have now been "found" (נמצא) in the Scriptures. In this connection, the idea that revelation has its epochs (עתים, καιροί) is prominent.[2]

In Paul—and not only Paul—we find ideas which are built up in somewhat the same way. The meaning of Scripture has been revealed in the new epoch inaugurated by the work of Christ; but it has been revealed principally to the Apostles, to those who are "stewards of the mysteries of God" (οἰκονόμοι μυστηρίων θεοῦ, 1 Cor. 4.1). We have already considered this topic.

The way in which Paul conceives of this alteration in the matter of the Holy Scriptures is perhaps seen most clearly in 2 Cor. 3.1–4.6, where we find a Christological midrash on Ex. 34. Paul naturally enough does not limit himself to the bare text of Scripture (*miqra*) in its Hebrew and Greek form; he is also familiar with the targumic and midrashic material which was connected, in the mind of a Torah scholar, with this text. It is even possible that he here takes up a fairly well-defined earlier Christian midrash, which he adapts for his purposes. This view has recently been expressed by S. SCHULZ.[3]

In this Pauline exposition, the ministry of the old Covenant is placed over against the ministry of the new. A foundation is provided by the description in Ex. 34 of how Moses, after having met with the Holy One on Sinai, and after having received the Torah, descended from the mountain, his face shining with the δόξα of God. Since the children of Israel could not bear to look upon this *doxa*, Moses veiled his face. The bearer of the Torah was thus hidden. Paul makes use of this for his own purposes. Moses is still hidden: when Moses is read aloud—note how Paul's thought oscillates between the person Moses, the bearer of the Torah, and the book of Moses, the Law of Moses—in the synagogues, a veil still separates the words of the Torah from the hearts of the hearers. (The thought here shifts from the idea that the veil hides the Torah to

---

[1] Note that Deut. 29.28 has been a point of departure; BETZ, *Offenbarung und Schriftforschung*, pp. 17 f.

[2] E.g. 1QS VIII.15, IX.13. For the whole problem, see BETZ, *op. cit.*

[3] Die Decke des Moses, in *Zeitschr. f. d. Neutest. Wiss.* 49 (1958), pp. 1 ff.

the idea that it hides the hearts of the hearers of the Torah.) But the veil is taken away in Christ. When the Jews are converted to Christ, the veil is removed, and the full and correct meaning of the Torah, the *doxa* of God, shines forth. Those who have the ministry of the new Covenant, ἔχοντες τὴν διακονίαν ταύτην, are able to present an unveiled message. For God has given them that divine instruction which consists of insight into the divine *doxa* in the face of Christ. This *doxa* is everlasting, in contrast to the temporary *doxa* which shone forth in the face of Moses when he was entrusted with the Torah in its O.T. version.[1]

The image which Paul uses here is full of subtle variations which we cannot stop to consider now. But we can state briefly that the Apostles— for the context shows clearly that it is principally these who are meant— are here said to have been given the ability to read the Holy Scriptures of the old Covenant (ἡ παλαιὰ διαθήκη) without the deepest meaning in the sacred words being hidden by a veil. The old veil is said to have been removed on conversion to Christ. From one point of view this is the same as the removal of "hardness of heart" (v. 14). To some extent Paul is here developing the same trains of thought as those which we find in the Qumran congregation. But the nearest parallel to this midrash (2 Cor. 3.4 ff.) is to be found in Lk. 24. (13 ff.) 36 ff. and in Acts 1.2 ff., where the Apostles, during a period of forty days (cf. Moses on the mountain) receive consummate knowledge of the Kingdom of God, and have their minds opened to understand the Scriptures.[2] On the other hand there are a number of differences between the Pauline and Lucan versions of these "events".

Paul, in his certainty of having received that gnosis which is necessary in order to interpret the Scriptures correctly in the new epoch, uses the ancient scrolls as a treasure-house of new and old material: "the unsearchable riches of Christ" (Eph. 3.8) in various aspects. From the technical point of view, his Christological midrash exegesis—like all midrash exegesis—takes somewhat varying forms. He sometimes keeps to what was traditionally considered to be the simple meaning of Scripture; he sometimes treats the contents of the Scriptures typologically; his exposition is occasionally more in the nature of allegory. We have no reason to go into this question here,[3] but we can nevertheless quote one

---

[1] Cf. H. ODEBERG, *Comm.*, ad loc., and J. JERVELL, *Imago Dei* (1960), pp. 183 ff.

[2] See above, pp. 229 ff. — Note Codex Bezae in Lk. 24.32.

[3] On Paul's attitude to the Scripture and use of the Scripture, see A. F. PUUKKO, Paulus und das Judentum, in *Studia Orientalia* 2 (1928), pp. 64 ff., O. MICHEL,

example. This is important, for two reasons: on the one hand, it shows the concern of the Apostle to uphold the Scriptures, i.e. to show that its word, rightly interpreted, is valid. On the other hand, it shows how he is able to draw from the Scriptures real support for his gospel of justification by faith, support which from the rabbinic point of view must appear to be very convincing indeed. His argument is technically advanced, and is worthy of a former pupil in *bet Hillel*.[1]

In Rom. 3.21 ff., Paul speaks of the way in which the righteousness of faith has now been revealed (πεφανέρωται) and witnessed by the Law and the Prophets. Both Jews and Gentiles are now—because of Christ's atonement—declared to be righteous without the works of the Law. The question then arises (v. 31): "Do we then abolish the Law (νόμον οὖν καταργοῦμεν) through faith?" The answer is: "By no means! We uphold the Law (νόμον ἱστάνομεν)." In Ch. 4 there then follows the argument by which Paul shows that the very Scriptures witness to the righteousness of faith. We recognize this type of exegetical procedure from the Rabbis. To show, by means of a process of exegesis, that a certain doctrinal statement does not abolish (בִּרטֵל) the Scriptures (or a passage of Scripture) is called by the Rabbis "to uphold", "to maintain" (קֵרֵים) the Scriptures (or a passage of Scripture).

Paul's argument, as JEREMIAS has shown,[2] is a sort of *gezera shawa*, a principle of exposition which was applied not least by Hillel and his school. The principle of exposition is based on the paralleling of two passages of Scripture having one term in common, and interpreting them in the light of each other; what is said in the first passage applies to the second, and vice versa.

Paul wishes to show that both circumcised and uncircumcised are declared righteous on a basis of faith (3.28 ff.). He first quotes Gen. 15.6, which tells how Abraham believed God and how that was accounted (ἐλογίσθη) to him as righteousness. Righteousness was thus not the reward of virtue, but was *accounted* to him by grace (4.3). Another passage of Scripture is then advanced, LXX Ps. 31.1 f. (TM 32.1 ff.), in which David blesses the man to whom the Lord does not account (λογίσηται)

Paulus und seine Bibel (1929), J. BONSIRVEN, *Exégèse rabbinique et exégèse paulinienne* (1939), E. ELLIS, *Paul's Use of the O.T.* (1957).

[1] On the hermeneutical principles used in *bet Hillel*, see the works mentioned above, p. 36, n. 2.

[2] Zur Gedankenführung in den paulinischen Briefen, in *Studia Paulina in honorem J. DE ZWAAN*, pp. 149 ff.

sin. The question which is then asked is (v. 9): does this apply only to the circumcised (David is of course addressing Israel), or does it apply to the uncircumcised as well? This question is settled by the passage from Genesis (v. 9 ff.): when Abraham was accounted righteous because of his faith, he belonged to the uncircumcised. He was later circumcised, but his circumcision only set the seal on the righteousness of faith he already had as uncircumcised. The benediction thus applies to *all* who believe, not only the circumcised but the uncircumcised as well. Abraham became the "father" of all who believe, both circumcised and uncircumcised (v. 11 f.). It is worth noting that "father" has approximately the same transferred meaning as has the word אב (πατήρ) in rabbinic Scripture exposition: prototype, basic example, precedent.[1]

In this context we need not discuss the continuation of Paul's argument (v. 13 ff.).

D. *Paul and Tradition — I*

In the New Testament documents as a whole, in the Gospels in particular, and in the Gospel of Mark most of all, we can observe the terms which were used in the *Greek-speaking* synagogue and Church to refer to the oral Torah of the Jews, its transmission and maintenance. We encounter a quite definite technical terminology here, and it may be of value, by way of introduction to our sketch of Paul's view of tradition, to take note of these terms. We shall also note in passing the Hebrew equivalents, as used by the Rabbis, though we shall not attempt to enter into a detailed discussion of the various alternatives which are possible in this connection.

The oral Torah is called ἡ παράδοσις τῶν πρεσβυτέρων (מסורת הזקנים), Mk. 7.3, 5, Matt. 15.2. When the early Church delimits its own position in relation to it, it is called ἡ παράδοσις ὑμῶν, Mk. 7.9, 13, Matt. 15.3, 6, and when its divine origin is denied it is called ἡ παράδοσις τῶν ἀνθρώπων, Mk. 7.7 f. (referring to Is. 29.13); cf. Col. 2.8. Paul speaks of αἱ πατρικαί μου παραδόσεις, Gal. 1.14.

The verb παραδιδόναι is used to refer to the "passing on" (מסר) of the oral Torah, Mk. 7.13; the term παραλαμβάνειν is used of the "receiving" (קבל) of the oral Torah as tradition, Mk. 7.4.

Further, we find the expression "to preserve" (שמר) the oral Torah, τηρεῖν τὴν π., Mk. 7.9, "to hold" (אחז) it, κρατεῖν τὴν π., Mk. 7.3, "to

---

[1] On the meaning of אב, see BACHER, *Terminologie* I, pp. 1 f. Cf. above, pp. 137 ff.

maintain" (קיים) the tradition, ἱστάναι τὴν π., Mk. 7.9 *var.* To "walk" (הלך, התהלך) after the oral Torah is περιπατεῖν κατὰ τὴν π., Mk. 7.5. We might also mention the phrase παραβαίνειν τὴν π., Matt. 15.2, referring to the "transgression" (עבר) of what is laid down in the oral Torah.

Paul in his epistles has remarkably little to say about the oral Torah of Pharisaic (Rabbinic) Judaism. In certain situations, however, he has reason to remind his congregations *anew* (sic!)[1] that he was once a Pharisee, and that he had been exceedingly zealous for the traditions of his fathers (περισσοτέρως ζηλωτὴς ὑπάρχων τῶν πατρικῶν μου παραδόσεων, Gal. 1.13 f., Phil. 3.5 ff.), by which, as a former Pharisee, he meant both the oral and the written Torah—interpreted in Pharisaic fashion. He himself bears witness to the fact that in the question of the observation of the Law he was a blameless man (Phil. *ibid.*). This implies of necessity that he had attempted, with an intensive thirst for knowledge, to absorb all that was available of the many-faceted wisdom of the Torah. Luke's evidence (Acts 22.3; cf. 7.58, 8.1 ff., 9.1 ff. with par.). that Paul had studied in Jerusalem in the college of Gamaliel (*bet Hillel*) is therefore certainly quite accurate.[2]

After his conversion, however, Paul broke deliberately with the "tradition of the elders", and with the Pharisaic interpretation of the Scriptures. This is part of that which he counted as loss for the sake of Christ, "because of the surpassing worth of the knowledge of Christ Jesus my Lord. For his sake I have suffered the loss of all things" (Phil. 3.7 f.). It is not impossible that Paul went so far as to take deliberate measures to free himself from that knowledge which he now considered to be misleading. We know that the Rabbis occasionally did so; not content with abandoning their customary repetition for long periods, they underwent fasting and other measures in order to get rid of knowledge which they had no further desire to keep in mind.[3] There has been much speculation as to what Paul did during the three years he spent in Arabia immediately after his conversion. Without the evidence of new source material we can never be sure. But the most

---

[1] On the way in which the Apostles mention themselves when teaching, see above, sec. C. On the meaning of this for the formation of traditions *about* the Apostles, see above, 259 f.

[2] Cf. above, p. 249. R. BULTMANN, Die Bedeutung des geschichtlichen Jesus für die Theologie des Paulus, in *Glauben und Verstehen* I (1933), p. 188, casts doubt upon Paul's having been a pupil of Gamaliel, and doubts that he can have been in Jerusalem at all. This is supported by Gal. 1.22—a remarkably flimsy support!

[3] See above, p. 168, n. 5.

likely possibility is that he spent the time in a new and intensive study of the Scriptures, working with the word of God in the light of the new conditions, and on a basis of the new knowledge he had "received", both by way of revelation and of teaching.

In our previous section we discussed the way in which Paul without reservation considered the Scriptures to possess undiminished validity, provided that they were interpreted christologically. We shall now proceed to consider the fact that Paul, having broken with the tradition of the elders, knows and recognizes, transmits and interprets *another tradition*.[1] Alongside the Scriptures he has an authoritative doctrinal substance which we must regard, though with certain reservations, as being the equivalent of the oral Torah.

Paul's terminology speaks for itself. We may make a comparison between his terminology and that used by his colleagues, the Evangelists, to denote the oral Torah, its transmission and maintenance, as we have just described it.

According to Paul, early Christianity has a body of authoritative material which he calls "tradition" (παράδοσις), 2 Thess. 3.6, and "the traditions" (παραδόσεις), 1 Cor. 11.2, 2 Thess. 2.15. The delivery of this tradition is indicated by the verb παραδιδόναι, 1 Cor. 11.2, 23, 15.3, its reception by παραλαμβάνειν, 1 Cor. 11.23, 15.1, 3, Gal. 1.9, Phil. 4.9, Col. 2.6, 1 Thess. 2.13, 4.1, 2 Thess. 3.6. When the congregations are exhorted to "stand fast by" and "hold fast" this tradition, the verbs used are κατέχειν, 1 Cor. 11.2, κρατεῖν, 2 Thess. 2.15, and ἑστηκέναι (עמד), 1 Cor. 15.1. To "walk after" the tradition is περιπατεῖν κατὰ τὴν π., 2 Thess. 3.6. In the Pastoral epistles the verbs τηρεῖν and φυλάσσειν are used to refer to the preservation of the early Christian tradition; the term παράδοσις is missing, however. The evidence of the Pastoral epistles is of particular importance for our understanding of the concept of tradition in the young Church,[2] but in this context we can leave them on one side, since our main interest lies in the earliest Pauline epistles.

What, then, was the extent of this tradition? Of what did it consist? What were the concrete forms in which it found expression? How was it transmitted? We are here faced by a series of extremely difficult questions. Paul had no reason to define what he meant by "tradition", or to describe what it was that was transmitted, or how this material was

---

[1] Cf. O. CULLMANN, *Die Tradition* (1954), pp. 12 ff.

[2] See e.g. C. SPICQ, Saint Paul et la loi des dépôts, in *Rev. Bibl.* 40 (1931), pp. 481 ff., RANFT, *Der Ursprung des katholischen Traditionsprinzips*, pp. 192 ff.

transmitted. In addition, he always expressly assumes in his epistles that the basic authoritative tradition has already been passed on *at an earlier stage* by himself, when the congregations in question were founded.

This latter statement is of course a truism, but a truism which must nevertheless be stressed extremely forcefully. The question of the content of the Pauline παράδοσις is often answered by means of a more or less rapid look at the information given by Paul in his epistles.[1] But Paul says clearly, time and time again, that *he has already transmitted* the basic authoritative tradition to his congregations;[2] over and over again we hear him appeal to what his listeners have already heard, or the information they have already received,[3] and an analysis of his arguments shows that he often builds on a number of doctrinal postulates which his listeners are assumed to share.[4] Any investigation of the contents of what Paul calls "tradition" must therefore have as its primary objective the answering of the question: *What was the nature of the fundamental authoritative material which Paul passed on to his congregations before writing his epistles to them?*[5]

Just as we have difficulty in finding exact terms with which to define tradition in its widest meaning,[6] so it is difficult for us to determine the outlines of the early Christian tradition as carried by Paul and his colleagues. Wherever they went, founding and instructing churches, they took with them a powerful spiritual impulse, which they communicated with the absolute and uncompromising claims of religious faith. From one point of view everything they said and did was delivery of tradition. This is not merely the judgement of the historian. They themselves were of the same opinion, as we can see from the writings of Paul in particular.

---

[1] See e.g. BULTMANN, *Die Bedeutung des geschichtlichen Jesus*, pp. 188 ff., and most recently H.-J. SCHOEPS, *Paulus* (1959), pp. 48 ff.

[2] E.g. 1 Cor. 11.2, 23, 15.1 ff.; Gal. 1.9, Phil. 4.9, Col. 2.6, 1 Thess. 2.13, 4.1, 2 Thess. 2.15, 3.6.

[3] E.g. Phil. 4.9, 1 Thess. 2.13, 4.1, 2 Thess. 2.15.

[4] In order to determine in more detail the extent of the tradition passed on by Paul, his argument must be analysed in detail on a basis of this view.

[5] SCHOEPS, *Paulus*, p. 49, is ironical, unjustly so, on the legitimate attempts to discover what Paul may have known about Jesus. It is really not enough to make note of what he has cause to discuss in his letters!

[6] See above, Ch. 6.

Paul appears in his epistles to be well aware of his apostolic *exousia*.[1] His estimate of his own position may be summarized as follows: He knows himself to have been chosen and set apart, even before his birth, to play a particularly important role in the history of salvation.[2] He has been entrusted with the task of carrying the gospel to the Gentiles.[3] He has been equipped, not only with the gospel of salvation, but with *sophia* and *gnosis* in good measure.[4] He has been granted unusually exalted revelations,[5] and is better equipped with charismatic gifts than others.[6] His message and his teaching can be seen to be filled with the Spirit and with power,[7] and their truth is confirmed by the "apostolic signs" which he performs.[8] To be sure, he is aware that this is all a result of pure grace, and of an election which he has done nothing to deserve, and he often speaks of his personal weakness,[9] but this is only in order to emphasize the great power with which God works in and through him.[10] He considers himself able to undertake his work with a clear conscience, and he attempts to be irreproachable in all things, in obedience to God and to his Lord Jesus Christ.[11] This implies that he is not one who interprets the work of the Spirit in him to be a commission to act as he pleases. His whole life is directed to one end, that the will of God and the work of Christ shall be fulfilled, to the glory of God and for the service of men.[12] Paul therefore has his authorities, "pneumatic" authorities, which we shall consider in more detail in the next section (E).

It is against this background that we must see the fact that Paul treats all he says, writes or does for a congregation as a kind of trans-

---

[1] Despite the exaggeration Paul's self-estimate is presented very instructively by H. WINDISCH, *Paulus und Christus* (1934). See further FRIDRICHSEN, *The Apostle*, W. D. DAVIES, *Paul and Rabbinic Judaism* (2nd ed. 1955), pp. 86 ff., 111 ff., and J. MUNCK, La vocation de l'Apôtre Paul, in *Studia Theol.* 1 (1947), pp. 131 ff.

[2] Rom. 1.1 ff., Gal. 1.1 ff., 15, etc.

[3] E.g. Rom. 15.15 ff., 16.25 f., Eph. 3, Col. 1.25 ff.

[4] E.g. 1 Cor. 2.6 ff., 2 Cor. 4.2, 5.11, 11.6 f., Eph. 3.4 ff.; see J. DUPONT, *Gnosis* (1949).

[5] 2 Cor. 12, 1 Cor. 2.8 ff.

[6] 1 Cor. 14.18 and elsewhere.

[7] E.g. 1 Cor. 2.4 f., 4.19 f., 1 Thess. 1.5.

[8] 2 Cor. 12.12; cf. Rom. 15.19.

[9] E.g. 1 Cor. 15.9, 2 Cor. 11.30, 12.5 f., Eph. 3.7 f.

[10] Rom. 15.17 ff., 1 Cor. 15.10, 2 Cor. 4.7 ff., 11.5–12.18, etc.

[11] E.g. 2 Cor. 1.12, 4.2, 5.10 ff., 1 Thess. 2.10. Cf. K. STENDAHL, Paulus och samvetet, in *Sv. Exeg. Årsbok* 25 (1960), pp. 62 ff.

[12] Rom. 6.1 ff., 14.6 ff., 2 Cor. 5.11 ff., Gal. 2.19 f., and passim.

mission: the passing on of revelation, of the message of joy, of teachings, recommendations and authoritative directions—all from God. He feels himself to be the father of those he has won for the gospel,[1] and of the churches he has founded.[2] He exhorts the congregations to be his imitators (μιμηταί) in all things, as he is of Christ.[3] In Phil. 4.9 we find the following exhortation, so indicative of his way of thinking: "The things which you learned and received (ἃ καὶ ἐμάθετε καὶ παρελάβετε) [from me] and heard and saw in me, do (καὶ ἠκούσατε καὶ εἴδετε ἐν ἐμοί, ταῦτα πράσσετε)." In 2 Thess. 2.15 the church in Thessalonica is exhorted: "So then, brethren, stand firm and hold to the traditions which you were taught by us, either by word of mouth or by letter (στήκετε, καὶ κρατεῖτε τὰς παραδόσεις ἃς ἐδιδάχθητε εἴτε διὰ λόγου εἴτε δι' ἐπιστολῆς ἡμῶν)." He thus regards all that he is, and all that he does, says or writes as tradition, in the widest meaning of the word.

The church in Corinth is praised (1 Cor. 11.1 f.) because they remember him in all things (ὅτι πάντα μου μέμνησθε) holding fast the traditions which he delivered to them (καὶ καθὼς παρέδωκα ὑμῖν τὰς παραδόσεις κατέχετε). And the church in Philippi is exhorted (Phil. 3.17 ff.) not only to imitate Paul, but to look to those who live in the same way as Paul. This expresses another aspect: that Paul is not alone in being an example; other early Christian authorities follow the same basic pattern of Christian behaviour, and are thus equally fitted to be *exempla ad imitandum*. Imitation is not only, or even primarily, an individual matter. The churches, too, are *imitatores*. In 1 Thess. 2.14 ff. we read that the church in Thessalonica has become an imitator of (the mother-church and) the mother-churches in Judaea.[4]

Paul thus considers that he is transmitting, not only in words, but also in his actions: on other words, with his whole life. We recognize this fact from the views of the Rabbis.[5] Occasionally he deliberately lays

---

[1] 1 Cor. 4.17, Philem. 10. On the concept of spiritual fatherhood, see above, p. 182, n. 5.

[2] 1 Cor. 4.14 ff., 2 Cor. 12.14, Gal. 4.19, 1 Thess. 2.11.

[3] See 1 Cor. 4.16, 2 Thess. 3.7, 9; 1 Cor. 11.1, 1 Thess. 1.6. Cf. 1 Thess. 2.14 and Eph. 5.1 ff. On the problem, see E. EIDEM, Imitatio Pauli, in *Teologiska studier tillägnade* E. STAVE (1922), pp. 67 ff., IDEM, *Det kristna livet enligt Paulus* I (1927), pp. 270 ff., D. M. STANLEY, "Become imitators of me": the Pauline Conception of Apostolic Tradition, in *Bibl.* 40 (1959), pp. 859 ff.

[4] The process of Paul's thought on this point is examined more closely in a coming dissertation by E. LARSSON, dealing with Christ as "example" in the Pauline writings.

[5] See above, Ch. 12 B.

down certain of the privileges he enjoys as an Apostle of Christ in order to be able to provide a halakic example (τύπος) for his churches, 2 Thess. 3.7 ff. (see below, section E). It is however clear that he places most emphasis upon his *preaching and teaching*, upon the methodical and painstaking transmission which takes place in his oral delivery. More than once it is evident that he is thinking primarily about the content of his teaching when he exhorts the churches to be his imitators. We thus see, e.g. in 1 Cor. 4.16, that the exhortation to be his μιμηταί is followed by the information that for that reason (διὰ τοῦτο) he is sending them his "child in the Lord", Timothy, in order to remind them of the "ways" which Paul teaches in Christ (ὑμᾶς ἀναμνήσει τὰς ὁδούς μου τὰς ἐν Χριστῷ): by which he seems to mean an extensive collection of text material, the contents of which are primarily ethical and paraenetic in character (see below).

When Paul in this way exhorts his congregations to receive and hold fast the sacred authoritative tradition in all its forms and aspects, he demonstrates that he is well aware of his exalted standing as a doctrinal authority. He is at the same time concerned to emphasize that he is not in himself the *ultimate* ideal, the *fons et origo* of the tradition. His mighty doctrinal authority has its limits! He must build on a given basis, to which he sees no alternative (1 Cor. 3).[1] He is himself a traditionist and imitator. He has received the tradition from the Lord (ἐγὼ παρέλαβον ἀπὸ τοῦ Κυρίου)[2] and is an imitator of Christ (μιμητὴς Χριστοῦ).[3] He is not free from the Law in every shape and form; he is ἔννομος Χριστοῦ.[4] Without going further into the complicated theme of imitation of Christ in Paul,[5] we must draw attention to the question: What was the attitude adopted by Paul to the early Christian tradition of the words and works of Jesus?

As we have seen, the concept of tradition in Paul is extremely complicated. All attempts to determine what were the various parts within the tradition must be regarded as risky. We shall therefore limit our-

---

[1] The fact that Christ is the foundation of the congregation also has a doctrinal side, and a quite concrete one: the fundamental λόγος τοῦ κυρίου is transmitted to the congregation.

[2] 1 Cor. 11.23; see further below.

[3] 1 Cor. 11.1: μιμηταί μου γίνεσθε, καθὼς κἀγὼ Χριστοῦ. Cf. 1 Thess. 1.6: ὑμεῖς μιμηταὶ ἡμῶν ἐγενήθητε καὶ τοῦ κυρίου.

[4] See below, pp. 308 ff.

[5] On this extensive theme, see the above-mentioned dissertation by E. LARSSON.

selves to a cautious sketch of the outlines of a possible grouping—outlines which we have deliberately schematized and simplified.[1] In the centuries following Paul, a certain amount of clarity was reached within the Church on the forms which tradition might take; we must not assume the existence of such clarity in the early material with which we are concerned here.

1. We must first state that, within the framework of the παράδοσις delivered by Paul and the authoritative διδαχή which he passed on, the core was provided by a corpus containing sayings of, and about, Christ. For the sake of simplicity we shall refer to this corpus as "the gospel tradition". It would be well to point out that ὁ λόγος, in common with הדבר, can denote the whole as well as each individual element. The gospel tradition is thus not to be regarded as a section within the tradition, but as a focus. We may make a comparison, though we do so fully aware of the dangers of using such a terminology, and say that this central corpus is the mishnah to which the rest of the Apostles' preaching, teaching and "legislation" is the talmud. At all events, this Christ-tradition seems to occupy a self-evident position as a basis, focus and point of departure for the work of the Apostle Paul. It is evident that he attempts to provide a firm basis in this centre even for what appear to be peripheral rules.[2] But he does not pass on this focal tradition in his epistles. He *presupposes* it constantly, since it has already been delivered, ἐν πρώτοις.

We have already pointed out that the content of the actual gospel (in its meaning of "missionary message") is *tradition*, in that it is received by the Apostles' disciples and other listeners, i.e. by such as can make no claim to have received it direct from the Lord. The contents of the gospel are thus described as having been "received" (παραλαμβάνεσθαι) in 1 Cor. 15.1 ff., and the term is without doubt used here in both its concrete and technical meaning as in the context of transmission. We may point out in passing that this does not mean that the contents of the gospel are thereby to be classified as the teachings of men: their divine origin is never disputed. In 1 Thess. 2.13, for example, the Apostle men-

---

[1] For a somewhat different division, see L. CERFAUX, La tradition selon saint Paul, in *Recueil* L. CERFAUX II (1954), pp. 253 ff.; cf. IDEM, Les deux points de départ de la tradition chrétienne, *ibid.*, pp. 265 ff.; cf. further L. GOPPELT, Tradition nach Paulus, in *Kerygma und Dogma* 4 (1958), pp. 213 ff., and A. BONNARD, La Tradition dans le N.T., in *Rev. d'Hist. et de Philos. Rel.* 40 (1960), pp. 20 ff.

[2] See 1 Cor. passim, and our account in the next section.

tions that the Thessalonians "received" the gospel (παραλαβόντες λόγον ἀκοῆς) from Paul (and his fellow-workers), not as the word of men, but as the word of God, "as it is in truth".[1]

We can make a particularly important observation from 1 Cor. 15.1 ff., where Paul does not speak merely about the fact of the Corinthians having received the gospel; he also reminds them *with what word* (τίνι λόγῳ)[2] he preached the gospel to them. He thus made use, when preaching the gospel, of a logos which he himself had received as authoritative tradition (ὃ καὶ παρέλαβον). How are we to reconcile this with his definite denial of having received the gospel by means of human mediation? Here we must draw a distinction between τὸ εὐαγγέλιον and ὁ λόγος τοῦ εὐαγγελίου.[3] When we read, in the passage of tradition which describes Peter's authorization as chief Apostle (Matt. 16.16 ff.), that his insight that Jesus was the Son of God was not due to flesh and blood, this does not imply that he received no instruction from Jesus or about Jesus. The same is true of Paul.[4] His declaration that he did not receive "his gospel" from man does not mean that he received no teaching, no tradition whatever, deriving from the Lord. Here he states expressly that he received the logos of the gospel as authoritative tradition. He says the same thing, as we shall see, about other parts of his *didache*. He has thus received authoritative tradition from, and about, the Lord.[5]

From whence did Paul receive this authoritative logos? As has already been pointed out, Paul accepts the statement that "the word of God" proceeds from Jerusalem, and treats the leaders of the Jerusalem congregation—i.e. the college of Apostles (or with his own term οἱ δοκοῦντες) —as the supreme (human) doctrinal authority of the Church. We read in 1 Cor. 15 that Paul received this logos as authoritative tradition

---

[1] Cf. Gal. 4.14, where the Apostle says that he was received by the Galatians as a messenger of God (ἄγγελος)—even as Jesus Christ!

[2] This translation is favoured by *inter alia* DIBELIUS, *Formgeschichte*, p. 17, FRIDRICHSEN, *The Apostle*, p. 19. W. G. KÜMMEL, in his supplement to LIETZMANN's commentary *An die Korinther* I–II (4th ed. 1949), translates: "mit welchem Wortlaut ich euch das Evangelium gepredigt habe" (p. 191).

[3] Cf. FRIDRICHSEN, *The Apostle*, pp. 20 f., and above, p. 273.

[4] See the comparison above, sec. A, between Matt. 16.16 ff. and Gal. 1.10 ff.

[5] In this fact A. SCHWEITZER sees a matter of inconsequence. "Paulus ... bleibt ... bei dem Prinzip, dass die Wahrheit über Christus und die Erlösung nicht aus überlieferten Nachrichten und Lehren, sondern aus Offenbarungen des Geistes Jesu Christi komme." ... "Natürlich ist Paulus nicht im Stande, die Theorie seiner Unabhängigkeit von der Tradition konsequent durchzuführen." *Die Mystik des Apostels Paulus* (1930), pp. 171 f.

(ἐγὼ παρέλαβον, מְקַבֵּל אֲנִי)[1] and that it reproduces what he and the other Apostles preach (v. 11). If we look more closely at the contents of this logos we find that it consists of a list of those who are witnesses of the resurrection, with the Jerusalem Apostles first and Paul last. And if we examine the language of the logos we find, as JEREMIAS has pointed out, that its phraseology is in many cases un-Pauline, and that certain expressions must be regarded as Aramaisms.[2] The only reasonable conclusion in this case is therefore that what we have here is a logos fixed by the college of Apostles in Jerusalem.[3] The hypothesis that Paul is here referring to what he had received as "revelation" is extremely improbable. The possibility that he is referring to something he had received from the vague entity usually called "the Hellenistic Community" is equally improbable.[4] It is quite out of the question that Paul would have recognized such an unqualified body as "die hellenistische Gemeinde" to be capable of delivering a tradition which he—as an Apostle—could call authoritative *paradosis*. (An appeal to tradition is always an appeal to *authoritative and valid* tradition.) Had Paul received the logos in question from "die hellenistische Gemeinde", this group must in turn have received it from Jerusalem and transmitted it as an authoritative tradition from Jerusalem ("in the name of the Apostles"). It is most likely that Paul was concerned as an Apostle to receive such *logoi* direct from the other Apostles, or at least to check such *logoi* with them.

From Paul himself we have the information that after his three-year "retreat" in Arabia he went up to Jerusalem in order to make the acquaintance of Cephas, "the Rock", and that he spent fourteen days in his company, Gal. 1.18. The expression ἱστορῆσαι Κηφᾶν gives us a

---

[1] On the expression, see below, p. 312.

[2] *Die Abendmahlsworte Jesu* (2nd ed. 1949), pp. 95 ff. — DIBELIUS, *Formgeschichte*, p. 18, supposes without valid reasons that this logos has been created by "hellenistischen Gemeinden".

[3] Correctly pointed out by e.g. NORDEN, *Agnostos Theos*, pp. 269 f.

[4] The hypothesis of "die hellenistische Gemeinde" as an intermediary between the Jerusalem church and Paul seems to have been seriously launched by W. HEITMÜLLER, Zum Problem Paulus und Jesus, in *Zeitschr. f. d. Neutest. Wiss.* 13 (1912), pp. 320 ff., and W. BOUSSET, *Kyrios Christos* (2nd ed. 1921), pp. 75 ff.; it was accepted as certain and worked out with great care by BULTMANN, in *Geschichte* and in *Theologie des N.T:s*. Cf. also DIBELIUS, *Formgeschichte*. SCHOEPS, *Paulus*, pp. 55 f., is right to place a question mark by the side of tendencies to reckon with "die vorpaulinische hellenistische Gemeinde als sichere Grösse".

[5] See BACHER, *Tradition*, pp. 1 ff.

hint as to why Paul wished to meet the one who was the leader of Jesus' disciples and Apostles. As KILPATRICK has shown, it seems to mean "to get information from Cephas".[1] We can do little more than make one *realistic* observation in this context. In their eagerness to create a wide gulf between the original Apostles and Paul, and in their fear of anything which might be termed "apologetics", many modern scholars have been driven to interpret this passage in a way quite different from that which lies closest at hand, historically speaking. We know what two Rabbis did when they had the opportunity of meeting: the word of the Torah "was between them". This does not apply merely to teachers; it was an ideal for all who were faithful to the Torah. Nor was it an unrealistic ideal: it was custom.[2] Further, we know how Jewish teachers and pupils sought out doctrinal authorities, pupils of such authorities, or others who were known to be able to transmit the doctrinal statements of a particular teacher, with or without interpretation, when their object was to "receive halakah" or to find out how some particular item of doctrine should be interpreted.[3] In Gal. 1–2 Paul is eager to stress his equality with Peter and the other Apostles. It is therefore in his interests to avoid giving his opponents an unfair advantage by dwelling on precisely what he did during his fortnight with Peter in Jerusalem. But if Paul in Jerusalem were the same man as the Paul of the epistles, we can almost guess what the two men did. A Paul does not go up to Jerusalem to Peter, "the Rock", merely in order to talk about the weather (DODD).[4] And a man with Peter's commission does not waste a fortnight talking rubbish. It can be little doubt that during this time the word of Christ "was between them" (cf. the exhortation given by Paul in Col. 3.16: ὁ λόγος τοῦ Χριστοῦ ἐνοικείτω ἐν ὑμῖν πλουσίως).[5] It is remarkable that critical scholars have ignored Paul's own statement

---

[1] G. D. KILPATRICK, Galatians 1:18 ΙΣΤΟΡΗΣΑΙ ΚΗΦΑΝ, in *N.T. Studies in memory of* T. W. MANSON (1959), pp. 144 ff. KILPATRICK's interpretation is doubted by KLEIN, *Galater 2,6–9*, p. 289, but on untenable grounds ("angesichts des fast völligen Fehlens von so etwas wie Jesusüberlieferung im Corpus Paulinum"). Cf. also O. BAUERNFEIND, Die Begegnung zwischen Paulus und Kephas Gal 1.18–20, in *Zeitschr. f. d. Neutest. Wiss.* 47 (1956), pp. 268 ff.

[2] Cf. above, pp. 168 f. and 228.

[3] Hillel travelled e.g. from Babylon to Jerusalem in order to receive halakah on certain questions (ועלה וקיבל הלכה), p Pes. VI.1; cf. e.g. T Neg. I.16. See further above, p. 101; cf. p. 206.

[4] *The Apostolic Preaching*, p. 16.

[5] Cf. also such texts as Lk. 24.13 ff., and Acts 20.7 ff., and above, p. 228.

about his fortnight's visit to Peter, speculating instead about Paul having received the tradition about Jesus from that more or less hypothetical entity, "the Hellenistic Community".

If we now return to the logos repeated by Paul in 1 Cor. 15.3 ff., we find it to be set out *as a series of simanim*:[1] each individual part is a short, heading-like designation for some passage of the tradition about Christ.

(a) ὅτι Χριστὸς ἀπέθανεν ὑπὲρ τῶν ἁμαρτιῶν ἡμῶν κατὰ τὰς γραφάς,

(b) καὶ ὅτι ἐτάφη,

(c) καὶ ὅτι ἐγήγερται τῇ ἡμέρᾳ τῇ τρίτῃ κατὰ τὰς γραφάς,

(d) καὶ ὅτι ὤφθη Κηφᾷ,

(e) εἶτα τοῖς δώδεκα·

(f) ἔπειτα ὤφθη ἐπάνω πεντακοσίοις ἀδελφοῖς ἐφάπαξ (ἐξ ὧν οἱ πλείονες μένουσιν ἕως ἄρτι, τινὲς δὲ ἐκοιμήθησαν)·

(g) ἔπειτα ὤφθη Ἰακώβῳ,

(h) εἶτα τοῖς ἀποστόλοις πᾶσιν·

(i) ἔσχατον δὲ πάντων (ὡσπερεὶ τῷ ἐκτρώματι) ὤφθη κἀμοί...

This passage, which has been much discussed, and rightly so, poses a number of problems, some of which we must indicate. (1) Is Paul quoting a passage of tradition from the beginning, or only those parts which he requires in this particular context? Paul's argument here has to do with the resurrection of the dead. He *needs* only this part of the tradition in question. Furthermore, we know that when he quotes Scripture he often cuts short his quotations, limiting himself to those parts which are relevant to his argument. Is that what he is doing here when he quotes the gospel tradition? (2) Where does the part which he took over as authoritative tradition (from Jerusalem) finish?[2] Are we to draw the line, as many scholars believe, after "the twelve" (e) or after "all the Apostles" (h)? Or did the Jerusalem Apostles also accept Paul's encounter with the Risen Lord (cf. i)? This is not so impossible as many scholars believe.[3] (3) Why does Paul introduce interpretative material into the passage of tradition (see parentheses above in f and i) and conclude it with an adaptation (v. 8 ff.)?

---

[1] On the matter, see above, pp. 143 ff., 153 ff.

[2] The Jewish parallel material gives us no right to decide such a question merely on the stylistic construction of a logos (*dabar*).

[3] If Paul is telling the truth in Gal. 2.7 ff., the Jerusalem leaders had recognized his apostolate. Such a fact implies that they recognized that he had been sent by Christ himself (see above, sec. A).

We shall not discuss these questions here.[1] It seems however to be of vital importance to note that the logos which we find in 1 Cor. 15.3 ff. seems to be built up in such a way that each individual element functions as a *siman* for a passage from the gospel tradition: (a) the passion narrative—in shorter or longer form?—in which it is a well-known fact that the whole and the details are seen in the light of Scripture, (b) the narrative of the burial (sic!) of Jesus, (c) a narrative telling that the resurrection took place on the third day according to the Scriptures (the tradition of the empty tomb!),[2] (d) the first revelation of the Risen Lord to Peter (cf. Lk. 24.34, John 21.15 ff., Matt. 16.16 ff.), (e) the revelation to the twelve (cf. Lk. 24.33 ff., John 20.19 ff.) and then to the others in chronological order (f–i). The problem posed by the dissonances between this logos and the description given by the Evangelists is well known; it is however difficult when estimating the evidence to avoid either to ignore or to explain away the differences.

1 Cor. 15.3 ff. is thus unambiguous evidence that Paul had received an authoritative tradition about the death and resurrection of Christ. We have good reason to suppose that he derived this tradition—directly or indirectly—from the college of Apostles in Jerusalem. And if the interpretation which we have advanced above be correct, that the catechetical logos quoted by Paul in 1 Cor. 15.3 ff. is arranged as, and intended to be, a (meaningful) chain of *simanim*, in which each link facilitates the recitation of a passage from the gospel tradition (and the proclamation of and the teaching on these matters), then Paul shows here that he has gained access to a good proportion of that tradition.

The terminology of transmission is used in a particularly interesting way in Col. 2.6 ff.: "As therefore you received (ὡς οὖν παρελάβετε) Christ Jesus the Lord, so walk in him (ἐν αὐτῷ περιπατεῖτε), rooted and built up in him and established in the faith, just as you were taught" (ἐρριζωμένοι καὶ ἐποικοδομούμενοι ἐν αὐτῷ καὶ βεβαιούμενοι τῇ πίστει καθὼς ἐδιδάχθητε...) What is said here is that "Christ" has been trans-

---

[1] See, apart from commentaries ad loc., E. L. ALLEN, The Lost Kerygma, in *New Test. Stud.* 3 (1956–57), pp. 349 ff., and BAIRD, *What is the Kerygma?*, P. WINTER, 1 Corinthians xv. 3b–7, in *Nov. Test.* 2 (1957–58), pp. 142 ff.

[2] This element ought not to be taken merely as indicating that there were passages of Scripture which said that the Messiah would rise on the third day. It is an important point here that the Scriptures support *what has happened*, according to the witness of the Apostles. Cf. J. MANÉK, The Apostle Paul and the Empty Tomb, in *Nov. Test.* 2 (1957–58), pp. 276 ff., J. DUPONT, Ressuscité "le troisième jour", in *Bibl.* 40 (1959), pp. 174 ff.

mitted to the congregation. They have been enabled to receive Christ in preaching and teaching, and are now exhorted to "walk in him". This expression need not necessarily have any mystical meaning; it seems quite simply to be a parallel to the phrase "walk in the Torah", (הלך(הת) בתורה, (e.g. Ps. 78.10, 119.1). The doctrinal material which is here passed on must be considered to be an rather well-defined and concrete entity. When we read in the same context that all the treasures of wisdom and insight (πάντες οἱ ϑησαυροὶ τῆς σοφίας καὶ γνώσεως) are hidden in Christ, this is also an example of a terminology drawn from the traditional sayings on the Torah.[1] As Paul was able to say, before his conversion, that all the secrets of wisdom are to be won by the intensive study of the Torah, so he can now say that they are to be won by the same intensive study of "the transmitted Christ". "The transmitted Christ" in this connection cannot be the same as the "gospel", in its meaning of "missionary message", but must be a comprehensive designation for the *tradition* of Christ as a whole. Here in Col. it seems as though Paul were referring to a collection of traditions which he regarded as being a unity: some oral or written equivalent of one of our Gospels. The supposition that "the transmitted Christ" is in fact a collected and redacted gospel is not made more difficult by the date of authorship of Col. In connection with the fact that this tradition of Christ is called simply "Christ", we may recall that the tradition of Isaiah (in its written or oral form) is called "Isaiah"—to name only one example.[2]

As we have already pointed out, the gospel tradition is not one section among many in the Pauline tradition. It forms a foundation and a focus: from one point of view, it has an even more central position than the Scriptures. Paul's teaching on various questions, his commandments, directions and advice—all are constantly being placed in relation to this centre or are motivated on this basis: not from some basic abstract principle contained in the tradition, but from the manifold divine secrets given, according to Paul, in the person of Christ, in his words and works.

It is an important task to determine the *extent* of the gospel tradition with which Paul was acquainted. It is a well-known fact that on this particular question, conflicting opinions are held with the utmost tenacity. One wing of scholarly opinion is formed by those who derive

---

[1] Such sayings as Prov. 2.1 ff., Is. 45.3 were interpreted during the centuries before and after Christ as referring to the wisdom of the Torah. See above, Ch. 1, beginning. Cf. also DUPONT, *Gnosis*, pp. 16 ff.

[2] See above, p. 198.

their views from the old Tübingen school, and who consider that Paul knew little or nothing of the historical Jesus;[1] on the other stands a group of exegetes who maintain that Paul was acquainted with practically the whole of the synoptic tradition.[2] We cannot here enter into the detailed analysis of the Pauline material which would be necessary for the taking up of a reasoned stand on this matter.[3] In our next section we shall however refer to a number of points in the Apostle's account, points at which he is quite evidently building on the gospel tradition; we shall also see how he accords the tradition from the Lord such decisive authority that he must have had every reason to attempt to gain the fullest possible access to the tradition. He seems to have regarded *sayings* of Jesus as being of particular importance. Very interesting is the fact that he seems to know gospel traditions peculiar to Matt.[4]

2. In an attempt to illustrate the central role which the tradition from and about the Lord—i.e. the gospel tradition—played for Paul, we have referred to it as a *mishnah*, with the Apostles' own teaching and "legislation" as a *talmud*. This terminology can easily be misleading, and so we must develop the theme.

Paul's foundation is provided by the Scriptures—Christologically interpreted—and the tradition about, and from, the Lord. However, he does not proceed like an anxious exegete or a mechanical traditionist, but rather in the manner of an astute and spiritually endowed *hakam*. Borrowing the imagery of Rabban Joḥanan ben Zakkai, we might say that Paul is not "a caulked cistern", but "a flowing spring".[5] He argues

---

[1] E.g. HEITMÜLLER, *Zum Problem Paulus und Jesus*, BOUSSET, *Kyrios Christos*, pp. 104 ff., BULTMANN, *Die Bedeutung des geschichtlichen Jesus*.

[2] E.g. A. RESCH, *Der Paulinismus und die Logia Jesu* (1904), which deserves to be thoroughly examined from another angle than that of the author himself, and O. MOE, *Paulus und die evangelische Geschichte* (1912).

[3] See e.g. C. H. DODD's observations, made in a number of works, on the connection between Paul and the synoptic tradition, *History and the Gospel* (1938), pp. 63 ff., *Gospel and Law* (1951), passim, *Matthew and Paul* (1947), in *N.T. Studies* (1953), pp. 53 ff., The primitive Catechism and the Sayings of Jesus, in *N.T. Essays in memory of* T. W. MANSON, pp. 106 ff.—On the connection between the eschatological-apocalyptic material in the synoptic tradition and Paul's presentation, mainly in Thess., see J. B. ORCHARD, Thessalonians and the Synoptic Gospels, in *Bibl.* 19 (1938), pp. 19 ff., and G. R. BEASLEY-MURRAY, *Jesus and the Future* (1954), pp. 232 ff. This theme will be dealt with in a forthcoming dissertation by L. HARTMAN.

[4] This has been emphasized in various contexts by DODD, e.g. *Matthew and Paul*.

[5] Ab II.8: בור סוד and מעין המתגבר. Cf. above, pp. 109 f.

with sovereign knowledge of the Scriptures and of what is cogent "in Christ"; as a rule the basic authoritative text material lies *behind* his actual argument, and provides the *conditions* for his teaching. We shall advance a number of examples in support of this statement below, in section E.

Paul's *talmud*, viz. that teaching which interprets and complements (the Scriptures and) the tradition from the Lord, may conveniently be divided into three sections: doctrinal, ethical and ecclesiastical, though the boundaries are fluid. It seems within each of these sections that we must take account of both solid and fluid elements; from another point of view, we must reckon with material having a more powerfully accentuated normative standing, and material having less emphatic authority (according to Paul himself).

(a) We must first say a few words on the doctrinal section.[1] Paul's teaching on every aspect of the faith, and his answers to questions of various kinds, are delivered with great authority. He claims to have *gnosis* and *sophia*, and the right (*exousia*) to give authoritative answers to the doctrinal problems of the Christian congregations: on eschatological matters, on the meaning and consequences of the work of Christ, etc. This teaching is often given in a fairly extended form in his epistles, but with remarkable factual unity and decisiveness. As we know, a number of quite definite doctrinal *topoi* appear in the Pauline literature.[2] It seems likely that Paul followed the same procedure in his oral teaching. It is not improbable that he linked his teaching with definite doctrinal statements, *logoi*, which were received, and *logoi* of his own formulation, which he repeated time and time again and then interpreted. We may recall such examples as 1 Cor. 15 on the resurrection, or 1 Cor. 7.19, Gal. 5.6, 6.15 on the invalidity of circumcision.[3] We encounter all manner of homiletical material on the periphery of the doctrinal tradition.

(b) The second section of the tradition is that which we have called the ethical section. It appears to have been the case in the young Church that various collections of texts were put together, for practical reasons,

---

[1] A. SEEBERG's works are, from our point of view, still worth of consideration: *Der Katechismus der Urchristenheit* (1903), *Das Evangelium Christi* (1905), *Christi Person und Werk nach der Lehre seiner Jünger* (1910). Cf. also RANFT, *Der Ursprung des katholischen Traditionsprinzips*, pp. 212 ff.

[2] Cf. D. G. BRADLEY, The *Topos* as a Form in the Pauline Paraenesis, in *Journ. of Bibl. Lit.* 72 (1953), pp. 238 ff.

[3] Cf. on this theme S. BELKIN, The Problem of Paul's Background, in *Journ. of Bibl. Lit.* 54 (1935), pp. 41 ff.

such as catechetical instruction on life "in the Spirit" or "in Christ". *These collections* do not seem to have consisted exclusively of collections of sayings of Jesus; they were not a pure ἱερὸς λόγος, but didactic tractates, "ways", groups of "commandments", etc. There can be little doubt that the material was drawn principally from the teaching of Jesus, but such sayings have been adapted for the end in view, being combined with other commandments, rules and regulations.[1]

We have a good example of a concrete collection of mainly ethical traditions in 1 Thess. 4.1 ff., in which Paul reminds the Thessalonian church about the rules for Christian living he (and his fellow-workers) passed on when the church was founded. Here we are dealing with a tractate, under the heading of τὸ πῶς δεῖ ὑμᾶς περιπατεῖν καὶ ἀρέσκειν θεῷ, and containing a series of commandments (παραγγελίαι) given on the authority of (διά)[2] the Lord Jesus. Paul reminds his readers about these, actualizing and stressing a number of these ethical directives by means of new formulations.[3] It is not easy to determine what were the detailed contents of this tractate. It was probably arranged according to some catechetical scheme similar to that which has proved to have been the basis of a number of New Testament passages.[4] It is difficult to say whether it contained lists of virtues and vices. Lists of this type do not however appear to have been so strictly fixed: the material is fairly definite, but is varied both in form and order from occasion to occasion.[5]

The "ways" (ὁδοί μου) which Paul taught everywhere in all congregations (καθὼς πανταχοῦ ἐν πάσῃ ἐκκλησίᾳ διδάσκω, 1 Cor. 4.17), seem to have been mainly ethical in character. It is possible, though, that these "ways" consisted of extensive summaries of the Apostle's *didache*, his τύπος διδαχῆς (Rom. 6.17),[6] divided up into various trac-

---

[1] Cf. DIBELIUS, *Formgeschichte*, pp. 234 ff.

[2] On the meaning of διὰ τοῦ κυρίου 'I.: "in der Vollmacht des Herrn Jesus", see L. NIEDER, *Die Motive der religiös-sittlichen Paränese in den paulinischen Gemeindebriefen* (1956), p. 7.

[3] Cf. B. RIGAUX, *Comm.*, ad loc.

[4] See P. CARRINGTON, *The Primitive Christian Catechism* (1940), E. G. SELWYN, *The First Epistle of St. Peter* (1946), pp. 369 ff., and cf. DAVIES, *Paul and Rabbinic Judaism*, pp. 111 ff.

[5] See A. VÖGTLE, *Die Tugend- und Lasterkataloge im N.T.* (1936), S. WIBBING, *Die Tugend- und Lasterkataloge im N.T.* (1959).

[6] On this crux interpretum, see A. FRIDRICHSEN, Exegetisches zum N.T., in *Coni. Neot.* 7 (1942), pp. 6 f., and J. KÜRZINGER, Τύπος διδαχῆς und der Sinn von Röm. 6,17 f., in *Bibl.* 39 (1958), pp. 156 ff., F. W. BEARE, On the Interpretation of Romans vi.17, in *New Test. Stud.* 5 (1958–59), pp. 206 ff.

tates, and dealing also with other than strictly ethical questions. The boundaries between ethical and doctrinal material are indistinct, and the ethical tractates also included doctrinal statements of other kinds, e.g. eschatological material.[1]

The remainder of the paraenetic material given by Paul in his epistles may be regarded as being an interpretative complement to the more definite and more authoritative elements in the ethical tradition.[2]

(c) The third of these sections may be characterized as consisting of rules and directions of ecclesiastical character: matters having to do with public worship, teaching, church discipline and the like. During the Apostolic Age, this type of tradition was hardly communicated in the form of tractates, containing rules and directions, but was given in accordance with the needs of the occasion (1 Cor. 11.34)—and in some cases was certainly taken over by means of imitation. The elements of this tradition vary in character. Some were called "commandments of the Lord" (ἐντολαὶ κυρίου), others "orders" (ἐπιταγαί), and some were known as "custom" (συνήθεια).[3] In this section, too, we must reckon with the existence of a flexible body of peripheral material of complementary and interpretative character.

It is clear from 1 Cor. 11.23 that Paul had already passed on to the Church the words of institution of the Eucharist. It is however improbable that this had taken place in connection with elementary instruction in the orders of public worship. One has the impression, from the Apostle's manner of dealing with this tradition, that he is basing his argument on a logos which is taken from its context in the gospel tradition, viz. as part of the passion narrative. This is however a moot point.

Paul gives the church at Corinth certain complementary instructions about forms of public worship and teaching in 1 Cor. 11 and 14. Here we see that when founding the congregation he had not regulated such matters in too much detail. Further, we note that he is eager for the establishment of common halakic practice in "all the congregations

---

[1] See the works mentioned on the foregoing page, n. 4.

[2] It is most important to note that the Pauline passages of paraenesis, without quoting a single saying of Jesus (it is not the nature of paraenesis to include direct quotation), still contain a large number of echoes of sayings of Jesus. Cf. DIBELIUS, *Formgeschichte*, pp. 239 ff., who is not able to produce even a single example to confirm his thesis that Paul *transmitted* sayings of Jesus amid other paraenetic material. DIBELIUS' examples show, however, that Paul *uses* sayings of Jesus.

[3] See below, pp. 308 ff.

of the saints", and that certain matters are laid down quite clearly in the logos which has proceeded from Jerusalem. When the church in Corinth had begun to apply local orders of worship and teaching (such as allowing women to act as teachers), Paul reminds them that they are not the centre and supreme doctrinal authority of the Church: "Did the word of God proceed from you, or are you the only ones it has reached?" The silence of women in church is thus a tradition from Jerusalem, and seems to be derived from the Lord himself. If the reading in 14.37 κυρίου ἐστὶν ἐντολή (P⁴⁶ ℵ ℵ*) is original, Paul must in fact be referring to a definite saying of Jesus.[1] The textual tradition is however divided on this point.[2]

We see in 1 Cor. 5 that Paul gave authoritative directions for the exercise of church discipline. He assumes here that the Corinthian church is acquainted with a procedure for such an exercise, similar to that in Matt. 18.15 ff.[3] We see, too, in other passages how Paul gives directives for the carrying out of church discipline against anyone placing himself outside that *paradosis* which he had passed on to the congregation, 2 Thess. 3.6 ff.

These simple observations should suffice to give a picture of the main types of tradition passed on by Paul. There remains to examine the relation of Paul to Jesus (the Lord), as estimated by Paul himself, and his relations with the college of Apostles in Jerusalem. Further, we must see how he regards his own rights, when it is a matter of mediating, or giving, authoritative tradition to the congregations.

E. *Paul and Tradition — II*

According to Acts 15 Peter, speaking at the council of Apostles in Jerusalem, had expressed the principle that it was illegitimate to put "a yoke (ζυγός) upon the neck of the disciples which neither our fathers nor we have been able to bear" (v. 10). The metaphor "yoke", "burden" (עֹל), denoting "obligations of the law", "subjection to religious duties", is rabbinic.[4] On this occasion James had also stressed the principle that

---

[1] On this, cf. DAVIES, *Paul and Rabbinic Judaism*, pp. 140 f. Different opinions are expressed by DODD, ΕΝΝΟΜΟΣ ΧΡΙΣΤΟΥ, p. 105, and E. SJÖBERG, Herrens bud i 1 Kor. 14:37, in *Sv. Exeg. Årsbok* 22–23 (1957–58), pp. 168 ff.

[2] D*G it read only κυρίου ἐστίν, ℵ vg sy read κυρίου εἰσὶν ἐντολαί.

[3] See DODD, ΕΝΝΟΜΟΣ ΧΡΙΣΤΟΥ, pp. 108 f., *Matthew and Paul*, pp. 60 f., STENDAHL, *The School*, p. 28.

[4] See BILLERBECK, *Comm.* I, pp. 608 ff.

Gentile Christians should not be troubled (παρενοχλεῖν) with the Law, they should, however, for practical reasons, be subject to a number of ordinances (v. 20). The two leaders of the college of Apostles in Jerusalem had thus maintained the Gentile Christians to be free from the Law, a freedom which was confirmed at a general session of the Jerusalem congregation. Luke states that the apostolic decretal was formulated on the same occasion: four rules of halakic character were laid down for the observance of Gentile Christians.[1]

Paul's account in Gal. 2 agrees with that of Luke on the decisive point: he states that the Apostles at a council in Jerusalem declared Gentile Christians to be free from the Law. According to Paul, however, he and Barnabas had no obligations imposed (προσανατίθεσθαι) upon them, apart from the collection for the poor in Jerusalem (2.9 f.). The apostolic decretal seems therefore to have been formulated and promulgated on some other occasion, as a practical solution to certain current questions.[2]

The important factors are, first and foremost, that the Gentile Christian congregations are declared not to be under the Law, i.e. under the Torah, as binding law, νόμος. That the sacred Scriptures maintain their position as "the word of God", containing wisdom, revelation, advice, prophecy and consolation, is another matter.

A further factor of importance is that according to Acts 15 the college of Apostles in Jerusalem laid down halakah for the Gentile congregations on only four points, otherwise imposing nothing upon them (... μηδὲν πλέον ἐπιτίθεσθαι ὑμῖν βάρος πλήν ...). We have even more important evidence on this point from Paul, according to whom the college of Apostles in Jerusalem accepted Paul's gospel, his apostolate and the *district* within which his mission was to be exercised. These are very important factors. His capacity and state as Apostle had been accepted and he had been declared free to exercise his ministry as ἀπόστολος καὶ διδάσκαλος[3] over the Christians within that area. They imposed only *one* condition upon him: that he should remember the poor in Jerusalem (2.10)—which was clearly not a direct *duty*.

---

[1] See above, Ch. 14 E.

[2] On the relationship between what is described in Acts 15 and what Paul relates in Gal. 2, see—apart from the commentaries on the chapters in question—above, p. 254, n. 2.

[3] Cf. 2 Tim. 1.11.—For a view of Paul's doctrinal activity which differs from ours, see H. Fr. von Campenhausen, *Die Begründung kirchlicher Entscheidungen beim Apostel Paulus* (1957).

This is the correct point of departure for our examination of this topic, since the high doctrinal and "legislative" authority and competence which Paul adopts when dealing with his churches is particularly striking.

We must point out, in order to avoid any misunderstanding, that we shall be using a terminology which is uncommon in works on the preaching and teaching of Paul. The authorized Torah colleges and Torah teachers had the power (רשות, ἐξουσία), derived from their divine commission, to promulgate authoritative and normative "teaching" of a doctrinal, ethical and legal nature. The main object here was to lay down the "law", halakah, for the everyday life of the people of God, though other doctrinal questions were also decided. Paul exercises an authority which from some points of view is similar: he answers questions, solves problems, and gives binding directions and "commandments". This is a communication of authoritative, normative teaching, and sometimes even a kind of pneumatic "legislation". A considerable part of this teaching is of ethical nature, though no clear lines of demarcation divide it from the more definitely doctrinal or ecclesiastical portions of the Apostle's teaching. We shall not in this context go into the question, which is so interesting from the point of view of dogmatics, of the kind of normativity possessed by the apostolic "legislation", and its relation to the gospel.[1]

Paul valued his office highly,[2] for two reasons. First, because he knew himself to have been entrusted with an office which had a high standing in the divine οἰκονομία;[3] he had great formal authority and extensive rights when building up, by word and deed, God's eschatological community among the Gentiles. This implied that he had to answer various burning questions, and produce correct rules for the solution of his congregations' problems. In other words, he had "authority to build up", ἐξουσία εἰς οἰκοδομήν (2 Cor. 10.8, 13.10),[4] and was able, within certain

---

[1] It is a well-known fact that the literature on Paul's concept of law is enormous. We shall not give any references.

[2] See e.g. Rom. 11.13, 12.3, 15.15 ff., Eph. 3, 1 Tim. 2.7, 2 Tim. 1.10 f.

[3] Eph. 1.8 ff., 3.2 ff., Col. 1.25 ff.; cf. 1 Cor. 4.1, 9.17.

[4] DODD has correctly pointed out that this definition of Paul's apostolic ministry has to do with Matt. 16.19, ΕΝΝΟΜΟΣ ΧΡΙΣΤΟΥ, p. 109. The formulation can be placed in an even wider context; see above, p. 220.

limits,[1] to *bind and loose*,[2] i.e. declare to be either forbidden or permissible (אסר והתיר). Secondly, because he knew that his office was not merely a matter of formal rights or legal power, but that it had been given with Spirit and wisdom, gnosis and power.[3]

Paul sometimes points out that he had a right to be an Apostle of Christ with authority (ἐν βάρει), and to use the rights and privileges given him as an Apostle. However, he abstains voluntarily from such rights, and instead aims at burdening (ἐπιβαρεῖν) his churches as little as possible (1 Thess. 2.6 ff., 2 Thess. 3.7 ff.). This applies to his *way of life*. He acts in accordance with the saying of Jesus, that the greatest in the Church of Christ must be the servant of all (Matt. 20.26 f. with par.; 1 Cor. 9.19), and other similar sayings. But it also applies to his authoritative *teaching*, his pneumatic "legislation". He sets a high value upon the Christian's freedom from the Torah in its old character of νόμος, and is unwilling to see his churches weighed down by too heavy duties, or staggering under a yoke of bondage (e.g. Gal. 2.4 f., 5.1).

Here we glimpse the heritage from his days as a pupil in the *bet Hillel*, sitting at the feet of Gamaliel. It was fundamental in this branch of Pharisaism to attempt, as far as possible, to "make easy" (היכל), i.e. to give moderate doctrinal judgements; this formed a sharp contrast with *bet Shammai*, where it was usual to "make heavy" (החמיר), i.e. to give strict and burdensome commandments and decisions. There are many cases preserved in the Mishnah in which *bet Shammai* forbids, "binds" (אסר), but *bet Hillel* permits, "looses" (התיר, Aram. שרא).[4]

But we have above all an unmistakeable heritage from Jesus, the doctrinal authority who had replaced all other teachers in Paul's estimation. Paul did not consider that what the earthly Jesus had said and done had been cancelled out by the cross and resurrection. The earthly Jesus, too, was Paul's Lord (κύριος).[5] It is certain that the sources

---

[1] It seems to be possible to draw a fairly clear picture, with the help of the comparative rabbinic material, of the relationship of the individual fully-qualified Apostle/teacher to his colleagues/college (חבורה/חברים), but we shall not attempt to discuss this matter here. Cf. above, p. 279.

[2] These two terms, which are so well able to clarify the categories which the Apostle works with, are not to be found in the Apostle's own vocabulary. This need not imply any special significance: the different schools often had different special expressions for the same thing.

[3] See above, p. 292.

[4] On this subject, see A. SCHWARZ, *Die Controversen der Schammaiten und Hilleliten* I (1893), BACHER, *Tradition*, pp. 54 ff.

[5] E.g. 1 Cor. 11.23. See L. CERFAUX, *Le Christ dans la Théologie de saint Paul*

are correct, and that Jesus criticized sharply the Pharisaic teachers *en bloc*—not only *bet Shammai* but also *bet Hillel* and other Pharisaic "schools"—accusing them of binding heavy burdens (δεσμεύουσιν φορτία βαρέα) and laying them on the shoulders of men (Matt. 23.4 with par.). By contrast, the early Church passed on a saying of Jesus directed to those who labour and are burdened (πάντες οἱ κοπιῶντες καὶ πεφορτισμένοι), inviting them to take the yoke of Jesus (ζυγός μου) and learn (μανθάνειν) of him, since his yoke is easy and his burden (φορτίον) light (Matt. 11.25 ff.). Other passages in the synoptic tradition also bear witness to the fact that Jesus both practised and proclaimed a halakah which, *from certain points[1] of view*, was light.

In Acts and Gal. we have certain indications that there were tensions in the Jerusalem church between a stricter group—undoubtedly inspired by the strict Pharisaism of the type of *bet Shammai*[2]—and a milder group, in which the lenient practice of Jesus was followed more faithfully. Both Acts and Gal. make it clear that Peter belonged to the latter group.

We cannot here go into the question of the *fundamental* background of Paul's "mildness" in his "legislative" activity. This naturally stems from his basic certainty that the Torah, in its aspect of νόμος, has been brought to an end in the Messiah (e.g. Rom. 10.4), and has been replaced by the messianic law (ὁ νόμος τοῦ Χριστοῦ, Gal. 6.2)[3] which, according to the prophet (Jer. 31.31), God was to write on the hearts of his people (2 Cor. 3.1 ff.). These are all concepts which Paul presumably encountered in embryonic form in the teaching he received before becoming a Christian, and which he certainly found in a developed form in the Christian tradition to which he was introduced after his conversion. To judge from the evidence, he seems to have been the personality in early Christianity who had to wrestle hardest with this problem, as he tried to find a solution during his work as an Apostle of Christ.[4]

(2nd ed. 1954), pp. 127 ff. The unreasonable idea that 2 Cor. 5.16 means that Paul regards the earthly Jesus as being insignificant dies hard. See against this view A. OEPKE, Irrwege der neueren Paulusforschung, in *Theol. Literaturzeit.* 77 (1952), col. 453 f.

[1] From another point of view, as is well-known, Jesus is stricter than any Rabbi.
[2] Cf. above, p. 249.
[3] Cf. 1 Cor. 9.21 and below.
[4] DODD has attempted in several works to determine the meaning of the "messianic law" which is evidently such an important concept for Paul. See e.g. *Gospel and Law*, partic. pp. 64 ff., and ΕΝΝΟΜΟΣ ΧΡΙΣΤΟΥ.

Paul has no wish to limit "the liberty which we have in Christ Jesus" (Gal. 2.4), a freedom which may be expressed in universal categories— as in the motto "all is lawful (for me)", πάντα (μοι) ἔξεστιν, 1 Cor. 6.12, 10.23—and which he praises in glowing terms.[1] Nor does he want to enslave his congregations, to bind what has been loosed, forbid what is allowed.[2] This attitude is typical of Paul's "legislative" activity, from which we shall later quote a number of examples.

It is nevertheless stated, clearly and definitely, that certain things are "bound", "forbidden". It is said of some deeds, that those who perform them shall not inherit the Kingdom of God (1 Cor. 6.9 ff., Gal. 5.21, Eph. 5.5), and of those who refuse to follow the authoritative *para-dosis* delivered by Paul, that the Christian congregation shall disassociate itself from them (2 Thess. 3.5 ff.; cf. 2 Cor. 6.14 ff.). The most unrepentant sinners are to be sharply disciplined: "delivered to Satan" (1 Cor. 5.3 ff.). All things are thus not allowed. Further, we see on the one hand how the Apostle delivers authoritative tradition, in which are to be found a number of unconditionally binding commandments, and on the other how he himself lays down and promulgates certain commandments, "enactments" (גזירות, תקנות): ἐπιταγαί, παραγγελίαι; διατάσσειν. This is worthy of our attention, since we see, first, the role played by Jesus as the Apostle's doctrinal authority, and secondly, the authoritative decisions and commandments for which he, Paul, is himself responsible.

The procedure followed by Paul when delivering decisions of halakic nature to his churches is set out with exemplary clarity in 1 Cor. 7. The church in Corinth has addressed a number of questions to the Apostle, questions which he here answers with the voice of authority.

In v. 1–7, the Apostle gives instructions on the sexual life.[3] He evidently starts with a phrase taken from the church's original letter (v. 1b),[4] that "it is well for a man not to touch a woman". He personally regards this to be the ideal (v. 7), but does not demand that all shall observe it; instead he gives directions concerning married life. He stresses, however, that he is not delivering these directives as halakic commandments (κατ' ἐπιταγήν), but as advice (κατὰ συγγνώμην). He also sets up

---

[1] E.g. Rom. 8.1 ff., Gal. 4.1 ff., 5.1 ff. See E. Esking, *Fri och frigjord. Det positiva innehållet i frihetstanken hos Paulus* (1956).

[2] Gal. 5.1 (cf. 2.4), 1 Cor. 6.12, Col. 2.16 ff.

[3] Cf. on this question E. Lövestam, *Äktenskapet i N. T.* (1950) and J.-J. von Allmen, *Maris et femmes d'après saint Paul* (1951).

[4] See Jeremias, *Zur Gedankenführung in den paulinischen Briefen*, pp. 151 f.

celibacy as his ideal in v. 8–9—the background is given in v. 25 ff.—
but stresses that those who lack the gift of continence are to marry, for
"it is better to marry than to be aflame with passion".[1] The same point
of view was expressed in v. 2: Christians should marry *in order to avoid
immorality*. As we shall soon see, Paul here has a collection of sayings
of Jesus at his disposal.[2] It is therefore probable that his attitude is
based essentially on two sayings of Jesus, both preserved in the synoptic
tradition: the saying that abstinence from marriage cannot be undertaken by all (Matt. 19.11 f.), and the strict saying that a man who looks
at a woman lustfully has already committed adultery with her in his
heart (Matt. 5.28). He cannot have encountered any equivalent of this
latter saying in *bet Hillel*.

In v. 10 he takes up a question, which he then answers by delivering
a definite commandment (παραγγέλλειν): "Unto the married I command,
not I but the Lord, that the wife ..." The question of the indissolubility
of marriage has already been decided by the Lord, and Paul does not
consider himself authorized to "loose" what has been "bound" by the
Lord. The Apostle here falls back upon the saying of Jesus preserved
in the synoptic tradition (Matt. 19.3 ff. with par.) on the permanent
nature of marriage. Paul does not quote the saying in its entirety, but
draws from it a short halakic statement (with interpretation inserted);
we recognize the procedure from the methods of the Rabbis who, when
drawing an actual statement of halakah from some tradition, did so
with the utmost brevity.[3]

When answering the next halakic question (v. 12 ff.), Paul distinguished
his own decision from that of the Lord. He delivers the statement in
his own name and on his own apostolic authority: "To the rest I say,
not the Lord (τοῖς δὲ λοιποῖς λέγω ἐγώ, οὐχ ὁ κύριος) ..."

It is worth our while when considering this saying to recall the procedure followed in the rabbinic doctrinal courts. During his time in *bet
Hillel* Paul learned to distinguish between questions which have, and
those which have not, been decided. To the former was said, "I have
heard" (שמעתי) or "it has been delivered to me" (מְקַבָּל אֲנִי or מְקֻבְּלָנִי): i.e.
we have in this question a decisive and final decision from some capable
doctrinal authority. To undecided questions was said, "I have not heard"

---

[1] For an interesting suggestion on the background of this formulation, see
D. DAUBE, Terms for Divorce, in *The N.T. and Rabbinic Judaism* (1956), pp. 368 f.

[2] This has often been pointed out, e.g. by CERFAUX, *Le Christ*, pp. 143 f.

[3] See above, p. 175.

(לא שמעתי); if the court in question had sufficient authority, they were then settled.

An important Tannaitic rule, transmitted as an old anonymous *baraita*[1] was in these words:

חכם שטמא אין	"If a doctrinal authority has
חברו רשאי לטהר	declared unclean, his colleague is
אסר אין חברו	not permitted to declare clean, if
רשאי להתיר.	he has forbidden, his colleague is
	not permitted to allow."

This rule was applicable in respect of an equal colleague: a decision made by another Torah scholar was not to be disavowed.[2] It was particularly applicable in the case of the great doctrinal masters, the great teachers of the past, whose words were transmitted.[3] We have no reason to be surprised that Paul applies this rule in those cases in which he is acquainted with what Jesus said on some question. Nor have we any reason for thinking that he disavowed what had been fixed by his apostolic colleagues in Jerusalem, if they really imposed something upon him (cf. Gal. 2.10). *If* he does not observe the apostolic decretal, it must be because it was never sent to him.[4]

Paul, when he has to adopt an attitude to doctrinal and halakic questions, makes a survey of what exists in the authoritative tradition and finds that the question has not been settled, whereupon he decides it in his own name. We might mention in passing that here his decision is *based* on the same saying of Jesus, but that he draws the consequences of the fact that the "legislative" authority of early Christianity cannot be extended to cover those who do not believe (cf. 2 Cor. 6.14 ff.). *Unbelievers* cannot be compelled by their Christian husbands or wives to obey the word of Jesus. (Cf. 1 Cor. 5.12f.)

When Paul writes, "To the rest I say" (λέγω ἐγώ, אומר אני), this is a commandment, just as the saying of Jesus was a commandment. It is not meant to be a piece of advice, like Paul's word on unmarried women in v. 25 ff., but is pronounced κατ' ἐπιταγήν.[5] Paul is aware that he has

[1] b Ber. 63b, b Nid. 20b; see further the explanation in b Ab. Zar. 7a, b Ḥul. 44b.

[2] This rule did not of course exclude the possibility of differences of opinion between one doctrinal authority and another, and that different decisions were in fact made by such authorities in their respective districts.

[3] Cf. above, p. 182 f.

[4] See above, p. 254, n. 2.

[5] Cf. CERFAUX, *La tradition*, p. 259. On the authoritative stringence in ἐπιταγή, ἐπιτάσσειν, διατάσσειν, see, apart from *Lexica*, DODD, ΕΝΝΟΜΟΣ ΧΡΙΣΤΟΥ, p. 104, and CERFAUX, *Le Christ*, p. 144.

the authority to pronounce binding halakah in his own name or, to be more accurate, in his capacity as an Apostle of Christ, and in line with Jesus' teaching.

In what follows, v. 17 ff., we are given new proof of the Apostle's own "legislative" authority. He has laid down (διατάσσειν) a halakah for *all* his churches, to the effect that each person is to remain in the state he was in when he was called. He interprets this *kelal* verse, which is repeated three times (v. 17, 20, 24), as being relevant to two cases: to the question of circumcision, and to that of freedom or slavery. The verse is interpreted and motivated.

In v. 25 ff., Paul considers a new problem: the position of unmarried women. Further light is here cast over his position as Apostle and *didaskalos*. "Now concerning the unmarried, I have no command of the Lord (ἐπιταγὴν κυρίου οὐκ ἔχω), but I give my opinion (γνώμην δὲ δίδωμι) as one who by the Lord's mercy is trustworthy." He returns to the same theme in v. 40: "But in my judgement ... And I think that I have the Spirit of God." Here Paul has no tradition of Jesus in which the question has been decided, to turn to. He must state, "I have not heard" (לא שמעתי). However, he gives no commandment on this point: something which might be taken to be an example of his principle, of avoiding imposing unnecessary burdens (cf. v. 35. For another example, cf. 2 Cor. 8.8 ff.). But he does give a piece of *advice*. And this is said to be given in the Holy Spirit. "I think that I have the Spirit of God", says Paul, with a conscious understatement.[1] We recall the situation described in Acts 15. There, too, they refuse to present their own halakic decisions as sayings of Jesus, but say instead, "It has seemed good to the Holy Spirit and to us ..." We need hardly dwell on the differences between the two cases.[2]

It has been suggested that Paul's advice may be based on the pericope of Martha and Mary (Lk. 10.38 ff.). This is not improbable, to judge from the language.[3]

In Ch. 8, Paul takes up the question of the Christian's attitude to meat which has been offered to idols. The struggle of early Christianity with the problem of the ritual cleanliness of food is reflected more than once in the New Testament documents, and gives us some extremely

---

[1] Paul does not doubt for one moment that he has the Spirit of God; see sub voce πνεῦμα in the concordances!

[2] Cf. above, 260 f.

[3] See C. F. D. MOULE, The Use of Parables and Sayings as Illustrative Material in Early Christian Catechesis, in *Journ. of Theol. Stud.* N.S. 3 (1952), p. 76.

interesting insights into the development of early Christian halakah, which did not proceed in one straight line, but was the result of a tension between two main tendencies.

There is a saying of Jesus preserved in the synoptic tradition (Mk. 7.14 with par.)[1] which says that there is nothing from without a man, that entering into him can defile him (οὐδέν ἐστιν ἔξωθεν τοῦ ἀνθρώπου εἰσπορευόμενον εἰς αὐτὸν ὃ δύναται κοινῶσαι αὐτόν.). This is interpreted by Mark, the disciple of Peter, to mean that all food has been declared to be clean: καθαρίζειν corresponds to the rabbinic טירהר, "to declare clean". In Matthew's version of this tradition (15.15) it is Peter who addresses Jesus with a request for teaching: "Explain (φράσον) the parable to us." In the answer given by Jesus the saying is interpreted as being a rejection of the demand for *the washing of hands* (נטילת ידים) *before meals*.[2] Does this mean that the school of Matthew interpreted this saying more narrowly: that it was not interpreted as being a declaration of the ritual cleanliness of all food?

According to Acts 10.9 ff., Peter learned in a revelation not to "declare unclean" (κοινοῦν, טימא) what God had "declared clean" (καθαρίζειν, טירהר).[3] In this connection, when we read that God "declared clean", this does not refer to something said by Jesus, but to words spoken by the voice from heaven (φωνή, בת קול), which invited Peter to kill and eat a number of "unclean" animals (v. 13). The question is decided by a *bat qol!*[4] Peter, the leader of the Apostles, is thus shown both in Matt. and in Acts to be the first to consider this problem. In Gal. 2.12 f. we also see how Peter observed a relaxed table-halakah, eating with uncircumcized men, but that he retracts when visited by emissaries from the Jerusalem church. That is why Paul is forced to take such drastic action, and to condemn Peter's behaviour before the assembled congregation.[5]

---

[1] For a formal analysis of this tradition, see D. DAUBE, Public Retort and Private Explanation, in *The N.T. and Rabbinic Judaism*, pp. 141 ff.

[2] See BILLERBECK, *Comm.* I, ad loc.

[3] This saying achieves its full overwhelming effect if it is placed together with the above-mentioned rule that when a doctrinal authority has declared clean, his colleague may not declare unclean.

[4] On the way in which *bat qol* could decide a halakic doctrinal question during the period of the Temple, particularly according to *bet Hillel*, see above, p. 213.

[5] GAECHTER, *Petrus* (pp. 242 ff.), finds Paul's procedure painful (peinlich) in the extreme, but has no wish to condemn the Apostle: "Er handelte und schrieb in gutem Glauben ..."!

We glimpse Paul's own attitude in this narrative. He is of the same basic opinion as Peter, but sees the question acutely, as a matter of principle. Paul returns to this topic several times in his epistles. In Rom. 14.20 we read: "All things are clean" (πάντα μὲν καθαρά ...), and in v. 14: "I know and am persuaded in the Lord Jesus that nothing is unclean (ὅτι οὐδὲν κοινόν ...) in itself ..." (It is not impossible that this certainty is based on the saying of Jesus we have just quoted[1] and/or on Petrine tradition.)[2] Here we also encounter the "stumbling-block" motif, as in the other early Christian texts we have mentioned. In the Matthaean version (15.12), the Pharisees are said to have been offended (σκανδαλίζεσθαι) by Jesus' words on the subject of what defiles a man; this he counters by saying: "Every plant which my heavenly Father has not planted will be rooted up." In Acts we see how Peter's way of dealing with this question offends the stricter, Pharisaically-inspired, members[3] of the Jerusalem church (11.3, cf. 15.1, 5, 12), which seems also to be confirmed by Gal. 2.12. In this way the offence aroused among Pharisaic Christians by the relaxation of the table-halakah is dismissed. Instead, Paul issues a warning against another stumbling-block (σκάνδα-λον): that which causes the weak (οἱ ἀσθενεῖς) to fall (Rom. 14.13 ff., 1 Cor. 8.9, 13). It is not improbable that Paul here bases his attitude on another saying of Jesus about σκανδαλίζειν: the warning against leading astray one of these least (οἱ μικροί) who believe (Matt. 18.6 with par.).[4]

In 1 Cor. 8 Paul does not quote the saying of Jesus to the effect that nothing which enters a man can defile him, when he wishes to convince the Corinthian church that it is legitimate to use meat which has been offered to idols as food. But he falls back upon the same halakic attitude as we have in this saying of Jesus, as interpreted by Mark, the disciple of Peter. Meat offered to idols, like all other meat, is "clean". But the

---

[1] Cf. Dodd, *Gospel and Law*, p. 49, ΕΝΝΟΜΟΣ ΧΡΙΣΤΟΥ, pp. 106 f., where he demonstrates further reminiscences of sayings of Jesus in this context (Rom. 14).

[2] The statement can possibly also have been drawn by Paul himself from the central doctrinal point that the Torah as νόμος has been terminated in Christ (Rom. 10.4). Cf. the rule πάντα (μοι) ἔξεστιν, 1 Cor. 6.12, 10.23.

[3] If these were, as we have supposed, former pupils of *bet Shammai*, the matter is even easier to understand. We ought in this connection also to remember that *bet Shammai* was somewhat sceptical about allowing a *bat qol* to decide a halakic question.

[4] Cf. Dodd, *Gospel and Law*, p. 50. On the problem, cf. further, S. Stein, The Dietary Laws in Rabbinic and Patristic Literature, in *Studia Patr.* 2 (1957), pp. 141 ff., and Y. M.-J. Congar, Die Kasuistik des Heiligen Paulus, in *Verkündigung und Glaube. Festgabe f. F. X. Arnold* (1958), pp. 16 ff.

liberty (ἐξουσία here means רשות) to eat all kinds of food can be a stumbling-block to the weak, and may cause him to fall, v. 9 ff. It may therefore be necessary for "the strong" (ὁ ἰσχυρός) to abstain from his rights and privileges.

Paul represents his own behaviour as an example, when illustrating this latter point. He is free; he is an Apostle: he has seen the Lord, and he has fulfilled his apostolic commission before the very eyes of the Corinthians in creating a church, and has thus set the seal on his apostolic office, 1 Cor. 9.1 ff. (cf. the argument with apostolic signs, τὰ σημεῖα τοῦ ἀποστόλου, 2 Cor. 12.12). He thus has the right (ἐξουσία) to food and drink in return for the carrying out of the work of an Apostle. Paul has not exercised this privilege; for the sake of the weak, for the sake of the gospel he has abstained from it (v. 15 ff.). This section on the exemplary conduct of the Apostle concluds with the parable of the athlete, who abstains from many things in order to win the prize (v. 24 ff.).

When examining Paul's methods of argument,[1] we must take note of the fact that he is not trying to lay down halakah for the apostolate: he has no authority to do this. What he is doing is to produce every available argument to convince the Corinthians of the privileges he has as an Apostle, so that he can then point out that he has voluntarily abstained from the exercise of these privileges. Like the Rabbis,[2] he produces arguments from *derek eres*: common behaviour,[3] v. 7 f. We must note here that the strength of his argument lies in the fact that these examples have metaphorical overtones: the situation of the soldier, the worker in the vineyard and the shepherd are suitable illustrations of what ought to apply to Christ's soldier, husbandman or shepherd. He argues from the *Scriptures*, from the Law itself (v. 9 f.) but, typically enough, interprets the statute allegorically; he cannot use the Scriptures as straightforward νόμος! He takes up new examples from *derek eres*: from common practice in education and Temple service, v. 11 ff. These arguments have subsidiary force, since they deal with work similar to that of the Apostles: sacral tasks, regarded with traditional religious reverence.[4] But Paul finally states, briefly and precisely, what is the real

[1] See also above, pp. 254 ff. Cf. MICHEL, *Paulus und seine Bibel*, pp. 159 ff.

[2] See above, p. 256.

[3] For a comparison with the Hellenistic popular philosophers' arguments, see R. BULTMANN, *Der Stil der paulinischen Predigt und die kynisch-stoische Diatribe* (1910), pp. 54 ff., 102 f.

[4] These examples must not be regarded as *halakic precedents* for legislation "in Christ". The Apostle would not have argued in such a way.

basis of the Apostles' right to be supported. This is independent of arguments which can be advanced on its behalf: the Lord has laid down (διέταξεν) that those who deliver the gospel shall live by the gospel, v. 14.[1] This is the decisive argument. Paul does not however quote a saying of Jesus; he produces a halakah based on such a saying. There can be no doubt as to the identity of the saying in question. In the synoptic Gospels, in a tractate of sayings of Jesus, put together as dealing with the instruction of Apostles[2] (Matt. 10.1 ff.; N.B. the verb διατάσσειν in 11.1; Lk. 10.1 ff.) we read that the Apostles are not to collect silver and gold in their belts, for "the labourer is worthy of his food" or, as Luke has it, "his wages" (10.7).

Another of Paul's privileges is that of taking a wife with him[3] on his missionary journeys, 9.5. For this privilege Paul does not refer to a saying of Jesus, but to the practice of the other Apostles, principally Peter. Here we see what were the origins of a certain type of halakah: the practice of the leading authorities constitutes the norm.[4] To judge from the evidence, this case has to do with a halakic practice which developed organically within early Christianity. According to Lk. 8.2 f., women were allowed to accompany the group of disciples even during Jesus' Galilean ministry. There we have the given basis.—If a master, when seeing his disciples doing something, did not forbid it, they considered that he had permitted the practice.

Incidentally, we can see how a similar case is reflected in Gal. 2.12 f., in connection with the table-halakah. Peter's position as halakic authority was so strong that Jewish Christians followed his practice even in Antioch, which lay in Paul's "district".[5] Peter is nevertheless responsible to the college of Apostles as a whole, and he refuses to stand up for his opinions when the emissaries from Jerusalem come to Antioch. Here we have an extremely interesting glimpse of the relations between an individual

[1] Cf. the tradition about Rabban Joḥanan ben Zakkai in Num. R. 19.8 with par.

[2] On this early tractate of sayings of Jesus, see L. CERFAUX, Les Unités littéraires antérieures aux trois premiers évangiles, in La Formation des Évangiles (1957), pp. 24 ff. — Cf. A. W. ARGYLE, St. Paul and the Mission of the Seventy, in Journ. of Theol. Stud. N. S. 1 (1950), p. 63.

[3] Cf. J. B. BAUER, Uxores circumducere (1 Kor 9.5), in Bibl. Zeitschr. N.F. 3 (1959), pp. 94 ff.

[4] For this phenomenon among the Rabbis, see above, Ch. 12 B. On the authoritative position of the Apostles, cf. C. K. BARRETT, The Apostles in and after the N.T., in Sv. Exeg. Årsbok 21 (1956), pp. (30 ff.), 43 ff.

[5] On this subject, cf. above, pp. 187 and 307 ff.

doctrinal authority and the *collegium* (חבורה). We cannot however stop to consider this topic now.

Paul thus relinquished the right, bestowed by the Lord himself, "to live off the gospel". It is interesting to note that Paul classified Jesus' commandment as a permission (ἐξουσία, רשות) for the Apostles, not as an obligation (ὀφείλημα, חובה).[1] Paul is therefore free to abstain from what is here laid down. In an earlier context we noted the same tendency with certain Rabbis: to abstain voluntarily from a privilege or voluntarily to impose upon themselves a stricter halakic practice than that which was laid down.[2] That is what Paul does here. He even motivates his behaviour: he has made himself the servant of all (cf. the saying of Jesus to the Apostles, Matt. 20.26 f.) in order to be able to win more. He has done this for the sake of the weak, in order that the weak might be won over, 9. 15 ff. In another epistle, Paul motivates the same behaviour by saying that in this way he wishes to provide an example (τύπος) *ad imitandum*: he is still thinking of the way in which his behaviour is imitated (2 Thess. 3. 7 ff.).[3]

It is in the midst of this account (1 Cor. 9.21), in which Paul presents a way of life which agrees point by point with transmitted sayings of Jesus or with halakah from the Lord, that we find his statement that he is not without law, but stands under the law of Christ (μὴ ὢν ἄνομος θεοῦ ἀλλ' ἔννομος Χριστοῦ). It is very difficult to interpret this otherwise than to mean that Paul accepts the concept of a messianic law (νόμος χριστοῦ), built on the foundation of a tradition of, and about, the Lord, i.e. the gospel tradition, to the extent and in the form in which he had received it.[4] We can at all events see from 1 Cor. that the demand that Gentile Christians should be taught to keep all that Jesus had commanded (διδάσκοντες αὐτοὺς τηρεῖν πάντα ὅσα ἐνετειλάμην ὑμῖν, Matt. 28.20) was not confined to some "legalistic" groups in early Christianity. In 1 Cor. we find several examples of the way in which even Paul acts on the same basis.[5]

Here we must draw a very important conclusion. We have seen that

---

[1] Also קבע. On this distinction among the Rabbis, see BACHER, *Terminologie* I, pp. 58 f., 167.

[2] Above, p. 186; cf. p. 117.

[3] Above, pp. 185 ff., on the way in which the Rabbis act with reference to "the disciples who follow after them" (Ab. I.11: התלמידים הבאים אחריכם).

[4] See DODD, ΕΝΝΟΜΟΣ ΧΡΙΣΤΟΥ, IDEM, *Gospel and Law*. Cf. also DAVIES, *Paul and Rabbinic Judaism*, pp. 111 ff.

[5] Cf. CERFAUX, *La tradition*, p. 260.

Paul subjects himself to the tradition from the Lord, and regards what Jesus bound as being bound indeed. One who argues in this way, and considers the commandments of Jesus, the Lord, as binding doctrine and precept, must regard it as his duty to gain access to as much as possible of what Jesus said and taught. If we assume consistency in the Apostle's thought, we must draw the conclusion from 1 Cor. 7 that Paul was extremely interested in receiving tradition from the Lord.[1]

If we proceed to consider 1 Cor. 11.2 ff., we there find how Paul insists that women shall wear a veil at prayer and prophecy. This is treated as being a general custom in all the churches of God (v. 16). But by "custom" (συνήθεια) is meant that type of halakah which, without direct "legislative" interference, developed into a normative pattern of behaviour: the rabbinic equivalent is מנהג.[2] Paul produces various arguments here for this early Christian halakah. On the one hand he bases his argument on certain essential points in his doctrinal *didache*: the order of creation, v. 3 ff. On the other he appeals to reason: "Judge for yourselves ..." v. 13. This is far from being an appeal to some vague quality of "commonsense"; it appeals to the reason as subject to the wisdom of Christ (cf. 2 Cor. 10.5); it has its counterpart in the Rabbis' appeal to *sebara*,[3] which is an appeal to reason as directed by the wisdom of the Torah. The argument, "Does not nature itself teach you ...?" v. 14 ff., also has a counterpart in the Rabbis' argument from *derek eres*. In addition we see once more how eager Paul is for the establishment of common halakic practice in all the congregations of the saints, v. 16.[4]

We have thus far been concerned to examine the Apostle's argument in connection with the settling of halakic questions or with homiletic-didactic teaching on such questions. In conclusion we shall now consider two texts in which Paul makes use of definite parts, definite *logoi* from the gospel tradition: not in order to support a commandment of halakah or a *didache* on halakic matters, but in order to provide a source for an authoritative, decisive doctrinal point of non-halakic nature.

In 1 Cor. 11.17 ff., Paul goes on to deliver a number of teachings on the nature of the Lord's Supper, and how it is to be celebrated. Paul

---

[1] Cf. how Hillel travelled all the way from Babylon to Jerusalem in order to receive tradition, above p. 298, n. 3.

[2] Cf. above, p. 182.

[3] Cf. above, p. 256.

[4] Cf. 4.17, 7.17.

refuses to dignify the common meals celebrated in the Corinthian church by the name of "the Lord's Supper" (τὸ κυριακὸν δεῖπνον); each eats what he has taken with him: as a result some eat and drink to excess while others go hungry. When Paul wishes to put things right, he repeats a tradition from the Lord, draws from it a point of doctrine (that the elements are the body and blood of Christ), and bases his argument on this.

First, a few words on the introductory phrase: ἐγὼ γὰρ παρέλαβον ἀπὸ τοῦ κυρίου, v. 23. It is the actual saying of Jesus in the quoted text, on which Paul wishes to base his argument. We therefore read that this logos comes from the Lord. Paul indicates the originator of the saying by using the preposition ἀπό[1] (Hebr. מִן or מפי).[2] It has been said that Paul was referring here to something he had received as "revelation". This possibility can be entertained only as a result of an active belief in miracles, or in an extremely peculiar development in early Christianity, crediting Paul with having received a revelation of what happened "in the night when the Lord Jesus was delivered (to death)". It would then be necessary to explain the agreement between the Pauline and the synoptic accounts of this event. Did this logos on the institution of the Eucharist begin as a revelation to Paul, spread to the whole of early Christianity and then become transformed into history at such an early stage that it could even become an intrinsic part of the passion narrative? Or did the miracle happen, and Paul receive the same message, in practically the same words, as that which the rest of early Christianity passed on as tradition from the twelve?[3] Other scholars have maintained that Paul was referring to a tradition received from the Hellenistic community.[4] But this idea, that Paul recognized the Hellenistic community as being capable of forming and promulgating authoritative tradition on what happened "in the night when the Lord Jesus was delivered to death", is extremely improbable. The only realistic possibility which remains is that Paul is here reproducing a tradition which he believed to have been derived from Jesus via the college of Apostles.

---

[1] Codex Claromontanus reads παρά. For the difference between π. and ἀπό, see J. WEISS, *Comm.*, ad loc., and CULLMANN, *Die Tradition*, pp. 17 f.

[2] Cf. e.g. M Zeb. I.3, the words of Simon ben Azzai: מקובל אני מפי ע״ב זקן, Sifra ad Lev. 10.1, the words of Eliezer ben Hyrkanos: כך מקובלני מרבותי, b Ab. Zar. 45b, the words of R. Aqiba: כך מקובלני אני ממך. See BACHER, *Tradition*, pp. 1 f.

[3] BULTMANN, *Theologie des N.T:s*, pp. 143 f., points out that Paul's version is more smooth and more theologically developed than Mark's!

[4] So BULTMANN, *op. cit.*, *ibid.*

Paul mentions only the first and last links in the chain of transmission; both are strongly emphasized: ἐγώ and ὁ κύριος. That the intermediate links have been omitted may possibly be because Paul considers himself to be a member of that group of Apostles who, as eyewitnesses, have received direct from the Lord.[1] But the matter is capable of another explanation. Since Paul has such a high position as a recognized doctrinal authority, he can himself guarantee that the tradition he is passing on as authoritative has been received from reliable sources. He therefore need name only the originator of the saying and the last recognized traditionist (himself). He is in fact responsible for the reliability of what he delivers as received authoritative tradition. We emphasize once more that the church in Corinth has already received this tradition, which Paul repeats again as a basis for his argument.

In the actual passage of tradition Paul concentrates on the saying of Jesus that the bread is "my body" and the wine "my blood". He is able to show from this that a person eating and drinking the elements unworthily (v. 27), "without discerning the body (of the Lord)",[2] v. 29, profanes the body and blood of the Lord, and draws judgement upon himself, *ibid*. On this doctrinal foundation—and we should note how literally the Apostle takes the saying of Jesus and the way he treats it as unquestionably authoritative—the Apostle then builds his instructions and exhortations on the worthy celebration of the sacred meal.

We are faced, finally, with 1 Cor. 15, in which the Apostle takes up the question of death and the resurrection.[3] His aim is to meet the objections of those in Corinth who have denied a future resurrection of the dead, v. 12. In order to confute this heresy, Paul builds his argument on an unshakeable foundation: the resurrection of Christ, confirmed both by the Scriptures and by eyewitnesses. He repeats for the benefit of the Corinthians the logos in which the death and resurrection of Christ, the Scriptural proofs and the evidence of the apostolic eyewitnesses are briefly summarized. He emphasizes that he has received this logos as authoritative tradition, and that both he and the other Apostles preach in accordance with it. The Apostles' standing

---

[1] So CERFAUX, *La tradition*, pp. 260 ff. Cf. IDEM, *L'unité du Corps apostolique dans le N.T.*

[2] For the interpretation of this crux interpretum, see *Comm.*, ad loc. — N.B. that 𝔓 D G vg^clem sy read τὸ σ. τοῦ κυρίου.

[3] For an analysis of Paul's thought in 1 Cor. 15, see H. RIESENFELD, Das Bildwort vom Weizenkorn bei Paulus, in *Festschrift* E. KLOSTERMANN (1961), pp. 51 ff.

as eyewitnesses, in the legal meaning of the word, is stressed in exactly the same way as in Luke: if their claim that Christ is risen be untrue, then they are "false witnesses" (v. 15).

The logos quoted here[1] by Paul serves as a solid basis for argument, since it shows that Christ has risen; this doctrinal fact is later used by the Apostle in support of his contention that there in fact will be a resurrection of the dead (v. 12 ff.).

---

[1] See further above, pp. 296 ff.

CHAPTER 16

The Origins and Transmission of the Gospel Tradition

IN THE COURSE of our attempt to discover how gospel material was transmitted in the young Church, we have so far examined the evidence of the earliest Fathers, in the Acts of the Apostles and in Paul. We ought now to proceed to the synoptic material, but this would require an independent monograph. We shall therefore conclude this study by offering a brief sketch of the picture we have obtained from our previous investigation of the origins and transmission of the gospel tradition in the earliest phase of the Church.

It is not possible historically to understand the origins of early Christian tradition by beginning with the *preaching* of the primitive Church. Such a procedure is both unhistorical and theologically dubious. Early Christian preaching claimed to pass on God's revelation for the last days. This revelation was not however presented as an isolated phenomenon, detached from tradition, history and the former revelation, but referred back to something which had already happened: to Jesus of Nazareth, his teaching, his works, and above all to his suffering and death, and to his disciples' remarkable experiences after having found his tomb to be empty. It also looked back to sacred history and to the Scriptures.

Nor is it possible to begin with Jesus. He claimed to stand in an extraordinary relationship to God, and therefore to be able to pass on to Israel the divine revelation appropriate to the "Aeon to come". But he, too, looked back to something which already existed: to the Torah tradition[1] in its written and oral forms, that holy and authoritative tradition which both he and his people believed to have come from God. When Paul says in Gal. 4 that in the fulness of time God sent forth His Son, born of a woman and subject to the Law, he is speaking dogmatically. But at the same time he is suggesting the existence of a fact which the historian cannot afford to neglect: that Jesus was born of a Jewish woman and brought up under the Torah. That means that he was familiar with, and subject to, the Torah. One of the main tasks facing any scholar who would trace the origins, development and transmission of the gospel

---

[1] For the conception of Torah, see above, pp. 19 ff.

tradition must therefore be to determine, in general and in detail, its relation to the Torah. Few factors have been so important for the formation of the gospel tradition as the belief that the words and works of Christ were the fulfilment of the Law and the Prophets. If we modern scholars knew our Old Testament (the Hebrew text, the Aramaic targum and the Greek translations) off by heart, we would be able to see this in its correct perspective. Least of all is it possible to understand the origins of the gospel tradition if Jesus be regarded as having no links whatever with the Torah tradition, and if all the ties which, according to the sources, bind him to that tradition be considered as secondary rejudaizing.[1] Jesus, as a historical figure, is placed in a tradition—a tradition which, according to the sources, he held to be sacred.

The synoptic tradition was transmitted and written down in the context of a Church which did not believe Jesus to be a mere earthly teacher. It believed him to be the Messiah: Christ, the Son of Man, the Servant of the Lord, the Son of God, the Lord—to mention only a few of the messianic epithets. This high Christology cannot be disconnected from the impression made by Jesus on his disciples, and furthermore it must have some original connection with Jesus' own view of his work, of his position, and of himself.[2] The opinion expressed by so many scholars, that the Christology of the N.T. is essentially a creation of the young Church, is an intelligent thesis, but historically most improbable.

But although the Church had such a developed Christology, it never

---

[1] E. STAUFFER, *Die Botschaft Jesu* (1959) maintains, "Jesus stand völlig allein in seiner Zeit, sterneneinsam in seinem Volk." The tradition of Jesus has, however, been judaized, re-judaized. "Dieser Rejudaisierungsprozess bereitet sich schon zu Lebzeiten Jesu in seinem Jüngerkreis vor, er kommt dann nach Ostern mit wachsender Macht zur Durchsetzung und wirkt alsbald zurück auf die Gestalt der Jesusüberlieferungen selbst." ... "Wir fragen heute mit neuem Ernst nach der Botschaft Jesu von Nazareth. Und wir haben heute neue Möglichkeiten, die Urbotschaft Jesu herauszuschälen aus der Jesusüberlieferung der ältesten Christenheit." ... "Nicht die jüdischen Herrenworte der Evangelien sind die echtesten, sondern die unjüdischen und antijüdischen. Noch einmal: Von 'antisemitischen' Worten kann keine Rede sein, wohl aber von antiqumranischen, antipharisäischen, antirabbinischen, antimosaischen Worten", pp. 9 ff. This way of isolating Jesus from his historical *milieu*, and from the tradition in which he stands, is impossible to accept from the point of view of the historian. And the theologian notes here a kind of docetism.

[2] See H. RIESENFELD, Observations on the Question of the Self-Consciousness of Jesus, in *Sv. Exeg. Årsbok* 25 (1960), pp. 23 ff.

lost sight of the fact that Jesus *taught*.[1] This means that although Jesus claimed so much, he was nevertheless a teacher. It is not possible to describe his ministry *only* in educational categories, but many of its characteristics may be traced to his teaching. And this is an original element in the tradition.[2] To be sure, there are exegetes who deny that Jesus taught at all, but this denial is based on dogmatic or subjective grounds—not on the evidence of the historical material.[3] Even such a sceptical scholar as BULTMANN reaches the result, after analysing the sources: "When faced with the evidence of the collected sources there can be little doubt that Jesus taught as a Rabbi, that he gathered 'disciples' and that he debated."[4]

The sources do not suggest that Jesus used any method radically different from that which was normal in his milieu. The existing terms for teaching, διδάσκειν, διδαχή; cf. διδάσκαλος, are used without further definition in the Gospels to refer to his activity. In a somewhat dogmatic saying we read that he taught ὡς ἐξουσίαν ἔχων, and not as the scribes (Matt. 7.29)[5]; this however says little about his method, and is scarcely a saying of such a kind as to be of use as a foundation for historical proof.[6]

Jesus' attitude in principle to the Torah can be described briefly only at the cost of considerable over-simplification. The problem is

---

[1] C. H. DODD, Jesus als Lehrer und Prophet, in *Mysterium Christi* (1931), pp. 69 ff., E. FASCHER, Jesus der Lehrer, in *Theol. Literaturzeit.* 79 (1954), col. 325 ff.; RIESENFELD, *The Gospel Tradition and its Beginnings*.

[2] DODD, *op. cit.*, p. 69 f., FASCHER, *op. cit.*, col. 327.

[3] E. SCHWEIZER, *Gemeinde und Gemeindeordnung im N.T.* (1959), p. 24: "Es wäre auch nicht einzusehen, was damit gerettet wäre, wenn sich nachweisen liesse, dass Jesus die Zwölf bewusst als Tradenten für eine spätere Gemeinde geschult hätte. Denn damit sänke Jesus nur auf die Stufe eines Rabbi hinunter, der durch seine Schüler in seiner Lehre weiterwirken will." Our task as historians is not to "save" Jesus or to "exalt" him but to attempt to find out—with the limited resources of historical research—"wie es eigentlich gewesen". Does not the mere truth about Jesus suffice?

[4] "Angesichts des Gesamtbestandes der Überlieferung wird man kaum bezweifeln, dass Jesus als Rabbi gelehrt, 'Schüler' gesammelt und disputiert hat," *Geschichte*, p. 52. See further IDEM, *Jesus* (1929), pp. 55 ff. On the other hand BULTMANN does not take sufficient account of the characteristics which distinguish Jesus from the Rabbis.

[5] Cf. Mk. 1.27: διδαχὴ καινὴ κατ᾽ ἐξουσίαν.

[6] For interpretation, see D. DAUBE, Rabbinic Authority, in *The N.T. and Rabbinic Judaism*, pp. 206 ff.

extremely complicated. It is evident that he accepted the written Torah (the Holy Scriptures) as the word of God. He also criticized sharply the regulations in the oral Torah, but it is not quite clear whether or not this is to be taken as a rejection in principle of the oral Torah in its entirety. It is however obvious that Jesus in fact adopted a number of elements of the oral Torah.

But Jesus' attitude to the Torah cannot be described merely in terms of acceptance and rejection. He obviously wished to *fulfil* (πληροῦν: קיים? מלא?) it, though in a different meaning from that of any Rabbi. His attitude is in all probability correctly described in the saying transmitted by Matthew, that he did not come in order to destroy the Law and the Prophets, but to fulfil them (Matt. 5.17). This does not mean merely that he deliberately related his ministry to the Torah; it also means that he wished his ministry to be the means of bringing about an alteration in the position of the Torah. He wished to transform the premessianic Torah into the messianic Torah. This took place, first, through his definite interpretation of the Torah: an interpretation which replaced the oral Torah, but on a considerably higher level. Secondly, he wished to carry out that work of salvation without which the position of the Torah could not be altered. The matter is perhaps to be interpreted in this way, though opinions on this central question differ sharply.[1]

The next question is how consciously Jesus linked his individual words and actions with the Torah, or with particular Torah texts. To what extent was there an *original* connection between the words and works of Jesus on the one hand, and definite texts in the Torah on the other?

In some cases the matter is quite simple. If Jesus taught in the Jews' synagogues, within the context of public worship, some of his sayings were delivered in direct relation to a text which had been read. The link thus existed from the very beginning. The same applies to those cases in which Jesus quoted, or made use of, sayings from the Holy Scriptures. There was therefore an original link between a saying of Jesus and a text from the written Torah. But to how much of the tradition of Jesus does this apply? The question cannot be decided by referring to the tendency of increase in the number of "Scriptural proofs" in the developing gospel tradition. We know from the Jewish parallel material that one and the same tradition is transmitted in forms of

---

[1] See further, LJUNGMAN, *Das Gesetz erfüllen*, W. D. DAVIES, Matthew, 5, 17–18 in *Mélanges Bibliques ... en l'honneur de* A. ROBERT (1957), pp. 428 ff.

varying extent—with or without midrashic element.[1] If we find one and the same tradition in both mishnaic and midrashic forms, we cannot without more ado assume the former to be the older.

Just as it is not possible to treat the actions of a Jewish Rabbi as historical events of a purely occasional character, lacking definite significance (*zufällige Geschichtswahrheiten*, in the words of LESSING),[2] so it is equally impossible to consider Jesus' works without first inquiring after the meaning Jesus laid in them, the pedagogical purpose behind them, and what Jesus wished to "teach" or "reveal" with them. The question is now, to what extent were his actions carried out with a view not only to the Scriptures and the prophetic message, to those hopes and expectations which were to be found in the tradition— or among those tradition-steeped individuals to whom he spoke— but also to definite texts in the written Torah. Can we be quite sure that links with O.T. texts were in every case first forged in the early Church?

We have good reason for believing that Jesus taught both in word and deed. Some of his works are didactic symbolic actions, and nothing more.[3] In most cases, however, the didactic symbolism is only one side of the picture: Jesus' works did not only fill a pedagogical function. At all events, the young Church saw all Jesus' works—in fact his whole life—as being teaching. This appears to agree in principle with the Master's intentions.

Turning to Jesus' oral teaching, we must reckon with the fact that he used a method similar to that of Jewish—and Hellenistic—teachers: the scheme of text and interpretation. He must have made his disciples learn certain sayings off by heart; if he taught, he must have required his disciples to memorize. This statement is not intended to be dogmatic or apologetic but is a consideration based on a comparison with the contemporary situation.[4] It can of course be used for dogmatic purposes, but the task of critical scholarship is only to estimate probability on the basis of the evidence of the source material.

We must now ask, how much of the tradition from Jesus gives us

---

[1] See above, 83 f., 136 ff., 175 f.

[2] Above, Ch. 12 B.

[3] Cf. above, p. 185.

[4] See above, Ch. 4, 6–12. — Cf. T. W. MANSON's observation, quoted above, p. 129, n. 2., that "the early Church remembered better than it understood".

the impression of being made up of condensed memory texts,[1] and how much of chance elements in his teaching as a whole? In the synoptic tradition we also find material which interprets sayings of Jesus, e.g. in the exposition (*talmud*) of parables.[2] Even though these expositions were not stressed by Jesus himself as being memory texts, and were therefore not delivered with a fixed wording, we must reckon with the fact that they derive *in principle* from Jesus' own interpretative exposition of his parables.[3]

If we now turn our attention to the young Church, we must account for the fact that the Torah tradition was still there—and that the young Church recognized at least the written Torah without reservation—and further, that Jesus' disciples were still there. The implication is that the words and works of Jesus were stamped on the memories of these disciples. Remembering the attitude of Jewish disciples to their master, it is unrealistic to suppose that forgetfulness and the exercise of a pious imagination had too much hand in transforming authentic memories beyond all recognition in the course of a few short decades.

The sources show that Jesus' closest disciples had a particularly authoritative position in the young Church. Luke's evidence[4] is supported not only by historical probability (the matter is virtually self-evident, seen against the background of the contemporary situation). Paul confirms it, directly and indirectly, and his evidence is particularly valuable, since it comes from a man who has had himself to fight for recognition as an Apostle of Christ.[5]

"The twelve" do not appear in the sources as particularly well-defined individual figures, but as a *collegium*. It is really only their leader, Peter, and the inner triumvirate of Peter, James and John who stand out as distinctive individuals. Their stay in Jerusalem was not the result of mere chance; important doctrinal considerations also played their part in the course of events.[6]

The *collegium* of Apostles was still in residence in Jerusalem in the forties

---

[1] See above, Ch. 11 C–D.

[2] After a linguistic analysis of the interpretation of the parable of the Sower, Joach. JEREMIAS concludes: "Die Deutung des Säemannsgleichnisses gehört der Urkirche an", *Die Gleichnisse*, p. 67.

[3] Cf. above, Ch. 12 A. Se also the remarks on the parables above, pp. 145, 177, and 315.

[4] See above, Ch. 14.

[5] See above, Ch. 15.

[6] See above, Ch. 14 A, E, 15 A, D–E.

and, to judge from the evidence, even as late as the fifties; they had thus been there between fifteen and twenty years.

We have comparative material from Qumran which shows what an authoritative *collegium* in an eschatologically self-conscious congregation did. Material from other contemporary groups is also extremely telling. It is no longer possible to under-estimate this evidence as the first form-critics did. We cannot find out how authoritative tradition originates if we ignore the tradition's authorities.

There can be no doubt that the twelve proclaimed a burning message about the atoning death and resurrection of Christ. But the poetic picture of ignorant men, suddenly delivering unprepared and unlearned sermons and speeches under the influence of powerful inspiration—and continuing the process for a generation or more—is a peculiar combination, arrived at on the basis of certain distinctly dogmatic tendencies in the sources and a number of romantic ideas in modern research. The historian, without neglecting the evidence for early Christian enthusiasm, must make up his mind on certain other elements in the picture painted for us by the sources.

Against the background of the Jewish milieu, it is evident that the early Christian Apostles were *compelled* to present their message as an eyewitness account, as "that which we have seen and heard", and in connection with the Holy Scriptures—even supported by a convincing exposition of the Scriptures.[1] There is no evidence that these needs were first felt at a later stage in the history of early Christianity. The eyewitnesses and the Scriptures were already there in the kerygma.[2]

In addition, the Apostles' preaching had an essential complement in their *teaching*. The aspect of the "eyewitness account" is also to be found there. They taught in the name of their Master, and bore witness to the words and works of their Teacher in a way which recalled—at least formally—the witness borne by other Jewish disciples to the words and actions of their teachers.[3]

It is unrealistic to try to sum up the varied activities of the young Church under one function, whether this function be identified as preaching or teaching. It is certain that in the life of the rapidly growing congregation there were a great number of varied activities: preaching, teaching, prayer, sacred meals, charitative activity, exor-

---

[1] See above, Ch. 14 C and 15 C.
[2] Above, Ch. 15 C.
[3] See above, Ch. 12 B and 14 B.

cism, healing, church discipline, jurisdiction, stewardship, and many more. Problems arose, and questions were asked. We may assume that in all these varied activities the members of the congregation "remembered" and made use of authoritative sayings, not only passages from the Holy Scriptures, but sayings of Jesus, and memories of what Jesus did. But the question is, which of these forms of activity provided *the essential Sitz im Leben* for the "actualization", collection and fixing of the tradition about Jesus? In the course of this present investigation we have come to the conclusion that the leading *collegium* in the Jerusalem church carried out a direct work on ὁ λόγος τοῦ κυρίου (i.e. the Holy Scriptures and the tradition from, and about, Christ). From certain points of view this work resembled the labours of Rabbinic Judaism on דבר יהוה (the Holy Scriptures and the oral Torah) and the work carried out in the Qumran congregation on דבר יהוה (the Holy Scriptures and the sect's own tradition, which was partly oral and partly written). This apostolic work on "the word of God" was thus the most important element in the comprehensive concept ἡ διδαχὴ τῶν ἀποστόλων (Acts 2.42) and the concept ἡ διακονία τοῦ λόγου (Acts 6.4).[1]

This work on "the word of the Lord" certainly took varying forms, but two of these forms demand our particular attention.

We must suppose, first, that an intensive study of the Scriptures took place. They "searched the Scriptures" in order to win deeper insight into "the secrets of the Kingdom of God". This study of the Scriptures was, formally speaking, midrash exegesis, similar in principle to that carried out by the Rabbis, the Qumran sect and the Apocalyptic groups. There were variations, but the technique employed was roughly similar.[2] The essential difference between the midrash exegesis of the Jerusalem church and that of the other groups is that the Jerusalem church interpreted the Scriptures in the light of the teaching of Jesus, given in word and deed, and in the light of the distinctive events experienced by the Apostles during and immediately after the first Easter. The early Christian Church had a new point of departure: one which was not shared by Rabbinic Judaism, and one which the Qumran sect possessed only in part. Several of the Scripture quotations which are to be found in Acts and in the synoptic tradition appear to be derived from this midrashic Scripture study in the young Jerusalem church. From these quotations we are able to see the way in which this study functioned.[3]

[1] Above, Ch. 14 D.
[2] See above, Ch. 2.
[3] Ch. 14 C. See further, STENDAHL, *The School.*

Secondly, we must take into account the discussions of doctrinal questions[1] raised by members of the *collegium*, by the Apostles' disciples—for there were certainly such—and by individual members of the congregation, as well as by opponents. When deciding such questions there were two natural authoritative sources from which answers might be drawn: the Scriptures and the tradition from Jesus. We have attempted in an earlier chapter to reconstruct the process followed here.[2]

In the course of this work on "the word of the Lord", sayings of Jesus were "remembered", repeated, expounded and applied. Such was the practice in rabbinic doctrinal debates, using sayings of the great teachers;[3] such was certainly the practice in early Christianity, too. Eloquent witness is borne by the fact that although sayings of Jesus in the Gospels are relatively few in number, they prove to have been used for many different purposes.[4] As in the rabbinic tradition,[5] one and the same "saying" appears in several different contexts. It is often extremely difficult to decide the "original" meaning of a saying of Jesus which has become separated from its situation.

In the course of this work, they also "remembered" how Jesus acted in various situations; narratives about Jesus' actions were formulated as answers to definite questions.[6] This does not mean that these narratives were mere inventions. The rabbinic comparative material does not favour such a view.[7]

Since Jesus was considered to be the Messiah, *the "only" teacher* (Matt. 23.10), his sayings must have been accorded even greater authority and sanctity than that accorded by the Rabbis' disciples to the words of their teachers. A fact which has been pointed out by a number of scholars is that the Jesus-tradition in the early Christian documents is *isolated* from the sayings of other authorities;[8] this shows that it had a distinctive

---

[1] Cf. BULTMANN, *Geschichte*, pp. 39 ff.

[2] 14 E; cf. 15 E.

[3] Ch. 12 A.

[4] See G. LINDESKOG, Logiastudien, in *Studia Theol.* 4 (1950, printed 1952), pp. 129 ff.

[5] Cf. above, p. 180.

[6] Cf. above, Ch. 12 B.

[7] Cf. above, p. 183.

[8] Thus already G. KITTEL, *Die Probleme des palästinischen Spätjudentums und das Urchristentum* (1926), p. 69: "Die Isolierung der Jesustradition ist das Konstitutivum des Evangeliums." — On the fact that *adapted* sayings of Jesus were, together with other maxims, incorporated into tractates which were compiled for various practical reasons, see above, pp. 303 f.

position among early Christian doctrinal authorities, and a peculiar dignity.

This brings us to the question of the grouping of the Jesus-tradition. Its arrangement among the disciples of Jesus is a matter of the psychology of memory, which we cannot consider in this context. We can, however, ask: How was this tradition grouped when it was to be taught to disciples? We might expect, on a basis of the Jewish parallel material, two different methods of grouping: the midrashic and the mishnaic.[1] In the former case, the grouping of the Jesus-traditions would have been based on their association with the consecutive text of Scripture: with passages or selections from the text. This method would seem to have been used to some extent in the young Church,[2] but it must have been somewhat unpractical. It is possible that traces of the much-discussed *testimonia* collections might be worth following in this context. Were these texts key-words to certain traditions about Jesus?

In the latter, mishnaic case, sayings of Jesus were grouped in more or less extensive blocks, "tractates", put together for various purposes and arranged on various principles: either factual or mechanical mnemotechnical. It is a well-known fact that we are able to catch glimpses of such "tractates" in the written Gospels. We may for example recall the instruction of the Apostles (or missionaries) in Matt. 10 with par.,[3] the parable tractate in Mk. 4 with par., and "the bread traditions" in Mk. 6.31–8.26 with par.[4] It is probable that relatively comprehensive "tractates" of Jesus-traditions had to be compiled at a fairly early stage for use of missionaries and teachers who went out from Jerusalem. But how early is the enigmatic traditional collection which we usually call "Q"? It is difficult to say whether or not Paul was acquainted with this extensive collection; but there is no doubt that Paul had access to a fairly comprehensive collection of traditions about Jesus, even though it is difficult to reach any definite conclusion as to the extent or the arrangement of this collection.[5]

---

[1] Above, pp. 151 ff.

[2] Cf. J. W. DOEVE, *Jewish Hermeneutics in the Synoptic Gospels and Acts* (1954), pp. 177 ff., IDEM, Le rôle de la tradition orale dans la composition des Évangiles synoptiques, in *La formation des Évangiles*, pp. 70 ff.

[3] Cf. e.g. L. CERFAUX, Les Unités littéraires, *ibid.*, pp. 24 ff.

[4] L. CERFAUX, La section des pains, in *Recueil* L. CERFAUX I, pp. 471 ff.—On the grouping, see also T. SOIRON, *Die Logia Jesu* (1916) and M. SMITH, *Tannaitic Parallels to the Gospels* (1951), pp. 115 ff.

[5] Ch. 15 D.

An intensive work on the logos was also carried on in other churches, but the Jerusalem church was the centre of the early Christianity and the leaders of this congregation was considered as the highest doctrinal authority of the whole Church.[1]

We have reason to suppose the Jesus-tradition to have been originally passed on by word of mouth—for ideological as well as for practical reasons. The distinction between written and oral Torah was familiar to the young Church;[2] the Jesus-tradition was a higher equivalent of the oral Torah. Furthermore, according to the prophetic word, God would in the last days write His Torah on the hearts of His Covenant people (Jer. 31.31), i.e. Israel was to memorize the Torah. When we remember the way in which such sayings were interpreted in contemporary Judaism, it is not improbable that such concepts as these were significant for the thought of early Christianity; we cannot however build too much on this assumption.

We must at all events take into account the fact that the actual transmission of such collections of traditions about Jesus was a distinct activity—a direct methodical delivery of the kind we have described in Chapters 9–12 of this work. The traditionist/teacher passed on the tractate, passage or saying to his pupil or pupils by means of continual repetition; he taught the pupil to repeat it, after which he gave the required interpretation. We catch glimpses in the synoptic material —particularly in Matt., "the rabbinic Gospel"[3]—of certain teaching situations which are worthy of our attention in this context, since they certainly reflect teaching practice in the Church in which the tradition in question was formed. But there is little point in stopping at such a statement. It was precisely the teacher's pedagogical measures which were the object of special observation and imitation. Jesus' teaching methods were certainly imitated by his disciples. It ought therefore to be possible, on the basis of the practice of these disciples, to draw certain conclusions as to the methods applied by their Master.

If the gospel tradition was carried in this way, how can there be variations between different parallel traditions? We must take a number of factors into consideration. First and foremost, we must make a very careful attempt to decide when we are actually dealing with variations

---

[1] On the relation between the leading *collegium* in Jerusalem and the other Christian Apostles and teachers, see my remarks above, in Ch. 14–15.

[2] Ch. 1, 11 E and 13.

[3] See STENDAHL, *The School.*

of one and the same basic saying, and when with sayings of Jesus, delivered by Jesus himself in more than one version. The ease with which many scholars explain all differences between related traditions as being secondary versions of one basic saying, seems most remarkable to anyone who has noted the role played by the category of "theme and variations" in Jewish teaching. Furthermore, we must take into account the fact that most of the gospel material is haggadic material, and that haggadic material is often transmitted with a somewhat wider margin of variation in wording than halakic material.[1] Nor must we overlook certain adaptations, carried out at an early stage, when the traditional material was gathered. Certain types of variation are due to the material having been translated—not only on one definite occasion, but in a process which was protracted and certainly complicated. Despite careful transmission, the occurrence of certain small alterations as a result of faulty memorization cannot be excluded. Finally, attention must be paid to the principles of redaction used by the different Evangelists.

We must distinguish in principle between this *transmission* in the strict meaning of the word, and the many *uses* to which the transmitted oral texts were put.[2] It is not impossible that the tradition of Jesus, as the special ἱερὸς λόγος of the early Church, was recited in the course of worship; this point of view has been advanced by RIESENFELD.[3] Further, we must take into account a number of other contexts in which the transmitted sayings were *used*: in preaching, in various forms of doctrinal debate and teaching, and others of the manifold activities of the young Church.

When the Evangelists edited their Gospels, however, they did not take their traditions from these forms of activity. They worked on a basis of a fixed, distinct tradition from, and about, Jesus—a tradition which was partly memorized and partly written down in notebooks and private scrolls,[4] but invariably isolated from the teachings of other doctrinal authorities.

We must be content with these suggestions as to the origins and transmission of the gospel tradition. A more detailed picture would require a thorough analysis of both the synoptic and the Johannine material; it has not however been possible to undertake such an analysis within the bounds of this investigation.

---

[1] Cf. above, pp. 96 f., and 146 ff.
[2] See above, Ch. 2.
[3] *The Gospel Tradition and its Beginnings.* — Cf. above, Ch. 5.
[4] Cf. above, Ch. 13.

Bibliography

A. Texts and Translations

Biblia Hebraica ..., ed. R. KITTEL, 8th ed. by P. KAHLE, A. ALT, O. EISS-FELDT. Stuttgart 1952.

Targum Onkelos ..., ed. A. BERLINER, I–II. Berlin 1884.

The Bible in Aramaic ... I: The Pentateuch according to Targum Onkelos, ed. A. SPERBER. Leiden 1959.

Septuaginta ..., ed. A. RAHLFS, I–II. Stuttgart 1943.

Novum Testamentum Graece ..., ed. Erw. NESTLE, K. ALAND, 23rd ed. Stuttgart 1957.

Synopse der drei ersten Evangelien, ed. A. HUCK, H. LIETZMANN. 9th ed. Tübingen 1936.

ספרי הברית החדשה, ed. F. DELITSCH. 7th ed. Berlin 1886.

Apocrypha and Pseudepigraphs of the Old Testament in English ..., ed. R. H. CHARLES, I–II. Oxford 1913.

Neutestamentliche Apokryphen in deutscher Übersetzung, ed. E. HEN-NECKE, W. SCHNEEMELCHER, I. 3rd ed. Tübingen 1959.

The Letter of Aristeas, A Linguistic Study with Special Reference to the Greek Bible, ed. H. G. MEECHAM. Manchester 1935.

The Greek Versions of the Testaments of the Twelve Patriarchs, ed. R. H. CHARLES. Oxford 1908.

The Zadokite Documents. I: The Admonition, II: The Laws, ed. C. RABIN. 2nd ed. Oxford 1958.

Documents of Jewish Sectaries I. Fragments of a Zadokite Work ..., ed. S. SCHECHTER. Cambridge 1910.

The Dead Sea Scrolls of St. Mark's Monastery. I: The Isaiah Manuscript and the Habakkuk Commentary. II:2: Plates and Transcription of the Manual of Discipline, ed. M. BURROWS, J. C. TREVER, W. H. BROWNLEE. New Haven 1950–1951.

Discoveries in the Judaean Desert I. Qumran Cave I, ed. D. BARTHÉLEMY, J. T. MILIK. Oxford 1955.

The Manual of Discipline ..., ed. P. WERNBERG-MØLLER. (Stud. on the Texts of the Desert of Judah I.) Leiden 1957.

Fragments of a Qumran Scroll of Eschatological Midrāšîm, ed. J. M. ALLEGRO, in *Journ. of Bibl. Lit.* 77 (1958), pp. 350–354.

A Midrash on 2 Sam. vii and Ps. i–ii (4Q Florilegium), ed. Y. YADIN, in *Isr. Explor. Journ.* 9 (1959), pp. 95–98.

338

Flavii Iosephi opera omnia, ed. S. A. NABER, I–IV. Leipzig 1888–1896.

Philonis Alexandrini opera quae supersunt, ed. L. COHN, P. WENDLAND, I–VII. Berlin 1896–1930.

Die sechs Ordnungen der Mischna. Hebräischer Text mit Punktation, ed. E. BANETH, J. COHN, D. HOFFMANN, M. PETUCHOWSKI, A. SAMMTER u. a., I–VI. Wiesbaden (1885) 1924–1933 (IV and I 2nd ed. 1924 and 1927 respectively).

Sanhedrin, Makkōt, ed. S. KRAUSS. (In Die Mischna, ed. G. BEER, O. HOLTZMANN.) Giessen 1933.

Der Mišna-Traktat Tamid ..., ed. A. BRODY. Diss. Uppsala. Uppsala 1936.

'Abōt ..., ed. K. MARTI, G. BEER. (In Die Mischna, ed. G. BEER, O. HOLTZMANN.) Giessen 1927.

The Mishnah. Translated from the Hebrew with Introduction and Brief Explanatory Notes by H. DANBY. Oxford 1933.

Tosephta, ed. M. S. ZUCKERMANDEL. Pasewalk, Trier 1879–1882.

The Tosefta ..., ed. S. LIEBERMAN, I ff. New York 5715–1955 ff.

Der babylonische Talmud mit Einschluss der vollständigen Mišnah, ed. L. GOLDSCHMIDT, I–IX. Berlin, Leipzig, Haag 1897–1935.

Talmud Babli I. Tractat Berachoth, ed. E. M. PINNER. Berlin 1842.

[The Babylonian Talmud translated into English, ed. I. EPSTEIN, I–XXXV. London (Soncino Press) 1935–1948.]

Der Jerusalemische Talmud nebst Glossar und Anhang. Krotoschin 1886. (I have given the passages of the Talmud Yerushalmi after this edition, which follows that of the Cracow edition.)

Talmud Yerushalmi (Title in Hebrew) I–II. Berlin 5689–1928.

[Le Talmud de Jérusalem traduit ... par M. SCHWAB, I–XI. Paris 1878–1890 (Nouvelle éd. photomécanique Paris 1932–1933).]

Masechet Soferim. Der talmudische Tractat der Schreiber ..., ed. J. MÜLLER. Leipzig 1878.

Der Traktat der Schreiber (Sopherim), in Auswahl übersetzt von H. BARDTKE, in Wissensch. Zeitschr. d. Karl Marx-Univ. Leipzig 3 (1953–54), pp. 31–49.

Aboth de Rabbi Nathan, ed. S. SCHECHTER. Wien 1887.

[The Fathers according to Rabbi Nathan, translated ... by J. GOLDIN. (Yale Judaica Ser. 10.) New Haven 1955.]

Mekilta de-Rabbi Ishmael, ed. J. Z. LAUTERBACH, I–III. Philadelphia 1933–1935.

Mechilta der älteste halachische und hagadische Commentar zum zweiten Buche Moses, ed. I. H. WEISS. Wien 1865.

Sifra. Commentar zu Leviticus aus dem Anfange des III. Jahrhunderts. Nebst der Erläuterungen des R. Abraham ben David (Rabed) und Masoret ha-Talmud von J. H. WEISS, ed. J. SCHLOSSBERG. Wien 1862.

Sifré debé Rab, ed. M. FRIEDMANN, I. Wien 1864.

Siphre d'be Rab, ed. H. S. HOROVITZ. Leipzig 1917. (Corpus Tann. III, III: 1.)

Pesikta, die älteste Hagada, redigiert in Palästina von Rab Kahana, ed. S. BUBER. Lyck 1868.

[Pesikta des Rab Kahana ... ins Deutsche übertragen, ed. A. WÜNSCHE. Leipzig 1885.]

Pesiqta Rabbati, ed. M. FRIEDMANN. Wien 1880.

Midrasch Tanchuma (Title in Hebrew), ed. S. BUBER, I–III. Wilna 1885.

Midrash Rabbah translated into English . . . , ed. H. FREEDMAN, M. SIMON, I–IX. London 1939.

Bibliotheca Rabbinica, ed. A. WÜNSCHE, I–XII. Leipzig 1880–1885.

Iggeret R. Scherira Gaon in der französischen und spanischen Version, ed. B. LEWIN. Haifa 1921.

Die apostolischen Väter. Neuberarbeitung der Funkschen Ausgabe, I, ed. K. BIHLMEYER, W. SCHNEEMELCHER. 2nd ed. Tübingen 1956. (Samml. ausgew. kirchen- u. dogmengesch. Quellenschr. II: 1: 1.)

S. Clementis I, ... opera omnia I. (Patrologiae cursus completus, Ser. Graeca, ed. J.-P. MIGNE, I.) Paris 1857.

Clementis Alexandrini opera quae exstant omnia ... I–II. (MIGNE Patr. Graec. VIII–IX.) Paris 1857.

Clemens Alexandrinus, Stromata, ed. O. STÄHLIN. (Die griech. christl. Schriftsteller d. ersten drei Jahrh. III:2, 3.) Leipzig 1906–1909.

Eusebii Pamphili ... opera omnia ... II–III. (MIGNE Patr. Graec. XX–XXI.) Paris 1857.

Eusebius Werke II: Die Kirchengeschichte, ed. E. SCHWARTZ. (Griech. Christl. Schriftst. 2: 1–3.) Leipzig 1903–1909.

Eusebius Werke VIII: Die Praeparatio Evangelica, ed. K. MRAS. (Griech. Christl. Schriftst. 8:1–2.) Berlin 1954–1956.

S. Eusebii Hieronymi opera omnia ... IV, VII. (Patrologiae cursus completus, Ser. Latina, ed. J.-P. MIGNE, XXIV, XXVI.) Paris 1845.

The Apostolic Tradition of Hippolytos. Translated into English ... by B. S. EASTON. Cambridge 1934.

Sancti Irenaei ... Contra Haereses. (MIGNE Patr. Graec. VII.) Paris 1857.

Evidence of Tradition. Selected Source Material for the Study of the History of the Early Church, Introduction and Canon of the New Testament, ed. D. J. THERON. London 1957.

Antilegomena. Die Reste der aussercanonischen Evangelien und urchristlichen Überlieferungen, ed. E. PREUSCHEN. 2nd ed. Gieszen 1905.

Antiquae musicae auctores septem. Graece et latine, VII, ed. M. MEIBOMIUS. Amsterdam 1652.

M. Tulli Ciceronis scripta quae manserunt omnia, fasc. 45: De natura deorum, ed. O. PLASBERG, W. AX. Leipzig 1933.

Dionis Chrysostomi Orationes. Post L. Dindorfium ed. G. DE BUDÉ, II. Leipzig 1919.

Q. Horati Flacci opera, ed. F. Klingner. Leipzig 1950.

Epicteti dissertationes ab Arriano digestae ..., ed. H. SCHENKL. Leipzig 1916.

Claudii Galeni Pergameni Scripta minora ..., ed. I. MARQUARDT, I. MÜLLER, G. HELMREICH, II. Leipzig 1891.

Philostratus and Eunapius. The Lives of the Sophists, ed. W. C. WRIGHT. London, New York 1921.

Platonis Dialogi sec. Thrasylli Tetralogias dispositi, ed. C. F. HERMANN. Leipzig 1904–1907.

M. Fabi Quintiliani Institutionis oratoriae libri XII, ed. L. RADEMACHER, I–II. Leipzig 1959.

B. *Literature*

AHLSTRÖM, G. W., *Psalm 89*. Eine Liturgie aus dem Ritual des leidenden Königs. Diss. Uppsala. Lund 1959.

AICHER, G., *Das Alte Testament in der Mischna*. (Bibl. Stud. 11:4.) Freiburg 1906.

ALBECK, C., *Untersuchungen über die Redaktion der Mischna*. (Veröffentl. d. Akad. f. d. Wiss. d. Judent. Talm. Sekt. 2.) Berlin 1923.

— Die Herkunft des Toseftamaterials, in *Monatsschr. f. Gesch. u. Wiss. d. Judent.* 69 (1925), pp. 311–328.

ALBRIGHT, W. F., A Catalogue of Early Hebrew Lyric Poems (Psalm LXVIII), in *Hebr. Un. Coll. Ann.* 23: 1 (1950–51), pp. 1–39.

— Notes on Psalms 68 and 134, in *Norsk Teol. Tidsskrift* 56 (1955), pp. 1–12.

ALEWELL, K., *Über das rhetorische* ΠΑΡΑΔΕΙΓΜΑ. Theorie, Beispielsammlungen, Verwendung in der römischen Literatur der Kaiserzeit. Diss. Kiel. Leipzig 1913.

ALLEN, E. L., The Lost Kerygma, in *New Test. Stud.* 3 (1956–57), pp. 349–353.

ALLEN, T. W., *Homer*. The Origins and the Transmission. Oxford 1924.

VON ALLMEN, J.-J., *Maris et femmes d'après saint Paul*. (Cahiers Théol. 29.) Neuchâtel, Paris 1951.

ANDRÆ, T., *Mystikens psykologi*. Besatthet och inspiration. (Modern religionspsykologi 4.) Stockholm 1926.

ANDRÉN, O., *Rättfärdighet och frid*. En studie i första Clemensbrevet. Diss. Uppsala. Uppsala 1960.

APTOWITZER, V., *Das Schriftwort in der rabbinischen Literatur* I–V (I, II: Sitz.-ber. d. Kais. Akad. d. Wiss. in Wien. Phil.-Hist. Kl. 153,6, 1906; 160,7, 1908. III–IV, 1911. V, 1915.) Wien 1906–1915.

ARGYLE, A. W., St. Paul and the Mission of the Seventy, in *Journ. of Theol. Stud.* N. S. 1 (1950), p. 63.

VON ARNIM, H., *Leben und Werke des Dio von Prusa*. Mit einer Einleitung: Sophistik, Rhetorik, Philosophie in ihrem Kampf um die Jugendbildung. Berlin 1898.

ARZT, M., The Teacher in Talmud and Midrash, in M. M. KAPLAN *Jubilee Volume*, New York 1953, pp. 35–47.

ASTING, R., *Die Verkündigung des Wortes im Urchristentum*, dargestellt an den Begriffen „Wort Gottes", „Evangelium" und „Zeugnis". Stuttgart 1939.

ATKINS, J. W. H., *Literary Criticism in Antiquity*. A Sketch of its Development, I–II. Cambridge 1934.

BACHER, W., *Abraham Ibn Esra's Einleitung zu seinem Pentateuch-Commentar*, als Beitrag zur Geschichte der Bibelexegese. (Sitz.-ber. d. Kais. Akad. d. Wiss. Phil.-Hist. Kl. 81, 3.) Wien 1876.

— *Die Agada der Tannaiten* I–II. Strassburg 1884–1890. (I, 2nd ed. Strassburg 1903.)

— Ein Räthsel in der Litteratur weniger, in *Mag. f. d. Wiss. d. Judent.* 17 (1890), pp. 169–172 and 18 (1891), pp. 50–51.

— *Die Agada der Palästinensischen Amoräer* I. Strassburg 1892.

— *Die Hebräische Sprachwissenschaft vom 10. bis zum 16. Jahrhundert.* Mit einem einleitenden Abschnitte über die Massora. Trier 1892.

— Ein alter Kunstausdruck der jüdischen Bibelexegese זֵכֶר לַדָּבָר, in *Zeitschr. f. d. Alttest. Wiss.* 18 (1898), pp. 83–98.

— Les trois branches de la science de la vieille tradition Juive, le Midrasch, les Halachot, et les Haggadot, in *Rev. des Ét. Juives* 38 (1899), pp. 211–219. (Expanded in *Die Agada der Tannaiten* I, 2nd ed. 1903, pp. 475–489.)

— Zum Verständnisse des Ausdruckes זֵכֶר לַדָּבָר, in *Zeitschr. f. d. Alttest. Wiss.* 19 (1899), pp. 166–168.

— Zur Geschichte der Schulen Palästina's im 3. und 4. Jahrhundert. Die Genossen (חַבְרַיָּא), in *Monatsschr. f. Gesch. u. Wiss. d. Judent.* 43 (1899), pp. 345–360.

— *Die exegetische Terminologie der jüdischen Traditionsliteratur.*
I. *Die bibelexegetische Terminologie der Tannaiten.* Leipzig 1899.
II. *Die bibel- und traditionsexegetische Terminologie der Amoräer.* Leipzig 1905.

— Academies in Babylonia, and Academies in Palestine, in *The Jew. Enc.* I, New York, London 1901, pp. 145–147 and 147–148 respectively.

— Die Gelehrten von Caesarea (רבנן דקיסרין), in *Monatsschr. f. Gesch. u. Wiss. d. Judent.* 45 (1901), pp. 298–310.

— Sanhedrin, in HASTINGS' *Dictionary of the Bible* IV, Edinburgh 1902, pp. 397–402.

— Das alt-jüdische Schulwesen, in *Jahrb. f. Jüd. Gesch. u. Lit.* 6 (1903), pp. 48–81.

— Gemara, in *Hebr. Un. Coll. Ann.* 1904, pp. 26–30.

— Talmud, in *The Jew. Enc.* XII, New York, London 1906, pp. 1–27.

— Ein bisher nicht erkanntes persisches Lehnwort im babylonischen Talmud, in *Zeitschr. d. Deutsch. Morgenl. Ges.* 67 (1913), pp. 268–270.

— *Tradition und Tradenten in den Schulen Palästinas und Babyloniens.* Studien und Materialien zur Entstehungsgeschichte des Talmuds. Leipzig 1914.

BAIRD, W., What is the Kerygma? A Study of I Cor. 15.3–8 and Gal. 1.11–17, in *Journ. of Bibl. Lit.* 76 (1957), pp. 181–191.

BALDUCELLI, P., Professor Riesenfeld on Synoptic Tradition, in *Cath. Bibl. Quart.* 22 (1960), pp. 416–421.

BALOGH, J., „*Voces Paginarum*". Beiträge zur Geschichte des lauten Lesens und Schreibens, in *Philologus* 82 (1926–27), pp. 84–109, 202–240.

BAMBERGER, B. J., Revelations of Torah after Sinai. An Aggadic Study, in *Hebr. Un. Coll. Ann.* 16 (1941), pp. 97–113.

BARDTKE, H., Der Traktat der Schreiber (Sopherim), in *Wissensch. Zeitschr. d. Karl Marx-Univ. Leipzig* 3 (1953–54), pp. 31–49.

BARRETT, C. K., Paul and the "Pillar Apostles", in *Studia Paulina in honorem* J. DE ZWAAN, Haarlem 1953, pp. 1–19.

— The Apostles in and after the New Testament, in *Sv. Exeg. Årsbok* 21 (1956), pp. 30–49.

BAUER, J. B., Uxores circumducere (1 Kor 9, 5), in *Bibl. Zeitschr.* N. F. 3 (1959), pp. 94–102.

BAUER, W., *Griechisch-Deutsches Wörterbuch zu den Schriften des Neuen Testaments und der übrigen urchristlichen Literatur.* 4th ed. Berlin 1952.

BAUERNFEIND, O., Die Begegnung zwischen Paulus und Kephas Gal 1, 18–20, in *Zeitschr. f. d. Neutest. Wiss.* 47 (1956), pp. 268–276.

BEARE, F. W., On the Interpretation of Romans VI.17, in *New Test. Stud.* 5 (1958–59), pp. 206–210.

BEASLEY-MURRAY, G. R., *Jesus and the Future.* An Examination of the Criticism of the Eschatological Discourse, Mark 13 with Special Reference to the Little Apocalypse Theory. London 1954.

BEILNER, W., *Christus und die Pharisäer.* Exegetische Untersuchung über Grund und Verlauf der Auseinandersetzungen. Wien 1959.

BELKIN, S., The Problem of Paul's Background, in *Journ. of Bibl. Lit.* 54 (1935), pp. 41–60.

BENOIT, A., Écriture et Tradition chez Saint Irénée, in *Rev. d'Hist. et de Philos. Rel.* 40 (1960), pp. 32–43.

BERGMANN, J., Die runden und hyperbolischen Zahlen in der Agada, in *Monatsschr. f. Gesch. u. Wiss. d. Judent.* 82 (1938), pp. 361–376.

BETZ, O., Felsenmann und Felsengemeinde. (Eine Parallele zu Mt 16.17–19 in den Qumranpsalmen), in *Zeitschr. f. d. Neutest. Wiss.* 48 (1957), pp. 49–77.

— *Offenbarung und Schriftforschung in der Qumransekte.* (Wissensch. Unters. z. N. T. 6.) Tübingen 1960.

BEUDEL, P., *Qua ratione Graeci liberos docuerint, papyris, ostracis, tabulis in Aegypto inventis illustratur.* Diss. Münster. [Münster] 1911.

BIALOBLOCKI, S., see KLEIN, S., BIALOBLOCKI, S.

BI(C)KERMAN(N), E. (J.), *Der Gott der Mackabäer.* Untersuchungen über Sinn und Ursprung der mackabäischen Erhebung. Berlin 1937.

— The Colophon of the Greek Book of Esther, in *Journ. of Bibl. Lit.* 63 (1944), pp. 339–362.

— La chaîne de la tradition pharisienne, in *Rev. Bibl.* 59 (1952), pp. 44–54.

— The Septuagint as a Translation, in *Proceed. of the Amer. Acad. for Jew. Research* 28 (1959), pp. 1–39.

BIETENHARD, H., ὄνομα, in *Theol. Wörterb.*, ed. G. KITTEL, V, Stuttgart 1954, pp. 242–281.

BILLERBECK, P., see STRACK, H. L., BILLERBECK, P.

BINDER, A. W., *Biblical Chant.* New York 1959.

BIRKELAND, H., *Zum Hebräischen Traditionswesen.* Die Komposition der prophetischen Bücher des Alten Testaments. (Avh. utg. av Det Norske Videnskaps-Akad. i Oslo II. Hist.-Filos. Kl. 1938, 1.) Oslo 1938.

BIRT, T., *Kritik und Hermeneutik nebst Abriss des antiken Buchwesens.* (Handb. d. klass. Altertumswiss. I:3). München 1913.

BJÖRCK, G., ΗΝ ΔΙΔΑΣΚΩΝ. Die periphrastischen Konstruktionen im Griechischen. (Skr. utg. av K. Hum. Vet.-Samf. i Uppsala, 32:2.) Uppsala, Leipzig 1940.

BLASS, F., DEBRUNNER, A., *Grammatik des neutestamentlichen Griechisch.* 9th ed. Göttingen 1954.

BLAU, L., *Zur Einleitung in die Heilige Schrift.* Budapest 1894.

— *Studien zum althebräischen Buchwesen und zur biblischen Litteraturgeschichte.* (In 25. Jahresber. d. Landes-Rabbinerschule in Budapest.) Budapest 1902.

— Ursprung und Geschichte des technischen Ausdrucks „Mündliche Lehre" nebst einigen Bemerkungen über die Sammlung der jüdischen Tradition, in J. WINTER, A. WÜNSCHE, *Mechiltha,* Leipzig 1909, pp. XVIII–XXV.

BLOCH, J. S., *Einblicke in die Geschichte der Entstehung der talmudischen Literatur.* Wien 1884.

BLOCH, R., Écriture et Tradition dans le Judaisme. Aperçus sur l'origine du Midrash, in *Cahiers Sioniens* 8 (1954), pp. 9–34.

— Quelques aspects de la figure de Moïse dans la tradition rabbinique, in *Cahiers Sioniens* 8 (1954), pp. 211–285.

— Midrash, in *Dict. de la Bible,* Suppl. V, Paris 1957, col. 1263–1281.

BOEHM, F., *De symbolis Pythagoreis.* Diss. Berlin. Berlin 1905.

BONNARD, P., La Tradition dans le Nouveau Testament, in *Rev. d'Hist. et de Philos. Rel.* 60 (1960), pp. 20–30.

BONSIRVEN, J., *Le judaïsme palestinien au temps de Jésus-Christ.* Sa théologie, I–II. (Bibl. de théol. hist.) 2nd ed. Paris 1934–1935.

— *Exégèse rabbinique et exégèse paulinienne.* (Bibl. de théol. hist.) Paris 1939.

BOSTRÖM, O. H., *Alternative Readings in the Hebrew of the Books of Samuel.* (Augustana Libr. Publ. 8.) Rock Island 1918.

BOUSSET, W., *Jüdisch-Christlicher Schulbetrieb in Alexandria und Rom.* Literarische Untersuchungen zu Philo und Clemens von Alexandria, Justin und Irenäus. (Forsch. z. Rel. u. Lit. d. A. u. N. T., N. F. 6.) Göttingen 1915.

— *Kyrios Christos.* Geschichte des Christusglaubens von den Anfängen des Christentums bis Irenaeus. (Forsch. z. Rel. u. Lit. d. A. u. N. T., N. F. 4.) 2nd ed. Göttingen 1921.

BOWMAN, J. W., Prophets and Prophecy in Talmud and Midrash, in *Evang. Quart.* 22 (1950), pp. 107–114, 203–220, 255–275.

BOYANCÉ, P., *Le culte des Muses chez les philosophes grecs.* Études d'histoire et de psychologie religieuses. (Bibl. des Écoles franç. d'Athènes et de Rome.) Paris 1937.

BOYD, W., *The History of Western Education.* 6th ed. London 1954.

BRADLEY, D. G., The *Topos* as a Form in the Pauline Paraenesis, in *Journ. of Bibl. Lit.* 72 (1953), pp. 238–246.

BRAUN, H., *Spätjüdisch-häretischer und frühchristlicher Radikalismus.* Jesus von Nazareth und die essenische Qumransekte, I–II. (Beitr. z. hist. Theol. 24:1–2.) Tübingen 1957.

BROWNLEE, W. H., Biblical Interpretation among the Sectaries of the Dead Sea Scrolls, in *The Bibl. Archaeol.* 14 (1951), pp. 54–76.

— *The Text of Habakkuk in the Ancient Commentary from Qumran.* (Journ. of Bibl. Lit. Mongr. Ser. 11.) Philadelphia 1959.

BRÜLL, J., *Die Mnemotechnik des Talmuds.* Wien 1884.

BRÜLL, N., Die Entstehungsgeschichte des babylonischen Talmuds als Schriftwerkes, in *Jahrb. f. Jüd. Gesch. u. Lit.* 2 (1876), pp. 1–123.

— Review of J. BRÜLL, Einleitung in die Mischna, and WEISS, Zur Geschichte der Tradition, in *Jahrb. f. Jüd. Gesch. u. Lit.* 4(1879), pp. 59–70.

BÜCHLER, A., Learning and Teaching in the Open Air in Palestine, in *Jew. Quart. Rev.* 4 (1913–14), pp. 485–491.

BULTMANN, R., *Der Stil der paulinischen Predigt und die kynisch-stoische Diatribe.* (Forsch. z. Rel. u. Lit. d. A. u. N. T. 13.) Göttingen 1910.

— *Jesus.* Berlin [1929].

— Die Bedeutung des geschichtlichen Jesus für die Theologie des Paulus, in *Glauben und Verstehen.* Gesammelte Aufsätze, I, Tübingen 1933, pp. 188–213.

— *Exegetische Probleme des zweiten Korintherbriefes.* Zu 2. Kor 5, 1–5; 5,11–6,10; 10–13; 12,21. (Symb. Bibl. Ups. 9.) Uppsala 1947.

— *Theologie des Neuen Testaments.* (Neue theol. Grundrisse.) Tübingen [1948–]1953.

— *Die Geschichte der synoptischen Tradition.* 4th ed. Göttingen 1958.

— Zur Frage nach den Quellen der Apostelgeschichte, in *N. T. Essays, Studies in Memory of* T. W. MANSON, Manchester 1959, pp. 68–80.

BURK, A., *Die Pädagogik des Isokrates als Grundlegung des humanistischen Bildungsideals*, im Vergleich mit den zeitgenössischen und den modernen Theorien dargestellt. (Stud. z. Gesch. u. Kult. d. Altert. XII, 3–4.) Würzburg 1923.

BURNEY, C. F., *The Poetry of Our Lord.* Oxford 1925.

BURR, V., Editionstechnik, in *Reallex. f. Ant. u. Christ.* IV, Stuttgart 1959, col. 597–610.

BURROWS, M., *More Light on the Dead Sea Scrolls.* More Scrolls and New Interpretations. With Translations of Important Recent Discoveries. London 1958.

CADBURY, H. J., The Purpose Expressed in Luke's Preface, in *The Expos.* 21 (1921), pp. 431–441.

— Commentary on the Preface of Luke, in *The Beginnings of Christianity* I:I, London 1920, pp. 489–510.

VON CAMPENHAUSEN, H. FREIH., Der urchristliche Apostelbegriff, in *Studia Theol.* 1 (1947), pp. 96–130.

— *Kirchliches Amt und geistliche Vollmacht in den ersten drei Jahrhunderten.* (Beitr. z. hist. Theol. 14.) Tübingen 1953.

— *Die Begründung kirchlicher Entscheidungen beim Apostel Paulus.* Zur Grundlegung des Kirchenrechts. (Sitz.-ber. d. Heidelb. Akad. d. Wiss. Phil.-hist. Kl. 1957: 2.) Heidelberg 1957.

CARRINGTON, P., *The Primitive Christian Catechism*. A Study in the Epistles. Cambridge 1940.

CERFAUX, L., Le Christ dans la théologie de saint Paul. (Lectio divina 6.) 2nd ed. Paris 1954.

— The following articles in *Recueil* L. CERFAUX: Études d'Exégèse et d'Histoire Religieuse, I–II (Bibl. Ephem. Theol. Lovan. VI–VII), Gembloux 1954: La section des pains (Mc., VI,31–VIII,26; Mt., XIV,13–XVI,12), I, pp. 471–485; Série IV: Les Actes des Apôtres et le Christianisme primitif, II, pp. 61–315, partic. Témoins du Christ d'après le Livre des Actes, pp. 157–174: L'unité du Corps apostolique dans le Nouveau Testament, pp. 227–237; La tradition selon saint Paul, pp. 253–263; Les deux points de départ de la tradition chrétienne, pp. 265–282.

— Les Unitées littéraires antérieures aux trois premiers évangiles, in J. CAMBIER, etc., *La Formation des Évangiles*. (Rech. Bibl. II.), Louvain 1957, pp. 24–33.

CHADWICK, H. M. and N. K., *The Growth of Literature* I–III. Cambridge 1932–1940.

CHROUST, A.-H., *Socrates: Man and Myth*. The Two Socratic Apologies of Xenophon. London 1957.

CLARK, D. L., *Rhetoric in Greco-Roman Education*. New York 1957.

CLAVIER, H., Πέτρος καὶ πέτρα, in *Zeitschr. f. d. Neutest. Wiss. Beih.* 21 (1954) (Neutest. Stud. f. R. BULTMANN), pp. 94–109.

CONGAR, Y. M.-J., Die Kasuistik des Heiligen Paulus, in *Verkündigung und Glaube. Festgabe f. F. X. ARNOLD*, Freiburg 1958, pp. 16–41.

CONZELMANN, H., Review of M. DIBELIUS, Botschaft und Geschichte, in *Verkündigung und Forschung* (1957), pp. 151–155.

— Die Mitte der Zeit. Studien zur Theologie des Lukas. (Beitr. z. hist. Theol. 17.) 3rd ed. Tübingen 1960.

COURCELLE, P., Source Chrétienne et Allusions Païennes de l'épisode du "Tolle, Lege" (Saint Augustin, Confessions, VIII, 12,29), in *Rev. d'Hist. et de Philos. Rel.* 32 (1952), pp. 171–200.

CROSS, F. M., *The Ancient Library of Qumrân and Modern Biblical Studies*. London 1958.

CULLMANN, O., *Petrus. Jünger — Apostel — Märtyrer*. Das historische und theologische Petrusproblem. 1st ed. Zürich 1952.

— Die Tradition als exegetisches, historisches und theologisches Problem. Zürich 1954.

— Parusieverzögerung und Urchristentum. Der gegenwärtige Stand der Diskussion, in *Theol. Literaturzeit.* 83 (1958), col. 1–12.

— πέτρα, Πέτρος, Κηφᾶς, in *Theol. Wörterb.*, ed. G. KITTEL, VI, Stuttgart 1959, pp. 94–112.

DAHL, N. A., *Das Volk Gottes*. Eine Untersuchung zum Kirchenbewusstsein des Urchristentums (Skr. utg. av Det Norske Videnskaps-Akad. i Oslo II. Hist.-Philos. Kl. 1941, 2.) Oslo 1941.

— Anamnesis. Mémoire et Commémoration dans le christianisme primitif, in *Studia Theol.* 1 (1947), pp. 69–95.

346

DAIN, A., *Les manuscrits*. Paris 1949.

DANIÉLOU, J., *Théologie du Judéo-Christianisme*. (Bibl. de théol. Hist. des doctrines chrétiennes avant Nicée 1.) Tournai 1958.

DAUBE, D., Rabbinic Methods of Interpretation and Hellenistic Rhetoric, in *Hebr. Un. Coll. Ann.* 22 (1949), pp. 239–264.

— Alexandrian Methods of Interpretation and the Rabbis, in *Festschrift H.* LEWALD, Basel 1953, pp. 27–44.

— The following articles in *The New Testament and Rabbinic Judaism* (Jordan Lectures 1952), London 1956: Principle and Cases, pp. 63–66; Precept and Example, pp. 67–89; Public Retort and Private Explanation, pp. 141–150; Rabbinic Authority, pp. 206–223; Basic Commandments, pp. 247–253; The 'I am' of the Messianic Presence, pp. 325–329; Terms for Divorce, pp. 362–372.

DAVIES, W. D., *Torah in the Messianic Age and/or the Age to Come*. (Journ. of Bibl. Lit. Monogr. Ser. 7.) Philadelphia 1952.

— *Paul and Rabbinic Judaism*. Some Rabbinic Elements in Pauline Theology. 2nd ed. London 1955.

— Matthew, 5, 17–18, in *Mélanges bibliques en l'honneur de A.* ROBERT (Travaux de l'Instit. Cath. de Paris 4.), Paris 1957, pp. 428–456.

DEBRUNNER, A., see BLASS, F., DEBRUNNER, A.

DELATTE, A., *Études sur la littérature Phythagoricienne*. (Bibl. de l'École des Hautes Études. Sciences hist. et philol. 217.) Paris 1915.

DENEFFE, A., *Der Traditionsbegriff*. Studie zur Theologie. (Münster. Beitr. z. Theol. 18.) Münster in W. 1931.

DHORME, É., *La poésie biblique*. Introduction à la Poésie Biblique et trente chants de circonstance. (Coll. "La vie chrét.") Paris 1931.

DIBELIUS, M., Rabbinische und evangelische Erzählungen, in *Theol. Blätt.* 11 (1932), col. 1–12.

— *Jesus*. (Samml. Göschen 1130.) Berlin 1939.

— Stilkritisches zur Apostelgeschichte, in *Aufsätze zur Apostelgeschichte*. 3rd ed. (Forsch. z. Rel. u. Lit. d. A. u. N. T., N. F. 42), Göttingen 1957, pp. 9–28.

— *Die Formgeschichte des Evangeliums*. 3rd ed. (ed. G. BORNKAMM). Tübingen 1959.

DIEZ MACHO, A., La cantilación protomasorética del Pentateuco, in *Estudios Bíblicos* 18 (1959), pp. 223–251.

— The Recently Discovered Palestinian Targum: its Antiquity and Relationship with the other Targums, in *Suppl. to Vet. Test.* 7 (1960), pp. 222–245.

DIX, G., *Jew and Greek*. A Study in the Primitive Church. London 1953.

DOBSCHÜTZ, L., *Die einfache Bibelexegese der Tannaïm* mit besonderer Berücksichtigung ihres Verhältnisses zur einfachen Bibelexegese der Amoraïm. Diss. Halle-Wittenberg. Halle 1893.

DODD, C. H., Jesus als Lehrer und Prophet, in *Mysterium Christi*. Christologische Studien britischer und deutscher Theologen, Berlin 1931, pp. 67–86.

— *The Apostolic Preaching and its Developments*. London 1936.

— *History and the Gospel*. London 1938.

— *Gospel and Law*. The Relation of Faith and Ethics in Early Christianity. (Bampton lect. in Amer. 3.) Cambridge 1951.

— *According to the Scriptures*. The Substructure of New Testament Theology. London 1952.

— ΕΝΝΟΜΟΣ ΧΡΙΣΤΟΥ, in *Studia Paulina in honorem J.* DE ZWAAN, Haarlem 1953, pp. 96–110.

— The following articles in *New Testament Studies*, Manchester 1953: The Framework of the Gospel Narrative, pp. 1–11; Matthew and Paul, pp. 53–66.

— The Primitive catechism and the Sayings of Jesus, in *N. T. Essays. Studies in memory of* T. W. MANSON, Manchester 1959, pp. 106–118.

DOEVE, J. W., Some Notes with Reference to ΤΑ ΛΟΓΙΑ ΤΟΥ ΘΕΟΥ in Romans III 2, in *Studia Paulina in honorem J.* DE ZWAAN, Haarlem 1953, pp. 111–123.

— *Jewish Hermeneutics in the Synoptic Gospels and Acts*. (van Gorcum's Theol. Bibl. 24.) Assen 1954.

— Le rôle de la tradition orale dans la composition des Évangiles synoptiques, in J. CAMBIER, etc., *La Formation des Évangiles* (Rech. Bibl. II.), Louvain 1957, pp. 70–84.

DOLLARD, J., see MILLER, N. E., DOLLARD, J.

DRAZIN, N., *History of Jewish Education from 515 B. C. E. to 220 C. E.* (During the Periods of the Second Commonwealth and the Tannaim.) (The Johns Hopkins Univ. Stud. in Education 29.) Baltimore 1940.

DUPONT, J., *Gnosis*. La connaissance religieuse dans les épîtres de saint Paul. (Univ. Cath. Lovan. Diss. II:40.) Bruges, Paris 1949.

— *Les problèmes du Livre des actes d'après les travaux récents*. (Anal. Lovan. bibl. et orient. 2:17.) Louvain 1950.

— L'utilisation apologétique de l'A.T. dans les Discours des Actes, in *Ephem. Theol. Lovan.* 29 (1953), pp. 289–327.

— Ressuscité "le troisième jour", in *Bibl.* 40 (1959), pp. 174–183.

DÜRR, L., *Das Erziehungswesen im Alten Testament und im antiken Orient*. (Mitteil. d. Vorderasiat.-aegypt. Ges. 36:2.) Leipzig 1932.

— *Die Wertung des göttlichen Wortes im Alten Testament und im antiken Orient*. Zugleich ein Beitrag zur Vorgeschichte des neutestamentlichen Logosbegriffes. (Mitteil. d. Vorderasiat.-aegypt. Ges. 42:1.) Leipzig 1938.

— Heilige Vaterschaft im antiken Orient. Ein Beitrag zur Geschichte der Idee des „Abbas", in *Heilige Überlieferung. Ausschnitte* ... I. HERWEGEN ... *dargeboten*, Münster 1938, pp. 1–20.

EBNER, E., *Elementary Education in Ancient Israel* During the Tannaitic Period (10–220 C. E.). New York 1956.

EHRMANN, P., *De iuris sacri interpretibus Atticis*. (Religionsgesch. Versuche u. Vorarb. IV:3.) Giessen 1908.

EIDEM, E., Imitatio Pauli, in *Teologiska studier tillägnade* E. STAVE, Uppsala 1922, pp. 67–85.

— *Det kristna livet enligt Paulus* I. Stockholm 1927.

EISSFELDT, O., *Einleitung in das Alte Testament* unter Einschluss der Apokryphen und Pseudepigraphen sowie der apokryphen- und pseudepigraphenartigen Qumrān-Schriften. (Neue theol. Grundrisse.) 2nd ed. Tübingen 1956.

ELBOGEN, I., *Der jüdische Gottesdienst in seiner geschichtlichen Entwicklung.* Leipzig 1913.

ELIADE, M., *Ewige Bilder und Sinnbilder.* Vom unvergänglichen menschlichen Seelenraum. Olten u. Freiburg im Breisgau 1958.

ELLIGER, K., *Studien zum Habakuk-Kommentar vom Toten Meer.* (Beitr. z. hist. Theol. 15.) Tübingen 1953.

ELLIS, E., *Paul's Use of the Old Testament.* Edinburgh, London 1957.

ENGNELL, I., *Gamla Testamentet. En traditionshistorisk inledning* I. Stockholm 1945.

— Profetia och tradition. Några synpunkter på ett gammaltestamentligt centralproblem, in *Sv. Exeg. Årsbok* 12 (1947), pp. 110–139.

— *Israel and the Law.* A review article. (Symb. Bibl. Ups. 7.) 2nd ed. Uppsala 1954.

— *Grammatik i gammaltestamentlig hebreiska.* Stockholm, Oslo, København, Helsingfors 1960.

— Methodological Aspects of Old Testament Study, in *Suppl. to Vet. Test.* 7 (1960), pp. 13–30.

— The following articles in I. ENGNELL, A. FRIDRICHSEN, *Sv. Bibl. Uppslagsverk,* I–II, Gävle 1948–1952: Gamla Testamentet, I, col. 645–670; Jesajas bok, I, col. 1029–1033; Litterärkritik 1., II, col. 89–97; Livets bok, II, col. 105–107; Profeter 1., II, col. 727–774; Söka Gud, II, col. 1322–1323; Traditionshistorisk metod 1., II, col. 1429–1437.

EPSTEIN, J. N., *Der gaonäische Kommentar zur Ordnung Tohoroth.* Eine kritische Einleitung zu dem R. Hai Gaon zugeschriebenen Kommentar. Diss. Bern. Berlin 1915.

— Zur Babylonisch-Aramäischen Lexikographie, in *Festschrift* A. SCHWARZ, Berlin, Wien 1917, pp. 317–327.

ESCHELBACHER, M., Probleme der talmudischen Dialektik, in *Monatsschr. f. Gesch. u. Lit. d. Judent.* 68 (1924), pp. 47–66, 126–150.

ESKING, E., *Fri och frigjord.* Det positiva innehållet i frihetstanken hos Paulus. Stockholm 1956.

VAN DEN EYNDE, D., *Les Normes de l'Enseignement Chrétien dans la littérature patristique des trois premiers siècles.* (Univ. Cath. Lovan. Diss. II:25.) Gembloux, Paris 1933.

FALKENSTEIN, A., Die babylonische Schule, in *Saeculum* 4 (1953), pp. 125–137.

FARMER, W. R., *Maccabees, Zealots, and Josephus.* An Inquiry into Jewish Nationalism in the Greco-Roman Period. New York 1956.

FASCHER, E., Jesus der Lehrer. Ein Beitrag zur Frage nach dem ,,Quellort der Kirchenidee'', in *Theol. Literaturzeit.* 79 (1954), col. 325–342.

— Theologische Beobachtungen zu δεῖ, in *Zeitschr. f. d. Neutest. Wiss. Beih.* 21 (1954) (Neutest. Stud. f. R. BULTMANN), pp. 228–254.

FESTUGIÈRE, A.(-)J., *L'idéal religieux des Grecs et l'Évangile*. Préface par M.-J. LAGRANGE. (Études bibl.) Paris 1932.
— *La révélation d'Hermès Trismégiste* I–II. (Études bibl.) Paris 1944–1949.
— Grecs et sages orientaux, in *Rev. de l'Hist. des Rel.* 130 (1945), pp. 29–41.
FIEBIG, P., *Altjüdische Gleichnisse und die Gleichnisse Jesu*. Tübingen, Leipzig 1904.
— *Der Erzählungsstil der Evangelien* im Lichte des rabbinischen Erzählungsstils untersucht, zugleich ein Beitrag zum Streit um die „Christusmythe". (Unters. z. N. T. 11.) Leipzig 1925.
— *Rabbinische Formgeschichte und Geschichtlichkeit Jesu*. Leipzig [1931].
FILSON, F. V., The Christian Teacher in the First Century, in *Journ. of Bibl. Lit.* 60 (1941), pp. 317–328.
FINKELSTEIN, L., Introductory Study to *Pirqe Abot*, in *Journ. of Bibl. Lit.* 57(1938), pp. 13–50.
— The Transmission of the Early Rabbinic Traditions, in *Hebr. Un. Coll. Ann.* 16 (1941), pp. 115–135.
FLUSSER, D., Two Notes on the Midrash on 2 Sam. VII, in *Isr. Explor. Journ.* 9 (1959), pp. 99–109.
FOERSTER, W., Die δοκοῦντες in Gal 2, in *Zeitschr. f. d. Neutest. Wiss.* 36 (1937), pp. 286–292.
FOHRER, G., Die Gattung der Berichte über symbolische Handlungen der Propheten, in *Zeitschr. f. d. Alttest. Wiss.* 64 (1952), pp. 101–120.
— *Die symbolischen Handlungen der Propheten*. (Abh. z. Theol. d. A. u. N. T. 25.) Zürich 1953.
FREEMAN, K. J., *Schools of Hellas*. An Essay on the Practice and Theory of Ancient Greek Education from 600 to 300 B. C. 3rd ed. London 1922.
FRIDRICHSEN, A., Die Apologie des Paulus Gal. 1, in *Norsk Teol. Tidsskrift Bihefte* 21 (1920), pp. 53–76.
— Exegetisches zum Neuen Testament, in *Coni. Neot.* 7 (1942), pp. 4–8.
— *The Apostle and his Message*. (Uppsala Univ. Årsskrift 1947:3.) Uppsala, Leipzig 1947.

GADD, C. J., *Teachers and Students in the Oldest Schools*. London 1956.
GAECHTER, P., *Petrus und seine Zeit*. Neutestamentliche Studien. Insbruck, Wien, München 1958.
GÄRTNER, B., Missionspredikan i Apostlagärningarna, in *Sv. Exeg. Årsbok* 15 (1950), pp. 34–54.
— The Habakkuk Commentary (DSH) and the Gospel of Matthew, in *Studia Theol.* 8 (1954), pp. 1–24.
— *The Areopagus Speech and Natural Revelation*. (Acta Sem. Neot. Ups. 21.) Diss. Uppsala. Uppsala, Lund, Copenhagen 1955.
GANDZ, S., The knot in the Hebrew literature, or from the knot to the alphabet, in *Isis* 14 (1930), pp. 189–214.
— The Robeh רוֹבֶה or the Official Memorizer of the Palestinian Schools, in *Proceed. of the Amer. Acad. for Jew. Research* 7 (1935 36), pp. 5–12.
— The Dawn of Literature. Prolegomena to a history of unwritten literature, in *Osiris* 7 (1939), pp. 261–522.

GEIGER, A., *Urschrift und Übersetzungen der Bibel* in ihrer Abhängigkeit von der innern Entwicklung des Judentums. 2nd ed. Frankfurt a. M. 1928.

GERHARDSSON, B., *The Good Samaritan — the Good Shepherd?* (Coni. Neot. 16.) Lund, Copenhagen 1958.

— Djuren vid Jesu krubba, in *Från bygd och vildmark* 47 (1960), pp. 23–34.

— Review of A. H. J. GUNNEWEG, Mündliche und schriftliche Tradition der vorexilischen Prophetenbücher, in *Sv. Exeg. Årsbok* 25 (1960), pp. 175–181.

GERLEMAN, G., *Synoptic Studies in the Old Testament*. (Lunds Univ. Årsskrift, N. F. I, 44:5.) Lund 1948.

GERTNER, M., The Masorah and the Levites, in *Vet. Test.* 10 (1960), pp. 241–272.

GINZBERG, L., Beiträge zur Lexikographie des Aramäischen, in *Festschrift* A. SCHWARZ, Berlin, Wien 1917, pp. 329–360.

— Tamid the Oldest Treatise of the Mishnah, in *Journ. of Jew. Lore and Philos.* 1 (1919), pp. 33–44, 197–209, 265–295.

— *Eine unbekannte jüdische Sekte* I. New York 1922.

GLAUE, P., *Die Vorlesung heiliger Schriften im Gottesdienste* I. Bis zur Entstehung der altkatholischen Kirche. Habilit.-schr. Giessen. Berlin 1907.

GOLDBERGER, I., Der Talmid Chacham, in *Monatsschr. f. Gesch. u. Wiss. d. Judent.* 68 (1924), pp. 211–225, 291–307.

GOPPELT, L., Tradition nach Paulus, in *Kerygma und Dogma* 4 (1958), pp. 213–233.

GORDIS, R., *The Biblical Text in the Making*: A Study of the Kethib-Qere. Diss. Philadelphia. Philadelphia 1937.

— The following articles in *The Univ. Jew. Enc.* I–II, New York 1948: Academies, I, pp. 63–67; Beruriah (Valeria), II, p. 243.

DE GRAAF, H. T., *De Joodsche Wetgeleerden in Tiberias van 70-400 n. C.* Bijdrage tot de Geschiedbeschrijving der School van Tiberias. Diss. Groningen. Groningen 1902.

GRANT, R. M., *The Letter and the Spirit*. London 1957.

GRASBERGER, L., *Erziehung und Unterricht im klassischen Alterthum*, mit besonderer Rücksicht auf die Bedürfnisse der Gegenwart, nach den Quellen dargestellt: II, Die Turnschule der Knaben. Würzburg 1866.

GRAY, G. B., *The Forms of Hebrew Poetry*. Considered with Special Reference to the Criticism and Interpretation of the Old Testament. London, New York, Toronto 1915.

GREENBERG, M., The Stabilization of the Text of the Hebrew Bible, Reviewed in the Light of the Biblical Materials from the Judean Desert, in *Journ. of the Amer. Orient. Soc.* 76 (1956), pp. 157–167.

GRONAU, K., *Poseidonios und die jüdisch-christliche Genesisexegese*. Leipzig, Berlin 1914.

GROSS, K., Archiv, in *Reallex. f. Ant. u. Christ.* I, Stuttgart 1950, col. 614–631.

GUDEMAN, A., The following articles in *Paulys Real-Encyclopädie d. class. Altertumswiss.*, Neue Bearb. beg. v. G. WISSOWA, hrsgeg. v. W. KROLL: Grammatik, VII, Stuttgart 1912, col. 1780–1811; Κριτικός, XI:2, Stuttgart 1922, col. 1912–1915.

GUNNEWEG, A. H. J., *Mündliche und schriftliche Tradition der vorexilischen Prophetenbücher als Problem der neueren Prophetenforschung*. (Forsch. z. Rel. u. Lit. d. A. u. N. T., N. F. 55.) Göttingen 1959.

GUTMANN, J., Archive und Archivwesen I, in *Enc. Jud.* III, Berlin 1929, col. 236–241.

GUTTMANN, A., *Das redaktionelle und sachliche Verhältnis zwischen Mišna und Tosephta*. Breslau 1928.

— The Problem of the Anonymous Mishna. A Study in the History of the Halakah, in *Hebr. Un. Coll. Ann.* 16 (1941), pp. 137–155.

— Akiba, "Rescuer of the Torah", in *Hebr. Un. Coll. Ann.* 17 (1942–43), pp. 395–421.

— The Significance of Miracles for Talmudic Judaism, in *Hebr. Un. Coll. Ann.* 20 (1947), pp. 363–406.

GUTTMANN, M., *Zur Einleitung in die Halacha* I–II. (In 32. and 36. Jahresber. d. Landes-Rabbinerschule in Budapest.) Budapest 1909–1913.

— Review of C. ALBECK, Untersuchungen über die Redaktion der Mischna, in *Monatsschr. f. Gesch. u. Wiss. d. Judent.* 69 (1925), pp. 387–393.

— Zur Entstehung des Talmuds, in *Entwicklungsstufen der jüdischen Religion* (Vorträge d. Inst. Judaicum an d. Univ. Berlin, I. Jahrg. 1925–26), Giessen 1927, pp. 43–60.

— Hantwerk II, in *Enc. Jud.* VII, Berlin 1931, col. 949–951.

HAENCHEN, E., *Die Apostelgeschichte*. (Krit.-exeg. Komm. ü. d. N. T. Begr. v. H. A. W. MEYER.) 3rd ed. Göttingen 1959.

— Quellenanalyse und Kompositionsanalyse in Act 15, in *Zeitschr. f. d. Neutest. Wiss. Beih.* 26 (1960) (Judentum, Urchristentum, Kirche. Festschrift f. Joach. JEREMIAS), pp. 153–164.

HAHN, A., ספר עוקרי הרים *The Rabbinical Dialectics*. A History of the Dialectians and Dialectics of the Mishnah and Talmud. Cincinnati 1879.

HAMMERSHAIMB, E., On the Method, Applied in the Copying of Manuscripts in Qumran, in *Vet. Test.* 9 (1959), pp. 415–418.

HANSON, R. P. C., *Origen's Doctrine of Tradition*. London 1954.

VON HARNACK, A., *Die Mission und Ausbreitung des Christentums* I. Die Mission in Wort und Tat. 4th ed. Leipzig 1924.

HAVET, L., *Manuel de critique verbale appliquée aux textes latins*. Paris 1911.

HEARD, R., The ᾿Απομνημονεύματα in Papias, Justin, and Irenaeus, in *New Test. Stud.* 1 (1954–55), pp. 122–129.

HEINEMANN, I., Die Lehre vom ungeschriebenen Gesetz in jüdischen Schrifttum, in *Hebr. Un. Coll. Ann.* 4 (1927), pp. 149–171.

— Die Kontroversen über das Wunder im Judentum der hellenistischen Zeit, in *Jubilee Volume in Hon. of* ... B. HELLER, Budapest 1941, pp. 170–191.

HEINISCH, P., *Das „Wort" im Alten Testament und im alten Orient*. Zugleich ein Beitrag zum Verständnis des Prologs des Johannesevangeliums. Münster 1922.

HEITMÜLLER, W., Zum Problem Paulus und Jesus, in *Zeitschr. f. d. Neutest. Wiss.* 13 (1912), pp. 320–337.

HELLER, B., Bet ha-Midrasch, in *Enc. Jud.* IV, Berlin 1929, col. 410–415.

HERMANIUK, M., *La Parabole Evangélique.* Enquête exégétique et critique. (Univ. Cath. Lovan. Diss. II: 38.) Paris, Louvain 1947.

HERMANN, A., Dolmetschen im Altertum, in K. THIEME, A. HERMANN, E. GLÄSSER, *Beiträge zur Geschichte des Dolmetschens* (Schr. d. Ausl.-u. Dolm.-inst. d. Joh. Gutenb.-Univ. Mainz I.), München 1956, pp. 25–60.

—, VON SODEN, W., Dolmetscher, in *Reallex. f. Ant. u. Christ.* IV, Stuttgart [1959], col. 24–49.

HIRSCHFELD, H. S., *Der Geist der talmudischen Auslegung der Bibel* I. Halachische Exegese. Berlin 1840.

HIRZEL, R., ΑΓΡΑΦΟΣ ΝΟΜΟΣ. (Abh. d. phil.-hist. Cl. d. kön. sächs. Ges. d. Wiss. 20: 1.) Leipzig 1900.

HOENIG, S. B., *The Great Sanhedrin.* A study of the origin, development, composition and functions of the *Bet Din ha-Gadol* during the Second Jewish Commonwealth. Philadelphia, New York 1953.

HOFFMANN, D., *Die erste Mischna und die Controversen der Tannaim.* (Beil. z. Jahres-Ber. d. Rabbiner-Sem. z. Berlin pro 1881-1882.) Berlin 1882.

— *Zur Einleitung in die halachischen Midraschim.* (Beil. z. Jahresber. d. Rabbiner-Sem. z. Berlin 5647, 1886–87.) Berlin [1887].

HOLSTEIN, H., La tradition des Apôtres chez saint Irénée, in *Rech. de Science Rel.* 36 (1949), pp. 229–270.

HOLTE, R., *Beatitudo och Sapientia.* Augustinus och de antika filosofskolornas diskussion om människans livsmål. Diss. Uppsala. Stockholm 1958.

HOROVITZ, J., Alter und Ursprung des Isnād, in *Der Islam* 8 (1918), pp. 39–47.

HOROVITZ, S., Midrash, in *The Jew. Enc.* VIII, New York, London 1904, pp. 548–550.

— Review of W. BACHER, Tradition und Tradenten in den Schulen Palästinas und Babyloniens, in *Monatsschr. f. Gesch. u. Wiss. d. Judent.* 60 (1916), pp. 66–73, 153–159.

HUNKIN, J. W., ,,Pleonastic" ἄρχομαι in the New Testament, in *Journ. of Theol. Stud.* 25 (1924), pp. 390–402.

HYATT, J. PH., The Dead Sea Discoveries: Retrospect and Challenge, in *Journ. of Bibl. Lit.* 76 (1957), pp. 1–12.

IBER, G., Zur Formgeschichte der Evangelien, in *Theol. Rundschau* N. F. 24 (1957–58), pp. 283–338.

IDELSOHN, A. Z., *Hebräisch-orientalischer Melodienschatz*, zum ersten Male gesammelt, erläutert und herausgegeben, I–III. *Gesänge der jemenitischen, babylonischen, persischen Juden.* Leipzig 1914–1922.

JAEGER, W., *Studien zur Entwicklungsgeschichte der Metaphysik des Aristoteles.* Berlin 1912.

— *Paideia*: the Ideals of Greek Culture. Trans. from the German Manuscript by G. HIGHET, I–III. Oxford 1939–1945. (I: 3rd ed. 1946.)

JASTROW, M., *A Dictionary of the Targumim, the Talmud Babli and Yerushalmi, and the Midrashic Literature* I–II. New York 1950.

JELSKI-GOLDIN, I., *Die innere Einrichtung des grossen Synedrions zu Jerusalem* und ihre Fortsetzung im späteren palästinensischen Lehrhause bis zur Zeit des R. Jehuda ha-Nasi. Ein Beitrag zum Verständnis und zur Würdigung der ältesten talmudischen Quellen. Diss. Leipzig. Breslau [1893].

JEREMIAS, Joach., *Golgotha*. (ΑΓΓΕΛΟΣ. Arch. f. neutest. Zeitgesch. u. Kulturkunde. Beih. 1.) Leipzig 1926.

— γραμματεύς, in *Theol. Wörterb.*, ed. G. KITTEL, I., Stuttgart 1933, pp. 740–742.

— *Die Abendmahlsworte Jesu*. 2nd ed. Göttingen 1949.

— Zur Gedankenführung in den paulinischen Briefen, in *Studia Paulina in honorem J.* DE ZWAAN, Haarlem 1953, pp. 146–154.

— *Die Gleichnisse Jesu*. 4th ed. Göttingen 1956.

— *Jerusalem zur Zeit Jesu*. Kulturgeschichtliche Untersuchung zur neutestamentlichen Zeitgeschichte. 2nd ed. Göttingen 1958.

— Paarweise Sendung im Neuen Testament, in *N. T. Essays. Studies in memory of* T. W. MANSON, Manchester 1959, pp. 136–143.

JERVELL, J., *Imago Dei*. Gen 1, 26 f. im Spätjudentum, in der Gnosis und in den paulinischen Briefen. (Forsch. z. Rel. u. Lit. d. A. u. N. T., N. F. 58.) Göttingen 1960.

— Til spørsmålet om tradisjonsgrunnlaget for Apostlenes gjerninger, in *Norsk Teol. Tidsskrift* 61 (1960), pp. 160–175.

JOHNSON, S. E., The Dead Sea Manual of Discipline and the Jerusalem Church of Acts, in *The Scrolls and the New Testament*, ed. K. STENDAHL, New York 1957, pp. 129–142.

JOUSSE, M., *Le style oral rythmique et mnémotechnique chez les verbo-moteurs*. (Archives de Philos. II:4.) Paris 1925.

— *Études sur la psychologie du geste. Les Rabbis d'Israel. Les Récitatifs rythmiques parallèles* I. Genre de la Maxime. Paris 1930.

JUSTER, J., *Les Juifs dans l'Empire romain*. Leur condition juridique, économique et sociale, I. Paris 1914.

JÜLICHER, A., *Die Gleichnisreden Jesu* I. Die Gleichnisreden Jesu im allgemeinen. 2nd ed. Freiburg in B. 1899.

KÄSEMANN, E., Die Legitimität des Apostels. Eine Untersuchung zu II Korinther 10–13, in *Zeitschr. f. d. Neutest. Wiss.* 41 (1942), pp. 33–71.

KAHLE, P., *Masoreten des Ostens*. Die ältesten punktierten Handschriften des Alten Testaments und der Targume. (Beitr. z. Wiss. v. A. T. 15.) Leipzig 1913.

— Die masoretische Überlieferung des hebräischen Bibeltextes, in H. BAUER, P. LEANDER, *Historische Grammatik der hebräischen Sprache des Alten Testaments* I, Halle a. S. 1922, § 9.

— *Masoreten des Westens* I–II. (I: Beitr. z. Wiss. v. A. T., N. F. 8; II: Beitr. z. Wiss. v. A. u. N. T., F. 3, 14.) Stuttgart 1927–1930.

— *The Cairo Geniza*. 2nd ed. Oxford 1959.

KAMINKA, A. *Studien zur Septuaginta* an der Hand der zwölf kleinen Prophetenbücher. (Schr. d. Ges. z. Förder. d. Wiss. d. Judent. 33.) Frankfurt a.M. 1928.

— Septuaginta und Targum zu Proverbia, in *Hebr. Un. Coll. Ann.* 8–9 (1931–32), pp. 169–191.

KAPLAN, J., *The Redaction of the Babylonian Talmud.* New York 1933.

KATZ, S., *Die mündliche Lehre und ihr Dogma* I–II. I: Leipzig 1922, II: Berlin 1923.

KENYON, F., *Books and Readers in Ancient Greece and Rome.* Oxford 1932.

KILPATRICK, G. D., Gal. 2.14 ὀρθοποδοῦσιν, in *Zeitschr. f. d. Neutest. Wiss. Beih.* 21 (1954) (Neutest. Stud. f. R. BULTMANN), pp. 269–274.

— Galatians 1:18 ΙΣΤΟΡΗΣΑΙ ΚΗΦΑΝ, in *N. T. Essays. Studies in memory of* T. W. MANSON, Manchester 1959, pp. 144–149.

KITTEL, G., *Die Probleme des palästinischen Spätjudentums und das Urchristentum.* (Beitr. z. Wiss. v. A. u. N. T., F. 3,1.) Stuttgart 1926.

KLAUSER, T., Auswendiglernen, in *Reallex. f. Ant. u. Christ.* I, Stuttgart 1950, col. 1030–1039.

— see KURFESS, A., KLAUSER, T.

KLEIN, G., Galater 2,6–9 und die Geschichte der Jerusalemer Urgemeinde, in *Zeitschr. f. Theol. u. Kirche* 57 (1960), pp. 275–295.

KLEIN, H., Gemara and Sebara, in *Jew. Quart. Rev.* 38 (1947–48), pp. 67–91.

— Gemara Quotations in Sebara, in *Jew. Quart. Rev.* 43 (1952–53), pp. 341–363.

— Some Methods of Sebara, in *Jew. Quart. Rev.* 50 (1959–60), pp. 124–146.

KLEIN, S., BIALOBLOCKI, S., Akademien, talmudische, in *Enc. Jud.* I, Berlin 1928, col. 1171–1216.

KLOSTERMANN, E., Zur Apologie des Paulus Galater 1,10–2,21, in *Gottes ist der Orient, Festschrift f.* O. EISSFELDT, Berlin 1959, pp. 84–87.

KLÜGER, H., *Über Genesis und Composition der Halachasammlung Edujot.* Diss. Leipzig. Breslau 1895.

KNOX, W. L., *St Paul and the Church of Jerusalem.* Cambridge 1925.

KOEP, L., *Das himmlische Buch in Antike und Christentum.* Eine religionsgeschichtliche Untersuchung zur altchristlichen Bildersprache. (Theophaneia. Beitr. z. Rel.-u. Kirchengesch. d. Altert. 8.) Bonn 1952.

— Buch I, and Buch IV (himmlisch), in *Reallex. f. Ant. u. Christ.* II, Stuttgart 1954, col. 664–688, and 725–731 respectively.

KÖSTER, H., *Synoptische Überlieferung bei den apostolischen Vätern.* (Texte u. Unters. z. Gesch. d. altchristl. Lit. 65; V. R., 10.) Berlin 1957.

KOTTEK, H., Die Hochschulen in Palästina und Babylonien, in *Jahrb. d. Jüd.-Lit. Gesellsch.* 3 (1905), pp. 131–190.

KRAMER, S. N., *Schooldays*: a Sumerian Composition Relating to the Education of a Scribe. (Museum Monogr.) Philadelphia [1949]. (Reprinted from *Journ. of the Amer. Orient. Soc.* 69, 1949, pp. 199–215).

KRAUSS, S., *Griechische und lateinische Lehnwörter im Talmud, Midrasch und Targum* II. Berlin 1899.

— Die Versammlungsstätten der Talmudgelehrten, in *Festschrift z.* I. LEWY, Breslau 1911, pp. 17–35.

— *Talmudische Archäologie* III. Leipzig 1912.

— Apostel, in *Enc. Jud.* III, Berlin 1929, col. 1–10.

— Outdoor Teaching in Talmudic Times, in *Journ. of Jew. Stud.* 1 (1948–49), pp. 82–84.

KREDEL, E. M., Der Apostelbegriff in der neueren Exegese. Historisch-kritische Darstellung, in *Zeitschr. f. Kath. Theol.* 78 (1956), pp. 169–193, 297–305.

KROLL, W., Rhetorik, in *Paulys Real-Encyclopädie d. class. Altertumswiss.* Neue Bearb. beg. v. G. WISSOWA, hrsgeg. v. W. KROLL u. K. MITTEL-HAUS. Suppl. VII, Stuttgart 1940, col. 1039–1138.

KUHL, C., Schreibereigentümlichkeiten. Bemerkungen zur Jesajarolle (DSIa), in *Vet. Test.* 2 (1952), pp. 307–333.

KUNKEL, W., *Herkunft und soziale Stellung der römischen Juristen.* (Forsch. z. Röm. Recht 4.) Weimar 1952.

KURFESS, A., KLAUSER, T., Akrostichis, in *Reallex. f. Ant. u. Christ.* I, Stuttgart 1950, col. 235–238.

KUTSCH, E., מִקְרָא, in *Zeitschr. f. d. Alttest. Wiss.* 65 (1953), pp. 247–253.

KÜBLER, B., Rechtsschulen, and Rechtsunterricht, in *Paulys Real-Encyclopädie d. class. Altertumswiss.* Neue Bearb. beg. v. G. WISSOWA, hrsgeg. v. W. KROLL u. K. WITTE. R-Z:l, Stuttgart 1914, col. 380–394, and 394–405 respectively.

KÜMMEL, W. G., Jesus und der jüdische Traditionsgedanke, in *Zeitschr. f. d. Neutest. Wiss.* 33 (1934), pp. 105–130.

— see LIETZMANN, H., *Comm. Cor.*

KÜRZINGER, J., Τύπος διδαχῆς und der Sinn von Röm. 6, 17 f., in *Bibl.* 39 (1958), pp. 156–176.

— Das Papiaszeugnis und die Erstgestalt des Matthäusevangeliums, in *Bibl. Zeitschr. N. F.* 4 (1960), pp. 19–38.

LAGRANGE, M.-J., *Évangile selon Saint Luc.* (Études bibl.) 7th ed. Paris 1948.

LALAND, E., Die Martha-Maria-Perikope Lukas 10,38–42, in *Studia Theol.* 13 (1959), pp. 70–85.

LANDERSDORFER, S., Schule und Unterricht im alten Babylonien (Ein Beitrag zur Geschichte des Schulwesens.), in *Blätter f. d. Gymnasial-Schulwesen* 45 (1909), pp. 577–624.

LAUTERBACH, J. Z., The following articles in *The Jew. Enc.* VII, New York, London 1904: Megillat Setarim, p. 427; Midrash Halakah, pp. 569–572; Mishnah, pp. 609–619; Mnemonics, pp. 631–632.

— The Name of the Rabbinical Schools and Assemblies in Babylon, in *Hebr. Un. Coll. Jubilee Volume,* Cincinnati 1925, pp. 211–222.

— The Belief in the Power of the Word, in *Hebr. Un. Coll. Ann.* 14 (1939), pp. 287–302.

— The following articles in *Rabbinic Essays,* Cincinnati 1951: The Sadducees and Pharisees, pp. 23–48; Midrash and Mishnah. A Study in the Early History of the Halakah, pp. 163–256.

VAN DER LEEUW, G., *Phänomenologie der Religion.* (Neue theol. Grundrisse.) 2nd ed. Tübingen 1956.

LEIPOLDT, J., MORENZ, S., *Heilige Schriften.* Betrachtungen zur Religionsgeschichte der antiken Mittelmeerwelt. Leipzig 1953.

— Buch II, in *Reallex. f. Ant. u. Christ.* II, Stuttgart 1954, col. 688–717.

LEVIAS, C., Word Studies, in *Hebr. Un. Coll. Ann.* 1904, pp. 147–153.

LEVY, J., *Wörterbuch über die Talmudim und Midraschim* I–IV. 2nd ed. Berlin, Wien 1924.

LEVY-BRÜHL, L., *Das Denken der Naturvölker.* Wien, Leipzig 1921.

LEWIT, J., *Darstellung der theoretischen und praktischen Pädagogik im jüdischen Altertume* nach talmudischen Quellen unter vergleichender Berücksichtigung des gleichzeitigen Schrifttumes. Diss. Erlangen. Berlin 1895.

LEWY, H., Aristotle and the Jewish Sage According to Clearchus of Soli, in *The Harv. Theol. Rev.* 31 (1938), pp. 205–235.

LEWY, I. (J.), *Über einige Fragmente aus der Mischna des Abba Saul.* (Zweiter Ber. üb. d. Hochschule f. d. Wiss. d. Judent. in Berlin.) Berlin 1876.

— *Interpretation des I. Abschnittes des paläst. Talmud-Traktats Nesikin.* (In Jahresber. d. jüd.-theol. Sem. Fraenckel'scher Stift.) Breslau 1895.

— [A lecture] in *Jahresber. d. Jüd.-Theol. Sem. z. Breslau* 1905.

LEWY, J., The Problems Inherent in Section 70 of the Bisutun Inscription, in *Hebr. Un. Coll. Ann.* 25 (1954), pp. 169–208.

LICHTENSTEIN, H., Die Fastenrolle. Eine Untersuchung zur jüdisch-hellenistischen Geschichte, in *Hebr. Un. Coll. Ann.* 8–9 (1931–32), pp. 257–351.

LIEBERMAN, S., *Hellenism in Jewish Palestine.* Studies in the Literary Transmission, Beliefs, and Manners of Palestine in the I Century B.C.E.– IV Century C.E. New York 1950.

LIETZMANN, H., *Geschichte der Alten Kirche* I. Die Anfänge. Berlin, Leipzig 1932.

— *An die Korinther* I–II. Vierte von W. G. KÜMMEL ergänzte Aufl. (Handb. z. N. T. 9.) Tübingen 1949.

LIGHTFOOT, R. H., *The Gospel Message of St. Mark.* Oxford 1950.

LINDESKOG, G., Logiastudien, in *Studia Theol.* 4 (1950), pp. 129–189.

LINTON, O., „Nicht über das hinaus was geschrieben steht", in *Theol. Stud. u. Krit.* 102 (1930), pp. 425–437.

— *Das Problem der Urkirche in der neueren Forschung.* Eine kritische Darstellung. Diss. Uppsala. Uppsala 1932.

— Paulus och juridiken, in *Sv. Teol. Kvartalskrift* 21 (1945), pp. 173–192.

— The Third Aspect. A Neglected Point of View. A Study in Gal. i–ii and Acts ix and xv, in *Studia Theol.* 3 (1949), pp. 79–95.

— Lag 2., in I. ENGNELL, A. FRIDRICHSEN, *Sv. Bibl. Uppslagsverk* II, Gävle 1952, col. 10–16.

LJUNGMAN, H., *Das Gesetz erfüllen.* Matth. 5, 17 ff. und 3,15 untersucht. (Lunds Univ. Årsskrift, N. F. I, 50:6.) Lund 1954.

LÖHR, M., Alphabetische und alphabetisierende Lieder im Alten Testament, in *Zeitschr. f. d. Alttest. Wiss.* 25 (1905), pp. 173–198.

— Psalm 7 9 10, in *Zeitschr. f. d. Alttest. Wiss.* 36 (1916), pp. 225–237.

Löw, L., *Graphische Requisiten und Erzeugnisse bei den Juden* II. (Beitr. z. jüd. Alterth.-Kunde v. L. Löw I, 2.) Leipzig 1871.

— Die Tradition, in *Gesammelte Schriften* I, Szegedin 1889, pp. 241–317.

LÖVESTAM, E., *Äktenskapet i Nya Testamentet.* Diss. Lund. Lund 1950.

LOEWINGER, S., The Variants of DSI II, in *Vet. Test.* 4 (1954), pp. 155–163.

MAASS, F., Von den Ursprüngen der rabbinischen Schriftauslegung, in *Zeitschr. f. Theol. u. Kirche* 52 (1955), pp. 129–161.

MACDONALD, D. B., *The Hebrew Literary Genius*, An Interpretation Being an Introduction to the Reading of the Old Testament. Princeton 1933.

MAIER, J., Zum Begriff יחד in den Texten von Qumran, in *Zeitschr. f. d. Alttest. Wiss.* 72 (1960), pp. 148–166.

MANÉK, J., The Apostle Paul and the Empty Tomb, in *Nov. Test.* 2 (1957–58), pp. 276–280.

MANN, J., *The Bible as Read and Preached in the Old Synagogue*. A Study in the Cycles of the Readings from Torah and Prophets, as well as from Psalms, and in the Structure of the Midrashic Homilies, I. The Palestinian Triennial Cycle: Genesis and Exodus. Cincinnati 1940.

MANSON, T. W., The Argument from Prophecy, in *Journ. of Theol. Stud.* 46 (1945), pp. 129–136.

— *The Church's Ministry*. London 1948.

— *The Servant-Messiah*. A Study of the Public Ministry of Jesus. Cambridge 1953.

— Review of Joach. JEREMIAS, Die Gleichnisse Jesu, in *New Test. Stud.* 1 (1954–55), pp. 57–62.

MANSON, W., The ΕΓΩ ΕΙΜΙ of the Messianic Presence in the New Testament, in *Journ. of Theol. Stud.* 48 (1847), pp. 137–145.

— *The Gospel of Luke*. (The Moffat N. T. Comm.) 6th impr. London 1948.

MARMORSTEIN, A., La réorganisation du doctorat en Palestine au troisième siècle, in *Rev. des Ét. Juives* 66 (1913), pp. 44–53.

MARROU, H.(-)I., ΜΟΥΣΙΚΟΣ ΑΝΗΡ. Étude sur les Scènes de la Vie Intellectuelle figurant sur les Monuments Funéraires Romains. Diss. Paris. Grenoble 1937.

— *Saint Augustin et la fin de la culture antique*. Paris 1938.

— *Histoire de l'éducation dans l'antiquité*. 4th ed. Paris 1958.

MARTIN, M., *The Scribal Character of the Dead Sea Scrolls* I–II. (Bibl. du Muséon 44–45.) Louvain 1958.

MARX, A., Strack's Introduction to the Talmud and Midrash, in *Jew. Quart. Rev.* 13 (1922–23), pp. 352–365.

MASSAUX, É., *Influence de l'Évangile de saint Matthieu sur la littérature chrétienne avant saint Irénée*. (Univ. Cath. Lovan. Diss. II: 42.) Louvain, Gembloux 1950.

MEISSNER, B., *Babylonien und Assyrien* II. (Kulturgesch. Bibl.) Heidelberg 1925.

MENOUD, PH.-H., Jésus et ses témoins. Remarques sur l'unité de l'œuvre de Luc, in *Église et Théologie* 23 (1960), pp. 7–20.

MENSCHING, G., *Das heilige Wort*. Eine religionsphänomenologische Untersuchung. (Unters. z. allgem. Relgionsgesch. 9.) Bonn 1937.

MENTZ, A., *Geschichte der Kurzschrift*. Wolfenbüttel [1949].

METZGER, B. M., The Formulas Introducing Quotations of Scripture in the NT and the Mishnah, in *Journ. of Bibl. Lit.* 70 (1951), pp. 297–307.

— The Furniture in the Scriptorium at Qumran, in *Rev. de Qumr.* 1 (1958–59), pp. 509–515.

358

MEYER, E., *Ursprung und Anfänge des Christentums* III. 1st–3rd ed. Stuttgart, Berlin 1923.

MEYER, R., Der 'Am hā-'Āreṣ. Ein Beitrag zur Religionssoziologie Palästinas im ersten und zweiten nachchristlichen Jahrhundert, in *Judaica* 3 (1947), pp. 169–199.

MICHEL, O., *Paulus und seine Bibel.* Gütersloh 1929.

— μιμνήσκομαι κτλ., in *Theol. Wörterb.*, ed. G. KITTEL, IV, Stuttgart 1942, pp. 678–687.

MIELZINER, M., *Introduction to the Talmud*, Historical and Literary Introduction, Legal Hermeneutics of the Talmud, Talmudical Terminology and Methodology, Outlines of Talmudical Ethics. 3rd ed. New York 1925.

MILIK, J. T., Le travail d'édition des manuscrits du Désert de Juda, in *Suppl. to Vet. Test.* 4 (1947), pp. 17–26.

— Review of P. WERNBERG-MØLLER, The Manual of Discipline translated and annotated, in *Rev. Bibl.* 67 (1960), pp. 410–416.

MILLER, N. E., DOLLARD, J., *Social Learning and Imitation.* New Haven [1941] 1946.

MIRSKY, S. K., Types of Lectures in the Babylonian Academies, in *Essays on Jewish Life and Thought Presented in Honour of* S. W. BARON, New York 1959, pp. 375–402.

MOE, O., *Paulus und die evangelische Geschichte.* Zugleich ein Beitrag zur Vorgeschichte der Evangelien. Diss. Norge. Leipzig 1912.

MOLLAND, E., Irenaeus of Lugdunum and the Apostolic Succession, in *The Journ. of Eccl. Hist.* 1 (1950), pp. 12–28.

MOORE, G. F., *Judaism in the First Centuries of the Christian Era.* The Age of the Tannaim, I–III. Cambridge, Mass. 1927–1930.

MORENZ, S., see LEIPOLDT, J., MORENZ, S.

MORGENTHALER, R., *Die lukanische Geschichtsschreibung als Zeugnis.* I: Gestalt, II: Gehalt. (Abh. z. Theol. d. A. u. N. T. 14–15.) Zürich 1949.

MORRIS, N., *The Jewish School.* An Introduction to the History of Jewish Education. London 1937.

MOULE, C. F. D., The Use of Parables and Sayings as Illustrative Material in Early Christian Catechesis, in *Journ. of Theol. Stud.* N. S. 3 (1952), pp. 75–79.

MOWINCKEL, S., Oppkomsten av profetlitteraturen, in *Norsk Teol. Tidsskrift* 43 (1942), pp. 65–111.

MULLINS, T. Y., Papias on Mark's Gospel, in *Vig. Christ.* 14 (1960), pp. 216–224.

MUNCK, J., La vocation de l'Apôtre Paul, in *Studia Theol.* 1 (1947), pp. 131–145.

— *Paulus und die Heilsgeschichte.* (Acta jutlandica 26: 1.) Aarhus, Copenhagen 1954.

— Presbyters and Disciples of the Lord in Papias. Exegetic Comments on Eusebius, Ecclesiastical History, III, 39, in *The Harv. Theol. Rev.* 52 (1959), pp. 223–243.

MURRAY, G., The Beginnings of Grammar, or First Attempts at a Science of Language in Greece, in *Greek Studies*, Oxford 1946, pp. 171–191.

NACHMANSON, E., *Der griechische Buchtitel.* Einige Beobachtungen. (Göteborgs Högskolas Årsskrift 47, 1941:19.) Göteborg 1941.

NIEDER, L., *Die Motive der religiös-sittlichen Paränese in den paulinischen Gemeindebriefen.* Ein Beitrag zur paulinischen Ethik. (Münch. theol. Stud. I: 12.) München 1956.

NIELSEN, E., *Oral Tradition.* A Modern Problem in Old Testament Introduction. (Stud. in Bibl. Theol. 11.) London 1954.

— *Schechem.* A Traditio-historical Investigation. Diss. Aarhus. Copenhagen 1955.

NILSSON, M. P., *Die hellenistische Schule.* München 1955.

NÖTSCHER, F., Himmlische Bücher und Schicksalsglaube in Qumran, in *Rev. de Qumr.* 1 (1958–59), pp. 405–411.

NORDEN, E., *Agnostos Theos.* Untersuchungen zur Formgeschichte religiöser Rede. Leipzig, Berlin 1913.

— *Die antike Kunstprosa* von VI. Jahrhundert v. Chr. bis in die Zeit der Renaissance, I. 3rd ed. Leipzig, Berlin 1915.

NYBERG, H. S., Das textkritische Problem des Alten Testaments am Hoseabuche demonstriert, in *Zeitschr. f. d. Alttest. Wiss.* 52 (1934), pp. 241–254.

— *Studien zum Hoseabuche.* Zugleich ein Beitrag zur Klärung des Problems der alttestamentlichen Textkritik. Uppsala 1935.

ODEBERG, H., Normativ judendom, in *Norsk Teol. Tidsskrift* 30 (1929), pp. 88–114.

— *The Aramaic Portions of Bereshit Rabba.* With Grammar of Galilæan Aramaic, I–II. (Lunds Univ. Årsskrift, N. F. I, 36:3.) Lund, Leipzig 1939.

— *Kristus och Skriften.* 3rd ed. Jönköping 1950.

— *Pauli brev till korintierna.* (Tolkning av N. T. 7.) 2nd ed. Stockholm 1953.

— *Skriftens studium, inspiration och auktoritet.* Stockholm 1954.

OEPKE, A., Irrwege der neueren Paulusforschung, in *Theol. Literaturzeit.* 77 (1952), col. 449–458.

ÖSTBORN, *Tōrā in the Old Testament.* A Semantic Study. Diss. Uppsala. Lund 1945.

OLIVER, J. H., *The Athenian Expounders of the Sacred and Ancestral Law.* Baltimore 1950.

ORCHARD, J. B., Thessalonians and the Synoptic Gospels, in *Bibl.* 19 (1938), pp. 19–42.

ORLINSKY, H. M., Problems of Kethib-Qere, in *Journ. of the Amer. Orient. Soc.* 60 (1940), pp. 30–45.

— Notes on the Present State of the Textual Criticism of the Judean Biblical Cave Scrolls, in *A Stubborn Faith, Papers ... Presented to Honor* W. A. IRWIN, Dallas 1956, pp. 117–131.

— The Origin of the Kethib-Qere System. A New Approach, in *Suppl. to Vet. Test.* 7 (1960), pp. 184–192.

OSBORN, E. F., Teaching and Writing in the First Chapter of the Stromateis of Clement of Alexandria, in *Journ. of Theol. Stud.* N. S. 10 (1959), pp. 335–343.

360

PARSONS, E. A., *The Alexandrian Library*, Glory of the Hellenic World, Its Rise, Antiquities, and Destructions. London 1952.

PAUTREL, R., Des abréviations subies par quelques sentences de Jésus dans la rédaction synoptique, in *Rech. de Science Rel.* 24 (1934), pp. 244–365.

— Les canons du mashal rabbinique, in *Rech. de Science Rel.* 26 (1936), pp. 5–45.

PEDERSEN, J., *Israel*. Its Life and Culture, I–II. London, Copenhagen 1926.

— *Den arabiske bog.* København 1946.

PERLER, O., Arkandisziplin, in *Reallex. f. Ant. u. Christ.* I, Stuttgart 1950, col. 667–676.

PERLOW, T., *L'éducation et l'enseignement chez les Juifs à l'époque talmudique.* Paris 1931.

PERLS, A., Der Minhag im Talmud, in *Festschrift z. I.* LEWY, Breslau 1911, pp. 66–75.

— Das Plagium, in *Monatsschr. f. Gesch. u. Wiss. d. Judent.* 58 (1914), pp. 305–322.

PERSSON, A. W., *Die Exegeten und Delphi.* (Lunds Univ. Årsskrift, N. F. I, 14: 22.) Lund 1918.

PETERSON, E., ΕΙΣ ΘΕΟΣ. Epigraphische, formgeschichtliche und religionsgeschichtliche Untersuchungen. (Forsch. z. Rel. u. Lit. d. A. u. N. T., N. F. 24.) Göttingen 1926.

— Zu Apostelgeschichte 13,1 f., in *Nuntius Sodal. Neot. Ups.* 2 (1949), col. 9–10.

PINNER, H. L., *The World of Books in Classical Antiquity.* Leiden 1948.

PROCKSCH, O., Der hebräische Schreiber und sein Buch, in *Von Büchern und Bibliotheken* ... E. KUHNERT ... *dargebracht*, Berlin 1928, pp. 1–15.

PUUKKO, A. F., Paulus und das Judentum, in *Studia Orientalia* 2 (1928), pp. 1–87.

RABIN, C., The Dead Sea Scrolls and the History of the Old Testament Text, in *Journ. of Theol. Stud.* N. S. 6 (1955), pp. 174–182.

— *Qumran Studies.* (Scripta judaica 2.) Oxford 1957.

RANFT, J., *Der Ursprung des katholischen Traditionsprinzips.* Würzburg 1931.

REICKE, B., A Synopsis of Early Christian Preaching, in A. FRIDRICHSEN et alii, *The Root of Vine*, Essays in Biblical Theology, London 1953, pp. 128–160.

— *Glaube und Leben der Urgemeinde.* Bemerkungen zu Apg. 1–7. (Abh. z. Theol. d. A. u. N. T. 32.) Zürich 1957.

— The Constitution of the Primitive Church in the Light of Jewish Documents, in *The Scrolls and the New Testament*, ed. K. STENDAHL, New York 1957, pp. 143–156.

RENGSTORF, K. H., The following articles in *Theol. Wörterb.*, ed. G. KITTEL, Stuttgart 1933 ff.: ἀπόστολος, I, 1933, pp. 406–44 8;διδάσκω κτλ., II, 1935, pp. 138–168; μανθάνω κτλ., IV, 1942, pp. 392–465.

RESCH, A., *Der Paulinismus und die Logia Jesu* in ihrem gegenseitigen Verhältnis untersucht. (GEBHARDT, HARNACK, Texte d. altchristl. Lit. N. F. 12.) Leipzig 1904.

REYNDERS, D. B., Paradosis. Le progrès de l'idée de tradition jusqu'à saint Irénée, in *Rech. de Théol. Anc. et Médiév.* 5 (1933), pp. 155–191.

RICHARDSON, H. N., Some Notes on lQSa, in *Journ. of Bibl. Lit.* 76 (1957), pp. 108–122.

RIESENFELD, H., Den nytestamentliga textens historia, in G. LINDESKOG, A. FRIDRICHSEN, H. RIESENFELD, *Inledning till Nya Testamentet.* Stockholm 1951.

— Tradition und Redaktion im Markusevangelium, in *Zeitschr. f. d. Neutest. Wiss. Beih.* 21 (1954) (Neutest. Stud. f. R. BULTMANN), pp. 157–167.

— Apostel, in *Die Rel. in Gesch. u. Gegenw.*, I, 3rd ed., Tübingen 1957, col. 497–499.

— The Gospel Tradition and its Beginnings. A Study in the Limits of 'Formgeschichte', in *Studia Evangelica* (=Texte u. Unters. z. Gesch. d. altchristl. Lit. 73; V. R. 18), Berlin 1959, pp. 43–65. Also printed separately, London 1957.

— Das Bildwort vom Weizenkorn bei Paulus (zu 1 Cor 15), in *Festschrift* E. KLOSTERMANN, Berlin 1961, pp. 51–63.

— Observations on the Question of the Self-Consciousness of Jesus, in *Sv. Exeg. Årsbok* 25 (1960), pp. 23–36.

RIGAUX, B., *Saint Paul. Les épîtres aux Thessaloniciens.* (Études bibl.) Paris, Gembloux 1956.

— Die „Zwölf" in Geschichte und Kerygma, in *Der historische Jesus und der kerygmatische Christus.* Beiträge zum Christusverständis in Forschung und Verkündigung. Hrsgeg. v. H. RISTOW, K. MATTHIAE, Berlin 1960, pp. 468–486.

RINGGREN, H., Oral and Written Transmission in the O. T. Some observations, in *Studia Theol.* 3 (1949), pp. 34–59.

ROBERTS, B. J., *The Old Testament Text and Versions.* The Hebrew Text in Transmission and the History of the Ancient Versions. Cardiff 1951.

— The Dead Sea Scrolls and the Old Testament Scriptures, in *Bull. of the J. Ryl. Libr.* 36 (1953–54), pp. 75–96.

— The Second Isaiah Scroll from Qumrân (IQIsb), in *Bull. of the J. Ryl. Libr.* 42 (1959), pp. 132–144.

ROBERTS, C. H., The Christian Book and the Greek Papyri, in *Journ. of Theol. Stud.* 50 (1949), pp. 155–168.

— The Codex, in *Proceed. of the Brit. Acad.* 40 (1954), pp. 169–204.

ROBINSON, T. H., *The Poetry of the Old Testament.* London 1947.

ROBSON, J., The *Isnād* in Muslim Tradition, in *Transactions from Glasgow Univ. Orient. Soc.* 15 (1955), pp. 15–26.

RÖSSLER, D., *Gesetz und Geschichte.* Untersuchungen zur Theologie der jüdischen Apokalyptik und der pharisäischen Orthodoxie. (Wissensch. Monogr. z. A. u. N. T. 3.) Neukirchen Kr. Moers 1960.

ROSENTHAL, L. A., *Über den Zusammenhang der Mischna* I–II. 2nd ed. Strassburg 1909.

— *Über den Zusammenhang, die Quellen und die Entstehung der Mischna* I–III. Berlin 1918.

ROSENZWEIG, A., Die Al-tikri-Deutungen. Ein Beitrag zur talmudischen Schriftdeutung, in *Festschrift z.* I. LEWY, Breslau 1911, pp. 204–253.

ROSSOWSKY, S., *The Cantillation of the Bible.* New York 1957.

SAHLIN, H., *Der Messias und das Gottesvolk.* Studien zur protolukanischen Theologie. (Acta Sem. Neot. Ups. 12.) Diss. Uppsala. Uppsala, Zürich 1945.

SANDYS, J. E., *A History of Classical Scholarship* I. 3rd ed. Cambridge 1921.

SCHADEWALDT, W., *Von Homers Welt und Werk.* Aufsätze und Auslegungen zur homerischen Frage. 2nd ed. Stuttgart [1951].

SCHEMMEL, F., Der Sophist Libanios als Schüler und Lehrer, in *Neue Jahrb. f. d. Klass. Altert.* 20 (1907), pp. 52–69.

— Die Hochschule von Konstantinopel im IV. Jahrhundert p. Ch. n., in *Neue Jahrb. f. d. Klass. Altert.* 22 (1908), pp. 147–168.

— Die Schule von Berytos, in *Philol. Wochenschr.* 43 (1923), col. 236–240.

SCHLIER, H., *Der Brief an die Galater.* (Krit.-exeg. Komm. ü. d. N. T. Begr. v. H. A. W. MEYER.) Göttingen 1949.

SCHMAUCH, W., *Orte der Offenbarung und der Offenbarungsort im Neuen Testament.* Göttingen 1956.

SCHMIDT, K. L., *Der Rahmen der Geschichte Jesu.* Literarkritische Untersuchungen zur ältesten Jesusüberlieferung. Berlin 1919.

— Die Stellung der Evangelien in der allgemeinen Literaturgeschichte, in ΕΥΧΑΡΙΣΤΗΡΙΟΝ, *Studien* ... H. GUNKEL ... *dargebracht*, Göttingen 1923, pp. 51–134.

— Die Kirche des Urchristentums. Eine lexikographische und biblisch-theologische Studie, in *Festgabe f.* A. DEISSMANN, Tübingen 1927, pp. 259–320.

— ἐκκλησία, in *Theol. Wörterb.*, ed. G. KITTEL, III, Stuttgart 1938, pp. 502–539.

SCHMITHALS, W., Die Häretiker in Galatien, in *Zeitschr. f. d. Neutest. Wiss.* 47 (1956), pp. 25–67.

SCHNIEWIND, J., Zur Synoptiker-Exegese, in *Theol. Rundschau* N. F. 2 (1930), pp. 129–189.

SCHOEPS, H. (-)J., *Theologie und Geschichte des Judenchristentums.* Tübingen 1949.

— *Paulus.* Die Theologie des Apostels im Lichte der jüdischen Religionsgeschichte. Tübingen 1959.

SCHOTT, S., *Die Deutung der Geheimnisse des Rituals für die Abwehr des Bösen.* Eine altägyptische Übersetzung. (Akad. d. Wiss. u. d. Lit. Abh. d. geistes- u. sozialwissensch. Kl. 1954, 5.) Wiesbaden 1954.

SCHUBART, W., *Das Buch bei den Griechen und Römern.* (Handb. d. staatl. Museen z. Berlin 12.) 2nd ed. Berlin, Leipzig 1921.

SCHUBERT, P., The Structure and Significance of Luke 24, in *Zeitschr. f. d. Neutest. Wiss. Beih.* 21 (1954) (Neutest. Stud. f. R. BULTMANN), pp. 165–186.

SCHULTHESS, O., Γραμματεῖς, in *Paulys Real-Encyclopädie d. class. Altertums-*

wiss. Neue Bearb. beg. v. G. WISSOWA, hrsgeg. v. W. KROLL, VII, Stuttgart 1912, col. 1708–1780.

SCHULZ, F., *Prinzipien des römischen Rechts.* Vorlesungen. München, Leipzig 1934.

— *History of Roman Legal Science.* Oxford 1946.

SCHULZ, S., Die Decke des Moses. Untersuchungen zu einer vorpaulinischen Überlieferung in II Cor 3.7–18, in *Zeitschr. f. d. Neutest. Wiss.* 49 (1958), pp. 1–30.

SCHÜRER, E., *Geschichte des jüdischen Volkes im Zeitalter Jesu Christi* I–III. (3rd and) 4th ed. Leipzig 1901–1909.

SCHWARZ, A., *Die Controversen der Schammaiten und Hilleliten* I. Die Erleichterungen der Schammaiten und die Erschwerungen der Hilleliten. Ein Beitrag zur Entwicklungsgeschichte der Halachah. Karlsruhe 1893.

— Die Hochschulen in Palästina und Babylon, in *Jahrb. f. Jüd. Gesch. u. Lit.* 2 (1899), pp. 83–102.

— *Die hermeneutische Quantitätsrelation in der talmudischen Literatur.* (23. Jahresber. d. Isr.-theol. Lehranst. in Wien.) Wien 1916.

SCHWEITZER, A., *Die Mystik des Apostels Paulus.* Tübingen 1930.

SCHWEIZER, E., πνεῦμα κτλ., E., in *Theol. Wörterb.*, ed. G. Kittel, VI, Stuttgart 1957, pp. 394–449.

— *Gemeinde und Gemeindeordnung im Neuen Testament.* (Abh. z. Theol. d. A. u. N. T. 35.) Zürich 1959.

VON SCHWIND, F. FREIH., *Zur Frage der Publikation im römischen Recht* mit Ausblicken in das altgriechische und ptolemäische Rechtsgebiet. (Münch. Beitr. z. Pap.-forsch. u. ant. Rechtsgesch. 31.) München 1940.

SEEBERG, A., *Der Katechismus der Urchristenheit.* Leipzig 1903.

— *Das Evangelium Christi.* Leipzig 1905.

— *Christi Person und Werk nach der Lehre seiner Jünger.* Leipzig 1910.

SEELIGMANN, I. L., *The Septuagint Version of Isaiah.* A Discussion of its Problems. (Mededel. en Verhandel. N° 9 van het vooraziat.-egypt. Genootsch. „Ex Oriente Lux".) Leiden 1948.

— Voraussetzungen der Midraschexegese, in *Suppl. to Vet. Test.* 1 (1953), pp. 150–181.

SEGAL, M. H., *Grammar of Mishnaic Hebrew.* Oxford 1927.

— The Promulgation of the Authoritative Text of the Hebrew Bible, in *Journ. of Bibl. Lit.* 72 (1953), pp. 35–47.

SELWYN, E. G., *The First Epistle of St. Peter.* The Greek Text with Introduction, Notes and Essays. London 1946.

SJÖBERG, E., Herrens bud i 1 Kor. 14:37, in *Sv. Exeg. Årsbok* 22–23 (1957–58), pp. 168–171.

SKEAT, T. C., The Use of Dictation in Ancient Book-production, in *Proceed. of the Brit. Acad.* 42 (1956), pp. 179–208.

SKEHAN, P. W., The Period of the Biblical Texts from Khirbet Qumrân, in *Cath. Bibl. Quart.* 19 (1957), pp. 435–440.

— The Qumran Manuscripts and Textual Criticism, in *Suppl. to Vet. Test.* 4 (1957), pp. 148–158.

SMITH, M., *Tannaitic Parallels to the Gospels*. (Journ. of Bibl. Lit. Monogr. Ser. 6.) Philadelphia 1951.

VON SODEN, W., see HERMANN, A., VON SODEN, W.

SOIRON, T., *Die Logia Jesu*. Eine literarkritische und literargeschichtliche Untersuchung zum synoptischen Problem. (Neut. Abh. VI:4.) Münster i. W. 1916.

SPICQ, C., Saint Paul et la loi des dépôts, in *Rev. Bibl.* 40 (1931), pp. 481–502.

SPIRO, A., Samaritans, Tobiads, and Judahites in Pseudo-Philo, in *Proceed. of the Amer. Acad. for Jew. Research* 20 (1951), pp. 279–355.

STÄHLIN, G., Die Gleichnishandlungen Jesu, in *Kosmos und Ekklesia, Festschrift f. W. STÄHLIN*, Kassel 1953, pp. 7–22.

STANLEY, D. M., "Become Imitators of me": the Pauline Conception of Apostolic Tradition, in *Bibl.* 40 (1959), pp. 859–877.

STARFELT, E., *Studier i rabbinsk och nytestamentlig skrifttolkning*. (Studia theol. Lund. Skr. utg. av Teol. Fak. i Lund 17.) Diss. Lund. Lund 1959.

STAUFFER, E., *Die Botschaft Jesu damals und heute*. (Dalp Taschenbücher 333.) Bern 1959.

STEIN, S., The Dietary Laws in Rabbinic and Patristic Literature, in *Studia Patr.* 2 (1957), pp. 141–154.

STENDAHL, K., Kerygma und Kerygmatisch. Von zweideutigen Ausdrücken der Predigt der Urkirche — und unserer, in *Theol. Literaturzeit.* 77 (1952), col. 715–720.

— *The School of St. Matthew* and its Use of the Old Testament. (Acta Sem. Neot. Ups. 20.) Diss. Uppsala. Lund, Copenhagen 1954.

— Paulus och samvetet, in *Sv. Exeg. Årsbok* 25 (1960), pp. 62–77.

STRACK, H. L., *Einleitung in Talmud und Midraš*. 5th ed. München 1930. (Eng. ed. *Introduction to the Talmud and Midrash*. New York, Philadelphia 1959.)

—, BILLERBECK, P., *Kommentar zum Neuen Testament aus Talmud und Midrasch* I–IV. München 1922–1928.

STRÖM, Å. V., *Vetekornet*. Studier över individ och kollektiv i Nya Testamentet med särskild hänsyn till Johannesevangeliets teologi Joh. 12:20–33. (Acta Sem. Neot. Ups. 11.) Diss. Uppsala. Stockholm 1944.

— Bibelns syn på arbetet, i *Ny Kyrkl. Tidskrift* 25 (1956), pp. 30–56.

SUNDKLER, B., *Jésus et les païens*. (Arb. u. Mitteil. aus d. neutest. Sem. z. Uppsala 6, pp. 1–38.) Uppsala 1937.

TABACHOVITZ, D., *Die Septuaginta und das Neue Testament*. (Skr. utg. av Sv. Inst. i Athen, 8°, 4.) Lund 1956.

TARDE, G., *Les lois de l'imitation*. Étude sociologique. 2nd ed. Paris 1895.

TCHERIKOVER, V., *Hellenistic Civilization and the Jews*. Trans. by S. APPLEBAUM. Philadelphia 1959 (Jerusalem 5719).

THACKERAY, H. ST. J., *The Septuagint and Jewish Worship*. A Study in Origins. (Brit. Acad. The Schweich lect. [13].) London, Oxford 1921.

The New Testament in the Apostolic Fathers, by a Committee of the Oxford Society of Historical Theology. Oxford 1905.

THEODOR, J., Midrash Haggadah, in *The Jew. Enc.* VIII, New York, London 1904, pp. 550–569.

TORREY, C. C., The Hebrew of the Geniza Sirach, in A. MARX *Jubilee Volume*, English Section, New York 1950, pp. 585–602.

DE VAUX, R., Les Grottes de Murabba'at et leurs documents. Rapport préliminaire, in *Rev. Bibl.* 60 (1953), pp. 245–267.

VERMÈS, G., *Les manuscrits du Désert de Juda.* Tournai 1953.

VAN VLIET, H., *No Single Testimony.* A Study in the Adoption of the Law of Deut. 19:15 par. into the N. T. (Studia Theol. Rheno-Traiectina 4.) Utrecht 1958.

VÖGTLE, A., *Die Tugend- und Lasterkataloge im Neuen Testament* exegetisch, religions- und formgeschichtlich untersucht. (Neutest. Abh. XVI:4–5.) Münster i. W. 1936.

— Messiasbekenntnis und Petrusverheissung. Zur Komposition Mt. 16,13–23 Par., in *Bibl. Zeitschr.* N.F. 1 (1957), pp. 252–272, 2 (1958), pp. 85–103.

DE VRIES, B., The Problem of the Relationship of the Two Talmuds to the Tosefta, in *Tarbiz* 28 (1959), pp. 158–170 (Hebr.; Eng. summary pp. III–IV).

WALDEN, J. W. H., *The Universities of Ancient Greece.* New York 1910.

WALLIS, P., Ein neuer Auslegungsversuch der Stelle I. Kor. 4, 6, τὸ μὴ ὑπὲρ ἃ γέγραπται, in *Theol. Literaturzeit.* 75 (1950), col. 506–508.

WEBER, F., *Jüdische Theologie* auf Grund des Talmud und verwandter Schriften gemeinfasslich dargestellt. 2nd ed. Leipzig 1897.

WEISE, M., Mt 5 21 f. — ein Zeugnis sakraler Rechtsprechung in der Urgemeinde, in *Zeitschr. f.d. Neutest. Wiss.* 49 (1958), pp. 116–123.

WEISS, J., *Der erste Korintherbrief* völlig neu bearb. (Krit.-exeg. Komm. ü. d. N. T. Begr. v. H. A. W. MEYER.) Göttingen 1910.

WENDEL, C., *Die griechisch-römische Buchbeschreibung verglichen mit der des Vorderen Orients.* (Hallische Monogr. 3.) Halle 1949.

— Bibliothek, in *Reallex. f. Ant. u. Christ.* II, Stuttgart 1954, col. 231–274.

WENGER, L., *Die Quellen des römischen Rechts.* (Österreich. Akad. d. Wiss. Denkschr. d. Gesamtakad. 2.) Wien 1953.

WERNBERG-MØLLER, P., Observations on the Interchange of ע and ח in the Manual of Discipline (DSD), in *Vet. Test.* 3 (1953), pp. 104–107.

WERNER, E., The Origins of Psalmody, in *Hebr. Un. Coll. Ann.* 25 (1954), pp. 327–345.

WIBBING, S., *Die Tugend- und Lasterkataloge im Neuen Testament* und ihre Traditionsgeschichte unter besonderer Berücksichtigung der Qumran-Texte. (Zeitschr. f. d. Neutest. Wiss. Beih. 25, 1959.)

WIDENGREN, G., *Literary and Psychological Aspects of the Hebrew Prophets.* (Uppsala Univ. Årsskrift 1948:10.) Uppsala, Leipzig 1948.

— *The Ascension of the Apostle and the Heavenly Book.* (*King and Saviour* III.) (Uppsala Univ. Årsskrift 1950: 7.) Uppsala, Leipzig 1950.

— Oral Tradition and Written Literature among the Hebrews in the Light of Arabic Evidence, with Special Regard to Prose Narratives, in *Acta Orient.* 23 (1959), pp. 201–262.

WIEDER, N., The Old Palestinian Ritual — New Sources, in *Journ. of Jew. Stud.* 4 (1953), pp. 30–37, 65–73.

WIESNER, L., *Die Jugendlehrer der talmudischen Zeit.* Wien 1914.

WIFSTRAND, A., Stylistic Problems in the Epistles of James and Peter, in *Studia Theol.* 1 (1947), pp. 170–182.

WIKENHAUSER, A., Die Belehrung der Apostel durch den Auferstandenen nach Apg 1, 3, in *Vom Wort des Lebens. Festschrift f.* M. MEINERTZ (Neutest. Abh. I Erg.-bd.), Münster i. W. 1951, pp. 105–113.

WILCKENS, U., Die Bekehrung des Paulus als religionsgeschichtliches Problem, in *Zeitschr. f. Theol. u. Kirche* 56 (1959), pp. 273–293.

WINDISCH, H., *Paulus und Christus.* Ein biblisch-religionsgeschichtlicher Vergleich. (Unters. z. N. T. 24.) Leipzig 1934.

WINTER, P., I Corinthians XV. 3 b–7, in *Nov. Test.* 2 (1957–58), pp. 142–150.

WOHLBERG, R., *Grundlinien einer talmudischen Psychologie.* Diss. Erlangen. Berlin 1902.

WOLFF, H. W., *Jesaja 53 im Urchristentum.* 3rd ed. Berlin 1952.

WOLFSON, H. A., *Philo.* Foundations of Religious Philosophy in Judaism, Christianity, and Islam, I–II. 2nd ed. Cambridge, Mass. 1948.

WRIGHT, L. E., *Alterations of the Words of Jesus* as Quoted in the Literature of the Second Century. (Harv. Hist. Monogr. 25.) Cambridge, Mass. 1952.

WÜST, E., Mnemonik, in *Paulys Real-Encyclopädie d. class. Altertumswiss.* Neue Bearb. beg. v. G. WISSOWA, hrsgeg. v. W. KROLL, XV: 2, Stuttgart 1932, col. 2264–2265.

ZAHN, T., *Geschichte des Neutestamentlichen Kanons* I. Das Neue Testament vor Origenes. Erlangen 1888.

ZEITLIN, S., The Halaka. Introduction to Tannaitic Jurisprudence, in *Jew. Quart. Rev.* 39 (1948–49), pp. 1–40.

ZIEBARTH, E., *Aus dem griechischen Schulwesen.* Eudemos von Milet und Verwandtes. 2nd ed. Leipzig, Berlin 1914.

ZIMMERMANN, H., Die Sammelberichte der Apostelgeschichte, in *Bibl. Zeitschr.* N. F. 5 (1961), pp. 71–82.

ZUCROW, S., *Adjustment of Law to Life in Rabbinic Literature.* Boston 1928.

ZUNZ, [L.], *Die gottesdienstlichen Vorträge der Juden,* historisch entwickelt. Ein Beitrag zur Altherthumskunde und biblischen Kritik, zur Literatur- und Religionsgeschichte. 2nd ed. Frankfurt a. M. 1892.

Index of Authors

Index of Passages

TRADITION AND TRANSMISSION IN EARLY CHRISTIANITY

Contents

Introduction

One of the basic assumptions of the form-critical school is that the early Christian Church was not interested in tradition or its transmission. Early Christianity had, of course, a tradition, as have all movements in history, but men can have and do a great deal without being conscious of it. The early Church, it is claimed, was inspired by a burning faith, and its primary concern was to spread, confirm and defend that faith. That it in fact created and preserved tradition was incidental to the real issue.

From this viewpoint the formation of tradition in early Christianity was a process, whose character was largely hidden from those who were concerned in it—i. e. the early Christians themselves. If we would examine and clarify that process we must therefore possess a degree of vision unknown in the early Church. The scholar must penetrate beneath the surface of early Christian history and lay bare the profound forces and 'motives' which gave rise, in the course of the early Church's preaching and teaching, to the formation of tradition. This is no easy task; the pioneer form-critics nevertheless undertook to solve the problem, and were in no way perturbed by its difficulties.

The process which the form-critics used, and use, is well known, and we need no more than recapitulate its main features briefly. They classify the Gospels as anonymous, popular *Kleinliteratur*. They adopt, extend and deepen the observations of the folklorists and sociologists as to the origins of such literature; they determine the laws according to which *geistiges Gut* may be born, under certain conditions, in a spiritually vital community: how it is formed and re-formed, preserved and fixed, or how it disappears—*eine Biologie der Sage*. They assume that general laws of this kind were equally effective in early Christianity, and that the growth of the early Christian *Kleinliteratur* followed the same principles.[1]

---

[1] The works of the pioneer form-critics need no introduction. The most important of these are M. Dibelius, *Die Formgeschichte des Evangeliums* (1st ed. 1919, 3rd ed. mit einem Nachtrag von G. Iber 1959, English trans. *From Tradition to Gospel*, 1934) and R. Bultmann, *Die Geschichte der synoptischen Tradition*

We are all deeply indebted to the form-critics and particularly to the pioneers of the school. Their attempt to describe and explain the origins of the early Christian Gospel tradition is bold, acute and penetrating. But the validity of its results depends on the validity of its first principles. And in this case a certain number of questions have been decided in advance. What happens, though, if certain basic assumptions prove to be unwarranted? They are by no means exempt from criticism. Is it quite certain that popular *geistiges Gut* does, in fact, originate in this way?[2] And that these conclusions apply in every conceivable situation—even the situation in which the synoptic tradition took form? Is it possible without further ado to classify the Gospels and the many different types of material in them as that type of popular *Kleinliteratur* which originates in this way? This will perhaps serve for the present. The point is that the form-critics' impressive creation has its Achilles' heel, and that is a highly vulnerable one. The ideas on which the entire programme of research is based, and which dictate the methods used and determine the results, are very far indeed from being beyond criticism. In fact they are open to serious objections.[3]

It is therefore a matter of some concern that other methods of examining the formation of early Christian tradition should be found: at least in order to subject the form-critics' work to critical examination,

---

(1st ed. 1921, 3rd—4th ed. mit Ergänzungsheft, 1958, English trans. *History of the Synoptic Tradition,* 1960). For a detailed introduction and bibliography of the extensive debate, see *Theol. Rundschau* N.F. 2 (1930), pp. 129—189 (J. Schniewind) and 24 (1957—58), pp. 283—338 (G. Iber). In the present work I refer not to the most recent form-critical studies, but to the classical basic works by Dibelius and Bultmann. The reason is of course that my criticisms are directed against *presuppositions* of the form-critical method. It is the foundations of the edifice which must be examined: not the top storey! My references are to the German editions of Dibelius' and Bultmann's books from 1959 and 1958 respectively.

[2] The early form-critics' views on the origins of popular *Kleinliteratur* must be compared with the results of modern folklore research, particularly on such questions as that of 'oral composition'. Comprehensive bibliographical references are given by Ch. H. Lohr in his article Oral Techniques in the Gospel of Matthew, in *The Cath. Bibl. Quart.* 23 (1961), pp. 403—435.

[3] In the present debate it is sometimes claimed that form-criticism is a purely *analytical* work on the problems of the Gospel tradition. As against this tendency we may advance Bultmann's excellent account in *Die Geschichte,* pp. 5—8, which makes it quite clear that form-criticism is both analysis and synthesis, and that certain synthetical attitudes form the basis of the analysis.

and to correct and complement that work. We shall discuss one such approach in the following pages. It may be briefly characterized in the following way: we shall limit our excursion into the wide fields of folklore and sociology by concentrating on the historical sphere in which the object of our investigation is located. We shall make no attempt—at least for the time being—to determine what the inner impulse may have been that actuated the unconscious minds of the persons concerned in the process. Instead we shall begin by considering the concrete framework of the historical process; we shall try to understand the customs, the methods and the main characteristics of teaching and transmission in the context in which the Gospel tradition was formed. Thus we shall be mainly concerned with the conscious element in the minds of those involved. Our aim is to work out a set of relatively reliable basic values; the attempt to lay bare the deeper secrets of the process of tradition-making must await some future occasion.[4]

Our point of departure, then, is the fact that early Christianity was born within a historical sphere in which tradition and transmission had already to some extent become conscious ideas and distinct activities. This was true of the Jewish milieu as well as the highly diversified Hellenistic world at the dawn of the Christian era. And in the New Testament, as early as in the Pauline Epistles, we find that terms like 'tradition', 'to pass on as tradition' and 'to receive as tradition' (παράδοσις, παραδιδόναι, παραλαμβάνειν) were used in connexion with sayings of Jesus, accounts of Jesus' work, and other matters of importance. This clearly gives us something like a comprehensible starting point. We might ask a simple and purely historical question: What was meant in this particular milieu by 'tradition' and how, practically speaking, did they set about transmitting this tradition—practical tradition (not expressed in words) and verbal tradition (articulated: oral or written)? It is with verbal tradition that we shall be chiefly concerned here.

To ask this question is to indicate the existence of a task for research. And it must be pointed out, in order to avoid misunderstanding, that as such it is a task having an intrinsic value as great as that of any other piece of scientific research. The history of early Christianity must

---

[4] We do not deny the need to penetrate to the deepest levels of the process of tradition. But we hold that a beginning must be made with the concrete facts of the case—with the things the people concerned do consciously, and which we can therefore see reflected most clearly in the sources.

be studied from various angles. One such approach is provided by the question we have posed here: How did the early Church proceed, technically speaking, with its work of teaching and transmitting?

The investigation of these techniques of the early Church is not an end in itself, however. It is carried out in order to provide, if possible, a foundation for a further task: that of determining the origins and early history of the Gospel material as we have it. Once we have a clear picture of the process followed by the early Church in the matter of teaching and transmission, we can turn to the synoptic material with a new question: Does this material (or any part of it) show signs of having been formed and transmitted in this deliberate, methodical way, or does it presuppose some other principle? Do there appear to be differences between material from different groups or milieus within early Christianity, or between different stages in the history of the Gospel material? Thus what is required is a new analysis of the synoptic material. The basis on which this analysis is made is not a general view of the creation of *geistiges Gut* in an anonymous collective, but concrete data on the technique of teaching and transmission in the early Christian milieu.

Once again we must emphasize that there are two separate and distinct tasks implied here, and that only by keeping them separate can we avoid the circular arguments of the form-critics. It is one thing to try to determine what the customs and methods were which set their mark on teaching and transmission in early Christianity; another to determine the extent to which the preserved traditions of Jesus were in fact formed and transmitted according to these principles.

In my book[5] *Memory and Manuscript: Oral Tradition and Written Transmission in Rabbinic Judaism and Early Christianity*[6] I have pub-

---

[5] Cf. H. Riesenfeld, The Gospel Tradition and its Beginnings, in *Texte und Unters.* 73 (1959), pp. 43—65, also printed separately (1957).

[6] Acta Semin. Neot. Upsal. 22, 1961. The second edition has appeared in 1964 (C. W. K. Gleerup Bokförlag, Lund).—Thanks to the interest shown by Professor J. G. H. Hoffmann there is a summary of the book in French: B. G-n, Mémoire et manuscrits dans le Judaïsme rabbinique et le Christianisme primitif. Adaptation française condensée de J. G. H. Hoffmann (*La Revue Réformée* No 54—1963/2, tome 14, 1963, 54 pp.).—Among sensitive and careful accounts I should like to mention in particular: J. A. Fitzmyer, Memory and Manuscript: the Origins and Transmission of the Gospel Tradition (in *Theol. Studies* 23, 1962, pp. 442—457), B. Brinkmann, review in *Scholastik* 37 (1962), pp. 426—430, and P. Benoit, Memory and Manuscript (in *Rev. Bibl.* 70, 1963, pp.

lished the results of my examination of the Jewish and early Christian techniques of transmission. It must be emphasized that this examination is still not complete. The field is so wide that it was impossible to deal with it all in a book of reasonable size. The account I have given is of an interpretation of a clearly defined area; other areas have been wholly or partially left. For instance, a broad and detailed study of popular 'pedagogics' in the various groups, trends and areas of life in the Hellenistic world would be desirable.[7] My studies have been concerned mainly with the Jewish and early Christian milieus. And in the Jewish section I have concentrated on that part which was unquestionably of most importance, viz. the Pharisaic-Rabbinic. (In my book I use, with due explanation, the simplified term 'Rabbinic Judaism'.)[8] Other groups have been dealt with only summarily, and largely in order to check whether or not the Pharisaic-Rabbinic teachers' methods were original and whether they were representative of the milieu as a whole.[9] My investigation of the early Christian stream of tradition begins with post-Apostolic Church, and then goes backward in time, via the Acts of the Apostles to Paul. This must be complemented by an analysis of the synoptic and Johannine traditions, but I have not been able to undertake such a task within the bounds of one book.[10] My investigation goes

---

269—273).—The Rabbinic section of the book has so far been reviewed by two Jewish scholars, both of whom were very positive; see the Israeli newspapers *Mitteilungsblatt* 29/9 1961 (K. Wilhelm, Christlich-theologische Doktorarbeiten zu jüdischen Themen) and *The Jerusalem Post* 18/9 1963 (A. Goldberg, Handing down tradition. Classic work on the transmission of the Written and Oral Law). [Cf. now below, n. 115.]—A number of other reviews will be mentioned below.

[7] *Memory*, pp. 15 and 193.

[8] The term 'Rabbinic Judaism' is an over-simplification in that the Pharisaic teachers of the time of the temple should not be called Rabbis (see *Memory*, p. 30). The fact that we use a simplified term for the Pharisaic-Rabbinic stream of tradition should not however be taken to mean that we are unaware of the development which separates Pharisaism of the temple period from later, fully stabilized Rabbinism. On this subject, see below, para. 2.

[9] See how the study is presented, *Memory*, pp. 30—32, 71—78, 193.

[10] Two tasks are involved here: (1) the completion of the study of the technique of teaching and transmission; (2) a comprehensive detailed study of the formal structure of the transmitted material. I hope in the not-too-distant future to be able to publish an attempt to deal with the first of these problems, by way of complement to *Memory*. As far as the second is concerned, the 'spade-work' involved is so enormous that one individual scholar can promise only a slight contribution. The field is wide open!

no further than to the threshold of the synoptic material. I have however sketched in a short final chapter some of the main lines of development which have so far appeared, and along which the study may be continued.[11]

This present monograph is a supplement to my earlier book. My aim here is to determine and discuss, against the background of certain critical articles, some of the points wherein I consider it particularly important that we should win a measure of clarity. I do not intend to try and solve the problems: only to try and define the questions.

The immediate cause of this essay is an article published by Professor M. Smith in *Journ. of Bibl. Stud.* 82 (1963), pp. 169—176, under the title *A Comparison of Early Christian and Early Rabbinic Tradition.*[12] This article passes adverse judgment on the results of my investigation, but its author criticizes without having determined the nature of the questions I am asking,[13] without taking note of the limitations of my study,[14] and without taking into account my attitude to the basic methodological issues involved.[15] In addition, his description of what I have said is very frequently incorrect.[16] In this way he has diverted attention from the special problem discussed in my book, and has instead dealt with a number of general questions.

My intention here is as follows: In the first part of this essay I shall determine the main problem and its three crucial points (para. 1), after which I shall discuss each crux in turn (para. 2—4). In the second part I shall make certain observations on the wider question of how Rabbinic tradition and early Christian tradition are to be com-

---

[11] Four times in *Memory* (pp. 15, 193, 324 and 335) I pointed out that this study must be completed by consideration of the synoptic material, but that this could not be undertaken within the bounds of the one book. This express limitation, and the fact that I closed my investigation on the threshold of the synoptic material, has been emphasized by a number of reviewers (e. g. P. Benoit, J. G. Davies and J. Dupont), but seems to have been overlooked by some of my critics. Some have called for comment on particular passages in the synoptic tradition (e. g. G. Widengren) or in the Gospel of Matthew (e. g. E. Lohse). M. Smith, too, seems to have misunderstood the course of my investigation (see below).

[12] Hereinafter referred to as *Comparison.*

[13] See below, para. 1—4.

[14] See below, especially n. 20 and 39.

[15] See the following pages with ref.

[16] See below, in particular n. 22, 30, 39, 58, 82.

pared, and what must be taken into account in this connexion (para. 5—7). The reader must excuse the many footnotes referring to *Memory and Manuscript*: the sole object of this is to answer criticism and clear away misunderstanding.[17]

I

1. The Task and its Three Crucial Points

The task we have set ourselves is that of trying to gain a concrete historical picture of the techniques of teaching and transmission used by Jesus and the early Church, in other words their 'pedagogics'.[18]

This task cannot be accomplished simply by recourse to the early Christian material, which is far too sparse. We must widen the perspective to include both Jewish and Hellenistic backgrounds. As far as the Jewish material is concerned, we do not have enough that is contemporary with Jesus and the early Church at our disposal to be able to start there. Nor does it seem possible to begin in the Old Testament documents and continue forwards in time, via the inter-testamental literature. The scattered references in the older sources are too fragmentary, and often of too uncertain interpretation, to serve as a solid basis of investigation. There seems in practice to be only one feasible method: *to move backward in time,* tracing critically the streams of tradition in the direction of their sources.[19]

There is in fact only one group of late Jewish sources in which the relevant material is clear and extensive enough to allow us to form *a sufficiently general, coherent and clear picture* of the Jewish peda-

---

[17] In this monograph I can consider only a selection of questions. A number of other important problems have been dealt with in reviews and articles. That I make no attempt to discuss them here should not be interpreted to mean that I have not taken note of them, or that I agree with the views therein put forward. Nor should the fact that I forbear to comment on those elements in Smith's account in which he has attempted to discredit my study be taken to imply that I accept his criticism on those points (e. g. *Comparison*, n. 2, p. 169 f.).

[18] In this monograph I use the term 'pedagogics' as a simplified substitute for 'technique of teaching and transmission'.

[19] Against E. Lohse's methodological criticism (review in *Theol. Zeitschr.* 18, 1962, pp. 60—62).

gogics of the time. That is the Rabbinic literature. The picture we gain
from these sources is primarily of the methods of fully developed
Rabbinism, that is from Rabbi Aqiba on. When we have determined
what the situation was at this particular time and in this particular
sphere we can trace a course backward in time to the Palestinian milieu
of the first century A. D., and then to early Christianity and Jesus.
(Then, if we wish, we may go even further back, to the OT sources,
the contents of which may conceivably stand out with a greater measure
of clarity when viewed in the light of tradition.) This retrospective
investigation must be constantly buttressed, complemented and checked
in detail by referring to the surroundings—and not least to the world
of Hellenism, from which Jewish teachers received many a fruitful
impulse.

This path leads from clarity into comparative obscurity, from a
developed form to a much less developed form. It goes without saying
that we must beware of a number of methodological snares. Anachronism and analogy based on inadequate premises must at all costs be
avoided, to mention only the worst.

It seems to me that we can best define the three crucial points in
the following three questions: (i) To what extent did the Pharisaic
teachers apply the Rabbinic principles of pedagogics during the first
century A. D.? (ii) To what extent are we justified in regarding the
pedagogics we find among the Pharisaic teachers as representative of
the normal practices of the Jewish milieu as a whole, i. e. even outside
the bounds of Pharisaism proper? (iii) To what extent did the teaching
and transmission of Jesus and the early Church follow the principles
of practical pedagogics which were common in their milieu, and to
what extent did they create new forms?

These seem to be the three foci of criticism. Smith, who has no clear
impression of the main problem I am discussing (the technique of
teaching and transmission),[20] has not himself defined these problems
with any clarity. In his criticism of my book the essential questions, as
I have defined them above, are lost amid such general problems as (i)
the relation of Rabbinism to Pharisaism, (ii) the situation of Pharisaism
in the contemporary Jewish milieu, and (iii) the relation of Jesus and

---

[20] My study is no attempt to investigate tradition as such; my concern has
been to describe the technical process by which tradition was transmitted. This
I have tried to express as clearly as possible: I have defined, motivated, repeated
myself and used italics (see pp. 14 f., 30, 71 f., etc.).

early Christianity to Pharisaism. This is to miss the significance of special problems by placing undue emphasis on general matters.

We may now proceed to a brief discussion of each of these three points in turn.

2. The Problem of Continuity

Scholars have long discussed—particularly since the publication of Moore's *Judaism*—the extent to which fully developed Rabbinism preserved the main characteristics of first-century Pharisaism. The problem has many facets. There is the question of the continuity of the various elements in religious outlook, of organization, of the efficacy of law in different areas of life, of custom and behaviour, of the techniques of Scripture exposition, and of teaching method. Examples might be multiplied. Separate questions of this kind cannot be viewed in isolation—I want to emphasize that—but they must be kept separate for the purpose of historical analysis, so as not to give rise to illegitimate general conclusions based on changes in only *one* area. Development and change in the various fields do not keep pace with one another. Pharisaism had in its care a rich and many-sided heritage from the fathers of the people. This heritage was preserved: but it was revised, corrected and enriched as well. Considerable changes took place during the revolutionary epoch between A. D. 65 and 135. But we cannot go so far as to claim that development was so uniform that changes in organization necessarily led to changes in other fields—in pedagogics, for instance—or that a change in the technique of instruction must necessarily reflect a changed organization or changes in religious belief. It is therefore wrong to allow the precise question we wish to investigate to be swallowed up by the general and diffuse question of the relationship between Pharisaism and Rabbinism. What we have to determine is the pedagogical methods they used, and the first crucial point is accordingly the question of the extent to which the Rabbis' technique of pedagogics was hereditary, traditional, and thus capable of being traced back to the first century.

My emphasis on continuity in the Pharisaic-Rabbinic stream of tradition (as far as pedagogics are concerned) has prompted Smith to issue a warning against the gross anachronism of reading back "into the period before 70 the developed rabbinic technique of ± 200".[21] I should like to

---

[21] *Comparison*, p. 169.

emphasize this warning still further. And in order to do so, and at the same time to dispose of Smith's criticism on this point, I shall give a rapid résumé of my earlier account of the development of pedagogical technique.

The methods of teaching and transmission used by Aqiba and his followers vary somewhat; there is ample evidence here of Talmudic variety. In my investigation I have however been mainly concerned to sketch the rough outlines of the Rabbinic pedagogics, and I have pointed out certain developments, divergencies, shifts and alterations by way of complementing this basic account. I have distinguished between the Tannaitic and Amoraic periods and taken pains, when quoting or using a dictum, to give the name of the Rabbi to whom it was first attributed. This enables the reader, with the help of an elementary Rabbinic index, to check the approximate age of each saying. I have also explained that it is the period from the time of Aqiba on which we see with some clarity in the Rabbinic sources. The criticism advanced against my work makes it necessary for me to re-emphasize these points.[22]

But I have also pointed out in my book[23] that we need not restrict ourselves to the period of fully stabilized Rabbinism, without the opportunity to trace a course backward in time to the Pharisaic teachers of the period of the temple. Continuity was not broken, in such matters as the basic elements of pedagogics, during the revolutionary epoch A. D. 65—135. Aqiba and his successors of course improved, developed and refined the teaching methods. But we need not penetrate to any great depth beneath the sophisticated surface in order to find that the pedagogics they practise is mainly hereditary and popular.

This is no forced and novel hypothesis. Such a view has a high degree of historical probability *a priori*. Pedagogics in Antiquity were generally characterized by a remarkable degree of conservatism. Reverence—often determined by religious considerations—for the universal religious and cultural heritage from the fathers, and for the fathers and

---

[22] Smith gives no account of the way in which I have attempted to reach a correct historical perspective: all I have said about development, changes, differences, dating, and the like. For instance, he has nothing to say about the way in which on pp. 122—170 I have indicated lines of development from Old Testament times down to the end of the Amoraic period. He seems to regard my book as merely an anachronistic comparison between "the developed rabbinic technique of ±200" and the primitive Christian tradition.

[23] See the discussion of principles in *Memory,* pp. 76—78 and 111 f.

teachers personally, left little room for pedagogical revolution. As far as Pharisaism and Rabbinism are concerned we must also remember that it was part of their conscious programme to preserve the words and the customs of the fathers inviolate. Reformers have little scope in a group of this kind. It is possible, with boldness and skill, to alter—for better or for worse—but this can only take place on a basis of what is already there; ostensibly at least it must conform to tradition.[24]

We need not confine ourselves to general observations of this kind. We claim that most of the characteristic features of Rabbinic pedagogics have a long history, *which can be traced far back into Old Testament times*.[25] I have several times in my book pointed out what the OT has to say about popular instruction, memorization and oral transmission in Palestine, centuries before Aqiba's first disciple learned his first text

---

[24] It is significant that when the Rabbis wanted to introduce something new or to alter an accepted custom they had to look for a precedent; this meant that they were often forced to strain the transmitted texts to the uttermost to find the motivation they wanted.

[25] For literature on the importance of oral tradition in ancient Israel, see references in *Memory*, p. 72. G. Widengren, in an article in *Numen* 10 (1963), pp. 42—83, entitled Tradition and Literature in Early Judaism and in the Early Church, has examined my thesis on a basis of the much-discussed question of the relationship between oral and written tradition (the relative importance of the two methods of transmission). Widengren finds that I have underestimated the importance of written tradition. My answer is that I was not concerned with that particular question. The object of my study was to examine practical methods of transmission, primarily of oral tradition, and only secondarily of written tradition (see *Memory*, p. 30). The question of the *relationship* between written and oral tradition in late Judaism and early Christianity seems to me to be extremely complex: see references in *Memory*, pp. 123 f., 27—32, 157—163 and 194—207. [Cf. now also R. A. Carlson, *David, the chosen King* (1964).]

Widengren suggests that more attention might have been paid to the Aramaic terminology of transmission. "Dr. Gerhardsson has very carefully examined the Hebrew terminology of transmission in Rabbinical circles, but he has hardly paid any attention at all to the corresponding Aramaic expressions," *Tradition*, p. 60 f. My answer is as follows. My problem is that of the *technique* of transmission. Analysis of the Hebrew terms—for Hebrew was the normal school language during the early Tannaitic period—has thrown very little light on that problem. It is therefore unlikely that analysis of the few Aramaic terms of transmission to be found in the oldest Rabbinic material or in other material from the first century B.C. to the first century A.D. will be particularly helpful. But the course of the debate on this question will show whether or not I am mistaken in this view.

by heart.[26] The methods of the Hellenistic teachers are also worth noting, having been established long before the beginning of the Christian era.[27] It is common knowledge that there were already Hellenistic schools in Palestine centuries before Christ,[28] and it is similarly worth recalling that every Jew who could read Greek must have had contact, direct or indirect, with the simple pedagogics of the Hellenistic elementary school teacher—pedagogics based on memorization.

We shall return in a moment to the question of what seems to be new in Rabbinic pedagogics. But first we must emphasize that we have never had the intention of merely antedating the fully developed, elaborate Rabbinic technique. All historical research demands a sense of history, or in other words a sensitivity to the historical process, its development and changes. Research otherwise loses touch with reality and becomes either a mechanical sorting out of phenomena or a mere analysis of images. Instead of reading back the fully developed Rabbinic technique we shall trace the course of development backward in history. It is possible to grasp the fundamentals in the oldest 'layers' of the Rabbinic tradition, and to find correspondences in older literature, often in the Old Testament. We are able to fix dates—at least to some extent—by referring to Josephus, the Dead Sea Scrolls and the remaining 'inter-testamental' literature. This however brings us to our next problem.

3. Pharisaic Practice or Popular Pedagogics?

When we find conflicting religious interests in a particular area of history, we cannot simply claim that the religious groups in question must hold conflicting views on everything, or that their practices must differ in all respects. A common heritage; a common milieu; common conditions of life; mutual influences—these are some of the factors which must be taken into account when forming a historical estimation. This means, for our present purposes, that we cannot postulate that everything connected with the Rabbis is *exclusively* Rabbinic, or that everything to do with the Pharisees is specifically Pharisaic. The Pharisaic-Rabbinic stream of tradition had a great deal in common

---

[26] See *Memory*, pp. 122—170 and *passim*. Cf. above, note 22.
[27] For references, see *ibid.*, pp. 56 and 124 f.
[28] Cf. 1 Macc. 1 :13 f., 2 Macc. 4 :9—12.

with the world of its day. It is therefore one thing to inquire how wide-spread certain customs and practices are, which we encounter in a religious party; another matter to ask how widespread the actual party is.

Smith criticizes me because, as he puts it, I "impose Rabbinism on the Pharisees and impose Pharisaism on the rest of first-century Judaism".[29] This objection is based on the assumption that the system of pedagogics I describe was *specifically* Pharisaic-Rabbinic. But was it?

It is true that the religious programme, the organization and the behaviour patterns of the Pharisees and Rabbis on the whole form an organic unity—though less a systematic unity than a mosaic. But it would be wrong to regard everything in that unity as uniquely Pharisaic or Rabbinic, derived from a specifically Pharisaic faith or Rabbinic body of opinion. When new religious parties are formed, new views may be launched; but this is not to say that all things become new, or that all hereditary customs and traditional professional practices are at one blow given new form. In my study I have been concerned with separate parts as well as with the whole. One long chapter is devoted to an attempt to analyse in turn the basic characteristics of Rabbinic pedagogics (*Memory*, pp. 122—170). The question now is how far these fundamentals can be regarded as specifically Rabbinic or Pharisaic techniques—the learning by heart of the basic texts; the principle that 'learning comes before understanding'; the attempt to memorize the teacher's *ipsissima verba;* the condensation of material into short, pregnant texts; the use of mnemonic technique, which was fairly simple in early Tannaitic times, but which by the end of the Amoraic period had become highly complex; the use of notebooks and secret scrolls; the frequent repetition of memorized material, aloud and with melodic inflexion; the retention of knowledge by these methods—not to mention the idea of the teacher as 'pattern' and the pupil as 'imitator' (*ibid.*, pp. 181—189). What could possibly justify the claim that the Pharisees or the Rabbis had *created* all this? The Rabbis' contributions to progress in this sphere are not difficult to see: methodical reflexion, systematization and formulation elevated the whole matter to a more sophisticated level. But in almost every case the basis is provided by hereditary, popular educational practice. The thesis that such concerns as the ones we have enumerated—and many others—should be the distinctive

---

[29] *Comparison*, p. 171 f.

property of Pharisaism or of advanced Rabbinism is contradicted by numerous analogies drawn from the surrounding milieu, before, during and after the periods in question. In my book I have referred to analogies from the Old Testament, from the Dead Sea Scrolls, and from the inter-testamental literature. Such examples might be multiplied.[30]

Further, we must try to do justice to the fact that Rabbinic sources throw light on wide areas of the contemporary Jewish world. In them we glimpse not only the specifically Rabbinic sphere in and around the school, but also life in the congregations and at home. Thus we read of, for example, the half-educated men of the people who served as elementary teachers: the *soferim* and *mashnim*. These were as a rule men with no Rabbinic training, in whom pilpulism and sophistry were unknown. The Rabbis looked down on them and criticized their teaching.[31] This phenomenon is of great significance for our subject, since here we can discern something of those features of popular education which aroused the Rabbis' displeasure. It was far from being the case that the Rabbis criticized these teachers for neglecting to practise memorization: on the contrary, it was the *one-sidedness* of their memorization that aroused the Rabbis' contempt. In a sense, Aqiba and his followers resemble Socrates, Isocrates and other educational pioneers in Greece in wanting to *deepen* traditional studies.[32] They oppose the popular error that memorization is an adequate form of education, and advocate energetically a deeper penetration and understanding of the written and oral tradition. We can see, in both the Greek-Hellenistic and the Jewish spheres, that learning by heart is not a new skill, abruptly introduced by an educational reformer, but an ancient didactic principle, the faults and failings of which are becoming more and more obvious. Whatever Aqiba and his trained disciples introduced, it was not memorization.[33] Nor was it the series of simple basic principles

---

[30] Smith gives no account of all the passages in my book which indicate that a similar practice was applied *outside* the bounds of the Pharisaic-Rabbinic stream of tradition. In his view I simply "impose Pharisaism on the rest of first-century Judaism" (*Comparison,* p. 171 f.).

[31] *Memory,* pp. 106—112; cf. pp. 59—62.

[32] On the development of the Greek-Hellenistic educational tradition, see H.-I. Marrou, *Histoire de l'éducation dans l'Antiquité* (4th ed. 1958).

[33] It would seem likely, remembering the role of memorization in 'primitive' teaching and in the teaching practice of Antiquity (both Oriental and Hel-

which come naturally to anyone whose teaching method is built on the principle of memorization.[34]

Apart from the fact that the Rabbis practised a great deal which was both common and natural in the Jewish milieu, they were able by their own efforts—within certain limits—to influence and form, or at least to stabilize, the practices of other Jewish teachers. It is generally accepted that this was the case during the second century A. D. and later. The position and influence of the Pharisaic teachers in the first century A. D. is however open to question. It is common knowledge that at this time Judaism comprised a number of different factions. Two questions suggest themselves. First, what united and what divided these groups? And secondly, which of them—if any—wielded the greatest influence? Smith claims that the period before the fall of the temple was a time of sectarian conflict. He calls the Pharisaism of that time "a small sectarian party", profoundly different from the Rabbinism

---

lenistic), that a good *a priori* case could be made out for this practice in the Jewish milieu in Jesus' day. Smith disagrees, claiming that halakah was probably not learnt by heart before the fall of the temple (*Comparison*, p. 169 f.). The only support he advances for this thesis is that the oldest textual material we have in the Mishnah was, in his view, fixed for the first time shortly after the fall of the temple. This is no argument. The fact that material has not been preserved is in no sense a proof that material has never existed. See below, para. 6.

[34] Smith (*Comparison*, p. 171) polemizes energetically on the basis of an unfortunate expression I used in a footnote to p. 131 of my book. I wrote, "The fact that the halakah verses from the time of the temple are mainly anonymous is due to the simple fact that at that time, Judaism had a unified doctrinal centre, from which halakah was issued." The wording here is admittedly unfortunate. By 'Judaism' I of course meant the main stream of Judaism which, according to the title of my book and the introductory chapter (pp. 30—32) I had set myself the task of describing.—However, the anonymity of the oldest halakah is a more complex problem than either my note or Smith's counter-proposal would indicate. A. Goldberg, in his review of *Memory*, has written, "What should be recognized is that our Mishnah is a definite Hillelite document, and only after that of Hillel became the one and only recognized House could division within it be given public expression. As long as it had to contend with the School of Shammai for supremacy the House had to stand united towards the outside, and all of its decisions—whatever the internal debate—had to be given an unanimous public appearance, and therefore the anonymity! This was the case in the united stand taken by both Houses of the Pharisaic school in the Temple times against the Sadducees and others." (Handing Down Tradition, in *The Jerusalem Post*, 18/9 1963.) Cf. below, para. 6.

of the third century.[35] I consider, however, that the Pharisaic teachers were clearly dominant in Palestine as early as the period of the temple, and I shall state briefly why I believe this to be so. The development of Judaism after A. D. 70 is evidence of the unremitting vitality of this very Pharisaism, and of the wide authority and leadership exercised by the Pharisaic teachers over the Jewish people. It is not only the Rabbinic literature that prompts this conclusion. The New Testament documents point in the same direction. The Acts, John, the synoptic tradition, the Corpus Paulinum—note how early this evidence is—reveal that the dominant, the strong, the 'dangerous' group within Judaism was Pharisaism. The early Christian sources say little about the Sadducees, the Essenes and other groups, although these were also the Church's opponents. It is a well-known fact that Josephus also stresses the influential position of the Pharisees.[36] It is clear that the position and influence of Pharisaism became *stronger* during the first century, and particularly after the fall of the temple, but it is highly unlikely that any sudden change took place at the end of the New Testament period. In other words, we have three separate groups of sources, all of which reveal, independently of one another, the dominance of Pharisaism during the first century.[37] We must therefore conclude that to call the Pharisees of the period of the temple "a small, exclusive, sectarian party" is mistaken.

It is important in this connexion that we should recall the Pharisees' ambitions as popular educators. The Pharisaic teachers, unlike those of the Qumran sect, were not content to spread esoteric doctrine. They worked in the synagogues and elsewhere—everywhere, in fact, where people thirsted after the wisdom of the Torah. They learned in order to be able to teach others, and this, too, tells us something about the potential range of their influence.

There is no reason to "impose Pharisaism on the rest of first-century Judaism". But we have seen that there is every reason to regard

---

[35] *Comparison*, p. 171: "the small, exclusive, sectarian Pharisaic party of the temple period".

[36] Ant. xiii. 10, 5 f., xviii.

[37] Smith rejects the evidence of the Rabbis and Josephus (*Comparison*, p. 172).—We do not deny that this evidence must be subjected to penetrating source criticism. But the evidence of three separate groups of sources, when they confirm each other, is not to be dismissed so lightly. The sceptical conjectures of modern scholars are of course valuable, but not necessarily more so than the facts and arguments on which they are based.

Pharisaism as "the leading, and most influential, current within Judaism" at this time.[38] And most important of all, the evidence points to the fact that the pedagogics of the Pharisaic teachers—leaving aside certain marks of sophistication—were *representative* of the methods common among Palestinian teachers during this period.[39] The many analogies point in the same direction—to the fact that the teaching methods used by a man trained in the Scriptures hardly varied, whether he was formally a Pharisee, merely influenced by Pharisaism, or a member of another group altogether. It is significant that the Jewish teachers ('the scribes', οἱ γραμματεῖς) are regarded in the New Testament as being a distinct class, worthy of mention alongside other groups such as the Sadducees, the Pharisees—and 'the high priests'. We conclude that for an observer *these men were noteworthy less as members of a particular party than as representatives of a professional teaching class!*[40]

There is ample room here for further research and debate. We can now replace the old general question of the influence of Pharisaism by more detailed questions of *specific* differences and resemblances between the pedagogical methods of the various parties, professional groups and classes of society. For example, in their attitude toward memorization, toward the principle of 'learning comes before understanding', and toward the conservation of the authentic words of the teacher.

We might point out in passing that the fact that it is now possible to ask questions such as these witnesses to the advantages of the method we have tried to apply (see above, para. 1). If we can determine what the situation was in the most easily accessible area of the milieu in question we can at least arrive at historically relevant *questions,* which we can apply to the rest of the material—e. g. the New Testament material. This principle is valid irrespective of the kind of *answers* we may find.

---

[38] *Memory,* p. 30.—Cf. Smith's presentation of the subject in the next note.

[39] Smith makes no mention of the complete title of my book, which indicates that my field of study is the Pharisaic-Rabbinic stream within Judaism. Nor does he give any account of the argument of my introductory chapter, pp. 30—32, where I take up the question of boundaries and describe why I take the Pharisaic-Rabbinic teachers as representative of their milieu. In Smith's view I claim to describe "the Jewish milieu", and regard this as predominantl\ Pharisaic.

[40] Cf. A. Schlatter's observations in the works of Josephus, *Die Theologie des Judentums nach dem Bericht des Josefus* (Beitr. z. Förd. Chr. Theol. 2 : 26, 1932), pp. 195—213.

4. Tradition and Innovation in Early Christian Pedagogics

This brings us to our main problem, that of the way in which Jesus and the early Church undertook their teaching and transmission. The crucial point is the extent to which the forms and practices of the milieu were made to serve Christocentric purposes, and the extent to which new wine demanded new bottles.

It is clear to every impartial observer that Jesus and the early Church made a profound impression on their times: they were original, eruptive and creative. But no historical person or group can be original in everything.[41] How does this judgment reflect on their formal pedagogical methods?

The sources as a rule tell us more about the original aspects of a movement than about those aspects they shared with their surroundings. New aspects are commonly set out deliberately, and are accordingly to be discerned in the group's own sources and, from another angle, in the sources of their opponents. We do not wish to make too much of this view here. The sources are not very extensive and it is risky to draw conclusions *e silentio*. But the observation seems nevertheless to be valid. If the teaching methods used by Jesus and the early Church had been radically new, it is only reasonable to suppose that something of this would have been seen in the documents which have been preserved. But there is no trace of this—a circumstance which prompts two conclusions. First, that formal teaching method was of minor interest to Jesus and early Christianity. They were by no means academic specialists, advocating one teaching method as against others: their goal was obviously not that of improving contemporary pedagogics. But the sources tell us, explicitly and implicitly, *that they in fact taught,* and it is therefore necessary to determine *how* they taught.[42] Secondly, that the methods they used, which neither they themselves nor their contemporaries regarded as being out of the ordinary, must for the most part have resembled those used by other teachers in the same milieu. The problem, therefore, is to place Jesus and the leaders of the early

---

[41] The attitude of Jesus to *language* is instructive. He appears not to have created a single one of his basic religious terms himself. He has adopted existing terms and used them for his own purposes; only occasionally has he needed to give them a new conceptual content.

[42] The fact that a teacher follows a certain method, and does so quite consciously, does not of course imply that he is preaching it!

Church in their original milieu, and to compare them and their activities with those of their contemporaries which appear to be the most relevant. At the same time it goes without saying that we must pay due attention to their distinctive features.

Here we must call in question three fairly common views. First, that there existed no positive relationship between the Pharisaic teachers on the one side and Jesus and the early Church on the other. Secondly, that Jesus, the twelve and the other leaders of the early Church were, and remained, simple and unlearned men of the people. And thirdly, that the spontaneous, charismatic aspect of Jesus and early Christianity ruled out acceptance of traditional forms, conscious technique and reasoned behaviour.

Some brief comments. From what circles or groups did Jesus, the twelve and the other leaders of the early Church come? And from which teachers did they derive the methods they used in their teaching? From the Pharisees, the Sadducees, the Essenes or from other lesser-known groups? We have already pointed out how strong was the influence of Pharisaism in that section of Judaism from which the young Church won its first followers; this we see from the New Testament documents. The relations between early Christianity and Pharisaism cannot be described in terms of a secondary confrontation between two elements which originally stood separate: so much is certain. Nor does it seem that early Christianity is to be regarded as a schism from Pharisaism. It seems that we ought rather to see the position as this, that the early Christian movement originated in a sphere in which Pharisaic teachers exercised great authority and great influence. It is also probable that the Jerusalemite church was more deeply influenced by Pharisaism than the Galilean church, or any of the churches outside Palestine.[43] But the question of what religious party the various teachers belonged to is of less significance than the question of the type of teaching they carried out. Important observations are sure to result if we concentrate on such problems as: Are Jesus and the leaders of the early Church more reminiscent of halakic or haggadic[44] teachers? Of

---

[43] Here we must generally be alive to the differences which existed between milieus and groups. The early Church included adherents with vastly differing backgrounds, and in no two places was the situation precisely identical.

[44] Here I am using the term 'haggadic' in the sense of 'non-halakic'. This rules out the possibility of a third category. Most apocalyptic material must therefore be comprehended under the category of 'haggadah'.

charismatic or non-charismatic teachers? Or of those who taught with scrolls or those who taught without? We shall return to a consideration of problems such as these in due course.

Smith criticizes my thesis that Jesus, the twelve and other prominent early Christian teachers taught according to methods which outwardly resembled those of the Pharisaic teachers. As NT evidence contrary to this thesis he advances Matt. 7:29, Jn. 7:15 and Acts 4:13. An elementary critical objection (*Memory*, pp. 12 f. and 326) he finds "amusing".[45] I trust he will be able to derive further amusement from what follows, since I now propose to repeat and develop that objection.

It is an incontrovertible fact that the Gospel tradition, even in its 'primitive' form, represents Jesus as behaving in a manner remarkably similar to that of a Jewish teacher.[46] He is said to have taught, and those of his words that have been preserved are characterized by a profound knowledge of the Scriptures. This is an original element in the tradition.[47] The conviction that Jesus was far more than an ordinary teacher is there in the oldest 'layers' of the tradition, but this conviction has not prevented his being represented in many respects as a teacher typical of the age he lived in. We are however able to follow a clear tendency in the developing ideology of the early Church: intensive Christological preoccupation leads to greater emphasis being placed on the unique character of Jesus; one result is the idea that Jesus could not have been taught by any ordinary teacher, since the Son of God must be taught by God himself, without human intervention. This tendency is a common one in the psychology of religion, and can be illustrated by many examples from the history of religion. That part of the competence and knowledge of a 'man of God', which is capable of rational appreciation, is set aside, in order that his religious insight and power might the more clearly be seen as coming direct from the deity, through an unmistakeable, direct, pure intervention. The extraordinary

---

[45] *Comparison*, p. 172.

[46] See e. g. K. H. Rengstorf, art. διδάσκω κτλ., in *Theol. Wörterb.* ed. Kittel 2 (1935), pp. 141—145, 154—160; cf. idem, μανθάνω κτλ., *ibid.*, 4 (1940), pp. 411 f., 447—460.

[47] See C. H. Dodd, Jesus als Lehrer und Prophet, in *Mysterium Christi* (1931), pp. 69 ff., and E. Fascher, Jesus als Lehrer, in *Theol. Lit.-zeit.* 79 (1954), cols. 325 ff.—Bultmann, after his detailed examination of the various 'layers' of the synoptic material, asks whether Jesus might not have come from the ranks of the scribes (*Jesus*, 1929, pp. 55 ff.).

power of a weak man, or the irresistible wisdom of an unlearned man, must come from above.[48] We can see in the New Testament material how this idea developed in the early Church around the figures of Jesus and the great apostles. Mark (1:22) and Matthew (7:29) state in the course of a 'frame' passage that Jesus taught with a (heavenly) *exousia*, and not like the scribes. John the Evangelist makes 'the Jews' ask whence Jesus derived his wisdom, since he had never been taught (7:15). In this way he prepares the ground for a discourse in which Jesus explains that he has been taught by God. The same phenomenon is to be discerned in Acts 4:13, though the subject there is not Jesus, but the apostles Peter and John. This tendency, which we see to have been operative within the bounds of the New Testament, is even more prominent in the history of the Church.[49] It became particularly marked after the Romantic period; Jesus came to be regarded by some as a natural genius, unspoiled by civilization. But historical research cannot dispense with source criticism. A 'dogmatic' passage in the editorial material of Mark and Matthew, a late formula in a Johannine narrative, a late tendentious passage in Acts—these must not be given precedence over the oldest 'layers' in the Gospel tradition without very good reason indeed. At all events they are not of themselves sufficient to absolve us from the task of historical examination and the attempt to find out "wie es eigentlich gewesen".

The Christian Church has always regarded the twelve as unlearned men of the people. What proof of this do we have in the sources? Irrespective of the answer, it is quite impossible to regard them as being as uneducated at the end of their lives as they were at the time of their call. For twenty, forty, sixty years they had led the work of the Church: they had preached, taught, searched the Scriptures, discussed doctrinal questions and passed judgment on them, exercised discipline and defended the belief of the Church.[50] The development of the specifically

---

[48] It is highly instructive to note Paul's argument in such passages as 2 Cor. 4:7, 1 Cor. 2:1—5, 2 Cor. 3:5, 12:9 f., 13:3 f.

[49] Cf. e. g. W. Bauer, *Das Leben Jesu im Zeitalter der neutestamentlichen Apokryphen* (1909), pp. 368—377. Cf. also pp. 426 ff.

[50] Many Christian scholars argue as though the Apostles were not only uneducated, but also unteachable. It is claimed, for example, that the simple fisherman John, son of Zebedee, could not have written the profound Johannine corpus. This argument is based on the assumption that John must have been as uneducated at the end of his life as he was at the time of his call by Jesus.—

Christian exegesis and theology down to the time when the Gospels were committed to writing is a problem we are unable to avoid. The large number of direct quotations from the OT Scriptures and the innumerable allusions to those same Scriptures in the Gospels are clear evidence that the problem of early Christian 'scholasticism' and that of the prehistory of the Gospels belong together.[51]

The task of trying to understand the distinctive features of Jesus and early Christianity is not made easier by making them appear original on points where they made no new contribution. This is to obscure their real originality. The *dominant* factors behind the growth of the new movement are easily overlooked if we lay too much emphasis on other factors.[52] It is therefore important that we should not draw sharper distinctions than the material permits.

Jewish scholars are as a rule more polite in their attitude to the great men of their tradition. According to the Rabbinic sources Joḥanan ben Zakkai and Eliezer ben Hyrcanus were illiterate at the respective ages of 22 and 28 (22); I think even Aqiba started his studies late. This is not however commonly regarded as sufficient reason for denying that they could have uttered the words of wisdom attributed to them.—Barrett (review in *Journ. of Theol. Stud.* N.S 14, 1963, p. 449), rejects, with a reference to H. Schlier, *Comm. ad Gal.* 1 : 18, the idea that Paul could have received any significant teaching from Cephas during his fourteen-day visit. This seems to me to set the Apostle's intelligence at a very low level. A person trained in a Rabbinic school could learn a great deal in a fortnight (cf. e. g. b Yeb. 72 b, in which Resh Laqish is said to have learned the Torat Kohanim midrash by heart in three days, *Memory*, p. 117). Furthermore it is unlikely that Paul was entirely destitute of knowledge of Jesus when he came to visit Peter.

[51] I hope soon to publish a detailed study of the midrash of Jesus' temptations in the desert, in which I have attempted to show the qualified knowledge of the Scriptures possessed at a quite early date by the young Church, and how this is reflected in the Gospel tradition.—See also K. Stendahl, *The School of St. Matthew* (Acta Sem. Neot. Ups. 20, 1954).

[52] A decisive role here was naturally played by certain definite *facts, events and experiences:* events connected with the life of Jesus and experiences of the risen Christ. We are here faced with phenomena which show up the limitations of purely historical research.—G. Kittel has expressed his view of the distinctive character of Jesus in the following words: "Derjenige Punkt, an dem das Neue und Andere im Urchristentum in die Erscheinung tritt, ist wieder nicht die Lehre Jesu, sondern die Person Jesu: sein persönliches Sendungsbewusstsein, das Bewusstsein der in seiner Person gegebenen Gegenwart der Sohnschaft und damit der in seiner Person gegebenen Gegenwart der göttlichen Gnade, darum aber: der Gottesgegenwart für den Sünder." *Die Probleme des palästinischen Spätjudentums und das Urchristentum* (1926), p. 135 f.

Anyone who has analysed the words spoken, according to the synoptic tradition, by Jesus knows that they are marked, as far as their *contents* are concerned, by a radical religious and ethical distinctiveness; *as a whole* they are both independent and original (though it is possible to find parallels from various teachers for most of the individual sayings). But are the *forms* in which they were spoken particularly original? In fact there are Jewish parallels for practically every style of teaching used by Jesus. It is not here that we must look for his uniqueness.

If we review the formal parallels which have been drawn, it is striking that most are derived from the Rabbinic literature (including the Wisdom literature) and not from the Prophets or Apocalyptic. Wilder, following Fuchs, has claimed that the teaching of Jesus showed originality in form: "The utterance and speech-forms of Jesus as proclaimer of the time of salvation are characterized by immediacy, directness and spontaneity." In Wilder's view this freedom and immediacy were such as to exclude a conscious concern with mnemonics and a catechetical purpose;[53] if the Gospel material is in fact characterized by didactic, polemical or institutional interest, these must be secondary elements in the tradition.[54] It seems clear to me that such characteristics came in time to occupy a more prominent role in the tradition, but are they absent from the oldest phases? This theory, it seems, falls with the fact that we have no objective criteria by which to prove that the more 'spontaneous' elements in the Gospel tradition are the more original, while the more didactic are secondary. The choice must be subjective: analysis depends in the last resort on a dubious *a priori* argument. It seems to me inescapable that we must pay close attention to the fact that the nearest formal equivalents of the sayings of Jesus are to be found in the Jewish *didactic* tradition.

It goes without saying that when we come to compare Jesus with contemporary Jewish teachers we must not lose sight of the fact that he was held to be one whose authority (ἐξουσία) was "from above",[55] and that his appearance was attended by miracles. There is no doubt that miracles played a much more important role in his case than in contemporary Pharisaism. But at the same time it is hardly just to

---

[53] A. N. Wilder, Form-History and the Oldest Tradition, in *Neotestamentica et Patristica* (dedicated to O. Cullmann, 1962), p. 8.

[54] *Ibid.*, p. 6.

[55] See below, n. 61 f. The distinction between prophet and teacher is far from simple.

enlarge the difference by deleting the resemblances that are in fact
there. History has not preserved the names of many Pharisaic teachers
from the first century, but two are said in the Rabbinic tradition to
have been acquainted with miracles. The two in question are Ḥanina
ben Dosa[56] (who worked in Galilee!) and Naḥum of Gimzo[57] (Aqiba's
teacher). The Pharisaic teachers of the time of the temple had more
scope for miracles than was the case a few generations later.[58] This
applies in particular to *bet Hillel,* in which we may note a number of
resemblances to early Christianity. We see in the Rabbinic tradition
that at the time of the temple a sign from heaven (a *bat qol*) was even
able to settle halakic disputes.[59] This is confirmed by the New Testament
sources.[60] The synoptic tradition represents the Pharisees and scribes as
trying to persuade Jesus to support his extraordinary claims by means of
a sign from heaven.[61] In John's Gospel a leading Pharisee, Nicodemus,
confesses that Jesus must be a teacher come from God (NB the category
in which Jesus is placed by an 'outsider'), *because he is able to provide
such signs.*[62] Thus we see that the Pharisaic teachers of Jesus' day had
a receptivity to miracles and signs from heaven—a receptivity which,
later in the Tannaitic period, came to be replaced by a measure of
scepticism to such things.[63] We do not have to make Pharisaism into
a charismatic or ecstatic movement in order to be aware that such

---

[56] b Ber. 33 a, Taan. 24 b, etc.

[57] b Taan. 21 a, Sanh. 109 a.

[58] See *Memory,* p. 212 f., where, following A. Guttmann (*vide* next note),
I point out that the Rabbis' attitude to miracles altered between the time of the
temple and the third Tannaitic generation. This Smith calls "an account the
reverse of the correct one" (*Comparison,* p. 173 f.), and supports his judgment
with an argument about the difference between Tannaitic and *Amoraic* Rabbis.

[59] See A. Guttmann, The Significance of Miracles for Talmudic Judaism, in
Hebr. Un. Coll. Ann. 20 (1947), pp. 363—406.

[60] *Ibid.*—Cf. Acts 10:13—16; 11:18.

[61] Matt. 12:38 ff., 16:1 ff., Mark 8:11 ff., Luk. 11:16, 29 ff.

[62] John 3:2. NB that according to the Evangelist the Pharisaic teacher Nicodemus does not confess Jesus as the Christ, but only as a teacher come from
God. Cf. John 5:36, 6:29 f., 9:30—33—all typical late Jewish ideas. It is a
well-known fact that John's view of the miracles of Jesus differed from that of
the synoptic writers. According to John they were precisely 'signs from heaven'.

[63] The important differences between the miracles worked by Jesus and those
worked by the Pharisaic teachers have been stressed—in my opinion over-
stressed—by A. Schlatter in his article *Das Wunder in der Synagoge* (Beitr. z.
Förd. Chr. Theol. 16:5, 1912, pp. 49—86).

attitudes were possible among its members. This applies equally to the contents of the traditions of Pharisaism, which were not limited to *halakah* statements. They were interested in every aspect of the inexhaustible wisdom given to the fathers. For example, Rabban Johanan ben Zakkai was said to have been acquainted not only with halakic tradition, but with all the other branches of the manifold wisdom of the Torah, including esoteric mysticism.[64] And he was not alone in that.

As far as early Christianity is concerned, it is hardly likely that there is any scholar who is still willing to claim that its history began in the spirit and ended in the law. Most agree that the spiritual and the legal existed side by side from the very beginning. On the other hand it seems likely that some teachers laid greater emphasis on the one element, while other teachers stressed the other; and similarly, that at times the course of events contributed to an intensification of the spiritual and apocalyptic atmosphere, at least in certain milieus. But the mere possibility that *some* early Christian teachers taught in accepted traditional forms is sufficient to motivate a detailed inquiry into the question of whether the Gospel tradition as we have it has been transmitted in this way.

W. D. Davies has stressed that the history of early Christianity must be studied with a view both to its historical background and, theologically, to its radical, kerygmatic newness.[65] This observation is of course correct, and it seems particularly worth emphasizing in respect of the question of tradition. But it is difficult to keep a correct balance. This may perhaps best be illustrated by an example. We know that Paul was a man who had been trained as a *talmid hakam* in a Pharisaic school. The question is, when he was converted and became a follower of Jesus Christ, what part of his pre-Christian life would he *want* to forget? And more important, how much *could* he forget? Was every thought and every behaviour-pattern he had derived from the past so tainted that he wanted to thrust it behind him? And was his conversion so miraculous that he was able to transform every element in his life into new-minted specifically Christian equivalents? Was the Apostle so logical in his theory and so gifted in his practice that he could base his entire thought and action on one doctrinal point, so that we are able

---

[64] See most recently J. Neusner, *A Life of Rabban Yohanan ben Zakkai* (Stud. post-bibl. 6, 1962), pp. 97—103.

[65] W. D. Davies, Reflections on a Scandinavian Approach to 'the Gospel Tradition', in *Neotestamentica et Patristica*, p. 27. [Cf. below, n. 115, end.]

to solve the historical problems connected with his life simply by a process of deduction from his soteriological focus?

A common methodological mistake in research into the history of early Christianity is to describe history on the basis of the documents' theological statements of principle, at the same time glossing over the real historical matter. This applies in particular to Pauline studies. Radical theological statements of the order of Gal. 1:11—17 and 2 Cor. 5:16 are, when interpreted in a certain way,[66] made to serve as proof that Paul had little or no connexion with the Jerusalem church or with Jesus, and that he neither received nor passed on tradition.[67] But against this we have Paul's own emphatic statement that ἐν πρώτοις he transmitted important textual material to the churches—texts which he himself had received as tradition.[68] And we see that Paul not only preaches the Gospel of the crucified and risen Lord, but also stresses the need of observing what 'the Lord' Jesus Christ 'said' and 'ordained'.[69] Some systematic theologians may feel compelled at this point to postulate a contradiction, and to choose between 'kerygmatic' and 'didactic' sayings. But the historian who wants to know how the man Paul of Tarsus actually behaved and taught cannot choose in this way. He has to take account of all the authentic material at his disposal. When Paul says that he in fact both received and transmitted tradition, certain of his interpreters may have theological doubts; at any rate they may find it hard to reconcile such statements with his most 'spiritual' assertions.[70]

---

[66] For a criticism of the common misinterpretation of Pauline passages of the order of the two mentioned here, see A. Oepke, Irrwege der neueren Paulus-forschung, in *Theol. Lit.-zeit.* 77 (1952), cols. 449—458.

[67] In Pauline research Gal. 1:11—17 and 2 Cor. 5:16 fill more or less the same function as Mark 1:22, Matt. 7:29 and John 7:15 in research into the life of Jesus. The former passages are used to prove that Paul had no connexion with the Jerusalem church or with Jesus: the latter to prove that Jesus had little in common with his milieu.

[68] 1 Cor. 15:3, 11:2, 23, Phil. 4:9, Col. 2:6, 1 Thess. 4:1, 2 Thess. 3:6.

[69] 1 Cor. 7:10, 9:14, 11:24 b—25, 1 Thess. 4:15; see further *Memory*, pp. 288—323.

[70] Many attempts have been made to reconcile the apparent contradictions in the Pauline material on this point. See e. g. *Memory*, p. 296, where I follow A. Fridrichsen in drawing a distinction between 'Gospel' and 'the *logos* of the Gospel'.—A. Schweitzer considers that the Apostle is simply inconsistent in his attempts to maintain an attitude of freedom from all tradition (*Die Mystik des Apostels Paulus*, 1930, p. 171 f.).

But anyone who is interested in the historical question of the Apostle's practical attitude to the tradition of Christ must regard them as being of the utmost importance.[71]

Here I have tried to point out the existence of a methodological pit, into which scholars have not infrequently fallen. Historical questions have often been over-simplified by starting with the idea that since all things were made new in Christ, every resemblance between the early Church and its milieu must be regarded as a secondary influence, and therefore condemned out of hand. The basic assumptions of the form-critics may all too easily give rise to an un-historical attitude toward the relationship of early Christianity and its milieu. The thesis "in the beginning was the sermon (kerygma)" is brilliant as a point of departure for Christian theology. But as a historical statement it is simply incorrect.

There must be a middle way. We need not represent Jesus and the early Church as more *unique* or more *conforming* than they were. To regard Jesus as a Jewish Rabbi among many Jewish Rabbis and the early Church as a Jewish sect among many Jewish sects is certainly as far from the historical truth as to call Jesus "völlig allein in seiner Zeit, sterneneinsam in seinem Volk".[72]

II

5. Comparison: Contrasting or Historical-genetic?

As anyone who has even a superficial acquaintance with comparative studies knows, there are great differences between the Rabbinic and the New Testament traditions. It is nevertheless necessary that the scientific

---

[71] Lohse advances a number of important points in Pauline *theology* as a criticism of my attempt to sketch Paul's actual relationship to the Christ-tradition (review, p. 61 f.). See also E. Käsemann's show of temper in *Verkündigung und Forschung* 1960/62 (1963), pp. 85—87.—Cf. Barrett's objection: "Paul, and the other New Testament theologians, did not proclaim the rabbi Jesus and his teaching, but Christ crucified and risen; the source of their proclamation was not a body of instruction but the fact of the resurrection faith" (review, p. 449). But is there any reason, on a basis of the sources, to draw this distinction? Is not the truth of the matter that Paul proclaims a Christ who not only acted (suffered, died, rose again) but also spoke (preached, taught, commanded)?

[72] The formula is taken from E. Stauffer, *Die Botschaft Jesu damals und heute* (1959), p.10.

task of comparison—at the deepest level—should be undertaken. Both streams of tradition derive from one and the same historical sphere, and both trace their descent from the same mother-tradition. And in matters of form it is true to say—as Schlatter said 65 years ago[73]—that early Christian tradition has no closer parallel than the Rabbinic tradition.

The task of comparing the two streams can be undertaken in one of two ways. One method concentrates on their differences, and points to the distinctive features of the two bodies. This is an important method, particularly as a corrective for over-bold analogy and identification. It is vital, though, that it should not be driven too far, and be made to cultivate differences and deny resemblances.

The other method seeks to penetrate behind the most striking differences and determine the resemblances, both in form and content, that are in fact there; this applies particularly to questions connected with period and background, with general customs and practices. That work has commenced on these lines may be regarded as a great step forward in the comparative study of religion and history. Thus light has been cast on many sides of the thought and historical development of early Christianity by comparing them with the Jewish material. And conversely, many obscure pages in the history of the Jews and Judaism have been interpreted in the light of early Christian sources. This method of course has its risks, too: the most dangerous is that of cultivating analogies and forgetting those discrepancies which are conditioned by the specific and central differences of the two streams.

Smith devotes the greater part of his article (*Comparison,* pp. 172—177) to a comparison according to the former method. And since it criticizes a comparison of the second type, we must examine it in some detail.

The task which Smith sets himself is "to compare the material preserved in the gospels with that in rabbinic literature." This comparison in his view reveals "differences which indicate that both the original natures of the material and the methods of transmission differed widely."[74] We note that in this case there is no question of outlining the basic features of traditional Rabbinic pedagogics and comparing

---

[73] *Jochanan Ben Zakkai, der Zeitgenosse der Apostel* (Beitr. z. Förd. Chr. Theol. 3 : 4, 1899), p. 8.

[74] *Comparison,* p. 172.

these with the methods of transmission used in the early Church. Instead Smith prefers to compare the Rabbinic *material* as we have it (thus the material as finally edited, written down and preserved) with the early Christian *material* as we have it (which was finally fixed and written down much earlier). By this method it is possible to make the best possible use of all the contrasts permitted by anachronistic comparison. How is this comparison made?

Smith presents the two groups of material as standing in striking contrast to each other; however, this effect is gained in two ways. In the first place he ignores all the material that shows any degree of resemblance. Most striking is the fact that he allows the halakic element alone to represent the Rabbinic stream of tradition, and the non-halakic element in the early Christian material alone to represent that tradition.[75] Secondly, he concentrates on the strictest legal aspect, the most scholastic attitude and the most advanced techniques to be found in the Rabbinic material. This means that for the most part he also makes use of the latest 'layers' of the different Rabbinic sources.

Let us consider some examples. The first element in this comparison is the Rabbinic literature. Smith, as we have suggested, ignores the whole of the vast body of haggadic material. But he does not even take into account the manifold halakic material as a whole. His simplified thesis is as follows: "The rabbinic material (is) predominantly expository. And the bulk of early rabbinic exposition has no apparent end save the exposition itself, is devoted to the exact determination of the sense of the particular laws, deals with regular sets of questions asked in regular succession about each successive law, and deals with them in fixed, legal formulae recurring again and again."[76]—There are serious objections to this view. There was a certain type of halakic exposition, which was reminiscent of an academic, systematic study of legal texts, and in which exposition was an end in itself, but by no stretch of imagination can this be called representative of "the bulk of rabbinic exposition". The picture must be widened: not with minor details, but with necessary material. The Rabbis' work of exposition was

---

[75] Smith states in a note on p. 173: "This is not to deny that there is much haggadic material in the tannaitic midrashim and that there are some traces of halakic disputes in the gospels... But these exceptions are not relevant to a discussion of the dominant characteristics of the two traditions."

[76] *Comparison*, p. 173.

motivated by one overpowering interest: they worked with God's Torah in order to participate in its wisdom, and in order to pass on that wisdom to God's people. Their exposition—the halakic not excepted— was almost always modernizing, practical and tendentious. The halakic material, such as we have it in the preserved collections, came into being at many different kinds of sessions, discussions, halakic lectures, etc. There were two main procedures: one was to follow the Scripture text and to proceed from thence to concrete questions; the other began with the questions and went on to consider text and tradition. There is no reason, when attempting to characterize Rabbinic exposition, to overlook such important factors.

If we go on to consider the second element in the comparison, we find Smith guilty of a similar over-simplification. Once more we give examples, to each of which has been added a short commentary. (a) According to Smith the Gospel material is "predominantly narrative";[77] this means that the non-narrative portions of the Gospels are left out when the dominant characteristics are to be stressed. And if we go to the tradition as it existed before the written Gospels we find that, for example, a collection like the 'Logia source' must be excluded from any comparison, as must all other blocks of sayings of Jesus. (b) The main concern of the Gospel material is claimed to be "to preach the Saviour".[78] In my view this is only part of the truth. The main concern of early Christianity in all its work with the Word was to spread and confirm faith in Christ as "the power and the wisdom of God". But the individual Gospel pericopes normally have a limited primary purpose: the concrete didactic purpose of giving the new people of God instruction on such matters as personal relationships, the practice of prayer, fasting, almsgiving and the like. Here the kerygmatic interest is in the background; the foreground is occupied by a didactic attitude toward concrete points in the Christian faith and life. (c) On the subject of the disposition of the early Christian traditional material Smith says that "the gospel material is connected by its relation to the life of Jesus".[79] This applies to the Gospels as we have them. But at the same time we must not overlook one of the best-attested results of modern Gospel research: that the grouping of the Gospel material on a basis of the life of Jesus came late, and is largely artificial.[80] Individual

---

[77] *Ibid.*   [78] *Ibid.*, p. 174.   [79] *Ibid.*

[80] Opinions differ only over the question of whether the early Church trans-

elements were previously grouped on entirely different principles: in blocks held together by a common topic, a key-word or some other principle, in other words, principles which we also find in the oldest blocks of the Rabbinic collections. (d) "The tannaitic material shows deliberate variation within a carefully memorized tradition; the gospels show the freer development of written material by editors of different schools."[81] Although we must admit that written versions were of greater significance for the final redaction of the Gospels than that of the Rabbinic collections, it is nevertheless impossible to draw a contrast in this way. Matthew and Luke both bear witness of the role played by oral tradition (alongside written versions) down to the last phase of the history of the synoptic Gospel tradition.

Though examples might be multiplied, these must suffice.

However, if we ignore the polemical exaggerations in Smith's comparison, we can accept and emphasize a number of his points. There are other differences which might be mentioned; there was a great deal which divided the Christocentric early Christianity from the Torah-centric Rabbinism. And close attention must of course be paid to these differences. But they must not be exaggerated to such an extent that genuine resemblances become obscured. Nor must they be used as arguments against an attempt *to compare what is comparable*. When all is said and done there remains the incontestable historical fact that Jesus and the early Church had a great deal in common with their milieu, including Pharisaism-Rabbinism. It is the extent of that common property that interests us here.

Jesus was no ordinary Rabbi; much less a Rabbinic lawyer of late Tannaitic or Amoraic type. But if we concentrate on the external forms in which his teaching was delivered we find that they are very similar to the practices of contemporary Jewish teachers. Why should an attempt not be made to trace the connexion, historically and structurally?

Early Christianity had no Rabbinic academy of the type we find in Judaism after the catastrophes of A.D. 132—135. But there is evidence which seems to show that at least some branches of the early Church

---

mitted, before the Gospels, a *summary* of the main events in the life of Jesus of the kind we find in Acts 10: 36 ff. and elsewhere.

[81] *Comparison*, p. 173.—NB that Smith here admits that the Gospels derived from different schools.

had leading *collegia*, similar to those in contemporary Pharisaism, the Qumran sect and probably other groups as well.[82] Why should we not examine the sources to see whether such was in fact the case?

The Rabbis' Oral Torah (we take the word in its widest sense)[83] included both halakah and haggadah. The greatest emphasis was normally placed on the halakah, though some teachers preferred the haggadah. There are many characteristics which are typical of both the halakic and the haggadic teaching and transmission: in my opinion these are common characteristics of contemporary Jewish pedagogics. It is thus not altogether pointless to compare the Rabbis' halakic tradition with the early Church's haggadic. But why should we not primarily compare the formation of Pharisaic-Rabbinic halakah with the formation of early Christian halakah, and haggadah tradition with haggadah tradition? If we were to compare Mekilta with the Gospels, should we concentrate on the strictly halakic elements in Mekilta, but ignore the mass of wisdom sayings, parables, narratives and the like, which are there *in the same collection of traditions* and which demand comparison with adequate parallel material? While on the subject of adequate comparative material it is worth mentioning that not all the material in the many-sided haggadah is commensurable with the sayings

---

[82] Smith, who consistently ignores the historical perspective in my study, attributes to me the thesis that the Apostles in Jerusalem "formed a rabbinical academy" (*Comparison*, p. 172, with reference to p. 201 [?] in *Memory*). But it is clear from my sketch of the development of the Jewish school system (*Memory*, pp. 85—92), and indeed from the book as a whole, that I do not claim that *any* institution in Palestine at the time of the temple was "a rabbinical academy". In my view colleges of the type of *bet Hillel* and *bet Shammai* were not sufficiently developed to be called academies. My actual thesis is that in the young Church, as in Pharisaism and the Qumran sect (and probably other groups at the time of the temple) there were leading "doctrinal *collegia*" in many congregations—principally in the Jerusalem congregation (*Memory*, p. 329 f.).

[83] I have defined the terms 'Torah', 'Written Torah' and 'Oral Torah' in chapter 1 of *Memory*, in the sense in which I use them in the book. Smith seems throughout to use these terms in a narrower sense. When he speaks of Oral Torah he usually means the *halakic* tradition. There are no linguistic objections to this usage. But a debate becomes easier to follow if the person criticizing a book uses the principal terms in the same sense as the author of the book in question, or defines his own use of the terms, when this is different from that of the author.

and narratives of Jesus, as contained in the early Christian tradition.[84] But the central religious and ethical elements in the haggadah: material accorded holiness, authority and supreme importance—such material from the haggadah is relevant. It seems that material of this kind was largely transmitted in the same way as the halakic material, with one difference, that its wording was as a rule more elastic[85]—a fact noted by the student of the Gospels with a measure of recognition.

6. The Interplay of Transmission and Redaction

We have seen that Smith compares the material which has been preserved from the two streams of tradition, and from it draws certain conclusions about the nature of the traditions and the method of their transmission. A comparison of this kind calls attention to two methodological problems, with which I propose to deal briefly.

Analysis of the mechanics of the process of oral transmission reveals three main functions: a *creative* function (traditions are created, grow and pass through fruitful changes), a purely *preservative* function (traditions are preserved and transmitted without either positive or negative changes) and an *annihilating* function (traditions lapse and become extinct, either by accident or design). The first two of these are naturally of the greatest interest from the historical point of view. The third is also worth attention. In one particular case—when it is decided to accept material as we have it as representative of what existed in an ancient stream of tradition—the problems it raises must receive the fullest consideration. It is true of all oral tradition that a good deal of it in time becomes obsolete and disappears; further, that historical circumstances are responsible for the disappearance of a certain amount: not only collective catastrophes (as when the Jerusalem

---

[84] A common methodological error is to lump together all kinds of haggadic material, classifying haggadah as 'preaching' and halakah as 'teaching'. It is obvious that methodical transmission of important haggadic material took place in more or less the same way as that of halakic material (see the next note); this can be seen from the mixture of material in the midrashim, in the Talmud and even in the Mishnah.

[85] Cf. *Memory*, pp. 96 f., 136—148, 177—179 and elsewhere. It is highly desirable that detailed research into the various types of material in the haggadah should be carried out.

scribes were virtually wiped out in A.D. 70), but private tragedies (the death of the individual traditionist) have this effect.[86] In addition, where there is a 'controlled tradition', material may be repressed consciously, either indirectly, by depreciation or silence, or directly, by censorship and purging.[87] If we fail to take account of this we may fall into the trap of regarding the preserved traditions as being the sum total of all traditions that ever existed.[88]

Another important complex of problems is intimately connected with this: the redactional history of the memorized material. The form-critics regarded the process of tradition as being one of gradual solidification of a hitherto plastic body of material. The final phase in this process, the actual transfer from memory to manuscript, they called the redac-

---

[86] Many expressive Rabbinic quotations could be advanced by way of illustration of this theme. The death of a learned man is compared to the burial or burning of a Torah scroll, T Sot. xv. 3, p Moed Qat. iii. 7, b Sot. 49 b, b Sanh. 68 a, 101 a, etc.

[87] See *Memory*, pp. 95—98.

[88] Smith's argument, *Comparison*, p. 169 f. (cf. above, n. 33), should be read with this in mind.—Those sayings which have been preserved from the time prior to the fall of the temple are largely transmitted anonymously. This is a well-known, much-discussed, but nonetheless enigmatic fact. From this Smith draws hasty and vulnerable conclusions: thus he can speak of "the general failure to preserve the *ipsissima verba* of the early teachers, and the free production of new legal texts to meet the new needs of the [Pharisaic] party," etc. But the phenomenon is not so easily explained. Certain questions might be asked. Why is the oldest halakah and haggadah anonymous? (Were they at this early period less interested in individuals? Or were they less anthropocentric? Or did they follow, without knowing precisely why, the principles of redaction handed down since the time of the Wisdom literature?) To what extent have definite historical events affected the situation? (e. g. the enormous losses of teachers, scrolls and oral texts in connexion with the destruction of Jerusalem in A.D. 70.) What changes are implied in the adoption of the rule that a saying is to be transmitted in the name of its originator? (That the oldest teachers are not mentioned by name need not *per se* mean that their teaching—or the words in which it was given—had been abandoned.) What was the nature of the redactional work carried out by the various teachers and colleges on the received collections of texts? (To what extent did they re-express, complement and re-group? What were the principles determining the gathering of new collections for definite purposes?) According to what principles were new legal texts formulated? (That new legal texts were in fact formulated need not *per se* imply that new words were placed in the mouth of older teachers, or that the transmission of older texts was abandoned.) Questions of this kind might be multiplied. Cf. next note.

tion-history of the material. This scheme cannot be applied to the Pharisaic-Rabbinic tradition. Here the basic material always had a 'fixed' form, being transmitted as memorized texts; during the period which preceded the final form taken by the material in its last redaction preservative transmission can however alternate with creative and annihilating treatment. Here the redaction-history cannot be restricted to the final phase in the process. The same applies to early Christian tradition: if its main sections were transmitted in the same way as the material in the Pharisaic-Rabbinic stream, here too we must take account of the *interplay* of traditio-history and redaction-history.

The decisive point is what 'work on the Word' means in this context. For the Rabbis, work on the Torah implied not only preservation and transmission, but also interpretation, adaptation, rearrangement, complementary creation, and the like. (In addition there were certain annihilating measures.) The Rabbis were thus not merely traditionists.[89]

When we speak of the Rabbis' Oral Torah (again using the word in its widest meaning) we must remember that this was not a coherent, *concrete unity*. Outwardly it was a plurality. In Pharisaic-Rabbinic Judaism the whole of the quantities of material which could be classified as Oral Torah had in Tannaitic times not been collated into a concrete unity; not even the halakic material was available in one collection. What did exist was a great number of larger or smaller collections of oral textual material (halakot and halakic midrashim, haggadot and haggadic midrashim), partly written down in unofficial notebooks and secret scrolls. Aqiba and his followers made creditable attempts to gather in and sort the material from the many oral collections. This was edited and complemented, time and time again, but not even R. Jehuda's Mishnah *kat' exochen* was, or claimed to be, complete. Other collections of halakic and haggadic material continued to exist. And the creative process continued.

A great deal of work remains before we can claim that the different sides of the Rabbis' work on the Torah have been clarified. One question of considerable interest which remains is how the Rabbis worked over and edited different kinds of oral textual material during

---

[89] In my study I concentrated expressly on one particular section of Rabbinic activity—the actual transmission of texts (see *Memory*, pp. 75—78 and 91 f.). Other important aspects of Rabbinic work on the Torah could be dealt with only in passing (*ibid.*, pp. 97 f., 103—112, etc.).

the period preceding that of the great collections.[90] The history of the form and redaction of Rabbinic tradition is a rich field for research.

A similar situation exists with respect to early Christian tradition. The study of the preservation and transmission of tradition is not enough, but must be supplemented by other studies, covering other aspects of early Christian work with the Word. This applies particularly to the nature and extent of the early Church's *creative* contribution. The early Church did not from the beginning have a unified oral *Urevangelium*, and the twelve and the other authoritative teachers and colleges were not traditionists only.[91] They worked with the Word. They worked on the Scriptures,[92] and on the Christ-tradition (which was originally oral): they gathered, formulated (narrative tradition), interpreted, adapted, developed, complemented and put together collections for various definite purposes.[93] This work does not provide a simple and perfect parallel to the Rabbis' work on the Torah tradition. There are a number of important differences, over and above those we have already mentioned, which must be taken into consideration.

7. The Distinctiveness of the Christ-tradition: some Observations

It goes without saying that we must beware of drawing false analogies when comparing the Rabbis' and the early Christian authorities' work on the Word. Attention must be paid to a number of significant differences, some of which we shall mention.[94]

---

[90] Cf. *ibid.*, pp. 77 f., 97 f., 111 f., 120 f., 152 f., etc. Goldberg (*Handing Down Tradition*) points out that I have not taken sufficient account of the various 'layers' of the Oral Torah: What happens when the tradition grows is not necessarily that the basic text tradition itself is 'reworked', but that it is given additional 'layers', representing the contributions of later generations.

[91] W. D. Davies advances arguments against the thesis that the Christ-tradition was originally a "single, clearly-defined 'Holy Word'" (*Reflections*, pp. 19 ff.). I never intended to suggest that it was (see *Memory*, p. 333 f.). Very much of Davies' criticism is due to this basic misunderstanding. Cf. E. Larsson, *Christus als Vorbild* (Acta Sem. Neot. Ups. 23, 1962), p. 46.

[92] For the work on *the Scriptures*, which I have not had the opportunity of discussing here, see *Memory*, pp. 324—335. Cf. also my attempt to clarify (a) how Luke describes early Christian work on the Scriptures, *ibid.*, pp. 225—234, and (b) how this matter is understood by Paul, *ibid.*, pp. 280—288.

[93] Cf. *Memory*, pp. 330—335.

[94] Cf. Davies, *op. cit.*, particularly pp. 31—34. I am a little surprised at

The Church's Christ-tradition was (if we may be permitted the expression) on a higher plane than the Rabbis' Oral Torah. The crux of the matter is that Jesus' followers did not regard him as a teacher among other teachers, but as the Messiah, the Ebed Jahwe, the Son of God. This means (i) that the early Church regarded Jesus as the eschatological saviour. The traditions of his suffering, death and resurrection were central. There is no equivalent to this in the accounts of any Rabbi; still less can such matters be regarded as standing at the centre of the Rabbinic tradition. This in turn implies (ii) that Jesus was regarded as the eschatological mediator of revelation, *the 'only' teacher* in the most qualified meaning of the word.[95] Many teachers were recognized in the Pharisaic-Rabbinic tradition: Hillel, Shammai, Gamaliel, Johanan ben Zakkai and many others. Their authority, their teaching and their decisions were held in the utmost respect. And the teachers respected one another. Their relative authority was only a matter of degree. But in early Christianity, though there were many revered teachers ('the twelve', Paul and others), one—Jesus—had a unique position *above* all these; he was the 'only' teacher. We must go back to Moses and the Exodus to find the closest equivalent of the person and work of Jesus.[96]

The idea of Jesus as the 'only' teacher is expressed in pregnant terms in a logion from the material peculiar to Matthew (23:8—10). But it

---

Davies' criticism on this point, since he seems to have overlooked two things: (1) that the oldest Rabbinic traditional material underwent changes during the Tannaitic and even during the Amoraic periods. The material was re-edited a number of times during the course of the Rabbis' work on the Oral Torah; new 'layers' of tradition were added and interpretative material was introduced. This is true even of the Mishnah *kat' exochen* (cf. above, para. 6, with the notes 88 and 90). (2) that in my view early Christianity not only transmitted the Christ-tradition, but also carried out work on it (cf. above, paras. 6—7).

[95] Cf. *Memory*, p. 332 f.

[96] The position of Jesus is thus unlike that of Hillel, Shammai or Gamaliel, but resembles that of Moses: he is a higher equivalent of Moses, who was God's *shaliah par excellence*. The comparison with Moses can in some respects be made on a fairly adequate basis; cf. e. g. Heb. 3:1—6 (where Christ is called the *apostolos* and high priest of our confession) and John 9:27—29 (where the Pharisaic scribes are called disciples of Moses and Jesus' followers *his* disciples). The comparison cannot however be carried out with full consistency. There is a great difference of perspective (Moses a figure of the past: Christ a near-contemporary), and further, Christ is regarded as being greater than Moses.

is of more importance to note that this same idea appears to lie behind the Gospel tradition as a whole. We know how great was the reverence accorded to the leaders of the early Church—'the three pillars' or 'the twelve'—by the Christians of the first century. Their authority was accepted, their teaching was listened to and their practice served as an example.[97] The sources indicate that Apostle-traditions grew up in the early Church.[98] But when these great men come to be compared with Jesus Christ, then no more is heard of their authority, their maturity, their knowledge, their wisdom and their insight. Never for one moment are we allowed to forget the distance between the 'only' teacher and these others. In the Gospels we see that only Jesus gave positive teaching; 'the twelve' are mentioned, as his disciples, servants and messengers, but never as mediators of their own teaching. The Evangelists are only interested in mediating the words and works of *Jesus;*[99] the traditionists have nothing to say—not even in passing—about any creative contribution made by a Peter, a James or a John to the teaching of Jesus Christ. So great is the concentration on the words and works of Jesus that even the contribution of these 'three pillars' is without interest.[100] It would be well to keep this in mind in face of sceptical scholars' attempts to show that the tradition of Jesus is a free compilation on the part of the early Church: that they took up sayings which were in circulation, and placed them in the mouth of Jesus;[101] that they them-

---

[97] Cf. *Memory,* p. 259 f. with ref.

[98] Davies (*op. cit.,* p. 28 f.) objects to my description of the account in Acts 10 as an apostolic *ma'asæh* (*Memory,* p. 259 f.). This criticism results from the fact that Davies uses the term *ma'asæh* in an unnecessarily narrow sense. This term denotes not only an action, but also an experience or any kind of event. *Ma'asæh* very often means simply 'a narrative tradition' (cf. *Memory,* p. 181).

[99] Cf. G. Kittel's pertinent remarks (*Die Probleme,* p. 68 f.) and see further *Memory,* p. 332 f.—When I there say that the tradition of Jesus is isolated from the sayings of other authorities I do not mean that it has been protected from undergoing certain adaptations; only that the early Christian collection of traditions of Jesus are exclusive in the sense that no attention is paid to the sayings of other doctrinal authorities; what is quoted is what is felt to be Jesus-tradition: words of *Jesus* and stories about *Jesus.*—Contra Davies, *Reflections.*

[100] Whether the Evangelists' claim to transmit only what Jesus said and did is *justified,* is quite another matter.

[101] Cf. M. Smith, The Jewish Elements in the Gospels, in *Journ. of Bible and Relig.* 24 (1956), p. 94 f.: "In general, good sayings went about the ancient world looking for good fathers, and it often happened that they found several"

selves freely created 'sayings of Jesus'; that they projected sayings of early Christian prophets back into the life of Jesus; and the like.[102]

It is perfectly clear that the preserved Jesus-traditions have been affected by the early Church's conviction that Christ had risen from the dead, and that the Holy Spirit had come; they are likewise marked by the use which was made of them in the many-sided activity of the young Church. Work on the Word has left distinct traces on these traditions.[103] But it is one thing to state that traditions have been *marked* by the milieu through which they passed; another to claim that they simply were *created* in this secondary milieu.[104] The evidence suggests that memories of Jesus were so clear, and the traditions with which they were connected so firmly based that there can have been relatively little scope for alteration.

We may take note of one such indication. It is often said nowadays that 'the twelve' were an institution in the early Church, later projected back into the life of Jesus.[105] Faced with this thesis one can only ask why the early Church failed to project their greatness, their authority,

---

(p. 94). This is also said to apply to the process of tradition in early Christianity: "Jesus' name may have attracted to itself a number of famous sayings which were current in the Judaism of that age ..." (p. 95). Theses of this kind are fascinating, but must be supported by facts and by valid arguments. Scepticism is no proof in itself.

[102] Bultmann, *Geschichte, passim.*—Against this, see the critical argument put forward by F. Neugebauer, Geistsprüche und Jesuslogien, in *Zeitschr. f. d. Neutest. Wiss.* 53 (1962), pp. 218—228.

[103] If we would determine the early Christian theology and *Selbstverständnis* it is of course of the greatest importance that we should observe how the early Church interpreted, and adapted, the Christ-tradition. But we are not concerned in this study with the religious views of early Christianity: only with their methods of teaching and transmission.

[104] The form-critics take the hypothesis that the Gospel material was created by the Christian congregation as their starting-point. The burden of proof is laid on whoever maintains that a tradition goes back to Jesus himself. This method seems to me to be wrong from the historical point of view. The burden of proof should rest on those who reject the statements contained in the sources: the commonsense, sound view is to start with *what the sources say* (that Jesus uttered the words attributed to him, etc.), but to criticize the sources and to reject what appears to be improbable.—It need scarcely be pointed out that the *narrative* traditions were normally first formulated by the Church.

[105] See most recently G. Klein, *Die zwölf Apostel. Ursprung und Gehalt einer Idee* (1961), pp. 34—49, and W. Schmithals, *Das kirchliche Apostelamt. Eine historische Untersuchung* (1961), pp. 56—77. On the other hand cf. my

their wisdom, their power and their creative force. Why, if that were the case, did they project their littleness, their immaturity, their incapability, their ignorance and their mere passivity? If this were a state of affairs which appeared only here and there in the Gospel tradition, then it might be possible to dismiss it as a tendentious interpretation of history.[106] But it characterizes the material as a whole, even when mentioned only in passing. We are forced to the conclusion that the early Church possessed an elementary sense of history, relatively firm memories from the time "when the Spirit was still not given" and relatively fixed traditions from that time; this applies at least to those circles of early Christianity, in which the Synoptic tradition was preserved and edited.

It therefore becomes necessary, when trying to determine the nature and extent of the early Church's creative contribution to the shaping of the tradition of Christ, to take account of the fact that the early Church regarded Jesus as the Messiah, the Christ, the 'only' teacher, and therefore had special cause to note, gather and keep what *he* said and did— he and no other. Early Christian work on the Christ-tradition seems to have taken place within fairly restricted limits, and thus to have had only limited freedom. The sole object was to keep and serve the 'words of Christ'—Christ and no other.

As far as the principles on which this work was carried out are concerned, we need not stop at speculation and synthetic statement. Careful analysis of the difference between parallel traditions can to some extent give definite results. In many cases—those in which we are sure we are in fact dealing with parallel traditions—the margin of variation can be deduced directly from the material: here we see how, and how much, the material has been changed.[107] It is not without significance that the sayings of Jesus vary much less than the narrative material and the redactional framework.[108] When sayings of Jesus are

---

article Die Boten Gottes und die Apostel Christi, in *Svensk Exeg. Arsbok* 27 (1962), pp. 89—131 (also available as offprint; Gleerup, Lund).

[106] Cf. what is said above in para. 4.

[107] We leave detailed comment for the time being. The importance of taking full account of the early Church's work on the tradition of Jesus has been emphasized by J. Fitzmyer (art. Memory and Manuscript, in *Theol. Stud.* 23, 1962, p. 455 f.) and others.

[108] Correctly pointed out by Dibelius, *Formgeschichte*, p. 31 f. (leaving aside the fact that he wrongly identifies the sayings-tradition with halakah and narrative tradition with haggadah).

reworked, it seems mainly to have been on a basis of what might be called 'interpretative adaptation'.

Early Christian work on the Christ-tradition seems to have been more creative on some points than on others. This applies in particular to those traditions which deal with the lesser-known periods in the life of Jesus. Here the principles of early Christian work on the Word stand out clearly in comparison with the principles for the formation of haggadic midrash in Judaism.[109]

It is a well-known fact that narratives of Jesus seldom have a halakic point: normally a Christological point. This does not however hinder their comparison with Rabbinic narrative tradition. The disciples' role as witnesses of the words and deeds of their master was not restricted to halakic contexts.[110]

The early Church's oral textual material was soon available in Greek (certainly even in Palestine), and was thus transmitted not only in Hebrew and Aramaic, but also in that language.[111] Written notes seem to have been in wider use among the more Hellenized Jews (and among proselytes, and 'Greeks') than in more conservative Hebrew circles. It took very few decades for the main parts of the Christ-tradition to be committed to writing, in comprehensive documents. On the other hand it is hard to say to what extent these documents were in circulation,

---

[109] Cf. above, n. 51.

[110] One aspect of teaching and transmission in the ancient world (including Pharisaism-Rabbinism) is that the pupil not only learned his teacher's words, but also his way of life. The pupil was regarded as a witness of what the teacher was, did and said (cf. *Memory*, pp. 181—187). Smith argues, on p. 174 f. of his article, as though this applied only in *halakic* contexts. This is incorrect. It would be possible to quote many examples showing that this is not merely a matter of witnessing *legally* relevant behaviour. One particularly illuminating example is found in b Ber. 27 b. In a learned discussion of the correct time for the reading of the Sabbath prayer R. Zeira quotes a tradition from Rab: "R. Ishmael b. R. Jose prayed the Sabbath prayer on the eve of the Sabbath beside that pillar." But when 'Ula came, he said, "It was beside a palm, not beside a pillar; it was not R. Ishmael b. R. Jose but R. Eleazar b. R. Jose; it was not the Sabbath prayer on the eve of the Sabbath but the prayer for the close of the Sabbath on the Sabbath day." Here we see how a well-informed traditionist corrects an ill-informed colleague, not only in respect of the halakic point in the narrative tradition but also on other elements of the tradition!

[111] See most lately L. Hartman, *Testimonium linguae* (Coniect. Neot. 19, 1963), pp. 5—56.

and whether they were used sufficiently widely to affect the life of the congregations. Probably the Christ-tradition was mainly an *oral* tradition in practice far into the history of the early Church.[112]

The process of purely oral transmission was nevertheless very brief, measured by Rabbinic standards. It is of the utmost importance that we should remember, when comparing Rabbinic and early Christian tradition, that in the latter case we are dealing with a very short process indeed, while the Rabbis' tradition stretches across several centuries.

These and other facts must be borne in mind when comparing Rabbinic and early Christian work on their respective traditions, and when estimating the earliest history of the Church's Christ-tradition. Particular attention must be paid to the final phase of redaction-history: to the circumstances and motifs which led each of the Evangelists to choose his material as he did, to interpret it, adapt it to his purposes and make a unity of it—a mosaic of Christ. In the past decade a number of scholars have drawn attention to the role of the Evangelists themselves in shaping the various Gospel documents, with many results of permanent value.[113]

One word more. The early Church regarded its work on the Word as a *charismatic* work. The early Christians uttered many sharp words on the subject of human wisdom, but they accepted 'the wisdom which is from above'—the wisdom granted to gifted teachers. They believed that it was this wisdom that enabled them to understand the Scriptures and the words of Christ, that enabled them to expound, to preach, to teach, to exhort—and to silence the objections and criticisms of outsiders. It would of course be a grave mistake if we were to regard the work carried out on the Word by the first Christians as a purely intellectual activity of the modern, secularized academic type. But we should

---

[112] *Memory*, pp. 194—207. Barrett (review, p. 446 f.) deduces from the statement in Luke 1:1 that "before Luke wrote Christianity had already become a literary phenomenon". This is a bold statement, since we know so little about the number and spread of Gospel documents at this early period, but the view deserves due attention. See also Widengren, *Tradition*, p. 60 f.—The fact that the extra-canonical tradition of Christ had declined so far, and was so decadent, when we encounter it e. g. in the writings of Irenaeus, of course has many causes. One such cause was probably that it was not protected by official written documents.

[113] For literature on the question of 'redaction-history', see Bultmann, *Ergänzungsheft* (1958), p. 5 f.

be almost equally mistaken if we were to underestimate the rational mechanisms which were obviously operative in the activity of the early Church. Early Christian enthusiasm was not without its logic; nor was zeal in preaching unaccompanied by its pedagogics.[114] Therefore, if we would gain a clear picture of the origins of the Gospel tradition, we must now, as I see it, concentrate less on 'the biology of the Saga' and more on the conscious methods and techniques applied by Judaism, Jesus and early Christianity in their Scriptural exposition, their teaching and their transmission.[115]

---

[114] Dibelius was able to write: "Wie sich im Urchristentum von Anfang an neben enthusiastischen auch nomistische Gedanken gezeigt haben, so steht neben dem pneumatischen Interesse, für das alle christliche Paränese den einen göttlichen Ursprung hat, die Wertschätzung der *Tradition,* der *Authentie* und der *Autorität*" (his italics), *Formgeschichte,* p. 243. This is however incidental. The programme of the form-critics was not based on this insight.

[115] *Additional note.* P. Winter, in his review in *Angl. Theol. Rev.* 45 (1963), pp. 416—419, takes a somewhat superficial view of the points at issue, and argues in far too general terms. I should like to make three comments. (i) Winter begins by saying, "Scandinavian biblical scholars, especially those of the Uppsala School, enjoy a reputation for interpreting Israel's customs, beliefs and traditions in the light of the traditions known from other civilisations but not attested—at least not directly—in the Old Testament itself... The author of the book under review, a pupil of Professor Harald Riesenfeld, resorts to the same procedure in his attempt to apply to the study of the formation and transmission of gospel traditions certain deductions he has drawn from the study of rabbinical methods of transmitting oral traditions" (p. 416 f.).—Is it not the case that the form-critical school—of which Winter is a representative (see his book *On the Trial of Jesus,* 1961, pp. 1—15)—subject the synoptic material to examination on the basis of observations made in *general folk-lore,* while I have attempted to compare early Christian pedagogics first with Jewish, and then with Hellenistic pedagogics? (ii) Winter questions "the validity of the method of simply transferring to the study of the growth of gospel tradition those deductions which Dr. Gerhardsson claims to have established by his examination of the methods of transmitting rabbinic records" (p. 417).—In this form I cannot recognize my thesis. (iii) Winter argues on the basis of a number of the postulates of form-criticism *as though these were established facts:* for example, the thesis that the kerygma was primary, the didache being only secondary, that early Christianity in its first phase was non-institutional, and that its pneumatic character excluded every interest in a more rational procedure (pp. 417 ff.).—It is my conviction that Gospel research must draw the consequences of the fact that over-simplified postulates of this kind have proved untenable (for references, see *Memory,* pp. 9—15).

Davies' article *Reflexions* has now been reprinted in his book *The Setting of the Sermon on the Mount* (1964), pp. 464—480.